Contents

QUICKSTART

If you can bear to delay your first footsteps into the world of Final Fantasy XIII for a moment or two, this brief introductory chapter offers observations, insights and advice that may help you to stride more purposefully through its opening hours.

COMMANDS

COMMANDS

PS3	XBOX 360	Field Controls	Battle Controls
L	L	Movement	Menu navigation; repeat previous command queue (L ➡ with Abilities menu highlighted)
R	R	Camera control	Camera control
D-pad	D-pad	Menu navigation	Menu navigation; repeat previous command queue (D-pad ➡ with Abilities menu highlighted)
⊗	A	Interact	Select menu option; enter sub-menu
◎	B	Return to previous menu; dismiss menu	Return to previous menu; cancel selection
△	Y	Enter Main Menu	Execute partial command queue before ATB gauge is filled
□	X	View map screen; view Mission list*	-
R1	RB	-	View enemy information
R2	RT	-	-
L1	LB	Enter Shrouds selection menu*	Change Paradigm*
L2	LT	-	-
L3	L	-	
R3	R	Center Camera	-
START	START	Pause	Pause
SELECT	BACK	Enable/disable mini-map; skip cutscenes or quit game (as applicable) on pause screen	-

* Note: This feature is not available from the opening stages of the story.

PLAYSTATION 3

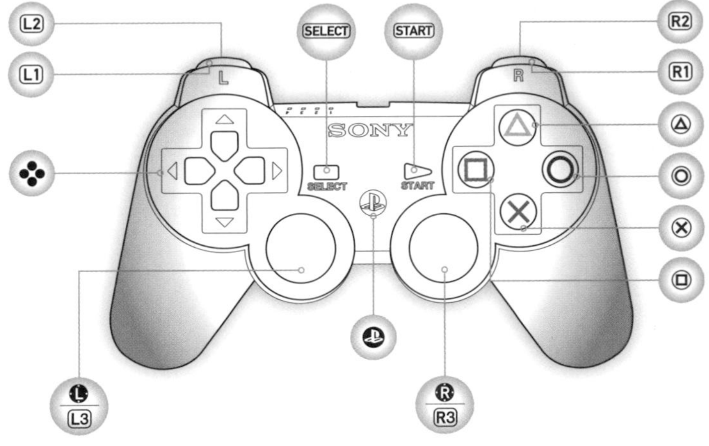

XBOX 360

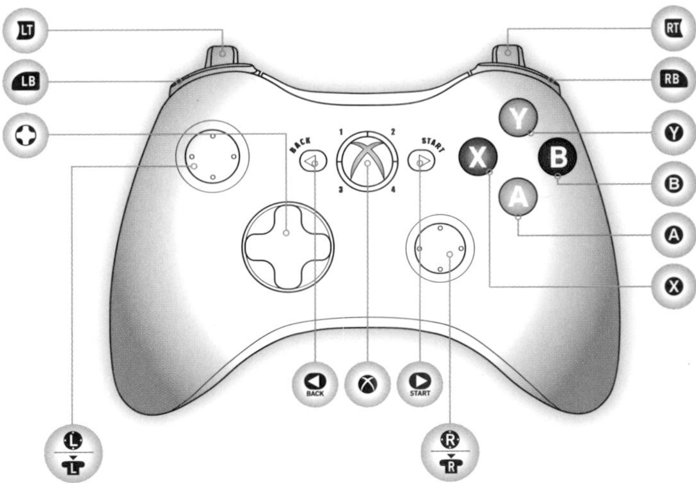

FIELD ONSCREEN DISPLAY

1 INTERACTIONS

Approaching any object that you can interact with in the game world (such as a Save Station or Treasure Sphere) triggers a pop-up instruction.

2 MINI-MAP

Offers information on the terrain in your immediate vicinity, including boundaries and assorted points of interest.

3 WAYPOINT COMPASS

Points towards your next destination.

MINI-MAP LEGEND

Icon	Description
	Party leader
	Path of your recent steps
	Ally
	Enemy
	Alerted enemy
	Recently defeated enemy
	Waypoint marker
	Save Station
	Recovered Treasure marker

BATTLE ONSCREEN DISPLAY

1 BATTLE MENU

Provides access to commands used during combat. New options are introduced later in the story. Disappears when your instructions are implemented.

2 ATB GAUGE (ACTIVE TIME BATTLE)

Fills gradually; once full, your commands will be performed by your current character (the party leader). Battle instructions (known as the "command queue") appear above this gauge once selected.

3 HELP DISPLAY

Offers information on highlighted menu options.

4 ENEMY NAME

The name of your currently targeted opponent.

5 ENEMY HP GAUGE

This green bar illustrates the current health ("hit points") of an opponent.

6 CHAIN GAUGE

Charts the increase of cumulative damage; at its highest point, an enemy enters "Staggered" status, which can lead to increased damage, new weaknesses and behavioral changes. The red marker shows your actual position on the gauge, while the orange bar is a timer. If the orange bar reaches the far left of the gauge before you or your allies land another attack, the Chain Bonus is reset.

7 CHAIN BONUS

Shows the current multiplier for damage inflicted on a targeted enemy. 100% is the default amount; this grows as the Chain Gauge is filled through successive attacks.

8 STAGGER THRESHOLD

Indicates the Chain Bonus level where an enemy will enter the Staggered state.

9 PARTY HP GAUGES

Shows the current health of your party.

10 STATUS EFFECTS

Various status ailments and enhancements can be applied to both allies and enemies; they always appear next to the corresponding HP gauge. These are fully introduced in the Walkthrough chapter of this guide, as they become available in the game.

EXPLORATION BASICS

MOVEMENT & NAVIGATION

Travelling from destination to destination in Final Fantasy XIII is extremely simple. The mini-map in the top right-hand corner of the screen features a compass marker on its outer edge. This always points towards your next destination. In more complicated environments, where perhaps the path doubles back on itself or there are two routes, you can also take a quick look at in-game maps by pressing ⊜/⊗, or study those printed in the Walkthrough chapter of this guide. As a general rule, though, you will find that it is combat encounters, not navigation, that complicate the process of moving from one waypoint to the next.

You will soon encounter swirling blue and red indicators. The former are used to mark areas where your party members can negotiate obstructions by jumping (Fig. 1). This occurs automatically once you move to preset positions. Red indicators highlight devices (such as control consoles) that must be used to progress further.

1

When present, other members of your active party will move independently of the character under your control, and may run ahead to scout or linger in a particular spot when the mood takes them. Your allies will not initiate combat or operate points of interactivity, so feel free to enjoy their company without feeling obliged to worry about their whims or whereabouts. Should you become separated from a companion, you will be automatically reunited once you enter combat – so there's no need to backtrack if you discover that you have left someone behind.

Party members may also engage in short conversations or pass comment on the current situation outside of cutscenes. These short snatches of dialogue are not central to the storyline, but it's nice to catch them when they happen. If you don't want to miss a single spoken line, remember to pause the game during breaks, however brief they may be. Pausing also freezes the game clock, which is useful if you would like the in-game timer available in the lower-left corner of the Main Menu to reflect the actual amount of time that you have played for.

2

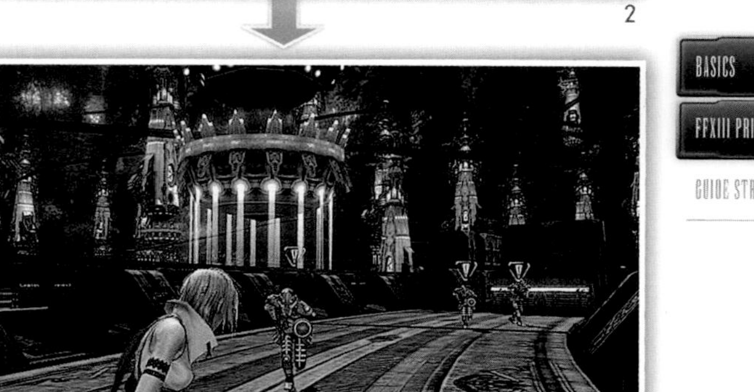

3

ENEMY ENCOUNTERS

Like its immediate forebear, Final Fantasy XIII eschews the old series tradition of random battles, with the vast majority of assailants appearing in plain view as you move on the field map (Fig. 2). Major combat encounters, however, are usually preceded by a cutscene. You'll soon learn to recognize when the placement of a Save Station at the end of a map area foreshadows such events.

There is a distinctive sound effect whenever you move within detection range of an enemy, or group of enemies; you will also notice the mini-map flash briefly. While you walk or run within this (invisible) zone, adversaries may notice your presence at any time. Once they espy the character under your control, another sound effect will be played, and special "warning" icons (Fig. 3) will appear over their heads (or whichever curious appendage is located in that general vicinity). At this point, they will move in to initiate combat. If you manage to take them by surprise, though, you can instead start the battle with a very profitable preemptive strike. This feature is properly introduced in the early pages of the Walkthrough chapter.

It's worth noting that combat with every enemy you meet is not mandatory. You can, if you wish, run past certain slow-moving assailants and escape their active range. Some will not be able to attack if your character is positioned at a different elevation, or is located behind a barrier of some description. That said, it's generally wise to confront the vast majority of prospective opponents you encounter. Winning battles leads to the reward of Spoils, post-battle rewards that may include valuable equipment and items. At a later date, victories also contribute towards character growth.

Save Stations

To store your current progress, you must interact with a Save Station (Fig. 4) and follow onscreen prompts. These devices are encountered at regular intervals, so you will rarely be much further than ten minutes away from the next one. Save Stations are also your only opportunity to buy and sell items and equipment via the "Shop" option. This becomes available from an early point in the story, with the number of available retail networks expanding as you progress. You will also eventually acquire the ability to upgrade weapons and accessories at these sites.

4

5

Treasure Spheres may also contain cold, hard cash. Unlike many other games in the Final Fantasy series, you do not obtain Gil automatically after combat encounters. In fact, finding raw currency is a fairly unusual event. Instead, your primary source of Gil is through selling plunder obtained through successful battles, or objects found in Treasure Spheres. Knowing when this is appropriate, and which stores offer valuable investments, is something that we cover in the Walkthrough chapter.

Treasure Spheres & Gil

Venturing slightly off the beaten path whenever you espy a curious cul-de-sac or alternative route may lead you to discover hidden Treasure Spheres (Fig. 5). Though not always concealed from view, these containers are a great source of equipment and items. They may also contain rare components, which have no use during early chapters, but become very important later in the game when they are used to upgrade equipment.

The maps in our Walkthrough chapter feature the locations of every last container. However, for players who would like to complete their first playthrough with minimal assistance, we would suggest the following tried-and-tested Treasure Sphere hunting tips:

- When presented with two paths, check the Map screen by pressing □/X and explore dead-ends first. These regularly feature a Treasure Sphere at the end.
- If entering a new area, you may sometimes find a Treasure Sphere located behind your starting position.
- Whenever there are two routes that lead to the same location, be sure to scrutinize both for hidden loot caches.
- Note that certain Treasure Spheres that lie off the beaten path may be guarded by an assortment of enemies – or, worse, be the site of an ambush by high-powered assailants. (Note that the latter scenario is rare during the first half of the story.)

Skipping Cutscenes

While most players will want to see every last story development, there are instances (particularly after failing a difficult boss battle) where the prospect of rewatching a lengthy cinematic sequence is less than enticing. To skip cutscenes, press START/▶ and then tap SELECT/◀.

COMBAT BASICS

INTRODUCTION

Final Fantasy XIII employs a new and quite radical interpretation of the classic Active Time Battle (ATB) system, which combines the tactical possibilities of a turn-based design with the dynamic flow and visual feel of an action game.

One of the most noteworthy changes is that you only have direct control over the current party leader during combat: any AI partners (if present) will always move and attack independently. You gain a degree of influence over their behavior once the powerful and intuitive Paradigm system is introduced (which we will cover later, both in the Walkthrough chapter and in a dedicated section of the Strategy & Analysis chapter) but, for now, your companions will always attack the target that is the current focus of your character's attention.

Another new feature is that the ATB gauge is now separated into segments, each of which is "spent" individually (Fig. 6). By pressing (△)/(Y) when at least one section is full, you can launch an early (yet truncated) attack. Most actions stacked via the Auto-battle option or Abilities menu take a single segment of the ATB gauge, but some (such as the Blitz physical attack used by Lightning) can take two or more. Different characters have varying numbers of ATB gauge segments, with additional sections introduced as they grow in power.

The number of attacks and abilities at your disposal is extremely small when the story first begins, but the options soon expand as you meet tougher and more sophisticated opponents. To avoid potential spoilers, this section is designed to act as a generalized introduction to key features of the battle system. Rest assured, though, that our exhaustive Walkthrough chapter will offer guidance on each new feature as it appears.

6

A simplistic step-by-step map of a combat encounter at a very early stage of the game would look something like this:

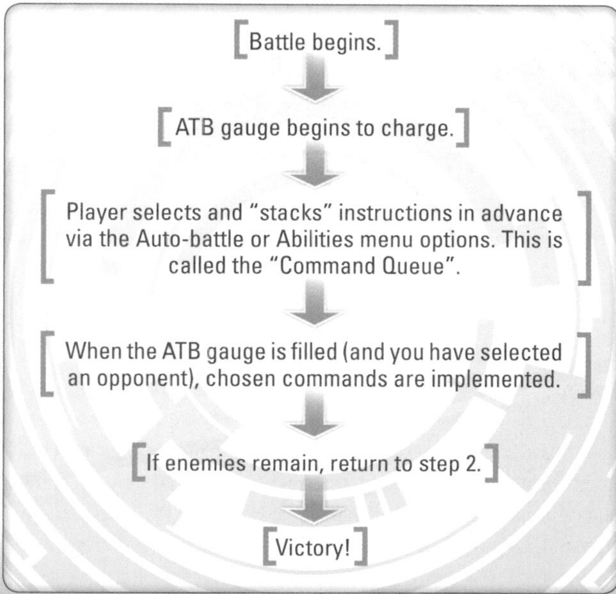

Battle begins.
ATB gauge begins to charge.
Player selects and "stacks" instructions in advance via the Auto-battle or Abilities menu options. This is called the "Command Queue".
When the ATB gauge is filled (and you have selected an opponent), chosen commands are implemented.
If enemies remain, return to step 2.
Victory!

Battle Menu

Once a battle starts and the ATB gauge begins to charge, the Battle Menu will appear (Fig. 7). During the first gameplay chapter, you will encounter the following options:

BATTLE MENU

Auto-battle	Automatically stacks the most appropriate attacks or actions for the targeted enemy.
Abilities	Choose abilities and attacks manually.
Items	Use objects – for example, a Potion to restore HP ("hit points") to your entire team, or a Phoenix Down to revive a fallen companion. Using the Items menu does not consume portions of the ATB gauge, but will nonetheless lead to a temporary break in your attack cycle.

After picking a menu option (and any subsequent selections), you will usually be directed to pick a target – an opponent for any form of assault, or a party member for a healing or support action. Your default approach should (with relatively few exceptions) be to focus on one enemy at a time, usually moving from weakest to strongest unless the situation calls for another strategy.

One of the first steps all players should take is to embrace the powerful and intuitive **Auto-battle** command. In essence, you could view it as a highly streamlined, automated version of the Gambits system used in FFXII. It picks what it believes to be the most appropriate selection of attacks for each particular enemy type and, by and large, does an excellent job of it.

Some players may recoil at the prospect of handing so much control of their tactics to the AI, but the sheer pace of battles actually makes regular use of the Auto-battle feature a time-saving necessity. This is especially true when additional systems introduced as you progress through the story add new and intriguing layers of complexity to combat. While early encounters do seem to comprise an awful lot of single button presses, rest assured that battles become much more involved as the hours fly by.

As a general rule, the **Abilities** menu is most useful when you have a very specific plan of attack that you suspect Auto-battle may not support. If, as a staunch traditionalist, you do choose to play exclusively via use of the Abilities menu, note that there is a special toggle on the Settings screen that enables you to specify that option as your default selection whenever the Battle Menu appears. You should also note that, by holding Ⓛ➡/✥➡, you can select "Repeat" to perform your previous set of commands.

The **Items** menu is unusual in that using objects does not consume any part of your current ATB bar – though, naturally, there is a brief pause as the ensuing action is performed. For this reason, it's usually prudent to access the menu straight after an attack sequence to make good use of time you might otherwise spend watching the ATB gauge fill.

HP, Healing & Game Over

Always pay close attention to the current state of HP gauges for all active party members. These change in color from green to yellow as damage is sustained, and eventually to an urgent red when reduced to a critical level. You will also notice the introduction of an angry red hue to the display when a character's HP is dangerously low (Fig. 8). During the opening stages of the adventure, you should consider this visual effect your final prompt to visit the Items menu to use a Potion. Unless a battle is almost at its end, it's usually wise to begin healing when the bar is still yellow.

Should the party leader (the individual under your direct control) be incapacitated, you will be taken to the Game Over screen. Selecting "Retry" will return you to a checkpoint just prior to the combat encounter, which is a great opportunity to adjust your equipment, apply upgrades (once available) and, naturally, formulate a new strategy.

When party members other than the leader are beaten into submission, the consequences are far less dire. You can either use a Phoenix Down via the Items menu to restore them to near full health if their presence is still required, or take a risk and attempt to finish the battle without them if you are fighting weaker opponents. Note that all party members are automatically revived (if necessary) and have their HP fully replenished once a battle ends.

Should a battle go disastrously awry at an early stage, you can press START/▶ and then tap SELECT/◀ to select the Retry option. This acts in much the same way as a visit to the Game Over screen (in that you restart at a checkpoint not too far away), and enables you to abandon a lost cause well in advance of an undignified defeat.

7

8

9

Battle Results & Spoils

Unless you are paying an unfortunate visit to the Game Over screen, each confrontation ends with a visit to the Battle Results (Fig. 9) and Spoils pages. Both warrant a brief introduction here.

Final Fantasy XIII features a new and novel Score system for each encounter, with an accompanying star rating acting as the true measure of your performance. Your grade at the Battle Results screen is primarily determined by the speed at which you slay aggressors. Beat opponents safely within a Target Time, and you can expect to obtain the full five stars. However, flounder awkwardly and at length, as you struggle to discern a particular adversary's weakness, and you might not receive any stars at all.

We will, of course, unveil the secrets of the underlying system later in the guide. Items obtained after combat will often be components (which are used at a future point to upgrade weapons and accessories), but you may also obtain useful items (particularly Phoenix Downs and Potions) and, on occasion, accessories and weapons.

CHARACTER EVOLUTION

In yet another departure from series mainstays, Final Fantasy XIII dispenses with the classic EXP system. For a fairly lengthy section of the early story you will experience very little character progression or growth (with the exception of narrative developments in cutscenes, of course). Without spoiling any surprises, though, we can assure you that you do eventually get to involve yourself in the development of your party, both through the spending of points to enhance abilities, and through acquiring and upgrading weapons and accessories.

For this reason, those accustomed to power-leveling should wait until later chapters before they even consider backtracking or picking fights with profit as the sole focus. We'll let you know when such activities are appropriate in the Walkthrough chapter.

WALKTHROUGH

This huge chapter is the heart of the guide, offering a considered blend of step-by-step guidance with in-depth advice and analysis. For those who wish to complete a first playthrough with a bare minimum of assistance, it can be used sparingly to find quick-fix solutions for tough battles, character development advice, and valuable tips on new gameplay features whenever they are introduced. Equally, though, it's also perfect for those who wish to plot the most optimal route through this huge adventure.

Gameplay Spoiler Level: Low

Story Spoiler Level: Low

STRATEGY & ANALYSIS

Designed primarily with later playthroughs in mind (but also doubtlessly a great temptation for those who seek first-time perfection), the Strategy & Analysis chapter exposes the hidden mechanics that drive Final Fantasy XIII. From practical advice (such as advanced battle tactics and character growth) to fascinating trivia, it combines expert advice with a wide variety of insights into how assorted gameplay systems actually work. Be warned: unless directed to visit sections of this chapter by page references in the Walkthrough, you may find that it reveals more than you care to know during your first run through the story.

Gameplay Spoiler Level: High

Story Spoiler Level: Low

INVENTORY

This chapter offers nothing less than an unabridged guide to every collectible item in Final Fantasy XIII. It also features complete lists of goods available for purchase from retail networks and – perhaps most importantly – demystifies and deconstructs the hugely important weapon and accessory upgrade system.

Gameplay Spoiler Level: Medium

Story Spoiler Level: Low

BESTIARY

From stock assailants to fearsome bosses, unusual opponents to extremely rare monsters, the Bestiary chapter offers a phenomenally detailed account of all enemies in Final Fantasy XIII. Need advance warning of a particular enemy's principle weakness, or the probability of obtaining a coveted component from a specific opponent? Such information, and *much* more, can be found in this authoritative reference section.

Gameplay Spoiler Level: Medium

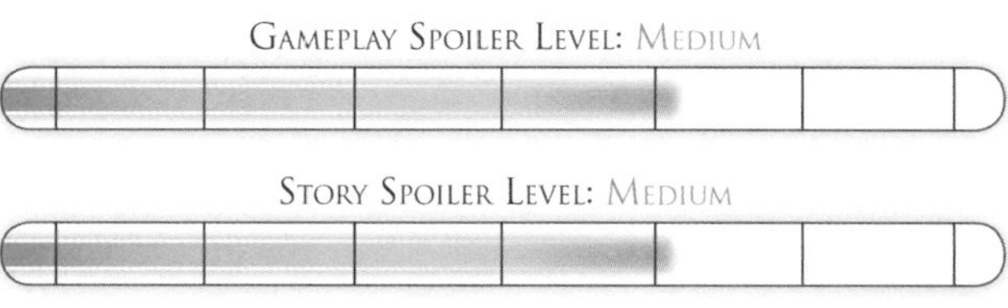

Story Spoiler Level: Medium

EXTRAS

Finally, the Extras chapter offers a round-up of features not covered elsewhere, such as a recap of side-quests, a checklist for Achievements and Trophies, and additional secrets. For this reason, we strongly advise that players avoid this section of the guide until they have completed their first playthrough.

Gameplay Spoiler Level: High

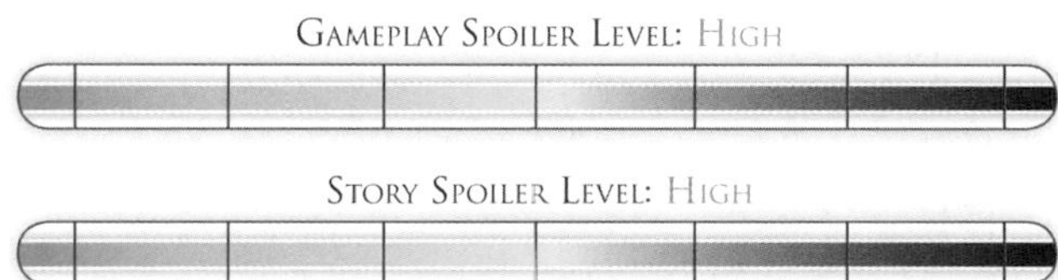

Story Spoiler Level: High

VERTICAL TAB

The vertical tab on the right-hand margin of each double-page spread is a navigational tcol designed to help you find your way around the guide. The top section lists individual chapters, while the lower section highlights which section of a chapter you are currently reading.

INDEX

If you are looking for specific information, our alphabetical index is just what you need. Simply search for the keyword you're wondering about, and turn to the relevant page number.

WALKTHROUGH

This chapter has been designed for first-time players and devoted fans of the Final Fantasy series alike, offering all the assistance and insight you will need to enjoy every last moment of the game. With story and situation spoilers kept to a bare minimum, you can safely use the walkthrough whether you need an occasional helping hand, or seek detailed step-by-step advice for a "perfect" playthrough.

Before you go any further, please take a few seconds to familiarize yourself with the structure of this chapter. The sample layout presented here illustrates all of the helpful features that will be available to you while using the walkthrough.

CHAPTER 01

THE HANGING EDGE

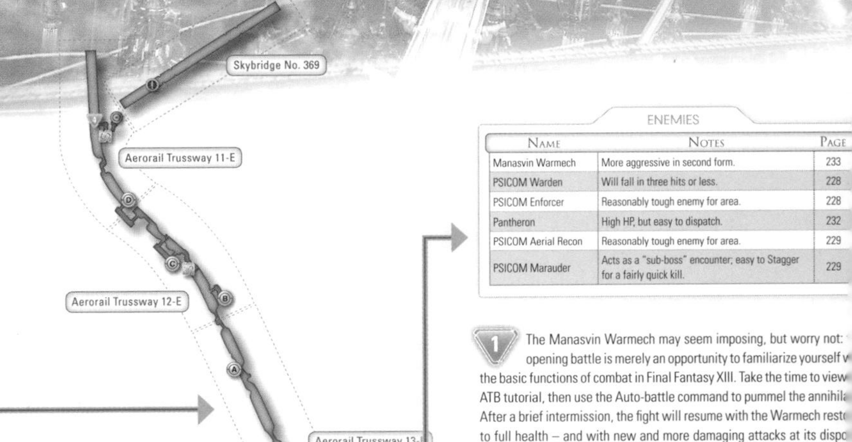

ENEMIES

Name	Notes	Page
Manasvin Warmech	More aggressive in second form.	233
PSICOM Warden	Will fall in three hits or less.	228
PSICOM Enforcer	Reasonably tough enemy for area.	228
Pantheron	High HP, but easy to dispatch.	232
PSICOM Aerial Recon	Reasonably tough enemy for area.	229
PSICOM Marauder	Acts as a "sub-boss" encounter; easy to Stagger for a fairly quick kill.	229

1 The Manasvin Warmech may seem imposing, but worry not: opening battle is merely an opportunity to familiarize yourself w the basic functions of combat in Final Fantasy XIII. Take the time to view ATB tutorial, then use the Auto-battle command to pummel the annihil After a brief intermission, the fight will resume with the Warmech rest to full health – and with new and more damaging attacks at its dispo Rapid use of the Auto-battle command (Fig. 1) will enable you to wh down its HP gauge before it can knock out Lightning.

TREASURE SPHERES

Sphere	Contents	Type
A	Potion	Item
B	Potion (x2)	Item
C	Iron Bangle	Accessory
D	50 Gil	Gil

20

1 Maps: Every double-page spread begins with a map that relates directly to the tips and advice covered on those pages. Designed as an aid to easy navigation, our maps feature all collectable treasures (as denoted by lettered icons) and other points of interest.

2 Treasure Spheres: For each location map, a table details the contents of all Treasure Spheres, with the object type represented by an easily identifiable icon. To locate a treasure, simply look for its lettered icon on the corresponding area map.

Icon	Represents
(item icon)	Item
(weapon icon)	Weapon
(accessory icon)	Accessory
(component icon)	Component
(gil icon)	Gil

3 Enemies: With each location map, you will also find a table listing all enemy types that you will encounter in the region covered. Read the corresponding notes for a quick description of each creature's strengths and weaknesses. If you need more information, the page references will lead you to detailed enemy data sheets in the Bestiary chapter.

4 **Main walkthrough:** The walkthrough has been designed to guide readers on an efficient and enjoyable path through the main storyline, offering just the right amount of information required to successfully beat every enemy encounter of consequence. We have also taken steps to avoid all unnecessary plot spoilers. For maximum clarity, the walkthrough text is structured in paragraphs that begin with reference numbers. These numbers also appear on the corresponding maps, acting as "walkthrough waypoints" to enable you to easily discover which challenges await in the indicated areas.

5 **Analysis, tactics and points of interest:** You will also find additional insights covering tactics, "power-leveling" suggestions, trivia and feature introductions throughout the walkthrough.

6 **Secrets and side-quests:** Final Fantasy XIII's optional challenges are all introduced as they are encountered in the game. All side-quests or non-essential activities that we recommend players should tackle immediately appear in box-outs on the appropriate pages. Those that are best left for endgame play are covered in a dedicated Side-Quests section at the end of the chapter.

MAP LEGEND

Most icons used on our maps should be instantly recognizable, as they are identical to those used in the game itself. If in doubt, you can refer back to this legend at any time.

Icon	Represents
	Starting Point
	Objective
	Walkthrough Waypoint
- - - - - - - -	Zone Outline
- - - - - - - -	Zone Link
	Stairway
	Save Station
	Treasure Sphere
	Point of Interest
	Temporary Obstruction
	Cie'th Stone
	Cie'th Waystone

THE HANGING EDGE

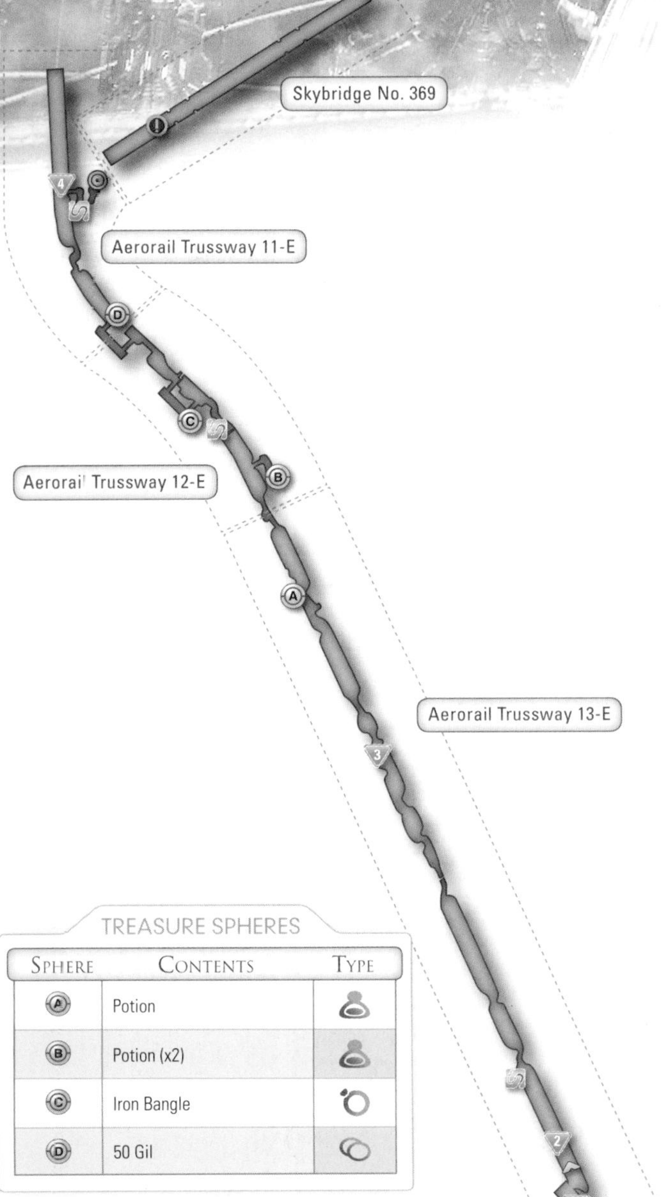

TREASURE SPHERES

Sphere	Contents	Type
A	Potion	
B	Potion (x2)	
C	Iron Bangle	
D	50 Gil	

ENEMIES

Name	Notes	Page
Manasvin Warmech	More aggressive in second form.	233
PSICOM Warden	Will fall in three hits or less.	228
PSICOM Enforcer	Reasonably tough enemy for area.	228
Pantheron	High HP, but easy to dispatch.	232
PSICOM Aerial Recon	Reasonably tough enemy for area.	229
PSICOM Marauder	Acts as a "sub-boss" encounter; easy to Stagger for a fairly quick kill.	229

1 The Manasvin Warmech may seem imposing, but worry not: this opening battle is merely an opportunity to familiarize yourself with the basic functions of combat in Final Fantasy XIII. Take the time to view the ATB tutorial, then use the Auto-battle command to pummel the annihilator. After a brief intermission, the fight will resume with the Warmech restored to full health – and with new and more damaging attacks at its disposal. Rapid use of the Auto-battle command (Fig. 1) will enable you to whittle down its HP gauge before it can knock out Lightning.

1

2 Run over to the Save Station, and select Save to create a new slot and store your progress. Move along the Aerorail platform, following the compass marker on the mini-map until you reach two soldiers, then run over to them to initiate combat. This may happen automatically if one of them makes contact with Lightning first. The two PSICOM Wardens are very weak, and will fall in no more than a few swift attacks. Just beyond them lies a seemingly impassable obstruction (Fig. 2). However, the nearby blue, swirling marker indicates that Lightning and Sazh can easily leap over this. Simply run into it to begin the climb and reach the other side.

2

3 Fight the next group of soldiers (this time including more resilient PSICOM Enforcers), then continue along the platform until you see a bobbing metallic device. This is a Treasure Sphere (Fig. 3): approach it and press ⊗/Ⓐ to obtain its contents. All Treasure Spheres are marked on area maps displayed throughout this walkthrough, so unless there is a specific need to talk about one – such as enemy guards, an ambush or notable rewards – we'll usually assume that you will diligently loot each one without further instruction.

3

4 Fight your way to the end of Aerorail Trussway 11-E where, after a cutscene, you will encounter three Pantherons and a PSICOM Warden. This is arguably the first battle where there is a very real danger of Lightning being knocked out if all four enemies focus their attacks on her. If you notice her HP gauge slip into the low yellow area (and especially so if red), quickly select the Items menu and use a Potion. Remember: you will invariably be taken to the Game Over screen if the party leader (that is, the character currently under your command) is incapacitated during combat. Judicious use of restoratives will always take less time than restarting from a prior checkpoint.

Once the battle is over, leap onto the nearby platform, then activate the control console to proceed. When you reach the PSICOM Marauder and his two cohorts, we strongly recommend that you carefully study and digest the excellent tutorial on the Chain Gauge and Stagger systems. The onscreen instructions will tell you all you need to know about this important aspect of combat in FFXIII at this stage of the story. For now, it's enough that you know that building Chain Combos by maintaining a steady flow of attacks (and inflicting the temporary Stagger status – Fig. 4) is the key to beating most enemies. We'll return to the subject to examine it in greater detail when all of its features are unlocked in the game.

4

Accessories

The third Treasure Sphere you encounter contains an Iron Bangle – the first accessory you receive in the game. Accessories are special pieces of equipment that confer a variety of bonuses on the wearer, from special resistances to improved attacking capabilities. In this instance, the Iron Bangle increases the user's total HP by 50 – a boost that you should give to party leader Lightning straight away. Visit the Equipment menu to place it in her single accessory slot.

Using the Blitz Attack

Blitz is a physical attack that inflicts damage on all enemies within a limited radius. It costs two segments of Lightning's ATB gauge. The early battle against two Pantherons and a single PSICOM Warden demonstrates how it is best used. As they are locked in close formation once combat begins, Lightning can inflict damage on all three in one hit, draining more total HP across three enemies than two standard Attack commands would on a single target. However, a Blitz assault on a solitary opponent is wasteful – though slightly stronger than a single Attack command, it is definitely less powerful than two. The Auto-battle AI is usually efficient at recognizing situations where Blitz is appropriate.

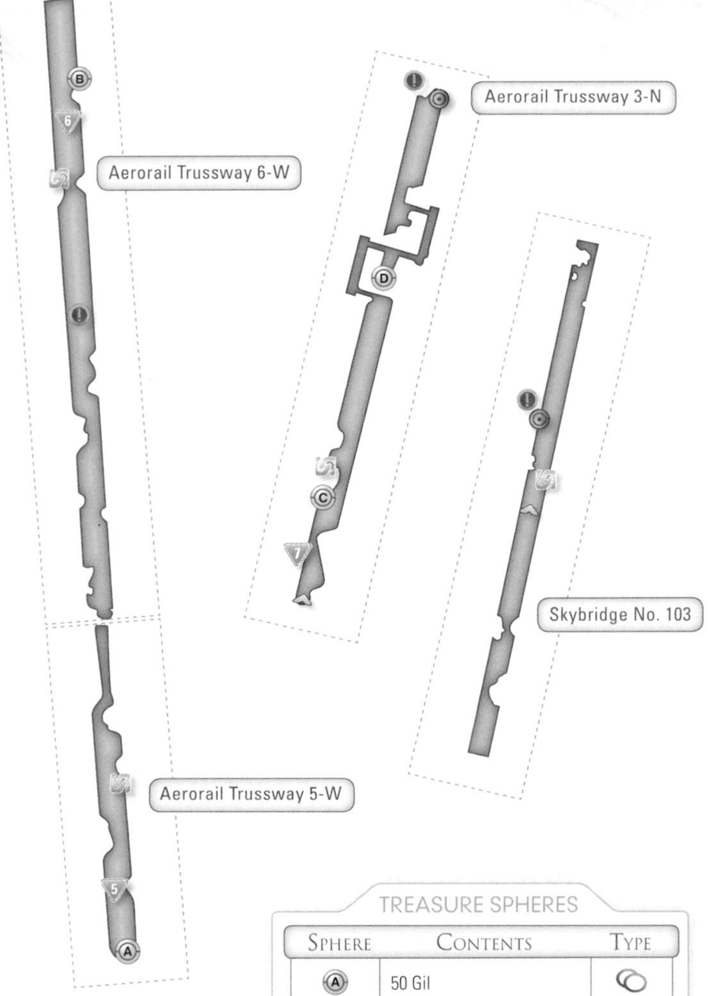

TREASURE SPHERES

Sphere	Contents	Type
A	50 Gil	
B	Iron Bangle	
C	Power Circle	
D	100 Gil	

ENEMIES

Name	Notes	Page
PSICOM Enforcer	Reasonably tough for area.	228
PSICOM Warden	Can be dispatched with great ease; good initial target whenever present.	228
Pantheron	High HP, but easily Staggered for a fairly quick kill.	232
Beta Behemoth	Sub-boss encounter; high HP, but difficulty reduced by presence of high-powered allies.	233
Myrmidon	Has strong attacks that damage both party members; be prepared to heal before the battle ends.	230
PSICOM Aerial Recon	Reasonably tough for area.	229

5 After the cinematic interludes, play resumes with a jump to a parallel storyline involving a new character known as Snow. For the time being, he will act as party leader. This switching of primary characters happens a lot during the opening chapters of the game. Run forward and save before scaling the debris; once play resumes, Snow will be accompanied by two allies (Fig. 5). Fight your way along the trussway until you reach a group of refugees from the destroyed train.

5

6

6 After the cutscene, collect the Iron Bangle from the nearby Treasure Sphere and equip it on Snow, then battle through to the waypoint marker where you will encounter a Beta Behemoth. This substantial monster is more striking than dangerous, especially as you have an ally poised to heal Snow once his HP falls below a certain level. Save your progress when prompted to do so. The story then briefly returns to Lightning and Sazh with a major enemy encounter. This time, however, you will need to be responsible for your own HP gauge, and should need to heal at least once using a Potion before the Myrmidon falls (Fig. 6).

7 Back to Snow, and you immediately face the largest (and strongest) group of generic opponents encountered so far. You should by now be acquiring a good sense of when it's appropriate to heal, and when it's better to push for a swift victory; the former is probably most prudent in this instance. Examine the vehicle (Fig. 7) once you reach the waypoint marker to initiate a cutscene, and a transition to a pair of new characters: Hope (who acts as leader), and Vanille. Once again, examine the vehicle when you reach the destination marked on your mini-map to continue.

7

Inventory Management

Items, equipment not in use, Gil and, eventually, components (used to upgrade weapons and accessories) are actually shared between different parties. Whether the story's main protagonists are separated by meters or miles, you can safely view all accumulated resources as actually "belonging" to you, the player. There is one notable exception. When the action switches to a new character or party, accessories worn by absent friends cannot be unequipped or otherwise transferred to your new group. If there is an instance where an accessory might be useful in a particular situation, we'll try to warn you well in advance.

Enemy Intel

Press R1/RB to view information on opponents during battles. On first encounter most fields will be blank, but additional data will appear during combat. After a few meetings with a particular enemy type, their page should be complete. Many of the facts presented have little relevance at this stage of the story, but you can still use them to identify weaknesses and formulate tactics. For example, enemy party members with low HP might be ripe for early dispatch (reducing the number of weapons directed against you), while an assailant with powerful attacks but easily Staggered, flanked by weak cohorts, might be a more astute choice of first target in another situation.

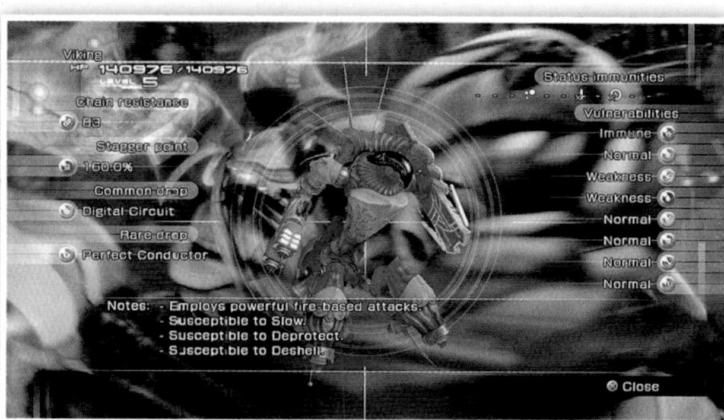

Potions

Potions are both plentiful and powerful at this stage of the adventure, fully restoring the HP gauges of all party members in combat. Don't feel the need to be frugal with them. If supporting characters are knocked out, a Phoenix Down will revive them instantly with an almost full health bar. These are less common, though. If you are confident that you can beat opponents without reviving a stricken ally, it's better to do just that. Remember that use of the Items menu does not consume segments of your ATB gauge.

Miscellany

- Snow's Hand Grenade attack works in a similar way to Lightning's Blitz – it's an area-effect physical assault that costs two ATB gauge segments, and is best employed when a group of enemies are standing in close proximity.
- Without wanting to burst anyone's bubble, the fact that you are almost certainly receiving a full five-star rating at each visit to the Battle Results screen is not especially meaningful. This feature only grows in importance when you reach Chapter 03. The principle calculation behind the score awarded is how quickly you dispatch all enemies. We'll return to this subject later in the guide, once the tactical options available to you begin to expand and enemies grow in strength and abilities, making it a far greater challenge to consistently beat the Target Time.
- The Datalog (accessed via the Main Menu) enables you to study intelligence acquired on different enemy types, but also features interesting entries that develop the FFXIII backstory. You will also find summaries of significant plot events that are updated at regular milestones.

THE PULSE VESTIGE

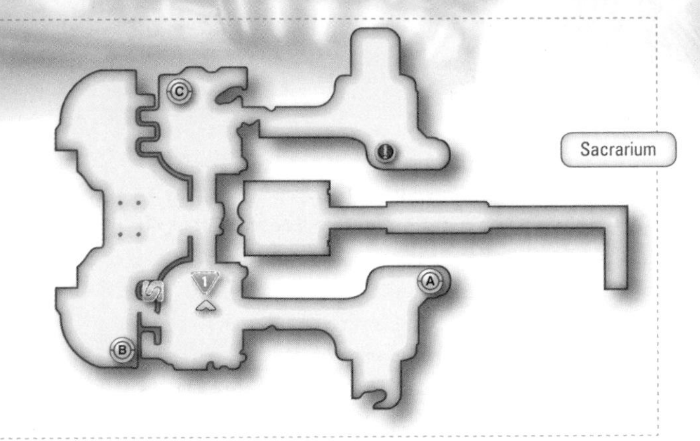

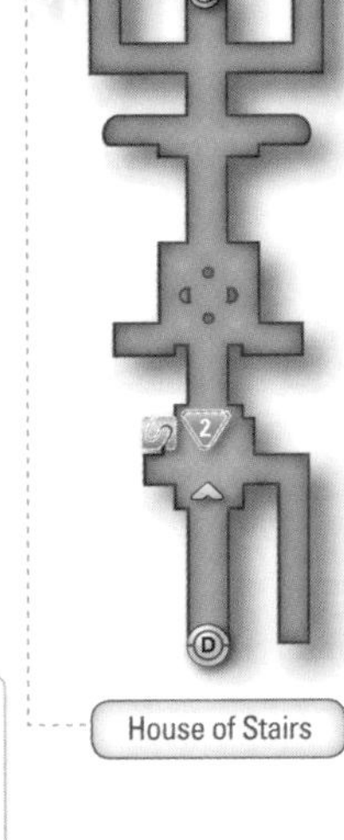

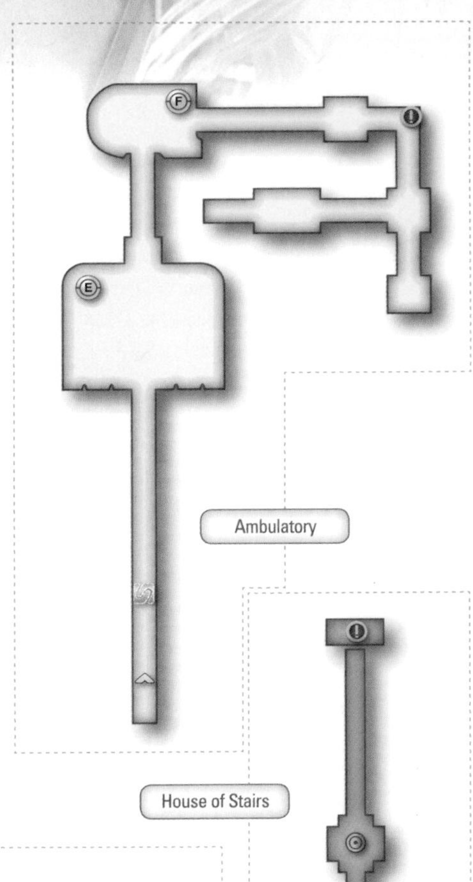

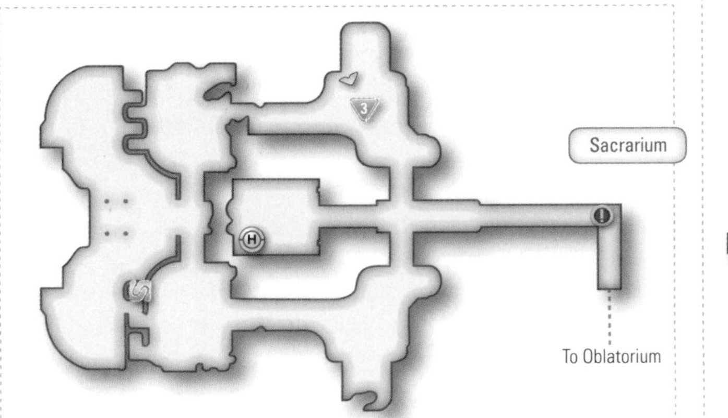

ENEMIES

Name	Notes	Page
Pantheron	Easily Staggered; mildly dangerous in large numbers.	232
Zwerg Scandroid	Limited detection ability makes preemptive strikes easy; very low HP.	232
Myrmidon	Tough enemy for area; dangerous if it focuses attacks on a single party member.	230

TREASURE SPHERES

Sphere	Contents	Type
A	30 Gil	
B	Potion (x4)	
C	Iron Bangle	
D	Potion (x2)	
E	Phoenix Down	
F	Gladius	
G	Potion (x2)	
H	Fortisol	

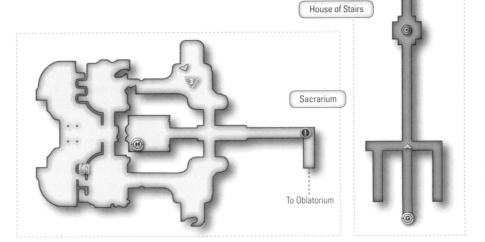

1 Once Hope and Vanille reach their destination, note that Vanille is now the party leader. Dispatch the sole Pantheron who foolishly chooses to greet them, then, after detouring to the container near the crashed vehicle, try to open each Treasure Sphere in turn on your way to the waypoint marker. There are no enemies in this area who will pose any real threat. You will also find that the Zwerg Scandroids, with their narrow field of vision, are ripe for devastating preemptive strikes (Fig. 1).

1

2 The story briefly returns to Snow for a short journey to a waypoint marker with one inconsequential battle. Activate the device when prompted to shift the focus of the action to Lightning and Sazh. Clear the area of Pantherons and Zwerg Scandroids, then attack the more dangerous Myrmidon. Dive straight in, but be ready to use a Potion to heal midway through the battle if required. After dispatching the enemies on the next level up, collect the Gladius from the Treasure Sphere, and equip it on Lightning to boost her Strength.

For the final battle before the waypoint marker (a Myrmidon supported by a Pantheron), you may wish to use a Deceptisol Shroud beforehand (Fig. 2), then dispatch the bigger opponent first for an easy fight.

2

3 After a brief interlude with Snow on the House of Stairs map (just defeat the small group of enemies, then activate the device to summon a platform), the story returns to Vanille and Hope. You have already explored most of the Sacrarium map, so all that remains to do here is to open the fourth and final Treasure Sphere of the area, then head through the large door (Fig. 3) to reach the Oblatorium.

Shrouds

Shrouds are a special class of single-use item that confers temporary benefits on your current party. They must be activated just prior to a confrontation: you cannot do so during battle. To use a Shroud, call up the menu at any time while exploring by pressing L1/LB. Their effects are temporary, so be sure to engage opponents before they dissipate. You will encounter two types during Chapter 02:

- **Deceptisol** shields the party from enemy eyes or senses, enabling you to perform a preemptive strike on potentially dangerous adversaries. It can be used to avoid many battles entirely, though skipping confrontations will cause your party to miss out on vital rewards from the start of Chapter 03.
- **Fortisol** casts various status enhancements on your party from the start of a battle. Status effects play little part in the events of Chapter 02, so for now it's enough to know that Fortisol makes your party faster and stronger.

Shrouds are usually obtained as spoils after battles, though some also appear in Treasure Spheres. They tend to be rare, so try to save them for times when you really need them. You will find advice on when to use Shrouds throughout the walkthrough.

Power Tip: If you wish, you can fight enemies in the Sacrarium area (second visit) with Hope and Vanille to farm for Deceptisol and Fortisol Shrouds, as both are common drops here. To make all opponents respawn, just exit to the Oblatorium then return to the Sacrarium.

Preemptive Strikes

If you can sneak up behind an enemy to stalk them silently, you have a chance to initiate a preemptive strike. When these take place, the current party leader will hit each enemy in turn once combat begins, causing no damage but filling their Chain Gauges to just below maximum. It also causes your party to begin a battle with full ATB gauges. If you are quick to attack, this will enable you to Stagger at least one opponent almost instantaneously – though you should note that the duration of the Stagger status is shorter than when triggered by traditional attacks.

Preemptive strikes are particularly effective against enemies with high HP, and may offer an opportunity to defeat the most threatening foe in a group very quickly. In some instances, it may be more efficient to take the opportunity to cut enemy numbers by defeating foes with low HP first (especially if multiple opponents can be Staggered with the first volley of attacks – Lightning's Blitz ability works well here). The most important thing is to act immediately – any delay will see enemy Chain Gauges drain rapidly, and you will lose your advantage.

3

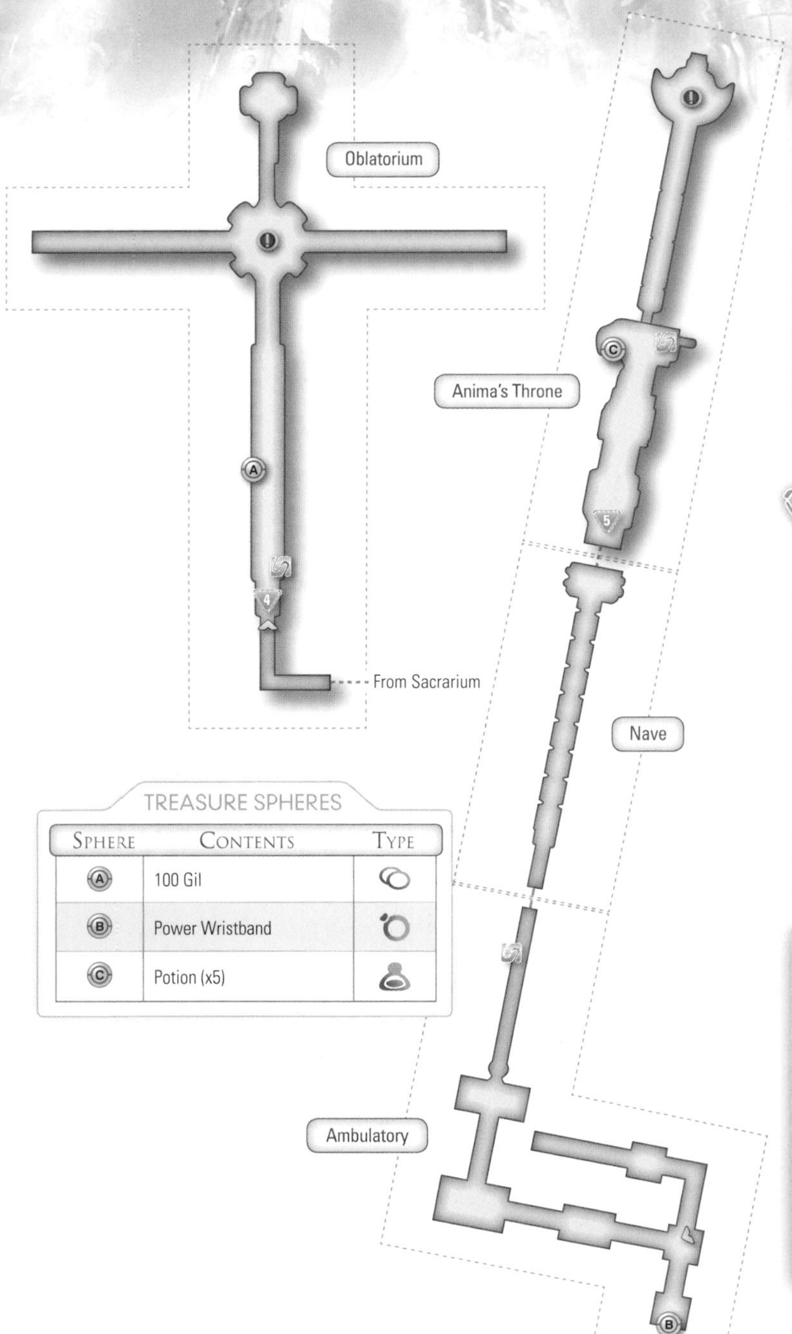

TREASURE SPHERES

Sphere	Contents	Type
A	100 Gil	
B	Power Wristband	
C	Potion (x5)	

ENEMIES

Name	Notes	Page
Pantheron	Easy to Stagger.	232
Ghoul	Slow, but possesses powerful attacks; can be dangerous in larger groups.	243
Ghast	Very high HP for area; uses powerful Fire attack; healing advisable when leader HP falls below 40%.	244
Wight	Low HP, but high attack evade rate.	244
Anima	High HP; becomes more aggressive later in battle.	245
Anima: Left Manipulator	Both act as separate entities during the Anima fight; destroy them to remove Anima's capacity to deal damage.	246
Anima: Right Manipulator		

4 Save your game before you travel to the waypoint marker. After the cutscene, Snow joins Vanille and Hope. The story then returns to Lightning and Sazh. Collect the Power Wristband from the nearby Treasure Sphere. You can equip this on Lightning to provide a notable boost to her Strength stat. Now head up the stairs and fight your way through the Ghouls en route to the destination marker, taking advantage of regular opportunities to launch preemptive strikes. The Ghast encountered later is a much tougher opponent, with a Fire attack that saps in the region of 100 HP. After fighting another sequence of Ghouls as you travel to the waypoint on the Nave map, you will need to confront two Ghasts at once. A quick application of Deceptisol just before you engage them could be a wise move; a swift Blitz attack from Lightning may Stagger them both from the start of the fight (Fig. 4).

4

5 With party leader Lightning accompanied by Snow and Sazh, fight your way through Ghasts and Wights to reach the final waypoint in this chapter. Don't neglect to store your progress at the Save Station before you enter the corridor.

Major Encounter – Anima: As boss encounters go, this is an undemanding confrontation once you know what to do. Target (and destroy) Anima's left and right Manipulators to remove its ability to inflict damage (Fig. 5), then grind away with Auto-battle commands on the main body until the appendages reappear. Anima becomes a little more ferocious when its HP falls below 50%, but will always cease its assaults once both Manipulators have been broken. It should take no more than three "rounds" of limb removal and a couple of Potions to see you safely through the battle.

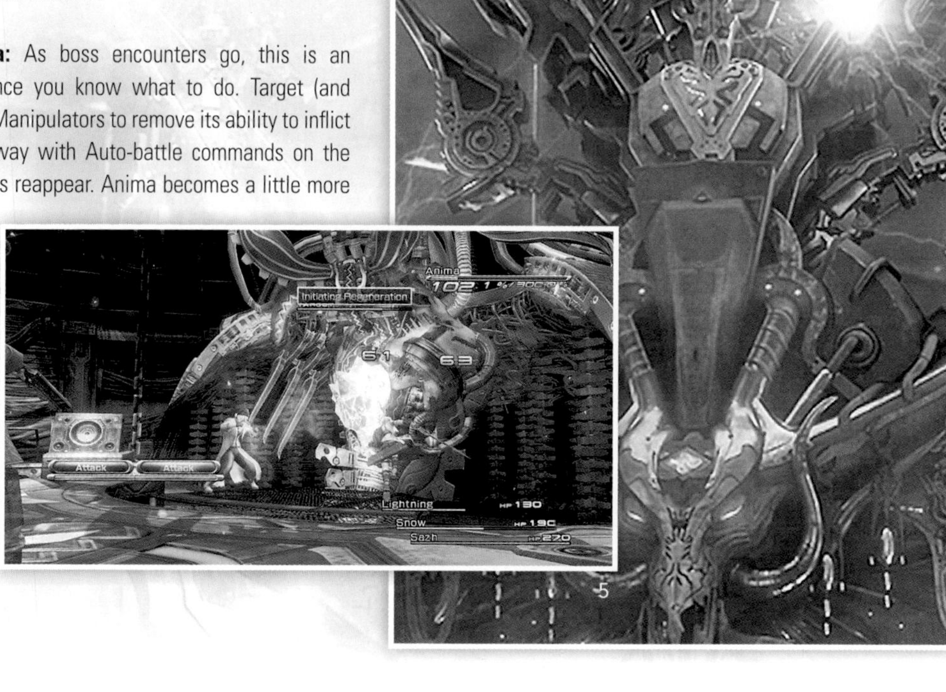

5

Tactics: Useful Button Commands

There are two button commands that will enable you to be much more efficient in combat, spending accumulated ATB gauge segments only where they are needed.

EARLY COMMANDS

To initiate an early attack before the ATB gauge is completely filled, press △/Ⓨ while the Auto-battle option is highlighted, or when you have a command queue in place. This has many applications. The most common is to use it to finish off an enemy with a mere sliver of HP remaining, perhaps to prevent a valedictory attack that might take place were you to sit and wait, or simply to shave a few seconds from the final battle time. Later in the game, this can enable you to cast healing or support magic in the instant it is required. It's also a great way to keep a Chain Bonus active when it might otherwise expire were you to apathetically watch the ATB gauge fill. Note that partially charged segments will always be preserved, and that attacks that require more than one segment (such as Lightning's Blitz assault) will be cancelled outright if the necessary bars are incomplete.

CANCEL COMMANDS

The tide of combat can change with a single enemy attack or unexpected new development, so the ability to revoke a full or partial command queue with ○/Ⓑ is also a great skill to master. Take the battle against Anima, for example. If its damage-dealing Manipulators regenerate at the very moment you commit to three strikes on its body, it makes sense to quickly cancel and choose either appendage as a new target. It can also enable you to use an emergency Potion (or, later, heal by other means).

Components

You will notice that you are acquiring many objects with exotic names from Treasure Spheres and as loot from vanquished opponents. These are components, unique items that are used to upgrade weapons and accessories later in the game. Don't feel tempted to sell them just yet – the Gil you will accrue may be far less useful than their future benefits. We'll offer advice on how best to profit from these objects all along the Walkthrough.

Miscellany

- The **Doctor's Code** accessory is awarded after the fight with Anima. When worn, it doubles the effect of Potions, so it may be worth equipping your party leader with this useful boon in certain situations in future – particularly if they are fighting alone with no other means of healing.

- You may have explored the **Shop** option available at Save Stations, but there's actually nothing of note that you can purchase right now. We'll let you know when genuinely unique or useful goods are made available. For now, it's better to save your limited Gil and stockpile all other items.

- The in-game tutorials freeze the battle clock while active, so don't ever feel the urge to skim-read (and potentially miss important hints and tips) in order to beat a deadline that doesn't exist.

LAKE BRESHA

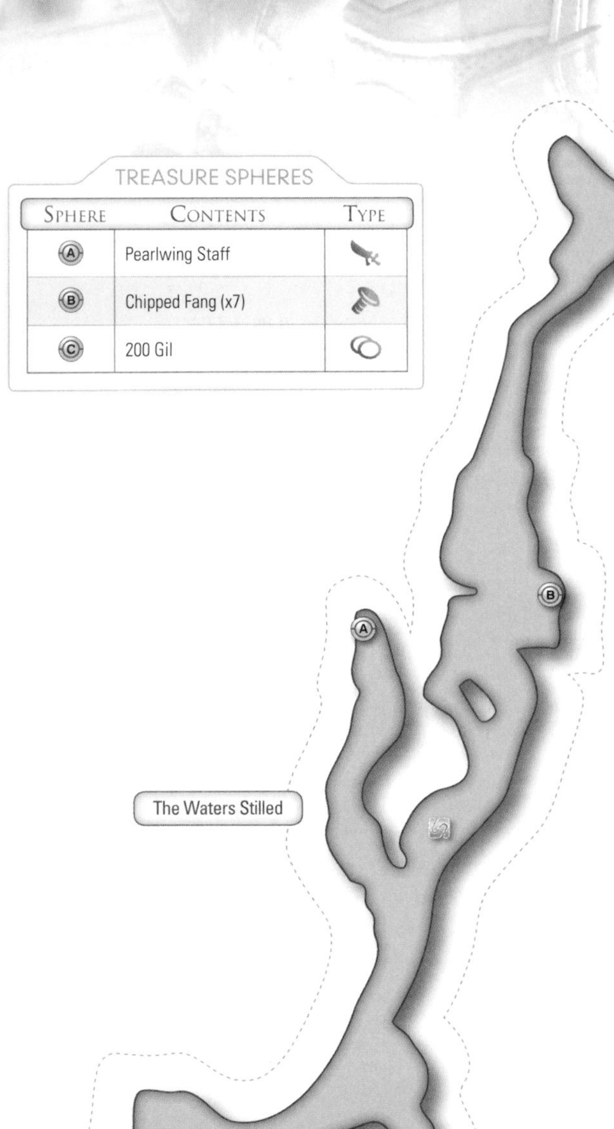

TREASURE SPHERES

Sphere	Contents	Type
A	Pearlwing Staff	
B	Chipped Fang (x7)	
C	200 Gil	

ENEMIES

Name	Notes	Page
Ghast	Both are little more than cannon fodder by this stage.	244
Ghoul		243
Wight	High evasion probability; falls easily once attacks land.	244

1 Pay close attention to the Paradigm tutorial and, once it ends, stay with the Relentless Assault option to obliterate the Ghasts with ease. That task complete, head down the slope for additional cutscenes and an introduction to the Crystarium. Now head left where the path forks (Fig. 1) and fight the four Ghouls and one Ghast to reach a Treasure Sphere containing a Pearlwing Staff that Vanille can use. This offers a slight boost to her Magic rating at the expense of a large drop in her (for the time being, unused) Strength stat. Continue forward until you reach a tutorial.

1

Paradigms & Roles

The introduction of the Paradigm system, character "roles" and several new abilities at the start of Chapter 03 marks a decisive step towards more tactical and challenging combat encounters. Final Fantasy XIII doesn't kick off the training wheels just yet, but this is the point where the shape and texture of the "true" battle engine first becomes apparent.

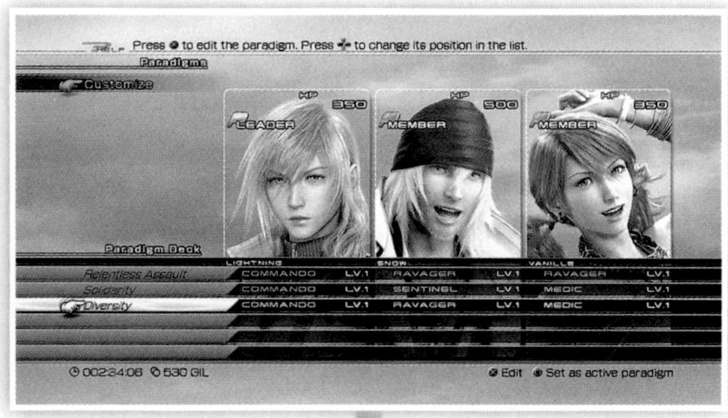

ROLES

As the Paradigm tutorial explains, every character can fight in one of six different roles. For now, only four are used in combat. The two further roles only become relevant during Chapter 04.

- **Commandos** specialize in physical assaults, though some of their abilities may have special properties. As a general rule they inflict greater damage than Ravagers. Their attacks slow down the depletion of the orange "timer" bar in the Chain Gauge, which is an invaluable contribution to the process of Staggering an opponent.

- **Ravagers** use magical attacks, many of which have elemental properties – such as Fire, Wind or Ice. After you have identified an opponent's elemental affinities and vulnerabilities (read "Enemy Intel and Libra" on page 33 for more details on this subject), allies operating as Ravagers (and, of course, a party leader entrusted to Auto-chain) will tailor their choice of spells to cause maximum harm. Their most significant contribution against stronger opponents is to drive their Chain Gauges and Chain Bonuses up at a rapid rate to cause the Stagger status and increase the damage inflicted with every blow.

- **Medics** are healers who use magic to restore HP and, eventually, remove negative status effects. They have no combat capabilities.

- **Sentinels** are the classic tank archetype, using their defensive bonuses and special abilities to attract and bear the brunt of enemy attacks. These "damage sponges" are capable of soaking up withering assaults that might cripple other party members.

PARADIGMS

After their transformation at the climax of Chapter 02, each protagonist can perform one or more roles. Different configurations of character roles are known as Paradigms. Each of these has a distinct tactical purpose, from raw aggression to pure defense, with many shades of gray in between. They are automatically assigned descriptive names that make them easy to identify on sight.

One vitally important feature of the Paradigm system is that characters can only use abilities specific to their current assigned role. For example, Vanille cannot use Cure while operating as a Ravager, or the Aero offensive magic while performing duties as a Medic. Press L1/LB during combat to bring up the Paradigm Deck, then make your selection with ⊗/Ⓐ to perform a Paradigm Shift. Your party leader and allies will automatically change their strategy in accordance with their new roles.

For the majority of this Chapter, you only need use two Paradigms: "Relentless Assault" for attack, and another featuring a Medic for healing. At first, the default Paradigm featuring a healer also has Snow operating as a Sentinel, a setup that is a little too defensive for your needs right now. This is, therefore, a good time to visit the Paradigm menu and create a more suitable configuration of your own. Select an empty slot in the Paradigm Deck and create a new setup that has Lightning as a Commando, Snow as a Ravager and Vanille working as a Medic. This is called "Diversity", and is a staple Paradigm that enables you to heal while maintaining a solid attack. While you're at it, feel free to change the order of your Paradigms as you see fit, and choose your active one.

It's always a good idea to check available setups in your Paradigm deck when your party changes and, if necessary, create new options of your own. Naturally, you should feel free to experiment. We examine Paradigm tactics throughout the walkthrough, and will always suggest useful combinations whenever it may be helpful to have them.

ENEMIES

Name	Notes	Page
Ghast	Both are little more than cannon fodder by this stage.	244
Ghoul		243
Wight	High evasion probability; falls easily once attacks land.	244
PSICOM Warden	Very low HP; may fall to a single blow.	228
Breshan Bass	Dangerous opponent in large groups; high HP; weak against Fire and Lightning elements, but halves Water damage.	235
Pantheron	A temporary inconvenience.	232
PSICOM Enforcer	Can be felled with a stern look.	228
Manasvin Warmech	Has a very distinct battle routine and two very powerful attacks that harm all party members; weak against Lightning and Water elements.	233

TREASURE SPHERES

Sphere	Contents	Type
A	Cie'th Tear (x5)	
B	Silver Bangle	
C	Phoenix Down	
D	50 Gil	
E	Strange Fluid (x8)	
F	Magician's Mark	

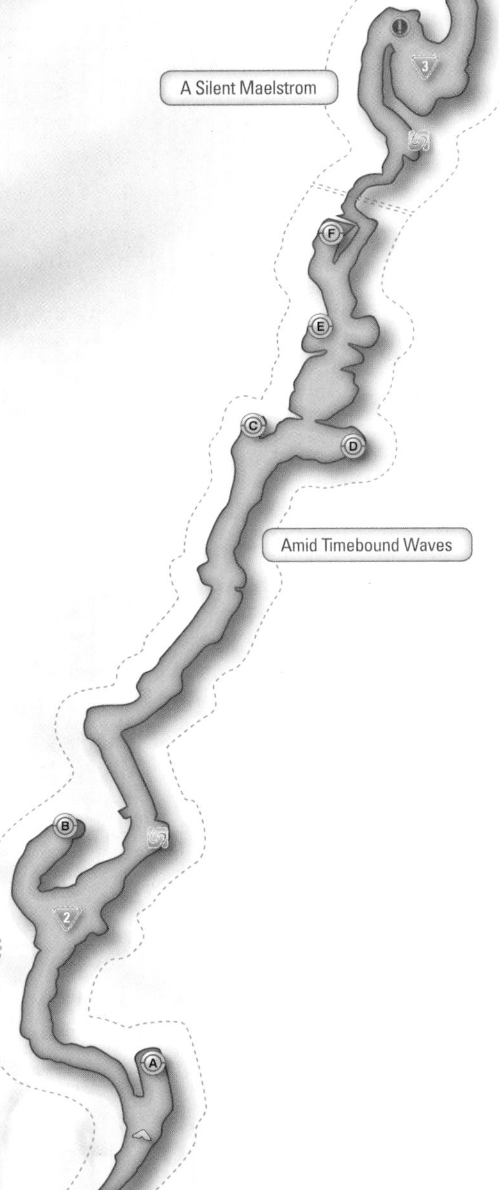

2 Breshan Bass seem an unassuming foe at first sight (Fig. 2), but are very hardy and pack a surprisingly vicious punch. Keep Relentless Assault as your default Paradigm until one or more party members slip below 50% HP, then switch to the newly created Diversity (see page 29) to have Vanille heal the party. Once the bars are back in the green, return to Relentless Assault to maximize your damage-dealing potential.

In the dead end that branches off to the left, there are another four Breshan Bass guarding a Treasure Sphere containing a Silver Bangle. Give this to party leader Lightning to increase her HP. The rest of the journey to the waypoint marker is blissfully uncomplicated. Don't neglect to pick up the Magician's Mark when you pass it – this is an excellent accessory tailor-made for Vanille.

2

3 **Major Encounter – Manasvin Warmech:** Invest CP (see "Using the Crystarium") in character upgrades if you have yet to do so, record your progress at the Save Station, then stride purposefully to the waypoint to meet a Manasvin Warmech. Unlike its comparatively sickly kin that you fought in the opening battle, however, this one has a massive total HP of 32,400 and boasts two special (and devastating) attacks that damage all party members. Stay with Relentless Assault until it unleashes its Wave Cannon (Fig. 3), then switch to Diversity (or the less efficient Solidarity if you did not create that custom Paradigm, see page 29) to have a Medic heal through the subsequent Crystal Rain attack. Failure to make this transition *will* lead to an abrupt end to the confrontation – the short tutorial beforehand really is an informative piece of foreshadowing.

Once all characters are looking healthy, with the Warmech performing vertical Plasma Bursts on individual party members, it's safe to switch back to Relentless Assault to accelerate the battle. Return to a more defensive Paradigm if a character's health falls below 60%, or if you notice visual cues for subsequent deployments of Wave Cannon and Crystal Rain. Using these tactics, you should beat it in less than two minutes, Staggering it twice.

3

Using the Crystarium

Those surprised by the absence of palpable character growth until this point will greet the introduction of the Crystarium with no small degree of happiness. From this point onward, all protagonists (whether in the active party or even temporarily gone) will be rewarded Crystogen Points (CP) at the end of almost every fight. The actual sum is determined by the CP value of each enemy (as revealed in the Bestiary chapter of this guide) and specified at the Battle Results screen. CP can then be spent at the Crystarium screen, a feature introduced in great detail by the in-game tutorial.

At this stage in the game, progression in the Crystarium is fairly linear, with no real opportunities or need to make informed choices on which role to invest in first. We would advise that you visit it to upgrade party members every time you accumulate 200-300 CP in Chapter 03 – though if a potentially useful Crystal is within your grasp (such as a large stat increase or a new ability) it's always worth paying an early visit.

Readers keen to "level up" the party straight away should note that Crystarium progression is capped, with new layers only introduced at fixed story milestones. Though there are instances where grinding for CP (by backtracking to fight enemies who respawn) can offer short-term advantages, this is not one of those occasions: there are just enough enemies between now and the chapter end to provide all the progress you need. You should also bear in mind that CP rewards (and Crystarium costs) actually grow with each passing chapter, so there's no real benefit in fighting in a single spot with long-term character advancement in mind.

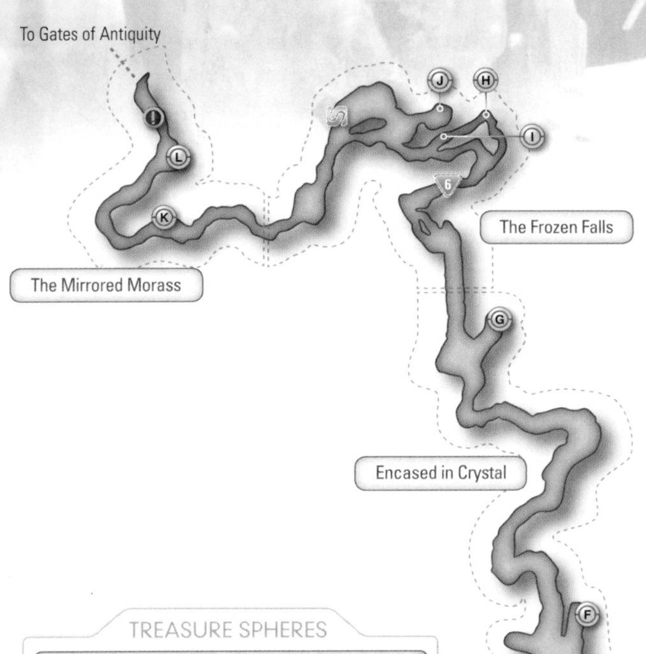

ENEMIES

Name	Notes	Page
Breshan Bass	Slightly less threatening after Crystarium upgrades, but still a strong foe.	235
Pantheron	Pose no danger whatsoever.	232
Bloodfang Bass	Very low HP; when mixed with their Breshan cousins, kill these first.	235
Alpha Behemoth	Powerful but very slow; easily Staggered.	233
PSICOM Tracker	Reasonable HP total, but no real threat.	228
Watchdrone	Extremely fast; in mixed groups, try to dispatch these before you turn to other enemies; weak against Lightning and Water elements.	230
PSICOM Ranger	Weak opponent; kill first to prevent them from casting Protect or Shell on their stronger allies.	228
Ciconia Velocycle	Halves physical and magic damage; sustains 10% of usual damage when in Charging status; loses resistances when Staggered.	231

TREASURE SPHERES

Sphere	Contents	Type
A	Strange Fluid (x6)	
B	240 Gil	
C	Deneb Duellers	
D	Enigmatic Fluid (x6)	
E	Wicked Fang (x7)	
F	Librascope	
G	Digital Circuit (x2)	
H	Paraffin Oil (x2)	
I	50 Gil	
J	Insulated Cabling (x3)	
K	30 Gil	
L	Begrimed Claws (x6)	

4 Sazh now joins the party to replace Snow, so ensure that you visit the Crystarium to unlock upgrades for him. Press on until the path separates into two bridges (Fig. 4), then take the leftmost of these to reach two otherwise inaccessible Treasure Spheres. The Deneb Duellers boost Sazh's Magic rating at the expense of a minor drop in Strength – a trade that is definitely worthwhile. Backtrack to the other bridge, then cross it to reach a large group of six enemies. Their appearance may suggest that a tough battle awaits, but five of these creatures are Bloodfang Bass (easily distinguished by their red legs): a far less dangerous adversary than its regional cousin, the Breshan Bass. Press forward and examine the vehicle overlooking the bridge to open the path ahead.

4

5 Don't underestimate the huge group of Breshan and Bloodfang Bass on the bridge (Fig. 5). Focus on the latter first, and be prepared to briefly switch to the Diversity Paradigm to heal midway through the battle. After the next Save Station you will encounter an Alpha Behemoth – and, usefully, a pertinent tutorial on the use of the Libra technique. The best tactic against this opponent is to stick with the Relentless Assault Paradigm and Stagger it for a quick victory. If you take too long, the Alpha Behemoth will charge its Extermination Mode attack, which enables it to inflict approximately 300 HP of damage with each blow.

5

6 While scaling the ice face at The Frozen Falls, take the right-hand route when the path branches (Fig. 6) to find two Treasure Spheres. You will encounter a Watchdrone and a powerful Ciconia Velocycle at the top. You should dispatch the former first, as the Ciconia Velocycle has very high HP. Don't be disheartened by the tiny shavings of damage that you inflict at first, as this enemy loses its high resistance to physical and magical attacks once Staggered.

6

Techniques

Techniques are special abilities that require Technical Points (TP) to activate. The TP cost of each Technique appears next to its name in the Battle Menu. Though you only have Libra right now, your repertoire will soon expand.

Like items, Gil and components, Technical Points are a resource that is shared between different parties – so even after changes in personnel and locale, your TP total will not change. They are replenished slowly during combat when you accumulate high Chain Combos, with additional increases awarded after battles. The higher your star rating, the bigger the reward – though the rise can be almost imperceptible after minor combat encounters.

You will discover later that judging when and where to spend TP on Techniques is an important skill. For the time being, feel free to use Libra whenever you need it.

Enemy Intel and Libra

As you should know by this stage, you can view information on enemies you face by pressing R1/RB during combat. Though all fields except an opponent's name are blank on first meeting, entries are gradually filled in during and after combat. It usually takes no more than three battles to build a complete picture of a particular adversary's strengths, weaknesses and special attributes.

Much of the data obtained for each enemy concerns their susceptibility or capacity to withstand elemental forces (Ice, Fire, et al) and status ailments (which do not matter just yet, but will do soon). With the introduction of magical attacks and physical assaults with elemental properties, this is vitally important.

Why? Actions chosen by the AI that controls your companions and the Auto-battle command (and indeed, all "auto" options for each role) are adjusted in accordance with the intelligence at your disposal. If you have not discovered that a foe has a high resistance to (or, worse, absorbs) Wind-based damage, for example, all party members will be oblivious to this fact until they learn otherwise. Furthermore, even if you know that an enemy is vulnerable to Water attacks after referring to the Bestiary chapter or a walkthrough tip, your allies (and Auto-battle) will not until this information is exposed in-game. In Final Fantasy XIII, knowledge really is power.

That is why the **Libra** technique and disposable **Librascope** item are genuinely essential – they can be used to immediately obtain a clearer picture of an opponent's attributes, though it may take two of the former to reveal every last secret. This is especially useful against stronger adversaries (particularly bosses) who pose a clear threat to your party. Note that whereas the Libra technique only reveals information about one target, the use of a Librascope item reveals the attributes of all opponents taking part in a battle at once.

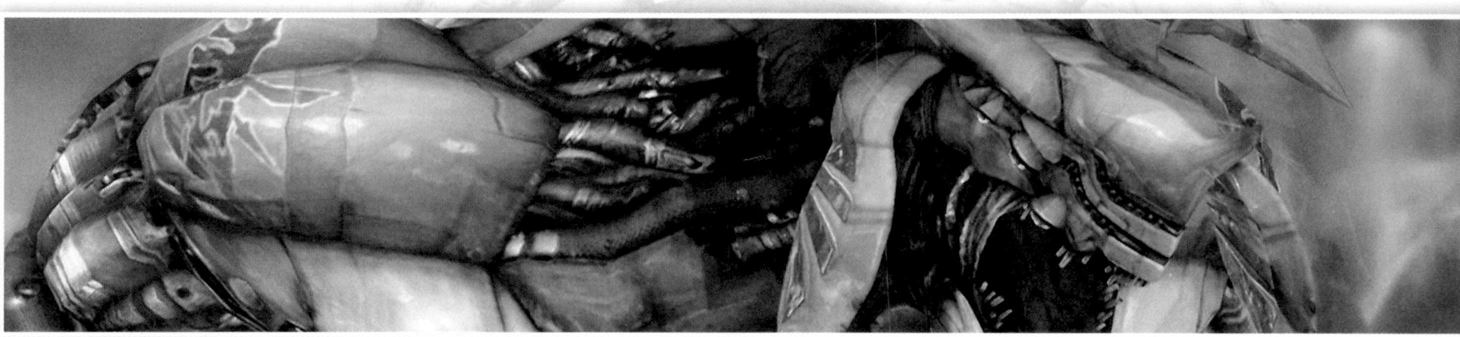

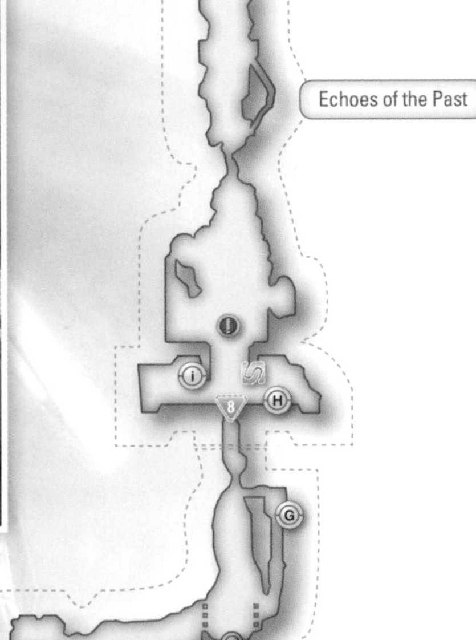

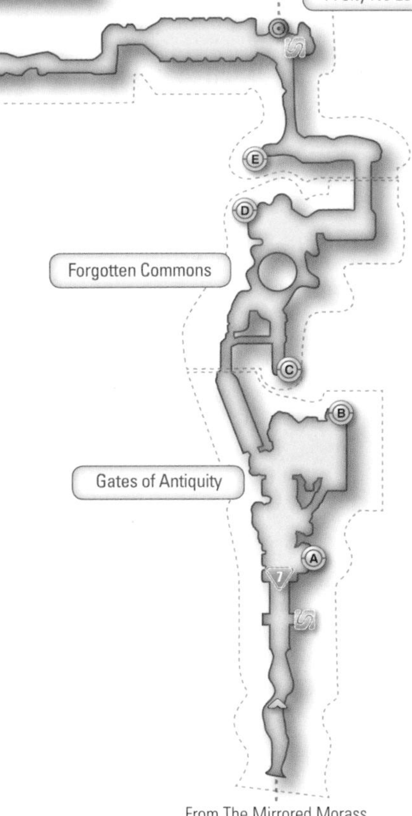

ENEMIES

Name	Notes	Page
PSICOM Tracker	May be awkward if buffed with Protect or Shell by an accompanying Ranger.	228
PSICOM Ranger	Weak opponent; kill first to prevent them from casting Protect or Shell on their stronger allies.	228
Watchdrone	Uses deadly combo attacks in conjunction with its allies - be ready to heal or revive victims.	230
Alpha Behemoth	High HP and Strength, but very slow; catch it with a preemptive strike for an easy fight.	233
Crusader	Sustains half usual damage from physical attacks; try to start battle with a preemptive strike.	231
Pantheron	Heels on command.	232
PSICOM Executioner	Fast and agile; sustains half usual damage on all attacks.	229
Garuda Interceptor	Sustains a tenth of normal damage while its Barrier is active; vulnerable to Wind-based magic.	233

TREASURE SPHERES

Sphere	Contents	Type
A	600 Gil	
B	Digital Circuits (x2)	
C	Begrimed Claws (x7)	
D	Spark Ring	
E	Potion (x3)	
F	Millerite	
G	Ferroelectric Film	
H	Phoenix Down	
I	Librascope (x2)	

7 Once you reach the Gates of Antiquity area, try to sneak up on the Alpha Behemoth. As you proceed through the ruins, aim to kill the weaker PSICOM Rangers first when you meet groups of enemies. They fall easily, but may cast Protect and Shell if left alive, which could be problematic if bestowed upon a stronger ally. The two Crusaders you fight are perhaps the most noteworthy foes – they are easy to Stagger, but have powerful attacks that are dangerous if directed at a single party member in an unbroken sequence. Starting the battles with preemptive strikes will make a big difference, though it's not worth wasting a Deceptisol Shroud to do so.

After the second Crusader falls, the journey to the Echoes of the Past map area is fairly uneventful. The PSICOM Executioners are worthy of respect, but soon fall once Staggered. When you reach the final Save Station, be sure to open the two Treasure Spheres before you approach the staircase (Fig. 7).

7

8 Equip the Spark Ring you just found and visit the Crystarium to spend accumulated CP before using the Save Station. If you haven't done so yet, unlocking Aero (Ravager magic) in Sazh's Crystarium will make the forthcoming battle a little easier.

Major Encounter – Garuda Interceptor: This fight is split into two sections – a short opening bout followed by a more involved second encounter. For the first, use Libra to reveal information about your opponent, then pound away with the Relentless Assault Paradigm until a cutscene begins. Your party's HP will be restored for the following stage, so there's really no need to heal.

For the final part of the fight the Garuda Interceptor is much stronger, as its Barrier status buff cuts all physical and magic damage to a tenth of its normal level. Don't be worried by the negligible effect you have on its HP bar at first: once this enemy is Staggered, its susceptibility to Aero magic (Fig. 8) will cause its health to plummet as the Chain Combo rockets upwards. Despite initial worries (and an occasional need to heal), you will find this a battle that ends satisfyingly quickly.

You receive several different rewards after the fight ends. In terms of spoils, you get a Silver Bangle and access to the Up in Arms store (accessed via the Shop option at Save Stations). Sazh and Vanille acquire the new Synergist and Saboteur roles respectively (more on which shortly), and all party members have their Crystariums expanded.

8

9 **Eidolon Battle – Shiva:** Once the story returns to Snow, you are launched straight into battle when the cutscene ends. If you equipped him with an accessory earlier it may be prudent to remove it now, as he has a limited role in combat encounters for the coming chapters. To do so, press START/▶ and then select Retry as soon as combat begins. This may seem like an unusual step, but it enables you to pay a quick automatic visit to the Main Menu before you resume.

Your first task is to fight a group of PSICOM soldiers. As Snow is fighting alone, you can dispatch individual Rangers efficiently and quickly by initiating Auto-battle after two ATB gauge segments are full (tap △/Ⓨ). When the tougher reinforcements arrive, use Potions to top up his HP level while you wait for his ATB gauge to fill between attacks.

In the second confrontation (against Shiva), you should immediately switch to the Sentinel Paradigm. While one of the sisters (Nix) will attack, the second (Stiria) will heal Snow at regular intervals. Select Auto-cover (the Sentinel equivalent of Auto-battle), and Snow will initially use Provoke on the aggressive Nix. She is actually immune to this ability, but what follows (and will be added to the command queue on every subsequent use of Auto-cover) is the key to completing the challenge: the Steelguard skill. This staple component of the Sentinel's repertoire enables its user to endure attacks with minimal HP loss.

All you need do here is engage Steelguard just before Nix attacks (Fig. 9). If its effects are active as she unleashes each assault, the Gestalt gauge will fill steadily. To ensure that all goes according to plan, use △/Ⓨ and ○/Ⓑ as required to rush or cancel Steelguard (with the latter being applicable when Nix stops to perform ATB Charge). Once the Gestalt gauge is sufficiently filled, press □/Ⓧ to end the confrontation.

9

Eidolon Battles

The fight against Shiva introduces a new gameplay feature: Eidolon Battles. As the in-game tutorial explains, beating these powerful opponents enables you to acquire their services for the rest of the game. Unlike traditional boss encounters, defeating them is rarely a simple matter of pummeling away until an HP gauge is depleted. Instead, the challenge is to discover what these creatures expect from you by using the Libra ability to obtain clues or learn weaknesses, then perform specific actions to increase the Gestalt gauge before the relentless Doom countdown reaches zero.

THE VILE PEAKS

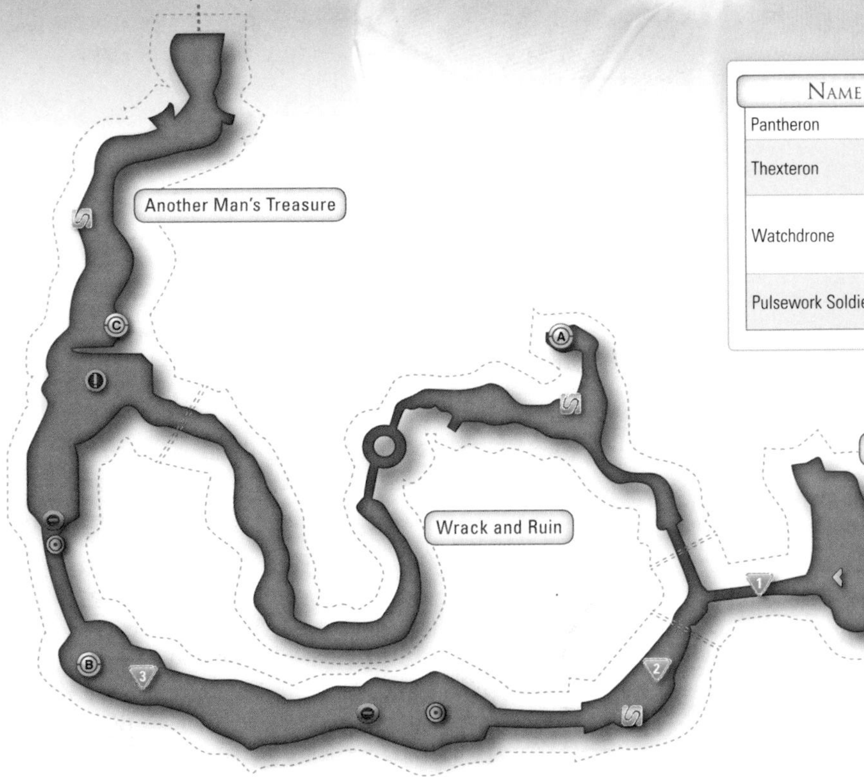

ENEMIES

Name	Notes	Page
Pantheron	A fleeting inconvenience.	232
Thexteron	Fairly high HP; aim for quick Stagger to kill it; casts Bravery to boost physical attacks.	232
Watchdrone	Very fast; hugely powerful combination attacks – switch to a Paradigm with a healer when these occur.	230
Pulsework Soldier	Weak against the Lightning element; high HP, but entirely passive once Staggered.	242

TREASURE SPHERES

Sphere	Contents	Type
A	Librascope	
B	Black Belt	
C	Ninurta	

1 Once you gain control of Sazh, run straight over the bridge. When play resumes, Lightning is now leader with Hope her supporting ally. Visit the Crystarium immediately to upgrade both characters. You will benefit from spending Hope's accumulated riches of CP on unlocking Aero (Ravager magic) and then Shell (a Synergist ability). Ensure that Lightning is wearing a Silver Bangle accessory, and give Hope an Iron Bangle; keep your second Silver Bangle (if collected earlier) free for Sazh.

After a couple of hours with three-person parties, going back to two can be a shock to the system. The Thexteron and two Pantherons pose no real danger, but the trio of Watchdrones are a sterner test. Be ready to Paradigm Shift to War & Peace should you notice two joining forces for a combination attack (which can instantly knock an injured party member out – Fig. 1).

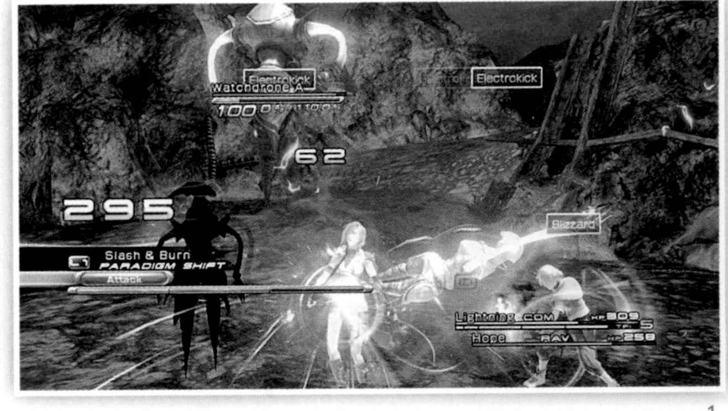

1

2 After reaching the waypoint, the story returns to Sazh and Vanille. Equip Sazh with the Silver Bangle, then visit the Crystarium. Upgrade Sazh's Synergist role until you reach the Vigilance crystal, then dedicate remaining points to his development as a Ravager. For Vanille, go for Fire (Ravager) and Deprotect (Saboteur), then concentrate on the Medic role. Until the next Crystarium level is unlocked, you can then proceed any way you please. Your final piece of preparation should be to create two new Paradigms: Synergist + Medic (Symbiosis) and Ravager + Saboteur (Undermine).

At the top of the slope you are introduced to your first three-way battle (Fig. 2), where two enemy groups are engaged in battle with one another, making it easier to initiate combat with a preemptive strike. Direct your aggression at the Watchdrones, as these are the most dangerous foes. When only the Pulsework Soldier remains, Paradigm Shift to Undermine. This will enable Vanille (now working in the Saboteur role) to inflict Deprotect and Deshell, weakening the final adversary and increasing its Chain Gauge. Once both are in place, return to Dualcasting to finish it off quickly. Activate the nearby device to continue.

2

3 In the next three-way battle, target the Thexteron, then repeat the tactic outlined previously to dispatch the Pulsework Soldier. The fight that follows is, for the unwary, potentially a very nasty trap (Fig. 3). As the Thexterons and Watchdrones are allied, it should be obvious that it makes sense to attack the Pulsework Soldier last – or suffer the consequences. For the final three-way battle, though, it's definitely best to kill one of the two Pulsework Soldiers first.

3

Once Hope joins the party, create the Smart Bomb Paradigm (Ravager + Saboteur + Ravager). This is perfect for Staggering strong enemies quickly; you can then switch to Tri-Disaster for increased damage.

Status Effects

With the introduction of more dangerous opponents and the Synergist and Saboteur roles, status effects will now play a greater part in future combat encounters. These "buffs" and "debuffs" add a whole new layer of strategy to combat, so you should familiarize yourself with the basic concepts straight away.

- A **status enhancement** is a beneficial condition conferred by an ability (or by wearing a special accessory), such as Haste (faster ATB gauge charging) or Protect (better resistance to physical damage). They are not the sole preserve of your party, which is why it remains important to learn as much about opponents as you can. An enemy who uses status enhancements could suddenly become much more powerful or bestow such boosts on their allies.
- **Status ailments** are debilitating conditions. These include Deshell (reduced resistance to magic damage) and Debrave (which reduces a target's strength).

Current status enhancements or ailments are represented by icons positioned next to HP gauges for both party members and enemies, and are only active for a limited period of time. For a complete list of status effects, turn to page 142.

Roles: Synergist & Saboteur

Synergist and Saboteur are the two final roles, completing the full set of six.

- **Synergist:** The Synergist's job is to imbue party members with useful status enhancements such as Bravery and Faith. They cannot attack enemies, and will simply recast existing effects on party members once all available buffs are active. It's best to parachute them in with a Paradigm Shift, then switch back to a more aggressive configuration once the desired enhancements are in place.
- **Saboteur:** An AI-controlled Saboteur (or the Auto-hinder command) will attempt to inflict status ailments on all enemies in a battle. These usually cause a small amount of additional magic damage. Like Synergists, Saboteurs serve no purpose once all potential status ailments are in place (until existing ailments have expired).

Interestingly, though, abilities used by Saboteurs have the effect of slowing down the depletion of the Chain Gauge in the same manner as Commandos. Potentially, a Ravager and Saboteur combination (Undermine or, with two Ravagers, Smart Bomb) could be as effective as a Commando and Ravager partnership at cooperating to inflict Stagger status.

TREASURE SPHERES

Sphere	Contents	Type
A	Metal Armband	
B	Phoenix Down	
C	Librascope	
D	Ember Ring	

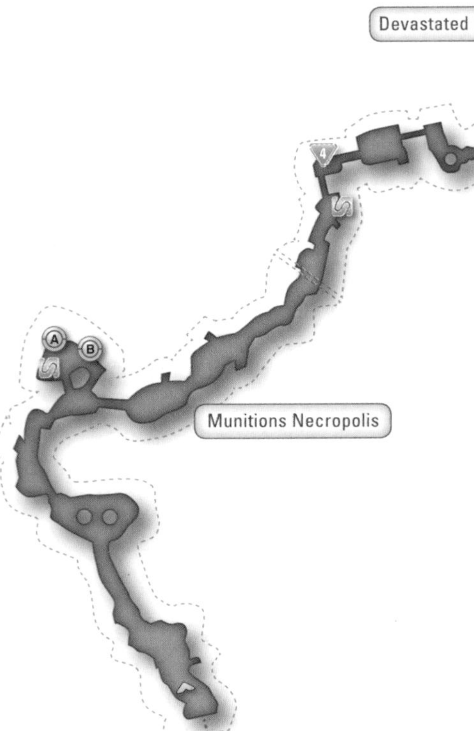

ENEMIES

Name	Notes	Page
Incubus	Weak against Water and Lightning elements; fast attack speed.	236
Pulsework Soldier	High HP; passive once Staggered.	242
Succubus	Makes its allies more dangerous when present; dispatch it first.	236
Dreadnought	Halves magical and physical damage, but weak to multiple status ailments.	243

4 Using the Smart Bomb/Tri-disaster tactic of exploiting the Saboteur's ability to reduce Chain Gauge depletion before pummeling with all-out magical attacks, there are no enemies that should cause you difficulties until you are reunited with Lightning in the Devastated Dreams map area. However, when you encounter groups containing a Succubus, be sure to kill it first. Though hardly blessed with colossal HP, its ability to cast Deprotect on your party and Bravery on its allies should not be ignored; equip the Metal Armband available in the nearby Treasure Sphere to increase your resistance to Deprotect.

Lightning replaces Hope in the party. Unless there is a pressing need to heal, the Relentless Assault Paradigm will suffice for the immediate future. Push on until you reach a control panel, then operate it to lower a bridge. After you fight the Incubus and two Succubi above, be careful not to miss the Treasure Sphere concealed just through an open doorway (Fig. 4). Further ahead there is a shortcut to the left that could enable you to skip a battle with two Pulsework Soldiers and a Succubus, but it's actually better to fight them for CP, spoils, and access to the nearby Treasure Sphere.

4

5 When you reach the third Save Station on the Devastated Dreams map area, stop and upgrade your party at the Crystarium, equip the Ember Ring from the last Treasure Sphere, then approach the ominous pile of junk to initiate a boss battle.

Major Encounter – Dreadnought: Due to its 50% reduction on both magical and physical attacks, your first action should be to switch to the Smart Bomb Paradigm to allow Vanille to cast Deprotect and Deshell. That done, switch back to Relentless Assault (Fig. 5). Dreadnought uses its Steam Clean ability to remove one status effect at a time, but don't worry about that for now. This is another two-part confrontation, and your only objective should be to Stagger your colossal opponent and deplete its HP gauge to meet its "true" form. You may need to heal once, but this first part is otherwise fairly simple.

After the short intermission, all party members are restored to full health. As Dreadnought's HP is so much higher this time, you should select the Bully Paradigm straight away. Use Sazh to apply the Faith and Bravery buffs while Vanille enfeebles the boss with her Saboteur skills. Switch to Diversity to heal, then use Relentless Assault to begin inflicting real harm. Some of Dreadnought's attacks can be highly unpleasant (particularly the Wrecking Ball assault), so be ready to cancel attacks and switch back to Diversity as required. When both status ailments expire or are removed, use Smart Bomb to quickly refresh them; this should occur just before your opponent's Chain Gauge reaches its limit. Dreadnought does not last long once Staggered.

After the battle, the party's Crystariums are expanded. Lightning acquires the Medic role, and Sazh can now operate as a Commando. You also receive the Omni-kit (which enables weapon and accessory upgrades) and access to Lenora's Garage, another retail outlet that you can visit at Save Stations.

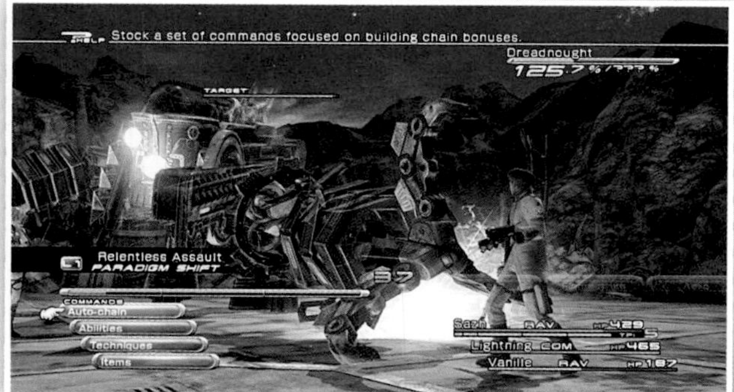

5

Upgrading Equipment

The ability to enhance weapons and accessories via the Upgrade option at Save Stations is obviously a major new feature. Strangely, though, we would advise that all but those willing to grind for spoils in an attempt to smash FFXIII's difficulty curve (see "Power Tip" below) should actually leave this feature alone until later, as it really won't put you at any form of disadvantage for the next chapter or so. We will, of course, return to the subject when the time is right.

As the game tutorial states, components can be used to upgrade equipment. Each component has an EXP value that determines how much experience it adds for each unit used (with a variation of up to +/-50% when applied to different weapons and accessories). However, components also have a hidden attribute that determines whether they increase or decrease a potential multiplier. The multiplier has a minimum value of 1.0x (no bonus), and a maximum value of 3.0x.

As a rule, components that offer large EXP boosts tend to decrease the multiplier, sometimes severely. The most efficient and cost-effective way to upgrade equipment, then, is to identify and use components that will maximize the multiplier, then use a huge batch of a single component type that offers the highest possible EXP yield. If you want to invest your resources wisely, it makes sense to wait until you have a much larger set of available components before you begin upgrading (hence our words of caution on starting straight away).

This introduction is merely a very quick and dirty appraisal of a complicated yet absorbing sub-game. We will return to the subject throughout the walkthrough, offering guidance on where notable components can be found (or farmed from local denizens), and when best to use them. Need to know more right now? Turn to page 216 to read our exhaustive guide to this fascinating and profitable diversion (but only if you don't object to unavoidable gameplay spoilers).

Power Tip: For those who really can't wait to begin upgrading, it's possible to run a route between the Devastated Dreams and Munitions Necropolis areas before you face Dreadnought to fight Pulsework Soldiers as they respawn. These drop the valuable Spark Plug (~90 EXP) and Passive Detector (~200 EXP) components.

ENEMIES

Name	Notes	Page
Corps Gunner	Weak against Fire and Ice; half damage from Lightning; low HP.	230
PSICOM Tracker	Standard grunt; no noteworthy features.	228
Corps Regular	Very similar to Corps Gunner.	230
Uhlan	Has Lightning and Water vulnerabilities; be wary of its Guided Missile area-effect attack.	231
PSICOM Ranger	Pitiful HP total; kill first to prevent them from casting Protect or Shell.	228

6 Follow the path until you reach a Save Station. At the waypoint just beyond it, the party will split again. Play resumes with Lightning and Hope fighting a group of four Corps Gunners and a PSICOM Tracker. These troops can inflict damage quickly, so choose Double Dose (Fig. 6) from the Paradigm Deck whenever the two protagonists' HP bars fall to around 50%, to have them heal each other.

Before you go any further, visit the Paradigm menu and create a War & Peace configuration (Commando + Medic). Double Dose may be great for healing quickly in an emergency, but it's lousy when you have Chain Combos to maintain. You should also spend available CP at the Crystarium. The priority for Lightning is to work towards Accessory (Medic – rewards a second accessory slot) and Launch (Commando – "air juggle" Staggered enemies). For Hope, work on the Ravager role first, then move on to Synergist (which also has an Accessory crystal) and, finally, Medic.

6

Scavenger's Trail

TREASURE SPHERES

Sphere	Contents	Type
A	Fiber-optic Cable (x3)	
B	Librascope	
C	Unique (see Pulse Armament minigame)	–
D	Unique (see Pulse Armament minigame)	–
E	Electrolytic Capacitor (x2)	
F	Spark Ring	
G	Phoenix Down	

7 The path through Scavenger's Trail is littered with tough Corps soldiers. Unless Lightning is grievously injured, though, it's usually safe to press on for a quick victory rather than heal. The same applies for the Uhlan you meet before the second Save Station of the zone.

After a brief quarrel with two PSICOM Trackers at the waypoint marker, a special gameplay sequence ensues. Once you've gained control of the Pulse Armament, use ⊗/Ⓐ to hit groups of foes. If you time this carefully, you can usually dispatch an entire group with one sweeping blow (Fig. 7). Trampling over them is also effective. As the tutorial states, breaking through fences recharges the machine's power reserves, allowing further attacks. There is no way that you can be harmed during this sequence, so feel free to bludgeon your way through in any way you see fit. There are, however, special bonuses available for fulfilling certain (unstated) requirements during this minigame. See Pulse Armament Minigame for further details.

7

8 The PSICOM Ranger makes a few cameo appearances in enemy groups here, so be sure to make these your priority target whenever you face them. If you don't, they will cast Protect or Shell on their allies. When the path splits (Fig. 8), take the right-hand route to find an Uhlan guarding a Treasure Sphere. After fighting an Uhlan and two PSICOM Trackers close to a Save Station, spend accumulated CP at the Crystarium and save your progress. Now create a new Paradigm featuring Medic + Synergist (known as Symbiosis) and set it as your default choice, then equip as many Spark Rings as you currently have.

8

9 **Eidolon Battle – Odin:** This is easily the hardest fight so far, even when you know what is required to beat this relentless opponent – consider temporarily switching the Battle Speed setting from Normal to Slow to buy yourself a little extra time. Your choice of Symbiosis as your active Paradigm should – *just* – get you through his opening onslaught. Odin yields to those who heal the wounded, and increase his Chain Gauge. Healing alone is not nearly enough to fill the Gestalt gauge, however, so you'll need to go on the offensive.

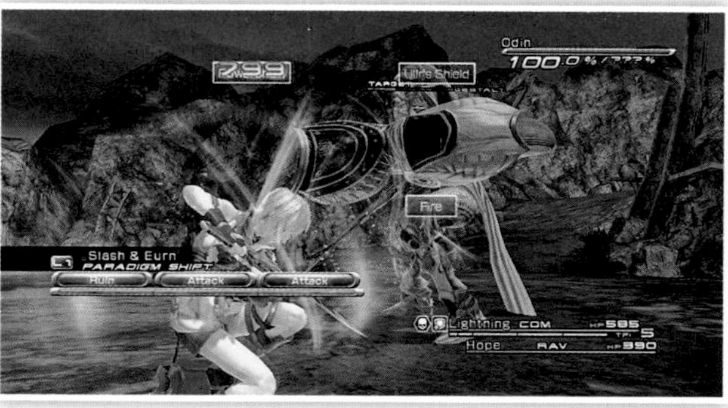

9

First, though, wait for Hope to cast Protect and Shell on both party members – without these, you stand no chance. With magical enhancements in place, switch to War & Peace. This enables Lightning to attack the Eidolon while Hope performs (vital) healing duties. Watch Odin carefully. As soon as he performs his Ullr's Shield ability (Fig. 9), switch to Dualcasting to have both Ravagers drive up his Chain Gauge. The moment he resumes his attacks, return to War & Peace. With this strategy, you should be able to defeat him before the Doom counter falls below 600 or so.

If you are ready to spend Aegisol and Fortisol Shrouds before the battle, you can actually skip the initial buffing step altogether, making the whole confrontation both easier and faster. This will allow you to fill Odin's Chain Gauge quickly with Dualcasting, switching briefly to Double Dose (Medic + Medic) whenever you need to heal.

When the fight is over, Lightning obtains the Odin Eidolith and an additional ATB gauge segment. Continue to the end of the path to reach a cutscene and, after that, a tutorial that explains the use of Eidolons. The instructions are straightforward (if in doubt, use the Autogestalt function – it works in the same way as Auto-battle), and the subsequent battle shouldn't cause you any difficulties – even if the Eidolon departs before all enemies have been defeated. You'll find a proper introduction to the system in "Using the Odin Eidolon", on page 45.

PULSE ARMAMENT MINIGAME

Once you finish the Pulse Armament minigame you will encounter two Treasure Spheres. The contents of these containers are altered in accordance with the number of Pulsework Soldiers destroyed with the ⊗/Ⓐ attack, and your overall kill total (which includes deaths by trampling). The best way to maximize both rewards is to be fast and purposeful as you approach each group with care, using the ⊗/Ⓐ attack to hit as many targets as you can before their formation breaks. Detailed tips can be found on page 127 in the (spoiler-heavy) Extras chapter of this guide.

Sweeping Blow Kills	Gil Reward
40+	999 Gil
25-39	300 Gil
24 or less	100 Gil

Total Kills	Item Reward
35+	Spark Ring
25-34	Thickened Hide (x20)
24 or less	Sturdy Bone (x10)

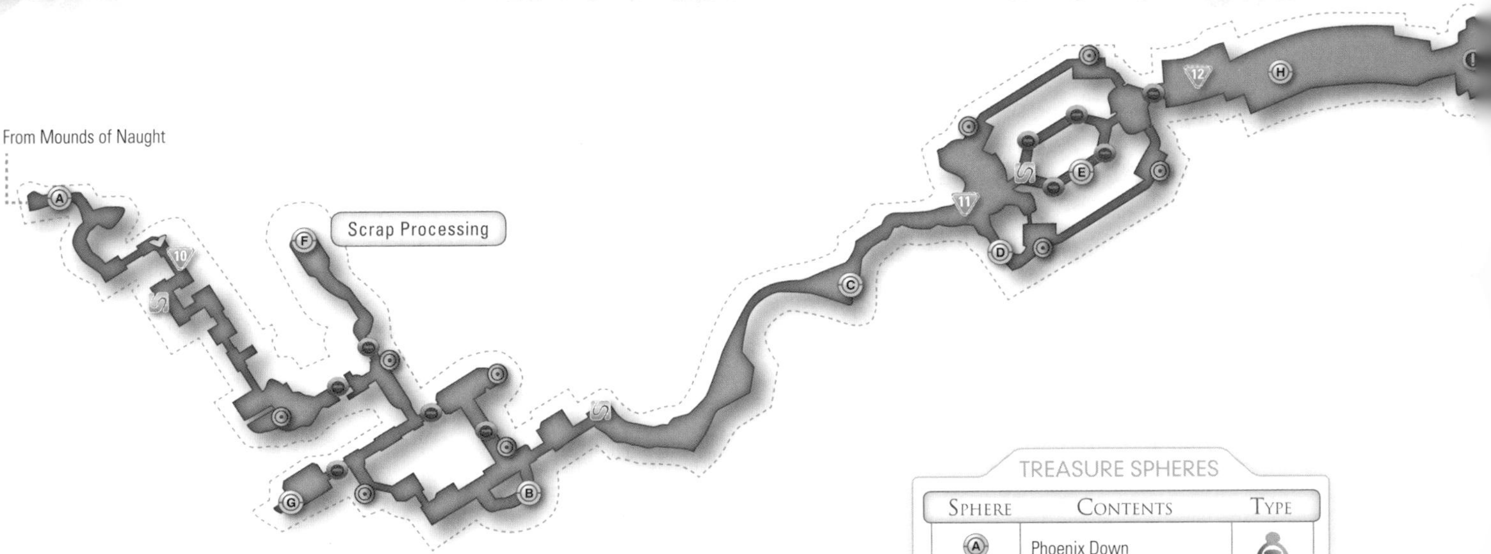

Sphere	Contents	Type
A	Phoenix Down	
B	Auric Amulet	
C	Ember Ring	
D	Phoenix Down	
E	Fortisol	
F	Iron Shell (x8)*	
G	Vibrant Ooze (x6)*	
H	300 Gil	

Treasure Spheres

* Special conditions apply. See "Scrap Processing Secrets".

Enemies

Name	Notes	Page
Bomb	May use Self-destruct, removing itself from battle for huge damage; absorbs Fire.	243
Pulsework Soldier	High HP; passive once Staggered.	242
Gremlin	Uses Fire attacks; low HP.	235

10 When the story resumes with Sazh and Vanille, your first action should be to create the Undermine Paradigm (Ravager + Saboteur), which can be highly effective against Pulsework Soldiers. Move forward and interact with the device marked on the map to extend the bridge. When you encounter mixed enemy groups that feature Bombs, be sure to destroy them first – their Self-destruct ability is utterly devastating (Fig. 10).

10

11 You will soon reach a large structure surrounded by four control panels (Fig. 11). Approach and activate each one of these to raise the central tower and open the way forward. Note that this also allows access to a Treasure Sphere on the inner walkway, and enables you to reach three new platforms in the area you have just travelled through. If you wish to backtrack to claim optional rewards, see "Scrap Processing Secrets" for more information.

11

12 Head to the gate that opened during the brief cutscene to fight two Bombs and a pair of Pulsework Soldiers. A preemptive strike will be useful here, though not strictly essential. Be ready to change to the War and Peace Paradigm if either Bomb prepares to Self-destruct before you can destroy it. The weaker Vanille may be knocked out by these attacks, so be sure to cancel stacked commands and quickly use a Phoenix Down should this occur. Sazh and Vanille do not fight in the next chapter, so you should remove valuable accessories before you reach the final waypoint if you would prefer to equip them on other party members.

There are no battles or potential rewards in the brief Bodhum interlude, so just head into the building at the centre of the area and talk to Lebreau (Fig. 12), then walk onto the pier to continue.

12

Miscellany

- If you are controlling the party's Medic, don't forget to use Ⓐ/Ⓨ to expedite the delivery of Cure magic when speed is of the essence, cr ◎/Ⓑ to cancel unnecessary repetitions.
- Performing a Paradigm Shift will cancel existing Command Queues for all party members, with charged ATB gauge segments available for use immediately.
- Certain combinations of weapons and accessories confer special bonuses (called "synthesized abilities") on the user. It's always good to see what potential benefits you might enjoy whenever you collect new equipment. If you can bear potential gameplay (though not story) spoilers, you can find information on all notable weapon and accessory interactions on page 194.

Scrap Processing Secrets

Activating the four control panels close to the end of the Scrap Processing map restores power to three consoles you may have noticed on your original journey through the area. Backtracking to activate these enables you to reach three optional battles and two additional Treasure Spheres on previously inaccessible platforms. The rewards are not spectacular, but the additional CP and spoils obtained probably make the journey worthwhile.

- The first platform (back near the start of the Scrap Processing area) is guarded by three Bombs and a Pulsework Soldier. This is a particularly nasty group, as a single Self-destruct attack can bring proceedings to a quick and frustrating halt. Consider using a Fortisol Shroud before you begin – the increased damage and Haste status will enable you to destroy the Bombs before this can happen.
- The second platform features a trio of Pulsework Soldiers. An application of Deceptisol will give you a good start, though patience and regular switches to the War & Peace Paradigm are enough to get you through this fight.
- The third console activates an elevator that takes you to a platform where two Pulsework Solders and three Gremlins await. There is no Treasure Sphere here, so engaging them is purely at your discretion. Interacting with the control panel here merely lowers a bridge that connects to the main map area, though you can also ride the elevator back down.

THE GAPRA WHITEWOOD

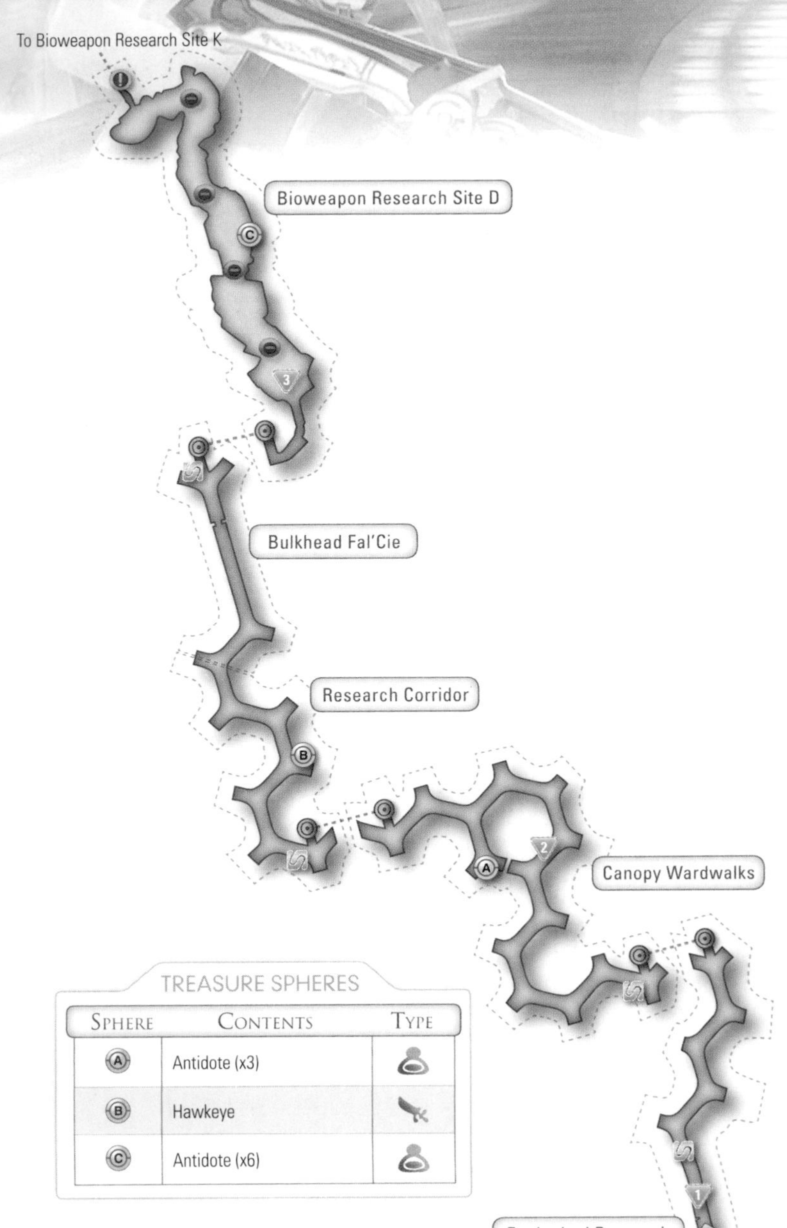

TREASURE SPHERES

Sphere	Contents	Type
A	Antidote (x3)	
B	Hawkeye	
C	Antidote (x6)	

ENEMIES

Name	Notes	Page
Frag Leech	Low HP; poses little threat.	232
Thexteron	Weak against Ice and Lightning elements.	232
Vespid	Beware its multi-hit Flurry of Fire attack – switch to a Paradigm with Medic when the caption appears.	232
Alpha Behemoth	Weak against Water and Fire.	233
Silver Lobo	Virulent Breath attack causes Poison; weak against Fire, but Ice damage is halved.	234
Crawler	Weak against Fire, but damage from Water-based attacks is halved.	237
Feral Behemoth	Sustains half damage from Fire and Lightning elements; weak against Water; can be Launched.	240

1 Visit the main menu to prepare for the chapter ahead before you set off. You have a relative fortune in CP to spend at the Crystarium, so do that straight away. You should now have sufficient points to unlock Lightning's Accessory (Medic) and Launch (Commando) crystals. For Hope, work on Synergist crystals to obtain Barfrost, Barfire (which respectively raise the target's resistance to ice and fire) and the extra accessory slot. At the Paradigm Deck, create War & Peace (Medic + Commando).

The Thexterons and Frag Leeches encountered on the path to the first waypoint present no real challenge. Once you reach the elevator, activate the controls to ride it to the next area (Fig. 1). There are several of these throughout this chapter.

1

2 The Vespid has high HP, but is only dangerous when it performs its (fairly rare) Flurry of Fire assault. Alpha Behemoths still have enormous endurance, but a combination of a preemptive strike, a quick Stagger and Lightning's Launch ability (Fig. 2) renders them completely toothless. If you can't get a preemptive strike, soften them up with Slash & Burn until the Chain Gauge reaches approximately 40%, then switch to Dualcasting to bring proceedings to a close.

2

3 You must defeat all monsters in the immediate area to unlock energy barriers that block your path. The first zone features a succession of Silver Lobo enemies. This opponent can inflict the Poison status ailment (Fig. 3). Rather than taking a break to cure it with an Antidote, it's better to aim for a quick kill, switching to War & Peace to heal only when necessary. Indeed all status effects automatically disappear at the end of each battle in Final Fantasy XIII. The Crawlers that follow are more nuisance than danger, especially once you identify their weakness to Fire.

The Feral Behemoth, however, is a different matter entirely. Soften it up first with Slash & Burn, then switch to Dualcasting for a fast Stagger. Return to Slash & Burn, and Lightning's Launch ability should prevent it from causing further damage – especially if you can time Hope's attacks to help "juggle" the monster while it is airborne.

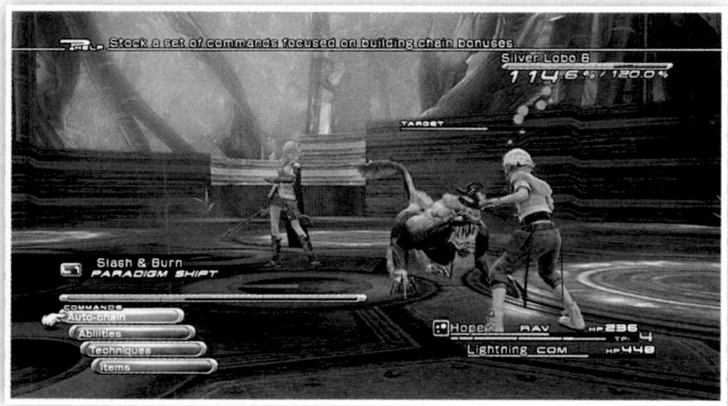

3

Using the Odin Eidolon

Once Lightning takes over as party leader midway through Chapter 05, you have the option of summoning Odin during combat, though this Technique requires three Technical Points (TP).

- Once Odin has been summoned and is fighting alongside Lightning, you should watch two gauges carefully: Odin's SP meter acts as an HP gauge and is depleted by enemy attacks, though it also drains steadily throughout; Lightning's Gestalt gauge gradually increases during combat (the more it fills, the longer Gestalt Mode will last and the more attacks you will be able to perform). Your objective in this first stage is always to build the Gestalt gauge as much as you can (increasing Chain Bonuses to high levels works best), then to switch to Gestalt Mode (press □/Ⓧ) just before the SP meter reaches zero (otherwise the Eidolon will leave straight away).

- Once you activate Gestalt Mode, you can either press ⊗/Ⓐ repeatedly to use the Autogestalt function (which works in the same way as Auto-battle), or perform abilities manually by following the onscreen prompts. Each ability removes a specific amount of units from the Gestalt Dial counter. Once the counter reaches "01", press △/Ⓨ to unleash a final attack before Odin departs.

- Remember that you can skip Eidolon cinematics (including Gestalt Mode transformations) with SELECT/◀.

- A character who summons an Eidolon has his or her HP replenished (which can be useful in a desperate situation where other party members have fallen and death is imminent). The HP of all party members is also replenished after an Eidolon departs; as an additional perk, all status ailments will also be removed.

- There is a downside to using Eidolons: when they leave, enemy Chain Gauges are reset, and any Staggered foes will immediately recover. Choosing the best moment to summon them is crucial.

- Ethersol (used via the Shrouds menu) replenishes your TP level, but it's a valuable commodity that you should not spend frivolously.

Miscellany

- Role Level crystals in the Crystarium cost more CP than others, but provide immediate (albeit invisible) upgrades that apply whenever a character uses that role – and there are small complimentary boosts for other party members, too. After key abilities, make Role Level crystals for commonly used roles (for example, Commando for Lightning) a priority whenever they are available. We have a complete breakdown of all level bonuses later in the guide, on page 154.

- Poison is a status ailment that reduces a victim's HP at a steady rate. In a protracted battle, where this might be a problem, you can heal the afflicted party member by using the Antidote item.

- **Power Tip:** There is a group of six Frag Leeches at the start of the Research Corridor area. The battle is not difficult, and earns you 156 CP. By riding the nearby elevator up and down to reset their position, you can "farm" these creatures to accrue thousands of CP in a fairly short space of time.

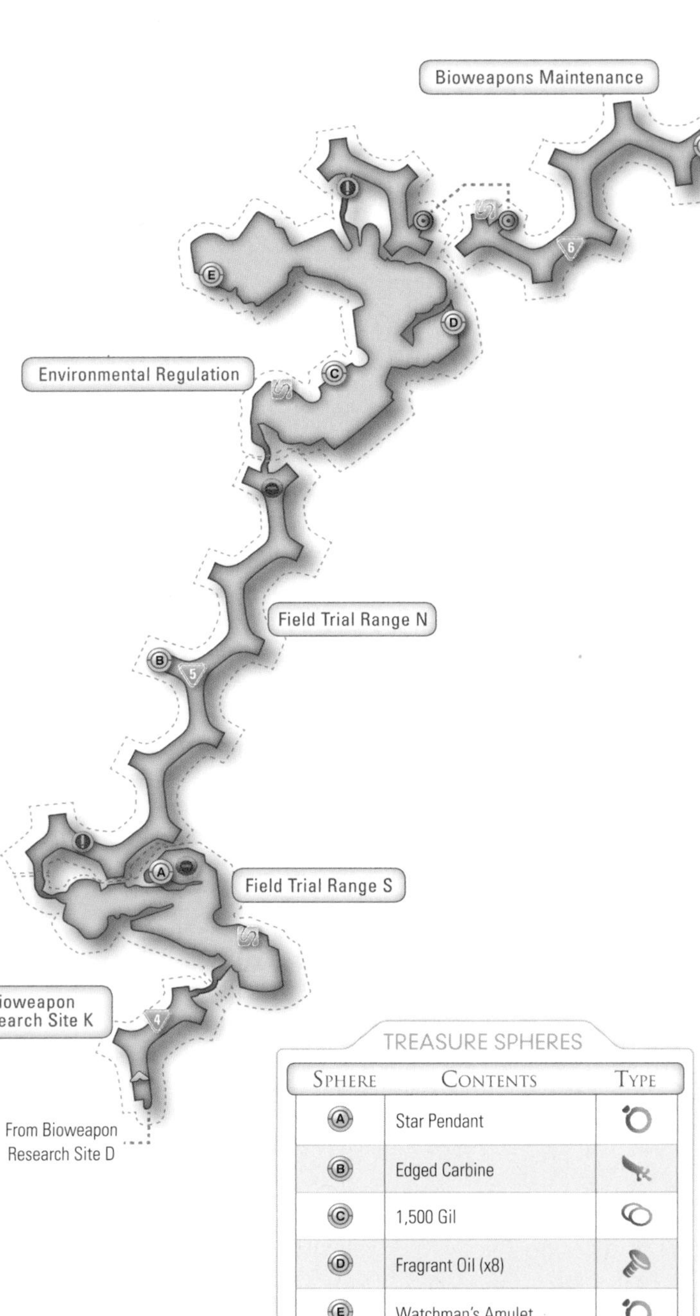

4 At the top of the climb, an enormous group of ten Crawlers awaits your arrival. After unleashing a first wave of attacks, switch to War & Peace and concentrate on healing while Lightning deals with them with her (tailor-made) Blitz attack.

When the cutscene ends, Lightning takes over as party leader. After the Save Station at Field Trial Range S, head right and kill the two Silver Lobos to remove a force field and gain access to a Treasure Sphere (Fig. 4).

4

5 You meet your first Barbed Specter at Field Trial Range N. The most efficient way to defeat these is to start with a quick round of Slash & Burn attacks, then immediately switch to Dualcasting. Another Feral Behemoth lies in wait in front of an energy barrier. The monster drops an electronic pass to the Magical Moments retail network, accessed via Save Stations.

As you enter Environmental Regulation, look at the energy barrier to your left. You can slip through small gaps at either end (Fig. 5) to fight another Feral Behemoth and open a Treasure Sphere. The next Treasure Sphere is the bait in a trap: the moment you enter the cul-de-sac, the Feral Behemoth charges forward to attack with a small army of Crawlers. Deal with the latter adversaries first, stop to heal, then employ the usual tactics against the bigger enemy. In the three-way battle that follows, kill two Silver Lobos before you attack the Feral Behemoth.

Another ambush lies in the large area to the left of the waypoint marker (before the climb), this time featuring a Feral Behemoth and a Barbed Specter. If you can start with a preemptive strike, the rest is a formality.

5

TREASURE SPHERES

Sphere	Contents	Type
A	Star Pendant	
B	Edged Carbine	
C	1,500 Gil	
D	Fragrant Oil (x8)	
E	Watchman's Amulet	
F	Ethersol	

ENEMIES

Name	Notes	Page
Crawler	Individually weak, but dangerous in large groups.	237
Silver Lobo	Inflicts the Poison status ailment; weak against Fire, but Ice damage is halved.	234
Barbed Specter	Weak against Fire, but Lightning element damage is halved.	237
Feral Behemoth	Sustains half damage from Fire and Lightning elements; weak against Water; can be Launched.	240
Corps Watchman	Immune against Fire; weak against Ice.	230
Corps Marksman	Immune against Fire; weak against Ice; low HP.	230
Milvus Velocycle	No specific weaknesses; be wary of its Triple Beam attack.	231
Aster Protoflorian	Changes elemental strengths and weakness during battle; powerful attacks; massive HP; can be Launched.	234

6 A group of four Silver Lobos lies in wait when you reach the Bioweapons Maintenance zone. Further ahead, after you dispatch a group of Corps soldiers, a Milvus Velocycle blocks your path (Fig. 6). Pummel it with Slash & Burn, then follow up with the Dualcasting Paradigm to achieve the all-important Stagger. With the four troops that follow, don't be too slow in your transitions to War & Peace to heal – especially if they all focus their attacks on a single party member.

6

7 Visit the Paradigm screen to create Symbiosis (Medic + Synergist), then activate the elevator at the waypoint marker to instigate a boss battle.

Major Encounter – Aster Protoflorian: Select the Supersoldier Paradigm to enable Hope to protect the party with a full set of vital buffs, then use Libra to scan your opponent. During this period, use Symbiosis whenever you need to heal (enabling Hope to continue applying status enhancements). This enormous creature has the ability to change its elemental strengths and weaknesses. In its first state, it halves all elemental damage. However, it will soon use one of four alternate Exoproofing states (Fig. 7) to slightly adjust its elemental affinities (absorbing one element and becoming weak against its opposite). Once Libra has built up a picture of the enemy's prowess, your party will automatically switch attacks to suit.

As soon as the party is sufficiently insulated by at least Protect and Shell, build the Aster Protoflorian's Chain Gauge to approximately 30% with the Slash & Burn Paradigm. When you reach that point, switch to Dualcasting to vastly accelerate its growth. You will need regular transitions to the War & Peace Paradigm to keep your party in good shape. Once your opponent is Staggered, change back to Slash & Burn. The Aster Protoflorian is susceptible to Lightning's Launch ability (only available in the Commando role), which offers a period blessedly free of incoming attacks.

Due to its colossal HP, you will not come close to destroying the boss with the first Stagger. Switch to Symbiosis as soon as it ends to have Hope reapply status effects before they expire while Lightning heals the party, then begin the process of building the Chain Gauge all over again. Once it reaches approximately 50% health, the Aster Protoflorian will become more aggressive. To be doubly safe, switch to War & Peace whenever a party member's HP falls to around 60%.

Your rewards for this battle are a Crystarium expansion, the Creature Comforts electronic pass (a components store), and a Tungsten Bangle. At the Maintenance Exit area, save your game then run over to the waypoint to end the chapter. Lightning and Hope do not take part in combat during Chapter 06, so you may wish to unequip certain accessories beforehand.

7

THE SUNLETH WATERSCAPE

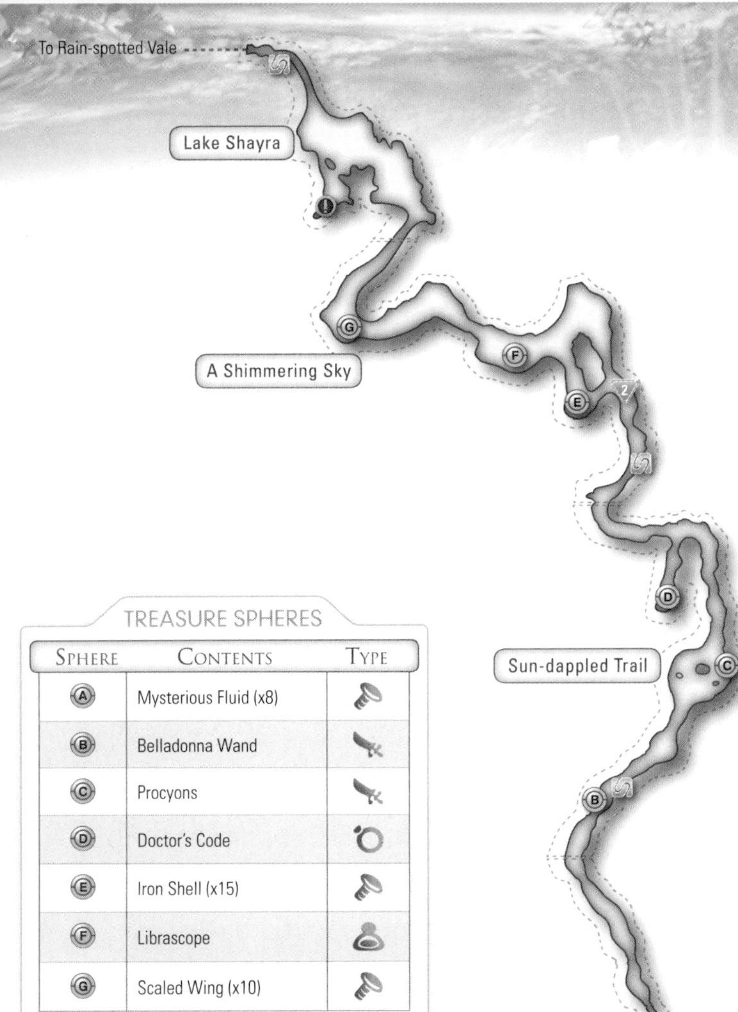

TREASURE SPHERES

Sphere	Contents	Type
A	Mysterious Fluid (x8)	
B	Belladonna Wand	
C	Procyons	
D	Doctor's Code	
E	Iron Shell (x15)	
F	Librascope	
G	Scaled Wing (x10)	

ENEMIES

Name	Notes	Page
Flandragora	Easy preemptive strikes; immune to physical damage and Water; easily Staggered.	239
Hedge Frog	Very low HP; may cast Deprotect.	235
Gremlin	Low HP; their Fire magic can be dangerous if you encounter large groups.	235
Scalebeast	Easy preemptive strikes; damage reduction or immunity until Staggered; difficult for area.	237

1 A quick trip to the Crystarium will reveal that you have a wealth of CP to invest. With Vanille, the new abilities offered by the top tier of the Ravager crystals (and Role Level) should probably be your first port of call, as they offer greater damage-dealing potential and tactical flexibility in battle. That achieved, your long-term goals should be to unlock Poison (Saboteur), Esuna and Cura (Medic) before targeting the final two Role Level enhancements.

For Sazh, aim for the Accessory crystal and Role Level for Synergist, followed by the Blitz ability (Commando), then favor Strength increases where possible to boost his Commando credentials. Last, but not least, you may wish to equip Vanille with the newly acquired Tungsten Bangle to boost her HP by 150, then create the Undermine Paradigm (Saboteur + Ravager). This (followed by Dualcasting) is excellent against the Flandragora (Fig. 1) you meet on the first map area, as they are immune to physical damage. Other enemies are easily dispatched with Slash & Burn.

1

2 Don't neglect to open the second and third Treasure Spheres of the chapter. The former contains a Belladonna Wand, a weapon for Vanille that offers the Improved Debuffing perk. The latter contains the Procyons for Sazh, which extend Stagger times.

If you are making good progress with the party's Crystariums, the Shocking Breath attack of Scalebeasts should drain approximately two thirds of an HP gauge on contact, so be ready to change to War & Peace whenever a party member's HP falls into the yellow area. The best strategy is to start with a preemptive strike, Stagger your opponent, then switch to Undermine to inflict status ailments (Fig. 2). Once its carapace regenerates, change to Slash & Burn until its Chain Gauge is 40% to 50% filled, then switch to Dualcasting to Stagger it a second time. It should fall halfway to a third Stagger, for a battle duration of around three minutes. Given the unremarkable Spoils and CP reward, you may prefer to just kill the one guarding a Treasure Sphere, then avoid the other three.

2

Miscellany

- Unlike other "magic" attacks Quake is classed as a Technique, and requires one block of your TP gauge to activate. It inflicts Earth element damage to all enemies within its effect radius. An interesting application of Quake is to use it after a successful preemptive strike to Stagger all opponents simultaneously.

- Enemy resistance to physical, magical and elemental damage becomes rather more complicated from this chapter forward. You should regularly study Enemy Intel report cards whenever you encounter new foes to get a better picture of their strengths and weaknesses. Not knowing that Flandragora are immune to physical damage, for example, might lead to battles against them becoming longer and harder than they need be. See the accompanying table for a description of possible damage modifiers.

DAMAGE MODIFIERS

Description	Effect
Normal	Standard damage
Weakness	200% damage
Halved	50% damage inflicted
Resistant	10% damage inflicted
Immune	No damage
Absorb	Attacks heal opponent

- While exploring, you can tell which enemies are going to attack when they detect you by looking at the alert icon above their head. When one doesn't appear, the opponent in question is actually a member of a separate party.

- The Esuna spell removes a single status ailment at a time. If a party member has more than one affliction, and you require a targeted cure for a specific illness, you can instead use specialist items. For example, an Antidote will immediately cure Poison.

- When you encounter mixed groups where you know one enemy to have a low ability to detect your party, it is sometimes worth waiting for these to stand alone before sneaking over for a preemptive strike attempt.

SPHERE	CONTENTS	TYPE
A	Metal Armband	
B	Aqua Ring	

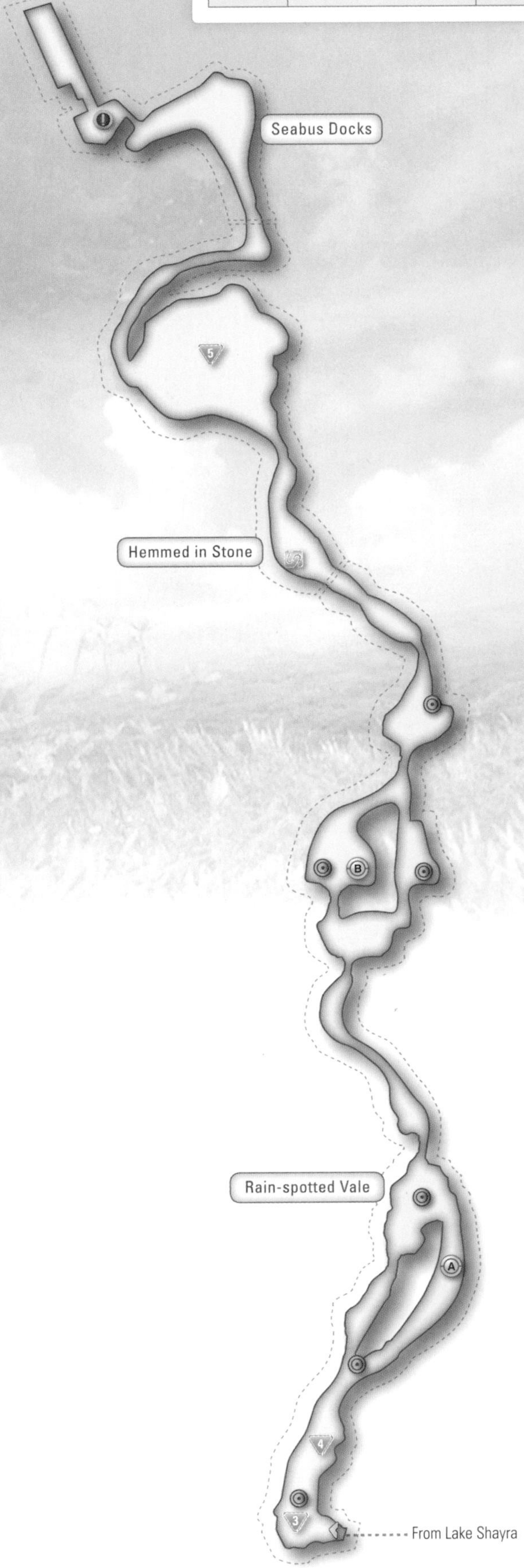

ENEMIES

NAME	NOTES	PAGE
Hedge Frog	Rain only; low HP; can inflict Deprotect.	235
Mud Frog	Rain only; Courtship Dance ability summons Hedge Frogs to the battle.	235
Scalebeast	Rain only; easy preemptive strikes; damage reduction or immunity until Staggered.	237
Gremlin	Fire attacks are dangerous in numbers; very low HP.	235
Garchimacera	Casts Fira; Magic, Ice and Water damage halved.	235
Wyvern	Dry only; immune against Earth; Magic damage halved.	237
Flandragora	Dry only; easy preemptive strikes; immune to physical damage and Water; easily Staggered.	239
Enki	Immune to Water but weak against Lightning element; uses status buffs.	238
Enlil	Immune to Lightning element but weak against Water; uses status buffs.	238

3 As the Climate Control Orbs (Fig. 3) act as a toggle between rain and shine, adjusting (and, you should note, respawning) the local fauna, the remainder of the journey through the Sunleth Waterscape is a puzzle of sorts. When it rains, you face Hedge Frogs, Mud Frogs, and Scalebeasts. Clement conditions, however, pit you against Wyverns and Flandragora. Whatever the weather, though, the Gremlins and Garchimacera can be seen frolicking around.

The Mud Frog is an unusual enemy. Its most noteworthy attribute is its Courtship Dance. This summons Hedge Frog reinforcements to the battle. Ignore these and focus exclusively on the Mud Frog, as it will simply repeat the trick if you kill the interlopers.

The Garchimacera has a Fira attack that can inflict damage on both party members if they are standing in close proximity, but it is easily Staggered. Again, this is another instance where it makes sense to destroy the most powerful enemy first. The Wyvern is rather stronger than the other local denizens. Casting Esuna to remove Deprotect is fairly pointless, as the status ailment can be restored by the monster within a matter of seconds. The best strategy is to inflict Poison, beef up your party with the Bravery and Faith status enhancements, then smash away with Slash & Burn and Dualcasting.

3

4 Stick to rainy conditions for the first orb, then switch to dry at the second and take the right-hand path. This pits you against six Flandragora split into two groups (repeat the tactics used earlier), and enables you to open a Treasure Sphere. Change to rainy conditions at the third orb. Take the left-hand path and operate the fourth orb before you approach the Treasure Sphere (a trio of Flandragora pose much less of a threat than a Scalebeast with several allies), then switch back to rain. You can bypass the next Scalebeast entirely (Fig. 4).

4

For the final orb, it's probably best to change to dry conditions. You'll need to fight three battles instead of two, but avoid a potentially nasty encounter against four Mud Frogs. If you have not reached the Role Levels for Vanille and Sazh at the Crystarium, you may profit from grinding through battles with the Flandragora and Garchimaceras here, though this is purely a suggestion.

5 **Major Encounter – Enki and Enlil:** Caution is key during this fight. Unless you make regular use of the War & Peace Paradigm to heal whenever a party member falls below 60% to 70% HP, Enki and Enlil possess the strength to end this battle with remorseless speed.

Switch to Tide Turner (Saboteur + Synergist) and inflict Deshell, Deprotect and Poison on Enlil straight away (Fig. 5). It's a good idea to use the Abilities menu to choose the debuffs manually, though, as the Auto-hinder option has an annoying effect of switching targets when you least expect it. Meanwhile, Sazh will buff the party with Bravery and Faith. From this point, use Slash & Burn until the Chain Gauge is 40% full, then switch to Dualcasting to Stagger the monster rapidly.

5

Once you see Enlil perform the Bellow ability, be ready for a sudden increase in difficulty. The cocktail of status enhancements it bestows makes him far more dangerous. Other abilities of note include Enraged (offers temporary heightened resistance to status ailments), and Trample (a dizzying physical attack that can leave either party member with precious little HP). Both monsters have an area-effect attack that is often cancelled if you hit them while the onscreen caption is present. Your assault should prevent Enlil from using Raging Tempest, but Enki's Raging Torrent will necessitate regular Paradigm Shifts to heal. Both creatures have attacks that inflict Deprotect, but we would advise against removing this status effect with Esuna – both occur too regularly to make such efforts worthwhile.

Once Enlil perishes, the battle becomes much less fraught. Stick to the same general tactics and you will win in no time. Your rewards are the Fulmen Ring, Riptide Ring and a Crystarium expansion. There are no further enemies en route to the final waypoint, so remove accessories if you would like to use them with your other party in the next chapter.

PALUMPOLUM

ENEMIES

Name	Notes	Page
Corps Tranquifex	Susceptible to Lightning element; water damage halved; easily Staggered.	230
Corps Pacifex	Susceptible to Lightning element; water damage halved.	230
Falco Velocycle	Physical and magical damage halved; weak against Lightning element.	231
Flanitor	Heals allies with its Rescue ability.	233
Lucidon	Massive damage resistance until Staggered; immune to status ailments.	232
Orion	Very fast attack speed; weak against Ice and Water.	231
PSICOM Bombardier	Huge Strength and high HP.	229
PSICOM Scavenger	Above-average HP.	228
PSICOM Predator	Inflicts the Curse status ailment.	228
PSICOM Warlord	High HP; dodges regularly; employs very dangerous attacks after using the Activate Manadrive ability.	229

TREASURE SPHERES

Sphere	Contents	Type
A	Fiber-optic Cable (x3)	
B	Holy Water (x3)	
C	Librascope	
D	Holy Water (x4)*	
E	Phoenix Down*	
F	Mobius Coil (x2)*	
G	Aqua Ring*	
H	Warding Talisman	
I	Fortisol	
J	Paladin	
K	Insulated Cabling (x4)	

*See "Nutriculture Complex Platforms" to learn how to reach these Treasure Spheres.

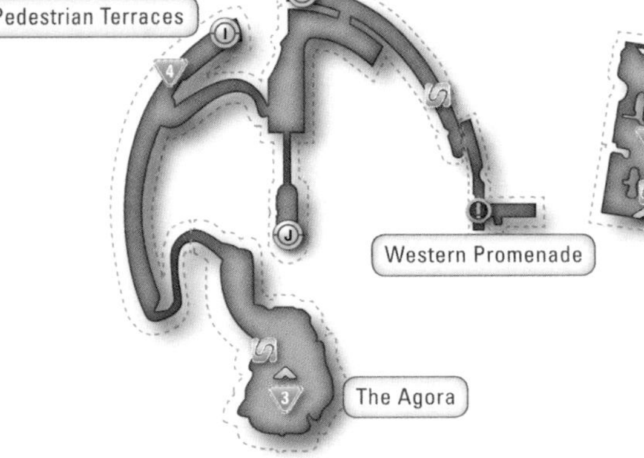

1 You have plenty of CP to invest at the Crystarium, so go there immediately. Lightning will spend more time working as a Ravager for a part of this chapter, so you'll benefit from unlocking Overwhelm, Thundara and Blizzard; after that, aim for Smite in the Commando role. Unlock Thundara and Watera for Hope, then complete the rings just above the three Role Level crystals before working on the uppermost rings of the Medic and Synergist roles. Your Paradigm Deck will be unchanged from the end of Chapter 05, so there is no need to make any adjustments there.

1

After defeating the two groups of Corps Tranquifex, drop down into the open pipe (Fig. 1). Both types of Corps enemies encountered in this area are easily defeated. The Falco Velocycle is tougher, but should fall during the first Stagger; to accelerate the battle, Paradigm Shift to Dualcasting when its Chain Gauge is 40% full.

2 There are four hidden Treasure Spheres in this area – see Nutriculture Complex Platforms for more details. Flanitors are more of an annoyance than a threat, but the Lucidon is a more demanding opponent. As its Photon Beam (Fig. 2) drains approximately half of Hope's HP bar and slightly less for Lightning, you will need to alternate between Slash & Burn and War & Peace as required until its Chain Gauge reaches 40%, then switch to Dualcasting to Stagger it in a timely manner. Robbed of its protective carapace, it is desperately weak – especially if you take advantage of its susceptibility to the Launch ability by changing back to Slash & Burn.

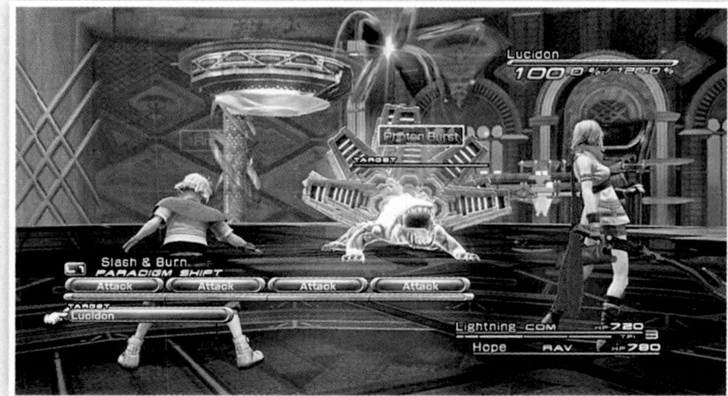

2

3 Play resumes with Snow fighting alongside Shiva in Gestalt Mode. Use Autogestalt to attack enemies – this should kill all with the exception of the stronger Orion (Fig. 3). This larger enemy may need to be finished off with physical attacks. If Snow is knocked out, select Retry, and you will this time be offered a chance to visit the main menu and work on his underdeveloped Crystarium. Purchase all available crystals for his Sentinel and Commando roles before you start on Ravager.

3

Once the battle is over, create the useful Dualcasting (Ravager + Ravager) and Supersoldier (Commando + Synergist) Paradigms, then press forward to engage the first group of troops. Dispatch the dangerous PSICOM Scavengers first. PSICOM Predators are also priority targets as they inflict the Curse status ailment (which increases the likelihood that actions attempted by an affected individual will fail, and also provides a success rate boost for assaults made by their opponents). When you encounter PSICOM Bombardiers, however, the opposite applies – due to their high HP, it's better to slay their companions before you direct attacks at them.

4 There are three Treasure Spheres that are easily missed on the way to the final waypoint. The first is guarded by a PSICOM Warlord, an opponent you will do well not to underestimate. If either party member is injured, the Activate Manadrive notification caption is your cue to heal – and fast. Stagger him quickly to put the Launch ability to good use. The second Sphere is at the top of a ramp to your right after you ascend the second ice path (Fig. 4). The size of this group of soldiers makes them a threat, so be prepared to switch to War & Peace regularly until you thin their numbers. The third Sphere is to your left when you jump down into the corridor after fighting a second Warlord; in this battle, aim to kill the PSICOM Predator swiftly to avoid the Curse debuff.

4

NUTRICULTURE COMPLEX PLATFORMS

There are two "secret" platforms in the Nutriculture Complex that you can reach to find Treasure Spheres.

- After riding the first moving platform on arrival in this map area, approach the floating switch on the left and activate it. Now step back onto the moving platform. You will be delivered to a location with two Treasure Spheres.
- Another secret area can be found when you reach a second moving platform. Again, activate the switch on the left-hand side to travel there. You must fight a Lucidon and a Flanitor to claim your prizes this time. Start with a preemptive strike if possible, and kill the latter target first to make the battle easier.

ENEMIES

Name	Notes	Page
Corps Tranquifex	Susceptible to Lightning element; water damage halved; easily Staggered.	230
Corps Pacifex	Susceptible to Lightning element; water damage halved; easily Staggered.	230
Orion	Very fast attack rate; susceptible to Slow; weak against Ice and Water.	231
PSICOM Predator	Inflicts Curse.	228
PSICOM Aerial Sniper	Powerful MLRS Volley causes multiple impacts for big damage.	229
Falco Velocycle	Physical and magical damage halved; weak against Lightning element; Gatling Gun attack is deadly.	231
Ushumgal Subjugator	Very high HP; vulnerable to Lightning element; immune to status ailments when its Overdrive ability is active.	234

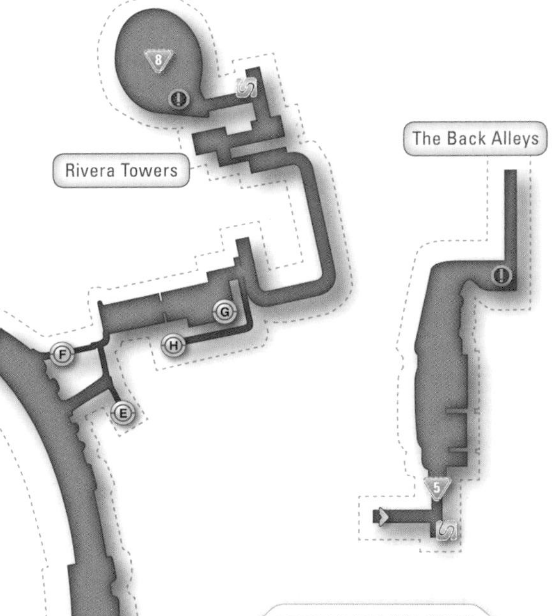

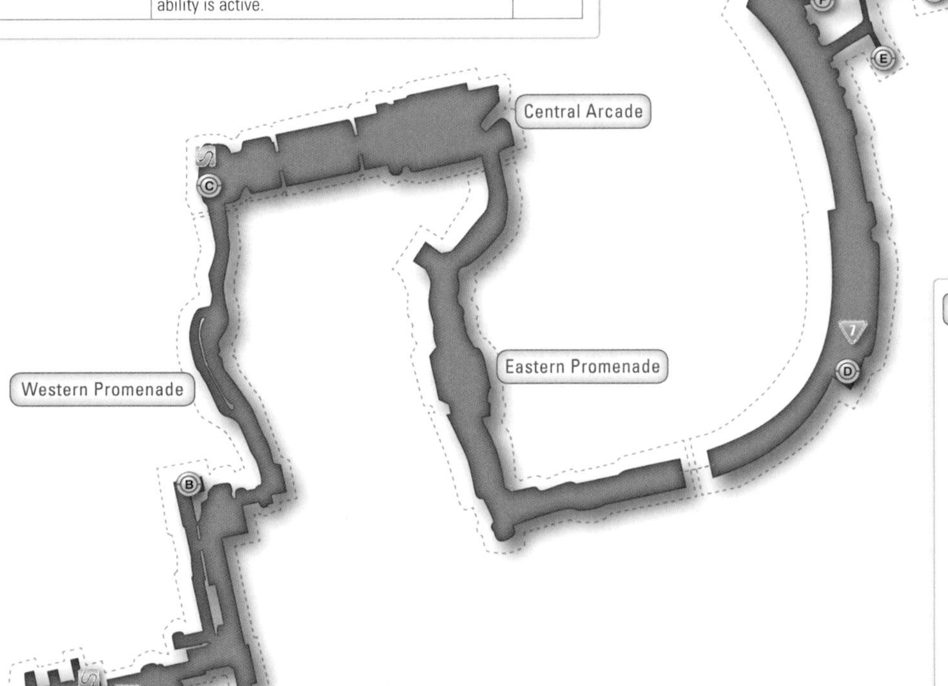

TREASURE SPHERES

Sphere	Contents	Type
A	Holy Water (x4)	
B	Incentive Chip (x2)	
C	Guardian Amulet	
D	Shaman's Mark	
E	Vidofnir	
F	Thrust Bearing (x3)	
G	Deceptisol	
H	2,000 Gil	

5 Lightning is joined by new party member Fang for the next section, so allocate her useful accessories and visit the Crystarium to upgrade both characters. Launch, Smite and Adrenaline (Commando) are the priorities for Fang, with Slowga and the Accessory crystal (Saboteur) your subsequent objectives. Create the War & Peace (Commando + Medic) and Divide & Conquer (Saboteur + Commando) Paradigms, then head straight into battle.

The Corps and PSICOM troops shouldn't be a trial, but the Orion can be difficult. It is susceptible to Slow (Fig. 5), so switch to Divide & Conquer straight away. With the status ailment in place, Slash & Burn is your best option.

5

6 Back with Snow and Hope, approach the first corner to the left (Fig. 6) to leap up and find a Treasure Sphere at the far end of the raised pathway; you can drop back down via the gap in the wall. The battles in the Western Promenade and Central Arcade maps are unremarkable. Though there are opportunities to avoid certain enemies, you should still try to engage them for CP and spoils. In the Eastern Promenade, though, you will meet a trio of PSICOM Aerial Snipers whose multi-hit MLRS Volley attack is rather vicious. For a rapid takedown of this enemy type, use one round of Slash & Burn attacks, immediately change to Dualcasting to Stagger, then return to the original Paradigm to finish them off.

6

7 You can equip on one character both the Shaman's Mark accessory found in the first Treasure Sphere of the Rivera Towers and the Magician's Mark for a massive 70 point Magic stat increase. The second Treasure Sphere encountered contains the Vidofnir, a weapon for Hope that extends the duration of his status enhancements. There are a number of Falco Velocycles in this area. Whenever the caption appears for their Gatling

7

Gun attack (Fig. 7), switch to the Lifeguard Paradigm without hesitation. This is the only way that Snow can survive this super-powerful assault, which will otherwise kill either party member in one burst.

As you jump up a sequence of platforms towards the end of the map area, consider using a Deceptisol Shroud before the battle against two PSICOM Aerial Snipers and a Falco Velocycle. If you cast Quake to stagger all three enemies straight away, then target the Velocycle first, this act turns a fraught four or five minute encounter into a minute of straightforward pounding.

8 **Major Encounter – Ushumgal Subjugator:** Spend CP at the Crystarium, record your progress at the Save Station, then head forward. Ushumgal Subjugator's Tail Hammer attack is a vicious physical assault that can hit both party members for massive damage (Fig. 8). For this reason, you should never allow either to fall below 50% HP. First, though, boost the party with Supersoldier (Synergist + Commando). Now use Slash & Burn to push your opponent's Chain Gauge up to just over a third full, then change to Dualcasting to Stagger it. With regular breaks for healing, and one further application of status enhancements once the original buffs wear off, this battle should take in the region of five minutes to complete.

8

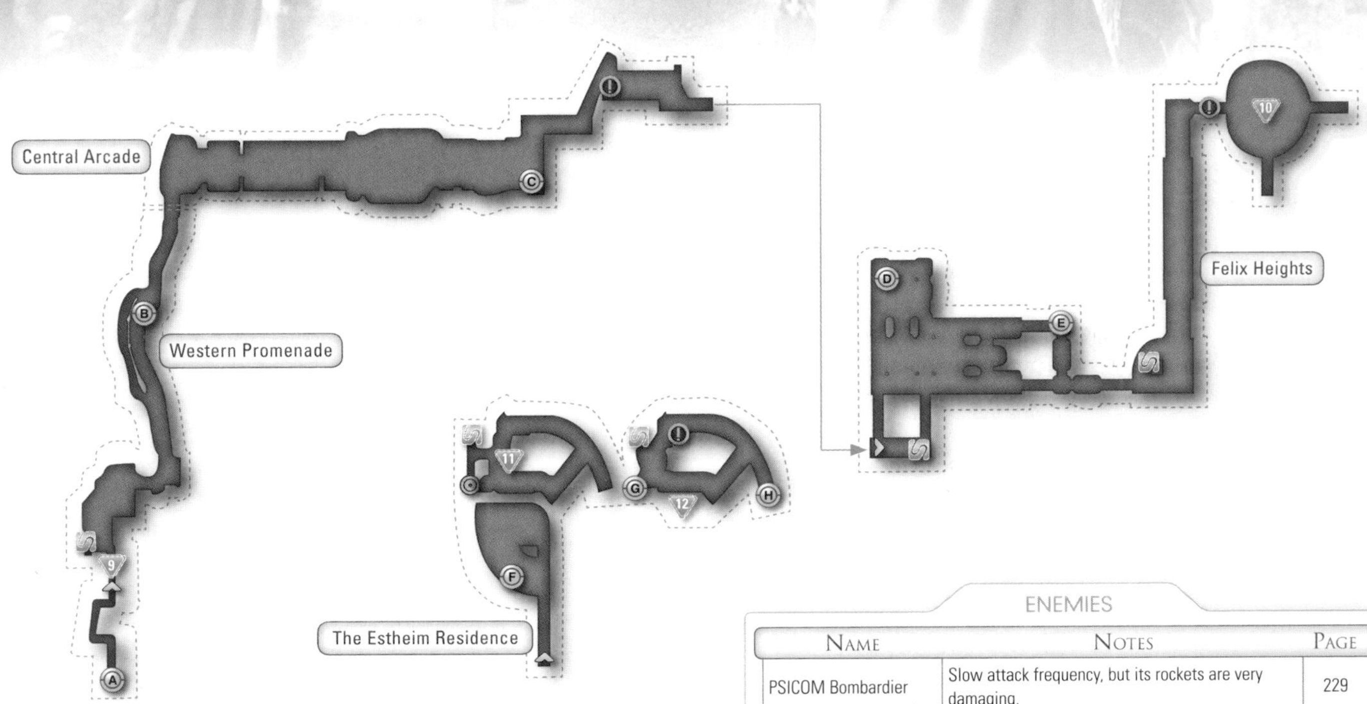

ENEMIES

Name	Notes	Page
PSICOM Bombardier	Slow attack frequency, but its rockets are very damaging.	229
Corps Pacifex	Weak against Lightning element; Water damage halved.	230
Orion	Fast attack speed; susceptible to Slow.	231
Lodestar Behemoth	Very strong attacks; possesses status ailment immunity in standing pose; susceptible to Slow.	233
Corps Tranquifex	Weak against Lightning element; Water damage halved.	230
PSICOM Scavenger	Uses its Manadrive Vigilance ability to prevent interruptions caused by your party's attacks.	228
PSICOM Predator	Inflicts Curse.	228
Ushumgal Subjugator (Walking)	Very high HP; swift attack speed; vulnerable to Slow.	234
PSICOM Aerial Sniper	Powerful MLRS Volley causes multiple impacts for big damage.	229
Havoc Skytank	Immune against status ailments and Wind; destroying sub-systems drains more HP than attacks on the body; very fast attack speed.	231

TREASURE SPHERES

Sphere	Contents	Type
A	Bestial Claw (x15)	
B	Gae Bolg	
C	Axis Blade	
D	Tungsten Bangle	
E	Black Belt	
F	Phoenix Down	
G	Ethersol	
H	Brawler's Wristband	

9

9 Spend CP to improve Fang and Lightning at the Crystarium, then engage the first group of soldiers. The most dangerous enemy types in this area are the Orion and Lodestar Behemoth. Paradigm Shift to Divide & Conquer to curb unwelcome enthusiasm with Slow; both enemies have very strong attacks, and will most likely fall before they are Staggered. Indeed, the Behemoth's Chain Gauge is reset when it rears up on its hind legs to fight in a standing posture (Fig. 9).

10 **Major Encounter – Ushumgal Subjugator (Walking):** When Hope faces this boss alone, cast Libra to learn about your foe and then stand by idly as your HP gauge is drained. The proper battle doesn't actually begin until Fang and Lightning join the fray, and there is no way you can begin to dent this monster's colossal HP before then.

Paradigm Shift to Evened Odds once the real engagement begins, inflict Slow with Fang, and wait until Hope has applied buffs before you commit to purposeful aggression. For a safe yet pedestrian victory, you can alternate between Solidarity and Delta Attack. Both feature a Sentinel, with Solidarity swapping Delta Attack's Ravager for a Medic. If you are seeking a faster finish, use bursts of Relentless Assault, but don't let your party's health fall too low, though – a single Medic will struggle to bring a party of three back from the brink of disaster against such a powerful opponent.

10

Once your huge foe is Staggered, use Relentless Assault for greater damage – the creature can be Launched, so it's perfectly safe to opt for all-out attack. It becomes more aggressive once the Chain Gauge is reset, though, so you'll need to be more patient than before. When the Ushumgal Subjugator uses its Targeting ability, ensure that your Paradigm is set to Solidarity or Delta Attack – the Pinpoint Beam (Fig. 10) or Photon Blaster attacks that can follow are very strong.

Your primary reward for winning this encounter is a Shield Talisman: an accessory that grants the wearer a Protect status enhancement from the start of each battle.

11 Once inside the Estheim Residence, interact with the television at the waypoint to continue. After further story development, play resumes with a fight against PSICOM soldiers. The halls of the gutted house are patrolled by a respawning supply of additional soldiers. Though this may seem a perfect place to generate extra CP, there is actually a far more lucrative power-leveling spot in the next chapter. Open the two Treasure Spheres (the one at the far end of the hall contains a Brawler's Wristband, which offers a Strength stat boost of 50 – Fig. 11), spend CP at the Crystarium, then head to the waypoint marker.

11

12 **Major Encounter – Havoc Skytank:** Paradigm Shift to Evened Odds immediately to enable Hope to cast status enhancements. Once everyone has Protect and Shell buffs active, your next task is to target each of the Skytank's four components in turn: Portside Hull, Starboard Hull, Portside Turret and Starboard Turret. Alternating between Solidarity and Delta Attack enables you to slowly but surely drain their HP gauges without putting the party at risk. Destroying the sub-systems also causes greater overall damage: as each one explodes, a large chunk of health is drained from the central body.

Destroying all sub-systems vastly reduces the Havoc Skytank's attack frequency. Reapply buffs when required, then continue as previously. When it permanently deploys the powerful Main Cannon, the end is in sight (Fig. 12). Once all party members are in a state of good health, use Relentless Assault to Stagger it, though be ready to return to Solidarity to heal. Once the battle ends, you are given an electronic pass for the Plautus's Workshop retail network and a Crystarium Expansion.

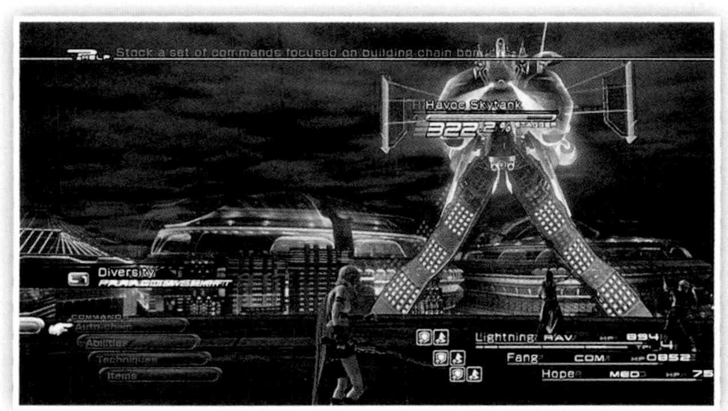

12

NAUTILUS

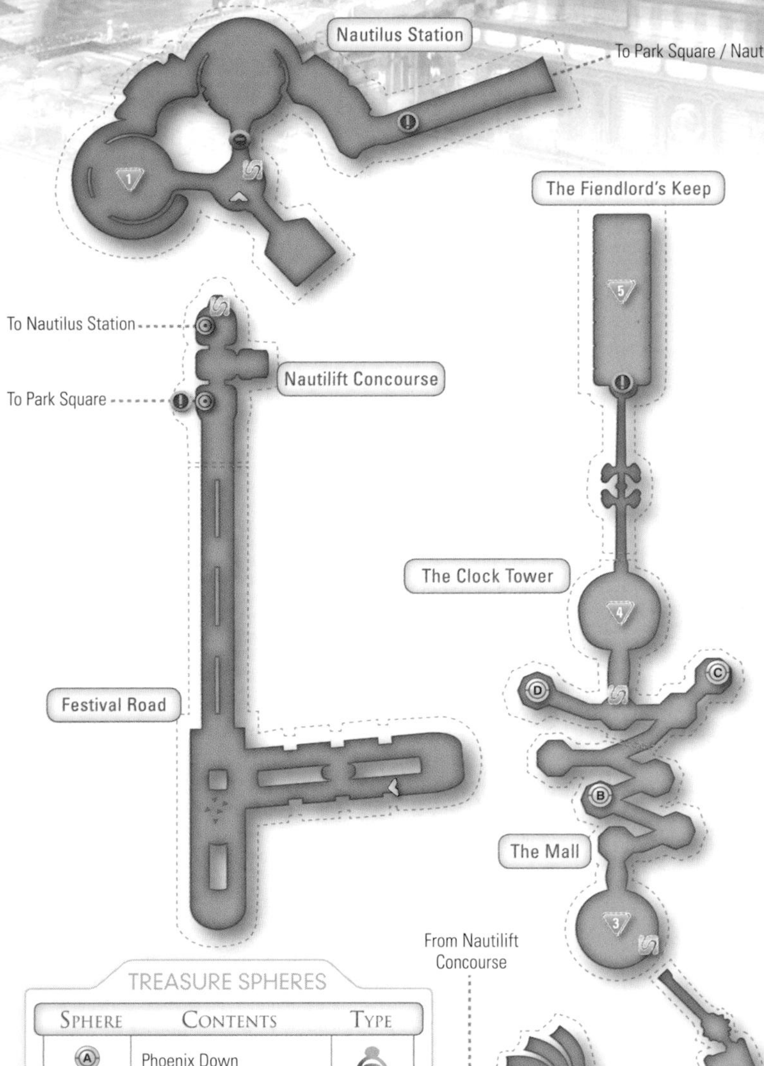

TREASURE SPHERES

Sphere	Contents	Type
A	Phoenix Down	
B	Spica Defenders	
C	Guardian Amulet	
D	Healer's Staff	
E	Star Pendant*	

* Only available after you've found the chocobo chick.

ENEMIES

Name	Notes	Page
Corps Gunner	Cannon fodder, though large groups can inflict worrying damage.	230
Orion	Fast attack speed; weak against Ice and Water.	231
Zwerg Metrodroid	Immune against Lightning and Water; weak against Wind and Fire.	232
Midlight Reaper	Magic and physical damage halved; immune to Lightning element, but weak against Fire and Ice.	231

1 Though you ostensibly have a fortune in CP to spend at the start of Chapter 08, anything more than a cursory examination of the Crystarium will reveal that the expense of purchasing crystals has skyrocketed. Unlock Haste (Synergist) for Sazh, then unlock all cheaper crystals (that is, those below 500 CP) in every role for both characters. With Vanille, you should then work towards Dispel (Saboteur) and Raise (Medic); Sazh's short-term objective should be to reach the next Commando Role Level.

There are no battles or Treasure Spheres in this opening section, so you only need to travel to each waypoint in turn. When you reach the Nautilift Concourse, jump into the marked Nautilift to reach Nautilus Park (Fig. 1).

1

2 You should have no problem finding the chocobo chick but just in case, here are its hiding places. Simply press ⊗/Ⓐ when the interaction notification pops up to find it.

- **Location 1:** In the large group of sheep to the right of the fountain.
- **Location 2:** On the stall.
- **Location 3:** By the fountain.
- **Location 4:** By the large group of chocobos (Fig. 2).

Open the Treasure Sphere to obtain a Star Pendant, then follow the newly-cleared path to reach the next waypoint.

2

3 You will meet various configurations of the Corps Gunner, Zwerg Metrodroid (Fig. 3) and Orion adversaries. Pounding away with Slash & Burn is generally the best tactic, though you can speed things up against an Orion by using Undermine (Ravager + Saboteur) to start, then switching to Dualcasting. (You should also note that if you run up to an Orion before its body parts are fully deployed, you may obtain a preemptive strike.)

3

4 **Major Encounter – Midlight Reaper:** Switch to Tide Turner and immediately use Libra to identify the Midlight Reaper's weaknesses. While Vanille attempts to inflict the Imperil status ailment (reducing your opponent's resistance to elemental damage), you should apply status enhancements. Haste, Bravery and Faith are all useful, though you can also cast Enfrost on Sazh (exploiting your opponent's weakness to the Ice element while in the Commando role). During this opening stage of the fight your opponent is fairly restrained, its Nerve Gas attack inflicts Poison, but this is no cause for alarm.

4

The Midlight Reaper is unusually easy to Stagger for a boss, so with the Chain Gauge gains made by Vanille's attempts to cast debuffs, you should be able to switch to Dualcasting and drive it up straight away. Once the first Stagger period is over, you should notice a caption that reads "Release Arms Restraints". From this point, whenever you see the Priming Main Cannon notification appear (Fig. 4), it's wise to ensure that your party is fully healed. You will need to Stagger the Midlight Reaper a few times to subdue it (using the standard Slash & Burn/Dualcasting tactic), with at least one break to reapply status enhancements and the Imperil ailment.

5

5 **Eidolon Battle – Brynhildr:** From the start of the fight, Paradigm Shift to Tide Turner (Synergist + Saboteur), then manually apply the Vigilance and Haste buffs to both party members (in that precise order). Vigilance reduces the likelihood that Brynhildr's frequent attacks will stun party members and interrupt their actions (Fig. 5), while Haste provides an essential boost to the ATB gauge charge rate. Switch to War & Peace to heal (which should be pretty urgent at this point), then alternate between this Paradigm and Dualcasting to drive up the Eidolon's Chain Bonus. If you can maintain and gradually increase this, your opponent should be ready to yield in just over two minutes. At the end of the fight, Sazh obtains the Brynhildr Eidolith and gains an ATB gauge segment.

Miscellany

- As the Crystarium now features more outlying "arms", you should note that you can complete these whenever you like – you are not obliged to unlock them as you pass. This means that you can bypass them initially in order to reach abilities on the inner circle a little earlier.
- **Power Tip:** When you reach the Clock Tower area, there is a group of five Zwerg Metrodroids arranged around a Treasure Sphere. These can be dispatched for 640 CP. To cause them to respawn, retrace your steps to the Treasure Sphere in the Mall area, then return.

CHAPTER 09

THE PALAMECIA

TREASURE SPHERES

Sphere	Contents	Type
A	Digital Circuit (x4)	
B	Millerite	
C	Incentive Chip (x3)	
D	Silicone Oil (x3)	
E	Lifesaber	
F	Ember Ring	
G	Pandoran Spear	

ENEMIES

Name	Notes	Page
PSICOM Raider	Inflicts Pain and Fog debuffs; can block damage with Guard ability; high HP, but not too difficult to Stagger.	228
PSICOM Infiltrator	Employs Esuna and Cura to heal itself and nearby allies.	228
Deckdrone	Weak against Fire and Ice; immune to Lightning element; wind damage halved.	230
PSICOM Dragoon	Wind damage halved; Missile Burst ability deals very high damage.	229
PSICOM Huntress	Magic and physical damage halved; uses status enhancements on herself and allies.	229
Viking	Immune to Fire, but weak against Water and Lightning; susceptible to Slow and Imperil; can be Launched.	231

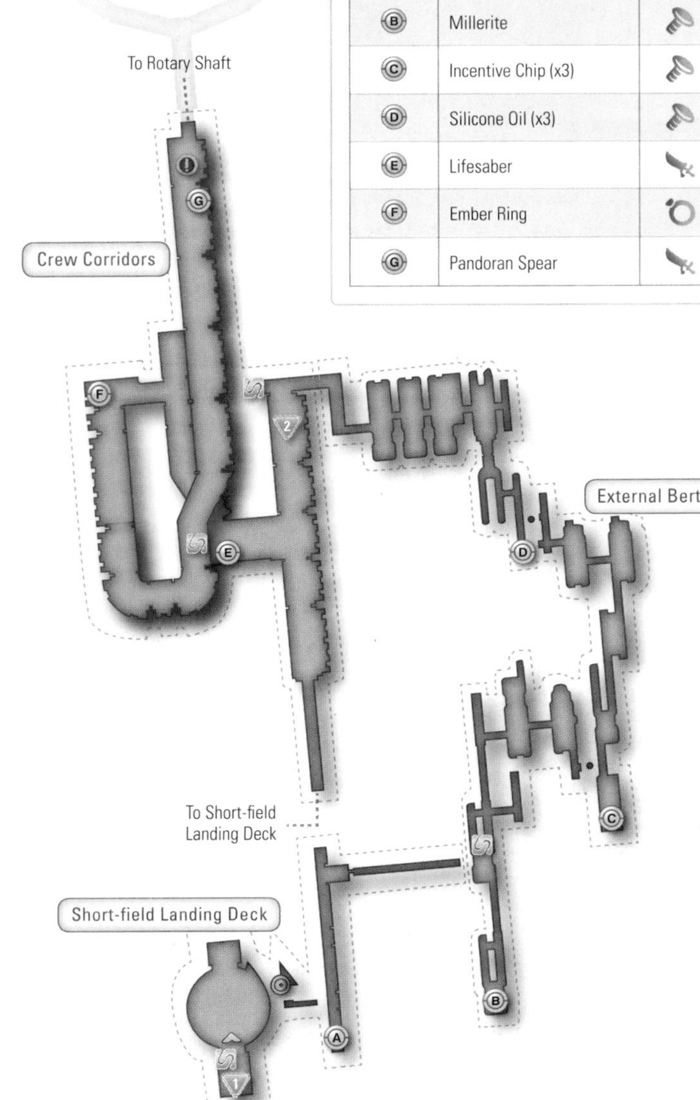

Aboard the Lindblum

Before you set off, visit the Crystarium. Unlock all crystals that cost less than 1,000 CP for each character, then focus on the following short and mid-term objectives:

- **Lightning:** As she will mostly operate as a Ravager for this chapter, unlock Aero and continue on to Watera. After that, spend CP to reach Raise and Renew (Medic).
- **Hope:** Unlock Veil and Boon (Synergist), grab Blizzara (Ravager), then aim to reach the Medic role level – this will make him more effective as your primary healer.
- **Fang:** Unlock Steelguard (Sentinel) and Dispel (Saboteur), then unlock the first three abilities in the Commando role. Once you have these, Curse and Cursega (Saboteur) should follow.

Snow doesn't play a major role in Chapter 09, so you can skip his upgrades for now. Your final acts of preparation should be to configure your accessories for the three active party members. Once you are ready to leave the Lindblum, speak to Rygdea at the waypoint marker to continue.

1 Two PSICOM Raiders and a PSICOM Infiltrator will attack after the cinematic sequence ends. While the Infiltrator is stronger and has lower HP, the Raiders inflict status ailments, so it's common sense to dispatch them first – especially as the Infiltrator will likely cease his assault in an attempt to cast Manadrive Cura. The same order of targets applies for the following battle.

The External Berths map area is patrolled by Deckdrones and PSICOM Dragoons. Though you might assume that a Sentinel may be advantageous here, this will slow each battle down to a crawl. Instead, stick with Relentless Assault for faster takedowns, switching to Diversity (Ravager + Medic + Commando) to have Hope heal when it becomes necessary. Make the Dragoons your priority – their Missile Burst attack can knock out an injured party member in a single flurry of explosions (Fig. 1).

1

2 Inside the Crew Corridors, you meet the PSICOM Huntress (Fig. 2) and Viking. Though the basic attack power and HP of the Huntress is not astonishing, their ability to cast four status enhancements at the start of every fight makes them a hardier foe than many of their allies. Due to the length of time it takes to pacify them, it's usually best to deal with their weaker companions first. The Viking is deceptively easy to dispatch on its own, as it is vulnerable to the Launch ability – rendering it toothless once Staggered. Though susceptible to Slow, Deprotect and Deshell, sticking with Relentless Assault should destroy it before the end of the first Stagger for a five-star rating.

2

At the first junction, head right – the path directly ahead returns you to the Short-field Landing Deck area. The two battles where you face a pair of PSICOM Huntresses backed up by Raiders are rather tricky, so use Diversity for the first part of the fight to be safe, then go back to Relentless Assault to speed things up when only the female warriors remain. When you reach the two Huntresses and a Viking, though, it's faster and safer to disable the female contingent first.

Miscellany

- Pain and Fog are status ailments that prevent the affected target from performing physical attacks or spell-casting respectively. This can have a disastrous effect on your battle tactics. They can be cured with Painkiller or Mallet items (which you don't have yet) or Esuna. A good short-term solution during this chapter is to set up a Discretion Paradigm (Medic + Medic + Commando). This will enable you to keep a party healthy under heavy fire while you remove a troublesome ailment inflicted by a PSICOM Raider for example.

- **Power Tip:** The External Berths and Crew Corridors areas are good locations for a spot of productive grinding for CP and spoils. Outside the ship, the Deckdrone drops two notable componenets, a Digital Circuit and Silicone Oil, and 141 CP for each one you destroy. PSICOM Dragoons sometimes surrender an Incentive Chip, a rare drop item with a value of 2,500 Gil. Once inside, the more dangerous enemies can be farmed for CP, Credit Chips (worth 500 Gil) and occasional Incentive Chips. To respawn all enemies in either area, move across the boundary between the two maps.

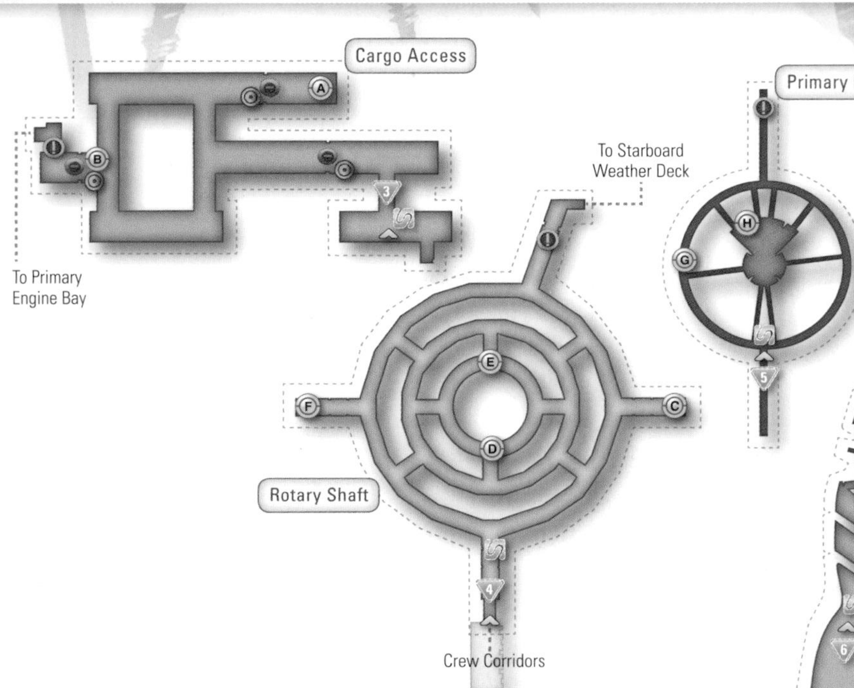

TREASURE SPHERES

Sphere	Contents	Type
A	Royal Armlet	
B	Murky Ooze (x12)	
C	White Cape	
D	Rhodochrosite	
E	Perfect Conductor	
F	Pain Dampener	
G	Segmented Carapace (x8)	
H	Phoenix Down	
I	Whistlewind Scarf	
J	Perfect Conductor	
K	Barbed Tail (x13)	
L	300 Gil*	
M	Spark Ring	

*Partially concealed – use the nearby moving "ramp" to reach it.

ENEMIES

Name	Notes	Page
Flanitor	Low HP; heals injured allies.	233
Flanborg	Immune to Lightning element, but double damage for Water; has Deshell and Deprotect vulnerability.	233
Vespid Soldier	Immune to Wind; has the dangerous Aeroga attack.	232
PSICOM Raider	Inflicts status ailments.	228
Thermadon	Massive damage resistance; powerful Photon Burst attack; weak when Staggered.	232
Viking	Immune to Fire, but weak against Ice and Lightning element; susceptible to Slow and Imperil; can be Launched.	231
PSICOM Infiltrator	Uses Cura to heal members of its battle party.	231
Deckdrone	Tornado Kick move is very dangerous if these enemies are numerous.	230
PSICOM Dragoon	Wind damage halved; Missile Burst ability deals very high damage.	229
Kalavinka Striker	Halves physical and Wind damage; absorbs Lightning element; susceptible to Slow and Curse.	233

3 You have CP to invest at the Crystarium, so go there now. For Sazh, unlock Boon (Synergist), Scourge and Jeopardize (Commando), then head for the Commando Role Level. With Vanille, go for Renew and Raise followed by the Medic Role Level. Now create the Undermine Paradigm (Ravager + Saboteur).

The Cargo Access area features bulkhead doors that must be opened by operating a switch next to them (Fig. 3). The ally-healing Flanitor is naught but a formality by this stage in your party's development, but the Flanborg can be quite tricky. Use Undermine to Stagger them rapidly.

3

4 After the brief intermission with Sazh and Vanille, the action returns to the main party. There are four Treasure Spheres in the Rotary Shaft (see map), but you'll need to fight to get them all. The enemies here may seem threatening, but they're all perfectly manageable if you use the strategies outlined previously, and guard against overconfidence when dealing with larger groups. The only new assailant here is the Vespid Soldier. It isn't especially strong, though its Aeroga attack (Fig. 4) necessitates caution (for which, read: use Diversity) if they are accompanied by a Thermadon, or if you meet them in groups of three or more.

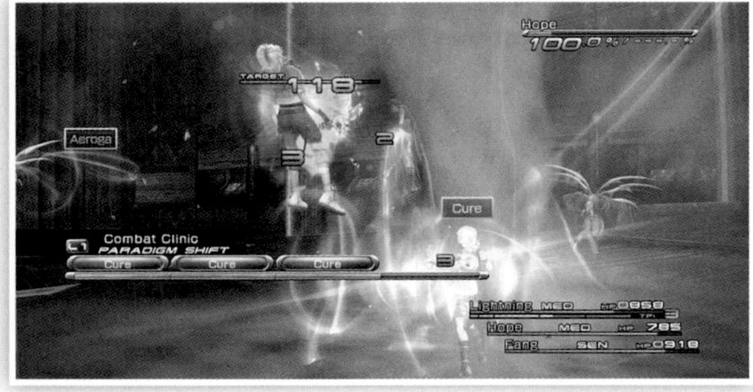

4

5 Back to Sazh and Vanille, the most efficient route through the Primary Engine Bay (Fig. 5) is to head left until you reach the Treasure Sphere, then take the second right to reach the second loot container in this area. Some of the enemies here are a little strong for a two-member party, so this route will provide easy access to the Thermadon guarding the path leading to the waypoint. The Undermine Paradigm (if you created it earlier) will enable you to Stagger it quickly. After the short cutscene, kill the Vespid Soldier first before you tackle the next Thermadon – again, Undermine works wonders against both foes.

5

6 Outside again with the main party, the Starboard Weather Deck features some sizable groups of familiar opponents. Against large collections of Deckdrones, the Delta Attack Paradigm (where Fang acts as a Sentinel) is the safest way to fight. If four or more of these enemies should combine to perform the Tornado Kick attack (Fig. 6), which spells instant death in such numbers, Fang will take the fall – and not Lightning. This Paradigm proves useful against other big groups (particularly four PSICOM Dragoons close to the last Treasure Sphere). For a faster finish, always switch back to Relentless Assault once the odds turn in your favor.

6

7 **Major Encounter – Kalavinka Striker:** Quickly inflict the Slow and Curse status ailments with the Bully Paradigm, then use Relentless Assault (with occasional switches to Diversity when party members are injured) to Stagger your opponent. You should be able to beat it within two minutes, which makes this a remarkably fast encounter (Fig. 7). Naturally, it's just a bit too easy...

7

On its second attack run, the Kalavinka Striker makes fairly regular use of its Hellstorm Bolt attack, which drains approximately one third to half of the target's HP gauge. Using the same tactics as before, though, the monster will this time fall in just over two minutes.

Your rewards are the Soulfont Talisman and Blessed Talisman accessories, which possess the Auto-Shell and Auto-Faith perks respectively. These status enhancements expire after a time like all others, but are advantageous in shorter battles. As Lightning is operating primarily as a Ravager, these may be a good combination for her until the final battle of the chapter.

TREASURE SPHERES

Sphere	Contents	Type
A	Librascope	
B	Pain Dampener	
C	Rune Bracelet (x2)	
D	Umbra	
E	3,600 Gil	
F	Gold Bangle	
G	Perfect Conductor	
H	Ethersol	

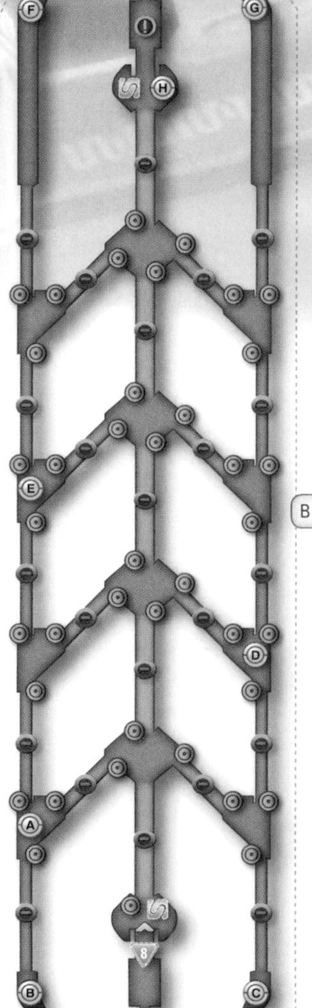

ENEMIES

Name	Notes	Page
PSICOM Infiltrator	Employs Esuna and Cura to heal itself and nearby allies.	228
PSICOM Destroyer	Powerful physical attacks; easily Staggered; dispatch first in mixed groups.	229
Thermadon	Massive damage resistance; powerful Photon Burst attack; weak when Staggered.	232
PSICOM Reaver	Very high HP; all magic and elemental damage other than Earth is halved; uses Dispel, Deshell and Deprotect.	229
PSICOM Huntress	Magic and physical damage halved; uses status enhancements at the start of a battle.	229
PSICOM Dragoon	Wind damage halved; Missile Burst ability deals very high damage.	229
Barthandelus	Massive damage and status effect resistance until armor is destroyed.	246

QUICKSTART
WALKTHROUGH
STRATEGY & ANALYSIS
INVENTORY
BESTIARY
EXTRAS
USER INSTRUCTIONS
CHAPTER 01
CHAPTER 02
CHAPTER 03
CHAPTER 04
CHAPTER 05
CHAPTER 06
CHAPTER 07
CHAPTER 08
CHAPTER 09
CHAPTER 10
CHAPTER 11
CHAPTER 12
CHAPTER 13
SIDE-QUESTS

8 **Note:** Even though you now have the option to change your party lineup, we strongly advise that you stay with the current group. We'll return to this topic shortly.

Activate the console left of the Save Station to extend a bridge to the next platform. You will need to use these throughout the Bridge Access area. The route you take rather depends on how much you value the rewards contained in the Treasure Spheres. We do, however, strongly recommend that you at least pick up the Gold Bangle – an accessory that offers an HP boost of 250.

Note that you can actually see which enemies lie ahead by peering over the edge of each vantage point (Fig. 8). You may decide to avoid certain foes. That said, if you use the Diversity Paradigm for uncomfortable early exchanges during confrontations with tougher or more numerous opponents, there is no one group that will cause you problems.

8

9 If you are not even close to the next Role Level crystals on the Crystarium for your three main characters, we strongly suggest that you spend time acquiring CP in the Bridge Access area to improve your party before you approach the next waypoint. Once satisfied with their progress, create a new Paradigm: Hero's Charge (Medic + Synergist + Commando). You should also equip the Gold Bangle accessory on Hope (the weakest member of your party), and give your two Tungsten Bangles to Lightning.

Major Encounter – Barthandelus: As with the Havoc Skytank encountered earlier, you must destroy this colossal opponent's armor to reduce its overall strength and the frequency of its attacks. Start by using Bully to bestow protective buffs (and, hopefully, the Slow debuff on your opponent's main body). Diversity is the safest Paradigm to choose thereafter, but you can briefly transfer to Relentless Assault to accelerate Chain Gauge growth when all party members are healthy – though this is a risk that you technically need not take.

Each Pauldron and Ailette has its own elemental weakness. To speed things up, use a Librascope or manually target the correct weakness with the Abilities option.

ARMOR VULNERABILITIES

Armor	Weakness
Left Pauldron	Lightning
Left Ailette	Fire
Right Pauldron	Ice
Right Ailette	Water

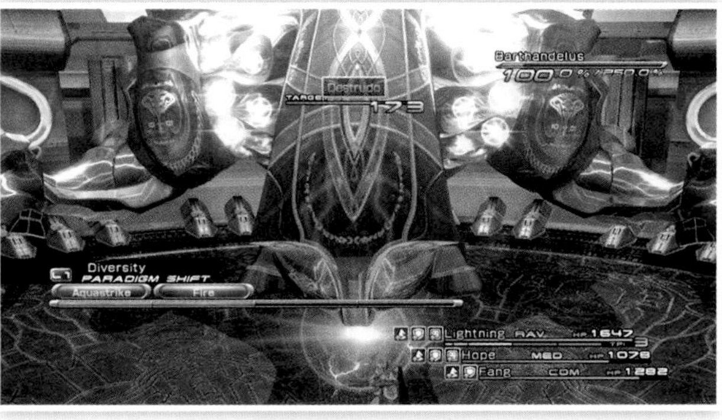

9

Once all Pauldrons and Ailettes have been destroyed, Barthandelus loses its damage resistance and blanket immunity to status ailments. Paradigm Shift to Bully straight away to strengthen party members with Shell, Protect and Veil, and (optimally) inflict a couple of debuffs. You can then use the Paradigm pairing of Relentless Assault and Diversity to Stagger your opponent and begin to deal significant damage.

The basic attacks employed by Barthandelus are strong enough, but its Destrudo ability – introduced after your opponent has been Staggered once – has the power to wipe out all party members in one fell swoop. It also completely resets the Chain Gauge, even if your foe is Staggered. This vicious assault is foreshadowed by a very loud and distinctive "power up" period (Fig. 9). It is absolutely vital that you ensure every party member is at full health before the attack is unleashed approximately 25 seconds later. This is where the Hero's Charge Paradigm proves invaluable. Change to it straight away once the attack notification caption appears, and Hope will refresh vital status enhancements while you manually heal with Lightning. Before the attack hits home, change to the Solidarity Paradigm. This will reduce the total damage sustained, and should see Hope heal Lightning in her moment of greatest need. You can then Paradigm Shift back to Diversity to have Hope continue healing while Lightning and Fang grind away at your resilient adversary.

Should things look grim, you always have the option of summoning Odin to facilitate a last-gasp escape from death. Near the very end of the battle, Barthandelus may cast the incurable Doom status ailment on your party leader. Don't be too alarmed: the deadline actually offers plenty of time to finish him off.

INTERMISSION

As you have reached the midway point in the story (though not, it must be said, the entire game), this is a good time to familiarize yourself with systems and features that become hugely significant over the coming hours of play. We also offer "Further Reading" suggestions that link to the chapters that follow the walkthrough. If you aspire to 100% completion and don't object to gameplay spoilers, these will enable you to plan a perfect playthrough.

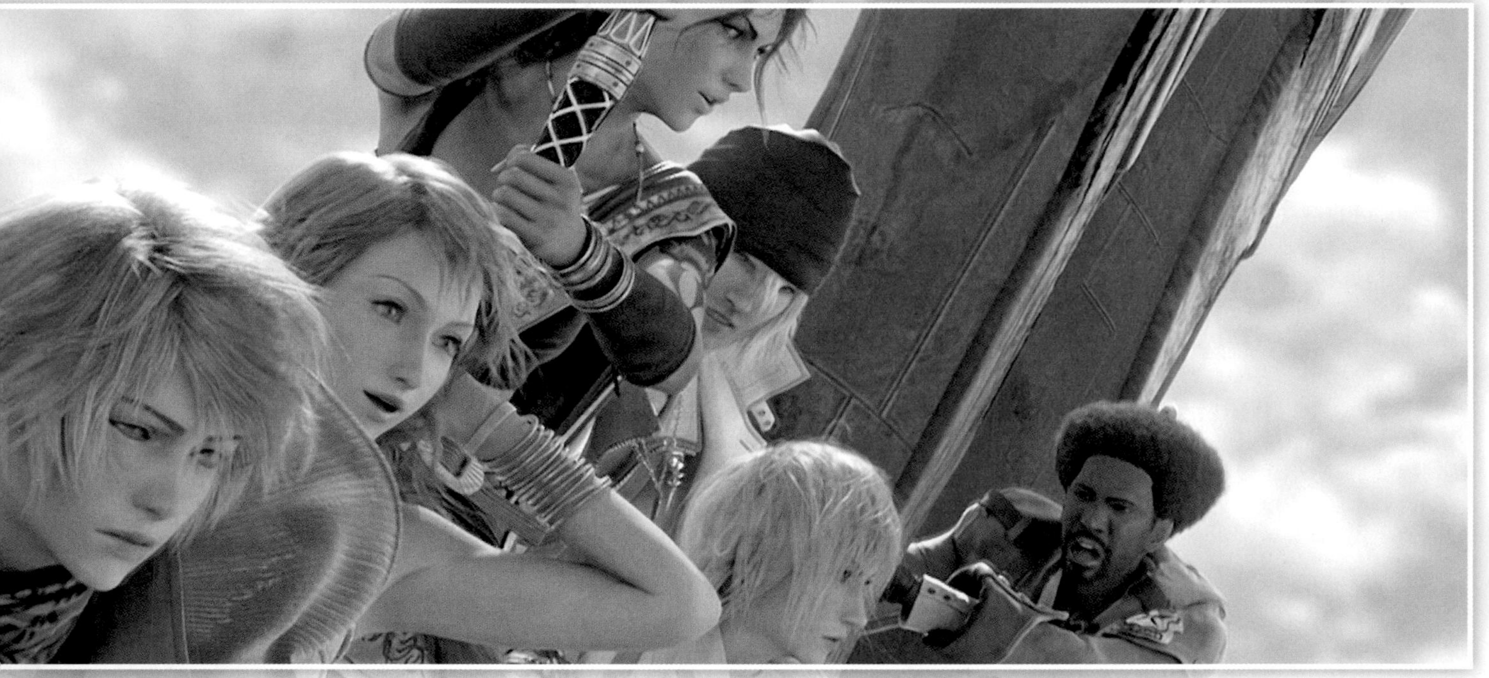

Battle Team Formation

Even though you now have the ability to change your party's composition and leader, we advise that you stay with your current line-up of Lightning, Fang and Hope. Indeed, there is a strong case to be made for sticking with this line-up for almost the entire adventure, as it not only gives you access to all six roles, but also features members that are strong in their specialist archetypes.

Our walkthrough will assume that you choose this party from this point forward. This doesn't mean that you can't, or won't, benefit from using other configurations, just that this setup offers one of the best all-round blend of strengths and abilities. Here's why:

- **Fang:** Sentinels have been mostly redundant so far, but become far more important in Chapter 10. From Chapter 11 onward, they are often invaluable. Snow may be a little stronger in this role than Fang (due to his high HP), but Fang's higher Strength stat (she eventually reaches heights that no other character can match) and proficiency as a Saboteur give her the edge.

- **Hope:** Having the highest possible Magic stat, he is a powerful Medic and Ravager. His Synergist abilities focus on defensive augmentation until later in the third level of his Crystarium, which is generally more useful than the offensive buffs that Sazh offers until later in his development.

- **Lightning:** Your choice of leader should be informed by the Techniques available to them, how many ATB gauge segments they have, and which roles they fulfill – playing as a Sentinel or Synergist really isn't a great deal of fun. Being an excellent all-rounder with access to a variety of abilities and Techniques, Lightning wins this particular face-off at a canter – she is arguably the most interesting character to play.

Having such a fixed primary group also offers a special benefit: it enables you to designate Vanille, Sazh and Snow as "super specialists". The cost of developing characters when you reach the final level of the Crystarium is astonishingly expensive. With your primary trio needing to be flexible in three roles, it will take a long time to reach the final Role Level crystals, which award a massive boost to a character's effectiveness. If you are aiming for 100% completion, and would like to complete side-quests and conquer optional foes, using all CP accrued to develop your reserves in a single role can be amazingly useful later in the game.

FURTHER READING

Topic	Page
Party composition	186
Paradigms	146
Character specialism	154
Optional role development	180

Weapons & Accessories

With generic enemies and major bosses becoming more deadly with each passing chapter, selecting and upgrading weapons and accessories is a decision with lasting repercussions.

Every character can use eight different types of weapons with unique characteristics; there are eight initial weapons that can be upgraded twice, for a total of 24 weapons per character. Some are balanced; others offer higher Strength and lower Magic, or vice versa; others have Passive Abilities that grant a special augmentation, but lower Strength and Magic as a consequence. Though you do not have access to all of these just yet, now is definitely the time to start paying more attention to the equipment that your characters use, and plan ahead.

Though stat boosts are important, weapons with Passive Abilities can offer a level of performance that compensates for their lower Strength and Magic totals. Every weapon and accessory in the game is part of a specific category. Combine two or more of these weapons or accessories on a character, and you will obtain a Synthesized Ability. This is often a minor yet disposable perk, but some Synthesized Abilities are remarkably powerful.

Take Lightning's Axis Blade and the Whistlewind Scarf accessory, for example. Individually, they are not especially impressive. The Axis Blade's Passive Ability is "ATB Charge", which slightly increases the ATB gauge when enemies are attacked; the Whistlewind Scarf is underwhelming, offering a single charged ATB gauge segment at the start of a battle. Combine the two, however, and you obtain the "ATB Rate +10%" Synthesized Ability, which makes a big difference. In an extended fight, that's one extra attack for every ten performed – and that's without factoring in existing Passive Abilities.

If you want to create the ultimate party, specialism is vitally important. Consider the primary role of each character, and then pick the weapons and accessories that complement their main focus with powerful augmentations.

FURTHER READING

Topic	Page
Weapons	207
Accessories	213
Synthesized Abilities	194
Weapon upgrades	218
Equipment setups	194
Components	216

Crystarium

The new upgrades made available when the Crystarium expands during Chapter 10 are extremely costly, with the paths to the next Role Levels littered with new crystals with a CP value of between 4,000 and 10,000 CP. That said, the rewards are commensurately higher. Tidy up loose ends by completing all crystals with a value of less than 2,000 CP first, then study the accompanying table and consider your options. We recommend that you focus on reaching the Role Level for each character's most important discipline first, with suggested detours or points of interest detailed in the Notes section.

If you are seeking individual abilities, remember that you can bypass outlying "arms" of the Crystarium and return to them later. You should also ignore optional Technique crystals for characters who do not operate as party leader.

CRYSTARIUM PRIORITIES

Party Member	Optimal Path	Notes
Fang	Commando, Sentinel, Saboteur	Vendetta and Accessory (Sentinel) offer a lot – but will cost a fortune to obtain early. Pain and Painga, however, are within easy reach for the Saboteur role, and could be worth an immediate investment.
Hope	Medic, Synergist, Ravager	The Accessory, Raise and Curasa abilities are just too good to ignore in the Medic role. Hope's ATB Level crystal is very close to the Synergist Role Level, which is why it may be best to develop that skill-set before the Ravager role.
Lightning	Ravager, Commando, Medic	Dispelga and ATB Level (Commando) are tempting targets prior to reaching the Ravager Role Level.

Other Topics of Interest

There are many other topics that are worth studying, such as:

- How to maximize Chain Gauge and Chain Bonus growth.
- How to appraise each status effect and the impact they have on an affected (or, indeed, afflicted) target.
- Finding out what you get for your CP investment at the Crystarium.
- How to accumulate or generate currency.
- How to farm CP and components to develop your party members.

The following table offers page references leading to the sections of the guide where you will find all the details on these subjects.

FURTHER READING

Topic	Page
Chain Gauge	140
Status ailments & enhancements	142
Ability analysis	188
Acquiring Gil	145
Power tips	144

CHAPTER 10

THE FIFTH ARK

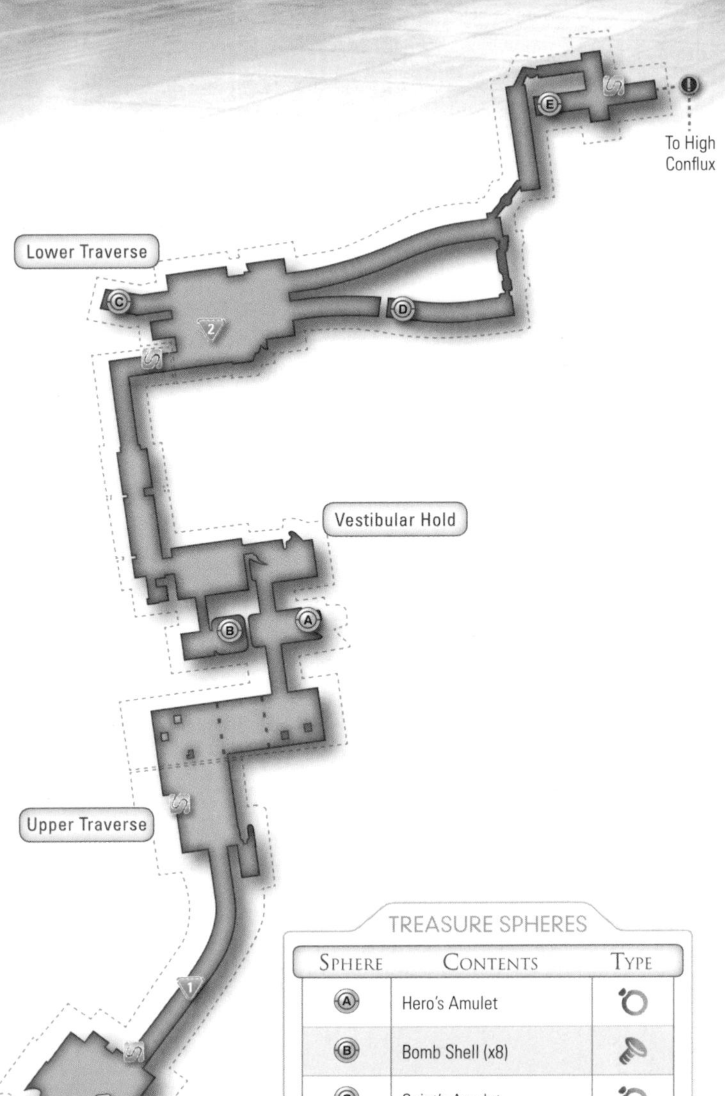

TREASURE SPHERES

Sphere	Contents	Type
A	Hero's Amulet	
B	Bomb Shell (x8)	
C	Saint's Amulet	
D	Medicinal Oil (x10)	
E	Rainbow Anklet	

ENEMIES

Name	Notes	Page
Pulsework Knight	High damage resistance until Staggered; weakness to Fire and Lightning element.	242
Circuitron	Physical damage halved; weak against Ice, but absorbs Lightning element; can self-destruct for devastating damage.	243
Noctilucale	Weak against Fire and Ice, but Water damage halved.	237
Phosphoric Ooze	Weak against Fire but absorb Water; inflicts Poison; two can merge to form Alchemic Ooze.	239
Alchemic Ooze	High HP; weak against Fire but absorbs Water; physical damage halved; very powerful attacks.	239

Battle Preparation

One of your first tasks should be to form a balanced party and configure its Paradigms. Once again, we strongly recommend Lightning, Fang and Hope as the best all-round group (if you haven't already, see "Battle Team Formation" on page 66 for advice on why this is necessary or advisable).

SUGGESTED PARADIGM DECK

Paradigm	Lightning	Fang	Hope
Relentless Assault	Ravager	Commando	Ravager
Diversity	Ravager	Commando	Medic
Delta Attack	Commando	Sentinel	Ravager
Solidarity	Commando	Sentinel	Medic
Protection	Medic	Sentinel	Synergist
Evened Odds	Medic	Saboteur	Synergist

At the Crystarium, the most important short-term consideration is that Fang complete all available Commando crystals and unlock the new abilities in the Sentinel role. Other than that, just work towards reaching Role Level crystals – these really make a huge difference to an individual's overall effectiveness. As regards the new Role Development feature (where you can develop characters in three "optional" disciplines), it's definitely in your best interests to only advance your three characters in their existing specialist roles until much later in the game.

1 Speak to all party members if you wish, then run along the tunnel until a prompt appears. Select "Yes" to continue – other than optional dialogue, there's nothing else for you to achieve in this area.

Pulsework Knights have incredible endurance until Staggered, but then fall rapidly to a concerted assault. In groups of two or more enemies, though, the sheer strength of their blows can severely weaken the party in an alarmingly short period of time. Circuitrons are close cousins of the Bombs encountered earlier. Unless you destroy them quickly, they may activate their Self-destruct ability, seriously injuring (or disabling) party members.

When you reach the group consisting of a Pulsework Knight and two Circuitrons, ignore the alert warnings and run onto the nearby walkway (Fig. 1). All three will instantly forget about your presence, which will enable you to sneak up behind the lumbering robot for an easy preemptive strike.

1

2 There are more new "old" faces in the Lower Traverse – but don't jump to conclusions based on your experiences with their distant relatives.

Noctilucale only have one attack but use it to absorb HP, which makes them threatening in large numbers. You can address this by using the Delta Attack Paradigm if you face more than five at once. The Phosphoric Ooze enemy seems to be a low-grade Flan enemy type with a rather weak attack that inflicts a short-term Poison ailment. Unless you defeat them swiftly, though, two of these will use their unique Merge ability to combine and form a larger, stronger foe: Alchemic Ooze (Fig. 2). With its high HP and resistance to physical damage, the appearance of this opponent will wreck your post-battle rating, so it's always prudent to take preventative measures. If you see a Phosphoric

2

Ooze performing a Merge, attack it immediately. It remains weak during the transformation process, meaning that you can devastate its HP gauge (which is transferred to its new form), or even destroy it before the morphing is complete.

Inside the left-hand tunnel, the battle with the combined forces of Noctilucale and Phosphoric Ooze may necessitate the use of a Sentinel – Delta Attack or, safer still, Solidarity – to weather the initial flurry of damage. Kill the slug-like enemies first. At the tunnel end, head right and jump up to find a group of ten Noctilucale surrounding a Treasure Sphere (see "Power Tip"), then continue towards the waypoint.

Power Tip: Leveling

There are a few interesting opportunities to farm enemies for CP and components in the Vestibular Hold and Lower Traverse areas. Circuitrons are easy to kill, but have the Bomb Shell component (worth around 250 EXP) as their rare drop item. Pulsework Knights take more time to beat, but offer 256 CP each and relinquish components with a good EXP value.

The most interesting opportunity is presented by a group of Noctilucale in the Lower Traverse area who guard a Treasure Sphere. These are easily defeated (especially if you achieve a preemptive strike – something they appear unusually susceptible to), respawn quickly (just backtrack four "jumps" down from the tunnel entrance), and offer a very respectable yield of 640 CP per battle. If you temporarily edit Relentless Assault to make Lightning a Commando (creating the Aggression Paradigm), a combination of a preemptive strike and a flurry of Blitz attacks from Lightning and Fang will enable you to kill all ten within 20 seconds. You can use this to generate thousands of CP in very little time.

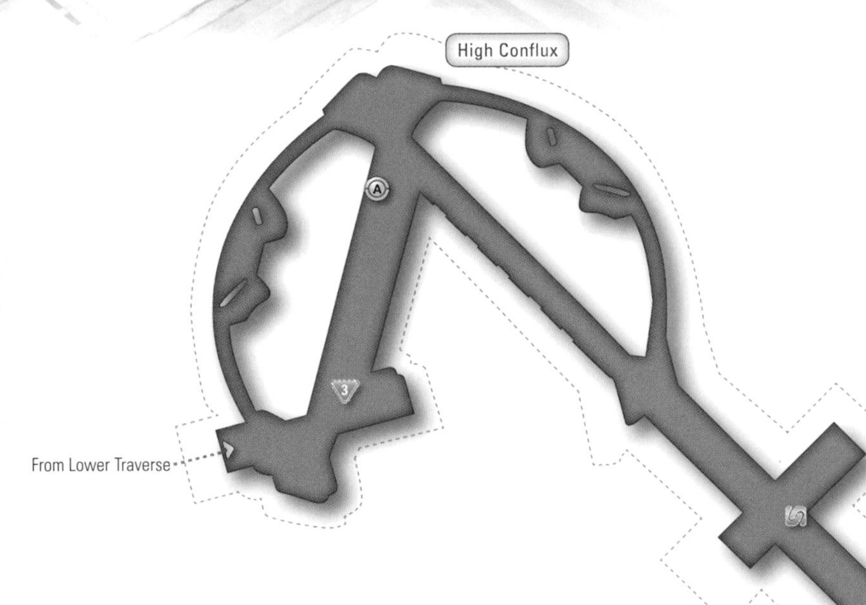

Sphere	Contents	Type
A	600 Gil	
B	Rigels	

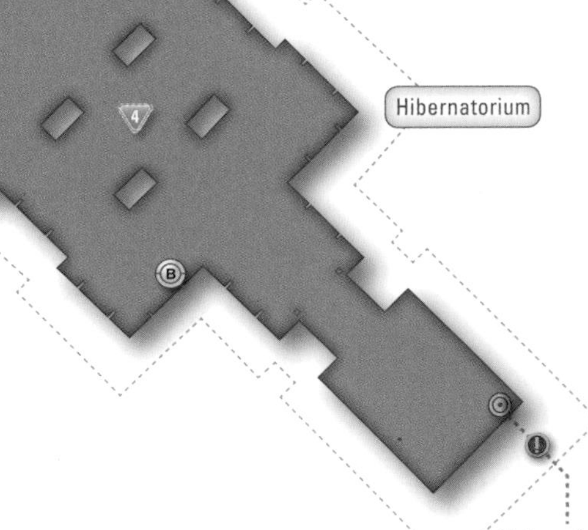

Name	Notes	Page
Skata'ne	Powerful attacks; coordinates attacks with others of its species; can be Launched.	236
Stikini	Inflicts Daze; coordinates attacks with others of its species; can be Launched.	236
Circuitron	Physical damage halved; weak against Ice, but absorbs Lightning element; can self-destruct for devastating damage.	243
Berserker	Immune to Fire, but weak against Lightning element; physical and magic damage halved; can use Forge ability to create Centaurion Blade.	242
Centaurion Blade	Only encountered when summoned during Berserker battles; immune to Fire, but weak against Lightning element; no spoils or CP reward.	243

3 Like the Succubus and Incubus enemy types encountered earlier in the adventure, Stikini and Skata'ne have complementary abilities: the former weakening your party while the latter bludgeon them into submission. Always target Stikini first: their ability to inflict Daze (though temporarily) can seriously disrupt your battle plan, while their lower HP and Chain Resistance means that they can be dispatched relatively quickly.

You can gain a preemptive strike on the second pair of Stikini and Skata'ne by (from your position at the entrance) following the path on the left-hand wall of the chamber, then sneaking up behind the one who is closest (Fig. 3). Continue down via the outer wall (rather than following the waypoint markers), and you can repeat the trick again with the third set, this time accompanied by a Circuitron (which you should only destroy after the Stikini has been neutralized).

3

4 The two Berserkers (who you fight alone in both instances) may have huge HP, high damage resistance and powerful physical and magical attacks, but they're also preposterously slow. Start with a preemptive strike for a ridiculously easy fight. If one should spot you beforehand, lure it over to a doorway and wait just over the threshold until its attention wavers, then sneak over and try again (Fig. 4). As soon as a Berserker is Staggered, you can juggle it with Launch. When the Chain Gauge is reset, throw everything into Staggering it a second time. Don't buff, or switch to any Paradigm other than Relentless Assault: just hammer away with Auto-chain until it falls.

If you do not start with a preemptive strike, the Berserker will almost certainly use its Forge ability, introducing a new enemy into the fray: the Centaurion Blade. The best strategy is to quickly Stagger the

4

Berserker, then kill its creation. Note that these Berserkers do not respawn once conquered: this is a one-time encounter. Through the next door, activate the switch to ride the elevator down.

Preemptive Strike Tactics

- Pay special attention to enemies who emerge from floors (such as foes in the Flan genus – like Phosphoric Ooze), or stationary foes that unfold and deploy body parts as you approach (such as Tilters – for example, the Orion). If you rush over and touch them before the animation is complete (or any nearby allies of theirs see you, of course) you may secure a preemptive strike.
- Though the aggression and tenacity of prospective opponents in their "alert" state can vary wildly, you'll often find that you can outrun all but the fastest foes. Put enough distance between your party leader and pursuing aggressors, and you can make a second attempt at gaining a perfect start to the fight.
- Enemies may not detect you if you are standing behind barriers, such as walls or low fences, or when you are positioned at a different elevation. There are even occasional instances where a slight transition between two surfaces (a bridge and a platform, for example, or by walking through a door) may render them incapable of seeing your party leader. An effective technique is to run out and lure an enemy to one of these boundaries, run and cross the invisible divide as they approach (which will reset the alert), then run back out to grab a preemptive strike before they return to their original position. Try to identify and exploit these "blind spots" whenever you can.

ENEMIES

Name	Notes	Page
Imp	Weak enemy that falls rapidly; can summon reinforcements if left long enough.	235
Phosphoric Ooze	Weak against Fire but absorbs Water; inflicts Poison; two can merge to form Alchemic Ooze.	239
Alchemic Ooze	High HP; weak against Fire but absorbs Water; physical damage halved; very powerful attacks.	239
Greater Behemoth	Magic damage cut to one tenth of usual level; slow Chain Gauge growth; inflicts Pain ailment when upright.	240
Noctilucale	Weak against Fire and Ice, but Water damage halved.	237
Cid Raines	Uses and inflicts various status effects; magic and physical damage halved during Guard, and permanently after transformation; Seraphic Ray attack hits all party members for life-threatening damage.	246

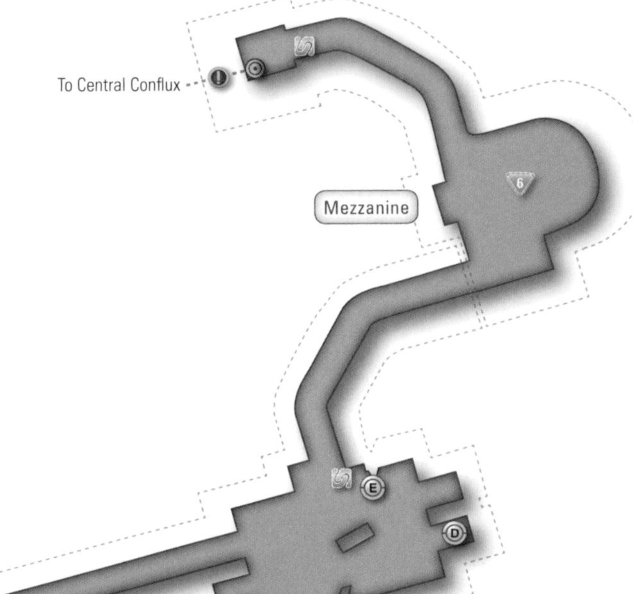

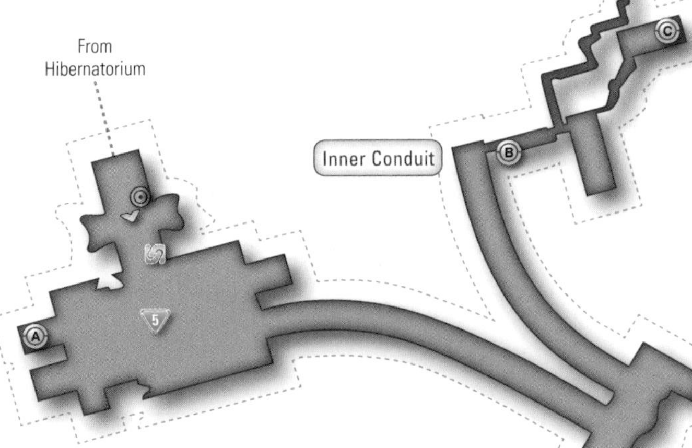

TREASURE SPHERES

Sphere	Contents	Type
A	Auric Amulet	
B	Alicanto	
C	Gargantuan Claw (x7)	
D	Metal Armband	
E	Ethersol	

5 The first two sets of enemies in the Inner Conduit area can be ambushed for easy preemptive strikes by leaping down from the raised platforms right next to them. When ambushed by four Phosphoric Ooze enemies, immediately switch to Diversity if you are unable to prevent two of them from merging to form a healthy Alchemic Ooze, then kill any remaining smaller foes first. When you reach the Greater Behemoth, try to sneak up behind it for a preemptive strike that will make the battle a brief formality. Should it detect you, retreat to the nearby platform to escape before you try again (Fig. 5).

Once you leave the tunnel to reach a large chamber, you can take a quick optional diversion leading to a Treasure Sphere. When you reach the glowing blue marker, jump up to fight ten Noctilucale. Beyond the next set of jumps, four Noctilucale and a Greater Behemoth await. Fighting the latter enemy without a preemptive strike is rather challenging. After dispatching its companions, start by inflicting the Deprotect and Curse status ailments, then grind away until it changes to a standing posture. This resets its HP total, but your accumulated Chain Bonus will probably cause you to kill it before the Chain Gauge has been filled. If, however, it uses its Painga ability beforehand, you will need to cure Fang with Esuna (tip – do this manually with Lightning on the Evened Odds Paradigm) to finish the fight without further delay. There are two further Greater Behemoths once you enter the tunnel leading to the next waypoint.

5

6 **Major Encounter – Cid Raines:** This is one of the most enjoyable battles so far, as it pits you against an opponent with a huge variety of attacks and abilities. The confrontation can be broadly divided into two parts: an opening exchange where Raines rather telegraphs his intentions, followed by a seamless transition to a longer (and more dangerous) second phase where you put your knowledge of his behavior to good use – but without onscreen prompts to guide you.

For the first part of the fight, look for the following three captions to judge his intentions:

- **Offensive Shift:** Raines will use a variety of attacks, including Launch during physical combos.
- **Defensive Shift:** Raines uses Guard to ward off damage.
- **Recovery Shift:** Raines will remove status ailments and heal himself. Don't panic about this: the Chain Gauge is your true prize.

Raines is susceptible to Slow and Curse, so your first task is to switch to Evened Odds to inflict both and have Hope buff the party. Rotate the

6

camera to maintain a clear view of when Fang successfully hits your opponent with the debuffs.

With these opening goals complete, and your party shielded by at least Protect and Shell, use Delta Attack while Raines is in the Offensive Shift state to have Fang bear the brunt of his ire. Defensive Shift mode is your opportunity to change to Relentless Assault and drive up his Chain Gauge, or to heal while reapplying lapsed status enhancements and ailments. Keeping your party in top condition is vital – use Solidarity when a Sentinel is called for, and Evened Odds while Raines defends. You can also use the Recovery Shift state to attack, heal and buff – but only until the Chain Gauge reaches approximately 60% full. At this point, you should use Delta Attack or Solidarity at all times other than when he is using his Guard ability.

The reason for this caution? At any point prior to the first Stagger, Raines will use his Metamorphose ability (Fig. 6), and begin the second stage of the conflict. This is followed by Seraphic Ray, a deadly attack that will reduce all party members to a seriously wounded state – even with a Sentinel offering protection. Switch to Solidarity straight away to heal. Raines will deploy this attack at random intervals for the rest of the fight when not using the Guard ability.

There is a clever technique that will enable you to cut down the battle duration. Just before his Chain Gauge is filled for the first time, Paradigm Shift to Relentless Assault. Once the Stagger takes place, wait until Fang uses the Launch ability, then carefully time attacks to "juggle" him in the air for as long as possible. The best technique is to delay your initial salvo of magic attacks until the last strike of Fang's opening aerial assault, then fire away. You can then use ⓐ/Ⓨ to issue advance attacks to keep him airborne when required. This prevents him from using Guard, which will drastically reduce the damage you inflict.

With the first Stagger over, Raines still has the same three discernable "modes", but you receive no special advance warning. Continue as before, but be vigilant in your use of Delta Attack and Solidarity at all times unless he is employing Guard. This will be your opportunity to buff and debuff with Evened Odds, then (albeit briefly) change to Relentless Assault until the caption disappears. He will eventually begin to use assorted status enhancements and ailments as the fight nears its conclusion – Solidarity may be your best defensive option at this point, even if it slows your progress to a crawl. When you finally achieve a second Stagger, use the same "air juggle" tactic as before to ward against the possibility of Guard.

At the end of the fight, you will receive the Tetradic Crown accessory, a Crystarium expansion, and gain access to the Moogleworks retail network from Save Stations.

TREASURE SPHERES

Sphere	Contents	Type
A	Feymark	
B	Electrode (x3)	

ENEMIES

Name	Notes	Page
Circuitron	Physical damage halved; weak against Ice, but absorbs Lightning element; can self-destruct for devastating damage.	243
Phosphoric Ooze	Weak against Fire but absorbs Water; inflicts Poison; two can merge to form Alchemic Ooze.	239
Alchemic Ooze	Potentially high HP; weak against Fire but absorbs Water; physical damage halved; very powerful attacks.	239
Pulsework Knight	High damage resistance until Staggered; weakness to Fire and Lightning element.	242
Stikini	Inflicts Daze; coordinates attacks with others of its species; can be Launched.	236
Imp	Weak enemy that falls rapidly; can summon reinforcements if left long enough.	235
Greater Behemoth	Magic damage cut to one tenth of usual level; slow Chain Gauge growth; inflicts Pain ailment when upright.	240
Skata'ne	Powerful attacks; coordinates attacks with others of its species; can be Launched.	236
Berserker	Immune against Fire, but weak against Lightning element; physical and magic damage halved; can create the Centaurion Blade enemy.	242
Centaurion Blade	Only encountered when summoned during Berserker battles; immune to Fire, but weak against Lightning element; no spoils or CP reward.	243

7 After exiting the Mezzanine via the elevator to reach the Central Conflux, be ready for an ambush by three Circuitrons that drop from above during the ride down. If you are quick to move, you can start with a preemptive strike and finish the fight in ten seconds. Inside the first large chamber, you can use the outer walkways (Fig. 7) and "steps" to avoid two three-way battles between flans and Pulsework Knights. We would suggest that you fight them for the CP gains. There is a catch, however: unlike similar confrontations of this type earlier in the game, you must sneak up on the warring factions to gain a preemptive strike and immunity to attack until one group has been eliminated – otherwise, both sets of enemies will attack you at once.

7

8 After the cutscene on entering the Synthrona, run forward slightly to engage the four Circuitrons straight away. If you remain perfectly still after this first battle, the three Pulsework Knights should take a few steps forward (Fig. 8), then turn around without detecting you – offering a perfect preemptive strike opportunity. Otherwise, you'll need to Paradigm Shift to Delta Attack or Solidarity to survive the first half of a tough confrontation. When you meet the Stikini and two Pulsework Knights, kill the former first to avoid the Daze status ailment.

8

9 It's exceedingly hard to get a preemptive strike against the two Pulsework Knights fighting Imps, though the reward of 1,024 CP makes diving into the confrontation worthwhile. Start with Relentless Assault and target the Imps, then change to Diversity until only one Pulsework Knight remains. You should definitely aim to start with a sneak attack on the Greater Behemoth on the bridge below, though.

9

Power Tip: The four Circuitrons in the first room of the Hypogeum (Fig. 9) have the Bomb Shell as a rare drop (worth approximately 250 EXP), take no more than 25 seconds to kill (less with a preemptive strike), and offer 512 CP per battle. They can be respawned in no time at all by running back out onto the Basement Conflux bridge.

10 When you reach a Stikini, two Skata'ne and a Greater Behemoth, tackle them in the order listed here, changing to Solidarity after the Stikini falls. In the event that you gain the element of surprise, try to Stagger and kill the Stikini and Greater Behemoth before their Chain Gauges deplete. Head left to reach a dead end that is the site of a Berserker ambush. This means that you will almost certainly experience its Forge ability, where it will create a Centaurion Blade. Stagger the Berserker and wait until Fang performs the Launch move, then focus your attacks on its ally. Once the summoned adversary falls, the rest of the fight should be fairly straightforward. Note that the enemies in the previous room may have respawned when you return en route to the waypoint, but there's no shame in making a dash for the exit if you do not wish to repeat the battle.

After activating the elevator, run to the center of the floor area and make contact with a Stikini or Skata'ne as the trio land for a valuable preemptive strike (Fig. 10).

10

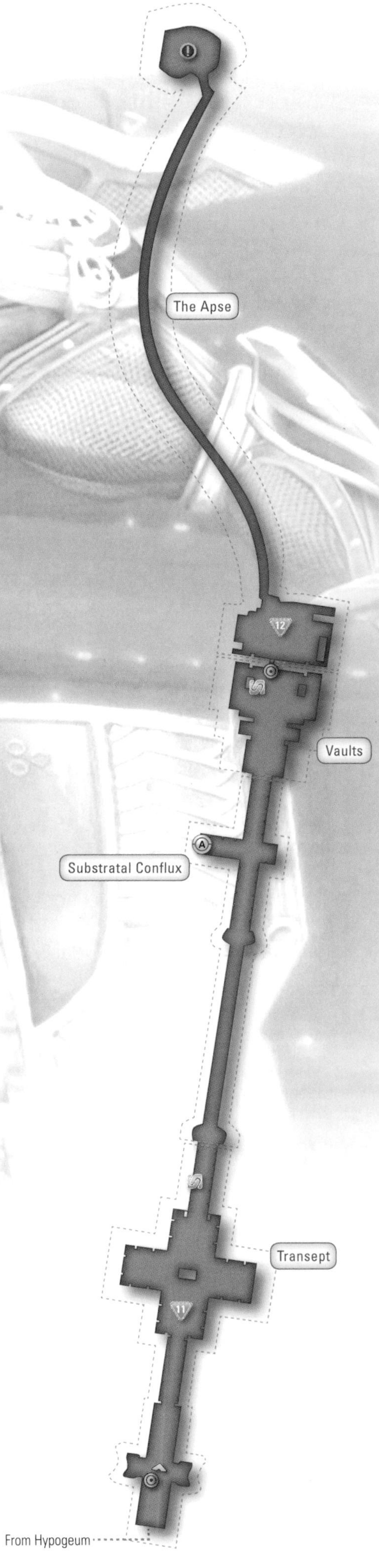

The Apse

Vaults

Substratal Conflux

Transept

From Hypogeum

TREASURE SPHERES

Sphere	Contents	Type
A	Otherworldly Bone (x2)	

ENEMIES

Name	Notes	Page
Skata'ne	Powerful attacks; coordinates attacks with others of its species; can be Launched.	236
Berserker	Immune to Fire, but weak against Lightning element; physical and magic damage halved; can create the Centaurion Blade enemy.	242
Centaurion Blade	Only encountered when summoned during Berserker battles; immune to Fire, but weak against Lightning element; no spoils or CP reward.	243

11 As with the similar confrontations earlier, ensure that you sneak up on the Berserker for a painless encounter that ends rapidly. On the bridge that follows, sprint back through the doorway to facilitate a preemptive strike against the two Skata'ne before they catch you. There are two further ambushes as you cross the Substratal Conflux, and both of these will end quickly if you can make contact with an enemy before they land and become truly "active".

When you reach the Vaults, there are two further Berserkers to fight. The first can be lured to the door, then approached when it turns away. The second is strangely shy in the company of steps, it seems, and will bashfully avert its gaze to enable a preemptive strike from the other side of the room if you run straight past it and bide your time (Fig. 11). Before you go through the door beyond the Save Station, equip Vanille with the Healer's Staff weapon (if you collected it earlier), and the Shield Talisman and Tetradic Crown accessories (though HP-boosting trinkets will suffice if you do not have one, or either, of these).

11

12 **Eidolon Battle – Bahamut:** You have a predefined party for this encounter, with Vanille joining Lightning and new leader Fang. To win this battle, all you need do at first is switch to the Combat Clinic Paradigm and use Auto-cover. Bahamut will assault the party and toss them around in a succession of savage attacks – and, for a time, things may look bleak (Fig. 12). Lighting and Vanillle will initially struggle to keep the party alive, but will gradually begin to assert a measure of control.

12

When the Doom counter reaches a point between 1,000 and 700, your party should be in remarkably good shape, with HP gauges in the green for each character. This is the moment to launch your counter-offensive. Wait until Bahamut finishes an attack and backs away, then Paradigm Shift to Delta Attack. Lightning and Vanille's sudden barrage will drive up the Gestalt gauge. Switching to Matador (Ravager + Sentinel + Saboteur) to cast debuffs on the Eidolon can help significantly too. Maintain this aggression for as long as you dare (we suggest you stop as soon as a party member falls below 50% HP), then switch back to Combat Clinic. Wait until both Medics rejuvenate the party, then repeat your attack. The Eidolon should be ready to yield not long after the Doom counter passes 300.

After the battle ends, Fang takes possession of the Bahamut Eidolith and gains an ATB gauge segment. Don't worry about rearranging your party just yet – it's better to do this at the start of the next chapter. To continue, simply run along the path until you reach the waypoint marker. The cinematic sequences that follow are fairly lengthy, so if you need to take a break, it might be a good idea to return to the Vaults to save.

VALLIS MEDIA

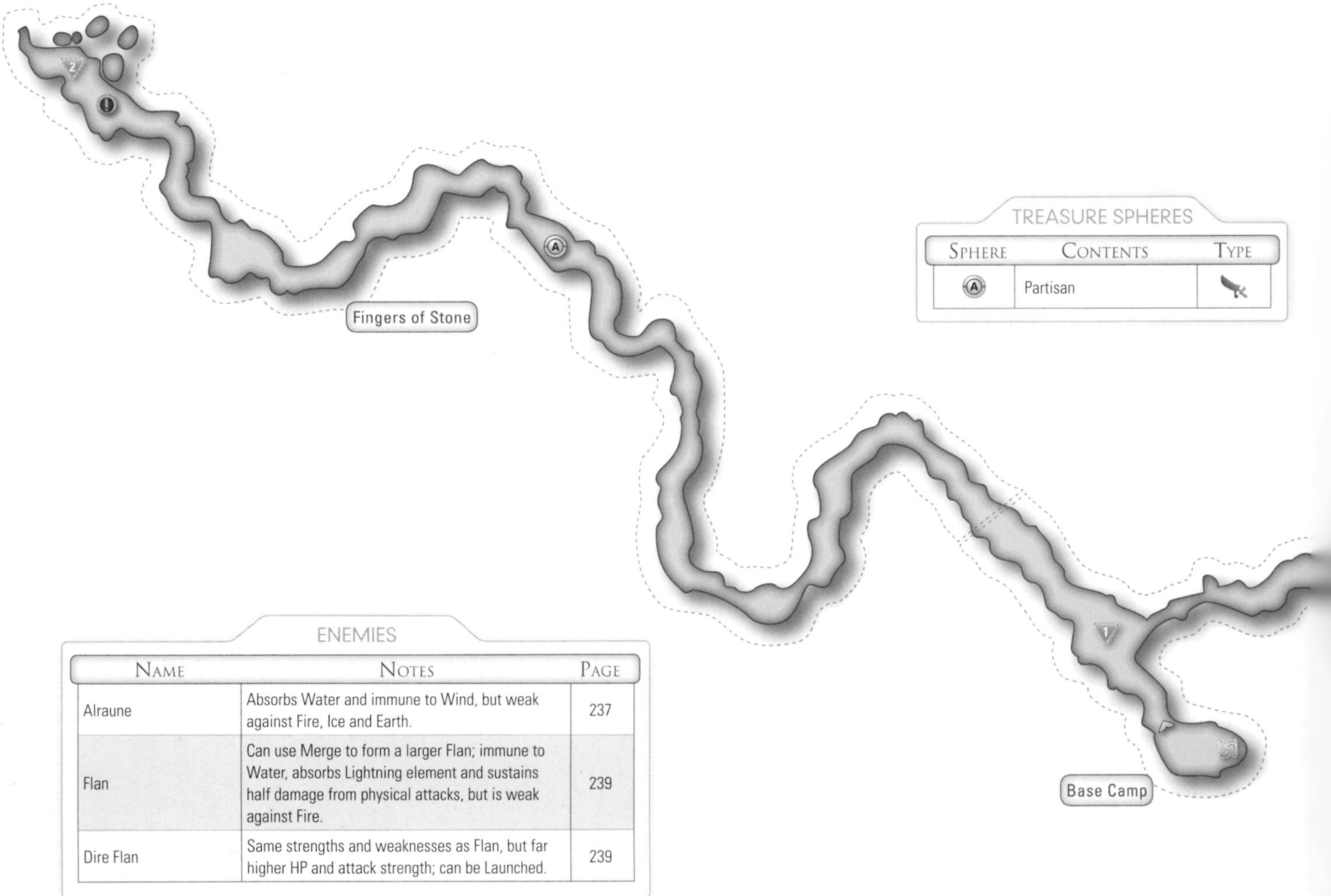

Fingers of Stone

Base Camp

TREASURE SPHERES

Sphere	Contents	Type
A	Partisan	

ENEMIES

Name	Notes	Page
Alraune	Absorbs Water and immune to Wind, but weak against Fire, Ice and Earth.	237
Flan	Can use Merge to form a larger Flan; immune to Water, absorbs Lightning element and sustains half damage from physical attacks, but is weak against Fire.	239
Dire Flan	Same strengths and weaknesses as Flan, but far higher HP and attack strength; can be Launched.	239

1 With Hope unavailable, create Paradigms for a party of Lightning, Fang and Vanille. In addition to the default three given, create Diversity (Ravager + Commando + Medic) and Delta Attack (Commando + Sentinel + Ravager). There's really no need to upgrade Vanille, though if you are following our strategy of creating "super specialists" for later, spending all available points on her Medic role is an option.

Ignore the path on the right at the start, as this is a dead-end (at least for the present time – see map). The route ahead is populated by Alraune, Flan and Dire Flan (Fig. 1): nothing, in short, that you can't cope with right now.

1

2 **Eidolon Battle – Alexander:** Hope returns to join Lightning and Fang for this confrontation, and acts as party leader throughout. The colossal Eidolon appears ponderous, but his combo attacks can bludgeon unprotected characters into submission with a handful of purposeful strikes (Fig. 2). For this reason, a Sentinel taking center stage is an absolute must.

Paradigm Shift to Delta Attack the moment the battle begins, then go straight on the offensive. As soon as anyone's HP falls below 50%, switch to Combat Clinic. Hope and Lightning can heal the party within seconds. Now return to Delta Attack to resume the offensive. You may need to make the switch between the two Paradigms several times over the course of the encounter, with Alexander yielding when the Doom counter reaches approximately 300. Hope will receive the Alexander Eidolith and the much-needed boost of an additional ATB gauge segment.

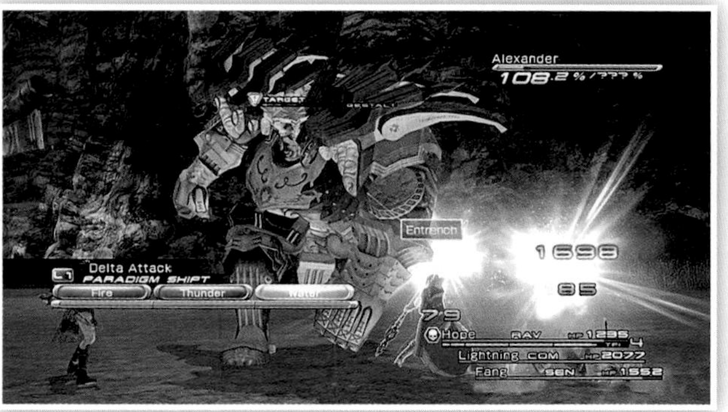

2

Miscellany

- We'll start with a warning for those who might feel tempted to browse the updated shop stock lists. If your eyes light up with a true power-leveler's joy at the sight of the **Collector Catalog** – an accessory that increases the item drop probability for post-battle spoils – pause before you sell everything of value to obtain it. Firstly, its effects are rather subtle, and you will not recoup its cost in many hours of grinding at this point in the game. Secondly, you actually obtain a free Collector Catalog before the end of Chapter 11. We suggest that you save your resources for more valuable purchases at a later date.
- Even though there is no option to "escape" from battle in FFXIII, don't forget that the "**Retry**" option in the pause menu acts in much the same way. It's consequence-free and near-instantaneous, and can be used to flee from an impossible (or just plain disastrous) battle, or to make another stealthy approach after an unsuccessful preemptive strike attempt.
- As Sentinels grow in importance over the coming hours, players seeking to maximize their efficiency in Staggering powerful enemies (and boost their Chain Combo damage multipliers to dizzy heights) should now consider using the Mystic Tower Paradigm (Ravager + Sentinel + Ravager) in conjunction with Delta Attack. This is essentially the same technique employed during earlier chapters to make two-man teams punch above their weight. After increasing the Chain Gauge to approximately 40% with Delta Attack, a quick change to Mystic Tower will enable your two Ravagers to Stagger an opponent far more rapidly. You can learn more about techniques for increasing your Chain Bonus – and other related topics of note – on page 140 of the Strategy & Analysis chapter.

THE ARCHYLTE STEPPE

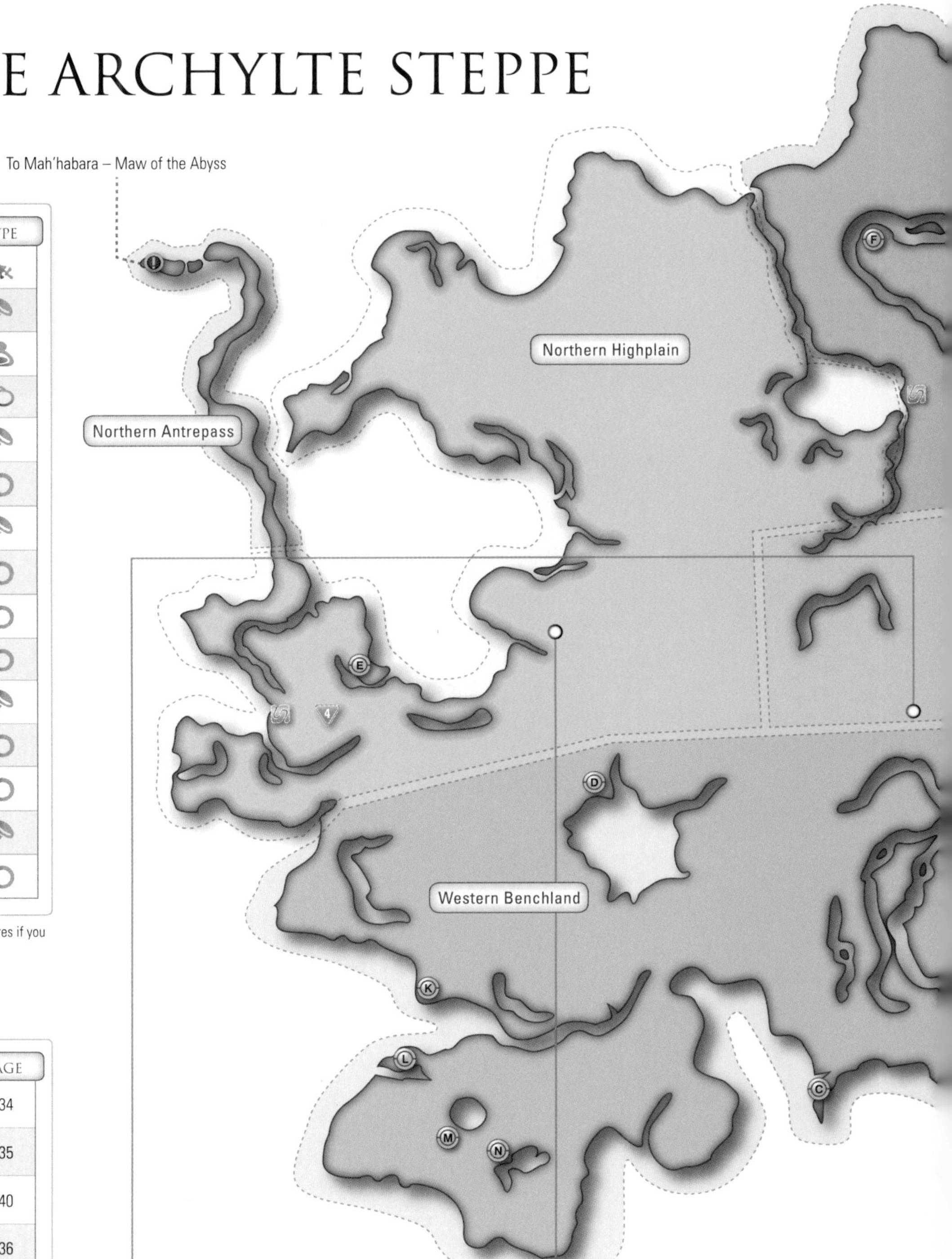

To Mah'habara – Maw of the Abyss

Northern Highplain

Northern Antrepass

Western Benchland

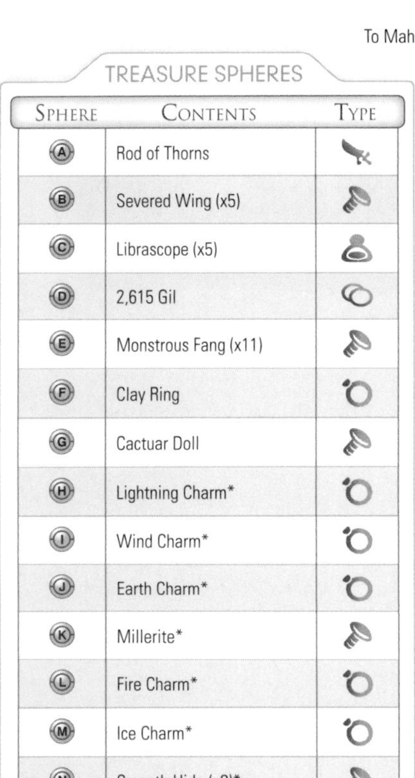

TREASURE SPHERES

Sphere	Contents	Type
A	Rod of Thorns	
B	Severed Wing (x5)	
C	Librascope (x5)	
D	2,615 Gil	
E	Monstrous Fang (x11)	
F	Clay Ring	
G	Cactuar Doll	
H	Lightning Charm*	
I	Wind Charm*	
J	Earth Charm*	
K	Millerite*	
L	Fire Charm*	
M	Ice Charm*	
N	Smooth Hide (x8)*	
O	Zephyr Ring*	

* You should only attempt to open these Treasure Spheres if you have a well-developed party.

ENEMIES

Name	Fight or Avoid?	Page
Gorgonopsid	Fight	234
Megistotherian	Avoid	235
Behemoth King	Possible	240
Leyak	Possible	236
Rangda	Possible	236
Flan	Fight	239
Dire Flan	Possible	239
Navidon	Fight	237
Amphisbaena	Avoid	238
Goblin	Fight	240
Adamanchelid	Avoid	238
Adamantoise	Avoid	238
Adamantortoise	Avoid	238
Cactuar	Avoid	241

The Archylte Steppe is a vast, untamed wilderness. Home to a diverse range of creatures, and with many secrets to uncover, it's a playground for future fun and profit. For now, though, it's an unforgiving and astonishingly dangerous location. Some of the indigenous species can kill your entire party with a first attack suffused with crushing disdain, while most notable features remain light years out of your reach until much later in the game. You can find a walkthrough for the area (including an introduction to a huge side-quest that begins here) on the double-page spread that follows.

There are well over 20 Treasure Spheres on this huge map, but only a fraction of these are available at this stage in the game. Some are inaccessible due to an obstruction, while others are guarded by powerful enemies that your party cannot hope to beat. Study the Treasure Spheres and Enemies tables to learn the locations and contents of the containers that you can open without risking life and limb.

There are several creatures on the Archylte Steppe that you cannot possibly triumph against, but the towering dinosaur-like creatures are the most spectacular of these. It's almost worth engaging them in battle once, if just to gain a sense of how far your party must progress over the coming chapters to beat them.

Yellow "jump markers" (as pictured here beside a pool near your starting point) cannot be traversed at this point in the story. This means that no matter how tantalizing the rewards or new paths may be, you'll just have to move on. Our Side-Quests section has a full map of the Steppe, which includes optional areas that are closed off until later.

This path near your starting point leads back to an expanded Vallis Media map, where you can find an entrance to an entirely optional area: Yaschas Massif. This large zone is packed with powerful foes and some rather nice opportunities to power-level for spoils and CP, but it's by no means mandatory that you visit it just yet. Again, this will be covered in detail at the end of our walkthrough (see page 116), when your chances of surviving most enemy encounters there will be much, much higher...

3 Before you set off (Fig. 3), your first step should be to restore Lightning as party leader and configure your Paradigms – see the accompanying table for our suggestions. You should also start to use Delta Attack as your active Paradigm.

SUGGESTED PARADIGM DECK

Paradigm	Lightning	Fang	Hope
Relentless Assault	Ravager	Commando	Ravager
Mystic Tower	Ravager	Sentinel	Ravager
Delta Attack	Commando	Sentinel	Ravager
Solidarity	Commando	Sentinel	Medic
Combat Clinic	Medic	Sentinel	Medic
Evened Odds	Medic	Saboteur	Synergist

3

4 Head northwest until you reach the Northern Highplain area. The path leading north here will take you to the next waypoint. The lone Behemoth King you pass on your way there can actually be defeated if you get a preemptive strike, then use a pre-stocked Aggression Paradigm (Commando + Commando + Ravager) before the Stagger expires. If you can't finish it within that time, things will end very badly – but 4,000 CP for a battle that might take no more than a minute to complete is worth the risk. Just before you reach the exit corridor, ignore the Megistotherian and Behemoth King (Fig. 4) – these are most likely too strong for you at this stage in the game, though a well-developed party could possibly beat them by making the most of a preemptive strike and by summoning Odin as a last resort.

Cast a wistful glance backwards before you leave, but worry not – you'll have ample opportunity to properly explore this vast expanse later in the adventure.

4

Hunt Side-Quest: Introduction

Interacting with Cie'th Stones enables you to begin special missions where you hunt very specific enemies known as "Marks". This huge side-quest actually continues beyond the end of the main story, and will take many, many hours to complete. For now, you can easily beat the first two Marks you encounter during your journey to the waypoint marker, then continue the side-quest later when your party is much stronger.

- Active Cie'th Stones are represented by flashing circles on the in-game maps, while "dormant" Cie'th Stones are black. Dormant Cie'th Stones are usually activated by successfully killing Marks, or sometimes by reaching a certain point in the story.
- To interact with an active Cie'th Stone, approach it and press ⊗/Ⓐ. Read the description, then choose to accept the challenge, or reject it. Note the "Class" letter: "D" is the easiest grade, with "A" being the hardest.
- If you take on a mission it will remain active until you complete it, or accept the challenge of another Cie'th Stone – you can only have one Mark mission active at any given time.
- Once a hunt has started, the Mark appears on the main map as a pink star.
- After a Mark has been slain, you can return to the Cie'th Stone to restart the mission at any time (which is useful if you are determined to obtain a five-star rating for each challenge). In the event that you defeat a Mark on multiple occasions, only your best star rating will be stored. Note that the unique reward offered at the conclusion of each battle is only given once – with future encounters, you will receive CP and lesser spoils (usually components).

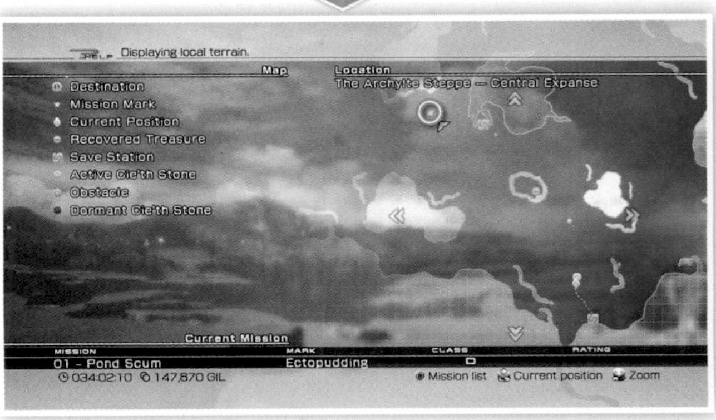

MISSION 01 – POND SCUM

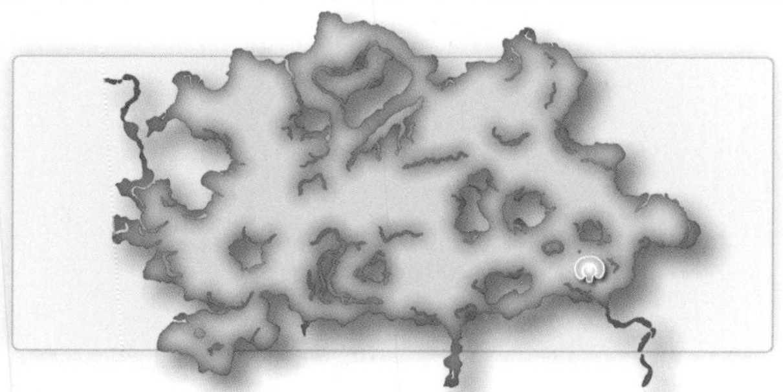

Mark:	Ectopudding
Cie'th Stone Location:	Archylte Steppe – Central Expanse
Mark Location:	Archylte Steppe – Central Expanse
Class:	D
Unlock Condition:	None
Reward:	Energy Sash

The Cie'th Stone that enables you to start the first hunt is located just in front of your starting position. Refer to the in-game map once you accept the commission: your quarry is represented by a pink star. When you reach it, start the battle with a preemptive strike. Should the Ectopudding see you, just run away and then carefully circle around behind it for another attempt. It is immune to physical damage, but characters acting as Commandos will adapt their strategy to use the magical Ruin attack once this is discovered. Select Relentless Assault to inflict huge damage before the opening Stagger ends. The Lightning element is its principle weakness, so you can manually select this via the Abilities menu if you wish. After the final Launch, switch to Delta Attack for a safe end to the battle.

MISSION 02 – GOODWILL HUNTING

Mark:	Uridimmu
Cie'th Stone Location:	Archylte Steppe – Central Expanse
Mark Location:	Archylte Steppe – Central Expanse
Class:	D
Unlock Condition:	Complete Mission 01
Reward:	Cobaltite

Interact with the Cie'th Stone that rose from the ground when you completed the previous mission, and accept the second hunt. As before, you can track your target down by looking for a pink star on the main map.

The second Mark, Uridimmu, is accompanied by a group of Gorgonopsids. If your party is at a fairly average stage of development for this stage in the game, you will have little chance of beating the Target Time. Start off with Delta Attack, then switch to Solidarity or Combat Clinic once your party looks worse for wear. You should then grind away with Lightning as your only offensive warrior (occasional counter-attacks from Fang notwithstanding) until only one or two Gorgonopsids remain. From this point, and with your party looking healthy, return to Delta Attack to end the confrontation. Your prize is Cobaltite, a rare transformational catalyst used to upgrade certain weapons (see page 218 for more details).

There are at least four further Mark missions that you can complete at this stage in your development, with some nice rewards for those who put in the effort. However, these require that you visit the optional (and rather dangerous) Yaschas Massif map, accessed via Vallis Media. The Cie'th Stone used to activate the third hunt is not far away from the site of your battle with Uridimmu. If you wish to leave the main storyline for now and continue this side-quest, refer to page 116 for guidance on beating each Mark.

MAH'HABARA

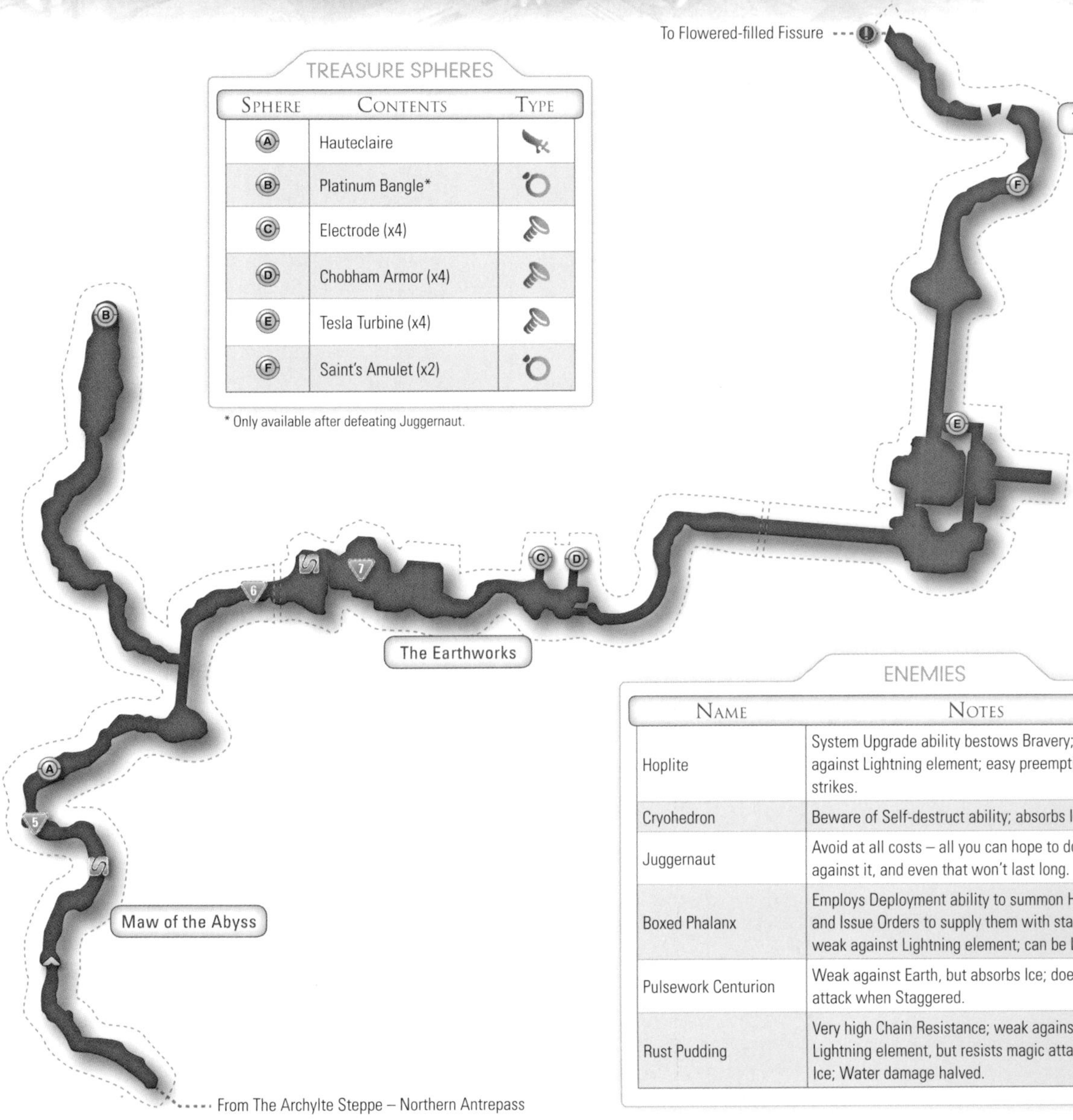

TREASURE SPHERES

Sphere	Contents	Type
A	Hauteclaire	
B	Platinum Bangle*	
C	Electrode (x4)	
D	Chobham Armor (x4)	
E	Tesla Turbine (x4)	
F	Saint's Amulet (x2)	

* Only available after defeating Juggernaut.

ENEMIES

Name	Notes	Page
Hoplite	System Upgrade ability bestows Bravery; weak against Lightning element; easy preemptive strikes.	242
Cryohedron	Beware of Self-destruct ability; absorbs Ice.	243
Juggernaut	Avoid at all costs – all you can hope to do is heal against it, and even that won't last long.	243
Boxed Phalanx	Employs Deployment ability to summon Hoplites, and Issue Orders to supply them with status buffs; weak against Lightning element; can be Launched.	242
Pulsework Centurion	Weak against Earth, but absorbs Ice; does not attack when Staggered.	242
Rust Pudding	Very high Chain Resistance; weak against Lightning element, but resists magic attacks and Ice; Water damage halved.	239

5 The Hoplite enemy type is easily defeated with Delta Attack, but your Battle Duration will be rather slow. To speed things up, switch your default Paradigm to Relentless Assault and secure a preemptive strike to defeat them in no time at all. When you reach a separate path to the left, go straight ahead – the Juggernaut guarding the Treasure Sphere at the end is far too powerful for your party at this stage (Fig. 5). You can return here later to defeat this enemy and claim the rewards it protects.

5

6 Not only can the Boxed Phalanx summon new Hoplites with its Deployment ability, it can also use Issue Orders to cause all Hoplites present to activate several status buffs at once. At a later stage in your development, it would be in your best interests to Stagger and dispatch this dangerous foe with great haste. Right now, though, it's unlikely that you can destroy it quickly enough.

As a preemptive strike isn't possible, you can either evade all three enemies and run straight past, or opt to use the Odin Eidolon to beat it (Fig. 6). If you don't have sufficient TP, backtrack along the corridor and fight Hoplites. You can use the Energy Sash accessory (if obtained from the first Mark) to accelerate the process. Once ready, set Relentless Assault as your active Paradigm, then direct your party to attack the larger foe straight away. As soon as Lightning is in danger of falling, summon Odin. The Boxed Phalanx should be Staggered before you enter Gestalt Mode, and will fall before the Eidolon departs. The Hoplites that remain are easily beaten with your renewed party.

6

7 The enemies in this area are all tough, but they're far from unbeatable. The four Cryohedrons are very tricky unless you secure a preemptive strike – if you don't, you'll expose yourself to their Self-destruct ability (Fig. 7). Rust Puddings are typical flan enemies with resistance to Chains and magic – but at least they don't possess the

7

Merge ability. The Pulsework Centurions, like other enemies of their ilk, have great strength and take time to Stagger – but fall quickly once this occurs. Individually, they succumb rapidly to Relentless Assault, but you will probably need to use Delta Attack if you face more than one, with Combat Clinic for rapid healing.

When you reach the second bridge, you will face a group of three Hoplites accompanying another Boxed Phalanx – and this is a battle that you cannot bypass. Once again, employ Relentless Assault until the latter enemy is Staggered, then summon Odin if necessary.

Miscellany

- **Power Tip:** The Maw of the Abyss area is a superb power-levelling spot. You can farm huge sums of CP there by running a route between (but not including) the first Boxed Phalanx and the dead-end where a Juggernaut guards a Treasure Sphere. In between five and ten minutes, you can amass a thoroughly respectable 22,400 CP in a sequence of fairly unremarkable battles – and these are even easier if you use the Relentless Assault Paradigm and obtain preemptive strikes whenever possible. If you fight here until you reach the Ravager, Commando and Medic Role Level crystals for Lightning, Fang and Hope respectively, you will put your party in a very powerful position for the battles to come. The additional spoils are also a welcome bonus.
- With crystals costing a fortune in the Crystarium, a great way to speed up your party's overall development is to ignore all crystals on "branches" that offer Magic, Strength or HP upgrades alone, as these are usually more expensive than those on the inner ring. This will enable you to reach Role Levels and useful abilities sooner during the course of Chapter 11. You can, of course, tie up these "loose ends" later.

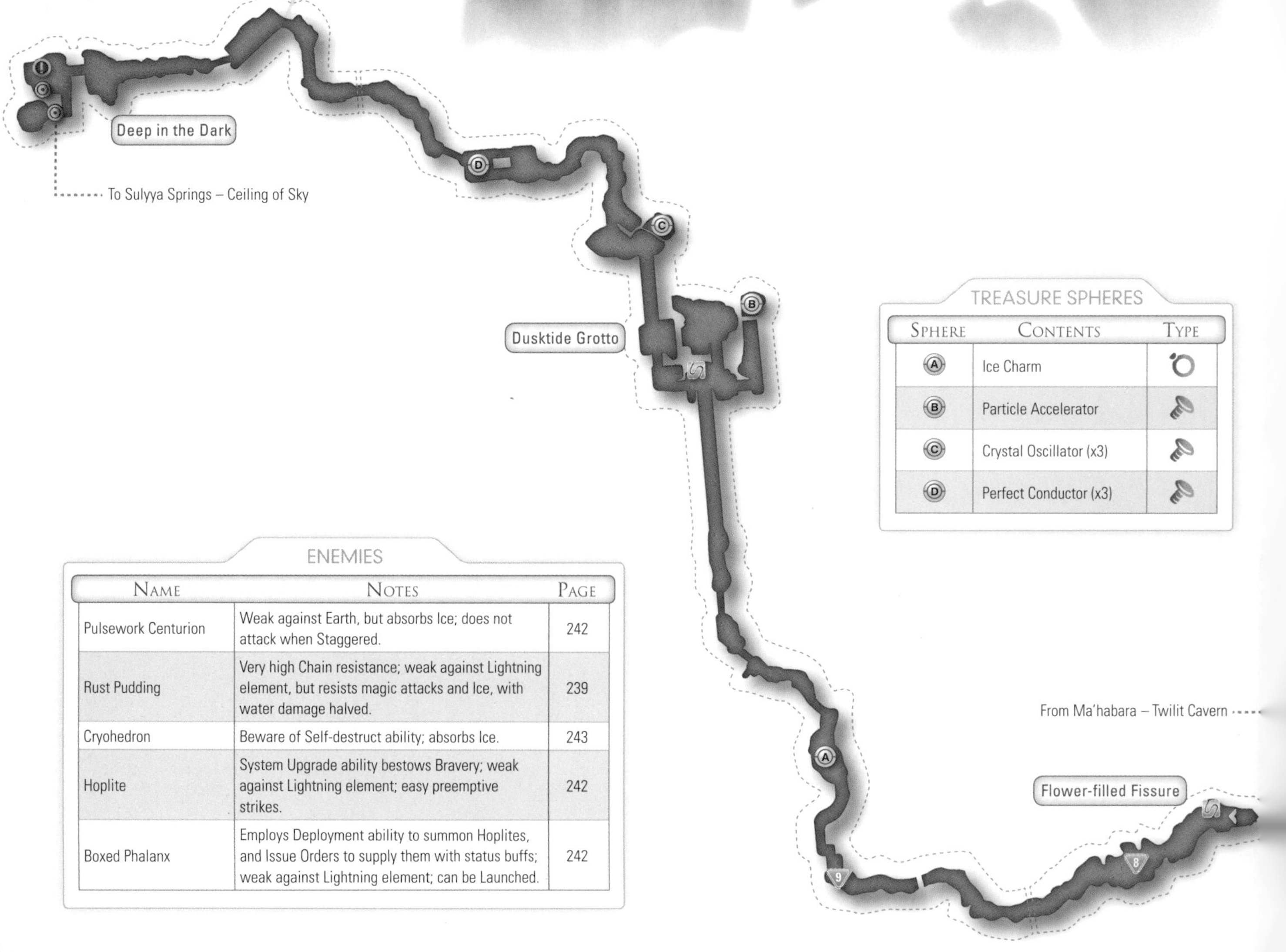

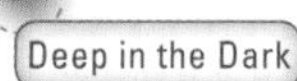

To Sulyya Springs – Ceiling of Sky

Dusktide Grotto

From Ma'habara – Twilit Cavern

Flower-filled Fissure

TREASURE SPHERES

Sphere	Contents	Type
Ⓐ	Ice Charm	
Ⓑ	Particle Accelerator	
Ⓒ	Crystal Oscillator (x3)	
Ⓓ	Perfect Conductor (x3)	

ENEMIES

Name	Notes	Page
Pulsework Centurion	Weak against Earth, but absorbs Ice; does not attack when Staggered.	242
Rust Pudding	Very high Chain resistance; weak against Lightning element, but resists magic attacks and Ice, with water damage halved.	239
Cryohedron	Beware of Self-destruct ability; absorbs Ice.	243
Hoplite	System Upgrade ability bestows Bravery; weak against Lightning element; easy preemptive strikes.	242
Boxed Phalanx	Employs Deployment ability to summon Hoplites, and Issue Orders to supply them with status buffs; weak against Lightning element; can be Launched.	242

8 If you have taken our advice to save all CP and keep Vanille, Sazh and Snow in reserve for "super specialist" roles, you will need to work on Vanille's Crystarium once you arrive at the Flower-filled Fissure. Vanille's best specialty is as a Medic, so purchase as many crystals in this role as you can afford (with Curasa and the ATB level crystals on the topmost tier being vitally important). Equip Vanille with the Healer's Staff, Blessed Talisman and Shield Talisman to boost her healing skill and provide additional protection.

Eidolon Battle – Hecatoncheir: Hecatoncheir fights in the same way throughout the battle: after standing still with the Looming Wrath caption visible, he will launch a furious combo attack (Fig. 8) before repeating this two-step sequence from the start. If you don't have a Sentinel in place when his assault begins, the battle will most likely end before he lands his final blow. For your first attempt at beating him, wait until Fang runs over to the Eidolon to perform her second batch of attacks with the Slash & Burn Paradigm (these have a purpose – they put distance between Fang and Vanille, at least partially shielding the latter from area-effect assaults), then immediately switch to Stumbling Block. Fang will protect the party while you, as Vanille, steadily increase the Gestalt gauge with constant Saboteur attacks. You should then alternate between Lifeguard and Stumbling Block for the rest of the battle.

8

If you fail on your first try (and this is likely), there are two ways to push the Gestalt gauge up to the necessary threshold on your second attempt. The first is to create the Arcane Defense Paradigm (Ravager + Sentinel). Start the battle as before, then alternate between Stumbling Block and occasional bursts of Arcane Defense when you have license to attack. This will have the effect of raising and maintaining Hecatoncheir's Chain Gauge – and the higher this is, the faster the Gestalt gauge will increase. The second trick is to use the Renew technique. You should have sufficient TP for at least one application, removing the need to use the Lifeguard Paradigm when the tide of the battle turns against you.

If you are but a sliver away from success when the Doom counter reaches approximately 100, try switching to Slash & Burn for the final moments in a last-gasp rush for victory. Once you force your opponent to yield, Vanille gains the Hecatoncheir Eidolith and a further ATB gauge segment.

9 The Rust Puddings, Pulsework Centurions and Cryohedrons that litter the first part of the Dusktide Grotto will pose no danger with the Delta Attack Paradigm; Relentless Assault, as ever, offers more speed at greater risk. When you reach the Juggernaut, walk right on by without a second glance. The mixed group of Pulsework Centurions and Cryohedrons that follow are difficult to defeat without a preemptive strike. You may find it easier to run straight past and attempt to sneak up from the bridge just beyond them.

9

The Boxed Phalanx just inside the Deep in the Dark area is the first that you can catch unawares, so be sure to do just that to spectacular effect. Press ⊗/Ⓐ to "Examine" when prompted at the end of the path, then approach and board the Atomos when the cutscene ends (Fig. 9).

MAH'HABARA: SECRET AREAS

After you ride the Atomos to Sulyya Springs, you have the option to get straight back on and backtrack to Mah'habara. The very act of returning opens up three new map areas, with the Atomos completing a "bridge" to these new locales. Feel free to visit if you would like to see the area for yourself – refer to page 116 of the Side-Quests section for a map and further details.

SULYYA SPRINGS

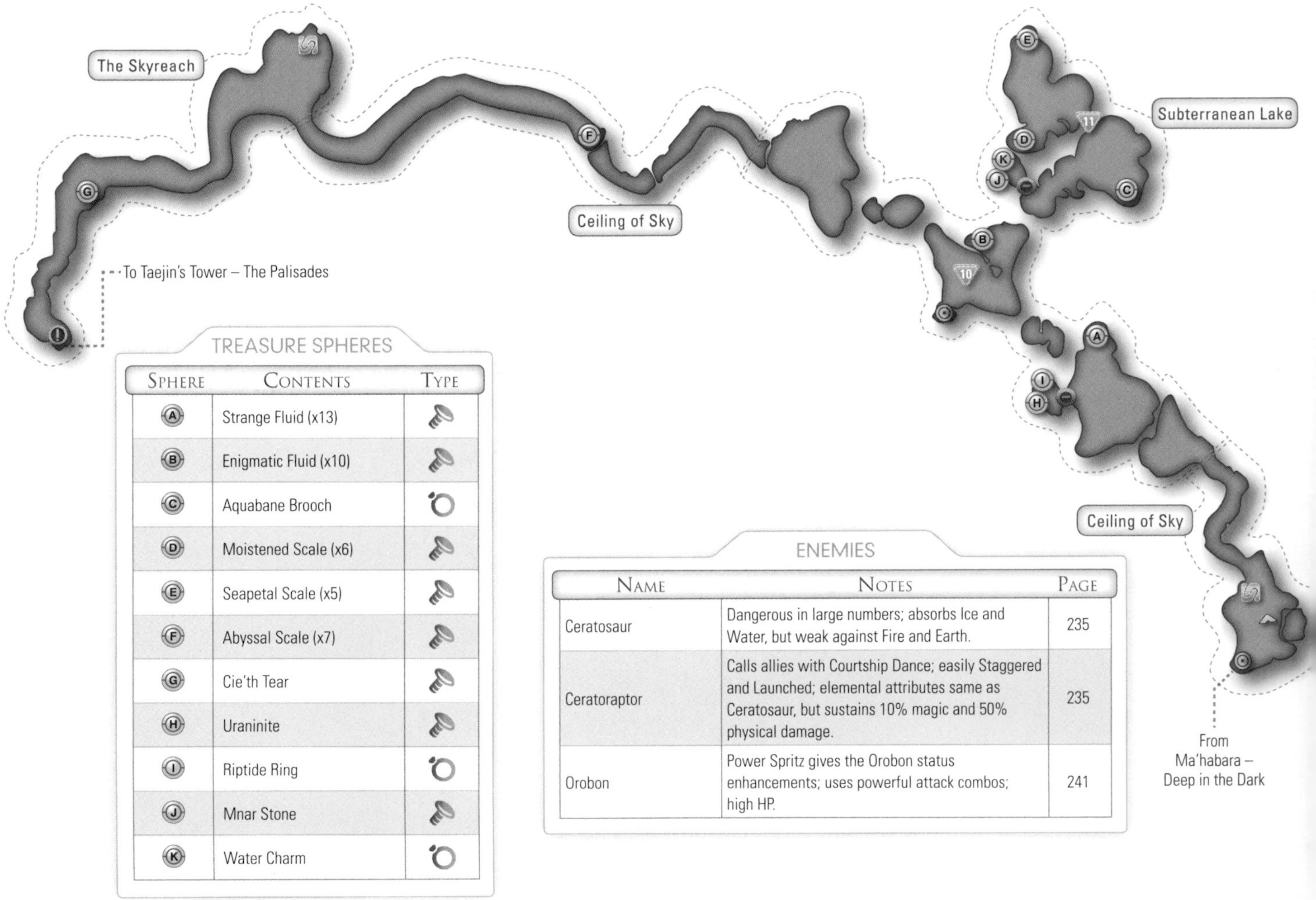

The Skyreach

Ceiling of Sky

Subterranean Lake

To Taejin's Tower – The Palisades

Ceiling of Sky

From Ma'habara – Deep in the Dark

TREASURE SPHERES

Sphere	Contents	Type
A	Strange Fluid (x13)	
B	Enigmatic Fluid (x10)	
C	Aquabane Brooch	
D	Moistened Scale (x6)	
E	Seapetal Scale (x5)	
F	Abyssal Scale (x7)	
G	Cie'th Tear	
H	Uraninite	
I	Riptide Ring	
J	Mnar Stone	
K	Water Charm	

ENEMIES

Name	Notes	Page
Ceratosaur	Dangerous in large numbers; absorbs Ice and Water, but weak against Fire and Earth.	235
Ceratoraptor	Calls allies with Courtship Dance; easily Staggered and Launched; elemental attributes same as Ceratosaur, but sustains 10% magic and 50% physical damage.	235
Orobon	Power Spritz gives the Orobon status enhancements; uses powerful attack combos; high HP.	241

10 The group of five Ceratosaurs may seem unassuming as you approach them, but they have the capacity to wipe out all but the most well-prepared party with indifference. Those who feel sufficiently powerful having explored optional areas and completed Mark missions may be able to go straight on the offensive with Relentless Assault to thin their numbers (and reduce the danger) very quickly. Players with less well-developed parties will benefit from Delta Attack (and a quick use of Libra to ascertain elemental weaknesses) or, should that fail, Solidarity for extra security.

When the battle ends, approach the water's edge and interact when prompted (Fig. 10). Two platforms will rise from the depths. Both carry a pair of Treasure Spheres – but, naturally, they are protected by large groups of the regional fauna. These are almost certainly too strong for you at this stage in the game, though a well-developed party could possibly beat them by summoning Odin before the Ceratoraptors call for reinforcements.

10

11 The raised area at the center of the Subterranean Lake zone (Fig. 11) is a dead-end, but features three Treasure Spheres. You will need to beat two Orobon and a pair of Ceratosaur to obtain the closest one. Defeat the latter enemies first, then turn your attention to the Orobon. These are potent adversaries before they are Staggered, with dizzying attack combos and the ability to inflict Daze and Slow. Oddly, though, they have a tendency to remain inactive for surprisingly long periods of time.

The next battle is against a group of Ceratosaurs and a single Ceratoraptor. Aim to start with a preemptive strike and deal with the new enemy first. Ceratoraptors can summon additional Ceratosaurs with their Courtship

11

Dance ability, so you should always dispose of them as a priority. The final Treasure Sphere is guarded by three Orobon. Their positions make a preemptive strike unlikely, so turtle up with Delta Attack and use Combat Clinic for rapid healing when the enemy onslaught begins to take a toll.

Party Improvements

Sulyya Springs acts as an acid test for the development of your party. If Lightning, Fang and Hope have yet to reach the Ravager, Commando and Medic Role Level crystals, you will definitely benefit from backtracking to Mah'habara to farm for CP to improve your party's durability and attacking prowess. See page 127 for further details.

Another idea is to improve your party with new accessories – a simple yet effective way to nudge characters ahead of the difficulty curve. Access the nearby Save Station and select the B&W Outfitters retail network. Sell all Incentive Chips and Credit Chips – these components offer negligible EXP in upgrades, but command a fine resale price. This should provide you with an enormous stock of Gil to spend. Sacrificing the Entite Ring for 60,000 Gil is an alternative option. Whatever you do, refrain from selling other high-value components – it's best to save these for weapon upgrades later in the game.

Visit the main shop page and purchase three Warrior's Wristbands and another three Sorcerer's Marks. Equip two Sorcerer's Marks on Hope, two Warrior's Wristbands on Fang, and give the remaining pair of accessories to Lightning. Add to this the best of the rest in your existing catalog of accessories for remaining slots, and you should be in perfect condition for the coming battles. If you really have no Gil or saleable assets, a party on a tight budget could instead opt for the Brawler's Wristband and Shaman's Mark – but with less impressive stat boosts.

TAEJIN'S TOWER

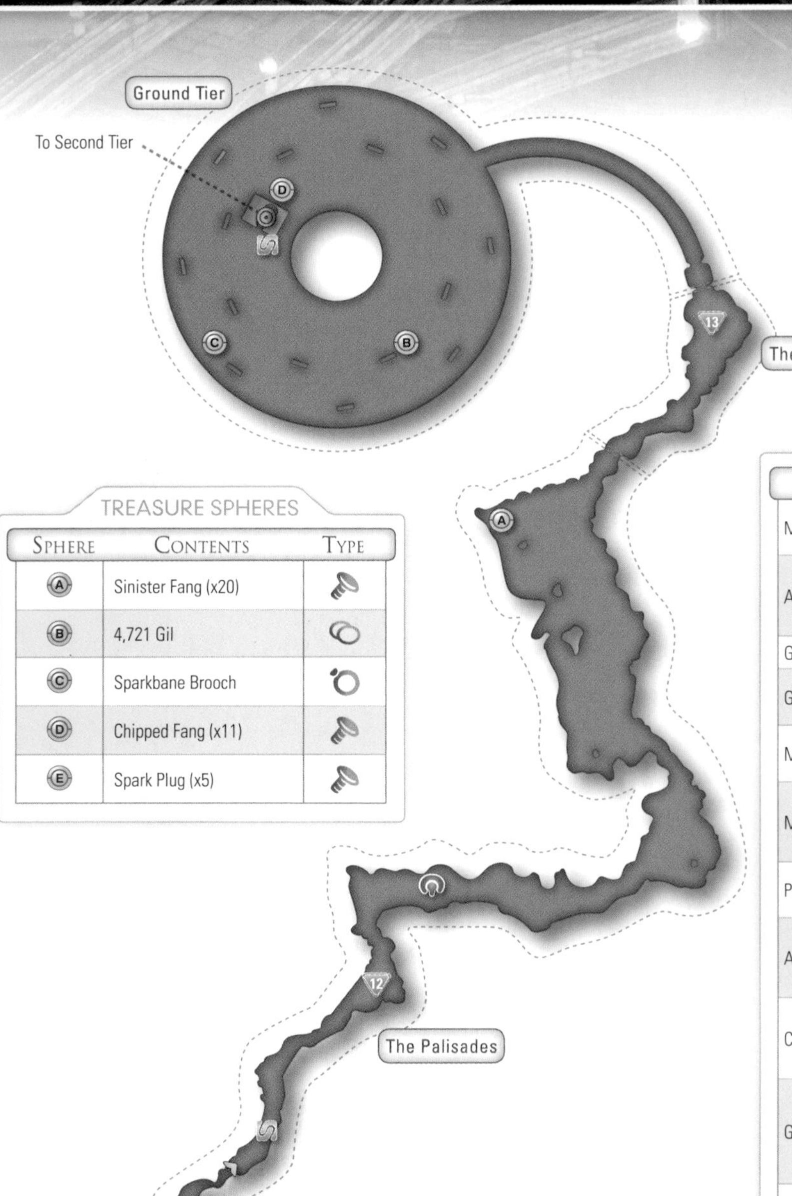

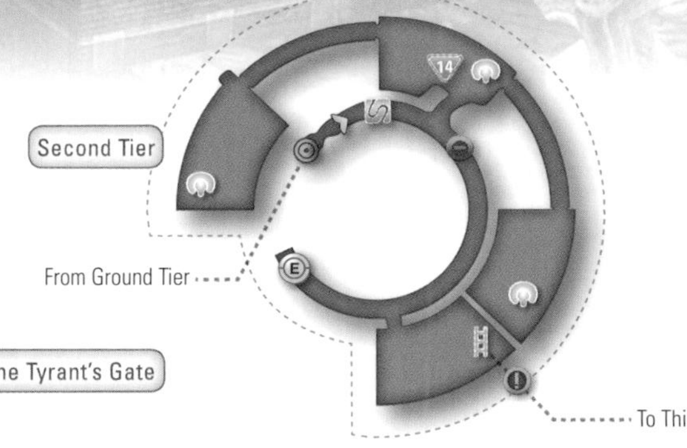

TREASURE SPHERES

Sphere	Contents	Type
A	Sinister Fang (x20)	
B	4,721 Gil	
C	Sparkbane Brooch	
D	Chipped Fang (x11)	
E	Spark Plug (x5)	

ENEMIES

Name	Notes	Page
Mánagarmr	Can inflict Imperil and Curse; powerful attacks; absorbs Lightning, but weak against Water.	235
Amphisbaena	Immune to Earth damage, but weak against Lightning and Wind; resistant to magic; high HP and assorted status immunities.	238
Goblin	Can morph into Goblin Chieftain.	240
Goblin Chieftain	Resistant to Lightning and Wind, immune to Earth and physical damage halved; can bestow Bravery.	240
Munchkin	Can morph into a Munchkin Maestro.	240
Munchkin Maestro	Weak against Ice and Wind, but immune to Lightning element; strong attacks, but falls quickly to a concerted assault; can bestow Bravery.	240
Pulsework Gladiator	Resistant to everything except Water; are incapacitated and easy to destroy once Staggered.	242
Ambling Bellows	Resistant to physical damage and Ice, with magic damage halved; weak against Lightning element, Water and Earth; can summon allies to battle.	242
Cryptos	Relatively weak unless it employs status buffs – when this happens, its attack power is worthy of respect.	242
Gurangatch	A typical Armadillon/Armadon-type enemy – enormously resistant to all forms of damage while its carapace is intact, but incredibly weak once Staggered.	237
Gelatitan	Fire, Ice and physical damage halved; Water absorbed, but weak against Lightning element; can inflict status ailments.	240

12 From this point forward, it's definitely provident to select Delta Attack as your active Paradigm. A Sentinel really is a mandatory fixture for many battles.

The two lone Mánagarmr you meet are easy to beat (especially with a preemptive strike), but the Amphisbaena that follows is a more stern opponent (Fig. 12). Take breaks for Solidarity or Combat Clinic healing when required – especially when party members are subject to the status ailments it inflicts.

12

13 On the approach to the tower, you will soon notice how two Mánagarmr can use their Accursed Breath status ailment attack to infect all three party members at once. Don't bother with Esuna or other ailment-removing mechanisms – just let Fang deal with the damage. The same applies with those found once you're inside as you move between the three Treasure Spheres. Once ready to continue, climb the ramp to reach the waypoint marker and ride the elevator up to the Second Tier.

Pulsework Gladiators may just be the quickest of all Pulsework soldiers to dispatch, so these should generally be your first targets when you encounter them in mixed groups. Be warned, though, that their attacks can knock party members over, temporarily halting the execution of any command queues.

13

There are three Menhirrim (Fig. 13) to activate on this floor, each one initiating a new Mark mission. Unlike all other challenges of this type, these are a mandatory part of the main story. Consult the following guides as you hunt each one in turn (Mission 21 to 23 – see paragraph 14), then head to the new waypoint marker once the flames blocking the path have been extinguished. Note that it is easier to obtain a preemptive strike against the five Pulsework Gladiators you meet there if you first lure them to the staircase.

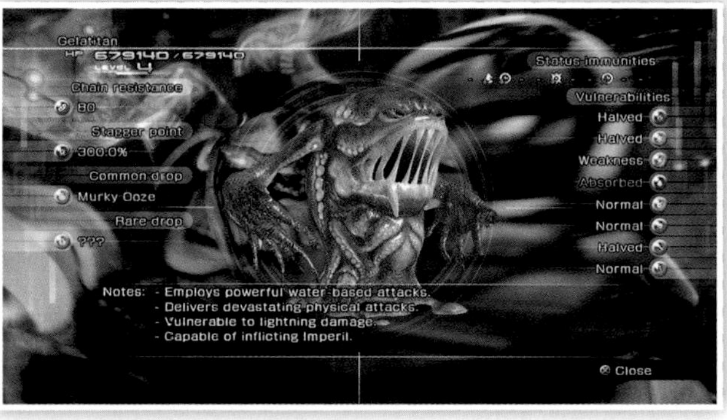

14

14 **Mission 21 – Gelatitan:** As this monster possesses a wide range of elemental resistances, it's a good idea to start the fight by casting Libra or using a Librascope to identify its weakness to the Lightning element (Fig. 14). With regular transitions to the Combat Clinic Paradigm, this should be a slow yet purposeful grind towards victory.

Mission 22 – Ambling Bellows: Stay out of range until a Cryptos approaches your position by the door, then run over to start the battle with a preemptive strike. Focus all aggression on the Ambling Bellows immediately in order to prevent it from summoning allies to the fray – continue to pummel away at the expense of healing until the Mark falls. If things go awry, the Odin Eidolon is your ace in the hole.

Mission 23 – Gurangatch: Gurangatch can be found by the central Menhirrim. Switch your default Paradigm to Relentless Assault, then sneak over carefully when its back is turned to secure a preemptive strike. If you fail, select Retry and attempt it again. Once the creature has been Staggered, it will fall within 40 seconds. Your reward, a Warrior's Wristband, can be equipped in Fang's third accessory slot to further increase her mighty Strength stat.

MISSION 20 – WORDS UNSPOKEN

Mark:	Goblin Chieftain
Cie'th Stone Location:	Taejin's Tower – The Palisades
Mark Location:	Taejin's Tower – The Palisades
Class:	C
Unlock Condition:	None
Reward:	Rhodochrosite

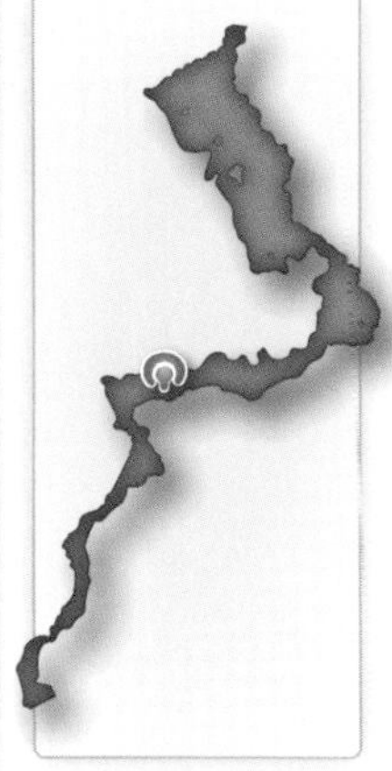

This optional hunt pits you against a robust gang consisting of a Munchkin, a Munchkin Maestro, two Goblins and a Goblin Chieftain. This is a straightforward battle if you use the Delta Attack Paradigm, but with one catch: the Munchkin and two Goblins can morph into their larger and more dangerous counterparts at any time. As the Munchkin Maestro can be killed more quickly than a Goblin Chieftain, it makes sense to direct your fire at the Goblins first, then kill the Munchkin.

With the Cie'th Stone that gave you this mission being a Waystone, completing the hunt allows you to teleport from and to the Palisades zone from now on (see page 128 for more details on this feature).

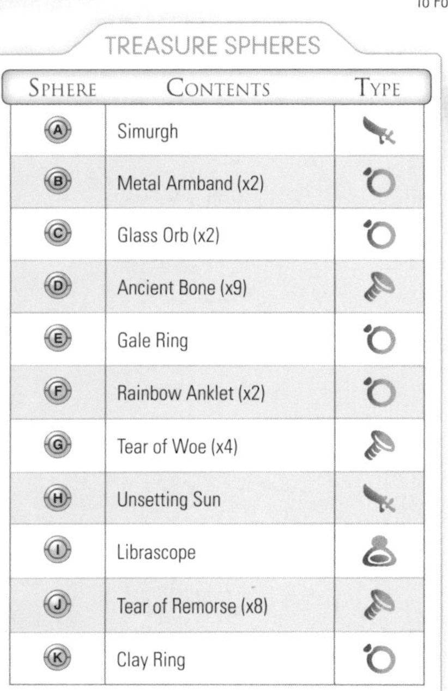

TREASURE SPHERES

Sphere	Contents	Type
A	Simurgh	
B	Metal Armband (x2)	
C	Glass Orb (x2)	
D	Ancient Bone (x9)	
E	Gale Ring	
F	Rainbow Anklet (x2)	
G	Tear of Woe (x4)	
H	Unsetting Sun	
I	Librascope	
J	Tear of Remorse (x8)	
K	Clay Ring	

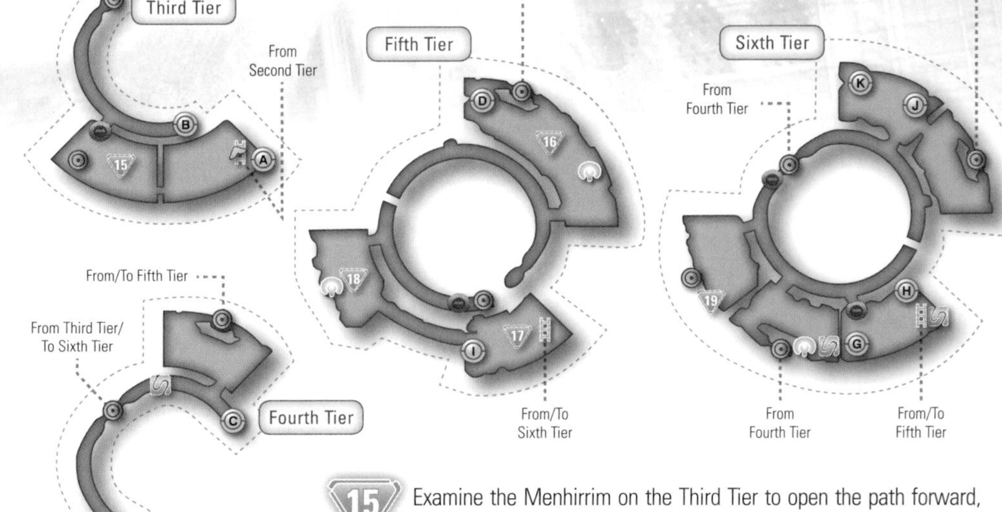

ENEMIES

Name	Notes	Page
Yaksha	War Dance attack packs a punch; physical damage halved, but weak against Water and Earth.	236
Varcolaci	Evades attacks; inflicts Poison; another relatively weak adversary.	244
Yakshini	Inflicts Deprotect; will use Bravery to enhance the attack power of all enemies present if left long enough.	236
Mushussu	Immune or resistant to all elements; inflicts status ailments; falls quickly once Staggered.	237
Vampire	Weak against all elements, but physical damage halved; huge HP; can inflict Daze and Deprotect.	244
Pulsework Gladiator	Resistant to everything except Water; is incapacitated and easy to destroy once Staggered.	242
Vetala	Massive damage resistance (though reduced when Staggered); inflicts many status ailments; high HP.	245
Chonchon	Low HP, but usually encountered in swarms; cannot be Provoked; inflicts Poison and Pain.	244
Tyrant	Uses Forge Blade ability to summon Centaurion Blade; very powerful attacks; high HP.	243
Centaurion Blade	Summoned by Tyrant; cannot be Provoked; very powerful attacks.	243

15 Examine the Menhirrim on the Third Tier to open the path forward, then approach the elevator and ride it to the Fourth Tier. Now run to the waypoint marker and ride the next elevator up to the Fifth Tier.

15

Yakshini and Yaksha guard the approach to the next Menhirrim (Fig. 15). The Yakshini inflicts Deprotect and bestows Bravery, which turns the Yaksha's War Dance attack into a far more potent weapon – so it naturally makes sense to always deal with the former first. With this minor distraction out of the way, interact with the Menhirrim to accept a fourth Mark mission.

Mission 24 – Mushussu: Accompanied by two Yakshini (which you should slay first), Mushussu has huge resistance to elemental damage. To speed things up, use Libra to identify its characteristics. With a quick break for healing after its allies have been slain, your Delta Attack formation will enable you to withstand Mushussu's attacks without difficulty.

16 Return to the Fourth Tier, then follow the waypoint marker. At the next elevator, ride up to the Sixth Tier. You can catch out the Vampire guarding the first room with a preemptive strike by luring it over to the doorway (Fig. 16). Accept the mission from the nearby Menhirrim, then approach another statue in the next room along to rotate the tower floor. Note that the swarm of Chonchon in this room are weak and cannot be Provoked, so feel free to change to Relentless Assault beforehand for a quicker finish.

Follow the waypoint marker then descend the staircase to reach the previously inaccessible portion of the Fifth Tier, where your next opponent awaits.

16

17 **Mission 25 – Vetala:** This opponent gains immunity to physical attacks and halves elemental damage when its Inertial Barrier ability is active (Fig. 17). Once Staggered, and its shield disabled, its physical immunity is removed – albeit only temporarily. It also has the ability to inflict a variety of long-lasting status ailments. There's no doubt about it: this is the most infuriating Mark you have encountered so far.

With a combination of Delta Attack and Combat Clinic – the latter employed for Esuna as much as basic healing – this will be a long fight, but not necessarily a difficult one. There are two principle tips that will make things easier. Firstly, ensure that Hope and Lightning are never inflicted with Fog at the same time (techniques help here: use Renew to heal in an emergency, or Dispelga, if you have it, to remove all ailments). Secondly, take care to remove the Pain debuff from Lightning if she has it before you Stagger Vetala.

Note that you can speed this battle up by employing the Mystic Tower Paradigm whenever Vetala's Chain Gauge reaches approximately 50%.

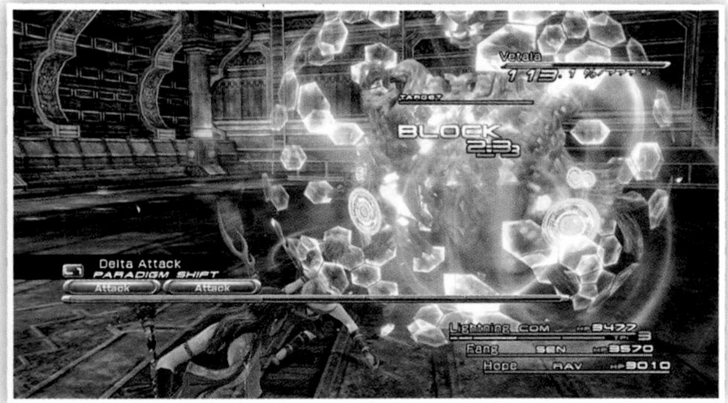

17

18

18 Accept the final mission from the Menhirrim in the next room. You may just be powerful enough to destroy the Tyrant here with Relentless Assault and a (difficult to obtain) preemptive strike. For the low sum of CP available, though, you will be better served by paying the Tyrant a wide berth. Backtrack to the Sixth Tier to face Penanggalan.

Power Tip: The five Pulsework Gladiators at the bottom of the Fifth Tier stairway (Fig. 18) can be destroyed within 40 seconds with a preemptive strike, and offer the princely gift of 8,000 CP. To force them to respawn, head up the staircase, run through the room to the outer walkway (the Vampire is easily avoided), then make the short return journey.

19

19 **Mission 26 – Penanggalan:** Defeat its Chonchon allies first, then use Combat Clinic to heal when its attacks seriously wound your party. Penanggalan may drop a Whistlewind Scarf when defeated, and you also get an excellent Diamond Bangle as a mission reward, making this a highly profitable skirmish.

Head to the waypoint marker to reach another Menhirrim on the Fifth Tier. Activate it, go to the elevator and ride it down to the Fourth Tier, then ride the main elevator up to the Sixth Tier. As the battle with the three Vampires outside the next elevator (Fig. 19) will take at least six minutes (with a reward of a fairly paltry 7,050 CP, all things considered), you may prefer to bypass them and ride straight up to The Cloven Spire at the top of the tower.

Treasure Spheres

Sphere	Contents	Type
A	Frostbane Brooch (x2)	
B	Ethersol	
C	Collector Catalog	

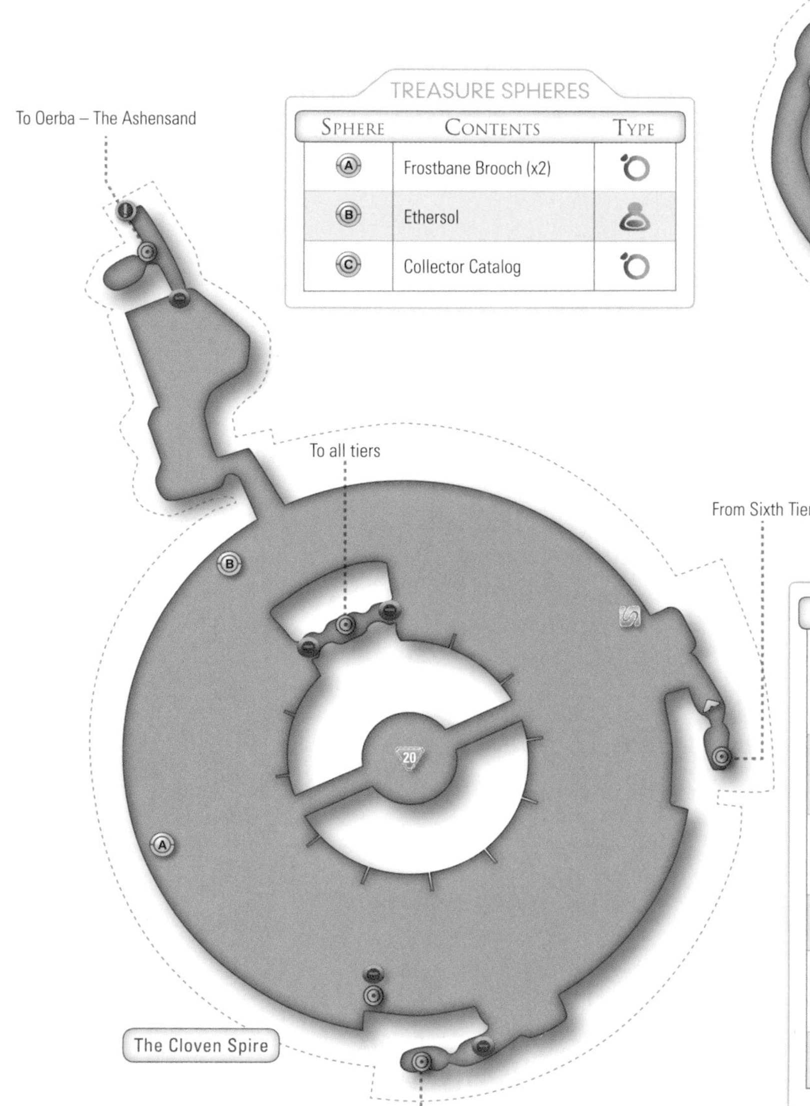

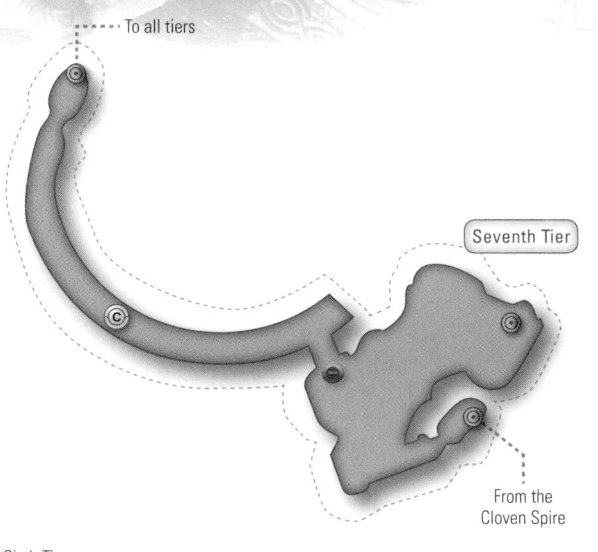

Enemies

Name	Notes	Page
Dahaka	Can inflict a devastating cocktail of status ailments; powerful attacks, but most are preceded by warnings; uses Faith and Haste to bolster attack.	246
Mánagarmr	Can inflict Imperil and Curse; powerful attacks; absorbs Lightning element, but weak against Water.	235
Amphisbaena	Immune to Earth damage, but weak against Lightning and Wind; resistant to magic; high HP and assorted status immunities.	238
Pulsework Gladiator	Resistant to everything except Water; incapacitated and easy to destroy once Staggered.	242
Yakshini	Inflicts Deprotect; will use Bravery to enhance the attack power of all enemies present if left long enough.	236
Yaksha	War Dance attack packs a punch; physical damage halved, but weak against Water and Earth.	236

20 Check your party setup (Delta Attack should definitely be your active Paradigm), then run to the central platform to initiate a boss encounter. If Lightning does not yet have the Dispelga technique (found in her Commando role at the Crystarium), consider backtracking to gain sufficient CP to unlock it. You can win the fight without this skill, but you may endure some fraught moments as a consequence.

Major Encounter – Dahaka: The key to conquering this opponent is to pay close attention to onscreen notifications. When you espy a caption for Fulminous Firestorm or Bone-chilling Breaker, immediately switch to the Combat Clinic Paradigm. After one highly powerful opening salvo (which you can heal from immediately), Dahaka will perform a handful of generally less powerful attacks. Stick with the defensive Paradigm until these end if you lack confidence, though you should at least make a brief switch to Delta Attack or Solidarity to avoid losing your progress on the Chain Gauge.

Another special attack is Diluvial Plague, which inflicts several different status ailments at once (Fig. 20). Dispelga is your savior here: with a quick visit to the Techniques menu, you can cure all of these instantly. If you don't have that ability, your only option is to switch to Combat Clinic and pray.

When you Stagger Dahaka, the beast will fall to the ground and be incapable of launching further attacks until the Chain Gauge depletes. This is your cue to switch to Relentless Assault and pound away. Interestingly, though, the monster is also susceptible to Deprotect, Imperil and Slow when Staggered. If you can Paradigm Shift and have Fang inflict Slow as the monster rises from its prone position (in other words, just before the Stagger ends), you can make the process of filling its Chain Gauge once again much faster. You will, however, need to quickly return to a Paradigm with a Sentinel before it resumes its assault – especially if any party members are injured.

If Dahaka casts Faith or Haste, note that you can employ the Dispelga technique to remove its buffs. If a Stagger is within reach, though, it's better to save your valuable TP for emergencies.

When the battle ends, you are awarded 33,000 CP and a Tetradic Tiara. You can go straight to the waypoint marker to proceed to the next area if you like, or stick around to collect an additional reward from a

20

previously inaccessible floor. See "Taejin's Tower – Seventh Tier" for more details. You can also take on a new Mark mission, though we advise against it – the foe in question is just too difficult at this stage. See "Mission 27: Mithridates, the Lone" on page 116 of the Side-Quest section if you would like to know more about this hunt.

TAEJIN'S TOWER – SEVENTH TIER

There is an additional Menhirrim on top of the Cloven Spire that you can activate after the fight with Dahaka. This summons the nearby elevator, which provides a route to the Seventh Tier. Interact with the final statue down below to rotate this floor: this will enable you to ride the central elevator between all levels.

On the walkway just outside the room you will find a Collector Catalog accessory in a Treasure Sphere. When equipped on a party member, this item increases the probability that you will receive spoils after combat. This is a beneficial tool if you are seeking to increase yields of components for weapon and accessory upgrades. You should equip this whenever you have the opportunity to power-level for CP against weak foes – the additional loot may not be significant for each and every battle, but the cumulative effect could be noteworthy.

OERBA

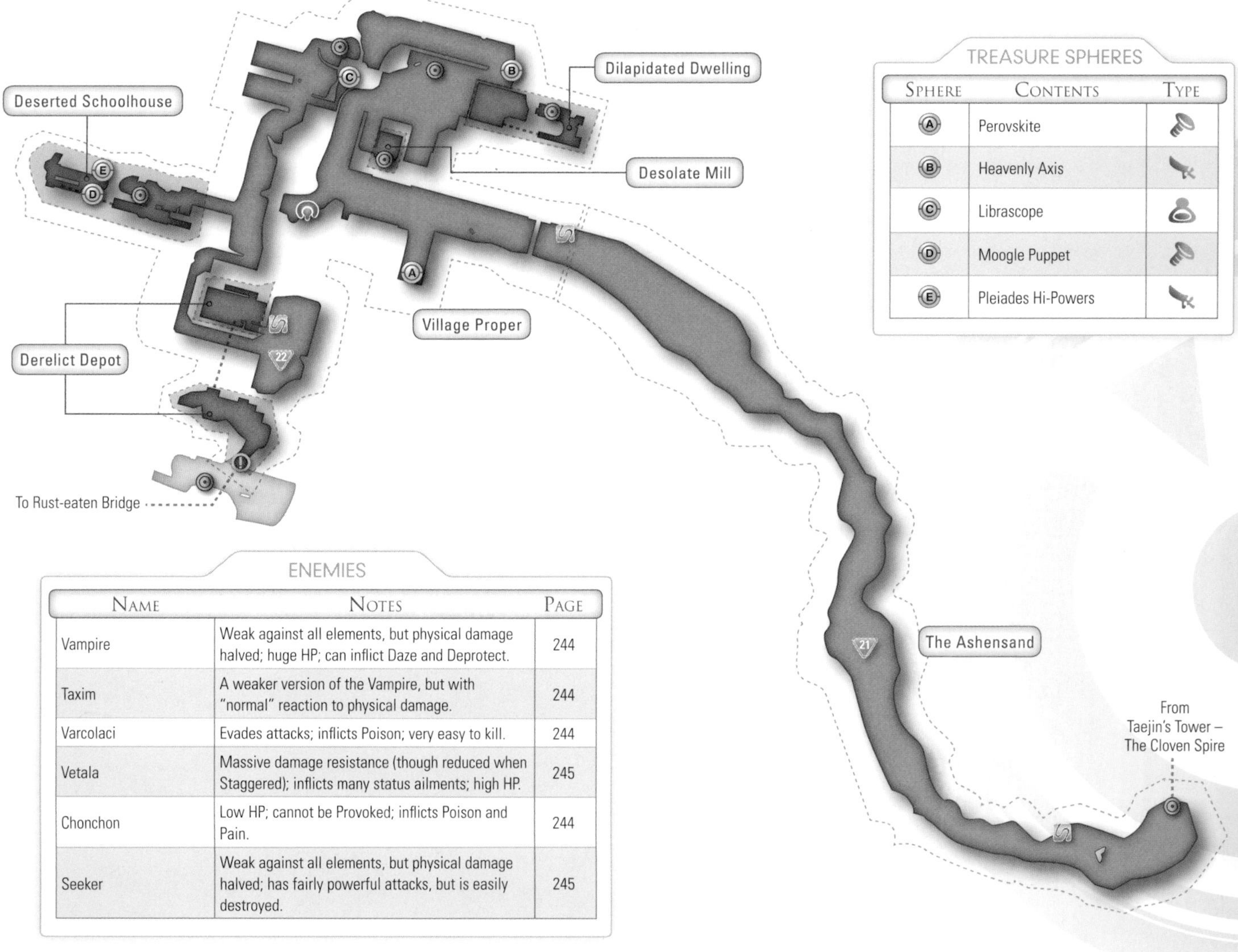

Dilapidated Dwelling

Deserted Schoolhouse

Desolate Mill

Village Proper

Derelict Depot

To Rust-eaten Bridge

The Ashensand

From Taejin's Tower – The Cloven Spire

TREASURE SPHERES

Sphere	Contents	Type
A	Perovskite	
B	Heavenly Axis	
C	Librascope	
D	Moogle Puppet	
E	Pleiades Hi-Powers	

ENEMIES

Name	Notes	Page
Vampire	Weak against all elements, but physical damage halved; huge HP; can inflict Daze and Deprotect.	244
Taxim	A weaker version of the Vampire, but with "normal" reaction to physical damage.	244
Varcolaci	Evades attacks; inflicts Poison; very easy to kill.	244
Vetala	Massive damage resistance (though reduced when Staggered); inflicts many status ailments; high HP.	245
Chonchon	Low HP; cannot be Provoked; inflicts Poison and Pain.	244
Seeker	Weak against all elements, but physical damage halved; has fairly powerful attacks, but is easily destroyed.	245

21 The initial paths and streets of Oerba are patrolled by Vampires and Taxim, with a single Varcolaci just before the path curves around to the right. Once you are further into the Village Proper area, though, things become a little more interesting. You should recall the Vetala from the most difficult mandatory Mark mission in Taejin's Tower. They can be found loitering with intent inside buildings (Fig. 21), so unless you are embarking on the Bhakti side-quest (see box-out), you may prefer to avoid them. If not, aim to Stagger this awkward opponent quickly with the Delta Attack/ Mystic Tower combination, and don't allow the status ailments to get out of hand – as before, use Combat Clinic for an early intervention, or Dispelga in an emergency. You should also be careful to cancel inappropriate attacks in your command queue to speed up the battle – so no Magic attacks when the Inertial Barrier is removed, or Attack commands once it is restored.

21

22 The linear path through this urban area holds no real surprises. At the end of the Village Proper map area, enter the building. The three Shambling Cie'th inside the Derelict Depot are actually Taxim, not the tougher Vampires, so dive in and dispatch them before you head up the stairs (Fig. 22).

22

Local Cie'th Stones

There are three Cie'th Stones in Oerba. The one on the route into the village activates Mission 28 (see page 132), which pits you against a group of ten Ceratosaurs. If you have reached Role Level crystals for each character's core disciplines, you should triumph within 40 undemanding seconds, with a Giant's Glove as your reward, and a new Waystone expanding further your teleportation network. The other two Cie'th Stones remain inactive until later in the game.

Repairing Bhakti

After reaching the waypoint marker at the center of a square in Oerba, head up the staircase next to a sand-filled dumpster to reach an abandoned bedroom. Now examine the small robot on the floor to start a special side-quest. Your first task is to locate five special parts, all found within the village. All five objects in this scavenger hunt are marked on our maps, so it's really not hard to find them.

1. The Battery Pack can be found in the upper room of the building next to Vanille's house – but you will need to slay the Vetala in order to collect it.
2. The Power Cable is obtained from the cart next to the large wind turbine on the square outside.
3. Head down the slope until you encounter a Vampire. Slay him to acquire the Trochoid Gear. This item is not marked on the in-game map, so be careful not to miss it.
4. The Aspheric Lens is just inside the Deserted Schoolhouse area, guarded by a Vetala and two Chonchons.
5. After making your way through the Derelict Depot, the Metal Plate is almost directly ahead as you reach the Rust-eaten Bridge map.

With all five parts in your possession, return to Bhakti to receive a special gift. The nature of the reward depends on the distance you have travelled on Grand Pulse. Depending on the total number of steps you have walked, you should receive ten vials of Deceptisol, and a range of components: two Ultracompact Reactors, a Gold Nugget, five vials of Perfume and three Platinum Ingots. The latter three have negligible EXP value, but can be sold for a massive 462,500 Gil whenever you need to raise currency for upgrades or purchases. Deceptisol is also highly valuable, but don't sell or waste this valuable resource on common opponents – if you save it for later in the game, it will give you a huge advantage when you face certain challenges.

You can speak to Bhakti repeatedly to read unique tips about the game world, and return here later for further interactions at a later date. If you would like to learn more about this, consult page 127.

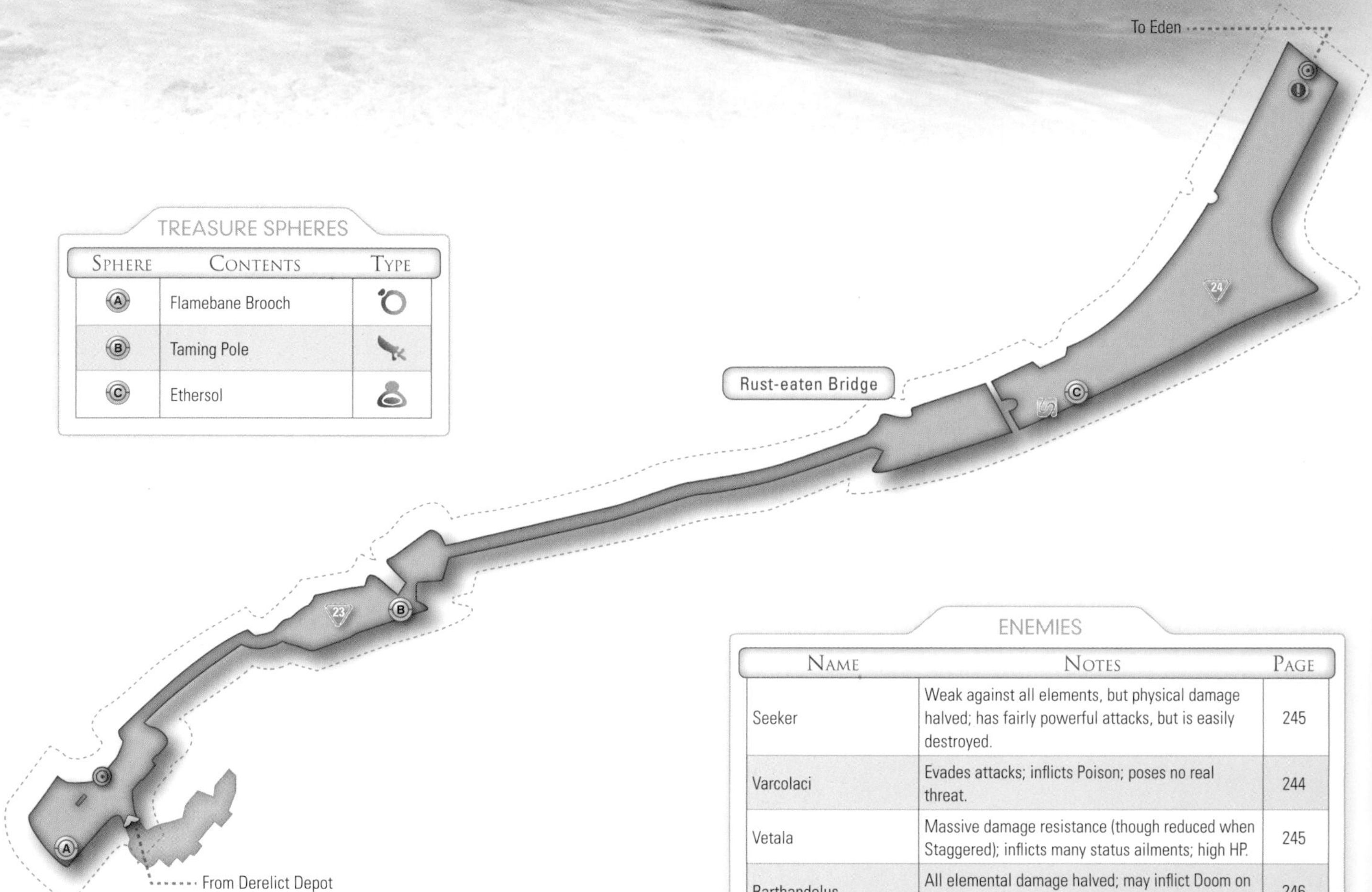

To Eden

Rust-eaten Bridge

From Derelict Depot

TREASURE SPHERES

Sphere	Contents	Type
A	Flamebane Brooch	
B	Taming Pole	
C	Ethersol	

ENEMIES

Name	Notes	Page
Seeker	Weak against all elements, but physical damage halved; has fairly powerful attacks, but is easily destroyed.	245
Varcolaci	Evades attacks; inflicts Poison; poses no real threat.	244
Vetala	Massive damage resistance (though reduced when Staggered); inflicts many status ailments; high HP.	245
Barthandelus	All elemental damage halved; may inflict Doom on party leader near the battle's end.	246

23 You may be tempted to bypass the Treasure Sphere guarded by a Vetala (Fig. 23), but it's better to fight it to obtain the Taming Pole weapon for Fang. Though not her most powerful weapon, it has useful applications later in the game. If you can't start the later battle against a Vampire and three Seekers with a preemptive strike, destroy the latter opponents first. If you have the element of surprise, Fang should be able to withstand the Seeker's assault until you dispatch the larger and more dangerous foe.

When you reach the Save Station at the end of the Rust-eaten Bridge area, spend all of your CP at the Crystarium and ensure that your party is prepared for a heavy encounter. Your characters should, as a baseline requirement, have reached Role Level crystals in all core disciplines; you also need a full TP gauge. If your party is lacking in either area, equip the Energy Sash accessory and backtrack to fight lesser enemies in Oerba before you continue to the waypoint.

23

24 **Major Encounter – Barthandelus:** Barthandelus is easy to Stagger (just use two rounds of Delta Attack, then switch to Mystic Tower), but his colossal HP means that you will need to achieve this many times during the course of this lengthy battle. One factor that slows things down immensely is your opponent's regular use of Cursega, Dazega and Poisonga, with occasional bursts of Fog and Pain. Though Fang will survive unaided for reasonably long periods against the basic (yet insistent) laser attack, you should nonetheless employ regular Combat Clinic breaks to cast Esuna.

Surprisingly, Barthandelus has no assaults with the potential to inflict massive, show-stopping damage. The Thanatosian Laughter hits all party members for a reasonably injurious HP drain (Fig. 24), but this shouldn't be an issue if you are making regular use of Combat Clinic.

As the battle progresses, the frequency of attacks that inflict status ailments increases. Don't rush to cure every last debuff, instead, focus on those that debilitate characters in significant ways, such as Fog on Hope or Pain on Lightning. You should also ensure that your party isn't overwhelmed by too many status ailments at once. You really need to save all Technical Points until the very last stage of the battle, so you cannot (or, strictly speaking, should not) rely on Dispelga or Renew to extract yourself from a difficult situation.

When he has 400,000 to 500,000 HP remaining, Barthandelus may inflict Doom on your party leader. If the rest of the battle is a grueling marathon, this final section is a desperately frantic sprint finish. The Delta Attack/Mystic Tower combination isn't aggressive enough to finish your obdurate adversary before the counter expires, and there really isn't enough time for regular healing with Combat Clinic either. Your only option is to go for broke with Relentless Assault.

24

With a full TP gauge, you have sufficient points for two applications of Renew, with one use of Dispelga if you are unfortunate enough to be hit by Fog or Pain on the wrong characters. Watch your party leader's HP gauge very carefully. If it falls near the red critical zone, weigh up your options quickly, and either use Combat Clinic then switch back to Relentless Assault as quickly as you can, or use one of your two opportunities to Renew. It's best to keep sufficient TP for one Renew in reserve for a genuine emergency, such as the Thanatosian Laughter attack. Without a Sentinel acting as a damage sponge, Barthandelus's attacks will take a terrible toll on your entire party.

At the end of the battle you receive 100,000 CP, a Goddess's Favor accessory and a Crystarium expansion. Examine the nearby Cie'th Stone to initiate a cutscene, then approach the vehicle and board it to return to Cocoon.

LEAVING GRAN PULSE

Returning to Cocoon means that you have no access to the various connected areas of Gran Pulse (and, of course, the assorted side-quests and optional adventures they contain) until Chapter 13. This is actually no great hardship – most Mark missions are far easier if you leave them until later, with many unavailable (or just plain impossible) at this stage. Travel between the areas of Gran Pulse is also an arduous slog right now, but soon a large network of Cie'th Waystones will give you access to a fast and convenient form of transportation.

EDEN

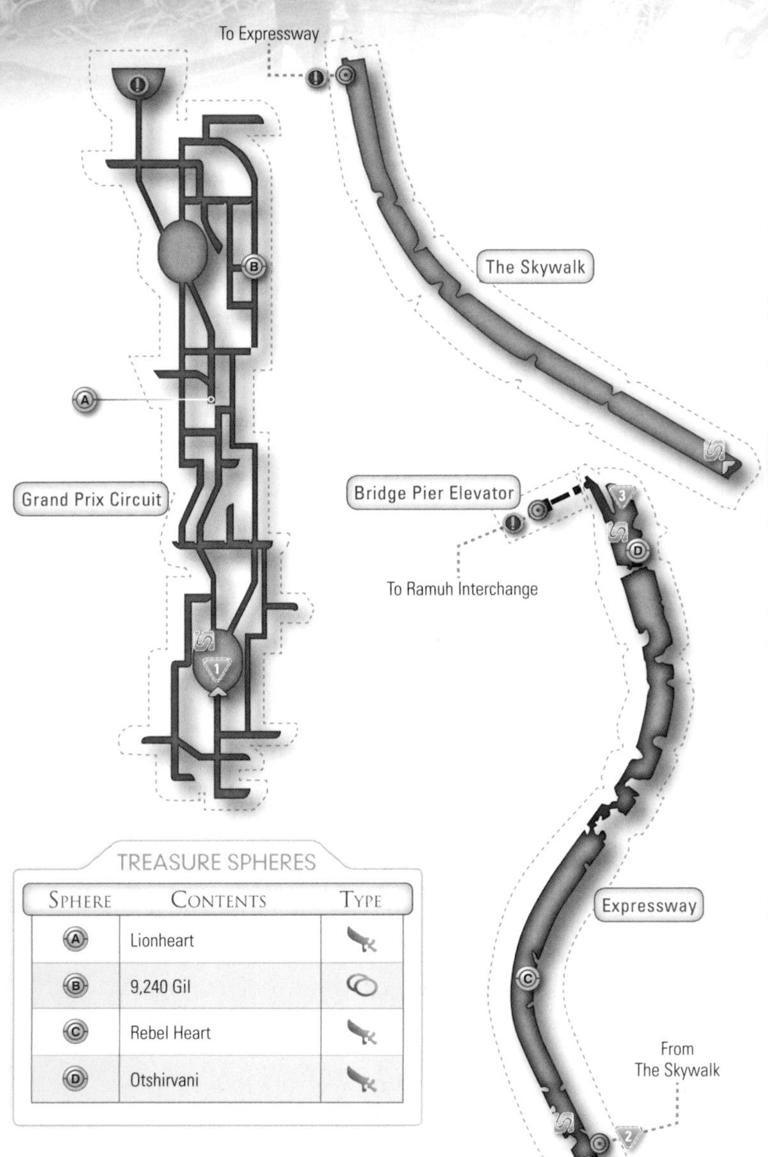

TREASURE SPHERES

Sphere	Contents	Type
A	Lionheart	
B	9,240 Gil	
C	Rebel Heart	
D	Otshirvani	

ENEMIES

Name	Notes	Page
Anavatapta Warmech	Not a "true" combat encounter – can be killed before Gestalt Mode expires.	233
Varcolaci	Evades attacks; inflicts Poison; can be killed in seconds.	244
Bulwarker	Only dangerous if it summons a Targeting Beacon to perform its Orbital Battery attack.	231
Targeting Beacon	Summoned by Bulwarker; does not attack; destroy to avert Bulwarker's Orbital Battery assault.	228
Corps Defender	Very low HP for this stage of the game; acts as cannon fodder in a few minor skirmishes.	230
Corps Steward	Ice and Water damage halved, but suffers a weakness to Fire.	230
Sanctum Archangel	Uses Guard ability to increase damage resistance; surprisingly powerful attacks.	228
Adamantheron	Can bestow Haste and Bravery.	232
Sanctum Seraph	Can bestow Bravery.	228
Behemoth King	HP gauge restored when it moves to an upright posture.	240
Orobon	Power Spritz gives the Orobon status enhancements; still rather slow to kill.	241
Amphisbaena	Immune to Earth damage, but weak against Lightning and Wind; resistant to magic; high HP and assorted status immunities.	238
Proto-behemoth	Fire and Lightning damage halved, but weak against Ice and Water; can change its form, regenerating HP and increasing attack power when it does so.	233
The Proudclad	Elemental damage halved; immune to all status ailments.	234

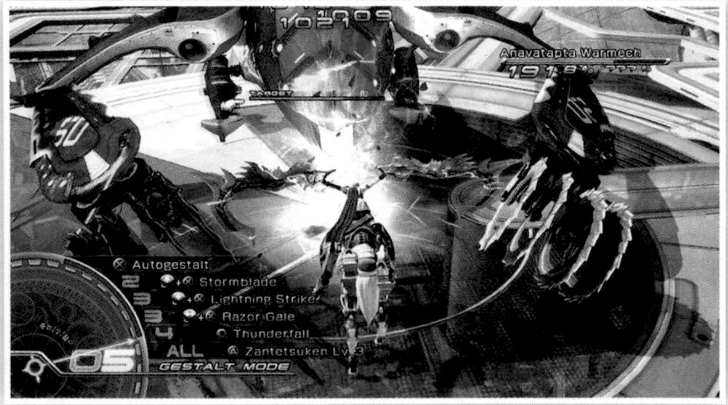

1

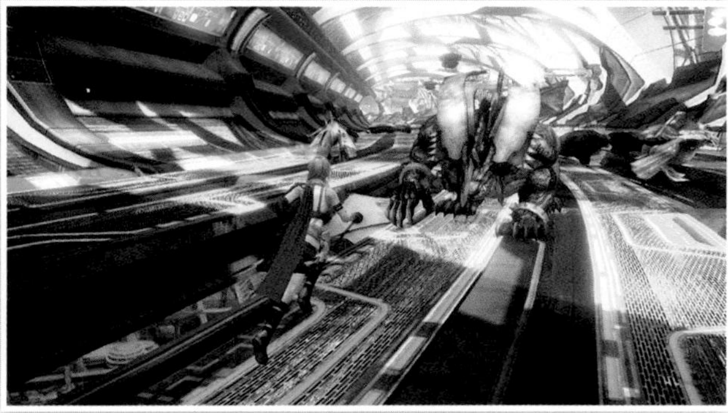

2

1 The Anavatapta Warmech can be defeated with Auto-gestalt commands alone (Fig. 1). This will add to your existing riches, so you should stop by at the Crystarium immediately to develop your party.

The Crystarium expansion given after the Barthandelus battle features some very useful abilities – but with CP costs starting at a minimum of 10,000, you'll need to pay a premium to reach them. Ignore the outer "arms" for now until you have picked up some interesting new skills. Lightning has the Thundaga and Army of One abilities (both Ravager) and the Stopga technique (Medic). Fang can now acquire the useful Reprieve auto-ability (Sentinel), Imperil (Saboteur) and Highwind (Commando). With Hope, aim for Curaja (Medic), Haste (Synergist) and Last Resort (Ravager) in that order. See page 188 for more information on abilities and techniques.

Once you have finished at the Crystarium, restore your default party, then configure their Paradigms as detailed in the following table.

SUGGESTED PARADIGM DECK

Paradigm	Lightning	Fang	Hope
Delta Attack	Commando	Sentinel	Ravager
Mystic Tower	Ravager	Sentinel	Ravager
Relentless Assault	Ravager	Commando	Ravager
Protection	Medic	Sentinel	Synergist
Evened Odds	Medic	Saboteur	Synergist
Combat Clinic	Medic	Sentinel	Medic

The Grand Prix Circuit area looks like a complicated maze, but you can actually collect both Treasure Spheres, defeat the three enemy groups and exit within a few minutes. The Varcolaci are no more than a momentary distraction and Bulwarkers are only dangerous if they spawn a Targeting Beacon, which enables them to perform their Orbital Battery attack. This can be prevented by destroying the beacon quickly.

The enemies who confront your party when you reach the Skywalk area can all be defeated rapidly with Delta Attack alone. When you encounter a second Bulwarker flanked by two Sanctum Seraphs, dispatch the mechanical adversary first.

2 Do not underestimate the Behemoth King: start with Delta Attack, then switch to Mystic Tower to accelerate the process of filling the Chain Gauge, and change to Relentless Assault once it has been Staggered. The Expressway map pits you against an assortment of foes from previous chapters. When facing the three Orobons that accompany a Behemoth King (Fig. 2), deal with the larger adversary first, using the tactics outlined earlier, but use Delta Attack instead of Relentless Assault once it is Staggered.

When you reach the second Treasure Sphere, the Proto-behemoth can be taken by surprise if you are patient. These behave in the same way as Behemoth Kings, but have greater resistance to physical and magical damage once they shift to their standing posture.

3 **Major Encounter – The Proudclad:** If Hope does not have the Haste ability yet (Synergist), it may be a good idea to go farm sufficient CP to unlock it. If you have not yet created the Protection Paradigm (Medic + Sentinel + Synergist), now would be a very good time to do so.

The Proudclad can be frustratingly difficult to beat unless you follow a very specific strategy. It uses a single attack repeatedly until the first Stagger ends, which you will no doubt find irritating but not particularly damaging. After the first Stagger, though, you will see the Limiters Deactivated notification (Fig. 3), which activates three permanent status enhancements. This is immediately followed by the Retaliatory Strike attack. This targets party members at random, draining significant sums of HP and briefly stunning afflicted characters. Even with Combat Clinic active, there is a high chance that your party leader could be hit by consecutive blasts and be knocked out before you have the chance to heal (unless of course you're playing with Fang as party leader).

3

The solution is to Paradigm Shift to Protection at the start of the battle, and keep it active until Hope has protected the party with a wide range of buffs. Once these are in place, go on the offensive with Delta Attack followed by Mystic Tower, then back to Delta Attack when your opponent has been Staggered. Approximately ten seconds before the Stagger period ends, change to Combat Clinic to heal party members prior to the imminent onslaught. Now let Lightning's ATB gauge fill, and save these for healing her, and her alone. If you begin healing after each impact, you should be able to keep her in good condition until the Proudclad returns to its standard attack routine.

After each Stagger, switch back to Protection to replenish and refresh status enhancements, then continue as before. The Proudclad drops a rare Particle Accelerator component once defeated.

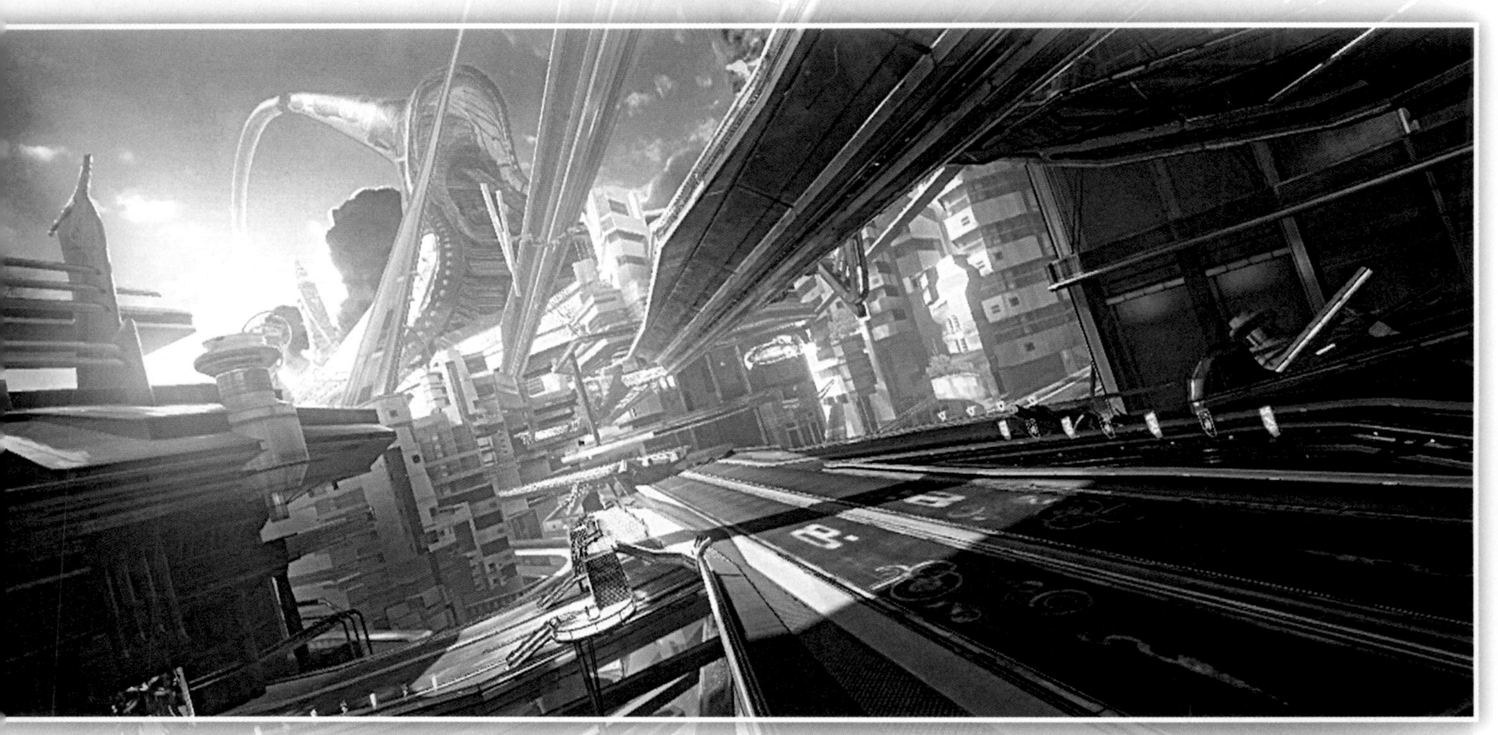

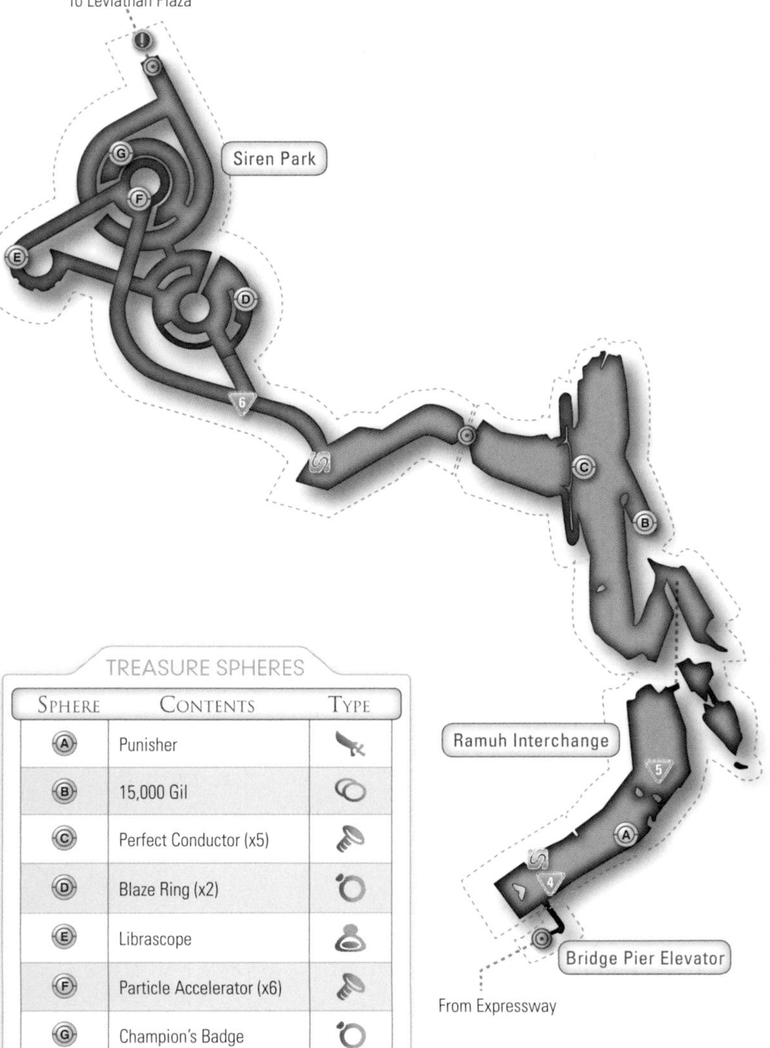

TREASURE SPHERES

Sphere	Contents	Type
A	Punisher	
B	15,000 Gil	
C	Perfect Conductor (x5)	
D	Blaze Ring (x2)	
E	Librascope	
F	Particle Accelerator (x6)	
G	Champion's Badge	

ENEMIES

Name	Notes	Page
Adamanchelid	Physical and magical damage halved, but weak against Ice; cannot be surprised by preemptive strikes; can inflict Daze with its Bay ability.	238
Corps Defender	Very low HP for this stage of the game; acts as cannon fodder in a few minor skirmishes.	230
Humbaba	Weak against Fire, immune to Water, and Ice damage halved; HP restored and attack power boosted significantly when it changes to a standing posture.	240
Corps Steward	Ice and Water damage halved, but suffers a weakness to Fire.	230
Sanctum Archangel	Has the lowest HP of all Sanctum troops, but performs regular attacks that cause surprisingly pernicious HP loss.	228
Proto-behemoth	Fire and Lightning damage halved, but weak against Ice and Water; can change its form, regenerating HP and increasing attack power when it does so.	233
Sanctum Seraph	High HP; can bestow Bravery.	228
Vampire	Weak against all elements, but physical damage halved; huge HP; can inflict Daze and Deprotect.	244
Tyrant	Uses Forge Blade ability to summon Centaurion Blade; very powerful attacks; high HP.	243
Centaurion Blade	Summoned by Tyrant; cannot be Provoked; powerful attacks.	243
Sanctum Inquisitrix	Uses status enhancements to vastly improve attributes; can be Launched.	229
Orobon	Power Spritz gives the Orobon status enhancements.	241
Adamantheron	Typical Pantheron-type enemy; should fall easily at this stage.	232
Vernal Harvester	Employs its Exoproofing abilities to switch its elemental strengths and weaknesses; hugely powerful attacks; can be Launched.	234

4 You may recall the Adamanchelid from your earlier journey through the Archylte Steppe (Fig. 4). Though it is now (obviously) within your power to defeat it, this is still a nasty opponent. Using Fang as a Saboteur to weaken the creature will make the battle much easier, though. If you can't survive without a Sentinel, switch to Protection instead to have Hope bestow status enhancements. The Adamanchelid attacks with relentless frequency, with both Stomp and Quake dealing notable damage with an accompanying brief stun effect. Worse still, its Bay ability inflicts Daze – usually just after you Stagger it. Don't take risks: make regular Paradigm Shifts to Combat Clinic, and ensure that your party has at least Haste active at all times.

4

5 You will encounter your first Humbaba not long after the Adamanchelid fight. This is a Behemoth in all but name, though it has more HP and massively increased attack power after changing to a standing posture. After a first round of Delta Attack commands, use Mystic Tower to build up its Chain gauge. Switch to Relentless Assault as soon as it is Staggered, and you should be able to prevent the transformation (and customary renewal) from taking place at all. Note that this tactic also works well against Proto-behemoths.

With the three-way battles that follow (where Humbaba fight Corps and Sanctum soldiers), always try to start the battle with a preemptive strike and kill the larger enemies first. Feel free to bypass the two Adamanchelids later on the Ramuh Interchange (Fig. 5) – the time and risk involved in defeating them really isn't worth the CP and spoils you might gain in return.

5

6 Siren Park features numerous opportunities to gatecrash existing conflicts for three-way battle opportunities (Fig. 6). With a preemptive strike, which are fairly easy to obtain, you always have the option of dispatching the most time-consuming or dangerous foes first. Other encounters are less attractive: a group of three Vampires is still a force that will take time and care to defeat.

6

Most opponents should already be familiar to you, though there are two new introductions. The Sanctum Inquisitrix is similar to the PSICOM Huntress. Though their base stats are not intimidating, their use of status enhancements turns them into extremely swift and powerful opponents, with their Somersault Kick capable of grievously wounding a party member in one attack. The Vernal Harvester is monstrously vicious, and should either be avoided or be your highest priority target in a three-way battle with a preemptive strike.

A Tyrant and a Vernal Harvester block the area exit. Sneak up on them, then Stagger and severely weaken the Vernal Harvester first – aim to pummel away until only a fraction of its HP gauge remains. Now do the same with the Tyrant. Destroy the summoned Centaurion Blade, and you should be able to end the battle rapidly and without injury.

Miscellany

- **Power Tip:** Siren Park is a great location to farm for CP and spoils. If you complete loops of the area fighting only those battles that promise high reward for minimal effort (particularly three-way battles), you can make great strides in the Crystarium prior to the closing battles of this chapter.

- Once a party member sitting in your "reserves" reaches 999,999 CP, all further Crystarium Points are wasted. As Snow, Sazh and Vanille may be nearing this point, this is a good time to invest their accumulated gains. To turn them into "super specialists", we suggest you simply spend points on going as far as you can with Sazh's Synergist role, Medic for Vanille and Sentinel for Snow. Pick up all abilities as you reach them, but don't worry about "optional" HP, Strength and Magic crystals for now.

- With certain three-way battle scenarios you may find that one enemy (or group of foes) detects you, while the other faction does not. If you can make contact with an opponent who hasn't seen your party leader, you will still get the usual bonus of a preemptive strike and immunity from attack until one side has been expelled from the battlefield.

- As you may have noticed, the first Paradigm Shift of a battle tends to take longer to perform than subsequent changes, unless your party leader is performing an aerial attack when you make the switch. This is a great way to make near-seamless transitions between Delta Attack and Relentless Assault against certain enemies – especially those who are best kept inactive with Launch juggling.

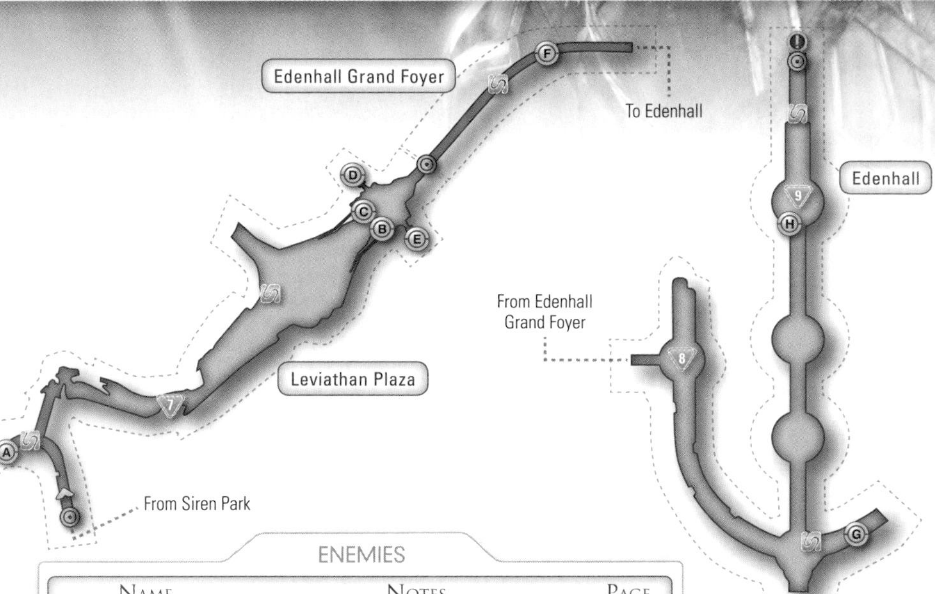

ENEMIES

Name	Notes	Page
Humbaba	Weak against Fire, immune to Water and Ice damage halved; HP restored and attack power boosted greatly when it changes to a standing posture.	240
Juggernaut	Physical and magical damage halved; very powerful attacks; extremely high HP.	243
Adamanchelid	Physical and magical damage halved, but weak against Ice; cannot be surprised by preemptive strike; can inflict Daze with its Bay ability.	238
Sanctum Archangel	Low HP, but powerful attacks and insistent strike rate.	228
Sanctum Celebrant	Fairly slow attack rate, but powerful when they do strike.	229
Adamantoise	Avoid at all costs – these can kill your party leader with a single blow.	238
Sanctum Inquisitrix	Uses status enhancements to vastly improve attributes; can be Launched.	229
Sacrifice	Physical damage halved; Anathema ability inflicts four status ailments on targeted party member; can inflict an instant KO.	244
Vernal Harvester	Employs its Exoproofing abilities to switch its elemental strengths and weaknesses; hugely powerful attacks; can be Launched.	234
The Proudclad (Second Encounter)	Can change between walking and aerial forms, with the former becoming more dangerous as the battle progresses; all elemental damage halved; immune to status ailments.	234

TREASURE SPHERES

Sphere	Contents	Type
A	Antares Deluxes	
B	Plush Chocobo*	
C	Particle Accelerator (x6)*	
D	Hellish Talon (x12)	
E	Hellish Talon (x17)	
F	Mistilteinn	
G	Power Glove	
H	Ethersol	

* Only one of these two Treasure Spheres can be opened – see "Treasure Sphere Secret" on the page to your right.

7 Leviathan Plaza acts as home to some of the largest and most dangerous "generic" enemies you have faced so far. For many players this will be the first realistic opportunity to kill a mighty Juggernaut. The most effective way to achieve this is to start with a preemptive strike, then go straight on the offensive with Relentless Assault. Paradigm Shift to Protection as soon as the first Stagger ends, then keep everyone healthy with Lightning, as Hope casts status enhancements. Stagger your adversary again with Delta Attack/Mystic Tower, and a ferocious barrage of Relentless Assault should at the very least reduce its HP gauge sufficiently for a safe Delta Attack finish.

If CP and spoils are your sole concern, and not individual challenges, you will actually be much better served by returning to Siren Park to fight in easy three-way battles, then return here and simply bypass all enemies positioned before the waypoint marker. Either way, the Adamantoise outside the building entrance (Fig. 7) should be avoided at all costs.

8 When the cutscene ends, run straight for the Juggernaut (Fig. 8) – there's really no reason to confront the Tyrant. The strategy outlined earlier will enable you to beat him with little difficulty. The fight against the three Sanctum Inquisitrices and a Sanctum Archangel actually has greater life-threatening potential. Kill the latter opponent first, then – after a brief pause for Combat Clinic – cautiously eliminate the three remaining foes.

The Sacrifice enemy can inflict a virulent battery of status ailments on a single party member. It also has a Death attack, which may kill a party member instantly. The only way to truly keep your party safe is to Stagger these opponents quickly and prevent them from acting by juggling them after a successful Launch. Though they drop valuable spoils, less dedicated players may prefer to run around them. When you reach the two fighting the Vernal Harvester, severely weaken the plant first, then kill both Sacrifices.

Power Tip: The Sacrifice's rare drop item is the Scarletite component, a transformational catalyst used for certain weapon upgrades. This costs 100,000 Gil to buy (though its resale value is substantially lower at 7,000 Gil). They also drop Perfume, which sells for a reasonable 12,500 Gil. Equip the Collector Catalog to increase your odds of obtaining these.

8

9 **Major Encounter – The Proudclad:** From the start, switch to Protection and wait until all three party members are protected and augmented by a wide range of buffs.

The Proudclad can transform itself between two forms (resetting the Chain Gauge as it does so). It starts the battle in Annihilation Mode on the ground. In this form, it uses the Muon Blaster attack (Fig. 9), and can be Launched when Staggered. In Aerial Defense Mode it hovers above the battlefield and benefits from a slight increase in Chain resistance. It will also use the powerful Retaliatory Strike attack after a Stagger period expires exclusively in this guise. Once again, you must change to Combat Clinic just before the gauge is depleted to heal and survive this onslaught.

9

Naturally, your opponent is holding back during the first part of the fight. When you see the Limiters Deactivated message, the Proudclad will activate status enhancements that improve its offensive prowess. It will also acquire a new attack in its walking form: Oneiric Maelstrom, which hits all party members for a variable (but often high) degree of HP loss. In short, Annihilation Mode begins to live up to its billing. You may need to stay with the Combat Clinic Paradigm constantly to keep your party alive.

The best time to inflict damage (and refresh buffs) is when the boss takes to the air. The fight soon settles into a comfortable rhythm: ultra-defensive tactics when the Proudclad is on the ground, followed by a quick Delta Attack/Mystic Tower/Delta Attack sequence to Stagger and deal damage once it takes off. Switch to Combat Clinic just before you endure the Retaliatory Strike, then refresh status enhancements with Protection before the cycle begins again.

It may take time and patience, but the Proudclad will eventually fall. Your reward is 100,000 CP, a Royal Armlet and access to the Eden Pharmaceuticals retail network. Interact with the elevator to continue when you are ready to progress to the next chapter.

TREASURE SPHERE SECRET

As you enter the main building you will notice two Treasure Spheres. For reasons that will soon become apparent, you can only open one of these. We strongly recommend that you pick up the six Particle Accelerators in the sphere on the left – their 4,800 EXP value far outweighs the monetary gain offered by the Plush Chocobo on the right (35,000 Gil).

ORPHAN'S CRADLE

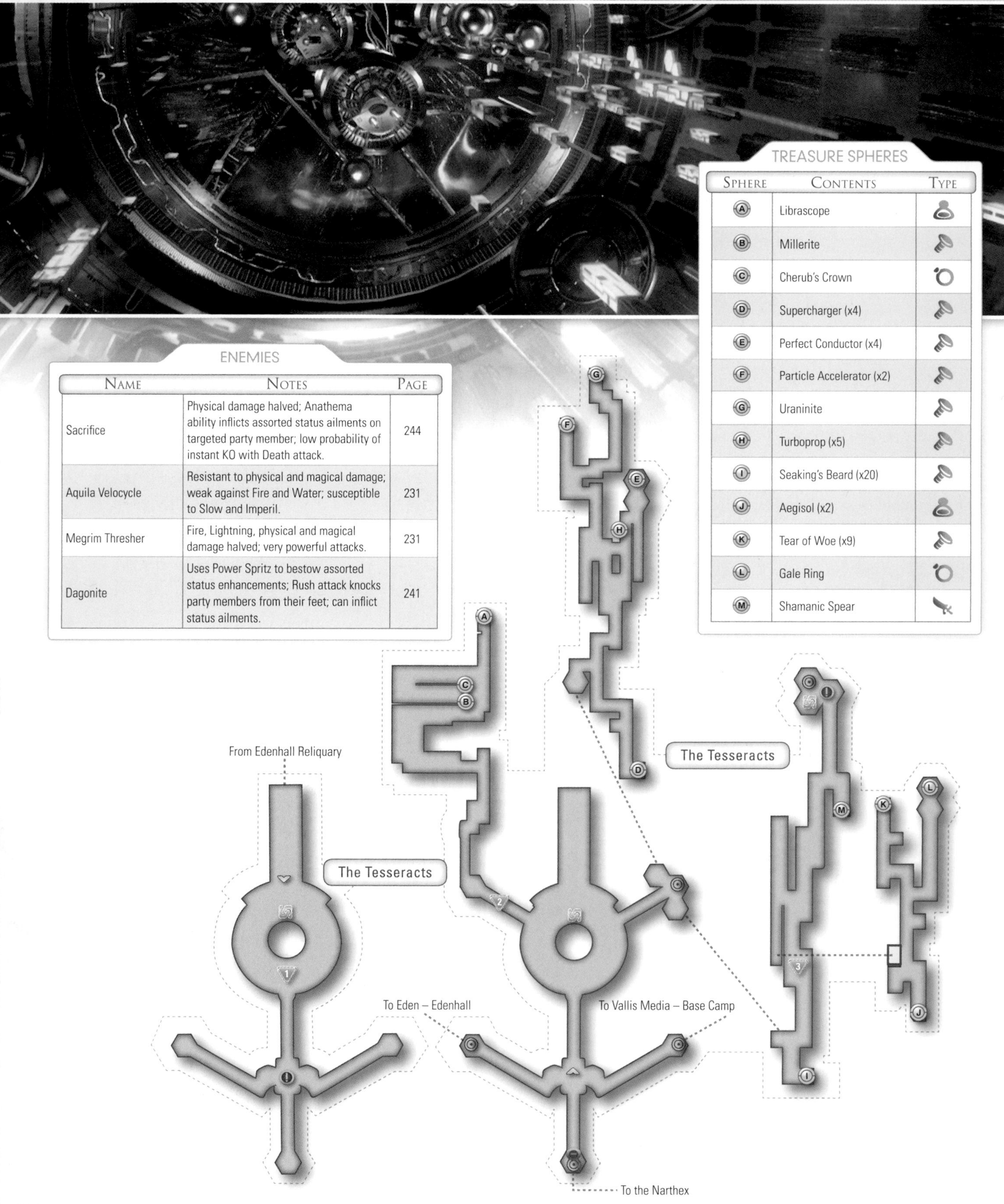

TREASURE SPHERES

Sphere	Contents	Type
A	Librascope	
B	Millerite	
C	Cherub's Crown	
D	Supercharger (x4)	
E	Perfect Conductor (x4)	
F	Particle Accelerator (x2)	
G	Uraninite	
H	Turboprop (x5)	
I	Seaking's Beard (x20)	
J	Aegisol (x2)	
K	Tear of Woe (x9)	
L	Gale Ring	
M	Shamanic Spear	

ENEMIES

Name	Notes	Page
Sacrifice	Physical damage halved; Anathema ability inflicts assorted status ailments on targeted party member; low probability of instant KO with Death attack.	244
Aquila Velocycle	Resistant to physical and magical damage; weak against Fire and Water; susceptible to Slow and Imperil.	231
Megrim Thresher	Fire, Lightning, physical and magical damage halved; very powerful attacks.	231
Dagonite	Uses Power Spritz to bestow assorted status enhancements; Rush attack knocks party members from their feet; can inflict status ailments.	241

1 Unless you are keen to acquire their Perfume and Scarletite drops, it may be better to avoid the two groups of Sacrifice enemies – even with a preemptive strike these can be draining battles that offer unspectacular sums of CP.

After the cutscene, two special "warp gates" are opened (Fig. 1). One enables you to travel instantly to Eden (specifically the Edenhall map), while the other takes you to the Base Camp in Vallis Media on Gran Pulse. There are, of course, gates in place in both destinations that enable an easy return journey. If you need to farm CP to strengthen an undernourished party, or have a hankering to hunt Marks and explore optional areas, this is one of your last opportunities to do so before the build-up to the final confrontation. You should note that Final Fantasy XIII does not end once you conquer the boss at the end of Orphan's Cradle. You can continue to explore the world and, indeed, only receive the final Crystarium expansion after the last story-oriented battle is complete. If you haven't struggled up until this point against most enemies, we suggest that you press forward. Besides, it's actually far more enjoyable (and practical) to explore after the closing cutscenes. Though the end of the main narrative is near, your journey through Final Fantasy XIII will not finish for many, many hours...

1

2 Before you head to the waypoint, explore the new arrangement of platforms opposite it to collect three Treasure Spheres. To speed up battles against the Aquila Velocycle, use the Evened Odds Paradigm to inflict Slow and Imperil while Hope applies a few status enhancements (Haste and Faith being the most important). This will enable you to drastically reduce the Battle Duration. Due to this opponent's magical and physical damage resistance, it is better to stay with Mystic Tower when it is Staggered. The same tactics work well against the Megrim Thresher, though its vulnerability to Launch when Staggered means that you can change to Relentless Assault to end the battle in just over two minutes.

2

Head to the waypoint marker and interact when prompted. Facing both moving platforms from the walkway (Fig. 2), the one on the left takes you to an optional area where you can find more Treasure Spheres guarded by Aquila Velocycles and another Megrim Thresher, while the one on the right leads towards the next waypoint.

3 The Dagonite is a close cousin to the Orobon. It uses its Power Spritz ability to bestow status enhancements at the start of each battle, though, which makes it a little more of a challenge. The groups you meet here can be slain easily if you take them by surprise. There are three Treasure Spheres on the upper level, so head up the ramp before you continue to the waypoint marker. This area is guarded by Sacrifices, though you only need engage the two that prevent you from opening the Treasure Sphere (Fig. 3).

Back down below, press ⊗/Ⓐ at the waypoint marker to reconfigure the platforms and explore the next part of Orphan's Cradle.

3

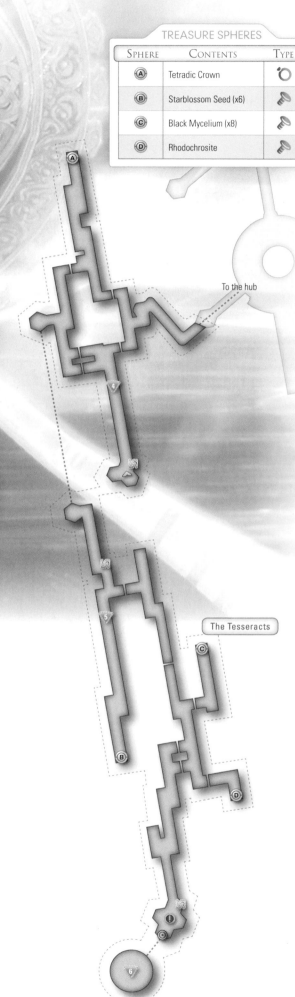

TREASURE SPHERES

Sphere	Contents	Type
A	Tetradic Crown	
B	Starblossom Seed (x6)	
C	Black Mycelium (x8)	
D	Rhodochrosite	

ENEMIES

Name	Notes	Page
Sacrifice	Physical damage halved; Anathema ability inflicts assorted status ailments on targeted party member; low probability of instant KO with Death attack.	244
Aquila Velocycle	Resistant to physical and magical damage; weak against Fire and Water; susceptible to Slow and Imperil.	231
Dagonite	Uses Power Spritz to bestow assorted status enhancements; Rush attack knocks party members from their feet; can inflict status ailments.	241
Sanctum Templar	All elemental damage halved; Charging Manadrive ability inflicts status ailments and massive HP loss; dangerous in groups of two or more.	230
Jabberwocky	Weak to all elements, but immune to magic damage; physical damage halved; susceptible to Deprotect and Poison.	238
Bandersnatch	Elemental damage halved; immune to physical damage, resistant to magic; susceptible to Deshell and Imperil.	238

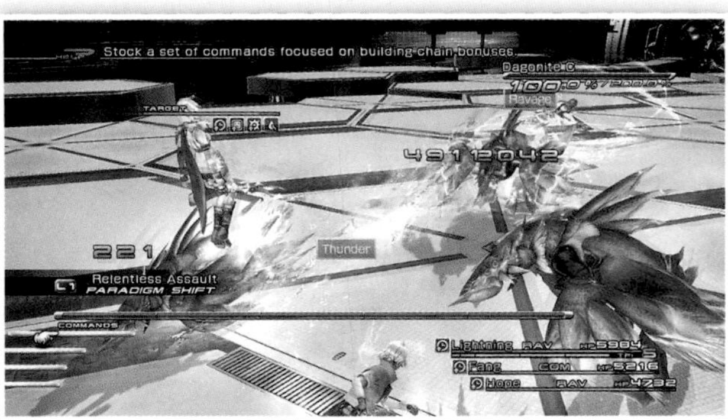

4

4 It may look as if the Sacrifice dead ahead is a straggler separated from a shambling pack and ripe for a contemptuous onslaught, but it is actually accompanied by an Aquila Velocycle. Status ailments and the Velocycle's Plasma Cannon attack are a winning combination for the wrong team, so aim to catch them out with a preemptive strike and dispatch the Sacrifice first. Another enemy party configuration you will encounter in this area of the Tesseracts has the Sacrifice accompanied by Dagonites. Unless you kill the latter enemies quickly, their coordinated Rush attacks will bowl party members off their feet (Fig. 4), making it difficult to attack, or to heal with Combat Clinic. Try to secure a preemptive strike against these groups, and – optimally – make a brief change to Protection to have Hope cast Haste on all party members.

The path to the right offers a route back to the "hub" where the two warp gates can be found. Unless you feel a pressing need to visit Gran Pulse or Eden, there is no reason to travel there. After you collect the Tetradic Crown from the Treasure Sphere, use the moving platform to travel to the next area.

5

5 Be prepared for a vicious fight against three Dagonites and an Aquila Velocycle to obtain the first Treasure Sphere on this floor level. Start by changing to Protection (or, better still, temporarily set it as your default Paradigm in advance) to have Hope cast Haste and Protect. You may need to switch to Combat Clinic to survive a barrage of Rush attacks and Plasma Cannon blasts. This is a long battle, but it becomes much easier as each Dagonite falls.

The Sanctum Templar that follows has strong physical attacks, but its Charging Manadrive ability is utterly devastating (Fig. 5). This inflicts status ailments prior to a catastrophic Lightning element attack which hits all party members for potentially fatal damage. However, this combined assault is rarely used during the first minute of battle, so you may find it more efficient to make the two Dagonites your opening targets. The Sanctum Templar can be Launched, so switch to Relentless Assault for a quick end to the battle once his Chain Gauge has been filled.

With the two separate Sanctum Templars that follow as you move towards the waypoint marker, a preemptive strike and Relentless Assault will enable you to kill them before they can land a single blow. The third is too vigilant for a surprise attack, so start with Evened Odds until all party members have Haste and Protect, then kill him before you attend to the Sacrifices. When you reach the Save Station, change your default Paradigm to Evened Odds before you proceed, and keep it that way for the foreseeable future. Note that you are about to pass a point of no return: you will not be able to come back to this section of the Tesseracts once you use the next warp gate.

6

6 **Major Encounter – Jabberwocky & Bandersnatch:** The Bandersnatch is immune to physical strikes, with magical damage cut to one tenth; the Jabberwocky is immune to magic, but physical damage is only halved. As the Jabberwocky is the stronger of the two (and employs Magic attacks that Sentinel Fang is less equipped to withstand), it makes sense to concentrate on it first (Fig. 6). Wait until Fang inflicts Deprotect on the monster, then stop to heal if required before using the Delta Attack/Mystic Tower combination to force up the Chain Gauge. Change back to Delta Attack once your target has been Staggered. Though Hope's attacks will cause no direct harm he will nonetheless drive up the Chain Bonus, enabling Lightning to inflict greater damage. Refresh the Deprotect debuff when required, and the Jabberwocky should expire during the third Stagger. For the Bandersnatch, use Evened Odds to inflict Deshell, then change to Relentless Assault for a direct and unproblematic end to the fight.

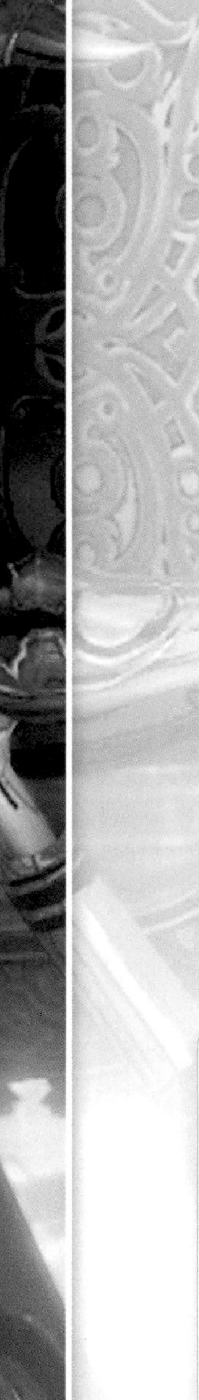

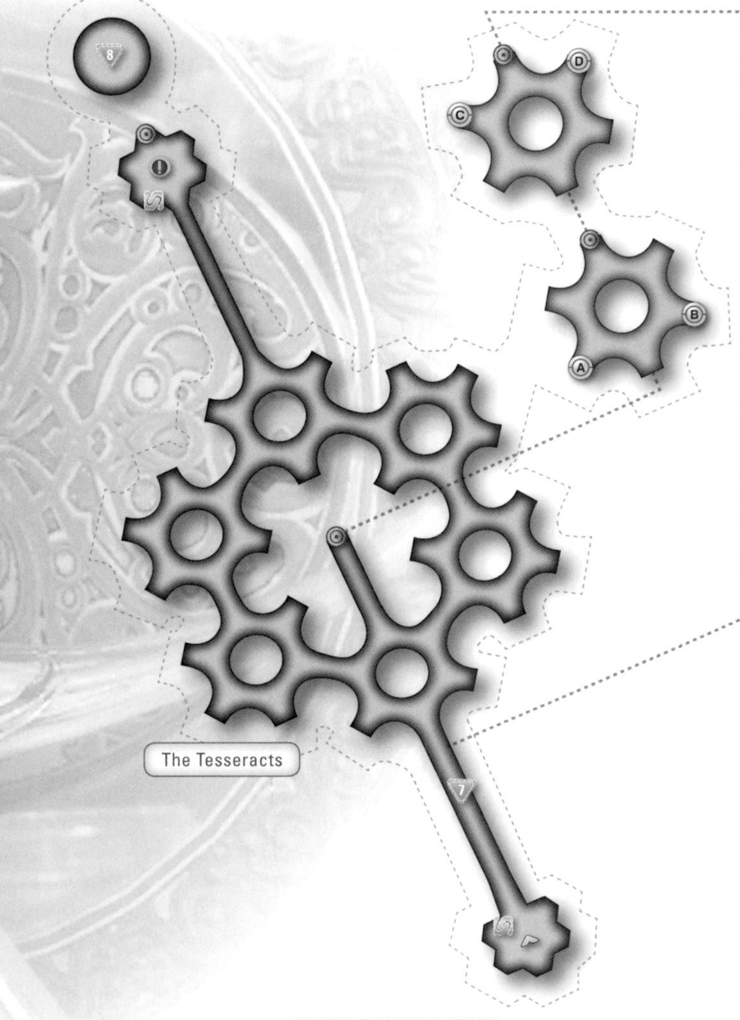

ENEMIES

Name	Notes	Page
Immortal	Uses Forge Blade ability to summon Centaurion Blade; very powerful attacks; high HP.	243
Centaurion Blade	Summoned by Immortal; cannot be Provoked; powerful attacks.	243
Sacrifice	Physical damage halved; Anathema ability inflicts four status ailments on targeted party member; very low probability of instant KO with Death attack.	244
Dagonite	Uses Power Spritz to bestow assorted status enhancements; Rush attack knocks party members from their feet; can inflict status ailments.	241
Aquila Velocycle	Resistant to physical and magical damage; weak against Fire and Water; susceptible to Slow and Imperil.	231
Sanctum Templar	All elemental damage halved; Charging Manadrive ability inflicts status ailments and massive HP loss; dangerous in groups of two or more.	230
Megrim Thresher	Fire, Lightning, physical and magical damage halved; very powerful attacks.	231
Wladislaus	Weak to all elements, but magic damage halved; Mounting Contempt attack can kill an unprotected party member instantly.	245
Jabberwocky	Weak to all elements, but immune to magic damage; physical damage halved; susceptible to Deprotect and Poison.	238
Bandersnatch	Elemental damage halved; immune to physical damage, resistant to magic; susceptible to Deshell and Imperil.	238

TREASURE SPHERES

Sphere	Contents	Type
A	Weirding Glyph	
B	Adamant Bangle	
C	Scarletite	
D	Elixir	

7 There are two routes through this area, with tough battles against awkward combinations of familiar foes on the left and right outer paths. The left-hand route (Fig. 7) is probably the easier of the two: you can evade the two Velocycles (there are less demanding opportunities to obtain CP shortly), then weaken the Sanctum Templar and Megrim Thresher with a preemptive strike, targeting the smaller enemy first. When you reach the Megrim Thresher blocking the path to the waypoint (a battle you face no matter which way you go), use the element of surprise once again and destroy the Sacrifices first.

Before you continue, spend available CP at the Crystarium and ensure that your default Paradigm is set to Protection.

7

8 **Major Encounter – Wladislaus:** This is another sub-boss where you must use a very particular strategy to achieve a comfortable victory. When the battle starts, stand by and wait as Hope bestows several status enhancements on each party member. With that task accomplished, switch to Delta Attack.

The Wladislaus has a very powerful physical attack, but this is nothing that Fang can't cope with. However, its Mounting Contempt ability inflicts Deprotect and/or Deshell before delivering a devastating blow that can kill a party member outright (Fig. 8). If you already have the corresponding buffs in place, Mounting Contempt will simply remove them. This is your cue to briefly return to Protection. Hope will reapply status enhancements while Lightning heals Fang. Even though the Wladislaus has a gigantic Stagger Point of 999%, you will defeat it not long after the Chain Bonus exceeds 200%.

HIDDEN TREASURE SPHERES

When you reach the Tesseracts level with hexagonal platforms, the warp gate at the center leads to four Treasure Spheres – but an Immortal blocks the path. Without a preemptive strike (impossible through standard sneaking here), this opponent will use its Forge Blade ability to summon a Centaurion Blade. These cannot be Provoked by a Sentinel, so will strike Lightning and Hope with impunity. Your best bet is to start with Evened Odds to inflict status ailments on the Immortal before its Forge Blade action is complete, switch to Protection to keep the party safe as Hope continues to cast buffs, then focus your attacks on the main enemy alone, with brief breaks for healing (or to restore the Haste buff when it expires). The Centaurion Blade will disappear once the main enemy is killed.

If you experience difficulties, an alternative strategy is to select Relentless Assault as your default Paradigm, then use a Deceptisol before you approach the Immortal. With a little good fortune, you should be able to fill its Chain Gauge a second time before it creates a Centaurion Blade. The rewards through the warp gate are more than worth the effort: the Adamant Bangle boosts HP by 800, while the Weirding Glyph boosts the wearer's Magic stat by 150. The Elixir is a uniquely valuable item, as it instantly restores the entire party to full health and replenishes TP.

8

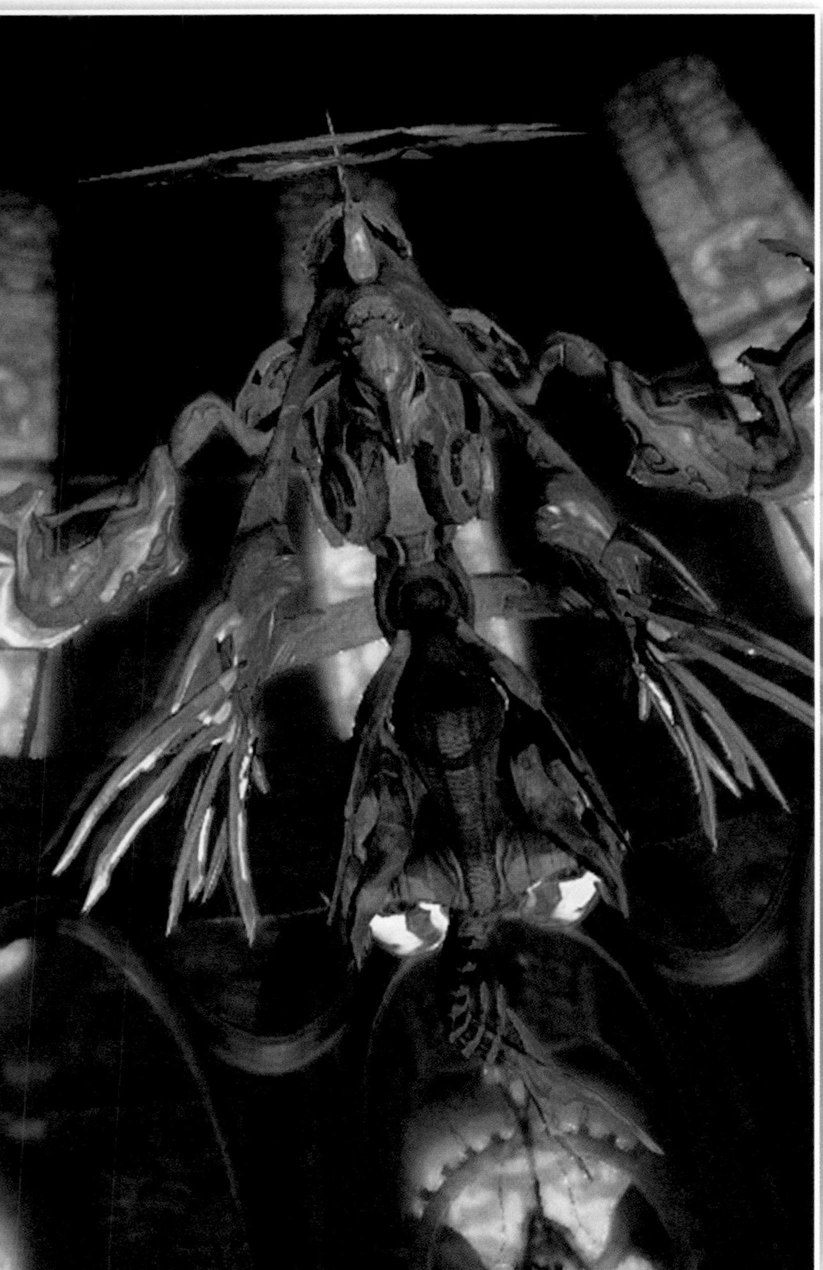

TREASURE SPHERES

Sphere	Contents	Type
A	3,000 Gil	
B	5,000 Gil	

The Tesseracts

ENEMIES

Name	Notes	Page
Sanctum Templar	All elemental damage halved; Charging Manadrive ability inflicts status ailments and massive HP loss; dangerous in groups of two or more.	230
Wladislaus	Weak to all elements, but magic damage halved; Mounting Contempt attack can kill an unprotected party member instantly.	245
Jabberwocky	Weak to all elements, but immune to magic damage; physical damage halved; susceptible to Deprotect and Poison.	238
Bandersnatch	Elemental damage halved; immune to physical damage, resistant to magic; susceptible to Deshell and Imperil.	238
Tiamat Eliminator	Immune to all status ailments; all elemental damage halved.	234

9 After the new platform has been constructed, ignore the hidden elevator platform in the corner (Fig. 9); instead, head up the ramp to meet another Wladislaus and a Sanctum Templar. Use the same tactics as in the previous battle. Once the necessary status enhancements are in place, kill the Templar first. At the top of the ramp, a Jabberwocky and a Bandersnatch await. You can avoid these, though 32,000 CP for a six-minute battle is a tempting reward. The same applies to the lone (and entirely optional) Wladislaus on the opposite "arm" of this floor level.

The three Sanctum Templars that block the route forward are an extremely dangerous group if you pay them too much respect – it's better to go for rapid kills. Start with the Evened Odds Paradigm, and simply keep all characters healthy as Hope and Fang apply status enhancements and ailments. Once you have approximately five or six per party member, switch to an all-out attack with Relentless Assault. Weakened by debuffs, the Templars should each fall quickly, though you will need Combat Clinic breaks whenever party members fall below 50% HP.

9

10 **Major Encounter – Tiamat Eliminator:** The build-up to the final story encounter begins with a fairly lengthy but leisurely grind against a boss who has no major attacks of note. The Tiamat Eliminator has two states: one aerial, one on land, with transitions usually occurring after a Stagger period expires.

In its flying form, the Tiamat Eliminator employs attacks that have a chance to inflict status ailments. The most common is Ice Grenades, which is of no real consequence, but Tail Hammer propels party members into the air (Fig. 10). Overdrive bestows status enhancements. While you could switch to Evened Odds to have Fang Dispel these prior to Staggering your opponent, it's safer to stick with a Sentinel. Use Protection just long enough for Hope to cast Haste on himself and Lightning, then use the Delta Attack/Mystic Tower combo for a quick Stagger.

When the Descent caption appears, the Tiamat Eliminator lands on the ground. In this form, all attacks remove status enhancements. Pinpoint Beam and Laser Rain are not especially damaging, but Photon Blaster can be worrying if your party is in poor condition. When you see the Lift-off caption, your opponent will take to the air again.

The principle difference between the two forms is that the Tiamat Eliminator can be Launched once you Stagger its walking form. This enables you to employ Relentless Assault and deplete a huge chunk of

10

its HP gauge. With a well-developed party, you should need very little healing time at all, with no more than a few quick Combat Clinic breaks. After four or five Stagger periods, your opponent should perish with little fanfare, surrendering 48,000 CP and an Imperial Armlet accessory as it dissolves into thin air.

Before you head through the warp gate to reach the Narthex area, be advised that you are poised to pass a point of no return. We suggest that you create a separate save file before continuing as a precaution. This way, you will have the option of loading it and returning here if you need to strengthen your party for coming challenges (see "Power Tip: Leveling").

Power Tip: Leveling

The Wladislaus, Jabberwocky and Bandersnatch enemies make repeat appearances in the final area of the Tesseracts, all yielding 32,000 CP per confrontation. As you can respawn these creatures by returning to the Save Station on the lower platform, this is one of the best power-leveling opportunities in the entire game. However this is positively the only time you can visit this area of the Tesseracts – once you pass through the final warp gate, there is no way to return unless you start FFXIII from the very beginning. Even an hour of patient grinding can set up your party for a triumphant start to the side-quests and optional adventures that wait after the final boss battle.

The Wladislaus accompanied by Sanctum Templar presents a very interesting opportunity. If you use a Deceptisol, you can start the battle with a preemptive strike – something that isn't usually possible with the Wladislaus. If you begin with the Relentless Assault Paradigm, you can kill the more dangerous enemy in an astonishingly short period of time due to an unusual "hidden Stagger" state. Given that Deceptisol costs 30,000 Gil per Shroud, though, the expense of doing this may be too high for the convenience of a fast battle. The lone Wladislaus on the upper platform level can be killed within two minutes every time if you adopt the (slightly risky) tactic of starting with Evened Odds, heal frantically until several buffs and debuffs have been applied, then switch to Relentless Assault. Best of all, this won't cost you a single Gil.

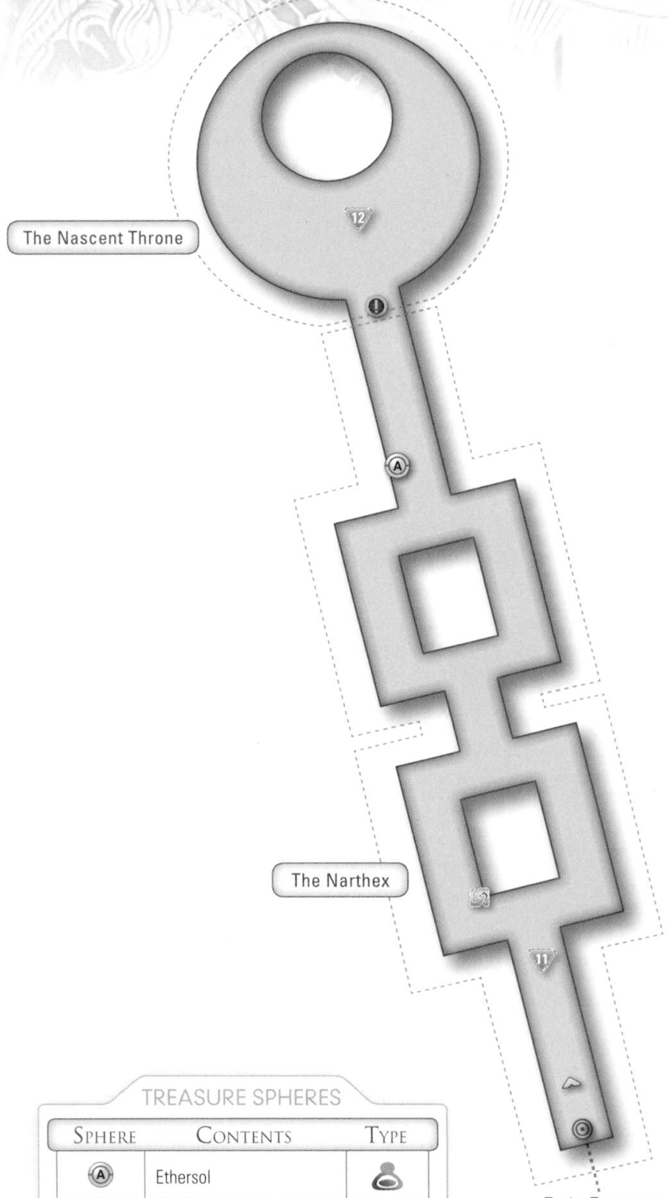

TREASURE SPHERES

Sphere	Contents	Type
A	Ethersol	

ENEMIES

Name	Notes	Page
Barthandelus	All elemental damage halved; Thanatosian Laughter can reduce all party members to critical status; may inflict Doom when near defeat.	246
Orphan	Physical and magical damage halved; can inflict instant KO on any party member; vulnerable to significant status ailments.	246
Orphan (Second Form)	Immune to all damage until Staggered.	246

11 At the final save point, purchase two Cherub's Crowns from B&W Outfitters and make sure you have at least five Phoenix Downs. If your party is found wanting in the climactic battles that lie ahead, note that you have the option of returning to the Orphan's Cradle entrance via the warp gate here (Fig. 11).

Major Encounter – Barthandelus: Stay with the Protection Paradigm until all party members have the Bravery and Faith status enhancements (for a total of five buffs), then set about this persistent foe with all your might.

In this final guise, Barthandelus has only three attacks. The first is an insistent but low-grade laser attack that will whittle away at Fang to little effect. The less common Ultima is an area-effect attack that hits for

11

moderate damage on well-protected characters. Last, but by *no* means least, Thanatosian Laughter hits the entire party for massive damage, which will regularly knock Lightning and Hope into critical status – even with status enhancements in effect. For this reason, ensure that all party members have green HP gauges at all times, and switch to Combat Clinic the moment the Thanatosian Laughter caption appears.

With the exception of breaks for healing and restoring buffs with Protection (we found that quick top-ups after each Ultima attack worked well), you only need to alternate between Delta Assault and Mystic Tower as applicable. Barthandelus may inflict Doom on your party leader if the battle goes on for 20 minutes. Time is of the essence, so after ensuring that your party is healthy, go for a quick Stagger then switch to Relentless Assault. Depending on how urgent matters become, you can use Renew to heal rather than Combat Clinic.

12 **Major Encounter – Orphan:** Once the battle begins, pause and select Retry; when the Main Menu appears, create the Aggression Paradigm (Commando + Commando + Ravager) to replace Protection, and set Combat Clinic as your active Paradigm. Now equip Lightning with as many Cherub's Crowns as you have. These will help prevent an instant-death attack that can otherwise make this climatic confrontation astonishingly frustrating.

Orphan has two "modes" during this battle, Consummate Light and Consummate Darkness. Every transition between these two states is followed by the Merciless Judgment special attack, which hits all party members for a massive HP drain. Always Paradigm Shift to Combat Clinic when you see the mode caption appear – once the attack begins, all button commands (bar the Pause button) are locked out until it is complete.

After you recover from this warm welcome, change to Evened Odds. If you wait until Hope bestows a total of six status enhancements on each character, Fang should have weakened your opponent with four or five ailments, including Slow. This is your cue to switch to Relentless Assault to start your onslaught, making short but purposeful breaks for Combat Clinic when any character's HP gauge nears 50%. When the first Stagger timer has almost expired, change to Combat Clinic to heal in anticipation of the imminent Merciless Judgment.

In its Consummate Darkness mode, Orphan performs reasonably strong attacks that have the added effect of inflicting status ailments, or removing existing buffs. Ignore this, and stick with Relentless Assault. Your task here is to fill the Chain Gauge as quickly as you can, with very occasional breaks for healing. Once Staggered, Orphan will not attack in this guise. It's an unusual step but, rather than redoubling your aggression, this is actually a very good time to return to Evened Odds to replenish buffs, renew debuffs, remove status ailments and heal your party. If you have time to resume your attack before the Stagger ends then by all means do so, but your absolute priority is to ensure that everyone is in excellent condition.

After recovering from the effects of Merciless Judgment, return to Relentless Assault. You should be making excellent progress on reducing Orphan's HP total, but this is the point when your opponent will break out two very dirty tricks. Merciless Assault suddenly

12

begins to happen at any time, necessitating swift Combat Clinic stops whenever Lightning's HP gauge falls into the yellow zone. Secondly, Orphan introduces a new attack: Progenitorial Wrath (Fig. 12). This can kill any party member instantly, no matter their status, and is why we earlier advised you to equip Lightning with Cherub's Crowns, which reduce the probability that she will die if targeted. If any other party member should fall, just use a Phoenix Down.

The latter stages of this battle have the feel of Russian roulette, with Orphan becoming more unpredictable and the deadly Progenitorial Wrath poised to strike at any moment. When you fill its Chain Gauge for a third time, wait until its Chain Combo reaches 999%, then change to Aggression to have dual Commandos wreak absolute havoc. With these tactics, Orphan should fall within eight minutes.

13

Major Encounter – Orphan (Second Form): With a Doom counter ticking away, go straight on the offensive with Relentless Assault. Orphan is immune to all damage until Staggered, so aim to reach that point as quickly as you can. Lightning's Army of One ability is a fantastic way to make great strides on the Chain Gauge in one attack; note that you must select this manually from the abilities menu. Naturally, you should also take regular breaks to heal.

Orphan can attack while Launched in this form, so keep a close eye on your party's HP levels. As with the first battle, switch to the Aggression Paradigm once the Chain Combo reaches 999% (Fig. 13). After each Stagger period ends, switch to Evened Odds to have Fang Dispel your opponent's status enhancements after Rebirth, then resume your assault. If all goes well during this brief final confrontation, Orphan will fall during the third Stagger period.

With your party's arrival in Gran Pulse at the start of Chapter 11, the world of Final Fantasy XIII suddenly abounds with opportunities to explore areas off the beaten track and take on challenges separate to the main storyline. In this final section of the walkthrough, we take a close look at these activities.

With a few exceptions (such as the mandatory Vile Peaks minigame), FFXIII is unusual in that most of its side-quests are best left until its final chapter. Indeed, its most significant non-story quest (the hunting of Marks) can only be played in earnest after a final Crystarium expansion is awarded once you beat the final boss battle – and even then, many hours of painstaking party development are required. In short, while the climax of FFXIII's main narrative acts as a full-stop to the story, it is but a comma if you view the game in its entirety.

Of course, we completely understand that many players will press on and hunt Marks or explore regardless of this advice, which is why we have included select tips and guidance that also apply to low-level parties. However, as character growth accelerates sharply over the final three chapters, hours of intensive play can be reduced to mere minutes if you attempt the same tasks at a later date.

Post-Story Instructions: Save your game when prompted to do so after the closing cutscene. When you reload this file, you will find your party by the Save Station in the final map area, with the final Crystarium stages unlocked. Turn around and travel through the warp gate. In the next area, you can use the warp gate on the right to return to Vallis Media on Gran Pulse, or the gate opposite to revisit Eden.

VILE PEAKS MINIGAME

To obtain the best rewards in the Pulse Armament minigame (introduced on page 41), follow these simple step-by-step instructions:

- The first wave consists of ten enemies. Take one or two steps forward and wait for the robots to congregate around you. Three sweeps should be more than enough to kill them all.
- The nine enemies of the second batch stand in a group right in front of a fence. You have three power charges to take them out, which is more than you really need.
- The last batch of enemies is where things become tricky. There are initially 12 of them in the area, but four more will join the fray via the nearby hatches as you approach. The hard part is to defeat these 16 enemies with only two sweeps. When you first jump down to the area, chase your targets towards the right side until they are grouped around you and use your first sweep. Unleash your second blow when the remaining automatons gather in a suitable position. This leaves you with one sweep for the final group of eight enemies on the bridge. Wait for them to retreat until they can move no further, as this will make it easier to kill them all in one mighty swipe.

VALLIS MEDIA

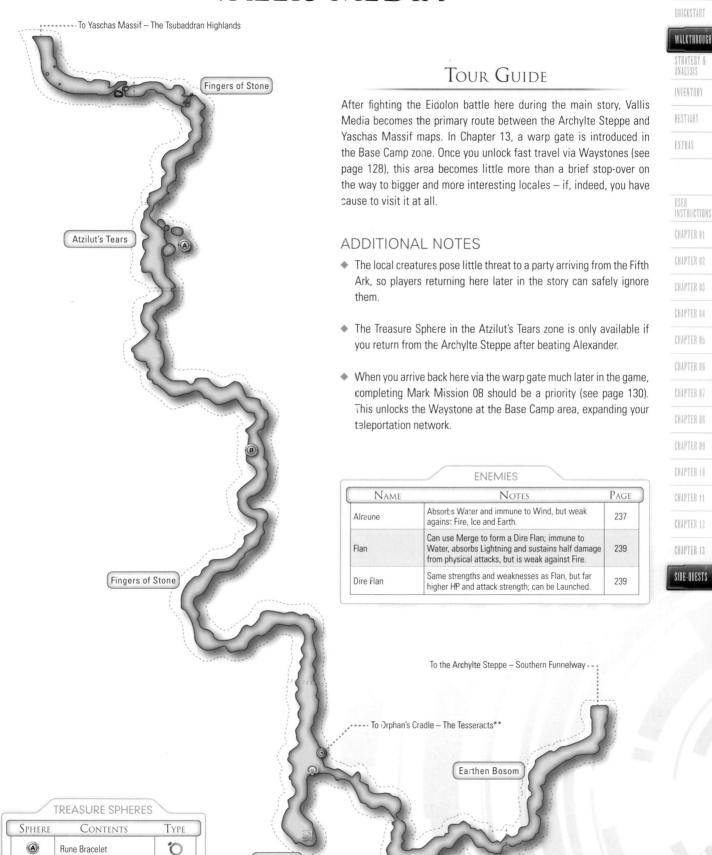

TOUR GUIDE

After fighting the Eidolon battle here during the main story, Vallis Media becomes the primary route between the Archylte Steppe and Yaschas Massif maps. In Chapter 13, a warp gate is introduced in the Base Camp zone. Once you unlock fast travel via Waystones (see page 128), this area becomes little more than a brief stop-over on the way to bigger and more interesting locales – if, indeed, you have cause to visit it at all.

ADDITIONAL NOTES

- The local creatures pose little threat to a party arriving from the Fifth Ark, so players returning here later in the story can safely ignore them.
- The Treasure Sphere in the Atzilut's Tears zone is only available if you return from the Archylte Steppe after beating Alexander.
- When you arrive back here via the warp gate much later in the game, completing Mark Mission 08 should be a priority (see page 130). This unlocks the Waystone at the Base Camp area, expanding your teleportation network.

ENEMIES

Name	Notes	Page
Alraune	Absorbs Water and immune to Wind, but weak against Fire, Ice and Earth.	237
Flan	Can use Merge to form a Dire Flan; immune to Water, absorbs Lightning and sustains half damage from physical attacks, but is weak against Fire.	239
Dire Flan	Same strengths and weaknesses as Flan, but far higher HP and attack strength; can be Launched.	239

TREASURE SPHERES

Sphere	Contents	Type
A	Rune Bracelet	
B	Partisan*	

* If not collected during first visit.

** Warp gate opens during Chapter 13.

YASCHAS MASSIF

TREASURE SPHERES

Sphere	Contents	Type
A	Diabolic Tail (x9)	
B	Watchman's Amulet	
C	Millerite	
D	Glass Orb	
E	Esoteric Oil (x8)	
F	Rune Bracelet	
G	1,827 Gil	
H	Millerite (x2)	
I	Mythril Bangle	
J	Rhodochrosite	
K	Spined Horn (x3)	
L	Whistlewind Scarf	

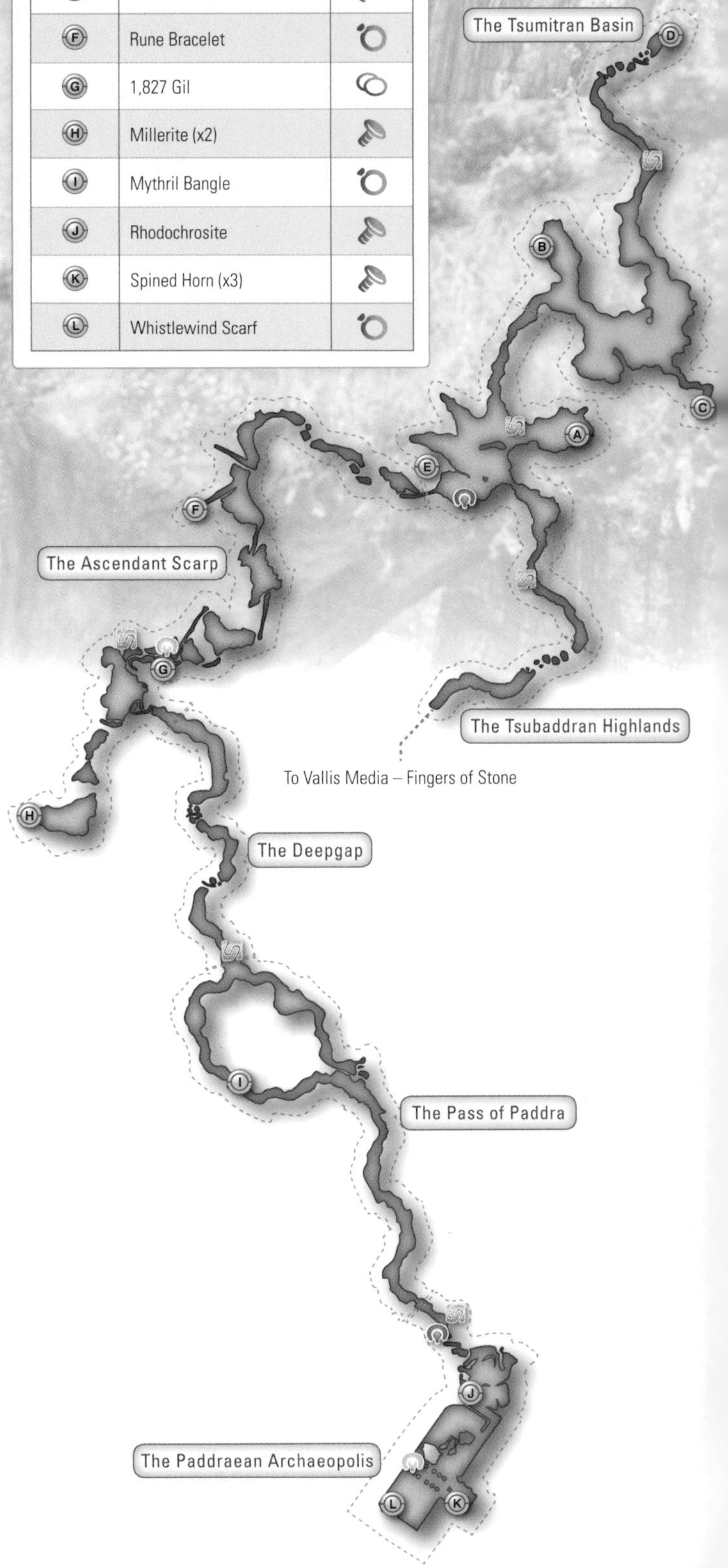

The Tsumitran Basin

The Ascendant Scarp

The Tsubaddran Highlands

To Vallis Media – Fingers of Stone

The Deepgap

The Pass of Paddra

The Paddraean Archaeopolis

ENEMIES

Name	Notes	Page
Rangda	Can summon reinforcements.	236
Leyak	Can summon reinforcements.	236
Gorgonopsid	Can inflict Poison.	234
Triffid	Inflicts Poison, Deprotect and Deshell; dangerous when accompanied by more powerful monsters.	237
Behemoth King	HP gauge restored when it moves to an upright posture; use a preemptive strike or avoid entirely if encountered early in Chapter 11.	240
Svarog	Resistant to physical damage, immune to Earth; can inflict Curse and Fog; difficult enemy in Chapter 11.	237
Alraune	Weak against Fire, Ice and Earth.	237
Hybrid Flora	Immune to physical damage, but susceptible to Deshell.	239
Munchkin	Can morph into a Munchkin Maestro.	240
Munchkin Maestro	Can bestow Bravery.	240
Nelapsi	High evasion rate.	244
Taxim	Weak against all elements; can be Launched.	244

Tour Guide

The Yaschas Massif is a large optional area that you can visit after you reach the Archylte Steppe in Chapter 11. It can be reached by travelling through the Vallis Media region. At that stage in the adventure, it's a harsh and unforgiving environment. Certain denizens will be far too tough for a party fresh from the Fifth Ark, and many battles will be uncomfortably long.

As the nearby Treasures table reveals, the rewards on offer are good but by no means spectacular. Are they worth hours of play to obtain? Probably not. Revisit later in Chapter 13 or after completing the story, though, and you can power through the entire map in a fraction of the time, casually swatting all opponents aside with the Relentless Assault Paradigm.

ADDITIONAL NOTES

- There is an optional cutscene in the Tsubaddran Highlands – look for the marker on the in-game map to locate it.
- If you visit the Yaschas Massif as soon as it becomes available, prepare your party's equipment and Paradigms with survival in mind. Delta Attack and Mystic Tower should be your primary attack options, with Combat Clinic and Protection at hand for healing and buffing your party.
- Take note of the colorful plants that abound throughout the region, as some of these are actually Triffids (Fig. 1) – an enemy type that inflicts dangerous status ailments. You can secure a preemptive strike against these foes if you make contact before they fully emerge from the ground.
- The most redoubtable enemies in the region are the Behemoth King and Svarog. Low-level parties will only conquer the former with a preemptive strike and a desperate rush to deplete its HP gauge before the Stagger period ends. The Svarog is less vicious, but still commands absolute concentration during lengthy confrontations. Both can thankfully be avoided with adept sneaking or judicious bouts of sprinting.
- Aim to dispatch Munchkins, Rangda and Leyak quickly. Munchkins can transform into the much more powerful Munchkin Maestro, while the other two enemy types can summon reinforcements.
- When you reach the Pass of Paddra, note that you can run a "loop" of the circular path to farm CP in a series of only mildly demanding battles.

1

THE ARCHYLTE STEPPE

TREASURE SPHERES

Sphere	Contents	Type
A	Lightning Charm	
B	Rod of Thorns	
C	Zephyr Ring	
D	Mnar Stone (x2) [1]	
E	Wind Charm	
F	Scarletite [1]	
G	Severed Wing (x5)	
H	Librascope (x5)	
I	Smooth Hide (x8)	
J	Ice Charm	
K	Fire Charm	
L	Millerite	
M	2,615 Gil	
N	Monstrous Fang (x11)	
O	Gold Nugget	
P	Platinum Bangle (x2)	
Q	Gold Nugget [1]	
R	Gold Nugget	
S	Speed Sash	
T	Cactuar Doll	
U	Clay Ring	
V	Earth Charm	
W	Diabolic Tail (x7) [1]	
X	Water Charm [2]	
Y	Seapetal Scale (x6) [2]	
Z1	Gloomstalk (x6) [1]	
Z2	Platinum Bangle [1]	
Z3	Collector Catalog [1, 3]	
Z4	Fractured Horn (x9) [1, 3]	
Z5	Witch's Bracelet [1, 3]	

[1] Chocobo required – complete Mark Mission 14 first.
[2] Inaccessible until Mark Mission 12 is complete.
[3] Inaccessible until Mark Mission 30 is complete.

	Chocobo position
!	Possible chocobo treasure location

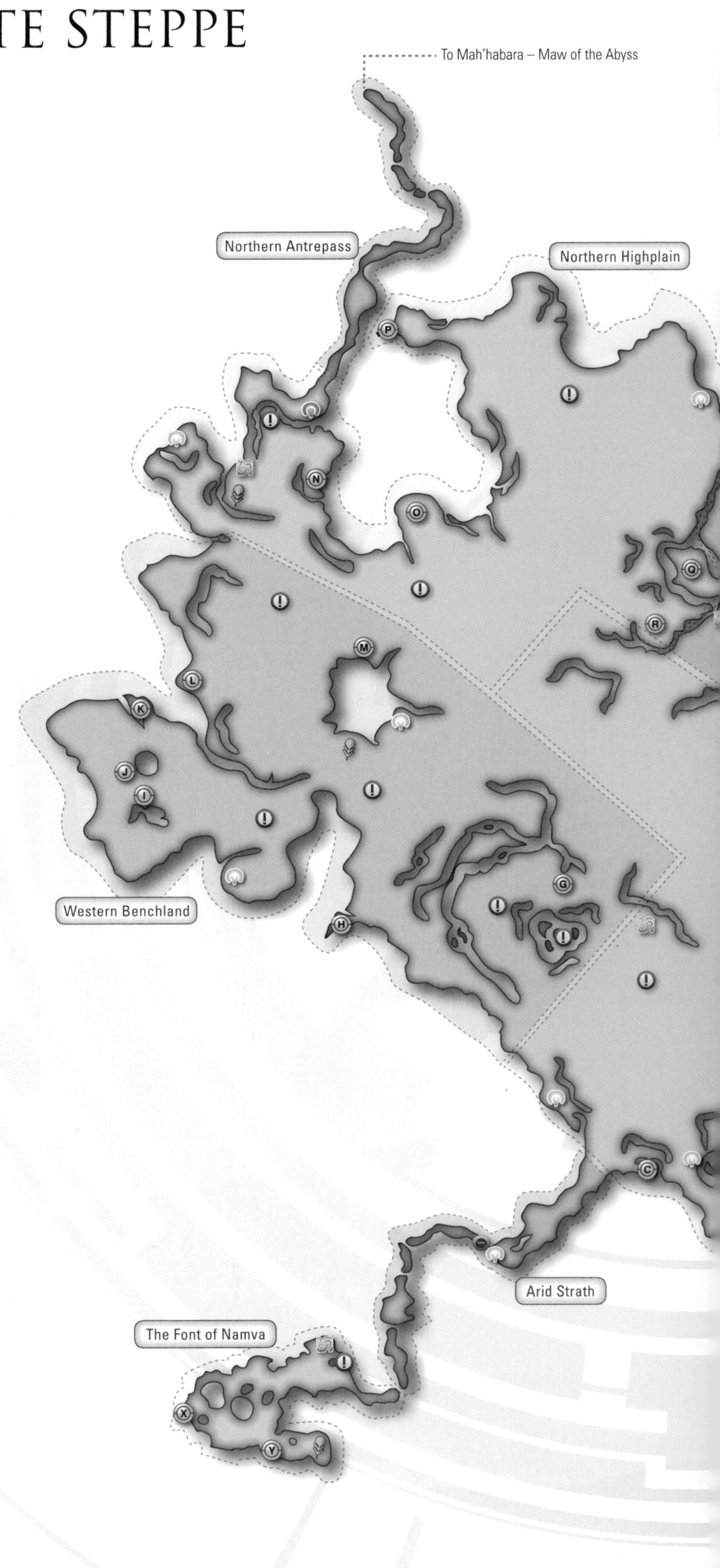

To the Faultwarrens – Truthseeker's Rise

Way of the Ancients

The Haerii Archaeopolis

The Haerii Oldroad

Aggra's Pasture

Aggra's Trough

Eastern Tors

Central Expanse

Southern Funnelway

To Vallis Media – Earthen Bosom

ENEMIES

Name	Primary Habitat	Page
Behemoth King	Various	240
Flan	Central Expanse	239
Dire Flan	Central Expanse	239
Gorgonopsid	Various	234
Rangda	Western Benchland	236
Leyak	Western Benchland	236
Navidon	Eastern Tors	237
Cactuar	Various	241
Amphisbaena	Western Benchland	238
Adamanchelid	Various	238
Adamantoise	Various	238
Adamantortoise	Various	238
Shaolong Gui	Various	239
Long Gui	Various	238
Megistotherian	Various	235
Goblin	Central Expanse, The Haerii Archaeopolis	240
Goblin Chieftain	Central Expanse, The Haerii Archaeopolis	240
Triffid	Aggra's Pasture	237
Ochu	Aggra's Pasture	241
Microchu	Aggra's Pasture	241
Strigoi	The Haerii Archaeopolis	244
Seeker	The Haerii Archaeopolis	245
Pijavica	The Haerii Archaeopolis	244
Orobon	The Font of Namva	241
Sahagin	The Font of Namva	241

Tour Guide

The Archylte Steppe is the largest contiguous map area in Final Fantasy XIII, and is suitably packed with optional adventures, unlockable features and opportunities for exploration. It is a perplexingly cruel and unforgiving locale when you first arrive on Gran Pulse, and will not surrender all of its potential rewards to a low-level party. As we state earlier in the Walkthrough chapter, it's advisable to complete the first two Mark Missions during your visit in Chapter 11, then immediately press on forward to Mah'habara. Even weaker groups of enemies may give your party a hard fight at this stage, which makes the mere process of looking around and opening Treasure Spheres much too time-consuming.

Players who don't shy away from a challenge can attempt to complete up to 20 Mark Missions here and in the neighboring Vallis Media and Yaschas Massif before they depart – see page 129 and onwards for our suggested order. Return to the Archylte Steppe during Chapter 13, though, and it's far easier to tame most of the regional monsters. As the primary location for Mark Missions (the majority of hunts begin or take place here), there are plenty of challenges to complete, many of which can be beaten with relatively little effort once your party has advanced to the end of the main storyline.

2

Additional Notes

- Though most enemies can be evaded with a little purposeful sprinting, certain adversaries (such as the Behemoth King and packs of Gorgonopsids) can be found moving at great speed along preset paths. Be very wary of these on your first visit.

- Yes, you *can* kill the colossal Oretoises that stride ponderously through the central areas of the Archylte Steppe (Fig. 2), but it's suicide to approach them unprepared. In fact, you will need to complete the story and beat a large proportion of Mark Missions before your characters are powerful enough to even survive their opening attacks (see page 144).

- When you return during Chapter 13 or later, most monsters should be reasonably familiar (and, moreover, simple to defeat) due to experience gained through battles with similar enemy archetypes during the main story. Exceptions include Cactuars and a single Ochu. Cactuars are introduced in a funny cutscene when you climb on the main rocky outcrop in the Eastern Tors zone using a chocobo. The Ochu enemy is worth a notable sum of CP, but is a more complicated opponent than most. Focus all your energies on killing him quickly, as he will simply summon more of his Microchu allies if you dispatch them.

- Though Mark Missions certainly contribute to your party's development, the Archylte Steppe offers remarkably few opportunities for efficient power-leveling. That said, the local creatures respawn very quickly, and there is no shortage of potential combat encounters.

- Certain areas of the Archylte Steppe are off-limits until you kill specific Marks – consult the table below for more information. Yellow ground markers indicate a jump that can only be made while riding a chocobo. We'll reveal how to acquire these shortly.

Unlockable Zones

Cie'th Paling Location	Unlock Condition	Unlocked Area	Recommended Chapter
Arid Strath	Complete Mark Mission 12	The Font of Namva	Chapter 13
The Haerii Oldroad	Complete Mark Mission 30	The Haerii Archaeopolis	Chapter 13 (at the earliest, but better post-story)
Way of the Ancients	Complete Mark Mission 34	The Faultwarrens (see page 124)	Post-story

Chocobos

For all dedicated players seeking to explore the Archylte Steppe with greater speed, safety and – of course – *style*, gaining access to chocobos will be a priority.

Completing Mark Mission 12 unlocks the red Cie'th Paling that prevents access to the Font of Namva area, which at least enables you to admire these signature birds up close. Complete Mark Mission 14, though, and you will acquire the Gysahl Reins. At this point, chocobos will appear in fixed positions throughout the Archylte Steppe. They're represented by yellow feathers on the in-game map when you're nearby.

(Note that a tiny Chocobo chick can be found flying over the main pool in the Font of Namva area – unlocked by completing Mark Mission 12. You can track its movements by studying the mini-map. When it moves within range, focus the camera on it and interact when prompted to claim a Chocobo Plume – though you can also receive a Chocobo Tail Feather component depending on the weather.)

To mount a chocobo, approach it and press ⊗/Ⓐ. Travelling on a chocobo is much faster than walking. It also increases your mobility, enabling you to jump over greater distances or heights whenever you espy a distinctive yellow marker (Fig. 3). You can interact with Save Stations, Cie'th Stones and Treasure Spheres as usual while riding, but cannot enter battle.

3

Instead, making contact with a monster will lead to the loss of one feather of Morale, as displayed at the bottom of the screen. These regenerate with time, but the chocobo will flee if all three feathers are depleted in quick succession. Note that making contact with an Oretoise will cause the chocobo to unceremoniously dump the party from its back and depart instantly.

To dismount a chocobo, press ◎/Ⓑ, but bear in mind that this will cause it to return to its starting location. You can only ride them in the Archylte Steppe – attempting to travel to another map via any one of the exits will cause them to leave as you approach the boundary.

4

Chocobo Treasure Hunting

Riding a chocobo enables you to hunt for treasure buried in secret caches throughout the Archylte Steppe. There are 20 potential treasure locations in total. Each time you enter the map (including reloads), five of these are chosen at random to hold a reward. Whenever an exclamation mark appears in a bubble above your chocobo's head (Fig. 4), this means that you are close to buried treasure. If you move closer the bubble will expand and contract more rapidly, which helps to pinpoint the reward's exact location. When you reach the correct position, an onscreen prompt will appear. Press ⊗/Ⓐ to begin excavating the loot.

There are two types of possible reward, as revealed by the nearby tables. Items in the "Infinite Treasures" category are limitless – you can obtain as many of these as you can bear to find. Items in the "Milestone Treasures" table, however, are awarded only once after you complete the specified number of digs.

INFINITE TREASURES

Treasure	Probability
Millerite	12.84%
Rhodochrosite	12.84%
Cobaltite	12.65%
Chocobo Plume	10.19%
Chocobo Tail Feather	9.94%
Gold Dust	9.52%
Dawnlight Dew	8.40%
Dusklight Dew	7.55%
Gold Nugget	6.32%
Moogle Puppet	5.00%
Plush Chocobo	4.75%

MILESTONE TREASURES

Digs	Reward
1	Gold Nugget
5	Tetradic Crown
10	Tetradic Tiara
15	Entite Ring
20	Ribbon

Sheep

You will encounter a herd of sheep (Fig. 5) in Aggra's Pasture, an area that can only be reached with a chocobo. Upon inspecting the grown sheep, a short cutscene will play. After it ends, you will receive a tuft of Fluffy Wool.

There are more sheep to be found throughout the Archylte Steppe. Depending on the weather conditions (which can be changed by touching certain Cie'th Stones, in particular the ones forming a circle in the Eastern Tors zones), you can obtain Thick Wool, Fluffy Wool, Rough Wool, or Scraggly Wool components. Keep in mind that only grown sheep will offer you a reward, though.

Grown sheep do not always appear, and re-entering an area resets opportunities to receive wool from them. They can be randomly found in four additional locations:

- On one of the small islands in the southeastern pond.
- On top of a hill southwest of the pond.
- On the right-hand side near the entrance to Aggra's Trough.
- Inside the ruined building in the far north of the The Haerii Archaeopolis.

5

THE FAULTWARRENS

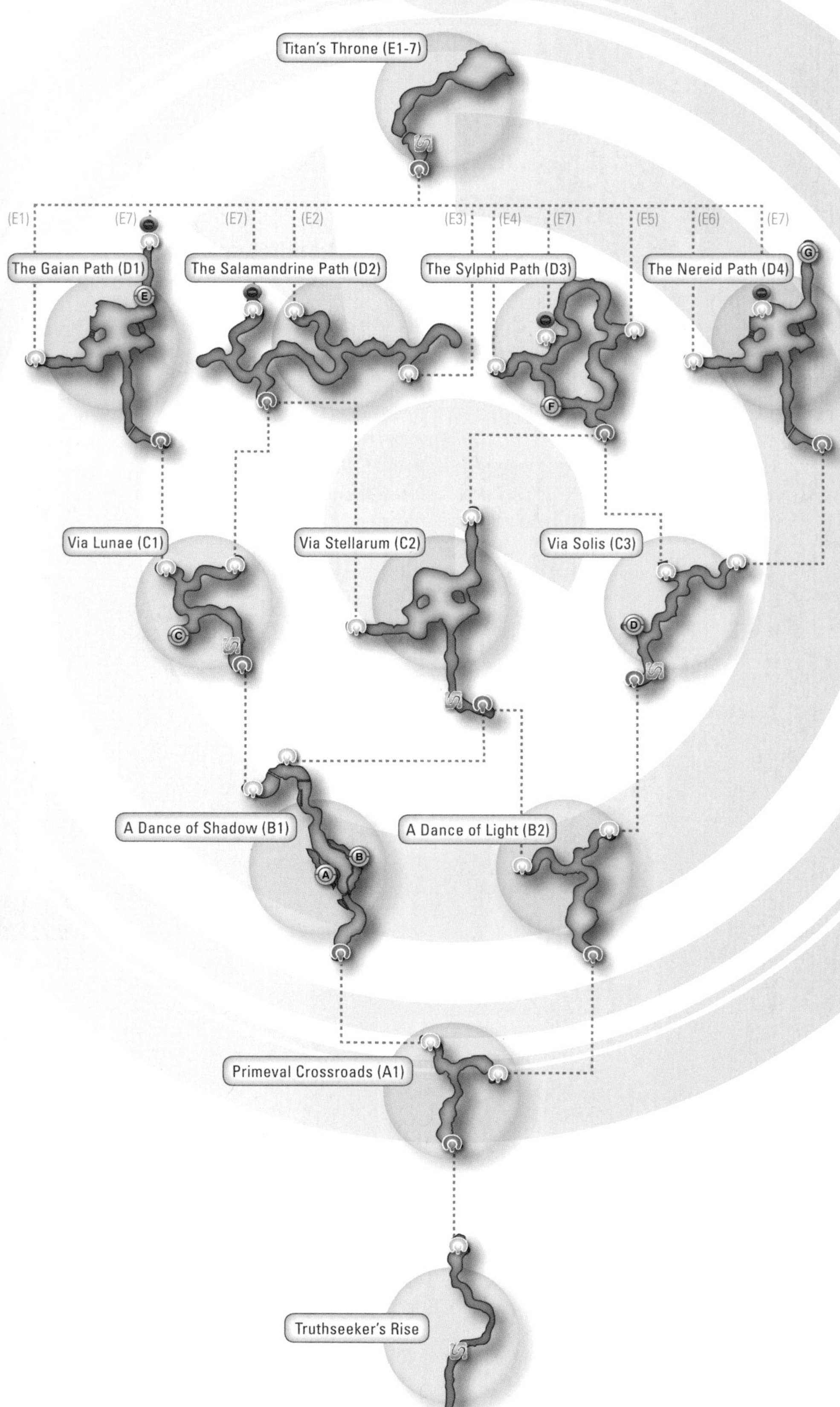

TREASURE SPHERES

Sphere	Contents	Type
A	Gold Dust	
B	Starblossom Seed	
C	Zealot's Amulet	
D	Starblossom Seed	
E	Warding Talisman	
F	Starblossom Seed	
G	Cactuar Doll	

ENEMIES

Name	Habitat	Page
Gurangatch	Primeval Crossroads	237
Amam	A Dance of Shadow	234
Rafflesia	A Dance of Light	237
Adroa	Via Lunae	236
Verdelet	Via Lunae, Via Solis, Titan's Throne	236
Ochu	Via Stellarum, The Gaian Path	241
Microchu	Via Stellarum, The Gaian Path	241
Tonberry	The Gaian Path	242
Flowering Cactuar	The Salamandrine Path	241
Borgbear	A Dance of Shadow, Via Lunae, The Salamandrine Path, The Sylphid Path	240
Borgbear Hero	The Salamandrine Path, The Sylphid Path	241
Munchkin	The Sylphid Path	240
Goblin	The Sylphid Path	240
Munchkin Maestro	The Sylphid Path	240
Goblin Chieftain	The Sylphid Path	240
Corrosive Custard	The Nereid Path	239
Monstrous Flan	The Nereid Path	239
Hybrid Flora	The Nereid Path	239
Neochu	Titan's Throne	241
Picochu	Titan's Throne	242
Zirnitra	Titan's Throne	238
Raktavija	Titan's Throne	245
Tyrant	Titan's Throne	243
Humbaba	Titan's Throne	240
Attacus	Titan's Throne	245

Tour Guide

The Faultwarrens is a maze of small map areas connected by a collection of Mark Missions known as the Titan's Trials. After accepting the first mission from the Cie'th Stone at Truthseeker's Rise, you will be teleported to the Primeval Crossroads. After defeating Gurangatch, you can pick your own route through this maze of caves and corridors, with each Cie'th Stone teleporting you to a specific area where a new Mark awaits. You can fight a maximum of five Marks on each journey through the Faultwarrens, necessitating six expeditions (and the repeat battles they entail) to conquer each of the 16 basic Marks. You must then make a seventh and final tour to kill one last adversary.

Sounds confusing? Trust us: navigation will be the least of your concerns. The Faultwarrens are home to some of the most powerful Marks in FFXIII. Don't even think about visiting until your characters are suitably equipped and trained to an impressive degree. We would suggest that you wait until your primary party has advanced to the very final level of the Crystarium in all three main roles, with their weapons upgraded to a very high level.

Additional Notes

- Examine the Cie'th Stone close to your starting position in each area to study your current progress in Titan's Trials. You can also use it to quit and return to Truthseeker's Rise.
- Accept each Mark Mission to proceed to the next area. The mission you choose will determine the location you will warp to next. See the nearby "Route Finder" diagram for more details.
- Borgbears and Flowering Cactuars (Fig. 6) offer a great opportunity for power leveling. A good route would be to complete Mark Missions 35, 36, 38, and then 42. This will bring you into contact with two groups of Flowering Cactuars, with each individual Cactuar yielding 7,500 CP. They have a tendency to flee, so try to defeat them quickly. The local Borgbears are also worth a decent sum of CP. You can then teleport back to the beginning of the Faultwarrens after completing Mission 42 and repeat the process. Depending on how well you do, this can net you over 100,000 CP in 15 to 20 minutes.

6

ROUTE FINDER

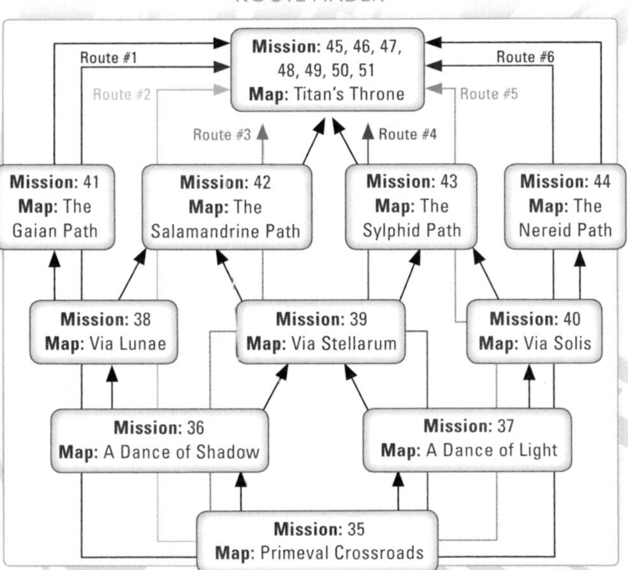

MAH'HABARA (OPTIONAL AREAS)

TREASURE SPHERES

Sphere	Contents	Type
A	Perfect Conductor (x3)	
B	Rainbow Anklet	
C	Metal Armband (x2)	
D	Particle Accelerator (x2)	
E	Moogle Puppet	
F	Perovskite	
G	Particle Accelerator (x2)	
H	Perfect Conductor (x4)	

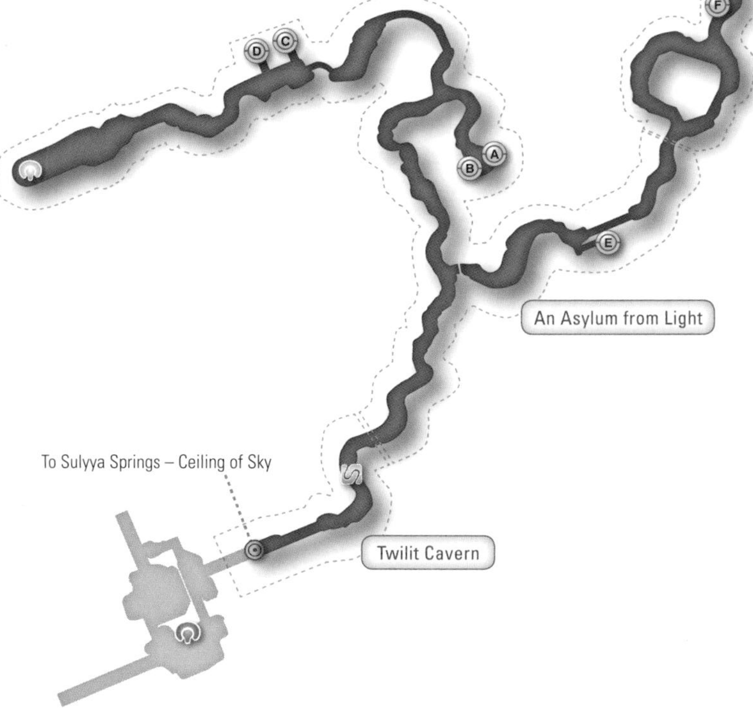

ENEMIES

Name	Notes	Page
Juggernaut	Physical and magical damage halved; very powerful attacks; extremely high HP.	243
Yaksha	Physical damage halved, but weak against Water and Earth.	236
Skata'ne	Powerful attacks; coordinates attacks with others of its species; can be Launched.	236
Yakshini	Inflicts Deprotect; will use Bravery to enhance the attack power of all enemies present if left long enough.	236
Rust Pudding	Very high Chain Resistance.	239
Ferruginous Pudding	Weak against Lightning element, and susceptible to Slow.	239
Cryohedron	Beware of Self Destruct ability; absorbs Ice.	243
Tyrant	Uses Forge Blade ability to summon Centaurion Blade; very powerful attacks; high HP.	243
Centaurion Blade	Summoned by Tyrant; cannot be Provoked; very powerful attacks.	243
Strigoi	Vulnerable to all elements, physical damage halved; can inflict Daze.	244
Vetala	Massive damage resistance (though reduced when Staggered); inflicts many status ailments; high HP.	245

Tour Guide

There are two "optional" zones in Mah'habara that can be accessed after you ride the Atomos to Sulyya Springs. If you make the return journey (or simply come back at a later date), you will find the Atomos positioned in the Twilit Cavern area, where it fills a previously impassable gap. Though many enemies encountered here can be beaten during Chapter 11, others will be too powerful until you have the opportunity to visit during or after completing Chapter 13.

ADDITIONAL NOTES

- When you return to Mah'habara after Chapter 11, don't forget to fight the Juggernaut in the Maw of the Abyss area – travel along the path to the dead-end, then approach the shuttered gate to reach it. This opponent can be defeated without difficulty from Chapter 13 onward. The Platinum Bangle inside the Treasure Sphere isn't really worth the journey by this point, but you also gain access to the Cie'th Stone used to initiate Mark Mission 29 – see page 133. You should also note that the Hoplites and Cryohedrons in this area are perfect for effortless post-story leveling. There are more lucrative ways to obtain CP and spoils, but few that require so little concentration for such solid rewards. If you are the type of player who can comfortably multitask while power-leveling, this is a great place to do just that.

- There is a dead-end with two Treasure Spheres guarded by a pair of Ferruginous Puddings and a Rust Pudding in the An Asylum from Light area. This is a seriously hard encounter during Chapter 11, but can be beaten in less than a minute from Chapter 13 onward.

- Six Cryohedrons emerge from two doors in the An Asylum from Light zone. These surrender 7,140 CP when destroyed, and have the valuable Bomb Core component as their rare drop item. Beating them takes less than 20 seconds during a post-story visit, making this a prime location for pain-free CP accumulation. If you have yet to fight the Tyrant at the end of the corridor, you can run an extremely profitable circuit between these and the shutter door, by route of assorted Daemons, selecting Retry every time the Tyrant battle begins to respawn all enemies.

- Beat the Tyrant behind the shutter door in the An Asylum from Light zone to access a Cie'th Stone where you can initiate Mark Mission 53 (see page 136).

- You must activate Mark Mission 30 to remove the barrier to the final part of the Abandoned Dig area and access the final two Treasure Spheres (see page 133).

OERBA:
REPAIRING BHAKTI

The core of the Repairing Bhakti side-quest involves finding and returning five special parts in Oerba (as detailed on page 97 of the walkthrough). Once he has been repaired, Bhakti has a wide assortment of hints to offer, with each "Bonus Byte" offering a useful tip or alluding to secrets that you can discover elsewhere on Gran Pulse.

BHAKTI'S BONUS BYTES

No.	Hint	Meaning
1	The Faultwarrens are home to some of Gran Pulse's most dangerous denizens. If you plan to challenge them, you had best go prepared.	Alludes to the optional Faultwarrens area where many Marks and powerful enemies can be found (see page 124).
2	Accepting a mission from a Cie'th Stone might remove a barrier impeding your progress.	There are red Cie'th palings that block certain paths until you complete corresponding missions (see page 122).
3	When riding chocobos, jumping at yellow map indicators will allow you to reach otherwise inaccessible areas.	You can only access some areas on the Archylte Steppe while riding a chocobo (see page 122).
4	Have you triumphed over all the challenges the Faultwarrens have to offer? Attempting the trial after doing so might draw the attention of a certain Cie'th.	Alludes to the multiple routes in the Titan's Trials side-quest, with the completion of all 16 Marks unlocking a confrontation with an extremely dangerous foe (see page 125).
5	Rumor has it that hitching a ride from Sulyya Springs on the fal'Cie Atomos will allow you to reach a secret stretch of Mah'habara.	A heavy hint that reveals the existence of Mah'habara's optional zones.
6	When it rains on the Archylte Steppe, it affects the wool of the resident sheep.	Relates to the secret where you can obtain different types of wool from sheep (see page 123).
7	Some Cie'th Stones on the Archylte Steppe take time to activate.	Certain Cie'th Stones remain dormant until you fulfill an unlock condition (see page 128 onwards).
8	Complete a top-secret mission on the Archylte Steppe and new varieties of Earth Shakers may emerge.	After you defeat the final Mark in Titan's Trials (Mark 51 – see page 136), the Adamanchelid and Adamantoise are replaced with the Shaolong Gui and Long Gui enemies.
9	Sulyya Springs is home to a whopper of a fal'Cie. Be careful when walking near the water's edge.	Alludes to the "secret" treasures in Sulyya Springs (see page 88).
10	If you climb to the seventh tier of Taejin's Tower, you will be able to rejoin all of the elevator's rail sections.	This is a required condition to complete Mark Mission 27 (see page 132).
11	The towering Adamantoise is the undisputed king of the steppe. Get too close, and even a chocobo will turn tail feather and run.	If you run into an Oretoise while riding a chocobo, it will depart instantly (see page 122).

Bhakti also awards you honorific titles that acknowledge certain milestones, as listed in the following table.

BHAKTI'S TITLES & REWARDS

Title	Condition	Reward
Pilgrim	Walked 4,999 steps or less in Gran Pulse.	Deceptisol (x10)
Sojourner	Walked 5,000 steps in Gran Pulse.	Ultracompact Reactor (x2)
Trailblazer	Walked 7,000 steps in Gran Pulse.	Gold Nugget
Cartographer	Walked 9,000 steps in Gran Pulse.	Perfume (x5)
Pulsian Pioneer	Walked 10,000 steps in Gran Pulse.	Platinum Ingot (x3), Pulsian Pioneer Trophy/ Achievement
Treasure Hunter	Collect all items available in the game. These do not need to be in your inventory at the same time – you simply need to have owned them once.	Treasure Hunter Trophy/ Achievement, Fang Theme/Gamer Picture

HUNT MISSIONS

For an introduction to the mechanics of this huge side-quest, please refer to page 82. In this section we offer information and advice for every last hunt (with enemy data sheets available in the Bestiary chapter). We have arranged all Mark Missions in an order that broadly represents a gradually rising difficulty curve, but also takes travel time between each Cie'th Stone and target into account.

As a rule, the best strategy for hunting Marks is to ensure that your party is as strong and well-equipped as it possibly can be. Even though almost half of the missions can be completed during your first visit to Gran Pulse, it's definitely easier to tackle them after you complete the main storyline. Later Marks can be quite astonishingly tough – far more dangerous than anything you encounter during the course of the main story. If you feel the need to strengthen your party, you can find power-leveling tips and suggestions on page 144.

As each player will develop their characters at different rates, our tips and tactics are designed for a "typical" developmental stage. They should at the very least inform your general approach to more powerful Marks. It will soon become apparent if your party is too weak for a particular hunt. If your characters are much stronger, though, you may be able to ignore specific strategies in favor of brute force.

Certain Cie'th Stones work as teleportation portals after you complete their missions. These "Waystones" join an interconnected travel network once activated, allowing instant transportation between convenient locations all over Gran Pulse. They appear as orange icons on our maps, making them easy to recognize.

Note that you can abandon a hunt by returning to its related Cie'th Stone. This can be useful if a particular Mark is too difficult to beat, but unfortunately blocks your party's safe passage to another area.

As you complete certain missions, you will receive titles that acknowledge your progress and prowess. These are listed in the "Hunting Titles" table.

HUNTING TITLES

Name	Condition
Good Samaritan	Complete Mission 01
Mercifex	Complete Mission 03
Archaeopolitan Idol	Complete Mission 07
Baneslayer	Complete Mission 12
Feathered Friend	Complete Mission 14
Dismantler	Complete Mission 18
Monumental Ally	Complete Missions 21 to 26
Grudge Settler	Complete Mission 27
Heartstriker	Complete Mission 30
Adamantine Knight	Complete Mission 33
Curse Lifter	Complete Mission 34
Righteous Avenger	Complete Mission 45
Protean Warrior	Complete Mission 46
Karmic Champion	Complete Mission 47
Walker of the Wheel	Complete Mission 48
Deus ex Machina	Complete Mission 49
Halcyonian Hero	Complete Mission 50
Guardian of Virtue	Complete Mission 51
Needleworker	Complete Mission 54
Hand of Wrath	Complete Mission 59
Adamantine Crusader	Complete Mission 63
Deliverer of Souls	Complete Mission 64
Great Redeemer	Complete all missions with a five-star rating

MISSION 01 – POND SCUM

Mark:	Ectopudding
Cie'th Stone Location:	The Archylte Steppe – Central Expanse
Mark Location:	The Archylte Steppe – Central Expanse
Class:	D
Unlock Condition:	None
Reward:	Energy Sash
Secondary Reward:	Bomb Core (x3)

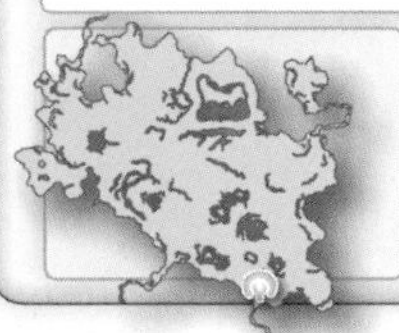

- An easy battle, even during Chapter 11 – and doubly so with a preemptive strike. See page 83 for more details.

MISSION 02 – GOODWILL HUNTING

Mark:	Uridimmu
Cie'th Stone Location:	The Archylte Steppe – Central Expanse
Mark Location:	The Archylte Steppe – Central Expanse
Class:	D
Unlock Condition:	Complete Mission 01
Reward:	Cobaltite
Secondary Reward:	Bomb Shell (x3)

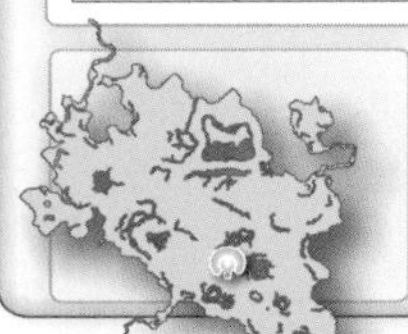

- Uridimmu is accompanied by four Gorgonopsids. On your first Steppe visit, the Mystic Tower Paradigm is a great way to Stagger enemies quickly while keeping your party safe at the start of this battle. See page 83 for further information.

MISSION 03 – MASSIF CONTAMINATION

Mark:	Ugallu
Cie'th Stone Location:	The Archylte Steppe – Central Expanse
Mark Location:	Yaschas Massif – Tsubaddran Highlands
Class:	D
Unlock Condition:	Complete Mission 02
Reward:	Platinum Bangle
Secondary Reward:	Bomb Core (x3)

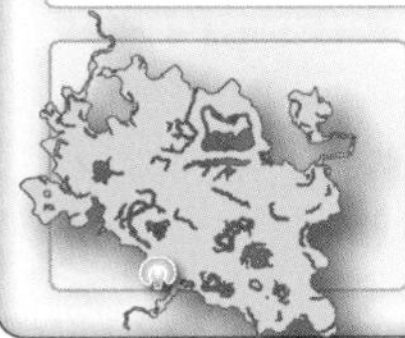

- Ugallu is capable of inflicting Poison and Curse.
- Stagger him with the Delta Attack/Mystic Tower combination, then immediately switch to a more offensive Paradigm such as Aggression (COM+COM+RAV).

MISSION 04 – A HERO'S CHARGE

Mark:	Adroa
Cie'th Stone Location:	Yaschas Massif – Tsubaddran Highlands
Mark Location:	Yaschas Massif – The Ascendant Scarp
Class:	D
Unlock Condition:	Complete Mission 02
Reward:	Pearl Necklace
Secondary Reward:	Bomb Shell (x3)

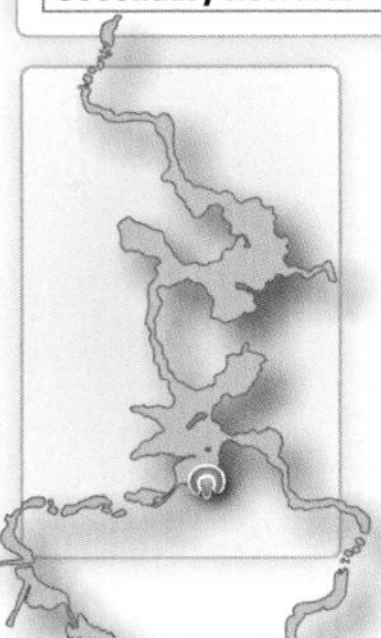

- Your foes consist of four Adroa and two Verdelet. The latter can summon other creatures into battle – including the previous Mark, Ugallu.
- Aim to stagger your opponents one by one, with the Verdelet your first priority.
- If Ugallu joins the fray, buff your party and heal as required, but keep focusing your efforts on the Verdelet to prevent them from summoning more enemies. Feel free to call an Eidolon in an emergency.
- Equipping your party leader with the Platinum Bangle from the previous mission may help low-level parties survive this encounter.

MISSION 05 – JOYLESS REUNION

Mark:	Edimmu
Cie'th Stone Location:	Yaschas Massif – The Ascendant Scarp
Mark Location:	Yaschas Massif – Tsumitran Basin
Class:	D
Unlock Condition:	Complete Mission 03
Reward:	Sorcerer's Mark
Secondary Reward:	Bomb Core (x5)

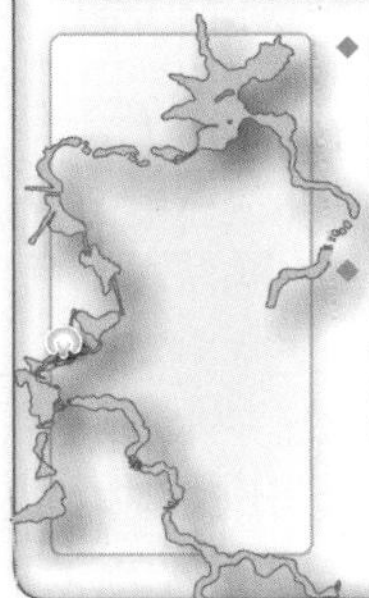

- Reaching the Cie'th Stone and backtracking to locate Edimmu requires that you travel through territory patrolled by powerful enemies, particularly the flying Svarog. It might be fair to say that the trials you face (or carefully evade) to meet this Mark are more challenging than your actual quarry.
- Edimmu inflicts status ailments with its Miasma ability and frequently evades attacks. Wind Slash damages all party members in range, though this is nothing that you can't address with a quick change to Combat Clinic. After the creature has been Staggered, switch to a Paradigm with more than one Commando for a quick finish.

MISSION 06 – NO PLACE LIKE HOME

Mark:	Munchkin Maestro
Cie'th Stone Location:	Yaschas Massif – Paddraean Archaeopolis
Mark Location:	Yaschas Massif – The Pass of Paddra
Class:	C
Unlock Condition:	Complete Mission 03
Reward:	Fulmen Ring
Secondary Reward:	Bomb Shell (x3)

- The Munchkin Maestro is accompanied by four smaller Munchkins.
- Dispatch these first with Relentless Assault before you turn your attention to the main Mark.

MISSION 07 – BITUITUS, THE PILLAGER

Mark:	Bituitus
Cie'th Stone Location:	Yaschas Massif – Paddraean Archaeopolis
Mark Location:	Yaschas Massif – Paddraean Archaeopolis
Class:	C
Unlock Condition:	Complete Mission 03
Reward:	R&D Depot retail network access
Secondary Reward:	Bomb Core (x5)

- This Mark is a much more challenging opponent than those you have faced so far. If you find that you cannot defeat Bituitus, return to the Cie'th Stone to cancel the hunt.
- Bituitus regularly evades attacks, inflicts status ailments with Miasma, and can cause significant Lightning-based damage with Levinbolt. The Fulmen Ring and Spark Ring accessories can be equipped beforehand to help party members (particularly your leader) to withstand this powerful attack.
- The Protection Paradigm will enable weaker parties to punch above their weight. Bituitus is easily dismissed if you return during Chapter 13 or after the story has been completed.
- As a reward for this mission you receive a pass to the R&D Depot retail network, which sells rare (and expensive) transformational catalysts.

MISSION 08 – THE ELEVENTH HOUR

Mark:	Rakshasa
Cie'th Stone Location:	Vallis Media – Base Camp
Mark Location:	Vallis Media – Atzilut's Tears
Class:	C
Unlock Condition:	Complete Mission 05
Reward:	Collector Catalog
Secondary Reward:	Bomb Shell (x3)

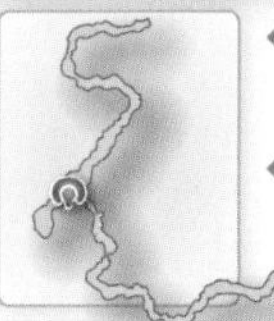

- Rakshasa is accompanied by three Flans. Dispose of these quickly with Relentless Assault to prevent them from merging to form a larger enemy, prolonging the battle.
- Your target can apply buffs with Fanatical Dance and inflict status ailments with Disastrous Dance, though it tends to wait until later in the battle before it uses these abilities. It is susceptible to Slow and vulnerable to Lightning damage.

MISSION 09 – HEAVE-HO

Mark:	Kaiser Behemoth
Cie'th Stone Location:	The Archylte Steppe – Central Expanse
Mark Location:	The Archylte Steppe – Central Expanse
Class:	C
Unlock Condition:	Complete Mission 04
Reward:	Rhodochrosite
Secondary Reward:	Bomb Core (x3)

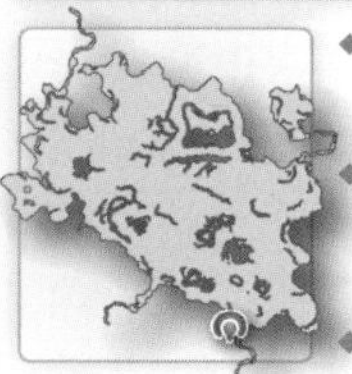

- Your characters should be close to role level 3 for their recommended disciplines at the Crystarium, and may benefit from being equipped with Fog-resistance accessories.
- Start the battle buffing your characters and debuffing your opponent; the Slow status ailment is especially useful. Evened Odds (SAB+SYN+MED) can do the trick. Note that you will need to cast these status ailments again once your foe moves to an upright position.
- Once all status effects are in place, try to quickly Stagger your opponent with Relentless Assault, switching briefly to Combat Clinic whenever you need to heal.

MISSION 10 – HOLLOW HOPE

Mark:	Ambling Bellows
Cie'th Stone Location:	The Archylte Steppe – Central Expanse
Mark Location:	The Archylte Steppe – Northern Highplain
Class:	C
Unlock Condition:	Complete Mission 05
Reward:	Superconductor (x4)
Secondary Reward:	Thrust Bearing (x3)

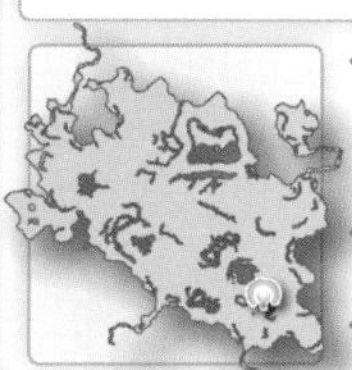

- As for the previous mission, immediately buff your party and debuff your opponent (Slow being extremely helpful again). As you should try to keep a Sentinel in your team at all times, Premeditation (SEN+SAB+SYN) is a good option.
- Work on building up a Chain with Delta Attack, with regular jumps to Combat Clinic to keep your Sentinel in the green.
- Switch to a more offensive Paradigm once you Stagger the creature to finish it off.

MISSION 12 – GEISERIC, THE PROFANE

Mark:	Geiseric
Cie'th Stone Location:	The Archylte Steppe – Arid Strath
Mark Location:	The Archylte Steppe – Western Benchland
Class:	C
Unlock Condition:	Complete Missions 05 and 07
Reward:	Royal Armlet
Secondary Reward:	Bomb Core (x5)

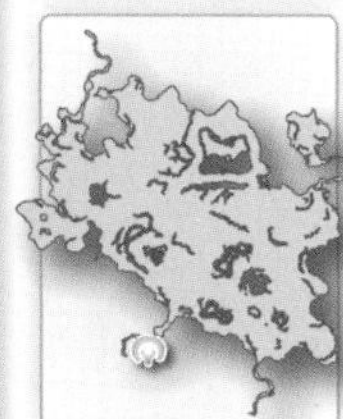

- Completing this mission removes the barrier close to the Cie'th Stone, allowing access to the Font of Namva.
- The area around the Mark is temporarily filled with Taxim for the duration of this hunt, but don't worry – you can bypass these and head straight for your target.
- The battle against Geiseric is fairly straightforward. The creature uses rather powerful physical attacks, so start by casting Protect at the very least. Use the Delta Attack/Mystic Tower combo to Stagger your opponent, then switch to Relentless Assault to make a serious dent in its huge HP total.

MISSION 13 – ETERNITY UNPROMISED

Mark:	Goblin Chieftain
Cie'th Stone Location:	The Archylte Steppe – Central Expanse
Mark Location:	The Archylte Steppe – Northern Highplain
Class:	C
Unlock Condition:	Complete Mission 12
Reward:	Cobaltite
Secondary Reward:	Bomb Shell (x4)

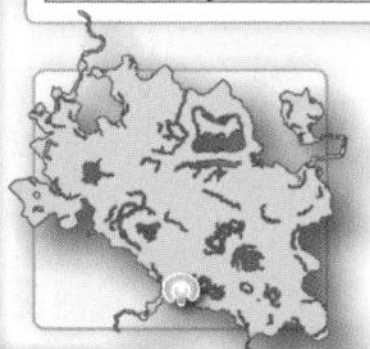

- The Goblin Chieftain is accompanied by three smaller Goblins, whom you should focus on first – secure a preemptive strike for a great start.
- The Chieftain will strengthen its henchmen with buffs, so a Sentinel will help less well-developed parties to survive.

MISSION 14 – DEFENDER OF THE FLOCK

Mark:	Sahagin
Cie'th Stone Location:	The Archylte Steppe – Western Benchland
Mark Location:	The Archylte Steppe – Font of Namva
Class:	C
Unlock Condition:	Complete Mission 13
Reward:	Gysahl Reins
Secondary Reward:	Bomb Shell (x3)

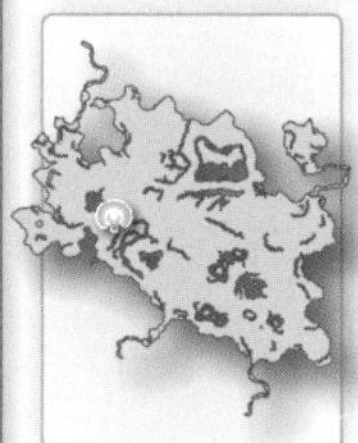

- This battle consists of two Sahagins and two Ceratosaurs; both can inflict status ailments. A wise approach would be to include a Sentinel if you attempt this mission during Chapter 11 – their attacks are fast and furious. If you experience difficulties, consider using an Eidolon (ideally Odin).
- By completing this mission you acquire the Gysahl Reins, which enable you to ride chocobos situated in various positions throughout the Archylte Steppe. See page 123 for further details.

MISSION 15 – TRIBAL WARFARE

Mark:	Goblin Chieftain
Cie'th Stone Location:	The Archylte Steppe – Central Expanse
Mark Location:	The Archylte Steppe – Northern Highplain
Class:	C
Unlock Condition:	Complete Mission 12
Reward:	Survivalist Catalog
Secondary Reward:	Bomb Shell (x4)

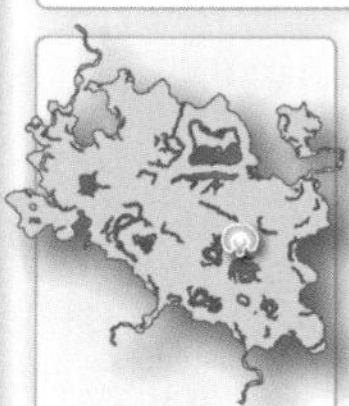

- This Cie'th Stone can only be accessed while riding a chocobo.
- Six Goblins and a Goblin Chieftain can be rather overwhelming. Start the battle with Strategic Warfare (COM+SEN+SYN) to set up basic status enhancements while your Sentinel protects the party.
- Now switch to Delta Attack and start dispatching the Goblins, ensuring that your Sentinel's HP does not drop too low. The fewer enemies you face, the easier the battle will become.

MISSION 11 – PRIDE BEFORE A FALL

Mark:	Adroa
Cie'th Stone Location:	The Archylte Steppe – Northern Highplain
Mark Location:	The Archylte Steppe – Central Expanse
Class:	C
Unlock Condition:	Complete Mission 05
Reward:	Frost Ring (x2)
Secondary Reward:	Bomb Shell (x3)

- You are confronted by four Adroa and two Verdelet who are likely to summon more enemies into battle (including Dire Flans).
- Use Delta Attack and dispatch one target at a time. If additional creatures are summoned, keep focusing on your initial targets, and deal with the interlopers afterwards.

MISSION 18 – SO CLOSE, YET SO FAR

Mark:	Ambling Bellows
Cie'th Stone Location:	Mah'habara – Twilit Cavern
Mark Location:	Mah'habara – Twilit Cavern
Class:	C
Unlock Condition:	Complete Mission 12
Reward:	Sorcerer's Mark
Secondary Reward:	Piezoelectric Element (x4)

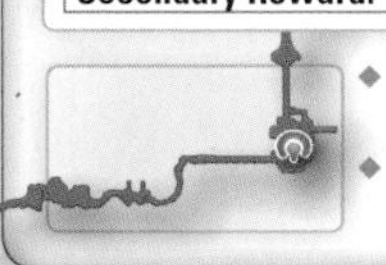

- An easy battle. Simply use Delta Attack/Mystic Tower to get rid of the Ambling Bellows, then dispatch the Hoplites.
- As long as you carefully heal your Sentinel with Combat Clinic, not much can go wrong.

MISSION 19 – TRIANGLE OF TRAGEDY

Mark:	Uridimmu
Cie'th Stone Location:	Sulyya Springs – Ceiling of Sky
Mark Location:	Sulyya Springs – Subterranean Lake
Class:	C
Unlock Condition:	Complete Mission 18
Reward:	Cobaltite
Secondary Reward:	Bomb Shell (x5)

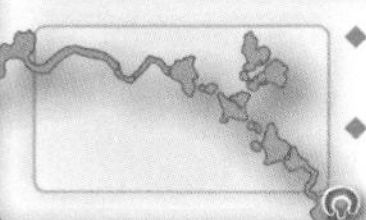

- The four Uridimmu pose no real threat if you stick to a balanced Paradigm such as Delta Attack.
- They can poison your party members, but just ignore this: stay offensive to end the battle quickly.

MISSION 20 – WORDS UNSPOKEN

Mark:	Goblin Chieftain
Cie'th Stone Location:	Taejin's Tower – The Palisades
Mark Location:	Taejin's Tower – The Palisades
Class:	C
Unlock Condition:	None
Reward:	Rhodochrosite
Secondary Reward:	Bomb Shell (x5)

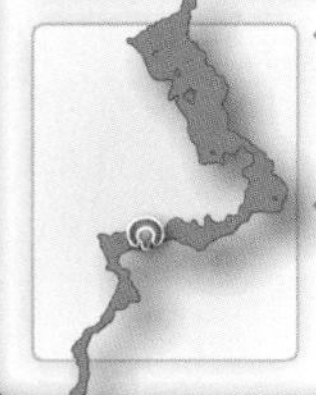

- As you face several enemies (a Goblin Chieftain, two Goblins, a Munchkin Maestro and a Munchkin), start with a Paradigm featuring a Sentinel to keep your party safe, and a Synergist to cast vital status enhancements such as Haste and Protect.
- Once your buffs are in place, switch to Delta Attack and deal with the smaller creatures first to prevent them from mutating into their larger and more dangerous forms.

MISSION 56 – A TOOTHY GRIN

Mark:	Ugallu
Cie'th Stone Location:	The Archylte Steppe – Eastern Tors
Mark Location:	Yaschas Massif – The Ascendant Scarp
Class:	C
Unlock Condition:	Reach Taejin's Tower
Reward:	Rhodochrosite
Secondary Reward:	Bomb Shell (x5)

- Ugallu is accompanied by four Munchkins.
- As previously, buff your party straight away, then use Delta Attack to defeat the weaker foes first.

MISSION 57 – WHAT'S YOURS IS BRINE

Mark:	Sahagin
Cie'th Stone Location:	The Archylte Steppe – Eastern Tors
Mark Location:	Vallis Media – Atzilut's Tears
Class:	C
Unlock Condition:	Reach Taejin's Tower
Reward:	Uraninite
Secondary Reward:	Bomb Shell (x5)

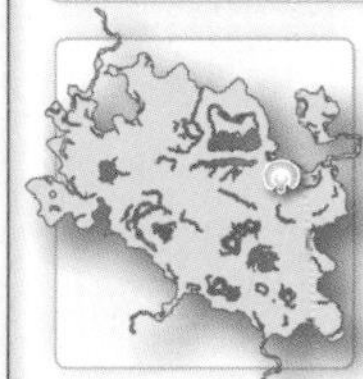

- This battle pits you against three Sahagin and two Alraune.
- Have a Sentinel present at all times and consider casting a few status enhancements on your party. You can then use Delta Attack to take on each enemy in turn, switching to Mystic Tower to speed up the Staggering process.

MISSION 58 – THE CULLER OF MANY

Mark:	Humbaba
Cie'th Stone Location:	The Archylte Steppe – Eastern Tors
Mark Location:	Mah'habara – The Earthworks
Class:	B
Unlock Condition:	Reach Taejin's Tower
Reward:	Speed Sash
Secondary Reward:	Bomb Shell (x5)

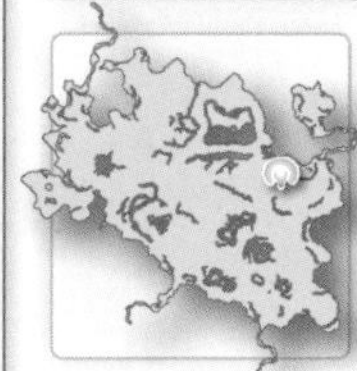

- The Humbaba is a Behemoth-type enemy, so has the ability to recover full HP and use new and more dangerous attacks when it rears up to stand on its hind legs.
- The safest strategy, then, is to prevent this transformation from taking place. Fill the Chain Gauge with the Delta Attack/Mystic Tower combo. As soon as the monster is Staggered, switch to a Paradigm with more than one Commando to keep the creature airborne until it dies. If necessary, use △/Y to issue advance attacks to keep it airborne when required.

MISSION 21 – A TREMULOUS TERROR

Mark:	Gelatitan
Cie'th Stone Location:	Taejin's Tower – Second Tier
Mark Location:	Taejin's Tower – Second Tier
Class:	C
Unlock Condition:	None
Reward:	Speed Sash
Secondary Reward:	Bomb Shell (x4)

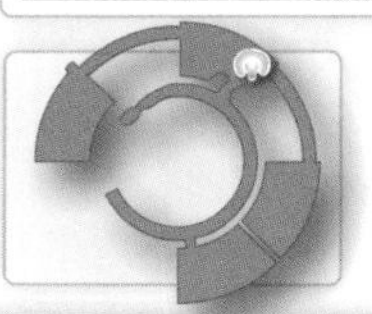

- See Walkthrough, page 91.

MISSION 22 – INFERNAL MACHINE

Mark:	Ambling Bellows
Cie'th Stone Location:	Taejin's Tower – Second Tier
Mark Location:	Taejin's Tower – Second Tier
Class:	C
Unlock Condition:	None
Reward:	Particle Accelerator (x3)
Secondary Reward:	Electrode (x3)

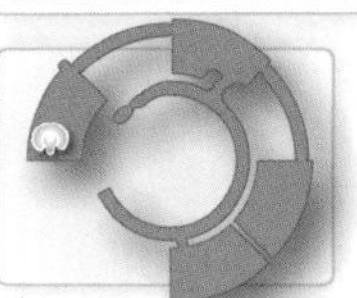

- See Walkthrough, page 91.

MISSION 23 – NATURAL DEFENSES

Mark:	Gurangatch
Cie'th Stone Location:	Taejin's Tower – Second Tier
Mark Location:	Taejin's Tower – Second Tier
Class:	B
Unlock Condition:	None
Reward:	Warrior's Wristband
Secondary Reward:	Bomb Shell (x4)

◆ See Walkthrough, page 91.

MISSION 24 – A POTENT STING

Mark:	Mushussu
Cie'th Stone Location:	Taejin's Tower – Fifth Tier
Mark Location:	Taejin's Tower – Fifth Tier
Class:	B
Unlock Condition:	Complete Missions 21 to 23
Reward:	Moonblossom Seed (x6)
Secondary Reward:	Moonblossom Seed

◆ See Walkthrough, page 92.

MISSION 25 – SPECTRAL HAUNT

Mark:	Vetala
Cie'th Stone Location:	Taejin's Tower – Sixth Tier
Mark Location:	Taejin's Tower – Fifth Tier
Class:	B
Unlock Condition:	Complete Missions 21 to 23
Reward:	Cobaltite
Secondary Reward:	Bomb Core (x6)

◆ See Walkthrough, page 93.

MISSION 26 – SO SHRILL, THE CRY

Mark:	Penanggalan
Cie'th Stone Location:	Taejin's Tower – Fifth Tier
Mark Location:	Taejin's Tower – Sixth Tier
Class:	B
Unlock Condition:	Complete Missions 21 to 23
Reward:	Diamond Bangle
Secondary Reward:	Bomb Core (x6)

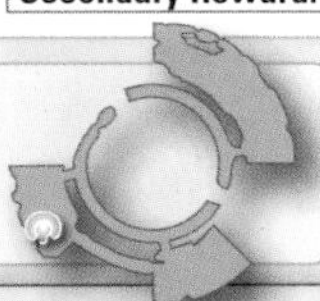

◆ See Walkthrough, page 93.

MISSION 28 – FADED GLORY

Mark:	Ceratosaur
Cie'th Stone Location:	Oerba – Village Proper
Mark Location:	Oerba – Village Proper
Class:	C
Unlock Condition:	None
Reward:	Giant's Glove
Secondary Reward:	Bomb Shell (x5)

- Have a Sentinel in your party to bear the brunt of the Ceratosaurs' attacks, and patiently dispatch them one at a time.
- Switch from Delta Attack to Combat Clinic when necessary.

MISSION 16 – SURROGATE SLAYER

Mark:	Sahagin
Cie'th Stone Location:	The Archylte Steppe – Eastern Tors
Mark Location:	The Archylte Steppe – Font of Namva
Class:	B
Unlock Condition:	Complete Mission 12
Reward:	Rhodochrosite
Secondary Reward:	Bomb Shell (x4)

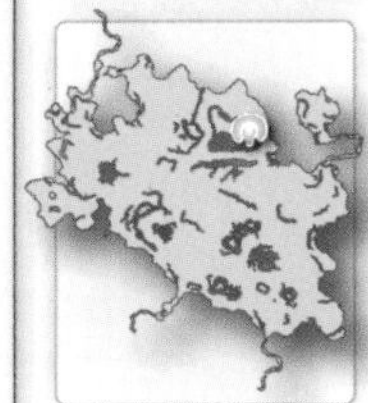

- This Cie'th Stone can only be reached while riding a chocobo.
- As you face a large group of four Ceratoraptors, four Ceratosaurs and two Sahagins, caution is advised for low-level parties. Buffs will help, and an immediate summon will offer a great start. Focus on the Ceratoraptors first to prevent them from calling allies into the fray.
- Use a Sentinel at all times until you defeat most of your enemies, healing as usual with Combat Clinic.
- If you struggle to get the upper hand, use a Paradigm that includes a Saboteur and a Synergist (such as Premeditation or, for stronger parties, Evened Odds).

MISSION 17 – A WIDOW'S WRATH

Mark:	Pulsework Champion
Cie'th Stone Location:	The Archylte Steppe – Northern Highplain
Mark Location:	The Archylte Steppe – Northern Highplain
Class:	B
Unlock Condition:	Complete Mission 12
Reward:	Perfect Conductor (x3)
Secondary Reward:	Piezoelectric Element (x4)

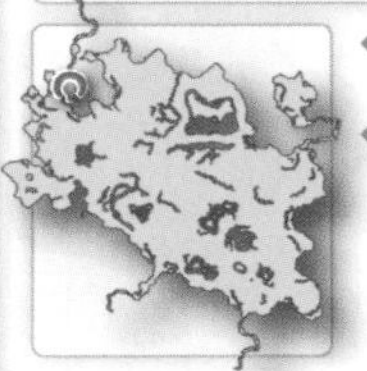

- The Pulsework Champion has high resistance to most attacks, but becomes much weaker once Staggered.
- The key, then, is to quickly build up a Chain with an offensive Paradigm such as Relentless Assault.

MISSION 27 – MITHRIDATES, THE LONE

Mark:	Mithridates
Cie'th Stone Location:	Taejin's Tower – The Cloven Spire
Mark Location:	Taejin's Tower – Ground Tier
Class:	B
Unlock Condition:	Defeat Dahaka
Reward:	Blaze Ring
Secondary Reward:	Bomb Core (x6)

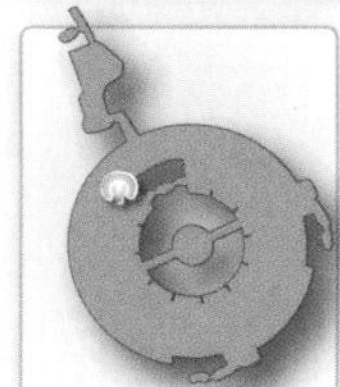

- To face this Mark you must activate the Menhirrim on top of the Cloven Spire. This provides access to the Seventh Tier, where you can interact with a final statue to rotate the floor and unlock central elevator access to all floor levels.
- Now make your way to the central elevator and ride it up to the tower's apex, then all the way down to the Ground Tier. The battle begins automatically after a short cutscene.
- Equip Lightning-resistant accessories and consider starting the battle with two Medics in anticipation of the Mark's Miasma attack, which inflicts multiple status ailments. The Medics can then immediately begin healing the party and curing status ailments (particularly Imperil, which exacerbates the injuries inflicted every time Mithridates casts its powerful Levinbolt assault).
- Buff your party after removing status ailments, then attack with an offensive Paradigm such as Relentless Assault. Once the creature is Staggered, go for all-out offense.

MISSION 29 – FALTERING FAITH

Mark:	Juggernaut
Cie'th Stone Location:	Mah'habara – Maw of the Abyss
Mark Location:	Taejin's Tower – The Palisades
Class:	B
Unlock Condition:	Complete Mission 20
Reward:	Uraninite
Secondary Reward:	Mobius Coil (x3)

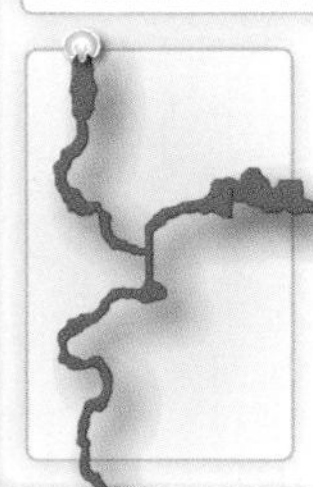

- The Juggernaut is susceptible to many status ailments. It will periodically attempt to remove them with its Steam Clean ability, which offers welcome respite from its powerful attacks (particularly the dizzying Wrecking Ball). Low-level parties can use bursts of Evened Odds (MED+SAB+SYN) to great effect, though more developed characters could leap straight in with Smart Bomb (RAV+SAB+RAV) for a quick Stagger.
- The Juggernaut can be Launched, so switch to an offensive Paradigm once the Chain Gauge has been filled.

MISSION 30 – SYPHAX, THE INSIDIOUS

Mark:	Syphax
Cie'th Stone Location:	The Archylte Steppe – Haerii Oldroad
Mark Location:	Mah'habara – Abandoned Dig
Class:	B
Unlock Condition:	Reach Sulyya Springs
Reward:	Uraninite
Secondary Reward:	Bomb Core (x6)

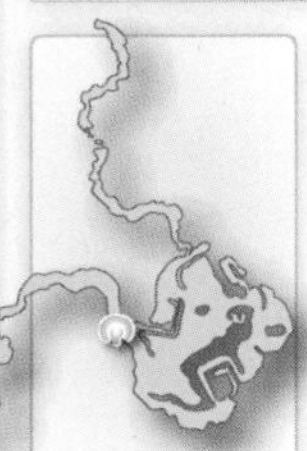

- This Cie'th Stone can only be reached with a chocobo.
- Your characters should have reached role level 4 crystals in their core specialties before you attempt this hunt.
- The battle initially pits you against a horde of Numidia. Once you destroy most of them, Syphax will enter the fray. Focus on the Mark from this point, as it will otherwise summon additional Numidia throughout the fight.
- Use Libra to reveal your opponent's weakness to Air, and Aeroga can then be employed to wreak havoc. Stay on the offensive to end the confrontation swiftly.

MISSION 31 – NEWFOUND PURPOSE

Mark:	Pulsework Champion
Cie'th Stone Location:	The Archylte Steppe – Haerii Archaeopolis
Mark Location:	The Archylte Steppe – Haerii Archaeopolis
Class:	B
Unlock Condition:	Complete Mission 30
Reward:	Perfect Conductor (x3)
Secondary Reward:	Crystal Oscillator (x2)

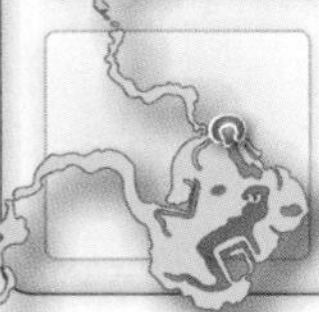

- This Waystone is located in the area behind the Cie'th Paling you removed by defeating Mark 30.
- The Pulsework Champion is accompanied by three Seekers. Dispatch the latter first, then launch an all-out attack on the Mark until you Stagger it.

MISSION 33 – A PARENT'S PLEDGE

Mark:	Adamanchelid
Cie'th Stone Location:	The Archylte Steppe – Haerii Archaeopolis
Mark Location:	The Archylte Steppe – Eastern Tors
Class:	B
Unlock Condition:	Complete Mission 30
Reward:	White Cape
Secondary Reward:	Bomb Shell (x5)

- The Adamanchelid is vulnerable to the Ice element. Use a Saboteur to inflict Imperil, Deprotect, Deshell and Slow on the creature to weaken it considerably.
- Offense is then the best form of defense in this fight, with quick healing sessions used only when necessary. The Mark should fall after no more than two Staggers.

MISSION 32 – AND THEN THERE WAS ONE

Mark:	Amam
Cie'th Stone Location:	Vallis Media – Earthen Bosom
Mark Location:	The Archylte Steppe – Western Benchland
Class:	B
Unlock Condition:	Reach Mah'habara
Reward:	Glass Buckle
Secondary Reward:	Bomb Shell (x5)

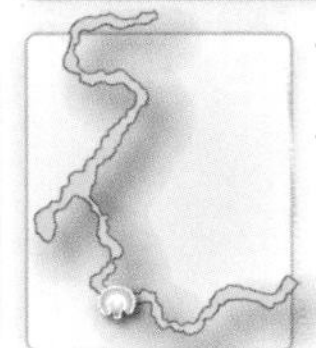

- The battle seems easy at first, but you will soon discover that Amam can heal itself with the Storm Conduction ability.
- Buff your party with Haste and pummel your opponent with a very aggressive Paradigm to inflict more damage than it can restore.

MISSION 34 – ZENOBIA, THE BUTCHER

Mark:	Zenobia
Cie'th Stone Location:	The Archylte Steppe – Way of the Ancients
Mark Location:	The Archylte Steppe – Haerii Archaepolis
Class:	B
Unlock Condition:	Complete Mission 30
Reward:	Hermes Sandals
Secondary Reward:	Bomb Core (x7)

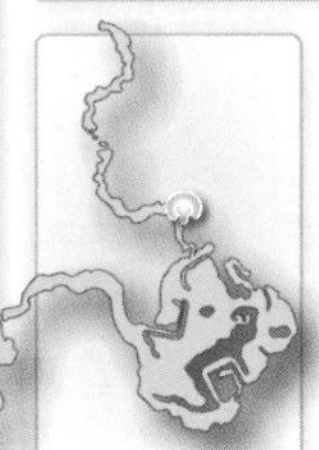

- This Cie'th Stone can only be accessed with a chocobo.
- Rather than fighting Zenobia, you instead face a famous Final Fantasy adversary: a Tonberry.
- The Tonberry's Knife ability can be wickedly painful, but its Grudge attacks are a far graver threat as the damage inflicted will increase throughout the confrontation. For this reason, an aggressive approach is definitely the best strategy.
- Quickly debuff the Mark (aim to inflict Deprotect at the very least), then attack relentlessly, healing only when party members are grievously wounded. This should enable you to end the battle before damage inflicted by each use of Grudge becomes unmanageable.

MISSION 35 – THE ROAD LESS TRAVELED

Mark:	Gurangatch
Cie'th Stone Location:	Faultwarrens – Truthseeker's Rise
Mark Location:	Faultwarrens – Primeval Crossroads (A1)
Class:	C
Unlock Condition:	None
Reward:	Witch's Bracelet
Secondary Reward:	Bomb Shell (x5)

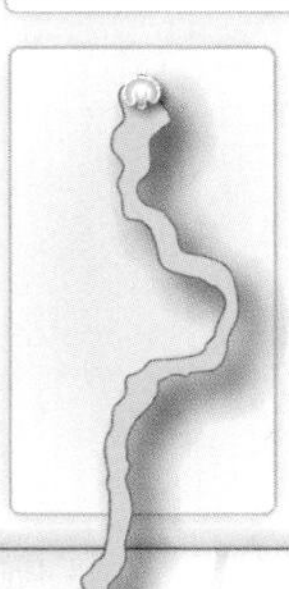

- This is the first mission of Titan's Trials, in which you pick a route through the Faultwarrens to fight a maximum of five Marks per visit. You will need to make six of these journeys to conquer the 16 Marks hidden there, then one final trip to fight against the area's ultimate foe. See page 125 for details.
- The battle against Gurangatch is an easy start, as you have defeated far more powerful Marks in order to reach this area. It's a typical Armadon enemy type – massively resistant with its carapace intact, slow to Stagger, but vulnerable to a quick finish once deprived of its armor.

MISSION 36 – DARK DELIVERANCE

Mark:	Amam
Cie'th Stone Location:	Faultwarrens – Primeval Crossroads
Mark Location:	Faultwarrens – A Dance of Shadow (B1)
Class:	C
Unlock Condition:	Complete Mission 35
Reward:	Uraninite
Secondary Reward:	Bomb Shell (x6)

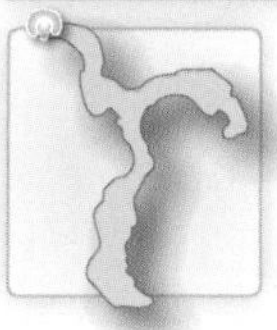

- It may help to equip accessories that enable party members to resist Pain (Pain Dampener) and Lightning (Fulmen Ring, Spark Ring).
- Cast Haste on your party at the start. The two Amam will use Accursed Breath to inflict status ailments, and heal themselves (and hurt you) with their Storm Conduction attack. Be ready to switch to Combat Clinic to remove debuffs and heal quickly.
- Your opponents are susceptible to Slow. For the rest, try to remain very aggressive.

MISSION 37 – DYING OF THE LIGHT

Mark:	Rafflesia
Cie'th Stone Location:	Faultwarrens – Primeval Crossroads
Mark Location:	Faultwarrens – A Dance of Light (B2)
Class:	C
Unlock Condition:	Complete Mission 35
Reward:	Star Pendant
Secondary Reward:	Bomb Shell (x5)

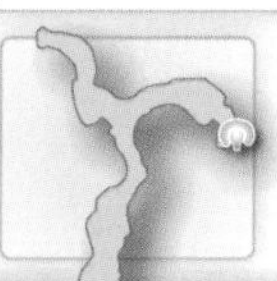

- You face five Rafflesia in this fight, but this is a rather easy battle.
- The creatures are immune to magic but weak against Fire, so a Ravager's Flamestrike works well.

MISSION 38 – MOONLIT MADNESS

Mark:	Verdelet
Cie'th Stone Location:	Faultwarrens – A Dance of Shadow
Mark Location:	Faultwarrens – Via Lunae (C1)
Class:	B
Unlock Condition:	Complete Mission 36
Reward:	Diamond Bangle
Secondary Reward:	Bomb Shell (x5)

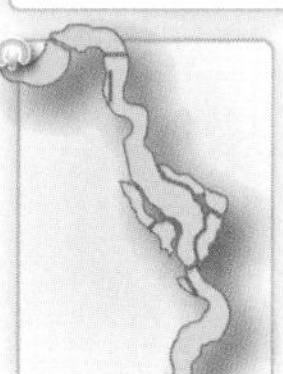

- In this Trial you face three Verdelet and one Adroa.
- Verdelet can summon powerful creatures to the battle, such as Juggernauts or Tonberries. The best way to prevent this is to enter the battle with the Cerberus Paradigm (COM + COM + COM) pre-selected and quickly execute a few Blitz moves with Lightning, specifically targeting Verdelet who are poised to call in reinforcements. With a little luck and a suitably powerful party, you can slay all three with no complications. If not, consider restarting the battle.

MISSION 39 – SEEING STARS

Mark:	Ochu
Cie'th Stone Location:	Faultwarrens – A Dance of Shadow/A Dance of Light
Mark Location:	Faultwarrens – Via Stellarum (C2)
Class:	C
Unlock Condition:	Complete Mission 36 or 37
Reward:	Siltstone Ring
Secondary Reward:	Moonblossom Seed (x2)

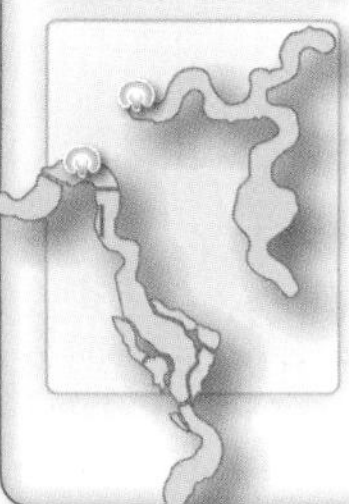

- Ochu is accompanied by Microchus and can create more during the battle, so your main priority is to defeat the Mark itself.
- Equipping your characters with accessories that resist Earth elemental attacks (such as the Clay Ring or Siltstone Ring) may help.
- Buff your party while you inflict Imperil on Ochu, then adopt a balanced approach. Delta Attack will enable you to survive the insistent pummeling delivered by the Microchus, though you will need regular Combat Clinic breaks to keep your Sentinel healthy.

MISSION 40 – SOLAR POWER

Mark:	Verdelet
Cie'th Stone Location:	Faultwarrens – A Dance of Light
Mark Location:	Faultwarrens – Via Solis (C3)
Class:	B
Unlock Condition:	Complete Mission 37
Reward:	Zealot's Amulet
Secondary Reward:	Bomb Shell (x5)

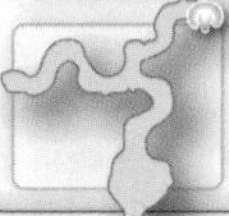

- The battle against these two Verdelet can be ridiculously easy if you use the Cerberus Paradigm (three Commandos).
- The Verdelet will attempt to summon reinforcements, but all-out aggression will enable you to kill both before any additional foes appear.

MISSION 41 – GAIAN GRUDGE

Mark:	Tonberry
Cie'th Stone Location:	Faultwarrens – Via Lunae
Mark Location:	Faultwarrens – Gaian Path (D1)
Class:	A
Unlock Condition:	Complete Mission 38
Reward:	Doctor's Code
Secondary Reward:	Tonberry Figurine

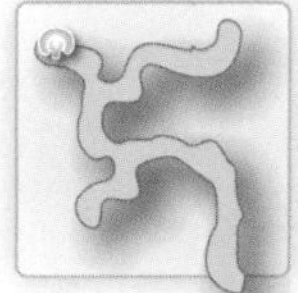

- This Trial pits you against three Tonberries, making it an extremely tough battle. Your characters should have progressed far into level 4 of their recommended roles, and their weapons should be upgraded to a high standard. Even then, this battle may prove to be too tough. Tonberries use Grudge attacks that cause ever greater damage as they escalate in scale, and they're fully healed after performing each one.
- A preemptive strike is essential, and is possible (though tricky) through a stealthy approach. Try to even the odds a little by using Shrouds beforehand. Aegisol and Fortisol will enable you to enter the battle with the Relentless Assault Paradigm. With a surprise attack, you should be able to kill two Tonberries fairly quickly.
- The final Tonberry may be preparing a second (or even third) Grudge attack by the time its companions fall. Your best bet is to opt for an all-out assault, slaying it as quickly as you possibly can.
- An alternative strategy is to make Vanille your party leader. Equip her with the Belladonna Wand and repeatedly cast Death on the Tonberries.

MISSION 42 – ANTIHERO

Mark:	Borgbear Hero
Cie'th Stone Location:	Faultwarrens – Via Lunae/Via Stellarum
Mark Location:	Faultwarrens – Salamandrine Path (D2)
Class:	B
Unlock Condition:	Complete Mission 38 or 39
Reward:	Witch's Bracelet
Secondary Reward:	Bomb Core (x7)

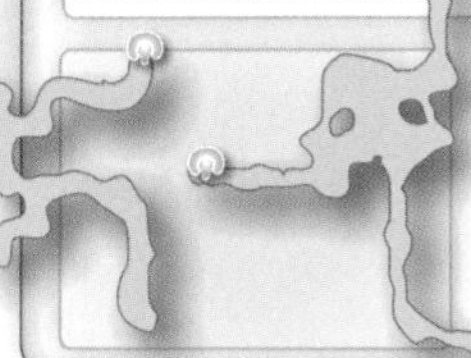

- You face a Borgbear Hero and four Borgbears in this battle. Start with a Sentinel (for safety) and a Synergist (to cast Haste on your party).
- You can then kill each Borgbear in turn with Delta Attack, and switch to Solidarity when healing is required. Compared to other battles on the "D" maps in Titan's Trials, this is a rather easy fight.

MISSION 43 – THE HERO NEVER DIES

Mark:	Borgbear Hero
Cie'th Stone Location:	Faultwarrens – Via Stellarum/Via Solis
Mark Location:	Faultwarrens – Sylphid Path (D3)
Class:	B
Unlock Condition:	Complete Mission 39 or 40
Reward:	Speed Sash
Secondary Reward:	Bomb Core (x7)

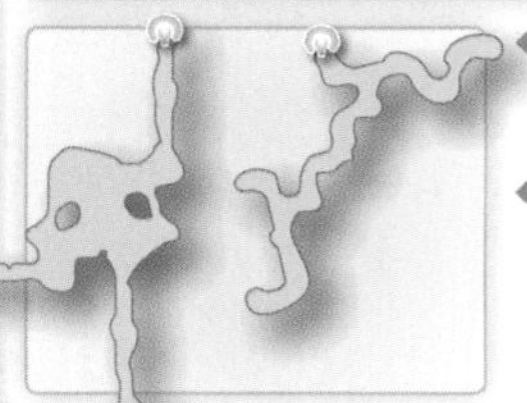

- This enemy party consists of a Goblin, a Goblin Chieftain, a Munchkin, a Munchkin Maestro, a Borgbear and a Borgbear Hero.
- Quickly dispatch the weaker foes first, using a Sentinel at the start of battle to keep your party safe – Delta Attack is as reliable as ever here. Later in the battle, switch to a more offensive Paradigm to speed things up.

MISSION 44 – THE OLD ONES GO TO RUST

Mark:	Corrosive Custard
Cie'th Stone Location:	Faultwarrens – Via Solis
Mark Location:	Faultwarrens – Nereid Path (D4)
Class:	A
Unlock Condition:	Complete Mission 40
Reward:	General's Belt
Secondary Reward:	Bomb Shell (x7)

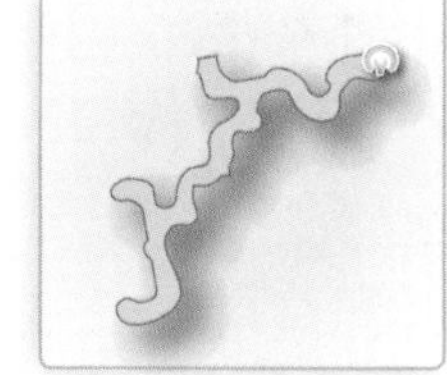

- The Corrosive Custard is accompanied by a Monstrous Flan and a Hybrid Flora. The Mark is by far the strongest of the bunch, though, so focus your attacks on it first.
- It might help to equip your party members with accessories that resist Earth elemental attacks (Clay Ring, Siltstone Ring), as the Corrosive Custard has a powerful Quake attack that can cause up to 3,500 HP of damage to all characters.
- Buff your team with several status enhancements (including Haste and Enthunder) while you debuff your opponents (Slow and Deshell work well). This will make the slaying of the Mark much easier. Once it falls, its allies are mere cannon fodder.

MISSION 45 – EMERGENT EVOLUTION

Mark:	Neochu
Cie'th Stone Location:	Faultwarrens – Gaian Path
Mark Location:	Faultwarrens – Titan's Throne (E1)
Class:	A
Unlock Condition:	Complete Mission 41
Reward:	Hunter's Friend
Secondary Reward:	Moonblossom Seed (x3)

- The easiest way to defeat Neochu is to have Vanille act as Saboteur and party leader. Make sure she has learned the Death spell and equip her with the Belladonna Wand. Your other two characters should act as a Medic and a Sentinel. You can then repeatedly cast Death on Neochu until it succumbs.
- An alternative strategy is to equip two Commandos with equipment that provides the Random: Instant Chain synthesized ability (see page 194), then buff them with Haste.
- If you decide to do this the hard way, you'll soon learn that Neochu is one of the strongest enemies in FFXIII. Though it only has a few attacks, these will enable it to dismiss an underpowered party with frustrating ease. Equipping your Sentinel with a Gaian Ring will help to reduce the power of its Earth-infused tentacle attack. Pollen inflicts numerous status ailments, while its powerful Screech ability dispels status enhancements and hits all party members for big damage.
- Other than Death, Neochu is only susceptible to Imperil, so inflict this on the creature first. Depending on your party's level, you could then work on building the Chain Bonus with Relentless Assault, or switch to a Paradigm that includes a Sentinel to reduce damage.
- The Tortoise Paradigm (three Sentinels) is very effective against the Screech attack if you have a trio of characters who can perform the necessary roles. Neochu will roar seconds before performing Screech, a warning that will give you sufficient time to make the Paradigm Shift.
- Try to maintain the Imperil status ailment throughout the battle. When Neochu is down to 50% HP, it will summon up to eight Picochu with its Seed Dispersal ability. This is the point where having a Sentinel present at all times becomes essential. Use Paradigms such as Solidarity, Combat Clinic and Delta Attack to keep your party healthy as it inflicts steady damage on Neochu. You will find it hard to maintain buffs during this stage. If everything goes awry, with all party members afflicted by assorted status ailments, consider summoning an Eidolon to wipe the slate clean.

MISSION 46 – ON SILENT WINGS

Mark:	Zirnitra
Cie'th Stone Location:	Faultwarrens – Salamandrine Path
Mark Location:	Faultwarrens – Titan's Throne (E2)
Class:	A
Unlock Condition:	Complete Mission 42
Reward:	Gilgamesh, Inc. (retail network)
Secondary Reward:	Bomb Core (x10)

- Zirnitra's most fearsome ability, Feeding Stoop, can inflict up to 10,000 HP of damage to an average party. It also has a very powerful area-effect attack.
- Have a Sentinel present at all times, and equip this character in advance with accessories that boost defense and possibly status ailment resistances – especially Deprotect.
- Start the battle by buffing your characters. An optimal approach is to pick a main party that enables you to use the Premeditation Paradigm (SAB+SEN+SYN) to inflict status ailments.
- Once fully prepared, switch to Delta Attack to Stagger your target. Lightning's Army of One ability is a great way to boost the Chain Gauge and seriously harm the creature.
- Follow this strategy, refreshing all status effects and healing with Combat Clinic when required, and you will make short work of your opponent.
- Note that Zirnitra is also vulnerable to Death. Equipping Vanille with a Belladonna Wand and casting Death repeatedly (with two other characters lending support as a Medic and a Sentinel) could also work well.

MISSION 47 – UNFOCUSED RAGE

Mark:	Raktavija
Cie'th Stone Location:	Faultwarrens – Salamandrine Path
Mark Location:	Faultwarrens – Titan's Throne (E3)
Class:	B
Unlock Condition:	Complete Mission 42
Reward:	Mnar Stone
Secondary Reward:	Bomb Core (x10)

- At this point, your party should ideally be in the tenth and final stage of the Crystarium in their recommended roles.
- The Random: Instant Chain synthesized ability is an extremely useful tool in this battle and can help you to Stagger Raktavija quickly.
- Your primary goal is to Stagger this Raktavija in order to remove its Inertial Barrier. To accelerate this process, inflict Imperil and Slow on the creature, and enhance your party with Haste and other buffs. Raktavija will dispel these, so be prepared to refresh them regularly.
- Raktavija only uses magical attacks, so equip suitable accessories beforehand. Though it's unlikely that you will be able to use it right now, the Magic Damper synthesized ability can make you virtually invincible here (see page 194).

MISSION 48 – THE ABYSS STARES BACK

Mark:	Verdelet
Cie'th Stone Location:	Faultwarrens – Sylphid Path
Mark Location:	Faultwarrens – Titan's Throne (E4)
Class:	A
Unlock Condition:	Complete Mission 43
Reward:	Twenty-sided Die
Secondary Reward:	Bomb Shell (x10)

- As with previous battles against Verdelet, favor brute force with the Cerberus Paradigm (three Commandos) and repeatedly perform area-effect moves such as Blitz. This will enable you to defeat your opponents before they can call for powerful reinforcements.
- Target the Verdelet that are in the process of summoning allies and dispatch them before they can finish. If you're too late and a Tonberry is brought into the fray, simply retry the battle.

MISSION 49 – TYRANNICIDE

Mark:	Tyrant
Cie'th Stone Location:	Faultwarrens – Sylphid Path
Mark Location:	Faultwarrens – Titan's Throne (E5)
Class:	A
Unlock Condition:	Complete Mission 43
Reward:	Particle Accelerator (x7)
Secondary Reward:	Crystal Oscillator (x2)

- The Tyrant is actually one of the easier enemies you fight during the last phase of Titan's Trials.
- Choose a very offensive Paradigm to Stagger your opponent quickly.

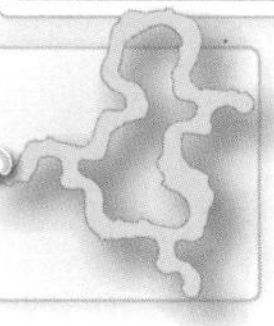

MISSION 50 – ROAD TO PREDATION

Mark:	Humbaba
Cie'th Stone Location:	Faultwarrens – Neired Path
Mark Location:	Faultwarrens – Titan's Throne (E6)
Class:	B
Unlock Condition:	Complete Mission 44
Reward:	Scarletite
Secondary Reward:	Bomb Core (x7)

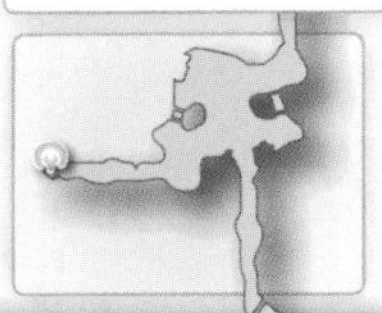

- The Humbaba is vulnerable to Imperil, Deprotect, Deshell, Slow, Curse, and even Daze in its first form. Casting these status ailments will make this a quick battle, especially if you buff your party at the same time.
- Once you're done with these preparations, switch to Relentless Assault to swiftly dispatch the beast.

MISSION 51 – ATTACUS, THE SOULLESS

Mark:	Attacus
Cie'th Stone Location:	Faultwarrens – Sylphid Path/Gaian Path/ Salamandrine Path/Nereid Path
Mark Location:	Faultwarrens – Titan's Throne (E7)
Class:	A
Unlock Condition:	Complete all previous Titan's Trials Missions (35-50)
Reward:	Genji Glove
Secondary Reward:	Bomb Core (x10)

- Attacus is susceptible to Deprotect, Deshell, Slow and Curse, so start the battle by casting these status ailments and refresh them as required during the remainder of the battle. Buffing your party with status enhancements will obviously be of benefit.
- This battle becomes increasingly difficult as time goes by. After losing approximately 22.5% of its HP, Attacus draws its Unrelenting Blade. Your opponent will then occasionally prepare a more powerful blow with the Concentrate ability. Paradigm Shift immediately to give a Sentinel sufficient time to Provoke the Mark and take the damage.

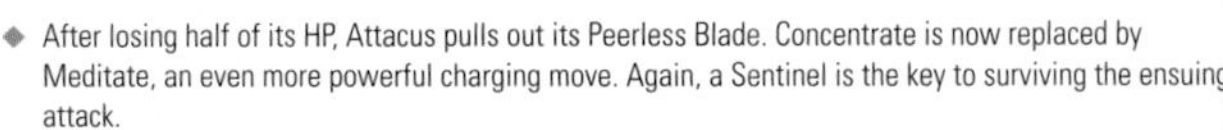

- After losing half of its HP, Attacus pulls out its Peerless Blade. Concentrate is now replaced by Meditate, an even more powerful charging move. Again, a Sentinel is the key to surviving the ensuing attack.
- Attacus cannot be Staggered, though increasing its Chain Bonus to 999% will significantly speed things up. Do your utmost to maintain the Chain at all times.

MISSION 52 – HEAD IN THE CLOUDS

Mark:	Zirnitra
Cie'th Stone Location:	The Archylte Steppe – Western Benchland
Mark Location:	The Archylte Steppe – Eastern Tors
Class:	A
Unlock Condition:	Reach Sulyya Springs
Reward:	Gale Ring
Secondary Reward:	Bomb Core (x7)

- Use the tactics suggested for Mission 46.

MISSION 53 – FREEDOM FROM FEAR

Mark:	Zirnitra
Cie'th Stone Location:	Mah'habara – An Asylum from Light
Mark Location:	Yaschas Massif – The Pass of Paddra
Class:	A
Unlock Condition:	None
Reward:	Blaze Ring
Secondary Reward:	Bomb Core (x10)

- Zirnitra is accompanied by four Alraune. Dispatch these quickly, then use the Mission 46 tactics.

MISSION 54 – THE BIGGER THEY ARE...

Mark:	Gigantuar
Cie'th Stone Location:	The Archylte Steppe – Northern Highplain
Mark Location:	The Archylte Steppe – Eastern Tors
Class:	B
Unlock Condition:	Find a Cactuar
Reward:	Cactuar Doll
Secondary Reward:	Chocobo Plume (x2)

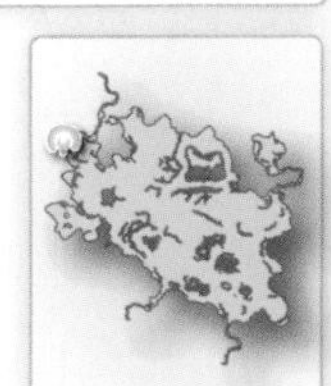

- This Mark can only be reached with a chocobo.
- Gigantuar can be extremely difficult to beat. It only uses one ability (10,000 Needles), but attacks very quickly.
- This battle is much more manageable if your characters have at least 15,000 HP (20,000 HP for your Sentinel). However there is a trick that can make it far less difficult. Choose Sazh as party leader, ideally equipping him with accessories that protect against Fog and Pain. Once the battle begins, repeatedly perform the Flamestrike/Fire/ Flamestrike/Fire/Flamestrike attack queue. Sazh will constantly step backwards as he executes these commands, and will eventually move out of Gigantuar's reach. If things look grim, summon Brynhildr and just keep repeating the same combo until you're safe from 10,000 Needles.
- An alternative strategy is to prepare characters with the Random: Instant Chain synthesized ability (see page 194), potentially offering you a "free" Stagger. This is particularly helpful if you are attempting to achieve a five-star rating for this Mark.

MISSION 55 – CAN'T WE ALL JUST GET ALONG?

Mark:	Neochu
Cie'th Stone Location:	Oerba – Deserted Schoolhouse (Roof)
Mark Location:	The Archylte Steppe – Aggra's Pasture
Class:	A
Unlock Condition:	Defeat Barthandelus in Oerba and complete Mission 14
Reward:	Growth Egg
Secondary Reward:	Moonblossom Seed (x2)

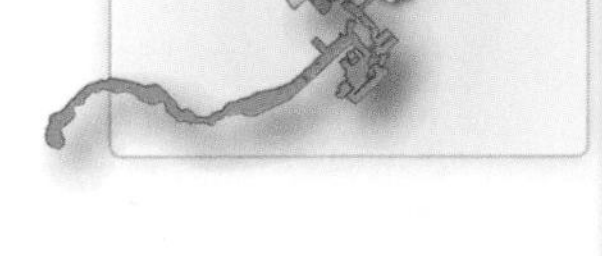

- The Neochu and its five Picochu allies can only be reached with a chocobo.
- If you want to defeat Neochu easily, refer to the first two tips offered for Mission 45.
- In a straight fight, this battle requires extensive preparation. Ideally, you should equip your characters with upgraded Super Ribbons and accessories that boost physical resistance. Your Sentinel will also benefit from a Gaian Ring.
- You will need to keep a Sentinel active at all times, so start the fight with a Paradigm such as Matador (RAV+SEN+SAB). Note that it is best to have your party leader working as a Saboteur. An AI-controlled SAB will constantly attempt to dispel status enhancements held by Picochus, which is a waste of time.
- Once you have inflicted Imperil on Neochu, switch to Delta Attack. The most important thing here is to keep the Chain active for as long as you can, so try to use very short bursts of Combat Clinic whenever you need to heal. Switching to a Paradigm with more than one Sentinel will also reduce the damage inflicted by Neochu's Screech attack.
- Time is of the essence in this fight, so only refresh the Haste status enhancement when it expires.

MISSION 59 – TWO-FACED FIEND

Mark:	Zirnitra
Cie'th Stone Location:	The Archylte Steppe – Eastern Tors
Mark Location:	Sulyya Springs – Subterranean Lake
Class:	A
Unlock Condition:	Reach Taejin's Tower
Reward:	Energy Sash
Secondary Reward:	Bomb Core (x6)

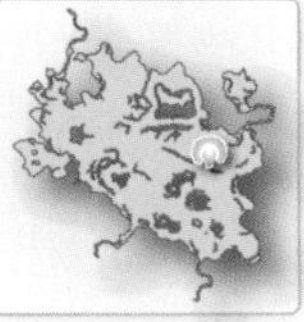

- Zirnitra is accompanied by three additional Ceratoraptors, who in turn call several Ceratosaurs. On top of that, the Mark's Feeding Stoop attack can inflict around 10,000 HP on a single target. A Sentinel is absolutely essential.
- Your initial goal should be to dispatch the Ceratoraptors, then deal with their Ceratosaur allies.
- That done, Paradigm Shift to Premeditation (SEN+SAB+SYN) to inflict Deprotect, Deshell and Imperil on Zirnitra, while you buff your party with at least Haste.
- Lightning's Army of One ability is great to build up the Chain Gauge or attack Zirnitra.

MISSION 60 – DÉGELÀ VU

Mark:	Gelatitan
Cie'th Stone Location:	The Archylte Steppe – Eastern Tors
Mark Location:	Taejin's Tower – The Cloven Spire
Class:	A
Unlock Condition:	Reach Oerba
Reward:	Mnar Stone
Secondary Reward:	Bomb Core (x7)

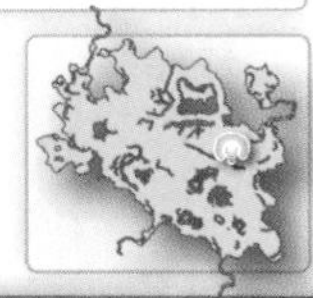

- The Gelatitans are vulnerable to the Lightning element, and susceptible to Deprotect and Imperil. Applying these two ailments seriously weakens them.
- Focus your attacks on one Gelatitan at a time, keeping a Sentinel in your team to maintain a solid defense, and this should be a slow yet purposeful grind towards victory.

MISSION 61 – I, JUGGERNAUT

Mark:	Juggernaut
Cie'th Stone Location:	The Archylte Steppe – Eastern Tors
Mark Location:	Oerba – Village Proper
Class:	A
Unlock Condition:	Reach Oerba
Reward:	Royal Armlet
Secondary Reward:	Crystal Oscillator (x2)

- By now, this should be a very easy battle. See Mission 29 for advice if you experience difficulties.

MISSION 62 – INDOMITABLE WILL

Mark:	Raktavija
Cie'th Stone Location:	The Archylte Steppe – Eastern Tors
Mark Location:	The Archylte Steppe – Central Expanse
Class:	A
Unlock Condition:	Reach Taejin's Tower
Reward:	Genji Glove
Secondary Reward:	Bomb Core (x10)

- The Raktavija only use magic attacks, so if you can activate the Magic Damper synthesized ability (see page 194) on your Sentinel, this will make this battle much, much easier. The Random: Instant Chain synthesized ability can also be extremely useful. In any case, equip your party with Magus's Bracelets and the like to boost your magic resistance – this will make a huge difference. Having an Elixir or two will also be of benefit.
- Buff your party with Aegisol and Fortisol, and inflict Imperil and Slow straight away.
- You should then aim to Stagger one of your enemies quickly. To speed things up, switch to Tri-disaster (three Ravagers). When the Inertial Barrier breaks, Paradigm Shift to Relentless Assault. Special abilities such as Lightning's Army of One will help you increase the Chain Bonus to 999% and inflict maximum damage. Repeat the process until your first target falls.
- You will need to regularly refresh your status enhancements and heal. Hero's Charge (COM+SYN+MED) will enable you to do that while maintaining the Chain Gauge.

MISSION 63 – CRUSHED BY DOUBT

Mark:	Adamantortoise
Cie'th Stone Location:	Sulyya Springs – Subterranean Lake
Mark Location:	The Archylte Steppe – Eastern Tors
Class:	A
Unlock Condition:	Reach the Faultwarrens
Reward:	Genji Glove
Secondary Reward:	Gold Nugget

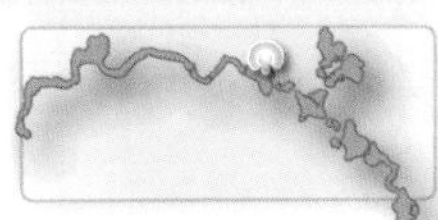

- At this point, your characters should have all reached the maximum role level in their recommended roles on the Crystarium, and possess fully upgraded equipment. Any degree of protection against the Earth element will also help – as will applications of Aegisol and Fortisol before the battle begins.
- The only way to lower the Mark's ridiculously high defense is to first defeat its left and right legs. To do so, weaken them with a Saboteur, then Stagger them and deplete their HP. As soon as the Mark falls to the ground, cast Slow, Deprotect and Deshell and pummel it with Tri-disaster (three Ravagers). When the Adamantortoise is finally Staggered, switch to Relentless Assault and use Chain-boosting abilities (such as Lightning's Army of One) to quickly bring the Chain Bonus up to 999%.
- Another approach is to select Vanille as party leader. Equip her with the Belladonna Wand and repeatedly cast Death on the Mark. This is a gamble, but one that could provide you with a fast and easy victory.

MISSION 64 – THE DOOMHERALD

Mark:	Vercingetorix
Cie'th Stone Location:	Oerba – Rust-eaten Bridge
Mark Location:	Yaschas Massif – Paddraean Archaeopolis
Class:	A
Unlock Condition:	Defeat Barthandelus in Oerba and complete Missions 27 and 51
Reward:	Gold Watch
Secondary Reward:	Bomb Core (x10)

- Vercingetorix is probably the toughest enemy in the entire game. You will need a party of very advanced characters who are at (or close to) maximum level for all roles at the Crystarium, and with all abilities unlocked.
- Having fully upgraded weapons and accessories helps tremendously. The sixth ATB slot offered by all ultimate weapons is a welcome bonus. A Genji Glove can increase the damage dealt by Commandos. Damage-reducing equipment such as the Imperial Armlet will also be handy.
- Use Aegisol and Fortisol before the battle begins.
- Vercingetorix follows a distinct attack routine. It begins with a series of powerful assaults that may include Wind Shear (which hits your entire party) and Putrescence (which inflicts damage and dispels two status enhancements).
- Impenetrable Aura comes next and makes Vercingetorix temporarily invincible. Your opponent will regenerate eight times, healing 1% of its lost HP – so the more HP you deplete, the more will be restored. As if this wasn't enough, this ability removes all status ailments from Vercingetorix, grants him status enhancements, and – last but by no means least – empties the Chain Gauge completely.
- Finally, Wicked Whirl, the Mark's ultimate move, deals horrendous damage to your entire party. Immediately Paradigm Shift to Tortoise (three Sentinels) the moment you see it coming.
- Vercingetorix sprouts additional sets of wings once it reaches thresholds of 90%, 60% and 30% HP, growing in strength on each occasion.
- If you are attempting to score a five-star rating on this mission, consider equipping the Gold Watch you receive for defeating Vercingetorix the first time.
- You will need a very specific set of Paradigms in order to even stand a chance in this battle. We suggest using a party consisting of Lightning, Fang and Hope, with the following Deck:

RECOMMENDED PARADIGM DECK

Paradigm	Setup	Notes
Infiltration	SAB + SAB + SAB	Enables you to dispel status enhancements from Vercingetorix quickly, and to inflict essential status ailments: Slow, Deshell, Deprotect, Imperil and Poison. Poison is invaluable given Vercingetorix's colossal HP total, so try to keep it active at all times.
Relentless Assault	COM + RAV + RAV	Used to inflict heavy damage after weakening Vercingetorix with ailments. Quick Stagger weapons might even enable you to Stagger him; if this happens, immediately make use of skills such as Lightning's Army of One to drive up the Chain Bonus.
Diversity	COM + RAV + MED	Switch from Relentless Assault to this whenever you need to heal during your attack phase. This will allow you to keep the Chain going.
Rapid Growth	SYN + SYN + SYN	The quickest way to buff your party whenever status effects have worn off or have been dispelled. Use this immediately after you've healed your characters during Impenetrable Aura.
Salvation	MED + MED + MED	Use this immediately when Vercingetorix performs Impenetrable Aura. As soon as your party is healed, switch to Rapid Growth to refresh your status effects, then to Infiltration to inflict status ailments again, and finally to Relentless Assault to resume your attack.
Tortoise	SEN + SEN + SEN	An absolute necessity to reduce damage incurred whenever Vercingetorix uses Wicked Whirl. Follow it with a bout of healing.

Strategy & Analysis

In this chapter we examine hidden gameplay mechanics and offer useful tips, proven strategies and tried-and-tested tactical concepts. If you are looking to improve your combat prowess, gain indispensable insights into the character development system, or learn how best to approach the Crystarium and Paradigm features, look no further.

Spoiler Warning: Though we have naturally taken steps to avoid references to plot events, this chapter does contain a wide variety of "gameplay spoilers".

CHAINS

Filling the Chain Gauge to Stagger enemies and increasing the Chain Bonus percentage are, naturally, the two key ways to maximize the damage your party inflicts during combat.

Chaining Basics

The Chain Gauge is accompanied by two percentages. The first one is the **Chain Bonus**, which reveals the current damage multiplier applied to all attacks. If the current Chain Bonus is 200%, for example, each attack will inflict double the "standard" damage. Maintaining a sustained assault will enable you to constantly increase this total. However, if the Chain Gauge is emptied, the Chain Bonus is reset to the minimum 100% immediately. The second percentage is the **Stagger Point** – the Chain Bonus percentage that must be reached for an opponent to be Staggered.

All enemies have an attribute called Chain Resistance. The higher this value is, the more slowly the Chain Bonus will grow. Enemies with a high Chain Resistance can be difficult to Stagger – particularly if they also have a very high Stagger Point.

Staggering an enemy can have many effects. Principle among these is an immediate Chain Bonus increase, with damage multiplier growth doubled while the enemy remains Staggered. The Chain Bonus can be built up to a maximum 999% during a Stagger (especially if you keep using Ravagers), though this is a rare occurrence until the later stages of the game. Once a Stagger period ends, the Chain Bonus is reset to 100%.

Chains and Roles

The Ravager, Commando, Saboteur and Sentinel roles all have a unique relationship with the Chain Gauge and Chain Bonus.

- **Ravagers** fill the Chain Gauge and increase the Chain Bonus damage multiplier rapidly. However, they also increase the rate at which the Chain Gauge depletes. They generally have lower damage-dealing potential than Commandos in most battles.
- **Commandos** are (broadly speaking) ineffective at increasing the Chain Gauge or Chain Bonus, but their attacks slow the rate of Chain Gauge depletion. As a rule, they inflict more injury per hit than Ravagers – especially when an opponent has been Staggered.
- **Sentinels** slow the rate of Chain Gauge depletion by successfully provoking opponents or landing counter-attacks. This can be beneficial when they fight alongside Ravagers (especially with the Mystic Tower Paradigm) but isn't something you can rely on.
- **Saboteur** abilities slow the rate of Chain Gauge depletion, but also increase it more than a Commando's attacks. Indeed, they can be used alongside Ravagers as a replacement for Commandos to debilitate an adversary prior to Staggering them. However, there are two drawbacks that you should take into consideration: their spells cause very little damage, and an AI-controlled Saboteur will cease to act once all possible status ailments have been inflicted.

POST-BATTLE RATINGS

Every time a battle ends you obtain a score, which is then translated into a final star rating that ranges from zero to five stars. Your score always begins at a fixed 10,000, and is then adjusted in accordance with how many seconds you are above or below a predetermined Target Time. This is the "par" time for a battle, and will result in the award of three stars.

Your Target Time is determined by your party's attributes (including enhancements conferred by weapons and accessories) and the relative strength of the adversaries they face. A battle-hardened party facing weak opponents will be expected to win in mere seconds; less experienced characters pitted against the same creatures might be allocated several minutes. Your score is further affected by an Initiative Bonus. This is set at 1.0x (no bonus) for most fights, but is increased to 1.2x (+20%) if you secure a preemptive strike.

As the following table reveals, your post-battle rating has an enormous influence on the spoils dropped by enemies. Essentially, better ratings will on aggregate reward you with a greater number of rare drop items, whereas lower ratings increase your chances of receiving Shrouds. Higher ratings also lead to greater TP gauge growth.

RATINGS & EFFECTS

Stars	Score	Rare Item Drop Rate	Shroud Drop Rate
0	≤ 6,999	None	x8
1	7,000-7,999	None	x4
2	8,000-8,999	None	x2
3	9,000-11,999	x1 (Normal)	x1 (Normal)
4	12,000-12,999	x3	x1 (Normal)
5	13,000+	x5	x1 (Normal)

SHROUDS

Shrouds form a special class of consumable items that confer temporary benefits on your party. They must be activated just prior to a confrontation and are unavailable during battle. Their effects last for 30 seconds. The Shroud icon will begin to blink three seconds before the effects expire, so be sure to engage opponents before they dissipate.

Shrouds can be obtained as spoils after battles (with the probability increased if you equip the Survivalist Catalog and obtain low scores), in Treasure Spheres and, later in the game, from the Eden Pharmaceuticals retail network. You can also obtain Shrouds by Dismantling certain pieces of equipment at the weapon upgrade screen.

SHROUD LIST

Name	Effect	Price	Notes
Aegisol	Casts Protect, Shell, Veil and Vigilance prior to battle.	12,000	◆ These two Shrouds activate the specified status enhancements at the start of a battle. Like all buffs, these will expire after a set period of time. ◆ Using these Shrouds enables you to augment your party with key buffs prior to a battle, removing the need to use a Synergist to prepare each character during the opening stages of a fight.
Fortisol	Casts Bravery, Faith and Haste prior to battle.	12,000	
Deceptisol	Makes you invisible to enemy eyes.	30,000	◆ Makes your party difficult to detect, allowing you to avoid difficult encounters or, more importantly, to trigger preemptive strikes. ◆ Deceptisol does not work on certain enemies – particularly bosses.
Ethersol	Restores the party's TP.	-	◆ Fully restores the party's TP, required for using Techniques and summoning Eidolons.

ELEMENTS

All attacks in Final Fantasy XIII are either physical or magical in nature. Both attack types can be imbued with an element from a sub-set of six elemental characteristics. In other words, an attack is either physical or magical, and all physical and magical attacks are either elemental or non-elemental.

ELEMENTS LIST

Icon	Represents
	Fire
	Ice
	Lightning
	Water
	Wind
	Earth
	Physical
	Magic

Each enemy has a set of elemental affinities, which determine the amount of damage they sustain from attacks.

ELEMENTAL AFFINITIES

Description	Damage Modifier
Normal	x1 (standard damage)
Weakness	x2 (200% damage)
Halved	x0.5 (50% damage inflicted)
Resistant	x0.1 (10% damage inflicted)
Immune	x0 (damage Blocked)
Absorb	Attacks heal opponent (30% of the usual damage)

There are many ways to exploit elements in your favor, both to defend yourself from enemy elemental attacks, and to add elemental properties to your assaults against enemies with corresponding weaknesses.

ENHANCING ELEMENTAL DEFENSE

Icon	Accessories	Abilities
	Ember Ring, Blaze Ring, Salamandrine Ring, Flamebane Brooch, Flameshield Earring, Fire Charm, Entite Ring	Barfire
	Frost Ring, Icicle Ring, Boreal Ring, Frostbane Brooch, Frostshield Earring, Ice Charm, Entite Ring	Barfrost
	Spark Ring, Fulmen Ring, Raijin Ring, Sparkbane Brooch, Sparkshield Earring, Lightning Charm, Entite Ring	Barthunder
	Aqua Ring, Riptide Ring, Nereid Ring, Aquabane Brooch, Aquashield Earring, Water Charm, Entite Ring	Barwater
	Zephyr Ring, Gale Ring, Sylphid Ring, Wind Charm, Entite Ring	-
	Clay Ring, Siltstone Ring, Gaian Ring, Earth Charm, Entite Ring	-

ENHANCING ELEMENTAL DAMAGE

Icon	Accessories	Abilities
	Ember Ring, Blaze Ring, Salamandrine Ring, Flamebane Brooch, Flameshield Earring, Fire Charm	Enfire, Imperil (on enemy target), Fire Damage (synthesized ability)
	Frost Ring, Icicle Ring, Boreal Ring, Frostbane Brooch, Frostshield Earring, Ice Charm	Enfrost, Imperil (on enemy target), Ice Damage (synthesized ability)
	Spark Ring, Fulmen Ring, Raijin Ring, Sparkbane Brooch, Sparkshield Earring, Lightning Charm	Enthunder, Imperil (on enemy target), Lightning Damage (synthesized ability)
	Aqua Ring, Riptide Ring, Nereid Ring, Aquabane Brooch, Aquashield Earring, Water Charm	Enwater, Imperil (on enemy target), Water Damage (synthesized ability)
	Zephyr Ring, Gale Ring, Sylphid Ring, Wind Charm	Wind Damage (synthesized ability)
	Clay Ring, Siltstone Ring, Gaian Ring, Earth Charm	Earth Damage (synthesized ability)

STATUS EFFECTS

Status Enhancements

Status enhancements (also called buffs) are beneficial conditions that improve the defensive or offensive prowess of the user – be that a party member or an enemy. They play a decisive role in determining the difficulty, duration and final outcome of many combat encounters, especially in the second half of the adventure.

Status enhancements can be bestowed by a Synergist, by equipping certain accessories, or by using Shrouds prior to a battle. Each buff has a specific purpose, such as increasing the user's physical strength, reducing magic damage, or heightening resistance to particular elemental attacks. Status enhancements can also be used to "cure" an opposing status ailment. There are instances where a capable Synergist will be more efficient at removing an unpleasant mix of debuffs than a Medic armed with the Esuna spell.

As a general rule, it makes sense to leave the control of a party's Synergist to the battle AI. It is faster and more decisive than most players could ever claim to be, and is usually more efficient at identifying less immediately apparent opportunities to strengthen your party (such as protecting against elements favored by opponents). However, as AI Synergists are slaves to invisible flow-charts, there are instances where taking manual control can make a big difference. For example, if you face a dangerous opponent who adopts a strategy of inflicting debuffs before following up with powerful assaults, you could manually select Veil and Vigilance as a priority at the start of a battle – something that an AI Synergist would never do.

Note that certain pieces of equipment can extend the duration of status enhancements. Augment Maintenance and Defense Maintenance are special properties conferred by weapons, while Buff Duration is a synthesized ability gained by using specific accessories.

STATUS ENHANCEMENTS LIST

Icon	Name	Description	Duration	Opposed Ailment
	Bravery	Raises target's Strength by 25%. A simple yet extremely effective way of increasing physical damage inflicted by the Attack, Blitz, and elemental "-strike" moves.		Debrave
	Bravera	Raises target's Strength by 75%. See Bravery.		Debrave
	Faith	Raises target's Magic by 25%, increasing the damage inflicted by Ravager and Saboteur spells, but also the Commando's Ruin and Ruinga attacks.		Defaith
	Faithra	Raises target's Magic by 75%. See Faith.		Defaith
	Haste	Accelerates target's ATB gauge recharge rate by 50%. Probably the best buff of all, as it increases the number of actions your party can perform.		Slow
	Protect	Raises target's physical resistance by 33%. An essential buff that reduces the amount of damage you take from physical attacks.		Deprotect
	Protectra	Raises target's physical resistance by 50%. See Protect.		Deprotect
	Shell	Raises target's magic resistance by 33%, reducing the damage sustained when opponents employ magic attacks.		Deshell
	Shellra	Raises target's magic resistance by 50%. See Shell.		Deshell
	Vigilance	Raises the success rate of the user's actions and defenses. A critical buff for Saboteurs.		Curse
	Veil	Raises target's status ailment resistance.		Imperil
	Enfire	These buffs add an elemental attribute to attacks. Perfect against enemies who suffer from an elemental weakness, and are outstanding in combination with Imperil.		-
	Enfrost			
	Enthunder			
	Enwater			
	Barfire	Raises target's elemental resistance. Very useful when an opponent favors attacks imbued with a specific element.		-
	Barfrost			
	Barthunder			
	Barwater			

Status Ailments

Status ailments (also called debuffs) are debilitating conditions that can afflict both your party and enemies. They become increasingly important as the game progresses, with opponents using them to weaken your party more regularly in later chapters. Some adversaries are extremely difficult to beat unless you weaken them with debuffs throughout the battle.

Status ailments can only be cast by Saboteurs. This means that you will often need to have Fang or Vanille in your main party, and that you should prepare at least one reliable Paradigm featuring a Saboteur. A staple example is Evened Odds (SAB + SYN + MED).

As more powerful enemies may resist the majority of conditions, using Libra or Librascope to quickly determine their vulnerabilities can be vital. What could be a long, protracted battle might become a formality the moment you hamper your opponent with the right debuff. Note that most status ailments have a duration that depends on the target type.

When your party is assailed by status ailments, you will need to quickly assess how dangerous they are. The "Status Ailments List" table reveals all possible remedies and protections against each ailment. The Medic's Esuna ability is the most obvious solution, but – once again – it's important to note that a Synergist can be more efficient in cancelling multiple afflictions. Consumable items are just as effective in removing ailments, though you will obviously need to purchase stocks of these beforehand. You can also remove debuffs by summoning an Eidolon or using the Dispelga Technique – and this cannot be prevented by Fog.

It's usually better to leave the casting of status ailments to an AI Saboteur – though, naturally, there may be instances where you could profit by taking manual control to inflict a very particular debuff. The most notable example is attempting to fell a powerful foe with Vanille's exclusive Death ability.

Status Ailments List

Icon	Name	Description	Remedy	Protection: Equipment	Protection: Abilities
	Debrave	Reduces target's physical power. A real nuisance when inflicted on party members with high Strength.	Bravery, Bravera, Esuna, Summon, Dispelga	Giant's Glove, Warlord's Glove, Tetradic Crown, Tetradic Tiara, Goddess's Favor, Ribbon, Super Ribbon	Veil, Debrave Duration (synthesized ability)
	Pain	Disables target's physical abilities. From a tactical perspective, very dangerous if inflicted at the same time as Fog.	Painkiller, Esuna, Summon, Dispelga	Pain Dampener, Pain Deflector, Tetradic Crown, Tetradic Tiara, Goddess's Favor, Ribbon, Super Ribbon	Veil, Pain Duration (synthesized ability)
	Defaith	Reduces target's magic power. A real nuisance when inflicted on party members with high Magic.	Faith, Faithra, Esuna, Summon, Dispelga	Glass Buckle, Tektite Buckle, Tetradic Crown, Tetradic Tiara, Goddess's Favor, Ribbon, Super Ribbon	Veil, Defaith Duration (synthesized ability)
	Fog	Disables target's spellcasting abilities. From a tactical perspective, very dangerous if inflicted at the same time as Pain.	Mallet, Esuna, Summon, Dispelga	White Cape, Effulgent Cape, Tetradic Crown, Tetradic Tiara, Goddess's Favor, Ribbon, Super Ribbon	Veil, Fog Duration (synthesized ability)
	Slow	Reduces target's ATB gauge recharge rate. Can be employed against the majority of enemies encountered – and a must against susceptible bosses and Marks.	Haste, Esuna, Summon, Dispelga	Glass Orb, Dragonfly Orb, Tetradic Crown, Tetradic Tiara, Goddess's Favor, Ribbon, Super Ribbon	Veil, Slow Duration (synthesized ability)
	Daze	Stuns target. A Dazed victim is paralyzed until the condition is removed; a subsequent attack will awaken them instantly. Could be used to halt an enemy prior to switching to a Paradigm dedicated solely to healing and buffs.	Foul Liquid, Esuna, Summon, Dispelga	Rainbow Anklet, Moonbow Anklet, Tetradic Crown, Tetradic Tiara, Goddess's Favor, Ribbon, Super Ribbon	Veil, Daze Duration (synthesized ability)
	Deprotect	Reduces target's resistance to physical attacks.	Protect, Protectra, Esuna, Summon, Dispelga	Metal Armband, Ceramic Armband, Tetradic Crown, Tetradic Tiara, Goddess's Favor, Ribbon, Super Ribbon	Veil, Deprotect Duration (synthesized ability)
	Deshell	Reduces target's resistance to magic attacks.	Shell, Shellra, Esuna, Summon, Dispelga	Serenity Sachet, Safeguard Sachet, Tetradic Crown, Tetradic Tiara, Goddess's Favor, Ribbon, Super Ribbon	Veil, Deshell Duration (synthesized ability)
	Curse	Renders target's actions more likely to fail. Very useful against enemies that cast status ailments.	Holy Water, Vigilance, Esuna, Summon, Dispelga	Warding Talisman, Hexbane Talisman, Tetradic Crown, Tetradic Tiara, Goddess's Favor, Ribbon, Super Ribbon	Veil, Curse Duration (synthesized ability)
	Poison	Causes target to gradually lose HP. Extremely effective on foes with very high HP, but not a big threat to party members.	Antidote, Esuna, Summon, Dispelga	Star Pendant, Starfall Pendant, Tetradic Crown, Tetradic Tiara, Goddess's Favor, Ribbon, Super Ribbon	Veil, Poison Duration (synthesized ability)
	Dispel	Removes target's most recent status enhancement and deals magic damage.	-	-	-
	Imperil	Reduces target's elemental resistances. One of the most useful ailments in the later game stages.	Veil, Wax, Esuna, Summon, Dispelga	Pearl Necklace, Gemstone Necklace, Tetradic Crown, Tetradic Tiara, Goddess's Favor, Ribbon, Super Ribbon	Veil, Imperil Duration (synthesized ability)
	Death	Causes magic damage, but also has a low probability of slaying a target immediately. Many opponents have immunity to the instant-kill effect, but some of the toughest creatures (including Marks) can be defeated this way.	-	Cherub's Crown, Seraph's Crown, Tetradic Crown, Tetradic Tiara, Goddess's Favor, Ribbon, Super Ribbon	Veil

USEFUL EQUIPMENT

Certain accessories can make power-leveling or grinding for valuable spoils far more effective. Note that certain pieces of equipment mentioned here only become available after you complete the main storyline.

- **Survivalist Catalog:** These increase the odds of obtaining Shroud drops. See page 141 for more information on farming for Shrouds.
- **Collector Catalog:** Increases the odds of obtaining an enemy's "normal" drop item. Very useful for acquiring common components.
- **Connoisseur Catalog:** Increases the probability that you will obtain rare drops. Extremely effective if you intend to battle specific enemies for high-value components.
- **Growth Egg:** Doubles CP rewards.
- **Sprint Shoes & Aurora Scarf:** Enable you to attack enemies immediately. Very handy when you are slaughtering weak enemies to farm CP quickly. All pieces of equipment in the "Boost" Synthesis Group will increase the speed at which ATB gauges fill. Turn to page 194 for more details on synthesized abilities.
- **Gold Watch:** Increases the Target Times for all battles, making it easier to obtain high post-battle ratings.

LEVELING SPOTS AND TIPS

Note: This section will only be of use to players who have reached Chapter 11 in the main story. If you are still at an earlier stage in the adventure, we advise you to return later to avoid potential gameplay spoilers.

For those who want to develop their party at an accelerated rate, Final Fantasy XIII has numerous locations where players can farm for CP, components and objects that can be sold for a high Gil return.

Leveling Spot #1: Yaschas Massif – Tsumitran Basin

Spot details:

- You can farm CP by focusing on Behemoth Kings fighting alongside Triffids.
- Can be attempted from Chapter 11 onwards – a good leveling spot for weaker parties.

Tactics:

- The Behemoth King is a powerful enemy when first encountered, but can be killed by a low-strength party if you secure a preemptive strike. The important thing is to use the Commando's Launch ability to prevent it from making its HP-replenishing transformation.
- There are two Behemoth Kings in the Tsumitran Basin that fight alongside Triffids that spring up from flowers as you approach. If you run straight into a Triffid as it emerges, you will automatically begin the fight with a preemptive strike.
- As you arrive from the Tsubaddran Highlands, one Behemoth King is very easy to surprise: you just have to run directly for the closest Triffid.
- The approach for the other Behemoth is rather tricky: there is a knack to moving around the first flower to reach the closest Triffid. This may take a little practice.
- If you fail to gain a preemptive strike, simply select Retry.
- You will receive more than 5,000 CP for each fight, and you can respawn all enemies by returning to the zone entrance.

Leveling Spot #2: The Archylte Steppe – Northern Highplain

Spot details:

- You can farm CP by fighting the Behemoth King and Megistotherian locked in combat close to the path leading to Mah'habara.
- Can be attempted from Chapter 11 onwards, though the battle takes less time if you return here later.

Tactics:
- Start this three-way battle with a preemptive strike.
- Stagger and Launch the Behemoth King, then "juggle" it until it expires. Do not allow the creature to land.
- Once the Behemoth King has been defeated, kill the weaker Megistotherian.
- Walk a few steps past the nearby Save Station to respawn both enemies.
- With Sprint Shoes and Aurora Scarf equipped, you could farm hundreds of thousands of CP per hour in this way.

Leveling Spot #3: Eden – Leviathan Plaza

Spot details:
- The Adamantoise offers some of the best rewards in the entire game: 40,000 CP, a Platinum Ingot as its normal drop (sell price 150,000 Gil), and a Trapezohedron as its rare drop. The latter component has a resale price of only 10,000 Gil, but is essential to create "ultimate" weapons and costs a massive 2,000,000 Gil to buy.
- A good leveling trick after completing the main storyline.

Tactics:
- Use Vanille as a Saboteur, with the Death ability available (stage 9 on the Crystarium). Equip her Malboro Wand for Improved Debuffing II. Any four accessories of the "Boost" Synthesis Group (including Sprint Shoes) are especially recommended for Auto-Haste and ATB +20%. Also make sure you have at least three TP.
- Your other two characters should be equipped with defensive accessories only (damage resistance and HP boosts). One should be a Sentinel (Snow is best at it) and the other a Medic (Hope ideally), forming the Attrition Paradigm.
- Summon Hecatoncheir at the beginning of the fight: Eidolons instantly disable the Oretoise's legs. Switch to Gestalt Mode and send Hecatoncheir back with Ⓐ/Ⓨ.
- Now cast Death repeatedly until the Adamantoise falls. The success rate is very low of course, so you will need both luck and patience. Potentially, though, a few minutes of effort could gain you some of the best possible rewards in the entire game. Note that it can help to cast Vigilance on Vanille.

Other Leveling Spots

The Walkthrough chapter contains many "Power Tips" that suggest lucrative power-leveling opportunities. The following table provides page links to locations that you may wish to visit during Chapter 13, or after completing the main storyline.

Map	Zone	Page	Notes
Mah'habara	Maw of the Abyss	85	◆ Great spot for effortless power-leveling – you will only need to look at the screen to move between battles. ◆ Expect to accrue over 20,000 CP every five minutes.
Mah'habara	An Asylum from Light	126	◆ A great location to obtain CP and valuable components. ◆ The six Cryohedrons surrender 7,140 CP when destroyed, and have the valuable Bomb Core component as their rare drop item.
Taejin's Tower	Fifth Tier	93	◆ Provides 8,000 CP per battle against Pulsework Centurions that can be defeated within 40 seconds with a preemptive strike.
Eden	Siren Park	103	◆ Features lots of easy three-way battles.
Eden	Edenhall	105	◆ The Sacrifice and Sanctum Inquisitrix enemies drop components with a high resale value.
Orphan's Cradle	The Tesseracts	113	◆ One of the best power-leveling spots in the entire game. ◆ The Wladislaus enemy surrenders 32,000 CP per battle, and is easy to defeat if you use a Saboteur-led strategy. ◆ You cannot return to this location during post-credits play.
The Fault-warrens	Various	125	◆ A strong party can gain a fantastic return of approximately 100,000 CP every 20 minutes by following a specific route through the Faultwarrens.

Gil Components

In addition to "premium" components that are designed purely to be sold, there are several standard components with a Gil value that far eclipses EXP or multiplier increases they may offer during weapon or accessory upgrades. Acquiring these can be a great way to generate funds for purchases.

Standard Components to Sell

Name	EXP Value	Multiplier Value*	Sale Price (Gil)
Gloomstalk	32	+46	1,000
Sunpetal	102	+21	1,000
Moonblossom Seed	73	+55	6,000
Starblossom Seed	230	+91	13,000
Succulent Fruit	10	+55	1,750
Malodorous Fruit	7	+21	4,000
Green Needle	60	+100	3,500
Perfume	180	+120	12,500

Shrouds and Rare Drops

As we discuss on page 140, your post-battle rating determines which spoils you are likely to receive once combat ends. A five-star result will multiply the base probability of obtaining a rare drop by five, while a no-star rating will make it eight times more likely that you will receive a Shroud. So: in addition to useful accessories, taking steps to cut short or artificially extend the Battle Duration can be extremely profitable.

COMMANDO: ROLE ANALYSIS

Overview

This offensive role makes use of physical attacks and non-elemental magic spells to deal massive damage.

Successful attacks by Commandos also cause enemy Chain Gauges to drain less rapidly when building towards a Stagger. This feature makes Commandos especially effective in combination with Ravagers.

Commandos cannot charge Chain Bonuses by themselves, however, as their attacks have little impact on the Chain Gauge. Instead, Commandos have access to various passive abilities that greatly enhance their combat performance.

A Commando who obtains a Role Level crystal through their Crystarium development will be awarded the bonus of Augmented Attacks. This causes physical and magical assaults to deal extra damage, with allies sharing a smaller bonus, as shown in the following table. The bonus increases with each Role Level crystal.

COMMANDO ROLE BONUS

Role Level	Damage Boost (Self)	Damage Boost (Allies)
1	x2.0	x1.05
2	x2.1	x1.05
3	x2.2	x1.10
4	x2.3	x1.10
Max	x2.5	x1.15

AI Behavior

AI Commandos select their own targets. If there is more than one Commando in the party, each will pick a different target when a choice exists.

An AI Commando will always opt to perform the attack that deals the maximum amount of damage, depending on the target's stats. They will use Attack and Blitz if the target is weak against physical attacks or strong against magic attacks; and they will switch to Ruin and Ruinga if the target is strong against physical attacks or weak against magic attacks.

RAVAGER: ROLE ANALYSIS

Overview

Ravagers excel at raising enemy Chain Bonuses, thereby increasing the damage done with each subsequent blow and leading the party to quicker Staggers. To achieve this, Ravagers have access to a wide variety of elemental magic and physical attacks.

The sudden hike in an enemy's Chain Bonus will drain away quickly after a Ravager's spell. This is why teaming Ravagers with Commandos works so well, as Commandos will prevent the Chain Bonus from slipping away while the Ravagers build it higher.

The Ravagers' armory of elemental attacks enables them to exploit the weaknesses of foes, which can be especially effective after lowering your enemy's elemental resistances with the help of a Saboteur. Indeed, a Saboteur can sometimes effectively replace a Commando and combine with Ravagers to "fix" those bonuses in place on your opponents' Chain Gauges.

When a Ravager advances sufficiently through the Crystarium to buy a Role Level crystal, they receive the bonus of Improved Chaining. This causes physical and magic attacks alike to impact on the Chain Bonus more significantly, with allies sharing a partial bonus, as shown in the following table.

RAVAGER ROLE BONUS

Role Level	Chain Boost (Self)	Chain Boost (Allies)
1	+1.0%	+0.1%
2	+1.5%	+0.1%
3	+2.0%	+0.2%
4	+2.5%	+0.2%
Max	+3.0%	+0.3%

AI Behavior

Unless they are the only attacker in the party, Ravagers will try to follow someone else's lead and so maximize the Chaining potential on a single target.

In choosing their attacks, Ravagers assess the target's strengths and weaknesses to determine the highest possible Chain Bonus within their ability. If your Datalog's Enemy Intel or a Libra scan happens to reveal that an opponent can nullify or absorb all elemental abilities, Ravagers won't waste attacks on targeting those enemies. When the enemy's details are unknown, the Ravager will unleash a variety of attacks to test for weaknesses and resistances.

SENTINEL: ROLE ANALYSIS

Overview

Sentinels act as "tanks", drawing the attention of enemies on themselves with Provoke. This ability has a tremendous additional benefit as it extends the duration of Staggers, allowing allies to inflict more damage during the process.

Keep in mind that when you switch your Sentinel to another role, the Provoke effect immediately wears off, freeing enemies to attack your other party members again.

Sentinels have access to numerous defensive skills that generally boost their (already high) resistance to damage. They are best placed in Paradigms that include Medics, Synergists and Saboteurs, as characters playing these roles tend to have lower HP and defense than more directly combative party members.

When a Sentinel advances sufficiently through the Crystarium to buy a Role Level crystal, they will be awarded the bonus of Damage Reduction. This increases their resistance to both physical and magic damage, with a partial bonus extended to allies, as shown in the following table.

SENTINEL ROLE BONUS

Role Level	Final Damage (Self)	Final Damage (Allies)
1	x0.65	x0.92
2	x0.63	x0.92
3	x0.60	x0.89
4	x0.56	x0.89
Max	x0.50	x0.86

AI Behavior

An AI Sentinel always starts by Provoking enemies. The Provoke ability is used against groups and has a 45% base chance of succeeding, while the stronger Challenge ability works against a single enemy, with a 99% base chance.

If the Sentinel has high HP, they will then perform guard abilities with a counter-attack effect (like Vendetta or Entrench). When the Sentinel has low HP, they will favor the use of a guard ability that greatly boosts defense (Steelguard) or that gradually regenerates HP while defending (Mediguard).

Sentinels repeat this cycle by keeping their enemies in a Provoked state.

MEDIC: ROLE ANALYSIS

Overview

A Medic focuses on healing duties, which naturally include restoring the HP of party members, reviving fallen allies, and removing status ailments.

Knowing that your party will be fully healed and cured after each battle, you will find yourself making frequent judgment calls on your chances of survival. Even in a critical predicament, you might want to keep attacking if you believe you're about to finish off your enemy and steal a victory. In all other cases – whether one of your essential characters is badly hurt, or you are hampered by status ailments – the Medic is your life-saver.

Take note that Medics cannot perform any actions at all once they are done with their healing tasks. In such situations, it's usually better to switch to a different role.

When a Medic advances sufficiently through the Crystarium to buy a Role Level crystal with their CP, they will be awarded the role-specific bonus of Augmented Healing. This increases the effectiveness of both healing abilities and items, with allies sharing a reduced bonus, as shown in the following table.

MEDIC ROLE BONUS

Role Level	Healing Eff.* (Self)	Healing Eff.* (Allies)
1	x1.20	x1.03
2	x1.23	x1.03
3	x1.26	x1.06
4	x1.29	x1.06
Max	x1.32	x1.10

* Healing Efficiency

Note: Bonus also applies to Sentinel's Mediguard.

AI Behavior

The most important tasks of an AI Medic are, in order of priority:

1. Heal characters with a red or yellow HP bar (prioritizing the party leader and Sentinels).
2. Raise KO'd party members.
3. Cure status ailments with Esuna.
4. Heal party members if their HP is not full.

If none of these actions are required, the Medic will do nothing at all. Note that Medics will always heal with the most efficient healing spell with regards to the amount of HP that needs to be restored.

SYNERGIST: ROLE ANALYSIS

Overview

The Synergist role empowers your characters with magic that improves the party's effectiveness. Status enhancements include increased damage, defense, speed and resistance to elements and status ailments. They can also imbue attacks with an elemental power.

These spells, also called buffs, enable your party to punch above its weight. They take time to apply and so they are sensibly reserved for a showdown with powerful enemies and bosses. In such instances, it's generally best to use Synergists at the start of the battle so that you can make the most of your enhancements. When you feel your party has been sufficiently buffed, switch to another Paradigm until your enhancements run out.

The Synergist is not required continuously throughout battle, but it's a role to enlist in bursts every time you need a temporary boost to your performance.

When a Synergist develops sufficiently to buy a Role Level crystal in the Crystarium, they will be awarded the bonus of Extended Enhancements. This increases the duration of all status enhancements cast by the character, with allies (including Saboteur's debuffs and Sentinel's Provoke) sharing a lesser bonus, as shown in the following table.

SYNERGIST ROLE BONUS

Role Level	Duration (Self)	Duration (Allies)
1	x1.20	x1.05
2	x1.35	x1.05
3	x1.50	x1.10
4	x1.65	x1.10
Max	x1.80	x1.15

AI Behavior

Synergists make their decisions based on information that has been obtained from the Datalog's Enemy Intel or scanned with Libra. Their tendency is to strengthen allies when facing only a few enemies, and to use defensive abilities when at least four enemies are in battle. The type of buff is also prioritized by the needs of the role, such that Ravagers get Faith before Bravery, and so on.

If the Synergist is strengthening allies, the following priority order of roles is applied: Commando, Ravager, Saboteur, Sentinel, Synergist, Medic.

If the Synergist is using defensive abilities on allies, the following priority order is applied: Sentinel, Commando, Ravager, Medic, Synergist, Saboteur.

If there are several characters with the same role, the Synergist will target the party leader and then the member closest to the party leader.

SABOTEUR: ROLE ANALYSIS

Overview

While Synergists cast status enhancements on your party to strengthen it, Saboteurs work to weaken your opponents by inflicting status ailments on them. Saboteurs also have access to Dispel, which cancels the last status enhancement of the target. Cancelling enemy status enhancements can also be done by casting the opposite status ailment on the enemy. For example, casting Deprotect (which lowers the enemy's defense) will negate their Protect status.

It is always worth casting Libra on new enemies to find out the status ailments to which they may be immune, as this will also improve the effectiveness of AI-controlled Saboteurs.

Saboteurs, like Synergists, are best used during the start of a tough battle that you believe will pose a challenge. Even though Saboteurs inflict damage with their spells, this cannot compare to the damage Commandos or Ravagers dish out in seconds. After inflicting sufficient status ailments on your opponent, switch your Saboteur to a more offensive role.

A Saboteur who advances through the Crystarium and buys a Role Level crystal will be awarded the bonus of Boosted Success Rates. This makes abilities more likely to succeed on enemies, with allies (including Sentinel's Provoke) sharing a similar but reduced bonus, as shown in the following table.

SABOTEUR ROLE BONUS

Role Level	Effect (Self)	Effect (Allies)
1	x1.20	x1.04
2	x1.24	x1.04
3	x1.28	x1.08
4	x1.33	x1.08
Max	x1.40	x1.12

AI Behavior

An AI Saboteur will always make use of Enemy Intel to weaken opponents by exploiting any vulnerabilities or eliminating advantages. If the Enemy Intel reveals that the enemy has high defense, for example, then the Saboteur will try to lower that defense with Deprotect and Deshell. If an enemy turns out to be immune to certain ailments, the Saboteur will not waste time casting the corresponding spells.

As a rule, if there are few enemies around, a Saboteur will use direct weakening abilities; if there are many enemies around, a Saboteur will use hampering abilities such as Pain and Fog.

CHARTS OF ALL PARADIGMS

2-ALLY PARADIGMS

Name	Composition
Double Trouble	COM + COM
Slash & Burn	COM + RAV
Misdirection	COM + SEN
Divide & Conquer	COM + SAB
Supersoldier	COM + SYN
War & Peace	COM + MED
Dualcasting	RAV + RAV
Arcane Defense	RAV + SEN
Undermine	RAV + SAB
Archmage	RAV + SYN
Yin & Yang	RAV + MED
Twin Shields	SEN + SEN
Stumbling Block	SEN + SAB
Building Block	SEN + SYN
Lifeguard	SEN + MED
Havoc	SAB + SAB
Tide Turner	SAB + SYN
Sap & Salve	SAB + MED
Rally	SYN + SYN
Symbiosis	SYN + MED
Double Dose	MED + MED

3-ALLY PARADIGMS

Name	Composition
Cerberus	COM + COM + COM
Aggression	COM + COM + RAV
Offensive Screen	COM + COM + SEN
Devastation	COM + COM + SAB
Strike Team	COM + COM + SYN
Tireless Charge	COM + COM + MED
Relentless Assault	COM + RAV + RAV
Delta Attack	COM + RAV + SEN
Ruthless	COM + RAV + SAB
Decimation	COM + RAV + SYN
Diversity	COM + RAV + MED
Guarded Assault	COM + SEN + SEN
Dirty Fighting	COM + SEN + SAB
Strategic Warfare	COM + SEN + SYN
Solidarity	COM + SEN + MED
Exploitation	COM + SAB + SAB
Bully	COM + SAB + SYN
Scouting Party	COM + SAB + MED
All for One	COM + SYN + SYN
Hero's Charge	COM + SYN + MED
Discretion	COM + MED + MED
Tri-disaster	RAV + RAV + RAV
Mystic Tower	RAV + RAV + SEN
Smart Bomb	RAV + RAV + SAB
Malevolence	RAV + RAV + SYN
Thaumaturgy	RAV + RAV + MED
Patient Probing	RAV + SEN + SEN
Matador	RAV + SEN + SAB
Riot Shield	RAV + SEN + SYN
Entourage	RAV + SEN + MED
Assassination	RAV + SAB + SAB
Guerilla	RAV + SAB + SYN
Variety	RAV + SAB + MED
Supernatural	RAV + SYN + SYN
Coordination	RAV + SYN + MED
Perpetual Magic	RAV + MED + MED
Tortoise	SEN + SEN + SEN
Overcaution	SEN + SEN + SAB
Conservation	SEN + SEN + SYN
Consolidation	SEN + SEN + MED
Countermeasure	SEN + SAB + SAB
Premeditation	SEN + SAB + SYN
Attrition	SEN + SAB + MED
Prudent Planning	SEN + SYN + SYN
Protection	SEN + SYN + MED
Combat Clinic	SEN + MED + MED
Infiltration	SAB + SAB + SAB
Espionage	SAB + SAB + SYN
Safe Subversion	SAB + SAB + MED
Superiority	SAB + SYN + SYN
Evened Odds	SAB + SYN + MED
Perseverance	SAB + MED + MED
Rapid Growth	SYN + SYN + SYN
Recuperation	SYN + SYN + MED
Convalescence	SYN + MED + MED
Salvation	MED + MED + MED

NOTABLE PARADIGMS

All suggested Paradigms in this section are based on the assumption that you will be using a party with access to all six roles, and that you will only be using your characters' primary roles. If you have already started exploring their secondary roles in the Crystarium during post-credits play, then you may consider using even more specialized configurations, such as Tortoise (SEN + SEN + SEN), Salvation (MED + MED + MED), Rapid Growth (**SYN** + **SYN** + **SYN**), and Infiltration (SAB + SAB + SAB). These are mostly useful when completing the toughest Mark missions in the game, though, and you will find all the advice required in the dedicated sections of this guide.

Offensive Paradigms

RELENTLESS ASSAULT **(COM, RAV, RAV)**: One of the most effective offensive Paradigms. The two Ravagers pummel the target to build Chain Bonuses while the Commando inflicts serious damage, contributing to the Bonus and preventing its decay. Once the enemy is Staggered, the Commando can immediately Launch it into the air while receiving magical support from the two Ravagers to keep the enemy soaring.

OFFENSIVE SCREEN **(COM, COM,** SEN**)**: This Paradigm is best used after Staggering a single enemy, the Sentinel offering extra Staggering time to the two Commandos. It can also be useful against a Staggered target that cannot be Launched.

AGGRESSION **(COM, COM, RAV)**: This Paradigm adds an extra Commando in place of a Ravager to Relentless Assault and is excellent for dealing high damage to a single target.

TRI-DISASTER **(RAV, RAV, RAV)**: This is the fastest way to send a Chain Bonus skyrocketing. It relies on each Ravager keeping the Chain going all the way to a Stagger without letting it drop, such that you will need to make deft use of their ATB gauge in issuing prompt attacks. It works best against single targets with a magical weakness, but fails terribly against groups of enemies who can interrupt the party's attack queues.

TIRELESS CHARGE **(COM, COM,** MED**)**: This Paradigm combines the sheer power of two Commandos with a Medic, healing them as they work their brutal craft. This is best used after Staggering a major enemy who cannot be Launched and will therefore keep attacking.

Defensive Paradigms

PROTECTION (SEN, **SYN**, MED): This Paradigm combines the three forces of defense with capabilities of healing, powering up your party with status enhancements and the deflective strength of a Sentinel. A secure retreat that's best used when you need to heal and refresh buffs simultaneously.

COMBAT CLINIC (SEN, MED, MED): A rapid recovery program, Combat Clinic effectively allows you to heal your party with two Medics while the Sentinel keeps the enemy off their backs. This emergency Paradigm is the smart way to crawl back from the brink after your entire party has been struck by a devastating attack.

CONVALESCENCE (**SYN**, MED, MED): The crisis variant of Protection, with an additional Medic replacing the Sentinel. A problem that may arise is when either the Medics or the Synergist are done sooner than the others, leaving them with nothing left to do. In such cases it's best to switch to a Paradigm that can finish the job while putting the other characters to good use in a different role.

CONSOLIDATION (SEN, SEN, MED): A situational Paradigm, only efficient when you need to dig in against enemies who can wipe out your party in mere seconds. Two Sentinels offer supreme defense, whilst the inclusion of a Medic allows you to heal wounds instantly and remove debilitating ailments until you're ready to fight again.

All-Round Paradigms

SOLIDARITY **(COM, SEN, MED)**: This Paradigm combines defense and offense in an interesting way. The Sentinel draws the attention of enemies and guards against their attacks. The Medic keeps your Sentinel in play, while your Commando has a free hand to damage the enemy, if only to keep a Chain Bonus active. This is an especially useful Paradigm if you need to heal during the chaining of a powerful enemy with a high Chain resistance.

MYSTIC TOWER **(RAV, RAV, SEN)**: This configuration allows you to build up Chain Bonuses with rapidity while enemies focus on your Sentinel. Switch quickly to an offensive Paradigm as soon as your target is Staggered.

DELTA ATTACK **(COM, RAV, SEN)**: An excellent all-round Paradigm, Delta Attack combines the best of offense and defense to build and maintain Chain Bonuses. The Sentinel functions as a damage sponge, freeing your other two characters to Stagger an opponent.

DIVERSITY **(COM, RAV, MED)**: Similar to Delta Attack, but with the Sentinel replaced by a Medic. In fact, switching from Delta Attack to Diversity is a great way to build Chain Bonuses when facing very resilient foes. To be most effective, this Paradigm demands a Medic with a high Role Level and Magic attribute to stay ahead of any injuries being sustained.

Buff/Debuff Paradigms

GUERILLA **(RAV, SYN, SAB)**: This Paradigm is best used at the start of battles and, as such, is best set as your active Paradigm. It allows you to quickly enhance your party, weaken the enemies, and start building Chains. When the desired status enhancements and ailments are in place, switch over to a more offensive damage-dealing Paradigm.

MATADOR **(RAV, SEN, SAB)**: This setup combines defense, Chain building (the Saboteur takes the Commando role here, preventing Chain Gauges from depleting too quickly), and the long-term advantage of inflicting debuffs on enemies. Switch back and forth to Protection whenever you need healing and your Sentinel will remain constantly active, making you very hard to beat. As soon as your enemies are weakened by the ailments, switch to something more belligerent and go in all guns blazing.

STRATEGIC WARFARE **(COM, SEN, SYN)**: The Commando takes care of maintaining the Chain Bonus while the Sentinel acts as a damage soak. The Synergist greatly improves your party's odds of winning by casting status enhancements on your characters, but loses usefulness when this has been achieved. Once buffed, it is better to switch the Synergist to another role.

ESPIONAGE **(SYN, SAB, SAB)**: While your allies gladly welcome their buffs, enemies don't take kindly to being debuffed and have a resistance to such magic. That's why Saboteurs will often cast the same spell several times in a row, in the hope that at least one of the ailments will "stick". Employing two Saboteurs greatly improves the odds of quickly inflicting all possible status ailments on your foe. Best used at the start of a long, hard battle, or when the ailments have worn out.

SAFE SUBVERSION **(SAB, SAB, MED)**: A mid-battle Paradigm, Safe Subversion should guarantee the survival of your party during the short period that your two Saboteurs inflict status ailments on your enemy.

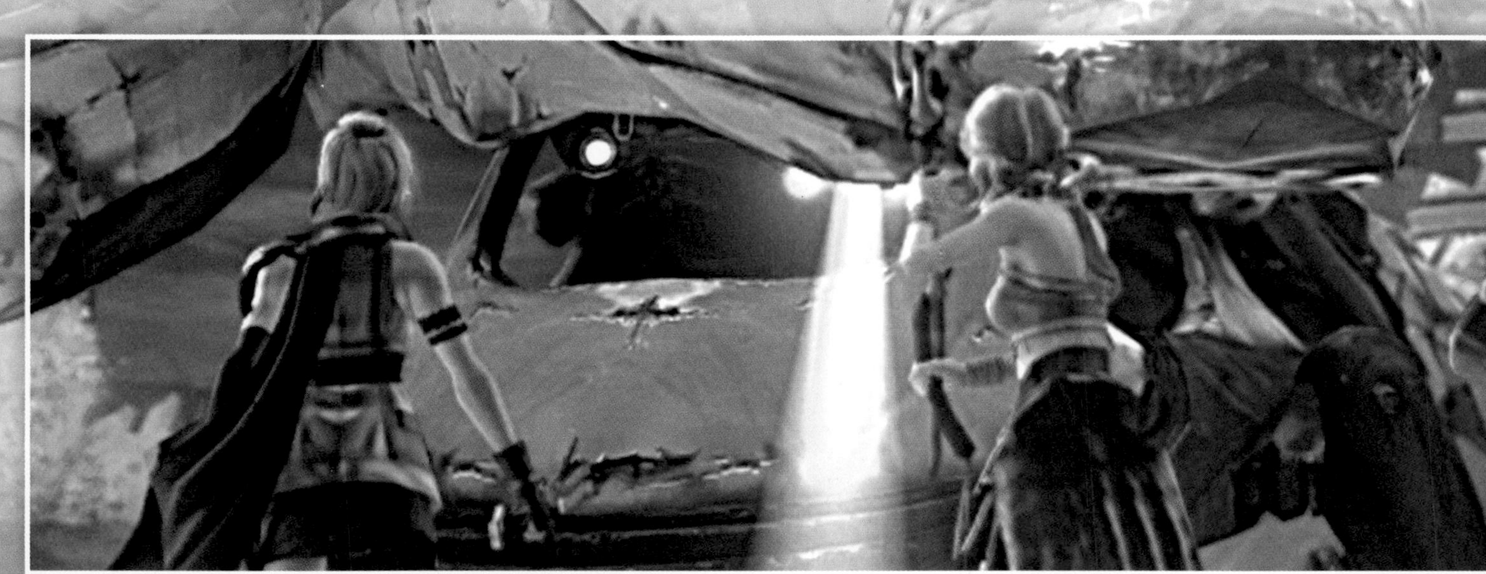

PARADIGM DECKS

The following Paradigm Decks are mere suggestions. There is no perfect combination as you always need to adapt to your current enemies, but these are meant to help you learn how to build a balanced configuration by taking into account the primary roles of your party members.

Lightning, Fang, Hope

Paradigm	Lightning	Fang	Hope
Relentless Assault	Ravager	Commando	Ravager
Delta Attack	Commando	Sentinel	Ravager
Combat Clinic	Medic	Sentinel	Medic
Solidarity	Commando	Sentinel	Medic
Mystic Tower	Ravager	Sentinel	Ravager
Evened Odds	Medic	Saboteur	Synergist

- You can safely start most battles with Delta Attack, a balanced formation, to assess the enemy's potential.
- If things go awry, switch to Solidarity to heal. Your Sentinel will keep protecting the team in the process (with Provoke still active), making this a very safe move. In addition, your Commando will maintain any Chain already established.
- Relentless Assault allows you to build Chains with considerable speed, and then to inflict solid damage on Staggered enemies.
- In case of emergency, Combat Clinic offers the chance to heal rapidly while still being protected by the Sentinel. As one Medic is most likely to be player-controlled, you may decide your own healing priorities without waiting for the AI.
- Mystic Tower enables you to speed up the process of building Chains while still benefitting from the defense of a Sentinel. It's more likely to succeed when the Chain Gauge is already partly filled.
- Evened Odds includes a Saboteur alongside your Synergist, both being healed by a Medic if necessary. A very useful combination in preparing yourself for a tough and lengthy battle.

Fang, Hope, Snow

Paradigm	Fang	Hope	Snow
Relentless Assault	Commando	Ravager	Ravager
Delta Attack	Commando	Ravager	Sentinel
Solidarity	Commando	Medic	Sentinel
Premeditation	Saboteur	Synergist	Sentinel
Guerilla	Saboteur	Synergist	Ravager
Consolidation	Sentinel	Medic	Sentinel

- A true staple of aggressive play, Relentless Assault not only builds quick, secure Chains but also deals solid mixed damage against Staggered enemies.
- Move to Delta Attack when you find yourself facing large groups, or if you need to shield your main attackers against enemies who boast particularly powerful attacks. Note that switching over to Delta Attack will only require Snow to change roles here.
- Solidarity calls a Medic to your team whenever things get rough, and when you require some healing, while the Commando keeps the ball rolling.
- Premeditation offers the defense of a Sentinel, while the other two characters simultaneously cast buffs on the party and debuffs on the enemy, making it highly useful for tougher battles.
- Guerilla can be used for speeding up regular, semi-hard battles. The Ravager can start building Chains between the Saboteur's casting of status ailments while the Synergist lays down a foundation of the most useful spells, such as Haste.
- Consolidation is this team's ultimate defensive Paradigm, combining two Sentinels with a Medic to effectively block enemy attacks while healing takes place.

Sazh, Snow, Vanille

Paradigm	Sazh	Snow	Vanille
Relentless Assault	Ravager	Commando	Ravager
Delta Attack	Commando	Sentinel	Ravager
Solidarity	Commando	Sentinel	Medic
Protection	Synergist	Sentinel	Medic
Premeditation	Synergist	Sentinel	Saboteur
Mystic Tower	Ravager	Sentinel	Ravager

- Again, Delta Attack is a very balanced Paradigm to start most battles. The Sentinel Provokes enemies while the others pound away.
- Solidarity is a single-role switch from Delta Attack to a team with a Medic for some quick curing.
- Protection is this team's entirely defensive Paradigm. The Synergist will effectively buff your party in preparation for tougher battles.

- Relentless Assault is the most aggressive stance, first building up Chains and then dealing mixed damage against Staggered enemies.

- Premeditation is a very defensive Paradigm, with both a Sentinel and a Synergist helping out, but it also weakens enemies via the Saboteur and makes subsequent use of offensive Paradigms more likely to succeed.

- Mystic Tower is one of the few Paradigms to build Chains while still benefitting from the defense of a Sentinel. Reaching a Stagger is easier when the Chain Gauge of an enemy is already partly filled, though.

Sazh, Vanille, Fang

Paradigm	Sazh	Vanille	Fang
Relentless Assault	Ravager	Ravager	Commando
Delta Attack	Commando	Ravager	Sentinel
Aggression	Commando	Ravager	Commando
Solidarity	Commando	Medic	Sentinel
Protection	Synergist	Medic	Sentinel
Evened Odds	Synergist	Medic	Saboteur

- As before, Relentless Assault instructs your team to build fast, steady Chains and is an excellent opening Paradigm when you're confident of victory.

- Delta Attack is another good Paradigm to open, considering the protection that your Sentinel provides your attackers.

- Solidarity takes care of your healing, while Protection throws a Synergist into the mix if you need additional magic defenses. This can be especially helpful during longer battles. Your Sentinel and Medic won't have to change roles.

- Evened Odds includes a Saboteur alongside your Synergist, both being healed by a Medic if necessary. A very useful combination while preparing yourself for a tough, recalcitrant foe.

- Aggression calls on two fighters to inflict heavy physical damage after Staggering a lone enemy.

Vanille, Hope, Fang

Paradigm	Vanille	Hope	Fang
Relentless Assault	Ravager	Ravager	Commando
Mystic Tower	Ravager	Ravager	Sentinel
Combat Clinic	Medic	Medic	Sentinel
Diversity	Ravager	Medic	Commando
Evened Odds	Medic	Synergist	Saboteur
Premeditation	Saboteur	Synergist	Sentinel

- Relentless Assault is usually a good offensive Paradigm to begin battle, being ideal for building Chains. In this party, especially, you have two strong magic talents and a supreme Commando.

- Mystic Tower is an excellent Paradigm to continue building up Chain Bonuses while under the protection of a Sentinel, allowing you to stay in this Paradigm for a while.

- A visit to the Combat Clinic takes care of all your healing needs while still under the safe protection of a Sentinel.

- Diversity is a balanced Paradigm that enables you to keep those Chains going while you heal more slowly.

- Evened Odds is a great Paradigm to soften up heavily defended enemies and improve your own stats after a few rounds.

- Premeditation replaces the Medic with a Sentinel, and is the better opening Paradigm when you know you're going to need assistance.

- This line-up grants access to the Saboteur skills of both Vanille and Fang, some being otherwise exclusive. It makes this party the indisputable queen of buffs and debuffs.

Hope, Vanille, Snow

Paradigm	Hope	Vanille	Snow
Relentless Assault	Ravager	Ravager	Commando
Tri-disaster	Ravager	Ravager	Ravager
Protection	Synergist	Medic	Sentinel
Combat Clinic	Medic	Medic	Sentinel
Attrition	Medic	Saboteur	Sentinel
Premeditation	Synergist	Saboteur	Sentinel

- Relentless Assault is your primary offensive strategy.

- Tri-disaster converts Snow into a Ravager, increasing the speed at which you can Stagger enemies.

- Protection is a safe and reliable way to defend and heal your party.

- Combat Clinic functions as your emergency healing Paradigm.

- Attrition focuses on healing and weakening your enemies with status ailments.

- Finally, Premeditation offers a chance to turn the tide with status effects.

Most traditional RPGs gradually award experience points as players progress through an adventure, with characters undergoing an automatic "level up" that increases core statistics and unlocks new abilities at key EXP milestones. With Final Fantasy XIII's Crystarium system, though, you must manually invest accumulated Crystogen Points (or "CP" – EXP in all but name) at the Crystarium screen to upgrade your party.

Though there is technically no right or wrong way to spend CP at the Crystarium, players will definitely profit by upgrading all six characters with a long-term strategy in mind. In this section, we study the Crystarium system as a whole before exploring each character's natural proficiencies – and the optimum developmental paths that these might suggest.

EXPANSIONS

The Crystarium is first introduced at the start of Chapter 03. Each role in the Crystarium has ten stages in total, initially limited to Stage 1, with access to higher tiers gradually unlocked through progression in the main storyline. During Chapter 10, all party members are also given three "secondary" roles. However, due to the enormous CP investment, we strongly advise that you focus on specialist disciplines alone until after the final boss battle.

CRYSTARIUM EXPANSIONS

Chapter/Event	Crystarium Stage
The Hanging Edge	-
The Pulse Vestige	-
Lake Bresha: become L'Cie	Stage 1
The Vile Peaks	Stage 2
The Gapra Whitewood	Stage 3
The Sunleth Waterscapes	Stage 4
Palumpolum	Stage 5
Nautilus Park/The Palamecia	Stage 6
The Fifth Ark	Stage 7
Gran Pulse	Stage 8
Eden	Stage 9
Final boss defeated	Stage 10

SPECIALIZATION

Each character has an initial allocation of three primary roles where you can invest CP. As a general rule, effective character development isn't a question of which crystals you obtain, but the order in which you unlock them after each Crystarium Expansion. When we talk of "specialization", then, we are referring to the act of focusing on a particular role or crystal purchase as a priority before spending points elsewhere.

As a general rule, you will acquire sufficient CP to maintain a balanced party if you diligently fight all battles that your party can conceivably win. A little power-leveling, though, can enable you to leap ahead of the difficulty curve for a particular area or even an entire chapter, making many fights far less difficult or time-consuming. You can find tips on suitable locations to farm CP throughout the Walkthrough chapter, and a dedicated power-leveling section on page 144.

CRYSTOGEN POINTS (CP)

The Crystogen Points total specified after the conclusion of a successful battle is the sum that is awarded to all characters, not merely those in the active party. This means that characters who rarely see front-line combat can potentially develop at the same rate as your more-favored warriors.

Crystogen Points are awarded for each enemy you defeat, with the following exceptions:

- You will receive no additional CP for defeating enemies that are summoned during the course of a battle. Only the original line-up of foes that you face when the fight commences are taken into account.
- There is no CP reward for enemies that escape from battle.
- In three-way battles you obtain CP for all enemies present at the start of the fight, even if your party did not land every finishing blow.

There is a 999,999 cap on unspent CP for each character, a sum that your reserves could reach from Chapter 11 onward if you are fighting with a fixed party. All further Crystogen Points are wasted after accumulating this total, so it is vital that you invest in suitable upgrades beforehand. This leads us neatly to a related topic: "Super Specialists".

SUPER SPECIALISTS

As we state in the walkthrough, staying with a fixed group of Lightning, Hope and Fang once you gain the ability to choose your own party can be advantageous in a variety of ways. Principle among these is the fact that it is a balanced line-up that boasts a great blend of roles and unique abilities. There are also secondary considerations that make this approach highly worthwhile – such as efficient use of resources for weapon upgrades, the ability to keep a fixed Paradigm Deck, and a reduction in the time spent engaged in administration at the Main Menu.

However, this strategy also offers a less obvious benefit that can be of great use during post-credits play. Once you complete the end-game boss battle and unlock the final tier of the Crystarium, you will find that the paths to the ultimate Role Level crystals are quite breathtakingly expensive. With your main trio developed as balanced all-rounders (with a degree of natural specialism), the perks offered by the fifth and final Role Levels could take many hours of play to obtain. However, the Crystogen Points accumulated by your reserves throughout the story will enable you to afford the 700,000+ CP required to max out one discipline immediately. This turns them into what we call Super Specialists who can be employed to beat opponents that your default group might struggle to overcome. Snow operating as a maxed-out Sentinel, for example, can become an indomitable damage sponge in all but the most difficult battles.

There are, of course, certain drawbacks to this strategy. Super Specialists will only truly excel in one role until you accumulate more CP and unlock important abilities and stat boosts in other disciplines. You will, therefore, need to tailor your Paradigm Deck carefully to take all relative strengths and weaknesses into account when you use them. Weapon upgrades are also a factor – as you will have almost certainly focused on your main trio, your three reserves will lack this advantage. Even with these considerations, though, the Super Specialists strategy can make the process of power-leveling, grinding for valuable spoils and hunting Marks much easier for many hours of post-story play.

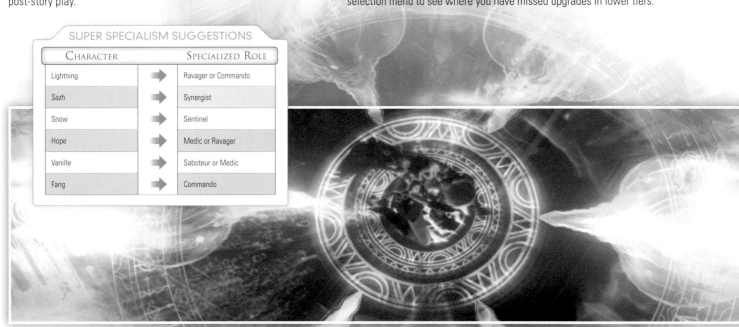

SUPER SPECIALISM SUGGESTIONS

Character		Specialized Role
Lightning	→	Ravager or Commando
Sazh	→	Synergist
Snow	→	Sentinel
Hope	→	Medic or Ravager
Vanille	→	Saboteur or Medic
Fang	→	Commando

BUYING PRIORITIES

For optimum party development, it is critical to prioritize the crystals you should acquire first. Indeed, some enhancements are far more valuable than others, regardless of what you pay for them:

- **ATB Crystals:** An extra ATB segment is one extra action point per round, and one of the best possible combat upgrades. A priority acquisition.
- **Accessory Crystals:** You can expand each character's accessory capacity up to a maximum of four slots. This crystal grants one extra slot, allowing you to equip another item and gain further protection or enhancement, with greater potential for experiencing useful synthesized abilities (see page 194).
- **Ability Crystals:** The early acquisition of powerful elemental attacks, status enhancements and debuffs, or multiple-target upgrades for all such spells, can make a serious difference to your performance in battle.
- **Role Level Crystals:** These are far more important than they may initially seem, as they offer a meaningful enhancement to a character's proficiency in the related role, plus a smaller boost to their companions. This (invisible) upgrade is applied immediately once you unlock the crystal. You can learn about the full benefits of reaching each Role Level on page 146.

It is of course equally important to ascertain which crystals can be left until later. For example, techniques – such as Quake, Renew and Dispelga – may not see much use if the character is never intended to be the party leader. With all primary roles, the Crystarium trees also feature branches of additional crystals that are effectively optional purchases. These often carry a higher CP price than crystals on the main crystogenesis paths, so it can often be preferable to leave non-essential improvements until they become more cost-effective.

Note that you can use the completion table that appears under the role selection menu to see where you have missed upgrades in lower tiers.

COMMANDO

0	HP +100				
0	Strength +15				
0	Magic +15				
0	Attack				
0	Blitz				
0	Ruin				
60	Strength +4	60	HP +20	60	Lifesiphon
60	HP +15				
60	Powerchain				
60	HP +15	60	Magic +6		
60	HP +25				
80	Magic +4				

90	HP +25		
90	Magic +10	90	Strength +7
90	Faultsiphon		
90	HP +25		
90	Strength +7		
120	HP +25		
120	Strength +4		

220	HP +20		
220	Launch	220	Strength +8
220	HP +20		
220	Strength +6	220	Ravage
220	Magic +4		
350	Role Level (LV2)		

230	Strength +3
230	HP +10
230	Magic +3
230	HP +10
330	Smite

400	HP +10				
400	Strength +3	400	Strength +3		
400	Magic +5	400	Magic +3	400	Quake
400	HP +10				
400	Strength +3				
400	HP +10				
600	Strength +3				

1,000	HP +20				
1,000	HP +30	1,000	HP +20		
1,000	Blindside	1,000	Strength +12	1,000	HP +30
1,000	Magic +5	1,000	Magic +5	1,000	HP +20
1,000	HP +30				
1,000	Strength +6				
1,000	Strength +5				
1,000	Scourge				
1,000	Magic +5				
2,000	Role Level (LV3)				

740	HP +50				
740	Strength +10	740	Strength +10	740	HP +50
740	Jeopardize				
740	Strength +8				
740	Magic +4				
2,000	HP +40				

4,000	Strength +18				
4,000	Strength +18	6,000	Strength +18		
4,000	HP +100	6,000	HP +100	6,000	HP +100
4,000	HP +100				
4,000	Magic +18	6,000	Dispelga		
6,000	Strength +18	8,000	Strength +18	8,000	HP +100
6,000	Ruinga				
6,000	Strength +18				
6,000	Magic +18				
8,000	ATB Level				
8,000	HP +100	10,000	HP +100		
8,000	Strength +18				
8,000	Magic +18				
8,000	Strength +18	10,000	Strength +20		
8,000	HP +100	10,000	Magic +24		
8,000	Role Level (LV4)				

10,000	Magic +20				
10,000	HP +180	18,000	HP +80	18,000	HP +80
10,000	Magic +20				
10,000	Strength +40	18,000	Strength +20	18,000	Strength +20
12,000	Magic +20				
12,000	HP +180	18,000	HP +100	18,000	HP +100
12,000	Magic +20				
12,000	Strength +30	18,000	Strength +30	18,000	Strength +30
12,000	HP +180				
12,000	HP +150				
12,000	Strength +40				
12,000	HP +150				

30,000	HP +250
30,000	HP +250
30,000	Strength +40
30,000	HP +250
30,000	HP +250
30,000	Magic +40
30,000	HP +250
30,000	Accessory
60,000	HP +250
60,000	Strength +40
60,000	HP +250
60,000	HP +250
60,000	Magic +40
60,000	HP +250
60,000	HP +250
60,000	Role Level (LV5)

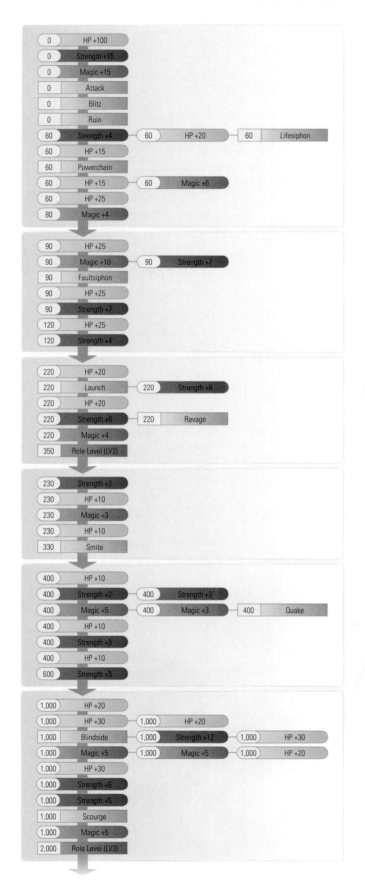

RAVAGER

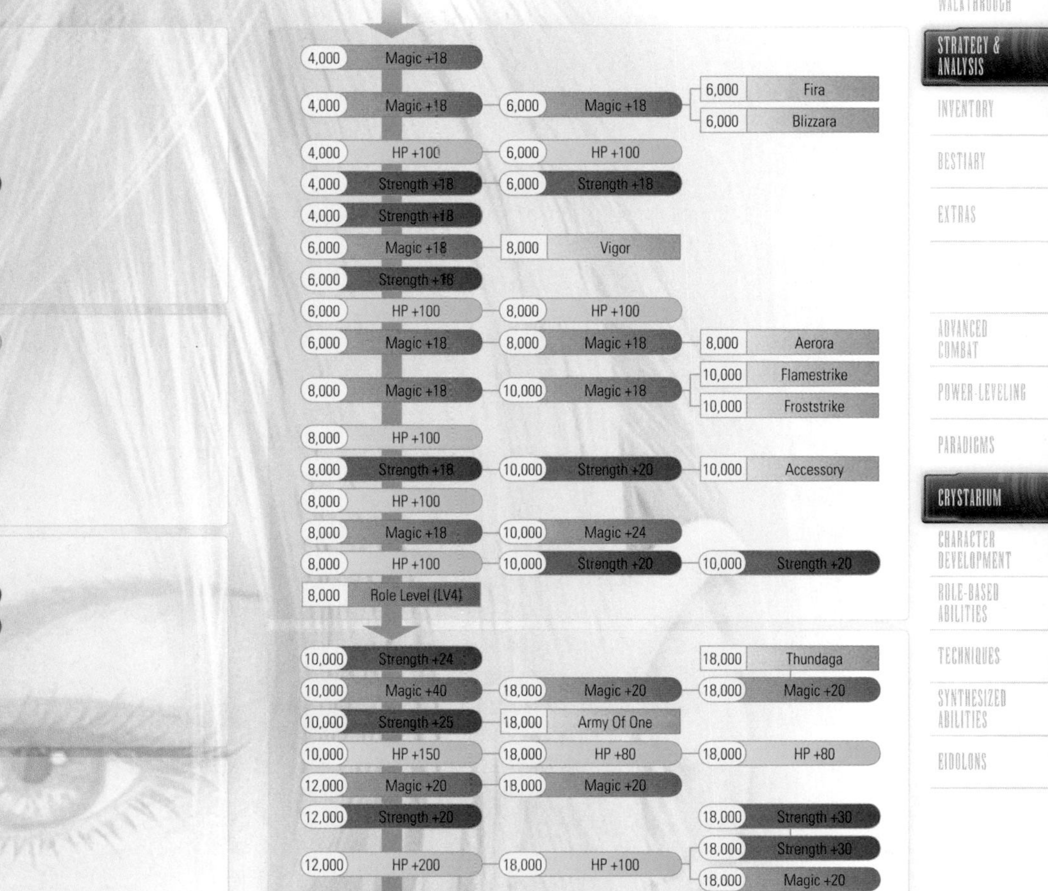

CP	Node	CP	Branch	CP	Branch
0	Libra				
0	Thunder				
60	HP +15				
60	Strength +4				
60	Magic +4	60	Strength +10		
60	Water				
80	HP +15				
80	Magic +4				

CP	Node	CP	Branch	CP	Branch
90	Magic +11	90	HP +25		
90	Sparkstrike				
90	Strength +3				
90	HP +10				
90	Aquastrike				
120	HP +10				

CP	Node	CP	Branch	CP	Branch
220	Magic +4				
220	Fire	220	Strength +5		
220	Strength +4	220	Magic +10		
220	HP +25				
220	Magic +4				
350	Role Level (LV2)				

CP	Node	CP	Branch	CP	Branch
230	HP +10				
230	Strength +3				
230	Magic +3				
230	Overwhelm				
330	HP +10				

CP	Node	CP	Branch	CP	Branch
400	Strength +3	400	Strength +3	400	HP +20
400	Thundera	400	Magic +3		
400	HP +20	400	HP +20		
400	Magic +3				
400	Blizzard				
400	Strength +3				
600	Magic +3				

CP	Node	CP	Branch	CP	Branch
1,000	Aero				
1,000	Magic +8				
1,000	HP +35	1,000	HP +20	1,000	Strength +5
1,000	Strength +5	1,000	Strength +4	1,000	HP +20
1,000	Magic +3				
1,000	HP +20				
1,000	Magic +5				
1,000	Watera				
1,000	HP +30				
2,000	Role Level (LV3)				

CP	Node	CP	Branch	CP	Branch
740	Strength +15				
740	Magic +20	740	Strength +5	740	HP +20
740	Magic +4				
740	Fearsiphon				
740	Strength +4				
2,000	HP +20				

CP	Node	CP	Branch	CP	Branch
4,000	Magic +18				
4,000	Magic +18	6,000	Magic +18	6,000	Fira
				6,000	Blizzara
4,000	HP +100	6,000	HP +100		
4,000	Strength +18	6,000	Strength +18		
4,000	Strength +18				
6,000	Magic +18	8,000	Vigor		
6,000	Strength +18				
6,000	HP +100	8,000	HP +100		
6,000	Magic +18	8,000	Magic +18	8,000	Aerora
8,000	Magic +18	10,000	Magic +18	10,000	Flamestrike
				10,000	Froststrike
8,000	HP +100				
8,000	Strength +18	10,000	Strength +20	10,000	Accessory
8,000	HP +100				
8,000	Magic +18	10,000	Magic +24		
8,000	HP +100	10,000	Strength +20	10,000	Strength +20
8,000	Role Level (LV4)				

CP	Node	CP	Branch	CP	Branch
10,000	Strength +24			18,000	Thundaga
10,000	Magic +40	18,000	Magic +20	18,000	Magic +20
10,000	Strength +25	18,000	Army Of One		
10,000	HP +150	18,000	HP +80	18,000	HP +80
12,000	Magic +20	18,000	Magic +20		
12,000	Strength +20			18,000	Strength +30
12,000	HP +200	18,000	HP +100	18,000	Strength +30
				18,000	Magic +20
12,000	Magic +20			18,000	Magic +19
12,000	Strength +20				
12,000	HP +150				
12,000	Magic +40				
12,000	HP +150				

CP	Node
30,000	HP +250
30,000	HP +250
30,000	Strength +40
30,000	HP +250
30,000	HP +250
30,000	Magic +40
30,000	HP +250
30,000	HP +250
60,000	HP +250
60,000	Strength +40
60,000	HP +250
60,000	HP +250
60,000	Magic +40
60,000	HP +250
60,000	HP +250
60,000	Role Level (LV5)

MEDIC

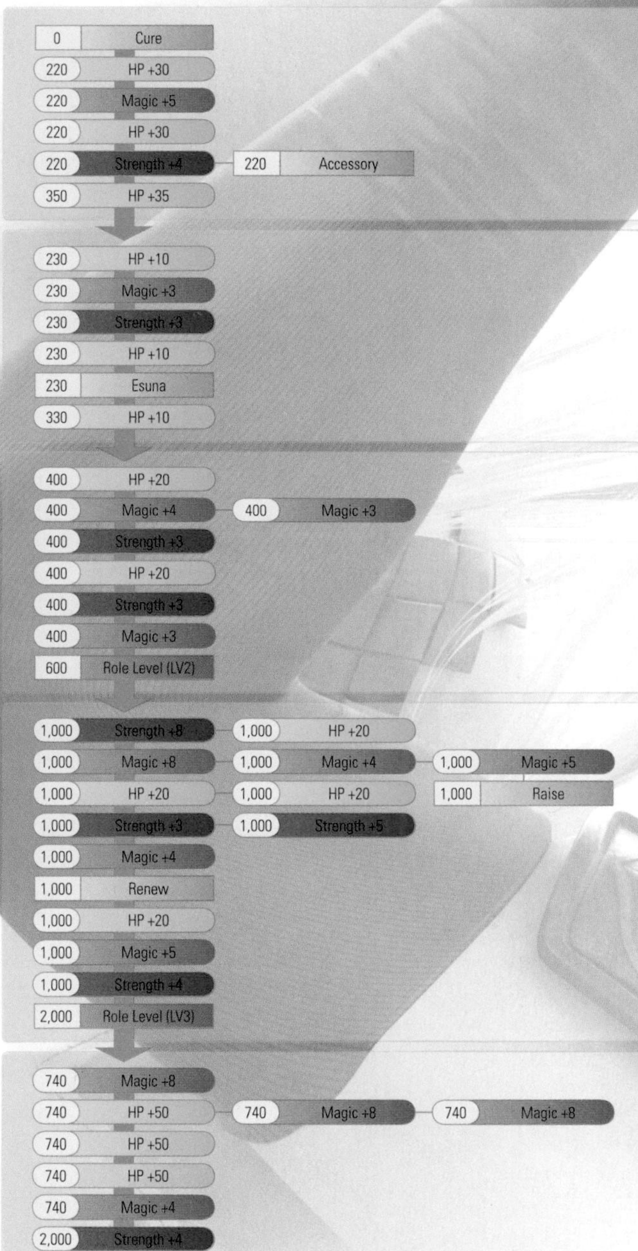

CP	Bonus	CP	Branch	CP	Branch
0	Cure				
220	HP +30				
220	Magic +5				
220	HP +30				
220	Strength +4	220	Accessory		
350	HP +35				

CP	Bonus	CP	Branch	CP	Branch
230	HP +10				
230	Magic +3				
230	Strength +3				
230	HP +10				
230	Esuna				
330	HP +10				

CP	Bonus	CP	Branch	CP	Branch
400	HP +20				
400	Magic +4	400	Magic +3		
400	Strength +3				
400	HP +20				
400	Strength +3				
400	Magic +3				
600	Role Level (LV2)				

CP	Bonus	CP	Branch	CP	Branch
1,000	Strength +8	1,000	HP +20		
1,000	Magic +8	1,000	Magic +4	1,000	Magic +5
1,000	HP +20	1,000	HP +20	1,000	Raise
1,000	Strength +3	1,000	Strength +5		
1,000	Magic +4				
1,000	Renew				
1,000	HP +20				
1,000	Magic +5				
1,000	Strength +4				
2,000	Role Level (LV3)				

CP	Bonus	CP	Branch	CP	Branch
740	Magic +8				
740	HP +50	740	Magic +8	740	Magic +8
740	HP +50				
740	HP +50				
740	Magic +4				
2,000	Strength +4				

CP	Bonus	CP	Branch	CP	Branch
4,000	HP +100				
4,000	Magic +18	6,000	Magic +18	6,000	Magic +18
4,000	HP +100	6,000	HP +100	6,000	HP +100
4,000	Magic +18				
4,000	Strength +18	6,000	Strength +18		
6,000	HP +100	8,000	HP +100		
6,000	HP +100				
6,000	Magic +18	8,000	Magic +18		
6,000	Strength +18				
8,000	HP +100	10,000	HP +120	10,000	HP +120
8,000	Magic +18			10,000	Cura
8,000	Strength +18	10,000	Strength +20		
8,000	Magic +18				
8,000	HP +100				
8,000	Magic +18	10,000	Strength +20		
8,000	Role Level (LV4)				

CP	Bonus	CP	Branch	CP	Branch
10,000	Strength +20				
10,000	HP +180	18,000	HP +80	18,000	Strength +20
10,000	Magic +40	18,000	HP +80	18,000	Strength +20
				18,000	Magic +20
10,000	Strength +20			18,000	Magic +20
12,000	HP +190			18,000	Stopga
12,000	HP +190	18,000	HP +100	18,000	HP +100
12,000	Magic +20	18,000	Magic +30	18,000	Magic +30
12,000	HP +200				
12,000	Magic +20				
12,000	Strength +20	18,000	Strength +30	18,000	Strength +30
12,000	HP +150				
12,000	Magic +40				
12,000	HP +150				

CP	Bonus
30,000	HP +275
30,000	HP +275
30,000	Strength +40
30,000	HP +275
30,000	HP +275
30,000	Magic +40
30,000	HP +275
30,000	HP +275
60,000	HP +275
60,000	Strength +40
60,000	HP +275
60,000	HP +275
60,000	Magic +40
60,000	HP +285
60,000	HP +275
60,000	Role Level (LV5)

SENTINEL

CP	Bonus
3,000	HP +10
3,000	Strength +3
3,000	HP +10
3,000	Magic +3
3,000	HP +10
6,000	Provoke
6,000	HP +10
6,000	Strength +4
6,000	HP +10
6,000	HP +10
12,000	Evade
9,000	HP +15
9,000	Magic +5
9,000	HP +15
9,000	Strength +5
18,000	Elude
12,000	HP +15
12,000	Strength +6
12,000	Magic +6
12,000	HP +15
12,000	HP +15
15,000	Strength +7
15,000	HP +20
15,000	HP +20
15,000	Magic +7
30,000	Counter
18,000	HP +20
18,000	Magic +8
18,000	HP +20
18,000	Strength +8
18,000	HP +20
21,000	HP +25
21,000	Magic +9
21,000	HP +25
21,000	Strength +9
42,000	Deathward

CP	Bonus
24,000	Strength +9
24,000	HP +25
24,000	Magic +10
24,000	HP +25
24,000	HP +25
60,000	Role Level (LV2)
30,000	HP +30
30,000	HP +30
30,000	Strength +9
30,000	HP +30
30,000	HP +30
30,000	Magic +10
30,000	HP +30
30,000	HP +30
30,000	Strength +9
30,000	HP +30
30,000	HP +30
30,000	Magic +10
30,000	HP +30
30,000	HP +30
60,000	Fringeward
120,000	Role Level (LV3)
60,000	HP +100
60,000	Strength +9
60,000	HP +100
60,000	HP +100
60,000	HP +100
60,000	Magic +10
120,000	Role Level (LV4)
60,000	HP +100
60,000	HP +100
60,000	HP +100
60,000	Strength +9
120,000	Reprieve
60,000	Magic +10
60,000	Strength +9
120,000	Role Level (LV5)

SYNERGIST

CP	Bonus
3,000	HP +10
3,000	Strength +3
3,000	HP +10
3,000	Magic +3
3,000	HP +10
6,000	Bravery
6,000	Magic +3
6,000	HP +10
6,000	HP +10
6,000	Strength +4
12,000	Faith
9,000	HP +15
9,000	Strength +5
9,000	HP +15
9,000	Magic +5
18,000	Enthunder
12,000	HP +15
12,000	Magic +8
12,000	HP +15
12,000	Strength +6
24,000	Enfire
15,000	Magic +7
15,000	HP +20
15,000	HP +20
15,000	Strength +7
30,000	Enwater
18,000	HP +20
18,000	HP +20
18,000	Magic +8
18,000	Strength +8
36,000	Enfrost
21,000	Strength +9
21,000	HP +25
21,000	Magic +9
21,000	HP +25
42,000	Protect

CP	Bonus
24,000	HP +25
24,000	Strength +9
24,000	HP +25
24,000	Magic +10
48,000	Shell
60,000	Role Level (LV2)
30,000	HP +30
30,000	HP +30
30,000	Strength +9
60,000	Boon
30,000	HP +30
30,000	Magic +10
30,000	HP +30
30,000	HP +30
30,000	Strength +9
30,000	HP +30
30,000	HP +30
30,000	Magic +10
30,000	HP +30
30,000	HP +30
30,000	HP +30
120,000	Role Level (LV3)
60,000	HP +100
60,000	Strength +9
60,000	HP +100
120,000	Vigilance
60,000	HP +100
60,000	Magic +10
120,000	Role Level (LV4)
60,000	HP +100
120,000	Haste
60,000	HP +100
60,000	Strength +9
60,000	HP +100
60,000	Magic +10
60,000	HP +100
120,000	Role Level (LV5)

SABOTEUR

CP	Bonus
3,000	HP +10
3,000	HP +10
3,000	Magic +3
3,000	HP +10
3,000	Strength +3
6,000	Deprotect
6,000	HP +10
6,000	Strength +4
6,000	HP +10
6,000	Magic +3
12,000	Deshell
9,000	HP +15
9,000	Magic +5
9,000	HP +15
9,000	Strength +5
9,000	HP +15
12,000	Magic +6
12,000	HP +15
12,000	HP +15
12,000	Strength +6
24,000	Imperil
15,000	HP +20
15,000	Magic +7
15,000	HP +20
15,000	Strength +7
30,000	Poison
18,000	HP +20
18,000	Magic +8
18,000	HP +20
18,000	Strength +8
18,000	HP +20
21,000	HP +25
21,000	Strength +9
21,000	HP +25
21,000	Magic +9
42,000	Deprotega

CP	Bonus
24,000	Magic +10
24,000	HP +25
24,000	Strength +9
24,000	HP +25
48,000	Jinx
60,000	Role Level (LV2)
30,000	HP +30
30,000	HP +30
30,000	Strength +9
30,000	HP +30
30,000	HP +30
30,000	Magic +10
30,000	HP +30
30,000	HP +30
30,000	Strength +9
60,000	Deshellga
30,000	HP +30
30,000	Magic +10
30,000	HP +30
30,000	HP +30
30,000	HP +30
120,000	Role Level (LV3)
60,000	HP +100
60,000	Strength +9
60,000	HP +100
120,000	Imperilga
60,000	HP +100
60,000	Magic +10
120,000	Role Level (LV4)
60,000	HP +100
60,000	HP +100
120,000	Poisonga
60,000	Strength +9
60,000	HP +100
60,000	Magic +10
60,000	HP +100
120,000	Role Level (LV5)

SYNERGIST

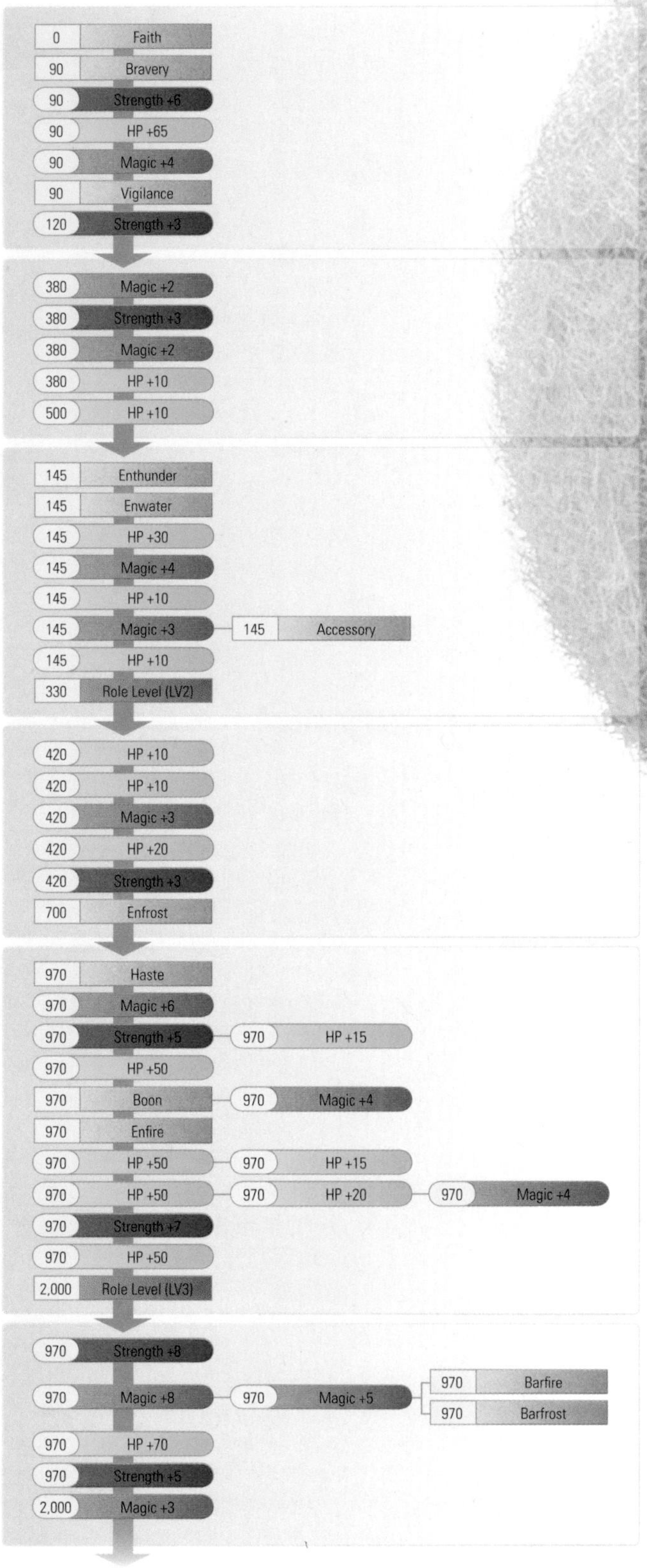
0 Faith
90 Bravery
90 Strength +6
90 HP +65
90 Magic +4
90 Vigilance
120 Strength +3
380 Magic +2
380 Strength +3
380 Magic +2
380 HP +10
500 HP +10
145 Enthunder
145 Enwater
145 HP +30
145 Magic +4
145 HP +10
145 Magic +3 / 145 Accessory
145 HP +10
330 Role Level (LV2)
420 HP +10
420 HP +10
420 Magic +3
420 HP +20
420 Strength +3
700 Enfrost
970 Haste
970 Magic +6
970 Strength +5 / 970 HP +15
970 HP +50
970 Boon / 970 Magic +4
970 Enfire
970 HP +50 / 970 HP +15
970 HP +50 / 970 HP +20 / 970 Magic +4
970 Strength +7
970 HP +50
2,000 Role Level (LV3)
970 Strength +8
970 Magic +8 / 970 Magic +5 / 970 Barfire / 970 Barfrost
970 HP +70
970 Strength +5
2,000 Magic +3

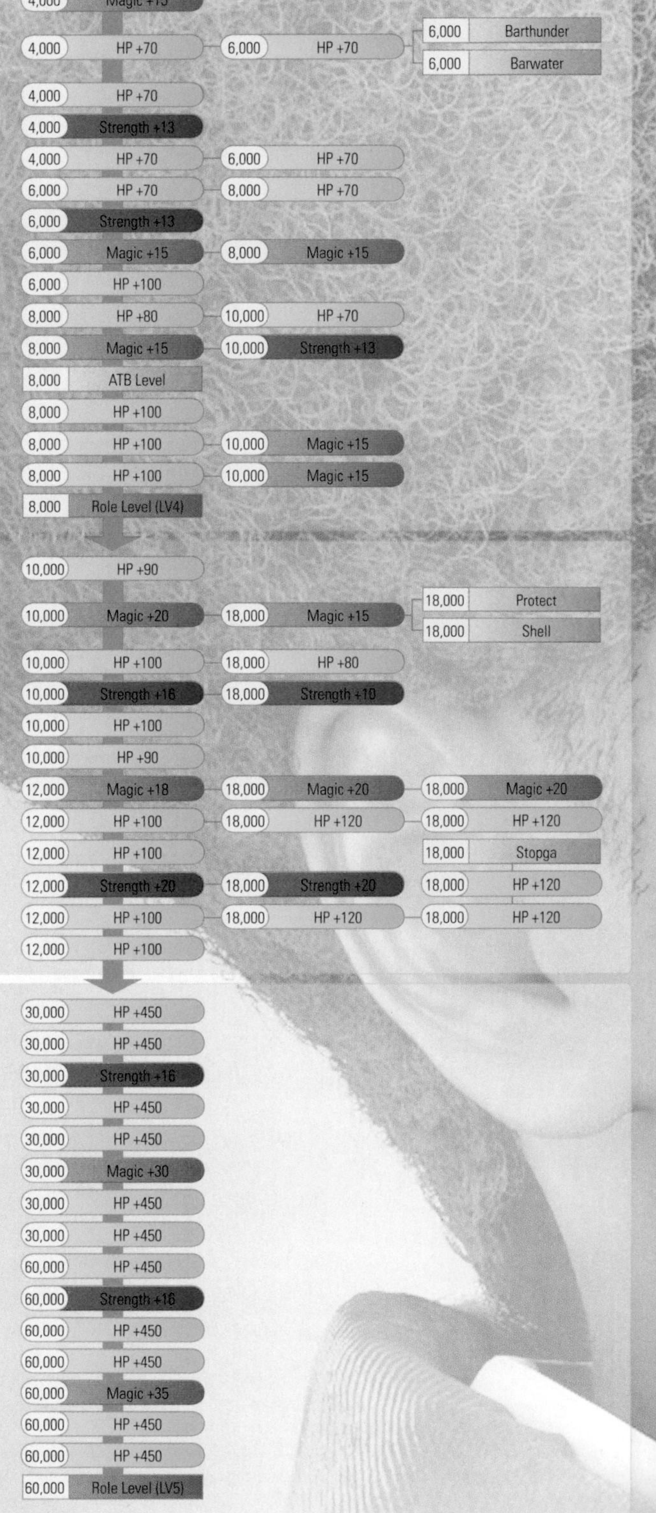
4,000 Magic +15
4,000 HP +70 / 6,000 HP +70 / 6,000 Barthunder / 6,000 Barwater
4,000 HP +70
4,000 Strength +13
4,000 HP +70 / 6,000 HP +70
6,000 HP +70 / 8,000 HP +70
6,000 Strength +13
6,000 Magic +15 / 8,000 Magic +15
6,000 HP +100
8,000 HP +80 / 10,000 HP +70
8,000 Magic +15 / 10,000 Strength +13
8,000 ATB Level
8,000 HP +100
8,000 HP +100 / 10,000 Magic +15
8,000 HP +100 / 10,000 Magic +15
8,000 Role Level (LV4)
10,000 HP +90
10,000 Magic +20 / 18,000 Magic +15 / 18,000 Protect / 18,000 Shell
10,000 HP +100 / 18,000 HP +80
10,000 Strength +16 / 18,000 Strength +10
10,000 HP +100
10,000 HP +90
12,000 Magic +18 / 18,000 Magic +20 / 18,000 Magic +20
12,000 HP +100 / 18,000 HP +120 / 18,000 HP +120
12,000 HP +100 / 18,000 Stopga
12,000 Strength +20 / 18,000 Strength +20 / 18,000 HP +120
12,000 HP +100 / 18,000 HP +120 / 18,000 HP +120
12,000 HP +100
30,000 HP +450
30,000 HP +450
30,000 Strength +16
30,000 HP +450
30,000 HP +450
30,000 Magic +30
30,000 HP +450
30,000 HP +450
60,000 HP +450
60,000 Strength +16
60,000 HP +450
60,000 HP +450
60,000 Magic +35
60,000 HP +450
60,000 HP +450
60,000 Role Level (LV5)

RAVAGER

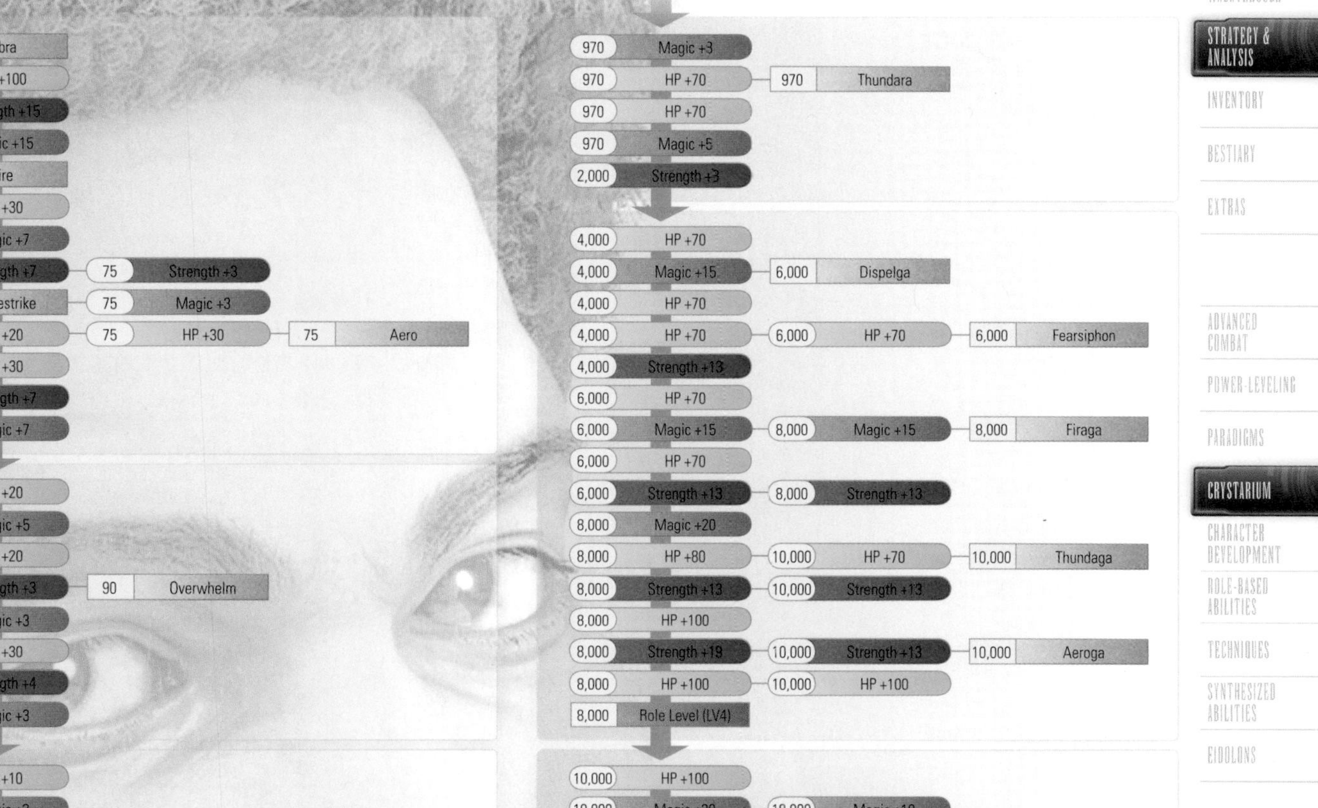

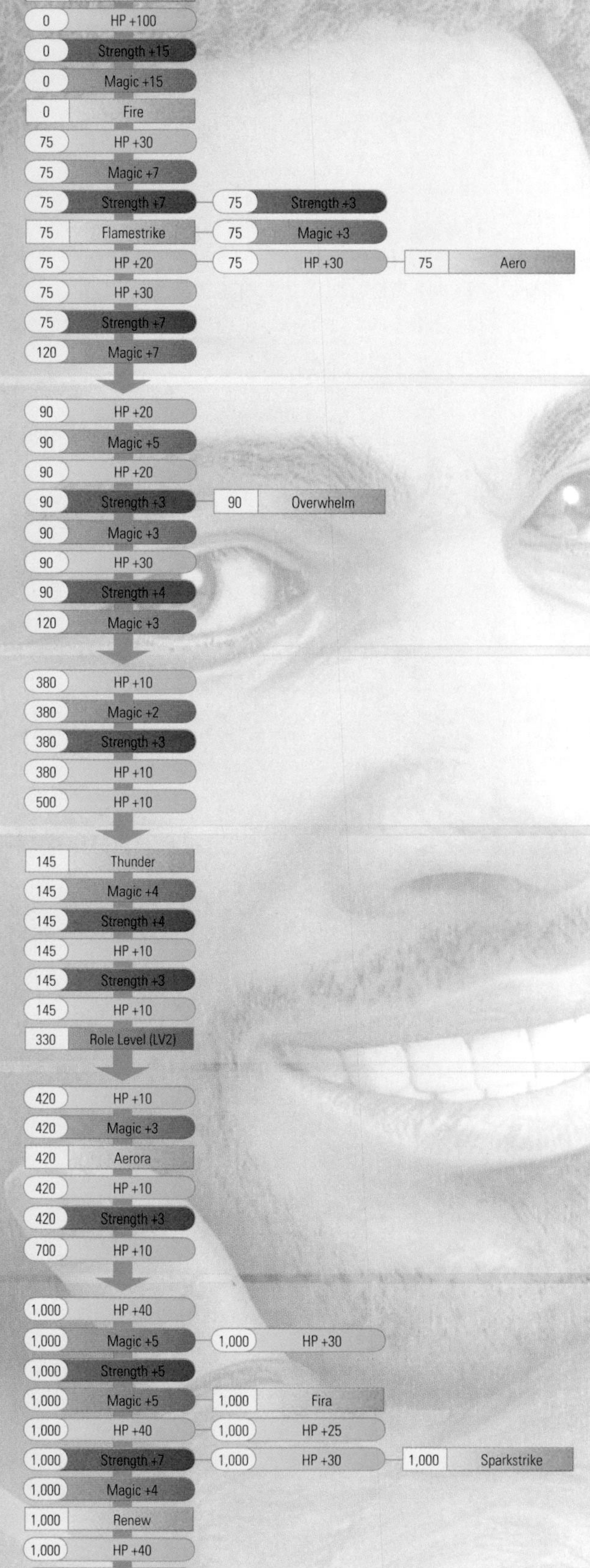

CP	Node	CP	Branch	CP	Branch
0	Libra				
0	HP +100				
0	Strength +15				
0	Magic +15				
0	Fire				
75	HP +30				
75	Magic +7				
75	Strength +7	75	Strength +3		
75	Flamestrike	75	Magic +3		
75	HP +20	75	HP +30	75	Aero
75	HP +30				
75	Strength +7				
120	Magic +7				

CP	Node	CP	Branch
90	HP +20		
90	Magic +5		
90	HP +20		
90	Strength +3	90	Overwhelm
90	Magic +3		
90	HP +30		
90	Strength +4		
120	Magic +3		

CP	Node
380	HP +10
380	Magic +2
380	Strength +3
380	HP +10
500	HP +10

CP	Node
145	Thunder
145	Magic +4
145	Strength +4
145	HP +10
145	Strength +3
145	HP +10
330	Role Level (LV2)

CP	Node
420	HP +10
420	Magic +3
420	Aerora
420	HP +10
420	Strength +3
700	HP +10

CP	Node	CP	Branch	CP	Branch
1,000	HP +40				
1,000	Magic +5	1,000	HP +30		
1,000	Strength +5				
1,000	Magic +5	1,000	Fira		
1,000	HP +40	1,000	HP +25		
1,000	Strength +7	1,000	HP +30	1,000	Sparkstrike
1,000	Magic +4				
1,000	Renew				
1,000	HP +40				
1,000	Magic +5				
2,000	Role Level (LV3)				

CP	Node	CP	Branch
970	Magic +3		
970	HP +70	970	Thundara
970	HP +70		
970	Magic +5		
2,000	Strength +3		

CP	Node	CP	Branch	CP	Branch
4,000	HP +70				
4,000	Magic +15	6,000	Dispelga		
4,000	HP +70				
4,000	HP +70	6,000	HP +70	6,000	Fearsiphon
4,000	Strength +13				
6,000	HP +70				
6,000	Magic +15	8,000	Magic +15	8,000	Firaga
6,000	HP +70				
6,000	Strength +13	8,000	Strength +13		
8,000	Magic +20				
8,000	HP +80	10,000	HP +70	10,000	Thundaga
8,000	Strength +13	10,000	Strength +13		
8,000	HP +100				
8,000	Strength +19	10,000	Strength +13	10,000	Aeroga
8,000	HP +100	10,000	HP +100		
8,000	Role Level (LV4)				

CP	Node	CP	Branch	CP	Branch
10,000	HP +100				
10,000	Magic +20	18,000	Magic +10		
10,000	HP +100	18,000	HP +80	18,000	HP +90
10,000	Strength +16				
10,000	HP +100	18,000	Cold Blood		
10,000	Strength +14				
12,000	Strength +20	18,000	Strength +20	18,000	Strength +20
12,000	HP +100				
12,000	HP +100	18,000	HP +120	18,000	HP +120
12,000	Magic +16	18,000	Magic +20	18,000	Magic +20
12,000	HP +100	18,000	HP +120		
12,000	Magic +18				

CP	Node
30,000	HP +400
30,000	HP +400
30,000	Strength +16
30,000	HP +400
30,000	HP +400
30,000	Magic +30
30,000	HP +400
30,000	Accessory
60,000	HP +415
60,000	Strength +16
60,000	HP +420
60,000	HP +420
60,000	Magic +35
60,000	HP +420
60,000	HP +420
60,000	Role Level (LV5)

COMMANDO

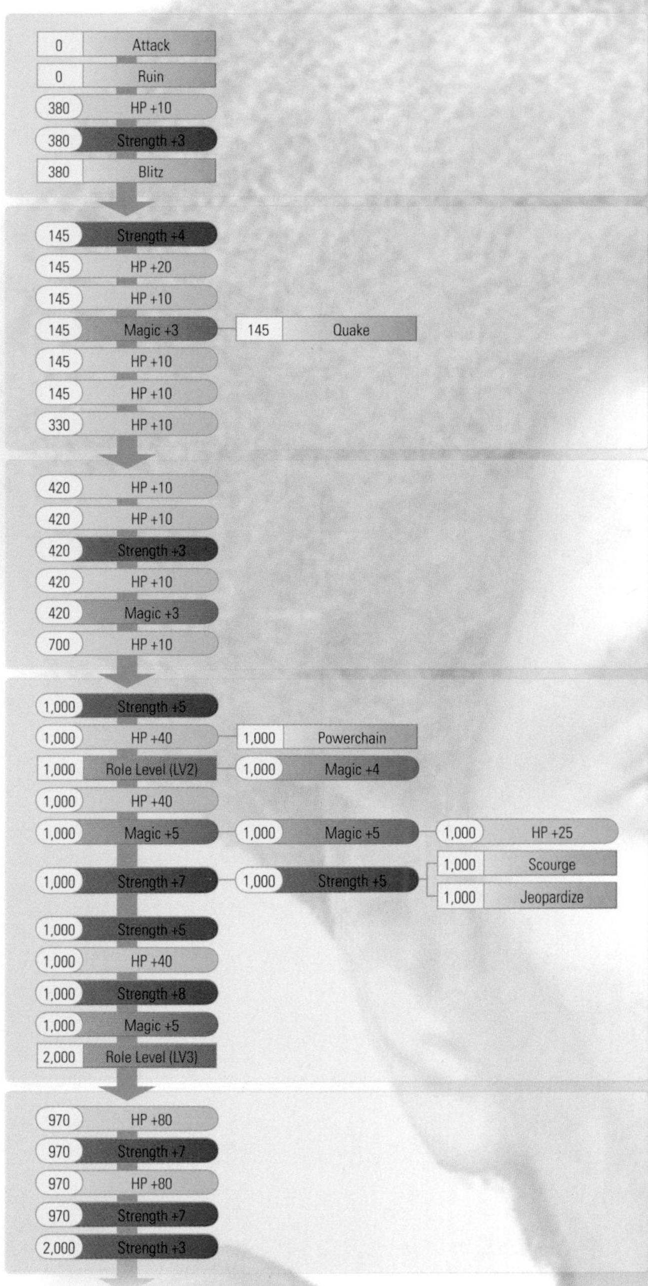
0 Attack
0 Ruin
380 HP +10
380 Strength +3
380 Blitz
145 Strength +4
145 HP +20
145 HP +10
145 Magic +3 — 145 Quake
145 HP +10
145 HP +10
330 HP +10
420 HP +10
420 HP +10
420 Strength +3
420 HP +10
420 Magic +3
700 HP +10
1,000 Strength +5
1,000 HP +40 — 1,000 Powerchain
1,000 Role Level (LV2) — 1,000 Magic +4
1,000 HP +40
1,000 Magic +5 — 1,000 Magic +5 — 1,000 HP +25
1,000 Strength +7 — 1,000 Strength +5 — 1,000 Scourge / 1,000 Jeopardize
1,000 Strength +5
1,000 HP +40
1,000 Strength +8
1,000 Magic +5
2,000 Role Level (LV3)
970 HP +80
970 Strength +7
970 HP +80
970 Strength +7
2,000 Strength +3

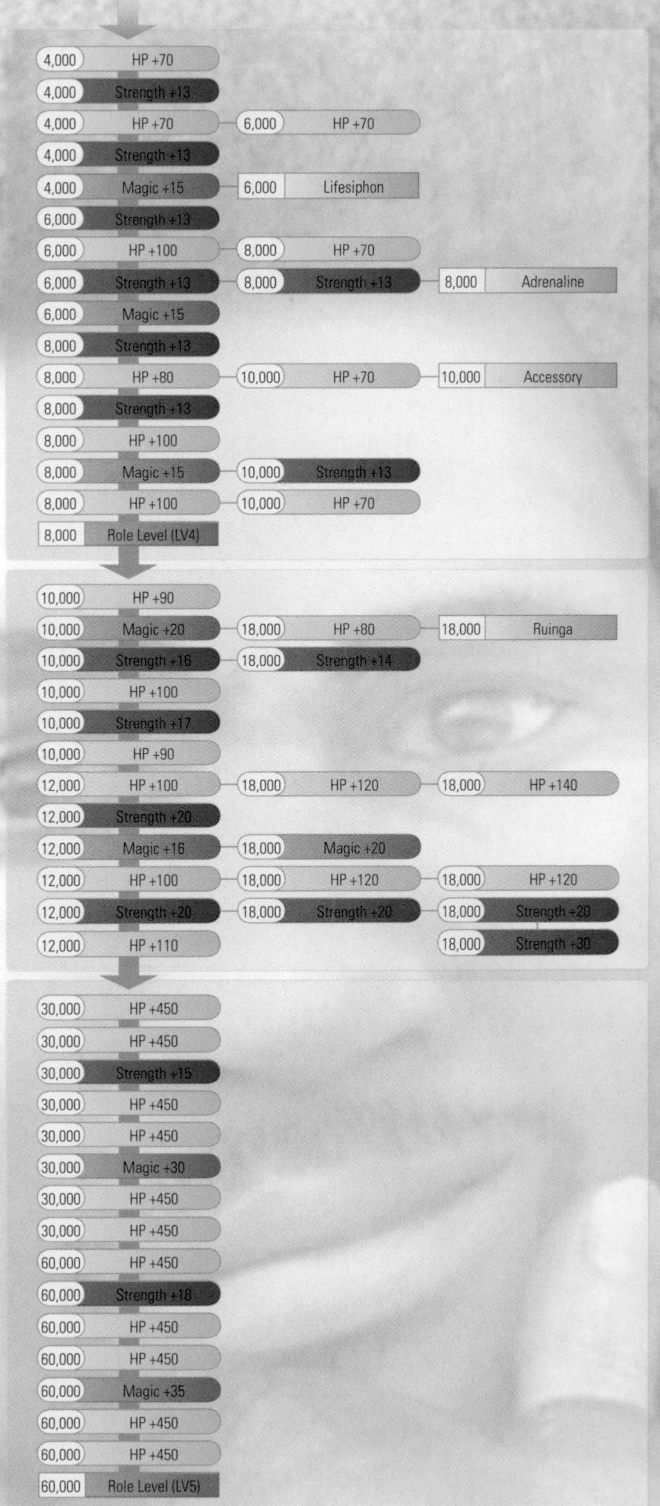
4,000 HP +70
4,000 Strength +13
4,000 HP +70 — 6,000 HP +70
4,000 Strength +13
4,000 Magic +15 — 6,000 Lifesiphon
6,000 Strength +13
6,000 HP +100 — 8,000 HP +70
6,000 Strength +13 — 8,000 Strength +13 — 8,000 Adrenaline
6,000 Magic +15
8,000 Strength +13
8,000 HP +80 — 10,000 HP +70 — 10,000 Accessory
8,000 Strength +13
8,000 HP +100
8,000 Magic +15 — 10,000 Strength +13
8,000 HP +100 — 10,000 HP +70
8,000 Role Level (LV4)
10,000 HP +90
10,000 Magic +20 — 18,000 HP +80 — 18,000 Ruinga
10,000 Strength +16 — 18,000 Strength +14
10,000 HP +100
10,000 Strength +17
10,000 HP +90
12,000 HP +100 — 18,000 HP +120 — 18,000 HP +140
12,000 Strength +20
12,000 Magic +16 — 18,000 Magic +20
12,000 HP +100 — 18,000 HP +120 — 18,000 HP +120
12,000 Strength +20 — 18,000 Strength +20 — 18,000 Strength +20
12,000 HP +110 — 18,000 Strength +30
30,000 HP +450
30,000 HP +450
30,000 Strength +15
30,000 HP +450
30,000 HP +450
30,000 Magic +30
30,000 HP +450
30,000 HP +450
60,000 HP +450
60,000 Strength +18
60,000 HP +450
60,000 HP +450
60,000 Magic +35
60,000 HP +450
60,000 HP +450
60,000 Role Level (LV5)

MEDIC

CP	Bonus
3,000	HP +10
3,000	Magic +3
3,000	HP +10
3,000	Strength +3
3,000	HP +10
6,000	Cure
6,000	HP +10
6,000	Magic +3
6,000	HP +10
6,000	Strength +3
6,000	HP +10
9,000	Magic +4
9,000	HP +15
9,000	HP +15
9,000	Strength +4
9,000	HP +15
12,000	HP +15
12,000	HP +15
12,000	Magic +4
12,000	Strength +4
24,000	Esuna
15,000	Strength +5
15,000	HP +20
15,000	Magic +5
15,000	HP +20
15,000	HP +20
18,000	HP +20
18,000	Magic +5
18,000	Strength +5
18,000	HP +20
18,000	HP +20
21,000	HP +25
21,000	Magic +6
21,000	Strength +5
21,000	HP +25
42,000	Cura

CP	Bonus
24,000	HP +25
24,000	HP +25
24,000	Strength +5
24,000	HP +25
24,000	Magic +6
60,000	Role Level (LV2)
30,000	HP +40
30,000	HP +40
30,000	Strength +5
30,000	HP +40
30,000	HP +40
30,000	Magic +6
30,000	HP +40
60,000	Curasa
30,000	Strength +5
30,000	HP +40
30,000	HP +40
30,000	HP +40
30,000	Magic +6
30,000	HP +40
30,000	HP +40
120,000	Role Level (LV3)
60,000	Magic +7
60,000	HP +100
60,000	HP +100
60,000	HP +100
60,000	Strength +5
60,000	HP +100
60,000	HP +100
120,000	Role Level (LV4)
60,000	Magic +7
60,000	HP +100
60,000	Strength +5
60,000	HP +100
60,000	HP +100
60,000	HP +100
120,000	Role Level (LV5)

SENTINEL

CP	Bonus
3,000	HP +10
3,000	HP +10
3,000	Strength +3
3,000	HP +10
3,000	Magic +3
6,000	Provoke
6,000	HP +10
6,000	HP +10
6,000	HP +10
6,000	Strength +3
12,000	Steelguard
9,000	HP +15
9,000	Magic +4
9,000	HP +15
9,000	Strength +4
18,000	Vendetta
12,000	HP +15
12,000	Magic +4
12,000	HP +15
12,000	HP +15
12,000	Strength +4
15,000	HP +20
15,000	Magic +5
15,000	HP +20
15,000	Strength +5
30,000	Challenge
18,000	Magic +5
18,000	HP +20
18,000	Strength +5
18,000	HP +20
18,000	HP +20
21,000	Strength +7
21,000	HP +25
21,000	HP +25
21,000	Magic +5
42,000	Fringeward

CP	Bonus
24,000	HP +25
24,000	Strength +7
24,000	HP +25
24,000	HP +25
24,000	Magic +6
60,000	Role Level (LV2)
30,000	HP +40
30,000	HP +40
30,000	Strength +9
30,000	HP +40
30,000	HP +40
30,000	Magic +6
30,000	HP +40
30,000	HP +40
30,000	Strength +9
60,000	Deathward
30,000	HP +40
30,000	Magic +6
30,000	HP +40
30,000	HP +40
30,000	HP +40
120,000	Role Level (LV3)
60,000	HP +100
60,000	Strength +5
60,000	HP +100
60,000	Magic +7
60,000	HP +100
60,000	HP +100
60,000	HP +100
120,000	Role Level (LV4)
60,000	HP +100
60,000	HP +100
60,000	Strength +5
60,000	Magic +7
60,000	HP +100
60,000	HP +100
120,000	Role Level (LV5)

SABOTEUR

CP	Bonus
3,000	Magic +3
3,000	HP +10
3,000	HP +10
3,000	Strength +3
3,000	HP +10
6,000	Deprotect
6,000	HP +10
6,000	HP +10
6,000	Magic +3
6,000	Strength +3
12,000	Deshell
9,000	Magic +4
9,000	HP +15
9,000	HP +15
9,000	Strength +4
9,000	HP +15
12,000	HP +15
12,000	Magic +4
12,000	HP +15
12,000	Strength +4
24,000	Imperil
15,000	Strength +5
15,000	HP +20
15,000	HP +20
15,000	Magic +5
15,000	HP +20
18,000	HP +20
18,000	Magic +5
18,000	Strength +5
18,000	HP +20
36,000	Poison
21,000	Strength +5
21,000	Magic +6
21,000	HP +25
21,000	HP +25
42,000	Jinx

CP	Bonus
24,000	Strength +5
48,000	Dispel
24,000	HP +25
24,000	Magic +6
48,000	Curse
60,000	Role Level (LV2)
30,000	HP +40
30,000	HP +40
30,000	Strength +5
60,000	Pain
30,000	HP +40
30,000	Magic +6
30,000	HP +40
30,000	HP +40
30,000	Strength +5
30,000	HP +40
30,000	HP +40
60,000	Fog
30,000	Magic +6
30,000	HP +40
30,000	HP +40
120,000	Role Level (LV3)
60,000	HP +100
60,000	Strength +5
60,000	HP +100
120,000	Daze
60,000	HP +100
60,000	Magic +7
60,000	HP +100
120,000	Role Level (LV4)
60,000	HP +100
120,000	Slow
60,000	Strength +5
60,000	HP +100
60,000	HP +100
60,000	Magic +7
120,000	Role Level (LV5)

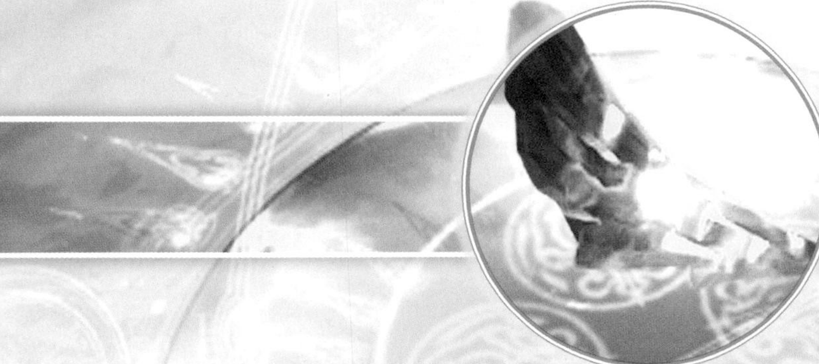

SENTINEL

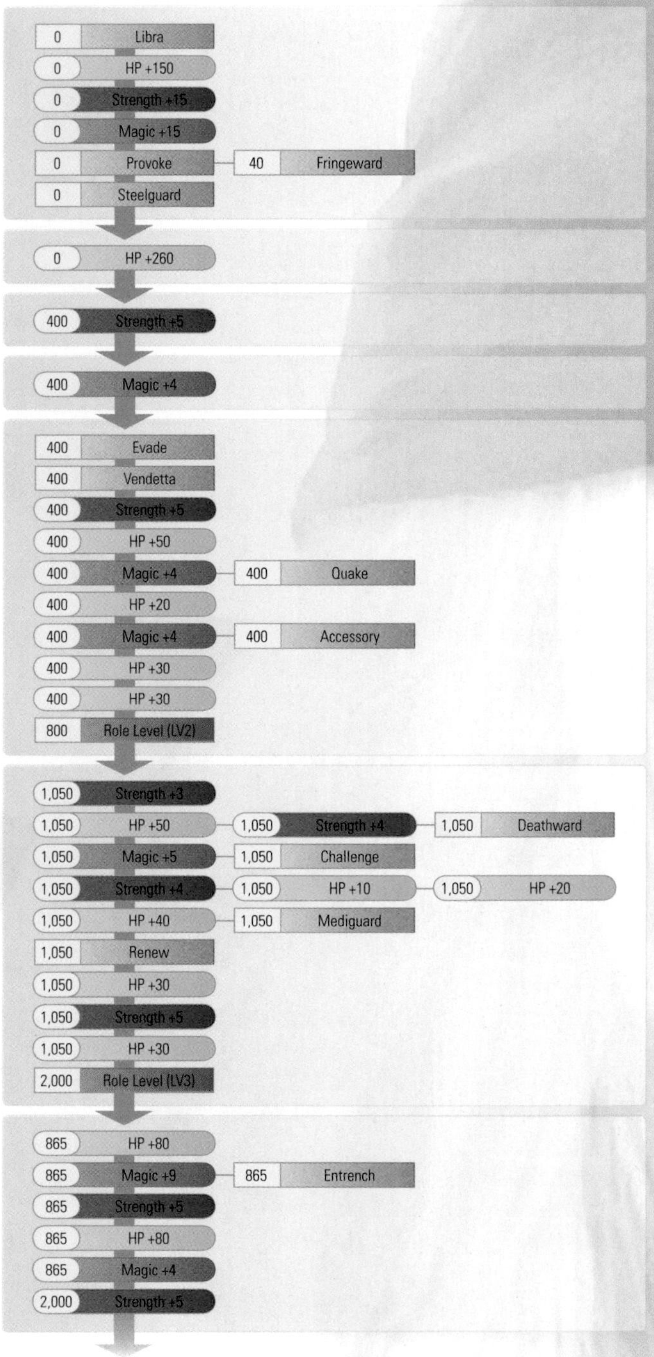
0 Libra
0 HP +150
0 Strength +15
0 Magic +15
0 Provoke
40 Fringeward
0 Steelguard
0 HP +260
400 Strength +5
400 Magic +4
400 Evade
400 Vendetta
400 Strength +5
400 HP +50
400 Magic +4
400 Quake
400 HP +20
400 Magic +4
400 Accessory
400 HP +30
400 HP +30
800 Role Level (LV2)
1,050 Strength +3
1,050 HP +50
1,050 Strength +4
1,050 Deathward
1,050 Magic +5
1,050 Challenge
1,050 Strength +4
1,050 HP +10
1,050 HP +20
1,050 HP +40
1,050 Mediguard
1,050 Renew
1,050 HP +30
1,050 Strength +5
1,050 HP +30
2,000 Role Level (LV3)
865 HP +80
865 Magic +9
865 Entrench
865 Strength +5
865 HP +80
865 Magic +4
2,000 Strength +5

4,000 HP +100
4,000 Strength +16
6,000 Strength +18
6,000 Dispelga
4,000 Magic +13
4,000 HP +100
6,000 HP +100
6,000 Counter
4,000 Magic +13
6,000 HP +100
8,000 HP +100
8,000 HP +100
6,000 Strength +18
6,000 Magic +14
8,000 Magic +13
6,000 Strength +18
8,000 HP +160
10,000 HP +100
10,000 HP +100
8,000 Strength +18
10,000 Strength +18
10,000 Reprieve
8,000 Magic +15
8,000 ATB Level
8,000 HP +200
10,000 Strength +18
8,000 Magic +15
8,000 Role Level (LV4)
10,000 HP +200
10,000 Strength +28
18,000 Strength +20
18,000 Strength +22
10,000 Magic +22
18,000 Magic +15
10,000 HP +200
18,000 HP +100
18,000 HP +100
12,000 Magic +25
18,000 HP +100
12,000 HP +240
18,000 HP +100
18,000 Strength +20
18,000 Magic +20
12,000 Strength +30
12,000 Magic +25
12,000 Strength +30
18,000 Strength +20
12,000 HP +200
18,000 HP +100
18,000 HP +100
12,000 Strength +30
12,000 HP +200
12,000 Magic +23
30,000 HP +450
30,000 HP +450
30,000 Strength +20
30,000 HP +500
30,000 HP +500
30,000 Magic +20
30,000 HP +500
30,000 HP +500
60,000 HP +500
60,000 Strength +24
60,000 HP +500
60,000 HP +500
60,000 Magic +20
60,000 HP +500
60,000 HP +500
60,000 Role Level (LV5)

COMMANDO

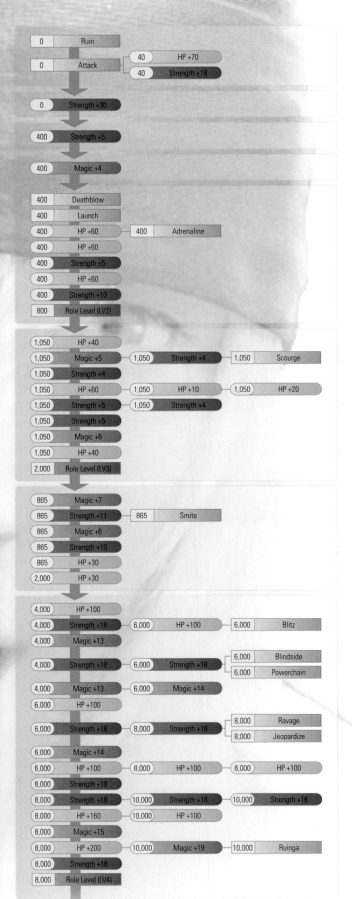

CP	Node	CP	Branch	CP	Branch
0	Ruin				
0	Attack	40	HP +70		
		40	Strength +18		
0	Strength +30				
400	Strength +5				
400	Magic +4				
400	Deathblow				
400	Launch				
400	HP +60	400	Adrenaline		
400	HP +60				
400	Strength +5				
400	HP +60				
400	Strength +10				
800	Role Level (LV2)				
1,050	HP +40				
1,050	Magic +5	1,050	Strength +4	1,050	Scourge
1,050	Strength +4				
1,050	HP +60	1,050	HP +10	1,050	HP +20
1,050	Strength +5	1,050	Strength +4		
1,050	Strength +5				
1,050	Magic +6				
1,050	HP +40				
2,000	Role Level (LV3)				
865	Magic +7				
865	Strength +11	865	Smite		
865	Magic +6				
865	Strength +10				
865	HP +30				
2,000	HP +30				
4,000	HP +100				
4,000	Strength +18	6,000	HP +100	6,000	Blitz
4,000	Magic +13				
4,000	Strength +18	6,000	Strength +18	6,000	Blindside
				6,000	Powerchain
4,000	Magic +13	6,000	Magic +14		
6,000	HP +100				
6,000	Strength +18	8,000	Strength +18	8,000	Ravage
				8,000	Jeopardize
6,000	Magic +14				
6,000	HP +100	8,000	HP +100	8,000	HP +100
8,000	Strength +18				
8,000	Strength +18	10,000	Strength +18	10,000	Strength +18
8,000	HP +160	10,000	HP +100		
8,000	Magic +15				
8,000	HP +200	10,000	Magic +19	10,000	Ruinga
8,000	Strength +18				
8,000	Role Level (LV4)				

RAVAGER

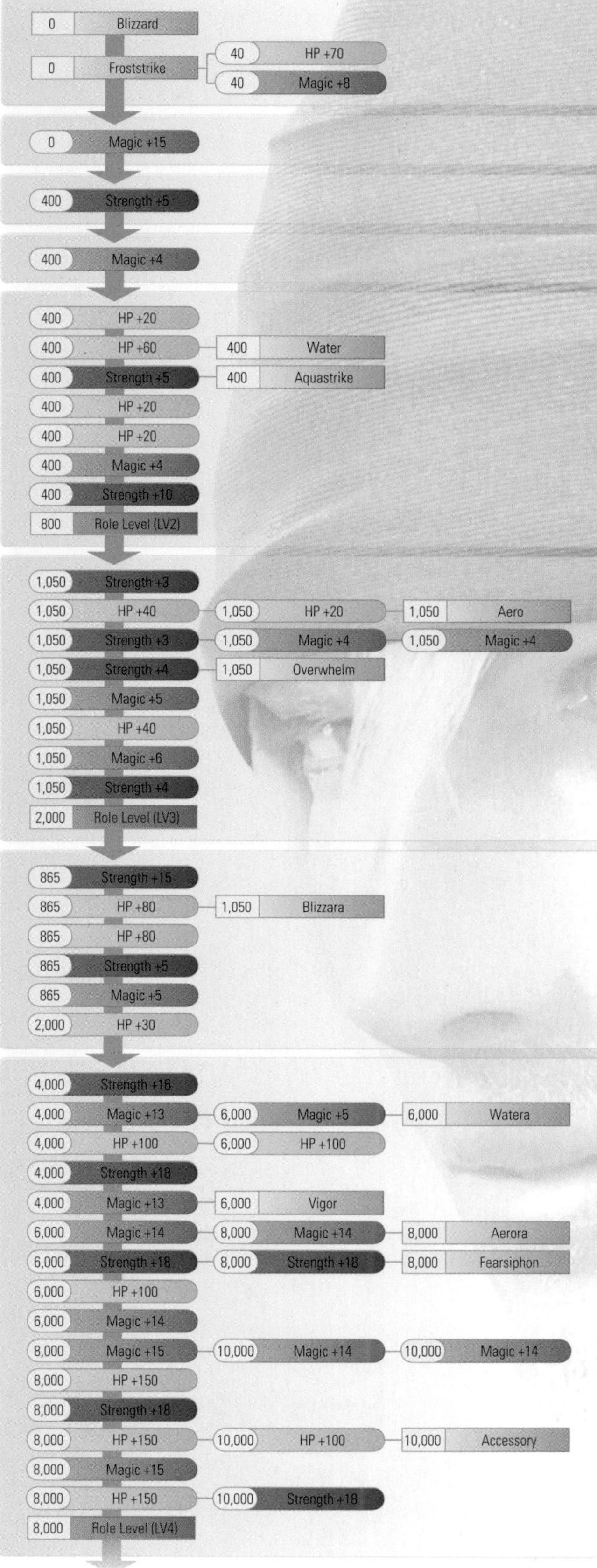

0 Blizzard
0 Froststrike — 40 HP +70
40 Magic +8
0 Magic +15
400 Strength +5
400 Magic +4
400 HP +20
400 HP +60 — 400 Water
400 Strength +5 — 400 Aquastrike
400 HP +20
400 HP +20
400 Magic +4
400 Strength +10
800 Role Level (LV2)
1,050 Strength +3
1,050 HP +40 — 1,050 HP +20 — 1,050 Aero
1,050 Strength +3 — 1,050 Magic +4 — 1,050 Magic +4
1,050 Strength +4 — 1,050 Overwhelm
1,050 Magic +5
1,050 HP +40
1,050 Magic +6
1,050 Strength +4
2,000 Role Level (LV3)
865 Strength +15
865 HP +80 — 1,050 Blizzara
865 HP +80
865 Strength +5
865 Magic +5
2,000 HP +30
4,000 Strength +16
4,000 Magic +13 — 6,000 Magic +5 — 6,000 Watera
4,000 HP +100 — 6,000 HP +100
4,000 Strength +18
4,000 Magic +13 — 6,000 Vigor
6,000 Magic +14 — 8,000 Magic +14 — 8,000 Aerora
6,000 Strength +18 — 8,000 Strength +18 — 8,000 Fearsiphon
6,000 HP +100
6,000 Magic +14
8,000 Magic +15 — 10,000 Magic +14 — 10,000 Magic +14
8,000 HP +150
8,000 Strength +18
8,000 HP +150 — 10,000 HP +100 — 10,000 Accessory
8,000 Magic +15
8,000 HP +150 — 10,000 Strength +18
8,000 Role Level (LV4)

10,000 Strength +28
10,000 Magic +22 — 18,000 Magic +20 — 18,000 Blizzaga
10,000 Magic +24 — 18,000 Magic +20 — 18,000 Waterga
10,000 HP +200 — 18,000 HP +100
12,000 HP +200
12,000 Strength +30 — 18,000 HP +100 — 18,000 Strength +20
18,000 Magic +20
18,000 Magic +20
12,000 Magic +25
12,000 HP +230
12,000 Magic +25
12,000 HP +200 — 18,000 HP +100 — 18,000 HP +100
12,000 Magic +30
12,000 Strength +30 — 18,000 Stopga
12,000 HP +200
30,000 HP +430
30,000 HP +430
30,000 Strength +20
30,000 HP +500
30,000 HP +500
30,000 Magic +20
30,000 HP +500
30,000 HP +500
60,000 HP +500
60,000 Strength +23
60,000 HP +500
60,000 HP +500
60,000 Magic +20
60,000 HP +500
60,000 HP +500
60,000 Role Level (LV5)

MEDIC

Stage	CP	Bonus
1	3,000	Strength +3
1	3,000	HP +10
1	3,000	HP +10
1	3,000	Magic +3
1	3,000	HP +10
1	6,000	Cure
2	6,000	HP +10
2	6,000	HP +10
2	6,000	Magic +3
2	6,000	Strength +4
2	6,000	HP +10
3	9,000	HP +20
3	9,000	HP +20
3	9,000	Strength +5
3	9,000	HP +20
3	18,000	Cura
4	12,000	HP +20
4	12,000	Magic +4
4	12,000	HP +20
4	12,000	Strength +5
4	12,000	HP +20
5	15,000	HP +30
5	15,000	Strength +5
5	15,000	HP +30
5	15,000	Magic +5
5	30,000	Esuna
6	18,000	Magic +5
6	18,000	HP +30
6	18,000	HP +30
6	18,000	Strength +5
6	18,000	HP +30
7	21,000	HP +40
7	21,000	HP +40
7	21,000	Magic +6
7	21,000	Strength +5
7	21,000	HP +40
8	24,000	HP +40
8	24,000	HP +40
8	24,000	Strength +5
8	24,000	Magic +6
8	24,000	HP +40
9	60,000	Role Level (LV2)
9	30,000	HP +40
9	30,000	HP +40
9	30,000	Strength +5
9	30,000	HP +40
9	30,000	HP +40
9	30,000	Magic +8
9	30,000	HP +40
9	30,000	HP +40
9	30,000	Strength +5
9	30,000	HP +40
9	60,000	Curasa
9	30,000	Magic +8
9	30,000	HP +40
9	30,000	HP +40
9	30,000	HP +40
10	120,000	Role Level (LV3)
10	60,000	Strength +5
10	60,000	HP +100
10	60,000	HP +100
10	60,000	HP +100
10	60,000	Magic +9
10	60,000	HP +100
10	60,000	HP +100
10	120,000	Role Level (LV4)
10	60,000	HP +100
10	60,000	HP +100
10	60,000	Magic +10
10	60,000	Strength +5
10	60,000	HP +100
10	60,000	HP +100
10	120,000	Role Level (LV5)

SYNERGIST

Stage	CP	Bonus
1	3,000	Magic +3
1	3,000	HP +10
1	3,000	HP +10
1	3,000	Strength +3
1	3,000	HP +10
1	6,000	Protect
2	6,000	HP +10
2	6,000	Strength +4
2	6,000	HP +10
2	6,000	Magic +3
2	12,000	Vigilance
3	9,000	HP +20
3	9,000	HP +20
3	9,000	HP +20
3	9,000	Strength +5
3	18,000	Shell
4	12,000	HP +20
4	12,000	Strength +5
4	12,000	HP +20
4	12,000	Magic +4
4	12,000	HP +20
5	15,000	Magic +5
5	15,000	HP +30
5	15,000	HP +30
5	15,000	Strength +5
5	30,000	Bravery
6	18,000	Strength +5
6	18,000	HP +30
6	18,000	Magic +5
6	18,000	HP +30
6	36,000	Faith
7	21,000	HP +40
7	21,000	Magic +6
7	21,000	HP +40
7	21,000	Strength +5
7	21,000	HP +40
8	24,000	Magic +6
8	24,000	HP +40
8	24,000	Strength +5
8	24,000	HP +40
8	48,000	Boon
9	60,000	Role Level (LV2)
9	30,000	HP +40
9	30,000	HP +40
9	30,000	Strength +5
9	30,000	HP +40
9	30,000	HP +40
9	30,000	Magic +8
9	60,000	Haste
9	30,000	HP +40
9	30,000	Strength +5
9	30,000	HP +40
9	30,000	Magic +8
9	30,000	HP +40
9	30,000	HP +40
9	30,000	HP +40
9	30,000	HP +40
10	120,000	Role Level (LV3)
10	60,000	HP +100
10	60,000	HP +100
10	60,000	Magic +9
10	60,000	HP +100
10	60,000	Strength +5
10	60,000	HP +100
10	60,000	HP +100
10	120,000	Role Level (LV4)
10	60,000	Magic +10
10	60,000	HP +100
10	60,000	Strength +5
10	60,000	HP +100
10	60,000	HP +100
10	60,000	HP +100
10	120,000	Role Level (LV5)

SABOTEUR

Stage	CP	Bonus
1	3,000	HP +10
1	3,000	Magic +3
1	3,000	Strength +3
1	3,000	HP +10
1	3,000	HP +10
1	6,000	Curse
2	6,000	Magic +3
2	6,000	HP +10
2	6,000	HP +10
2	6,000	Strength +4
2	12,000	Pain
3	9,000	Magic +4
3	9,000	HP +20
3	9,000	HP +20
3	9,000	Strength +5
3	18,000	Fog
4	12,000	HP +20
4	12,000	HP +20
4	12,000	Magic +4
4	12,000	Strength +5
4	24,000	Jinx
5	15,000	HP +30
5	15,000	HP +30
5	15,000	Strength +5
5	15,000	Magic +5
5	30,000	Daze
6	18,000	HP +30
6	18,000	Magic +5
6	18,000	HP +30
6	18,000	Strength +5
6	36,000	Slow
7	21,000	HP +40
7	21,000	HP +40
7	21,000	Strength +5
7	21,000	Magic +6
7	42,000	Cursega
8	24,000	Strength +10
8	24,000	HP +40
8	24,000	Magic +6
8	24,000	HP +40
8	48,000	Dazega
9	60,000	Role Level (LV2)
9	30,000	HP +36
9	30,000	HP +36
9	30,000	Strength +5
9	30,000	HP +36
9	30,000	HP +36
9	30,000	Magic +8
9	30,000	HP +36
9	30,000	HP +36
9	30,000	Strength +5
9	30,000	HP +36
9	30,000	HP +36
9	30,000	Magic +8
9	30,000	HP +36
9	30,000	HP +36
9	60,000	Slowga
10	120,000	Role Level (LV3)
10	60,000	HP +30
10	60,000	Strength +5
10	60,000	HP +30
10	120,000	Fogga
10	60,000	HP +30
10	60,000	Magic +9
10	60,000	HP +30
10	60,000	HP +30
10	120,000	Role Level (LV4)
10	60,000	HP +30
10	120,000	Painga
10	60,000	Strength +5
10	60,000	HP +30
10	60,000	Magic +10
10	120,000	Role Level (LV5)

MEDIC

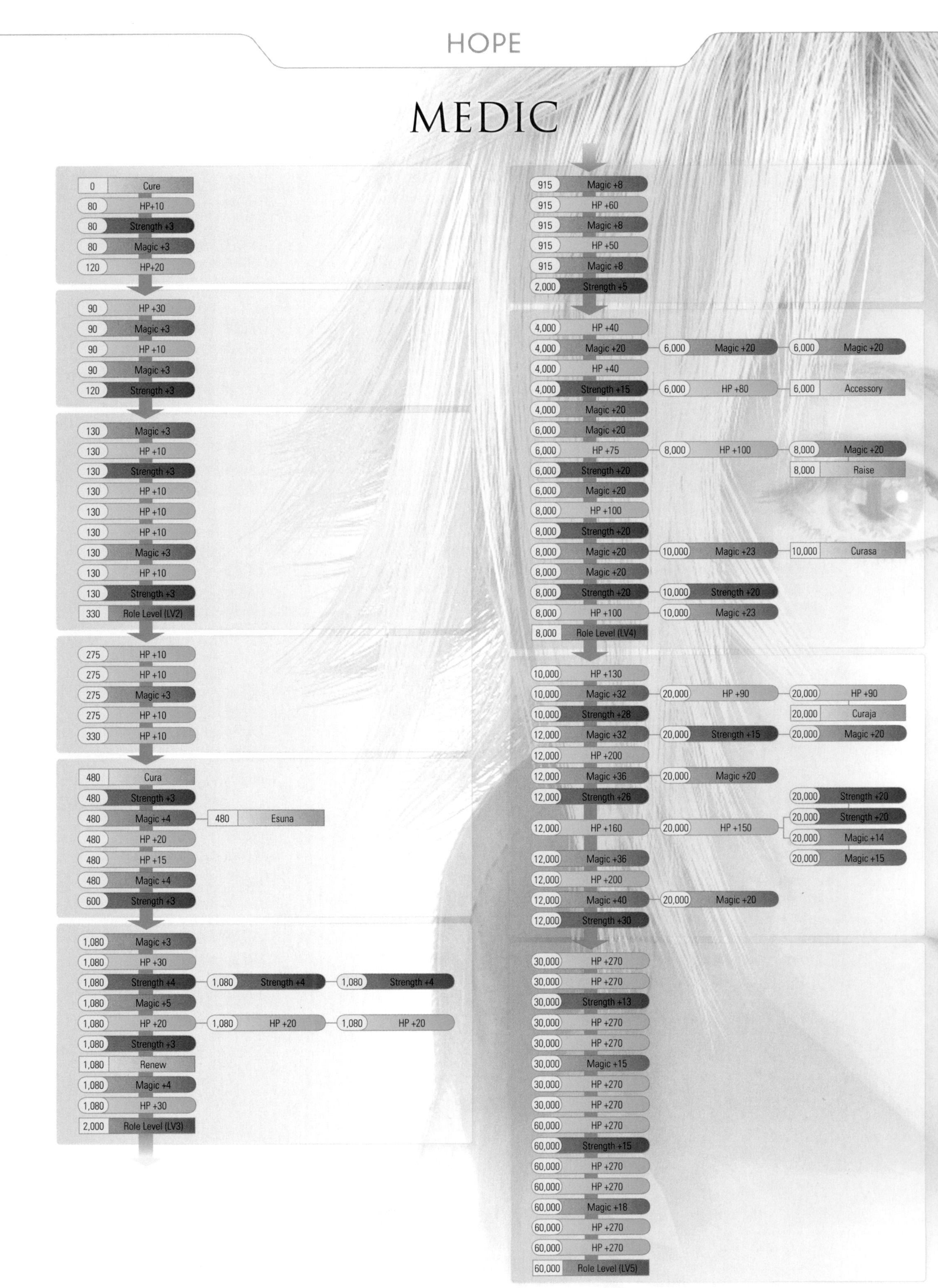
0 Cure
80 HP+10
80 Strength +3
80 Magic +3
120 HP+20
90 HP +30
90 Magic +3
90 HP +10
90 Magic +3
120 Strength +3
130 Magic +3
130 HP +10
130 Strength +3
130 HP +10
130 HP +10
130 HP +10
130 Magic +3
130 HP +10
130 Strength +3
330 Role Level (LV2)
275 HP +10
275 HP +10
275 Magic +3
275 HP +10
330 HP +10
480 Cura
480 Strength +3
480 Magic +4
480 Esuna
480 HP +20
480 HP +15
480 Magic +4
600 Strength +3
1,080 Magic +3
1,080 HP +30
1,080 Strength +4
1,080 Strength +4
1,080 Strength +4
1,080 Magic +5
1,080 HP +20
1,080 HP +20
1,080 HP +20
1,080 Strength +3
1,080 Renew
1,080 Magic +4
1,080 HP +30
2,000 Role Level (LV3)
915 Magic +8
915 HP +60
915 Magic +8
915 HP +50
915 Magic +8
2,000 Strength +5
4,000 HP +40
4,000 Magic +20
6,000 Magic +20
6,000 Magic +20
4,000 HP +40
4,000 Strength +15
6,000 HP +80
6,000 Accessory
4,000 Magic +20
6,000 Magic +20
6,000 HP +75
8,000 HP +100
8,000 Magic +20
8,000 Raise
6,000 Strength +20
6,000 Magic +20
8,000 HP +100
8,000 Strength +20
8,000 Magic +20
10,000 Magic +23
10,000 Curasa
8,000 Magic +20
8,000 Strength +20
10,000 Strength +20
8,000 HP +100
10,000 Magic +23
8,000 Role Level (LV4)
10,000 HP +130
10,000 Magic +32
20,000 HP +90
20,000 HP +90
20,000 Curaja
10,000 Strength +28
12,000 Magic +32
20,000 Strength +15
20,000 Magic +20
12,000 HP +200
12,000 Magic +36
20,000 Magic +20
12,000 Strength +26
20,000 Strength +20
12,000 HP +160
20,000 HP +150
20,000 Strength +20
20,000 Magic +14
20,000 Magic +15
12,000 Magic +36
12,000 HP +200
12,000 Magic +40
20,000 Magic +20
12,000 Strength +30
30,000 HP +270
30,000 HP +270
30,000 Strength +13
30,000 HP +270
30,000 HP +270
30,000 Magic +15
30,000 HP +270
30,000 HP +270
60,000 HP +270
60,000 Strength +15
60,000 HP +270
60,000 HP +270
60,000 Magic +18
60,000 HP +270
60,000 HP +270
60,000 Role Level (LV5)

FINAL FANTASY XIII

SYNERGIST

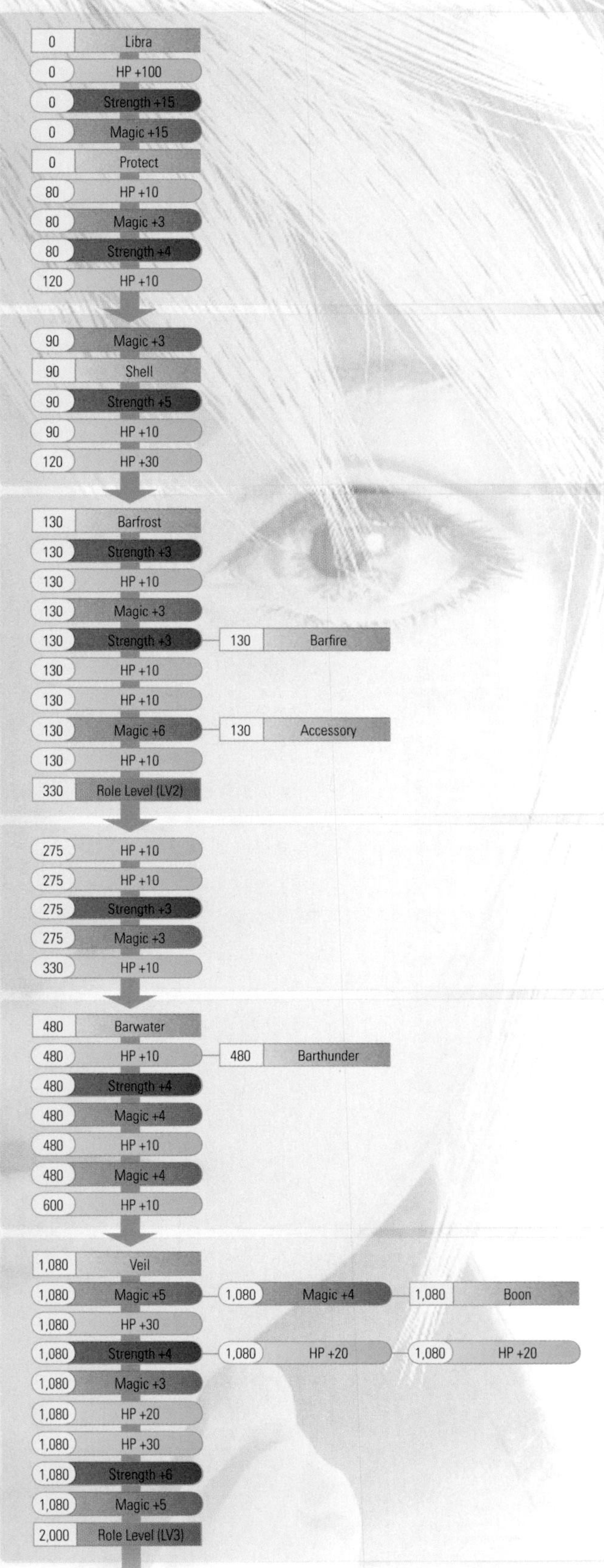
0 Libra
0 HP +100
0 Strength +15
0 Magic +15
0 Protect
80 HP +10
80 Magic +3
80 Strength +4
120 HP +10
90 Magic +3
90 Shell
90 Strength +5
90 HP +10
120 HP +30
130 Barfrost
130 Strength +3
130 HP +10
130 Magic +3
130 Strength +3
130 Barfire
130 HP +10
130 HP +10
130 Magic +6
130 Accessory
130 HP +10
330 Role Level (LV2)
275 HP +10
275 HP +10
275 Strength +3
275 Magic +3
330 HP +10
480 Barwater
480 HP +10
480 Barthunder
480 Strength +4
480 Magic +4
480 HP +10
480 Magic +4
600 HP +10
1,080 Veil
1,080 Magic +5
1,080 Magic +4
1,080 Boon
1,080 HP +30
1,080 Strength +4
1,080 HP +20
1,080 HP +20
1,080 Magic +3
1,080 HP +20
1,080 HP +30
1,080 Strength +6
1,080 Magic +5
2,000 Role Level (LV3)

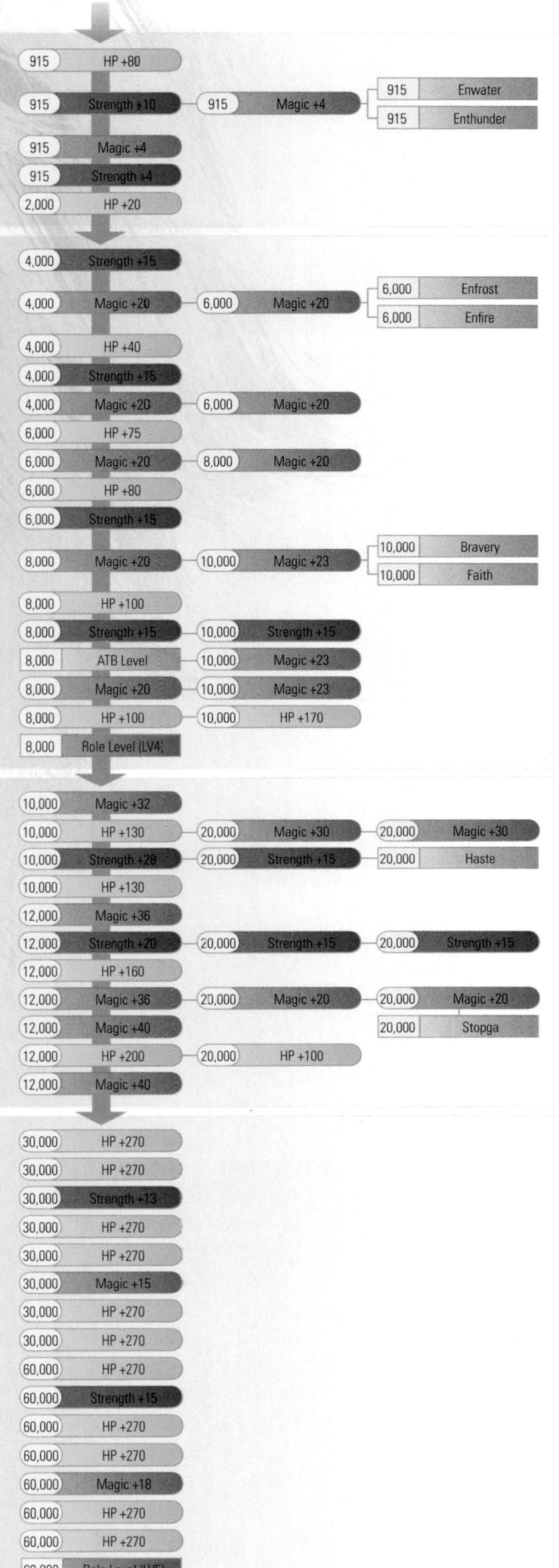
915 HP +80
915 Strength +10
915 Magic +4
915 Enwater
915 Enthunder
915 Magic +4
915 Strength +4
2,000 HP +20
4,000 Strength +15
4,000 Magic +20
6,000 Magic +20
6,000 Enfrost
6,000 Enfire
4,000 HP +40
4,000 Strength +15
4,000 Magic +20
6,000 Magic +20
6,000 HP +75
6,000 Magic +20
8,000 Magic +20
6,000 HP +80
6,000 Strength +15
8,000 Magic +20
10,000 Magic +23
10,000 Bravery
10,000 Faith
8,000 HP +100
8,000 Strength +15
10,000 Strength +15
8,000 ATB Level
10,000 Magic +23
8,000 Magic +20
10,000 Magic +23
8,000 HP +100
10,000 HP +170
8,000 Role Level (LV4)
10,000 Magic +32
10,000 HP +130
20,000 Magic +30
20,000 Magic +30
10,000 Strength +20
20,000 Strength +15
20,000 Haste
10,000 HP +130
12,000 Magic +36
12,000 Strength +20
20,000 Strength +15
20,000 Strength +15
12,000 HP +160
12,000 Magic +36
20,000 Magic +20
20,000 Magic +20
12,000 Magic +40
20,000 Stopga
12,000 HP +200
20,000 HP +100
12,000 Magic +40
30,000 HP +270
30,000 HP +270
30,000 Strength +13
30,000 HP +270
30,000 HP +270
30,000 Magic +15
30,000 HP +270
30,000 HP +270
60,000 HP +270
60,000 Strength +15
60,000 HP +270
60,000 HP +270
60,000 Magic +18
60,000 HP +270
60,000 HP +270
60,000 Role Level (LV5)

RAVAGER

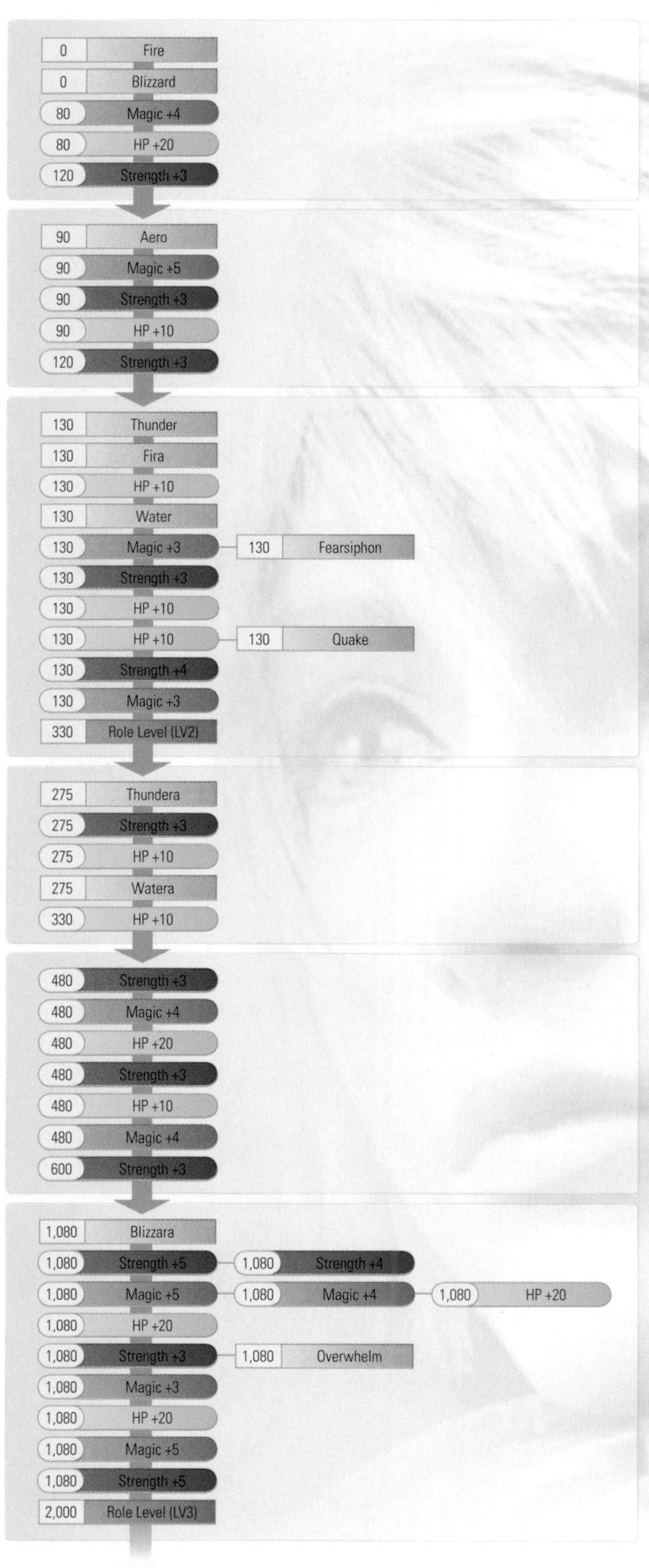

CP	Node	Branch	Branch
0	Fire		
0	Blizzard		
80	Magic +4		
80	HP +20		
120	Strength +3		

CP	Node	Branch	Branch
90	Aero		
90	Magic +5		
90	Strength +3		
90	HP +10		
120	Strength +3		

CP	Node	Branch	Branch
130	Thunder		
130	Fira		
130	HP +10		
130	Water		
130	Magic +3	130 Fearsiphon	
130	Strength +3		
130	HP +10		
130	HP +10	130 Quake	
130	Strength +4		
130	Magic +3		
330	Role Level (LV2)		

CP	Node	Branch	Branch
275	Thundera		
275	Strength +3		
275	HP +10		
275	Watera		
330	HP +10		

CP	Node	Branch	Branch
480	Strength +3		
480	Magic +4		
480	HP +20		
480	Strength +3		
480	HP +10		
480	Magic +4		
600	Strength +3		

CP	Node	Branch	Branch
1,080	Blizzara		
1,080	Strength +5	1,080 Strength +4	
1,080	Magic +5	1,080 Magic +4	1,080 HP +20
1,080	HP +20		
1,080	Strength +3	1,080 Overwhelm	
1,080	Magic +3		
1,080	HP +20		
1,080	Magic +5		
1,080	Strength +5		
2,000	Role Level (LV3)		

CP	Node	Branch	Branch
915	Strength +10		
915	Magic +15	915 Aerora	
915	HP +25		
915	Strength +7		
2,000	Magic +4		

CP	Node	Branch	Branch
4,000	Magic +20		
4,000	Strength +15	6,000 Dispelga	
4,000	HP +40	6,000 HP +80	
4,000	Strength +15	6,000 Strength +15	6,000 Strength +15
4,000	Magic +20		
6,000	HP +75		
6,000	Magic +20	8,000 Magic +20	8,000 Thundaga
6,000	Strength +15	8,000 Strength +15	8,000 Waterga
6,000	Magic +20		
8,000	HP +100	10,000 HP +180	10,000 Vigor
8,000	Strength +15		
8,000	Magic +20	10,000 Magic +22	10,000 Firaga / 10,000 Blizzaga
8,000	HP +100		
8,000	Strength +15	10,000 Aeroga	
8,000	HP +100	10,000 HP +180	
8,000	Role Level (LV4)		

CP	Node	Branch	Branch
10,000	Strength +28		
10,000	Magic +32	20,000 Magic +15	20,000 Strength +20
10,000	HP +130	20,000 HP +90	20,000 Last Resort
12,000	Magic +32		
12,000	Strength +26		
12,000	HP +160	20,000 HP +100	20,000 Strength +20 / 20,000 Strength +20 / 20,000 Magic +15 / 20,000 Magic +15
12,000	Magic +36		
12,000	Magic +36		
12,000	Strength +26	20,000 Strength +12	
12,000	HP +150		
12,000	Magic +40		

CP	Node
30,000	HP +270
30,000	HP +270
30,000	Strength +15
30,000	HP +270
30,000	HP +270
30,000	Magic +15
30,000	HP +270
30,000	Accessory
60,000	HP +270
60,000	Strength +15
60,000	HP +270
60,000	HP +270
60,000	Magic +18
60,000	HP +270
60,000	HP +270
60,000	Role Level (LV5)

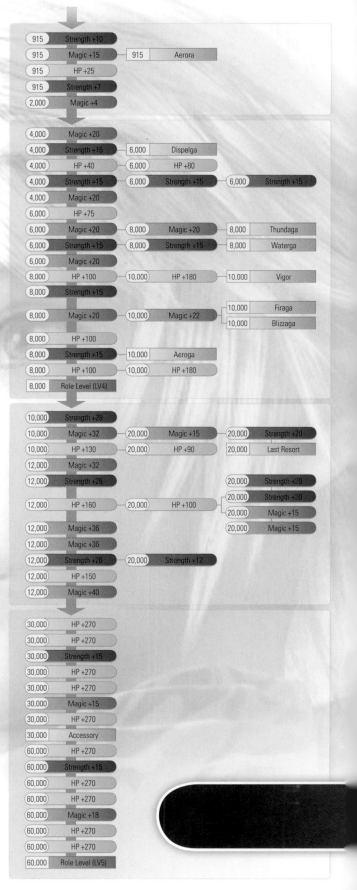

COMMANDO

6,000	Ruin
6,000	Attack
3,000	HP +10
3,000	Strength +3
3,000	HP +10
3,000	HP +10
6,000	HP +10
6,000	Magic +4
6,000	HP +10
6,000	Strength +4
6,000	HP +10
9,000	HP +15
9,000	HP +15
9,000	Magic +5
9,000	Strength +5
18,000	Faultsiphon
12,000	HP +15
12,000	Strength +5
12,000	Magic +5
12,000	HP +15
24,000	Blitz
15,000	HP +20
15,000	HP +20
15,000	Strength +5
15,000	Magic +5
30,000	Lifesiphon
18,000	HP +20
18,000	Strength +5
18,000	Magic +5
18,000	HP +20
36,000	Ravage
21,000	Magic +5
21,000	Strength +5
21,000	HP +25
21,000	HP +25
42,000	Scourge

24,000	HP +25
24,000	Strength +5
24,000	HP +25
24,000	Magic +5
48,000	Jeopardize
60,000	Role Level (LV2)
30,000	HP +25
30,000	Magic +5
30,000	Strength +5
30,000	HP +25
30,000	HP +25
30,000	Magic +5
60,000	Ruinga
30,000	Magic +5
30,000	Strength +5
30,000	Magic +5
30,000	HP +25
30,000	Magic +5
30,000	HP +25
30,000	HP +25
30,000	Magic +5
120,000	Role Level (LV3)
60,000	HP +100
60,000	Strength +5
60,000	HP +100
60,000	HP +100
60,000	Magic +5
60,000	HP +100
60,000	HP +100
120,000	Role Level (LV4)
60,000	HP +100
60,000	HP +100
60,000	Strength +5
60,000	HP +100
60,000	Magic +5
60,000	HP +100
120,000	Role Level (LV5)

SENTINEL

3,000	Strength +3
3,000	HP +10
3,000	HP +10
3,000	Magic +3
3,000	HP +10
6,000	Provoke
6,000	HP +10
6,000	HP +10
6,000	Magic +4
6,000	Strength +4
12,000	Evade
9,000	HP +15
9,000	Strength +5
9,000	HP +15
9,000	Magic +5
18,000	Entrench
12,000	Strength +5
12,000	HP +15
12,000	HP +15
12,000	Magic +5
12,000	HP +15
15,000	HP +20
15,000	Strength +5
15,000	HP +20
15,000	Magic +5
30,000	Elude
18,000	Strength +5
18,000	HP +20
18,000	Magic +5
18,000	HP +20
36,000	Counter
21,000	HP +25
21,000	Strength +5
21,000	Magic +5
21,000	HP +25
21,000	Magic +5

24,000	HP +25
24,000	HP +25
24,000	Strength +5
24,000	Magic +5
48,000	Vendetta
60,000	Role Level (LV2)
30,000	HP +30
30,000	Magic +5
30,000	Strength +5
30,000	HP +30
30,000	HP +30
30,000	Magic +5
30,000	HP +30
30,000	Magic +5
30,000	Strength +5
60,000	Reprieve
30,000	HP +30
30,000	Magic +5
30,000	HP +30
30,000	HP +30
30,000	Magic +5
120,000	Role Level (LV3)
60,000	HP +100
60,000	Strength +5
60,000	HP +100
60,000	HP +100
60,000	Magic +5
60,000	HP +100
60,000	HP +100
60,000	HP +100
120,000	Role Level (LV4)
60,000	HP +100
120,000	Deathward
60,000	Strength +5
60,000	HP +100
60,000	Magic +5
120,000	Role Level (LV5)

SABOTEUR

3,000	HP+10
3,000	Magic +3
3,000	HP+10
3,000	HP+10
3,000	Strength +3
6,000	Deprotega
6,000	Magic +4
6,000	HP +10
6,000	HP +10
6,000	Strength +4
12,000	Deshellga
9,000	HP +15
9,000	HP +15
9,000	Strength +5
9,000	Magic +5
9,000	HP +15
12,000	Magic +5
12,000	HP +15
12,000	HP +15
12,000	Strength +5
24,000	Dispel
15,000	HP +20
15,000	Magic +5
15,000	HP +20
15,000	Strength +5
30,000	Cursega
18,000	HP +20
18,000	Magic +5
18,000	HP +20
18,000	Strength +5
36,000	Jinx
21,000	HP +25
21,000	Strength +5
21,000	Magic +5
21,000	HP +25
42,000	Poisonga

24,000	HP +25
24,000	Magic +5
24,000	HP +25
24,000	Strength +5
48,000	Slowga
60,000	Role Level (LV2)
30,000	Magic +5
30,000	HP +25
30,000	Strength +5
30,000	HP +25
30,000	HP +25
30,000	Magic +5
60,000	Painga
30,000	HP +30
30,000	Strength +5
30,000	HP +30
30,000	HP +30
30,000	Magic +5
60,000	Fogga
30,000	Magic +5
30,000	HP +30
120,000	Role Level (LV3)
60,000	HP +100
60,000	Strength +5
60,000	HP +100
60,000	Magic +5
60,000	HP +100
120,000	Dazega
60,000	Magic +5
120,000	Role Level (LV4)
60,000	HP +100
60,000	Strength +5
120,000	Imperilga
60,000	HP +100
60,000	HP +100
60,000	Magic +5
120,000	Role Level (LV5)

SABOTEUR

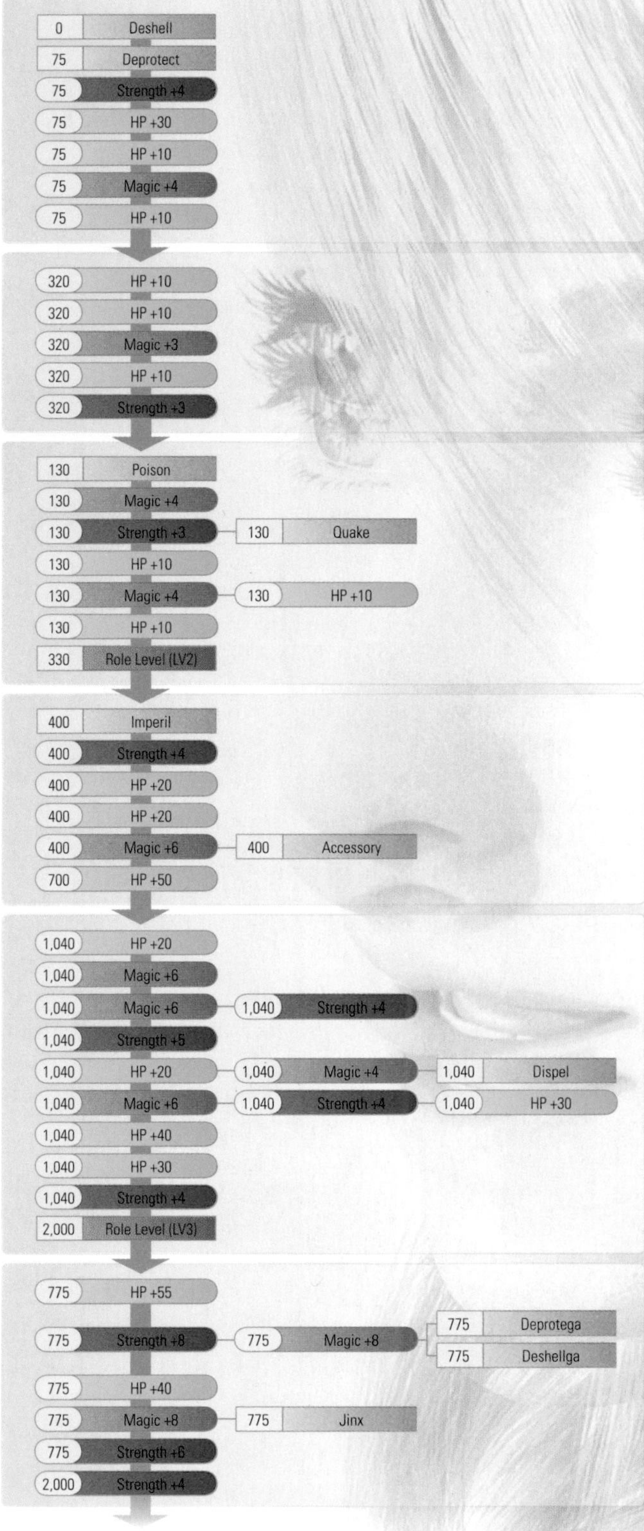
0 Deshell
75 Deprotect
75 Strength +4
75 HP +30
75 HP +10
75 Magic +4
75 HP +10
320 HP +10
320 HP +10
320 Magic +3
320 HP +10
320 Strength +3
130 Poison
130 Magic +4
130 Strength +3
130 Quake
130 HP +10
130 Magic +4
130 HP +10
130 HP +10
330 Role Level (LV2)
400 Imperil
400 Strength +4
400 HP +20
400 HP +20
400 Magic +6
400 Accessory
700 HP +50
1,040 HP +20
1,040 Magic +6
1,040 Magic +6
1,040 Strength +4
1,040 Strength +5
1,040 HP +20
1,040 Magic +4
1,040 Dispel
1,040 Magic +6
1,040 Strength +4
1,040 HP +30
1,040 HP +40
1,040 HP +30
1,040 Strength +4
2,000 Role Level (LV3)
775 HP +55
775 Strength +8
775 Magic +8
775 Deprotega
775 Deshellga
775 HP +40
775 Magic +8
775 Jinx
775 Strength +6
2,000 Strength +4

4,000 Strength +15
4,000 Magic +18
6,000 Poisonga
4,000 HP +100
6,000 HP +100
6,000 HP +100
4,000 Strength +14
4,000 Magic +18
6,000 Magic +18
6,000 Imperilga
6,000 Magic +18
6,000 HP +100
6,000 Strength +15
8,000 Strength +15
6,000 Magic +18
8,000 Strength +15
10,000 Fog
8,000 Magic +20
10,000 Magic +18
10,000 Strength +18
10,000 Pain
8,000 HP +100
8,000 Magic +20
8,000 Magic +20
10,000 Strength +18
8,000 HP +100
10,000 HP +100
8,000 Role Level (LV4)
10,000 HP +50
10,000 HP +80
10,000 Magic +26
10,000 HP +130
16,000 HP +80
16,000 HP +80
12,000 Strength +20
12,000 Magic +26
16,000 Magic +20
16,000 Magic +20
12,000 Magic +36
16,000 HP +100
16,000 Strength +20
12,000 Magic +36
16,000 Death
12,000 Strength +28
16,000 Strength +20
12,000 HP +200
16,000 HP +100
16,000 Strength +20
16,000 Magic +20
12,000 Strength +20
16,000 Magic +20
12,000 Magic +30
12,000 HP +200
12,000 Strength +20
30,000 HP +290
30,000 HP +290
30,000 Strength +20
30,000 HP +290
30,000 HP +290
30,000 Magic +20
30,000 HP +290
30,000 HP +290
60,000 HP +290
60,000 Strength +23
60,000 HP +290
60,000 HP +290
60,000 Magic +24
60,000 HP +290
60,000 HP +300
60,000 Role Level (LV5)

MEDIC

CP	Bonus	CP	Bonus	CP	Bonus
0	Libra				
0	Cure				
70	HP +30				
70	Magic +3				
70	Strength +3				
70	Magic +5				
70	Strength +4				
120	HP +20				

CP	Bonus	CP	Bonus	CP	Bonus
75	HP +30				
75	Magic +5				
75	HP +10				
75	Magic +3				
130	Strength +3				

CP	Bonus	CP	Bonus	CP	Bonus
320	HP +10				
320	Strength +2				
320	HP +10				
320	Magic +3				
500	HP +10				

CP	Bonus	CP	Bonus	CP	Bonus
130	Esuna				
130	Cura				
130	Magic +3				
130	HP +10				
130	Strength +2				
130	HP +10				
330	Role Level (LV2)				

CP	Bonus	CP	Bonus	CP	Bonus
400	HP +10				
400	HP +10				
400	Magic +5				
400	HP +10				
400	Strength +4				
700	HP +10				

CP	Bonus	CP	Bonus	CP	Bonus
1,040	HP +30				
1,040	HP +10	1,040	Strength +4		
1,040	Renew				
1,040	HP +40				
1,040	Strength +4	1,040	HP +30		
1,040	Magic +5	1,040	Magic +4	1,040	Strength +4
1,040	Strength +5	1,040	HP +30	1,040	Raise
1,040	Magic +5				
1,040	Strength +4				
2,000	Role Level (LV3)				

CP	Bonus	CP	Bonus	CP	Bonus
775	Strength +10				
775	Magic +10				
775	Magic +9				
775	Magic +8				
775	HP +40				
2,000	Strength +4				

CP	Bonus	CP	Bonus	CP	Bonus
4,000	ATB Level				
4,000	HP +100	6,000	HP +100	6,000	HP +100
4,000	Magic +18				
4,000	Strength +14	6,000	Strength +15	6,000	Magic +18
4,000	Magic +13			6,000	Curasa
6,000	HP +100				
6,000	Magic +18	8,000	Magic +18		
6,000	Strength +15				
6,000	HP +100	8,000	HP +100	8,000	Accessory
8,000	HP +100				
8,000	Magic +18	10,000	Magic +18	10,000	HP +125
8,000	HP +100				
8,000	Strength +18				
8,000	HP +100	10,000	Strength +21		
8,000	Magic +20	10,000	Magic +22	10,000	Curaja
8,000	Role Level (LV4)				

CP	Bonus	CP	Bonus	CP	Bonus
10,000	HP +50				
10,000	HP +80				
10,000	Strength +20	16,000	HP +80	16,000	Magic +20
10,000	Strength +25			16,000	Strength +20
12,000	Magic +26	16,000	HP +80	16,000	Magic +20
12,000	HP +150	16,000	HP +50	16,000	Stopga
12,000	HP +200	16,000	HP +100		
12,000	Magic +36				
12,000	Strength +28	16,000	Strength +20	16,000	Strength +20
12,000	HP +200				
12,000	Magic +36	16,000	Magic +20	16,000	Magic +20
12,000	Magic +30				
12,000	HP +200	16,000	HP +100		
12,000	Strength +20				

CP	Bonus	CP	Bonus	CP	Bonus
30,000	HP +290				
30,000	HP +290				
30,000	Strength +20				
30,000	HP +290				
30,000	HP +290				
30,000	Magic +20				
30,000	HP +290				
30,000	HP +290				
60,000	HP +290				
60,000	Strength +23				
60,000	HP +290				
60,000	HP +290				
60,000	Magic +23				
60,000	HP +290				
60,000	HP +300				
60,000	Role Level (LV5)				

RAVAGER

Main Path	Branch	Branch
0 Aero		
70 Strength +3		
70 Water	70 Magic +4	
70 Strength +2		
70 HP +30		
70 Strength +4		
120 Magic +5		

Main Path	Branch	Branch
75 Magic +5		
75 Strength +3	75 Fire	
75 HP +10		
75 Strength +4		
130 HP +10		

Main Path	Branch	Branch
320 HP +10		
320 Magic +3		
320 HP +10		
320 HP +10		
500 Strength +3		

Main Path	Branch	Branch
130 Aerora		
130 HP +5	130 Thunder	
130 Strength +3	130 Overwhelm	
130 Magic +2		
130 Strength +2	130 Fira	
130 HP +5		
330 Role Level (LV2)		

Main Path	Branch	Branch
400 Magic +2		
400 Magic +3		
400 HP +10		
400 HP +10		
400 Strength +4		
700 HP +10		

Main Path	Branch	Branch
1,040 Blizzard		
1,040 HP +30	1,040 Watera	
1,040 Strength +4	1,040 Magic +4	
1,040 Magic +5		
1,040 HP +30	1,040 HP +30	
1,040 Strength +4	1,040 Strength +5	1,040 Magic +4
1,040 Magic +5	1,040 Magic +4	1,040 Blizzara
1,040 HP +30		
1,040 Magic +4		
2,000 Role Level (LV3)		

Main Path	Branch	Branch
775 Magic +10		
775 HP +30	775 HP +30	
775 Thundara		
775 Strength +9		
775 HP +30		
2,000 HP +60		

Main Path	Branch	Branch
4,000 HP +100		
4,000 Magic +18	6,000 Dispelga	
4,000 Strength +14		6,000 Magic +18
4,000 HP +100	6,000 HP +100	6,000 Magic +18 / 6,000 Strength +15
4,000 Strength +15		6,000 Strength +15
6,000 Strength +15	8,000 HP +100	8,000 Firaga
6,000 HP +100		
6,000 Magic +18	8,000 Fearsiphon	
6,000 Strength +15		
8,000 Strength +15		
8,000 Magic +20	10,000 Magic +18	10,000 Blizzaga
8,000 HP +100		
8,000 Strength +15		
8,000 Strength +15	10,000 Strength +18	10,000 Strength +18
8,000 Magic +20	10,000 HP +100	
8,000 Role Level (LV4)		

Main Path	Branch	Branch
10,000 Magic +10		
10,000 Magic +16		
10,000 Strength +20	16,000 Strength +20	16,000 Strength +20
10,000 Magic +26	16,000 Magic +20	
12,000 HP +120	16,000 HP +80	16,000 HP +80
12,000 Strength +20		16,000 Strength +20
12,000 HP +200	16,000 HP +100	16,000 Strength +20 / 16,000 Magic +20
12,000 Strength +28		16,000 Magic +20
12,000 Magic +36		
12,000 Strength +28		
12,000 HP +200	16,000 HP +100	16,000 HP +100
12,000 HP +200		16,000 Magic +30
12,000 Magic +30		
12,000 Strength +30		

Main Path
30,000 HP +290
30,000 HP +290
30,000 Strength +20
30,000 HP +290
30,000 HP +290
30,000 Magic +20
30,000 HP +290
30,000 Accessory
60,000 HP +290
60,000 Strength +23
60,000 HP +290
60,000 HP +290
60,000 Magic +24
60,000 HP +290
60,000 HP +290
60,000 Role Level (LV5)

COMMANDO

CP	Bonus
3,000	Magic +3
3,000	HP +10
3,000	HP +10
3,000	Strength +3
3,000	HP +10
6,000	Attack
6,000	HP +10
6,000	HP +10
6,000	Magic +4
6,000	Strength +4
12,000	Ruin
9,000	HP +20
9,000	Strength +5
9,000	HP +20
9,000	Magic +5
18,000	Jeopardize
12,000	Magic +5
12,000	HP +20
12,000	HP +20
12,000	Strength +5
24,000	Faultsiphon
15,000	HP +25
15,000	HP +25
15,000	Strength +5
15,000	Magic +5
30,000	Blindside
18,000	HP +25
18,000	Magic +5
18,000	HP +25
18,000	Strength +5
18,000	HP +25
21,000	Magic +5
21,000	HP +30
21,000	Strength +5
21,000	HP +30
42,000	Scourge

CP	Bonus
24,000	Strength +5
24,000	Magic +5
24,000	HP +30
24,000	HP +30
48,000	Adrenaline
60,000	Role Level (LV2)
30,000	HP +40
30,000	Magic +5
30,000	Strength +5
30,000	HP +40
30,000	Strength +5
30,000	Magic +5
30,000	HP +40
60,000	Deathblow
30,000	Strength +5
30,000	Magic +5
30,000	HP +40
30,000	HP +40
30,000	Strength +5
30,000	Magic +5
30,000	HP +40
120,000	Role Level (LV3)
60,000	HP +100
60,000	Strength +10
60,000	HP +100
60,000	HP +100
60,000	Magic +10
60,000	HP +100
60,000	HP +100
120,000	Role Level (LV4)
60,000	HP +100
60,000	Strength +10
120,000	Ruinga
60,000	HP +100
60,000	Magic +10
60,000	HP +100
120,000	Role Level (LV5)

SENTINEL

CP	Bonus
3,000	Strength +3
3,000	HP +10
3,000	HP +10
3,000	Magic +3
3,000	HP +10
6,000	Provoke
6,000	HP +10
6,000	Strength +4
6,000	HP +10
6,000	Magic +4
6,000	HP +10
9,000	HP +20
9,000	Magic +5
9,000	HP +20
9,000	Strength +5
18,000	Mediguard
12,000	HP +20
12,000	Strength +5
12,000	HP +20
12,000	Magic +5
12,000	HP +20
15,000	Magic +5
15,000	HP +25
15,000	Strength +5
15,000	HP +25
30,000	Steelguard
18,000	Strength +5
18,000	HP +25
18,000	HP +25
18,000	Magic +5
18,000	HP +25
21,000	Magic +5
21,000	HP +30
21,000	HP +30
21,000	Strength +5
42,000	Reprieve

CP	Bonus
24,000	Magic +5
24,000	HP +30
24,000	HP +30
24,000	Strength +5
24,000	HP +30
60,000	Role Level (LV2)
30,000	HP +40
30,000	Magic +5
30,000	Strength +5
30,000	Strength +5
30,000	HP +40
30,000	Magic +5
60,000	Entrench
30,000	HP +40
30,000	Strength +5
30,000	HP +40
30,000	HP +40
30,000	Magic +5
30,000	Strength +5
30,000	HP +40
30,000	Magic +5
120,000	Role Level (LV3)
60,000	HP +100
60,000	HP +100
60,000	Strength +10
60,000	HP +100
60,000	HP +100
60,000	Magic +10
60,000	HP +100
120,000	Role Level (LV4)
60,000	HP +100
60,000	Strength +10
60,000	HP +100
60,000	HP +100
60,000	Magic +10
60,000	HP +100
120,000	Role Level (LV5)

SYNERGIST

CP	Bonus
3,000	HP +10
3,000	Magic +3
3,000	HP +10
3,000	Strength +3
3,000	HP +10
6,000	Vigilance
6,000	HP +10
6,000	Strength +4
6,000	Magic +4
6,000	HP +10
12,000	Veil
9,000	HP +20
9,000	Magic +5
18,000	Barwater
9,000	Strength +5
18,000	Barfrost
12,000	HP +20
12,000	Magic +5
24,000	Barfire
12,000	Strength +5
24,000	Barthunder
15,000	HP +25
15,000	HP +25
15,000	Strength +5
15,000	Magic +5
15,000	HP +25
18,000	HP +25
18,000	Magic +5
18,000	Strength +5
18,000	HP +25
36,000	Boon
21,000	Magic +5
21,000	HP +30
21,000	Strength +5
21,000	HP +30
42,000	Protectra

CP	Bonus
24,000	HP +30
24,000	Strength +5
24,000	HP +30
24,000	Magic +5
24,000	HP +30
60,000	Role Level (LV2)
30,000	HP +40
30,000	Magic +5
30,000	Strength +5
30,000	HP +40
30,000	HP +40
30,000	Magic +5
60,000	Shellra
30,000	HP +40
30,000	Strength +5
30,000	HP +40
30,000	Strength +5
30,000	Magic +5
30,000	HP +40
30,000	Magic +5
30,000	HP +40
120,000	Role Level (LV3)
60,000	HP +100
60,000	Strength +10
60,000	HP +100
120,000	Bravera
60,000	Magic +10
60,000	HP +100
120,000	Role Level (LV4)
60,000	Strength +10
60,000	HP +100
60,000	HP +100
60,000	Magic +10
120,000	Faithra
60,000	HP +100
60,000	HP +100
120,000	Role Level (LV5)

COMMANDO

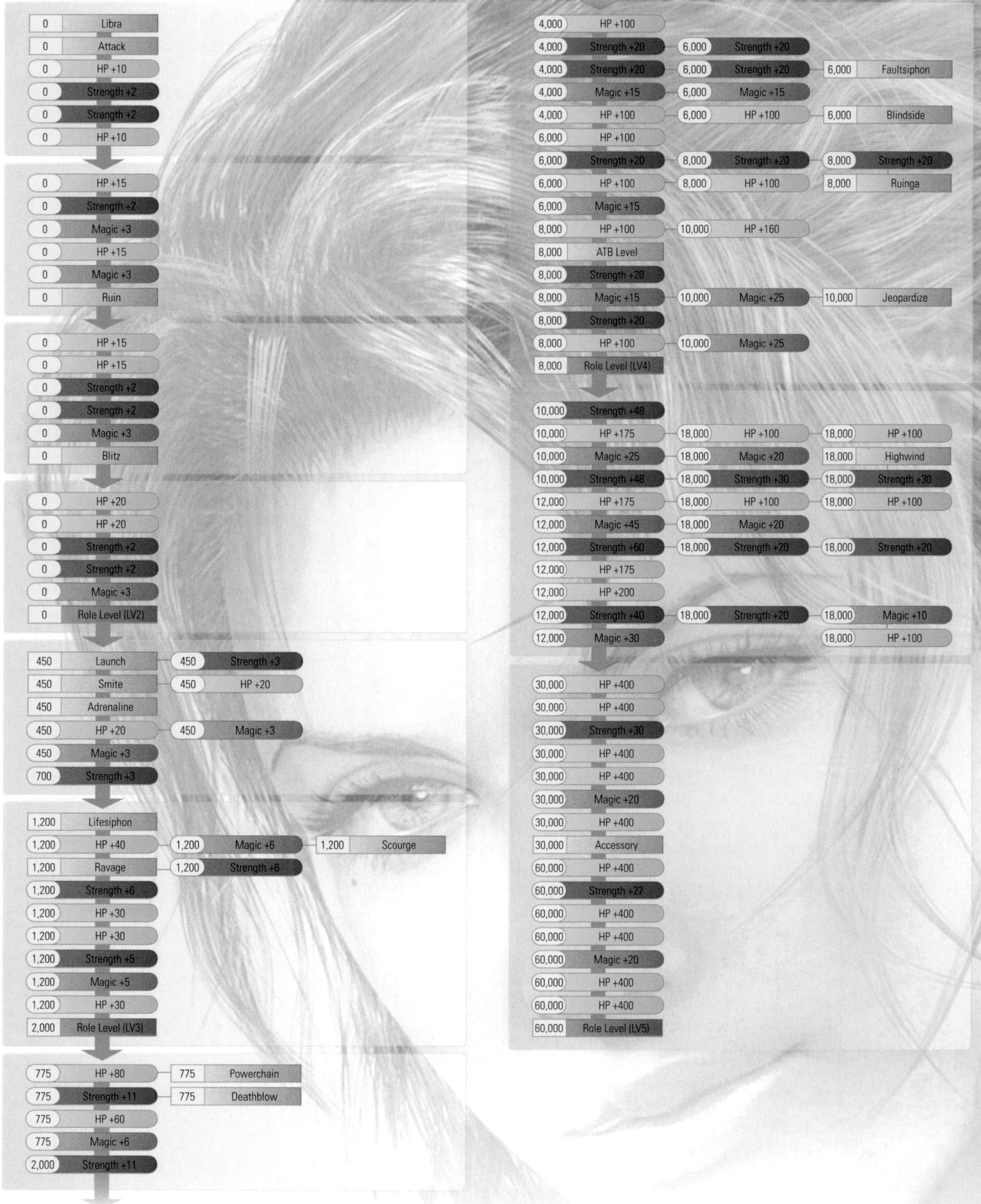
0 Libra
0 Attack
0 HP +10
0 Strength +2
0 Strength +2
0 HP +10
0 HP +15
0 Strength +2
0 Magic +3
0 HP +15
0 Magic +3
0 Ruin
0 HP +15
0 HP +15
0 Strength +2
0 Strength +2
0 Magic +3
0 Blitz
0 HP +20
0 HP +20
0 Strength +2
0 Strength +2
0 Magic +3
0 Role Level (LV2)
450 Launch — 450 Strength +3
450 Smite — 450 HP +20
450 Adrenaline
450 HP +20 — 450 Magic +3
450 Magic +3
700 Strength +3
1,200 Lifesiphon
1,200 HP +40 — 1,200 Magic +6 — 1,200 Scourge
1,200 Ravage — 1,200 Strength +6
1,200 Strength +6
1,200 HP +30
1,200 HP +30
1,200 Strength +5
1,200 Magic +5
1,200 HP +30
2,000 Role Level (LV3)
775 HP +80 — 775 Powerchain
775 Strength +11 — 775 Deathblow
775 HP +60
775 Magic +6
2,000 Strength +11
4,000 HP +100
4,000 Strength +20 — 6,000 Strength +20
4,000 Strength +20 — 6,000 Strength +20 — 6,000 Faultsiphon
4,000 Magic +15 — 6,000 Magic +15
4,000 HP +100 — 6,000 HP +100 — 6,000 Blindside
6,000 HP +100
6,000 Strength +20 — 8,000 Strength +20 — 8,000 Strength +20
6,000 HP +100 — 8,000 HP +100 — 8,000 Ruinga
6,000 Magic +15
8,000 HP +100 — 10,000 HP +160
8,000 ATB Level
8,000 Strength +20
8,000 Magic +15 — 10,000 Magic +25 — 10,000 Jeopardize
8,000 Strength +20
8,000 HP +100 — 10,000 Magic +25
8,000 Role Level (LV4)
10,000 Strength +48
10,000 HP +175 — 18,000 HP +100 — 18,000 HP +100
10,000 Magic +25 — 18,000 Magic +20 — 18,000 Highwind
10,000 Strength +48 — 18,000 Strength +30 — 18,000 Strength +30
12,000 HP +175 — 18,000 HP +100 — 18,000 HP +100
12,000 Magic +45 — 18,000 Magic +20
12,000 Strength +60 — 18,000 Strength +20 — 18,000 Strength +20
12,000 HP +175
12,000 HP +200
12,000 Strength +40 — 18,000 Strength +20 — 18,000 Magic +10
12,000 Magic +30 — 18,000 HP +100
30,000 HP +400
30,000 HP +400
30,000 Strength +30
30,000 HP +400
30,000 HP +400
30,000 Magic +20
30,000 HP +400
30,000 Accessory
60,000 HP +400
60,000 Strength +27
60,000 HP +400
60,000 HP +400
60,000 Magic +20
60,000 HP +400
60,000 HP +400
60,000 Role Level (LV5)

SENTINEL

0 Provoke
0 HP +10
0 Strength +3
0 HP +10
0 Strength +3
0 Mediguard
0 Strength +3
0 HP +15
0 Magic +2
0 Strength +3
0 HP +15
0 Deathward
0 Strength +3
0 Strength +3
0 HP +15
0 HP +15
0 Magic +3
0 Fringeward
0 Evade
0 Strength +3
0 Strength +3
0 HP +20
0 HP +20
0 Role Level (LV2)
450 HP +40
450 Strength +8
450 HP +40
450 Magic +4 — 450 Quake
450 Strength +6
700 HP +10
1,200 Steelguard
1,200 Magic +5
1,200 HP +40 — 1,200 HP +30
1,200 Strength +6 — 1,200 Strength +5
1,200 Strength +6
1,200 Renew
1,200 Strength +5
1,200 Magic +5
1,200 HP +30
2,000 Role Level (LV3)
775 Magic +10 — 775 Strength +10 — 775 Counter / 775 Challenge
775 HP +80 — 775 Entrench
775 HP +60
775 Strength +10
2,000 Magic +5

4,000 Strength +20
4,000 HP +100 — 6,000 HP +100 — 6,000 Dispelga
4,000 Strength +20 — 6,000 Strength +20 — 6,000 Strength +20
4,000 HP +100
4,000 Magic +15 — 6,000 Magic +15
6,000 Strength +20 — 8,000 Strength +20 — 8,000 Strength +20 / 8,000 Vendetta
6,000 HP +100
6,000 HP +100 — 8,000 HP +100
6,000 Magic +15 — 8,000 Magic +15
8,000 Strength +20
8,000 HP +100 — 10,000 HP +160 — 10,000 Accessory
8,000 Magic +15
8,000 Strength +20 — 10,000 Strength +34
8,000 HP +100 — 10,000 HP +160
8,000 Strength +20 — 10,000 Magic +30
8,000 Role Level (LV4)
10,000 HP +195
10,000 Strength +48 — 18,000 Strength +20 — 18,000 Strength +20
10,000 HP +195 — 18,000 HP +100 — 18,000 Reprieve
10,000 Magic +25 — 18,000 Magic +20
12,000 HP +195
12,000 Strength +60 — 18,000 Strength +20 — 18,000 Strength +20
12,000 Magic +45
12,000 HP +195 — 18,000 HP +100 — 18,000 HP +100
12,000 HP +200
12,000 Strength +40 — 18,000 Strength +20 — 18,000 Magic +10
12,000 Magic +30
30,000 HP +400
30,000 HP +400
30,000 Strength +30
30,000 HP +400
30,000 HP +400
30,000 Magic +17
30,000 HP +400
30,000 HP +400
60,000 HP +400
60,000 Strength +27
60,000 HP +400
60,000 HP +400
60,000 Magic +20
60,000 HP +400
60,000 HP +400
60,000 Role Level (LV5)

SABOTEUR

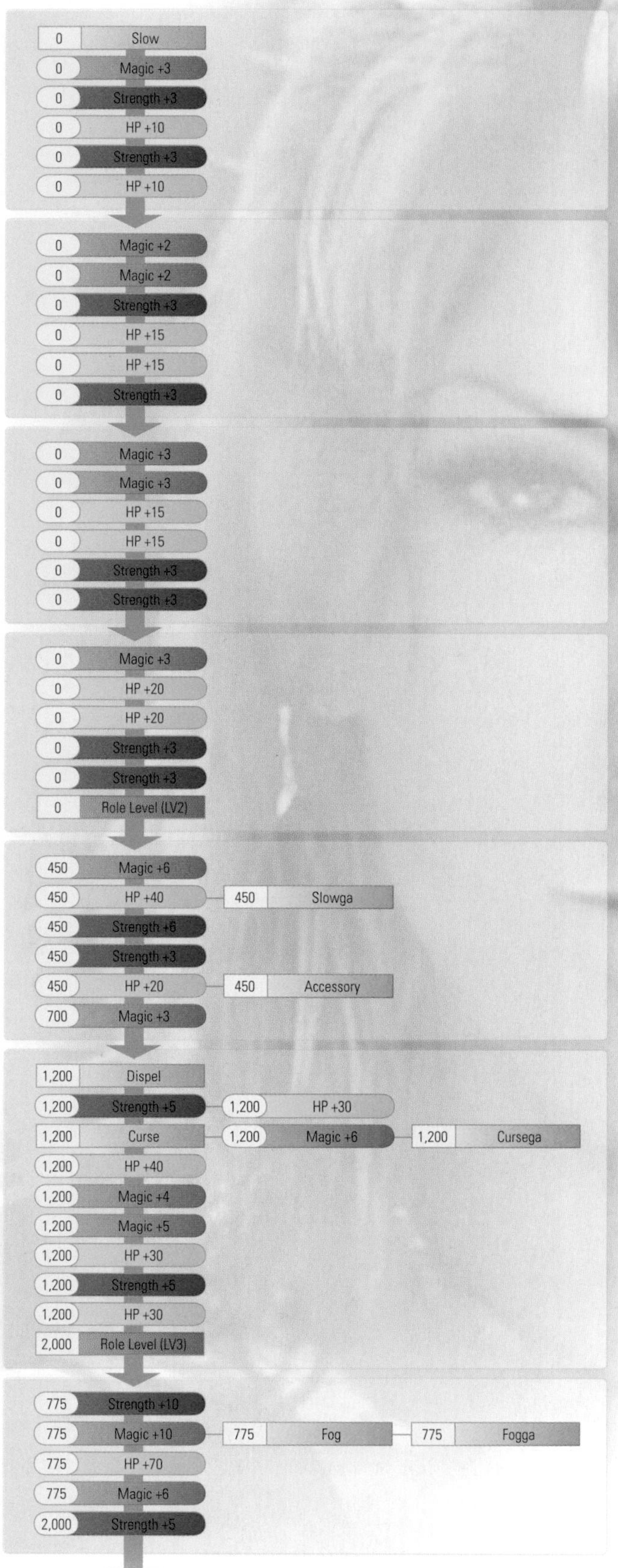

0 Slow
0 Magic +3
0 Strength +3
0 HP +10
0 Strength +3
0 HP +10
0 Magic +2
0 Magic +2
0 Strength +3
0 HP +15
0 HP +15
0 Strength +3
0 Magic +3
0 Magic +3
0 HP +15
0 HP +15
0 Strength +3
0 Strength +3
0 Magic +3
0 HP +20
0 HP +20
0 Strength +3
0 Strength +3
0 Role Level (LV2)
450 Magic +6
450 HP +40 | 450 Slowga
450 Strength +6
450 Strength +3
450 HP +20 | 450 Accessory
700 Magic +3
1,200 Dispel
1,200 Strength +5 | 1,200 HP +30
1,200 Curse | 1,200 Magic +6 | 1,200 Cursega
1,200 HP +40
1,200 Magic +4
1,200 Magic +5
1,200 HP +30
1,200 Strength +5
1,200 HP +30
2,000 Role Level (LV3)
775 Strength +10
775 Magic +10 | 775 Fog | 775 Fogga
775 HP +70
775 Magic +6
2,000 Strength +5

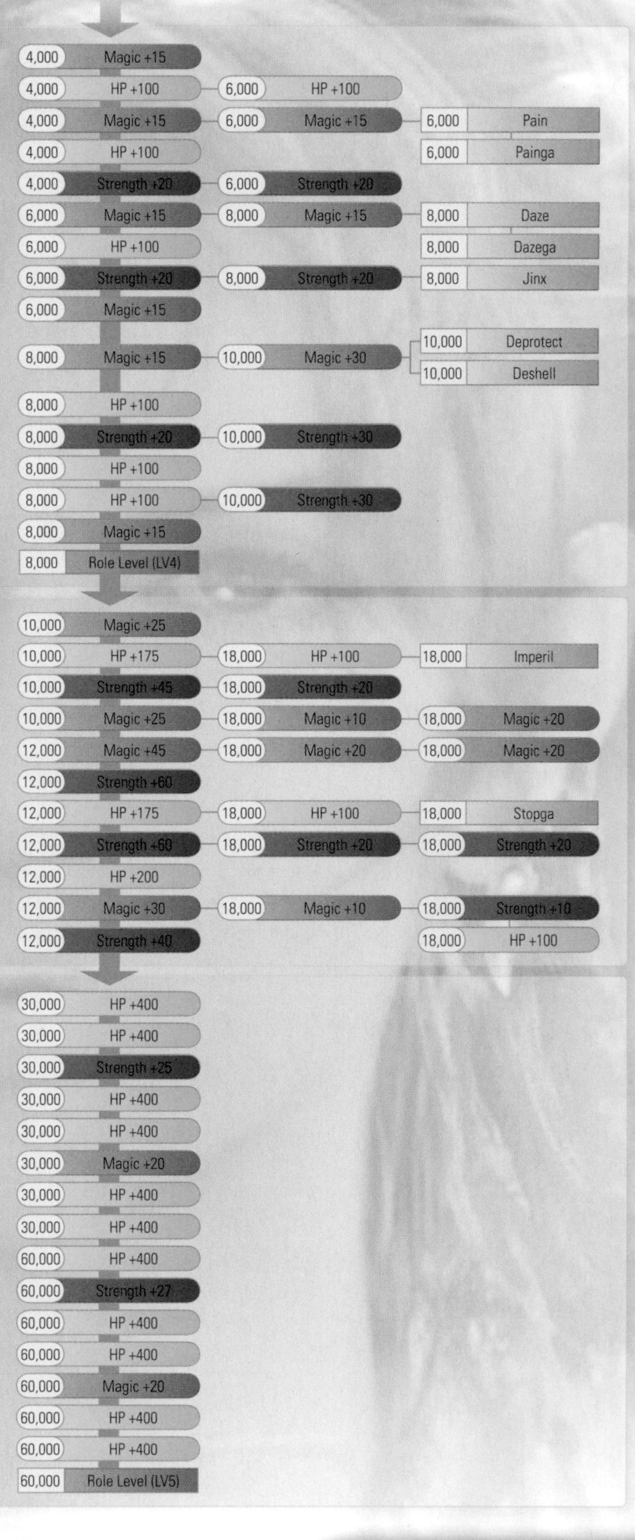

4,000 Magic +15
4,000 HP +100 | 6,000 HP +100
4,000 Magic +15 | 6,000 Magic +15 | 6,000 Pain
4,000 HP +100 | 6,000 Painga
4,000 Strength +20 | 6,000 Strength +20
6,000 Magic +15 | 8,000 Magic +15 | 8,000 Daze
6,000 HP +100 | 8,000 Dazega
6,000 Strength +20 | 8,000 Strength +20 | 8,000 Jinx
6,000 Magic +15
8,000 Magic +15 | 10,000 Magic +30 | 10,000 Deprotect
10,000 Deshell
8,000 HP +100
8,000 Strength +20 | 10,000 Strength +30
8,000 HP +100
8,000 HP +100 | 10,000 Strength +30
8,000 Magic +15
8,000 Role Level (LV4)
10,000 Magic +25
10,000 HP +175 | 18,000 HP +100 | 18,000 Imperil
10,000 Strength +45 | 18,000 Strength +20
10,000 Magic +25 | 18,000 Magic +10 | 18,000 Magic +20
12,000 Magic +45 | 18,000 Magic +20 | 18,000 Magic +20
12,000 Strength +60
12,000 HP +175 | 18,000 HP +100 | 18,000 Stopga
12,000 Strength +60 | 18,000 Strength +20 | 18,000 Strength +20
12,000 HP +200
12,000 Magic +30 | 18,000 Magic +10 | 18,000 Strength +10
12,000 Strength +40 | 18,000 HP +100
30,000 HP +400
30,000 HP +400
30,000 Strength +25
30,000 HP +400
30,000 HP +400
30,000 Magic +20
30,000 HP +400
30,000 HP +400
60,000 HP +400
60,000 Strength +27
60,000 HP +400
60,000 HP +400
60,000 Magic +20
60,000 HP +400
60,000 HP +400
60,000 Role Level (LV5)

RAVAGER

CP	Bonus
3,000	HP +10
3,000	HP +10
3,000	Strength +3
6,000	Fire
3,000	Magic +3
6,000	Thunder

CP	Bonus
6,000	HP +10
6,000	Magic +4
12,000	Blizzard
6,000	Strength +4
12,000	Water

CP	Bonus
9,000	HP +20
9,000	Strength +5
9,000	HP +20
9,000	Magic +5
18,000	Aero

CP	Bonus
12,000	Magic +5
12,000	HP +20
24,000	Sparkstrike
12,000	Strength +5
24,000	Flamestrike

CP	Bonus
15,000	HP +20
15,000	Strength +5
30,000	Froststrike
15,000	Magic +5
30,000	Aquastrike

CP	Bonus
18,000	HP +30
18,000	Magic +5
36,000	Thundara
18,000	Strength +5
36,000	Blizzara

CP	Bonus
21,000	Strength +5
21,000	HP +40
42,000	Watera
21,000	Magic +5
42,000	Fira

CP	Bonus
24,000	HP +40
24,000	HP +40
24,000	Strength +5
24,000	Magic +5
48,000	Aerora

CP	Bonus
60,000	Role Level (LV2)
30,000	Strength +5
30,000	HP +50
30,000	Strength +5
60,000	Aeroga
30,000	HP +50
30,000	Magic +5
30,000	HP +50
30,000	HP +50
30,000	Strength +5
60,000	Overwhelm
30,000	HP +50
30,000	Magic +5
30,000	HP +50
30,000	Strength +5
30,000	HP +50

CP	Bonus
120,000	Role Level (LV3)
60,000	Strength +5
60,000	HP +50
120,000	Vigor
60,000	HP +50
60,000	Magic +5
60,000	HP +50
120,000	Fearsiphon
120,000	Role Level (LV4)
60,000	Magic +5
60,000	HP +50
120,000	Waterga
60,000	HP +50
60,000	Strength +5
60,000	HP +50
120,000	Role Level (LV5)

MEDIC

CP	Bonus
6,000	Cure
3,000	Magic +3
3,000	HP +10
3,000	Strength +3
3,000	HP +10
3,000	HP +10

CP	Bonus
6,000	HP +10
6,000	Strength +4
6,000	HP +10
6,000	HP +10
6,000	Magic +4

CP	Bonus
9,000	Magic +5
9,000	HP +20
9,000	HP +20
9,000	Strength +5
9,000	HP +20

CP	Bonus
12,000	Magic +5
12,000	HP +20
12,000	Strength +5
12,000	HP +20
24,000	Esuna

CP	Bonus
15,000	HP +30
15,000	Strength +5
15,000	Magic +5
15,000	HP +30
15,000	HP +30

CP	Bonus
18,000	Magic +5
18,000	HP +30
18,000	HP +30
18,000	HP +30
18,000	Strength +5

CP	Bonus
21,000	HP +40
21,000	HP +40
21,000	Strength +5
21,000	Magic +5
42,000	Raise

CP	Bonus
24,000	HP +40
24,000	HP +40
24,000	Strength +5
24,000	Magic +5
24,000	HP +40

CP	Bonus
60,000	Role Level (LV2)
30,000	Magic +5
30,000	Strength +5
30,000	HP +50
30,000	Strength +5
30,000	Magic +5
30,000	HP +50
30,000	HP +50
30,000	Strength +5
30,000	HP +50
30,000	HP +50
30,000	Strength +5
30,000	Magic +5
60,000	Cura
30,000	Magic +5
30,000	HP +50

CP	Bonus
120,000	Role Level (LV3)
60,000	HP +50
60,000	Strength +5
60,000	HP +50
60,000	Magic +5
60,000	HP +50
60,000	HP +50
60,000	HP +50
120,000	Role Level (LV4)
60,000	HP +50
60,000	HP +50
60,000	HP +50
60,000	Strength +5
60,000	HP +50
60,000	Magic +5
120,000	Role Level (LV5)

SYNERGIST

CP	Bonus
3,000	Magic +3
3,000	HP +10
3,000	HP +10
3,000	Strength +3
3,000	HP +10
6,000	Veil

CP	Bonus
6,000	HP +10
6,000	Magic +4
6,000	HP +10
6,000	Strength +4
12,000	Bravera

CP	Bonus
9,000	HP +20
9,000	HP +20
9,000	HP +20
9,000	Strength +5
18,000	Faithra

CP	Bonus
12,000	Magic +5
12,000	HP +20
12,000	HP +20
12,000	Strength +5
12,000	HP +20

CP	Bonus
15,000	HP +30
15,000	Strength +5
15,000	Magic +5
15,000	HP +30
30,000	Protectra

CP	Bonus
18,000	Magic +5
18,000	HP +30
18,000	Strength +5
18,000	HP +30
36,000	Shellra

CP	Bonus
21,000	HP +40
21,000	Strength +5
21,000	Magic +5
21,000	HP +15
21,000	HP +40

CP	Bonus
24,000	Magic +5
24,000	HP +40
24,000	Strength +5
24,000	HP +40
48,000	Haste

CP	Bonus
60,000	Role Level (LV2)
30,000	HP +50
30,000	Magic +5
30,000	Strength +5
30,000	HP +50
30,000	Strength +5
30,000	Magic +5
30,000	HP +50
30,000	HP +50
30,000	Strength +5
60,000	Boon
30,000	HP +50
30,000	Magic +5
30,000	Strength +5
30,000	Magic +5
30,000	HP +50

CP	Bonus
120,000	Role Level (LV3)
60,000	HP +50
60,000	HP +50
60,000	Strength +5
60,000	HP +50
60,000	HP +50
60,000	HP +50
60,000	Magic +5
120,000	Role Level (LV4)
60,000	HP +50
60,000	Magic +5
60,000	HP +50
60,000	Strength +5
60,000	HP +50
60,000	HP +50
120,000	Role Level (LV5)

LIGHTNING

- **Primary Roles:** Ravager, Commando, Medic
- **Secondary Roles:** Saboteur, Synergist, Sentinel

LIGHTNING: ROLE EFFICIENCY

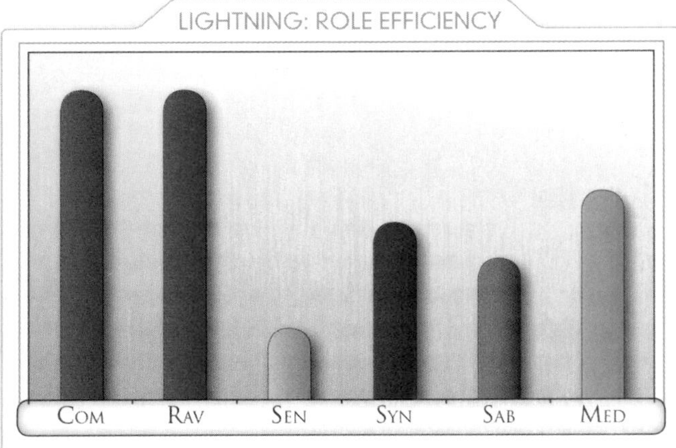

The purpose of these diagrams is to offer a general indication of each character's relative strength in all six disciplines. They have been calculated with complex formulas that take the most important attributes for every role into account, including HP, Strength, Magic, abilities and weapons.

Overview

Lightning is a great all-round character, a versatile aggressor with a useful sideline in combat medicine. With Odin as her Eidolon and the Thundaga spell becoming her one area-effect magic through Ravager development, her nickname is entirely appropriate. She's very much attuned to that element, and works especially well as a Ravager when confronted by Pulse Automata and certain beast types.

Development Paths

You will probably find that you use Lightning as a Commando at first, then make more of her Ravager potential later in the adventure. Once unlocked, her unique Ravager ability, Army of One, is an excellent way to raise the Chain Bonus to 999% during a Stagger – but even before then, Chaining is her forte.

Indeed, Lightning's true strength is in Chain-building as either a Commando (Chain-fixing) or Ravager (Chain-boosting). Her versatility makes her a good bet for strategies that require changes between all-out and more cautious offensive Paradigms (Relentless Assault to Delta Attack/Diversity, for instance). Naturally, though, the disadvantage of being an all-rounder is that she's not the most effective character in any of her duties.

In a pinch, she makes a very handy back-up Medic – for example, as a secondary healer in Combat Clinic, or in a Paradigm where she temporarily watches over allies (such as Evened Odds).

Secondary Development

Not particularly strong as either a Synergist or Saboteur, Lightning has a pared-down skillset in both of these roles. Worse still, she makes a terrible Sentinel, only possessing the ability to draw enemy attacks and attempt to dodge rather than counter.

SAZH

- **Primary Roles:** Synergist, Ravager, Commando
- **Secondary Roles:** Sentinel, Saboteur, Medic

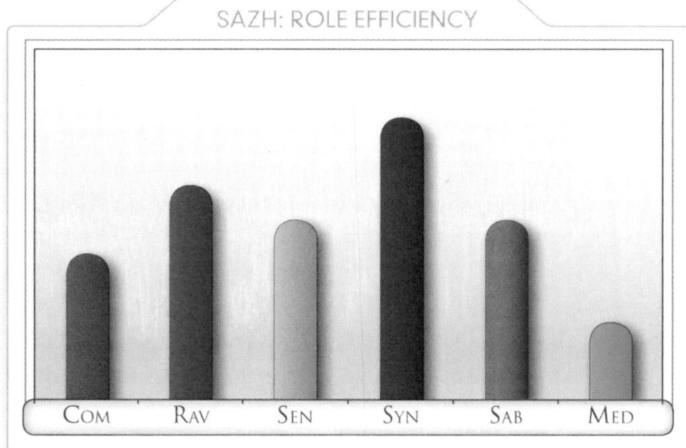

Overview

Sazh's HP growth through parameter crystal acquisitions is steady and generous, so he transforms from a rather weak fighter into a much tougher prospect by the end of the game.

The important thing to note about him, though, is that his basic attributes are fairly low but can be boosted significantly through weapon upgrades, so the equipment you give him can make a profound difference – choosing the right gear will affect him more than other characters. He also has weapons with some highly interesting additional effects (such as Stagger Maintenance).

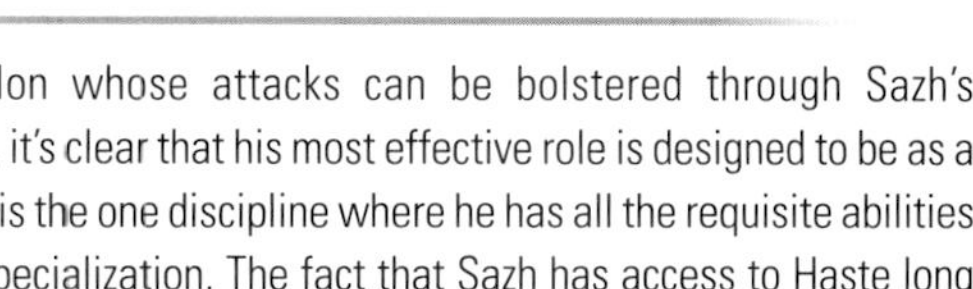

Development Paths

With an Eidolon whose attacks can be bolstered through Sazh's enhancements, it's clear that his most effective role is designed to be as a Synergist. This is the one discipline where he has all the requisite abilities for profitable specialization. The fact that Sazh has access to Haste long before other characters is very nice during earlier chapters; later on, he is also suited to providing elemental enhancements and protections. If you intend to turn Sazh into a Super Specialist, this is definitely his best role.

As a Ravager, Sazh can count on Firaga as a good area-effect spell against many plants and animals, and he also gets Aeroga – so this is clearly his best secondary role, building Chains for the real heavy-hitters. His special Cold Blood attack, in particular, turns him into a one-man Chaining machine. Your choice of equipment here can make a big difference.

Sazh's main problem is that he is a lousy Commando, which means that he never shines when called upon to inflict decisive damage. He can only realistically replace Lightning if you wish to maintain a balanced party, but lacks her outstanding flexibility. In short, he is a highly "technical" character with great potential – but identifying situations where his prowess can be exploited without encountering irksome drawbacks can be a real challenge.

Secondary Development

As a Saboteur, Sazh only obtains the single-target version of every ability – but by the later stages of the game, you really need the speed and convenience of debuffs that debilitate entire groups. As a Medic, he's just as hopeless as Snow in needing Phoenix Downs or the Renew technique to revive KO'd colleagues. Thanks to his high HP, he's not a bad Sentinel, though he doesn't have the self-sufficiency of Mediguard.

SNOW

- **Primary Roles:** Sentinel, Commando, Ravager
- **Secondary Roles:** Saboteur, Synergist, Medic

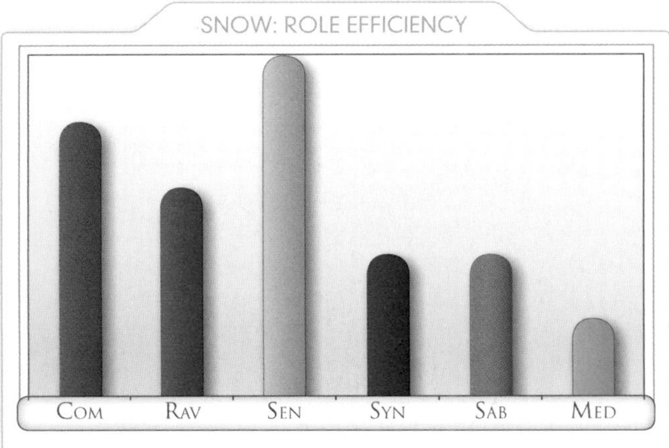

Overview

Snow starts with the best Strength value of all characters, but this advantage slowly decreases as others catch up later in the game. His natural HP total is unparalleled, though, which makes him a peerless Sentinel who can retaliate effectively as a Commando. These qualities make him an excellent choice in a wide variety of scenarios.

Development Paths

As with Fang, Snow's presence in your party enables you to have a good blend of offensive and defensive Paradigms within one deck, which is useful in areas where you encounter groups of weak yet numerous enemies and tough big-hitter types in quick succession. Though not as strong as Fang, his superior HP makes him the natural choice as a Super Specialist Sentinel.

As a Ravager, Snow has no capacity for Fire or Lightning spells. This makes him less effective against many enemy types encountered early in the main storyline, including robots and plants. That said, his Shiva Eidolon (Ice) and later acquisition of Waterga and Blizzaga means that he is not without merit as a dealer of high elemental damage against the right opponents. He can work very effectively as a replacement for Fang in certain Mark missions, offering greater security in defensive Paradigms and the benefit of the all-Ravager Tri-disaster when allied with Lightning and Hope.

Secondary Development

Snow is a terrible Medic, and cannot even Raise KO'd allies. You should unlock these crystals last to obtain endgame parameter boosts. As a Saboteur he lacks the oft-vital Imperil and Imperilga skills. He must also rely on another character to weaken enemies to the Water and Ice elements if you intend to make the best use of his Ravager skills. His Synergist abilities, meanwhile, are essentially limited to offering a quick and dirty early-battle boost.

HOPE

- **Primary Roles:** Ravager, Synergist, Medic
- **Secondary Roles:** Commando, Sentinel, Saboteur

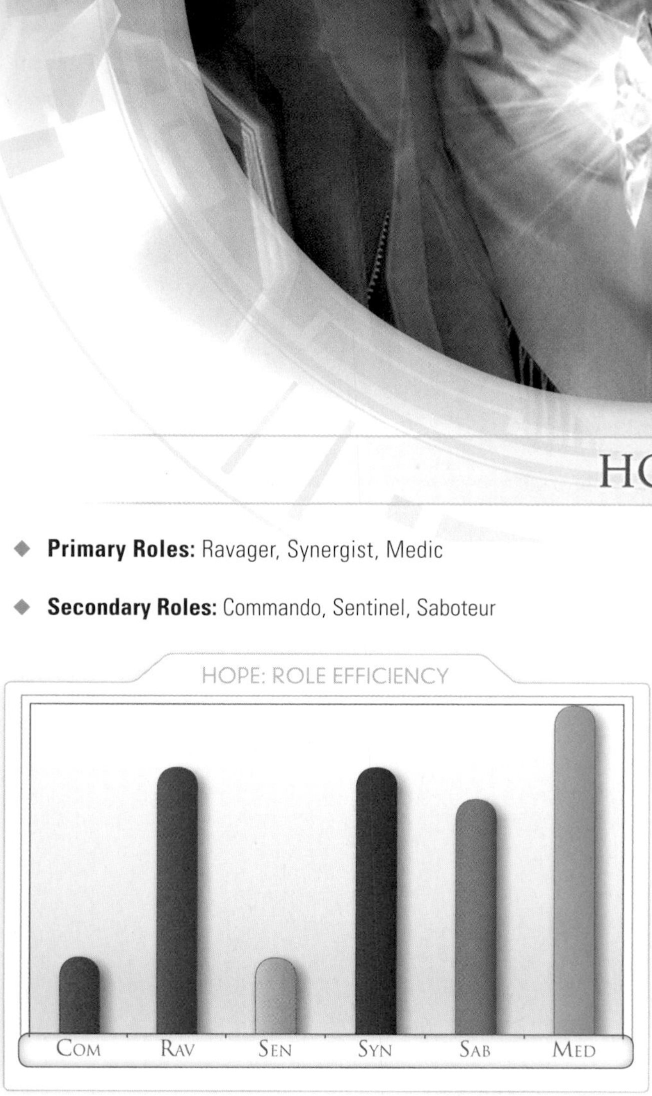

HOPE: ROLE EFFICIENCY

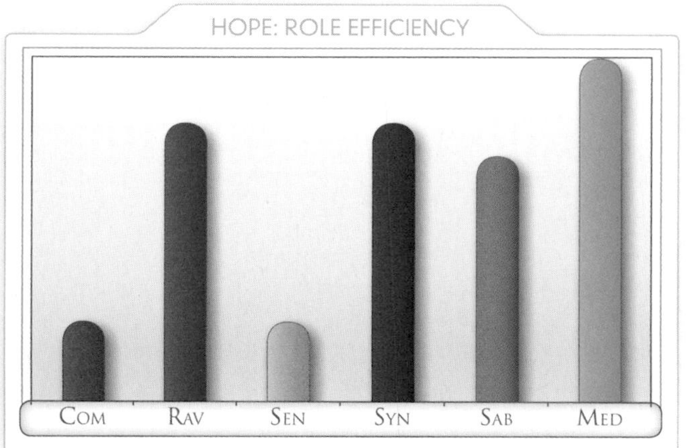

Overview

Hope has the lowest HP of all characters, so he really needs a Sentinel or frequent switches to healing Paradigms to protect him during difficult or protracted battles. The good news is that he starts with a solid Magic stat and finishes the game as your most powerful spellcaster, with all his main roles relying heavily on his magical prowess. He is a highly effective yet fragile party member.

Development Paths

Hope works well in a supporting role, having exactly the right primary disciplines to enable you to create a strong Paradigm Deck. As a Ravager he has access to all major offensive spells, including those that affect multiple targets. Take his incredible Magic stat and his Last Resort special skill into consideration, and this is clearly a powerful combination. Like Vanille, his only drawback in this role is that he lacks the "-strike" attacks, which means that he has no physical alternative to his spells.

As a Synergist, Hope is equally effective: equivalent to Sazh in terms of his skillset, but with better Magic stat potential. Having access to all healing abilities, Hope is also your best Medic. The only question is: will Hope's low HP allow him to survive long enough during the toughest battles to live up to his enormous potential?

Secondary Development

Amazingly, as a Saboteur Hope gets all of the area-effect abilities for group target debilitation, including Dazega and Fogga, even though it's a secondary role. This is the route you should take with him after completing his primary disciplines. Commando and Sentinel should obviously be left until last for final stat boosts.

VANILLE

- **Primary Roles:** Saboteur, Medic, Ravager
- **Secondary Roles:** Synergist, Commando, Sentinel

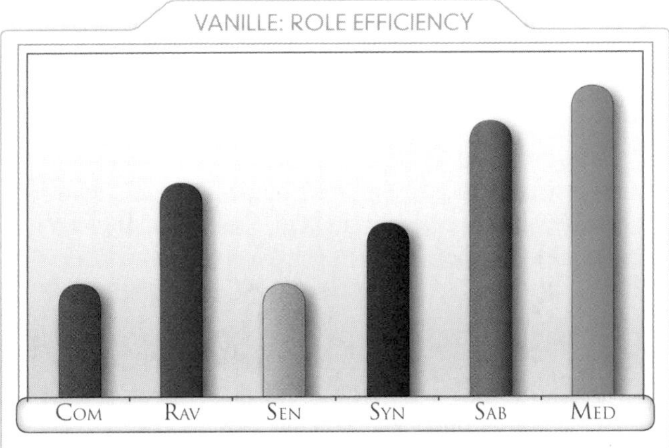

OVERVIEW

Vanille starts out as a strong magical character, and becomes more balanced as the game progresses – though her final Magic stat is second only to that of Hope. Hope is probably the better choice in many situations, but Vanille's superior HP and unique Death skill make her an extremely interesting character during certain tough battles and bouts of specialist leveling.

As with Sazh, equipment makes a big difference to her performance. If you have a particular purpose in mind while developing her, look for a weapon that will complement your goals. She can be quite a strong attacker during the early stages of her stat growth, but you may wish to take advantage of her very high Magic for the greatest long-term gain.

DEVELOPMENT PATHS

Vanille starts out as a great Ravager, but lacks both -strike abilities and area-effect spells such as Thundaga, Waterga and Aeroga, which is a great shame. Nonetheless, she will still make an excellent second Ravager in Paradigms that feature two.

As a Saboteur, Vanille has all the spells that are effective in the early game stages (Deprotect, Deshell, Poison and Imperil – all in their area-effect form too), which are also the debuffs that the majority of enemies are susceptible to. Her main drawback is that she doesn't learn more advanced spells (such as Slow, Fog and Pain), which are essential abilities for numerous major encounters later in the adventure. What she does have, though, is the singular Death spell. This deals serious damage to a single target even if it fails, but will kill a susceptible adversary instantly if successful. Most enemies enjoy blanket immunity to its main effect, but those that don't can offer some very interesting power-leveling opportunities. See page 144 for more information.

Where Vanille really shines is as a Medic. She rivals Hope in this area, and her superior HP means that she's less likely to be incapacitated by powerful attacks. If you are looking to cast her as a Super Specialist, it's a close call between this and Saboteur.

SECONDARY DEVELOPMENT

Vanille can unlock most status enhancements in their more powerful forms – but unfortunately, she's the one Synergist who can't cast Haste. Obviously, with her relatively low Strength and HP, don't expect her to thrive or survive if employed as a Commando or Sentinel.

FANG

- **Primary Roles:** Commando, Sentinel, Saboteur
- **Secondary Roles:** Ravager, Synergist, Medic

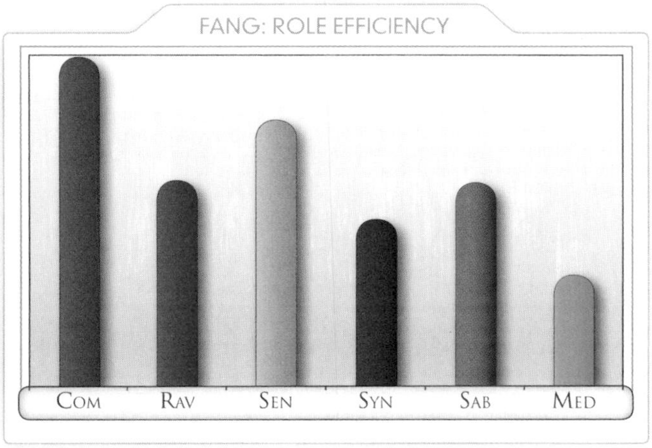

FANG: ROLE EFFICIENCY

COM RAV SEN SYN SAB MED

Overview

Fang has the highest natural Strength attribute of all, and is therefore your physical attack expert. A key party member throughout her involvement in the main storyline, her versatility and all-round ability improve enormously during post-story play.

Development Paths

Fang is such a strong fighter that Commando is really the way to go in terms of early specialization. A quick look at her Auto-ability list will confirm this: she has access to all of them. Because the path of the Commando is slightly less complex in terms of decision-making, Fang makes an excellent AI Commando to accompany a player-controlled Ravager. Her AI routines are better equipped to cope with her speed, and are usually swift to take advantage of a Launch opportunity to set up juggles for other battle team members.

Play her as leader during late game stages and post-story play, and you can employ her vicious Highwind attack. This is a killing blow that wipes the Chain Bonus in order to calculate its damage – so you really need it to be at or close to 999% to make it worthwhile.

Though a less redoubtable Sentinel than Snow, she can nonetheless excel in this role throughout the main storyline. It is her capacity to act as a Saboteur, however, that confirms her as the ideal partner to Lightning and Hope in your core party. Fang eventually obtains powerful debuffs for disabling tougher enemies, which means that she becomes increasingly valuable as time goes by.

Secondary Development

For those who might expect Fang's secondary roles to be underwhelming to compensate for her natural ability in her core disciplines, a surprise: it also transpires that she is an accomplished Ravager, only lacking Firaga, Blizzaga and Thundaga. She can obtain every elemental attack type and all four "-strike" abilities. If you make this her fourth discipline, there's really nothing in the game world that she can't hurt effectively.

It's only fair that she's not much of a Synergist, but Haste, Bravera, Faithra, Protectra and Shellra are handy enough for most battles. In a worst-case scenario, she can even Raise and Cure a KO'd ally as a Medic – possibly serving as the second character donning scrubs in a switch to the Combat Clinic Paradigm.

CHARACTER COMPARISONS

In order to help you to decide which characters you would rather play with, or how to specialize your party members, we have prepared the following visual comparison of all protagonists during a typical playthrough. The table and graphs show each character's evolution in the main three attributes: HP, Strength and Magic. This information is based on a standard and direct route through the main game, with no specific power-leveling and "average" equipment upgrade levels.

You will also find it beneficial to read the Inventory chapter to learn about weapon-specific perks or attributes that might enhance each individual's performance in their strongest roles.

STAT DEVELOPMENT

Character	Stat	Beginning of the Game	The Pulse Vestige	The Vile Peaks	The Sunleth Waterscape	Palumpolum	The Palamecia	The Fifth Ark	The Archylte Steppe	Mah'habara	Taejin's Tower	Oerba	Eden	Orphan's Cradle	End of the Game
Lightning	HP	200	300	389	505	656	851	1,104	1,433	1,860	2,415	3,135	4,069	5,281	7,603
	Strength	30	55	70	101	137	184	245	318	409	526	676	869	1,118	1,560
	Magic	30	45	60	101	137	184	245	318	409	526	676	869	1,118	1,560
Snow	HP	350	450	584	758	983	1,276	1,626	2,037	2,552	3,197	4,006	5,112	6,635	9,551
	Strength	32	57	72	113	152	201	261	334	433	562	730	949	1,233	1,718
	Magic	22	30	37	58	79	106	141	184	245	326	434	584	796	1,142
Sazh	HP	220	320	416	550	739	993	1,335	1,730	2,168	2,716	3,403	4,342	5,636	8,113
	Strength	27	42	62	98	130	169	219	278	353	449	572	729	962	1,354
	Magic	30	45	59	95	127	167	214	269	339	427	539	680	892	1,245
Hope	HP	170	270	338	423	540	701	893	1,119	1,428	1,854	2,407	3,067	3,843	5,439
	Strength	26	41	52	83	98	131	170	218	283	368	478	621	806	1,128
	Magic	32	47	55	92	134	175	228	295	402	561	785	1,072	1,429	2,033
Vanille	HP	-	300	376	480	623	809	1,031	1,316	1,708	2,217	2,878	3,736	4,937	7,227
	Strength	-	41	52	73	97	127	168	224	298	397	529	705	940	1,338
	Magic	-	47	75	108	141	184	241	316	415	545	716	942	1,241	1,745
Fang	HP	-	-	-	-	750	940	1,199	1,557	2,021	2,624	3,406	4,341	5,439	7,697
	Strength	-	-	-	-	140	183	239	318	427	575	775	1,048	1,420	2,036
	Magic	-	-	-	-	90	118	155	206	276	372	502	671	885	1,251

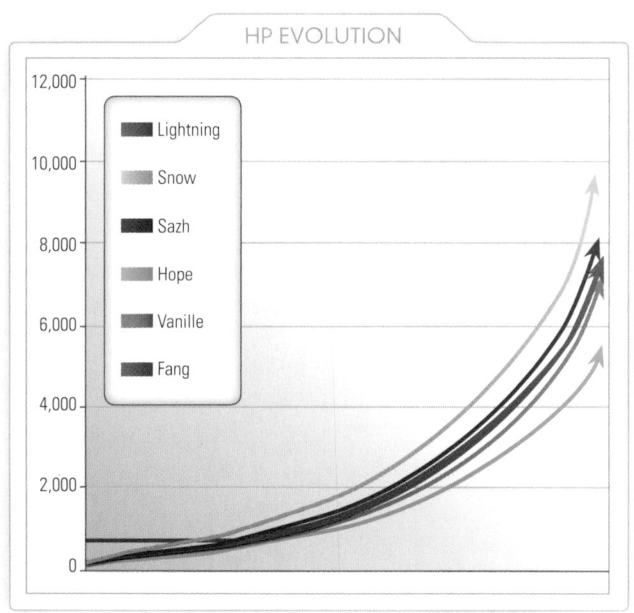
HP EVOLUTION
12,000
10,000
8,000
6,000
4,000
2,000
0
Lightning
Snow
Sazh
Hope
Vanille
Fang

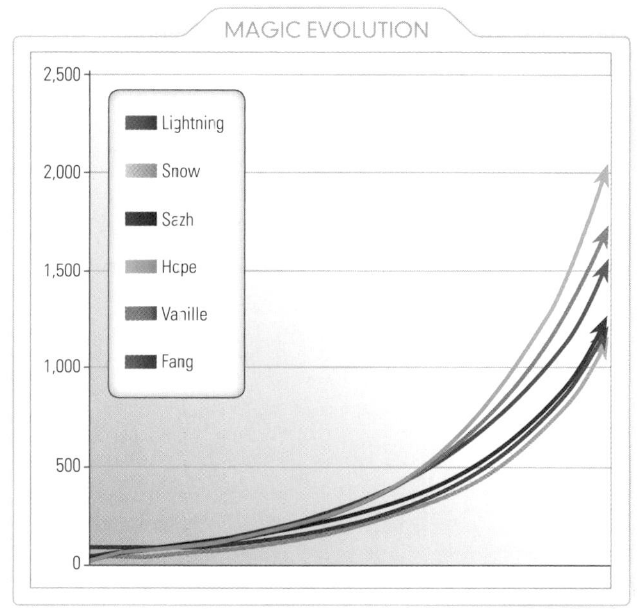
MAGIC EVOLUTION
2,500
2,000
1,500
1,000
500
0
Lightning
Snow
Sazh
Hope
Vanille
Fang

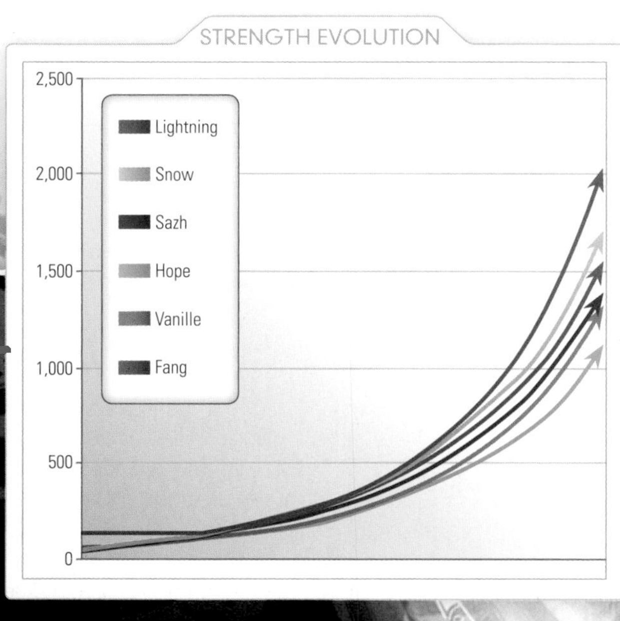
STRENGTH EVOLUTION
2,500
2,000
1,500
1,000
500
0
Lightning
Snow
Sazh
Hope
Vanille
Fang

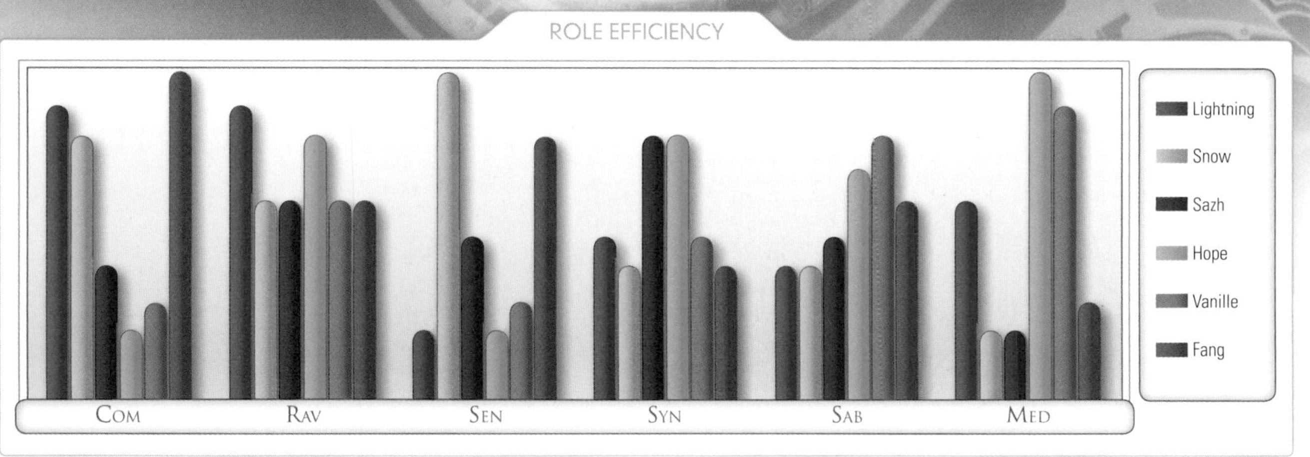
ROLE EFFICIENCY
COM
RAV
SEN
SYN
SAB
MED
Lightning
Snow
Sazh
Hope
Vanille
Fang

In this section we examine the abilities that can be unlocked via Crystarium progression in all six roles. There are, broadly speaking, two forms of abilities: actions that can be added to the command queue manually, and Auto-abilities that are performed automatically at the AI's discretion.

Before we continue, we should take a moment to clarify how the context-sensitive Auto-abilities operate in a battle situation. These passive enhancements or advanced skills are implemented by the combat AI whenever it deems it appropriate to use them, even if you are choosing actions manually via the Abilities menu. For example, if an enemy has been Staggered, the first Attack instruction in a (suitably trained) Commando's command queue will be automatically changed to Launch.

Once you have committed to a command queue, the AI will interpret your orders and check to see which Auto-abilities are applicable and of benefit to your current situation. While many of these operate transparently in the background, acting as subtle boosts to your party's performance, it's worth familiarizing yourself with the activation conditions for certain Auto-abilities. If you really need to Launch a Staggered enemy to gain respite from powerful attacks, a command queue filled with the Ruin ability is not the way to obtain it.

SENTINEL ABILITIES

The Sentinel role is unique in the way that abilities are employed. After a command queue has been selected, each ability remains active for a set duration until its effect expires and the next action begins. This continues until all ATB gauge segments have been used. As a party leader, the best tactic is to create a long queue of actions of the same type to form an effective defense. If circumstances should change, you can cancel outstanding commands at any time.

Name	ATB Cost	Notes	Lightning	Snow	Sazh	Hope	Vanille	Fang
Evade	AUTO	Enables the user to occasionally avoid enemy attacks. It can be improved with specific accessories.	✓	✓		✓		✓
Counter	AUTO	Occasionally counterattacks enemies after evading an attack. Fang can improve this ability by equipping a weapon with the Improved Counter special property.	✓	✓		✓		✓
Deathward	AUTO	Boosts physical and magic resistance when HP is low. Can be improved by equipping accessories that have critical triggers (such as casting buffs), the Low HP: Power Surge synthesized ability, and Snow's weapons with the Improved Ward special property.	✓	✓	✓	✓		✓
Fringeward	AUTO	Reduces damage to nearby allies when the Sentinel is the target of an area-effect attack.	✓	✓	✓			✓
Reprieve	AUTO	If HP is above a certain threshold, the Sentinel retains 1 HP after an attack that would otherwise lead to an instant KO. This is enormously useful once unlocked, and offers the opportunity to make an instant switch to Combat Clinic.	✓	✓		✓	✓	✓
Provoke	1	Attracts the attention of all enemies in range for 50 seconds, with a 45% base chance of success against each one. You can tell which opponents have been successfully Provoked by looking for the hazard triangle hovering above them.	✓	✓	✓	✓	✓	✓
Elude	1	Defend with a high probability of evading enemy attacks.	✓			✓		
Challenge	1	A refinement of Provoke, targeted at a single opponent with a 99% base chance of success and a duration of 150 seconds.		✓	✓			✓
Vendetta	1	Counterattack after defending, dealing increased damage if the Sentinel was attacked regularly.		✓	✓	✓		✓
Entrench	1	Counterattack after defending, dealing damage determined by how long the Sentinel maintained the defensive stance.		✓		✓	✓	✓
Steelguard	1	A strong and purely defensive posture, with physical and magic resistance increased each time the Sentinel is attacked.		✓	✓		✓	✓
Mediguard	1	Defend while gradually recovering HP. This can lead to fewer Paradigm Shifts for healing purposes.		✓			✓	✓

COMMANDO ABILITIES

Name	ATB Cost	Notes	Lightning	Snow	Sazh	Hope	Vanille	Fang
Powerchain	AUTO	If the enemy's Chain Gauge is empty when the Commando's attack lands, Powerchain strengthens the blow, granting significantly greater damage.	✓	✓	✓			✓
Lifesiphon	AUTO	Recharges one ATB gauge segment after slaying a target. You obtain an ATB segment for every enemy killed, so this becomes more powerful once your party acquires area-effect attacks.	✓	✓	✓	✓		✓
Faultsiphon	AUTO	Slightly charges the ATB gauge when a character attacks a target suffering from status ailments. Once you start making use of a Saboteur, party members with this Auto-ability will be more effective against afflicted enemies.	✓			✓	✓	✓
Launch	AUTO	Used automatically when the Attack command is selected against a Staggered enemy. By Chaining moves on an opponent while they are airborne, it is possible to "juggle" them with further hits.	✓	✓				✓
Ravage	AUTO	A staple of Chain-building, used to enable Ravagers to blast the Chain Gauge high and Commandos to reduce the rate of gauge depletion.	✓	✓		✓		✓
Smite	AUTO	Enhances a Commando's standard Attack command when an enemy is poised to recover from a Stagger.	✓	✓				✓
Blindside	AUTO	Enhances normal attacks when a non-Staggered adversary is not targeting a party member who has this skill. Working alongside a Sentinel increases the likelihood of obtaining a regular Blindside bonus.	✓	✓			✓	✓
Scourge	AUTO	Enhances a Commando's normal Attack when an enemy is about to recover from a Stagger.	✓	✓	✓	✓	✓	✓
Jeopardize	AUTO	Boosts the amount by which an attack raises a Staggered enemy's Chain Bonus, increasing the damage of all subsequent hits while it remains Staggered.	✓	✓	✓	✓	✓	✓
Deathblow	AUTO	Instantly slays a target with low HP.		✓			✓	✓
Adrenaline	AUTO	Boosts Strength and Magic when HP is high. You can enhance this effect with equipment that provides the High HP: Power Surge synthesized ability.		✓	✓		✓	✓
Attack	1	The basic assault move of the Commando. The Strength stat determines the level of damage inflicted. If a target is out of range, a Commando may move in close to perform it. Advanced players can exploit this feature to break up a party locked in close formation and under fire from area-effect attacks. (Example: using a single Commando attack to move Fang close to a powerful opponent and away from her allies at the start of a battle, then switching to a Paradigm where she acts as a Sentinel.)	✓	✓	✓	✓	✓	✓
Blitz	2	Inflicts damage on all adversaries in range, best used against targets at or near the center of tightly-packed groups of enemies. Highly effective when employed to Stagger multiple opponents after a preemptive strike.	✓	✓	✓	✓		✓
Ruin	1	Inflicts non-elemental magic damage on a single target. Effective when enemies are resistant to physical assaults or vulnerable to magic. It's also efficient against distant, airborne or fast-moving opponents – the Ruin projectiles automatically home in on a target, and do not require the Commando to move.	✓	✓	✓	✓	✓	✓
Ruinga	3	Same effects as Ruin, but acts as a more powerful area-effect upgrade. Ruinga can interrupt enemy actions, blasting smaller or Staggered enemies into the air.	✓	✓	✓	✓	✓	✓
Highwind	All	Unique to Fang. Releases a catastrophic blast with damage determined by the current Chain Bonus – the higher the percentage, the more effective it will be. However, it then resets your chaining progress, so it's best used as a finishing move, or just before a Stagger period ends.						✓
Sovereign Fist	All	Same as Highwind, but unique to Snow.		✓				

RAVAGER ABILITIES

Name	ATB Cost	Notes	Lightning	Snow	Sazh	Hope	Vanille	Fang
Vigor	AUTO	Boosts the Chain Bonus effect of attacks when HP is high. Similar to the Commando's Adrenaline Auto-ability, but even more useful for a Ravager.	✓	✓		✓		✓
Overwhelm	AUTO	Boosts Chain Bonus increases for each ally targeting the same enemy. Use Paradigms with more than one Ravager to make best use of its effects – particularly the all-RAV Tri-disaster.	✓	✓	✓	✓	✓	✓
Fearsiphon	AUTO	Slightly charges the ATB gauge after attacking a Staggered target. Becomes more effective once your Ravagers acquire area-effect magic – especially during instances where you secure preemptive strikes against large groups.	✓	✓	✓	✓	✓	✓
Fire	1	Deals Fire damage to target.	✓		✓	✓	✓	✓
Fira	2	Deals Fire damage to targets in range.	✓		✓	✓	✓	✓
Firaga	3	Deals Fire damage to targets within a wide radius.			✓	✓	✓	
Blizzard	1	Deals Ice damage to target.	✓	✓		✓	✓	✓
Blizzara	2	Deals Ice damage to targets in range.	✓	✓		✓	✓	✓
Blizzaga	3	Deals Ice damage to targets within a wide radius.		✓		✓	✓	
Thunder	1	Deals Lightning damage to target.	✓		✓	✓	✓	✓
Thundara	2	Deals Lightning damage to targets in range.	✓		✓	✓	✓	✓
Thundaga	3	Deals Lightning damage to targets within a wide radius.	✓		✓	✓		
Water	1	Deals Water damage to target.	✓	✓		✓	✓	✓
Watera	2	Deals Water damage to targets in range.	✓	✓		✓	✓	✓
Waterga	3	Deals Water damage to targets within a wide radius.		✓		✓		✓
Aero	1	Deals Wind damage to target and temporarily stuns it.	✓	✓	✓	✓	✓	✓
Aerora	3	Deals Wind damage to targets in range, tossing them up and drawing them in.	✓	✓	✓	✓	✓	✓
Aeroga	5	Deals Wind damage to targets within a wide radius, drawing them up into a tornado.			✓	✓		✓
Flamestrike	1	Physically attacks a target with a blow infused with the Fire, Ice, Lightning or Water element. The important point to note about the four elemental weapon "-strike" abilities is that they use the Ravager's Strength stat to calculate damage, not Magic. This greatly suits characters such as Lightning, Snow, and much later in her development, Fang.	✓		✓			✓
Froststrike	1		✓	✓				✓
Sparkstrike	1		✓		✓			✓
Aquastrike	1		✓	✓				✓
Army of One	All	This ability packs numerous attacks into a focused assault, driving up the Chain Gauge and Chain Bonus. Hugely effective against tough opponents, particularly those with high Chain Resistance. With Haste active, you can repeat this special skill several times before a Staggered enemy recovers.	✓					
Cold Blood	All	Sazh's equivalent of Army of One.			✓			
Last Resort	All	Hope's equivalent of Army of One.				✓		

SABOTEUR ABILITIES

For a full list of status ailments and their effects, refer to page 143. Note that all Saboteur spells have a base success chance, which is then affected by several factors: the target's susceptibility to the ailment; the Chain Bonus; the Vigilance buff; the Role Level of the caster; if the caster is wielding a weapon with Improved Debuffing or Improved Debilitation (I = x1.2, II = x1.4); finally if the target is protected by Veil (x0.5).

Name	ATB Cost	Notes	Lightning	Snow	Sazh	Hope	Vanille	Fang
Jinx	AUTO	Extends the duration of a target's existing status ailments once new debuffs are inflicted.	✓	✓	✓	✓	✓	✓
Deprotect	1	Reduces a target's physical resistance and deals magic damage, augmenting Commando Attacks and Blitzes (but not Ruin and Ruinga), and Ravager "-strike" attacks (but not spells). Base success chance: 40%.	✓		✓		✓	✓
Deprotega	3	Reduces physical resistance and deals magic damage within a wide radius. Base success chance: 30%.	✓			✓	✓	
Deshell	1	Reduces a target's magic resistance and deals magic damage, increasing the level of injury inflicted by Ravager spells, and the Ruin and Ruinga Commando abilities. Base success chance: 40%.	✓		✓		✓	✓
Deshellga	3	Reduces magic resistance and deals magic damage within a wide radius. Base success chance: 30%.	✓			✓	✓	
Poison	1	Poisons target and deals magic damage. Base success chance: 30%.	✓		✓		✓	
Poisonga	3	Poisons and deals magic damage to targets within a wide radius. Base success chance: 24%.	✓			✓	✓	
Imperil	1	Reduces a target's elemental resistance and deals magic damage. One of the most useful spells of all in the later stages of the game. In some battles it may be worthwhile to designate your Saboteur as leader to prioritize its use. Base success chance: 30%.	✓		✓		✓	✓
Imperilga	3	Reduces elemental resistances and deals magic damage within a wide radius. Base success chance: 24%.	✓			✓	✓	
Slow	1	Reduces target's ATB gauge recharge rate and deals magic damage. An immensely useful spell for reducing an enemy's rate of attack, it works on a high proportion of adversaries. Some of the most dangerous Marks can be slowed, which significantly reduces the amount of damage they can inflict during the course of a long battle. Base success chance: 30%.		✓	✓			✓
Slowga	3	Reduces ATB gauge recharge rate and deals magic damage within a wide radius. Base success chance: 24%.		✓		✓		✓
Fog	1	Disables a target's spellcasting abilities and deals magic damage. A great way to silence an enemy who favors magical attacks. Base success chance: 20%.		✓	✓		✓	✓
Fogga	3	Disables enemy spellcasting and deals magic damage within a wide radius. Base success chance: 15%.		✓		✓		✓
Pain	1	Disables a target's physical abilities and deals magic damage. Pain is the physical counterpart to Fog. Base success chance: 20%.		✓	✓		✓	✓
Painga	3	Disables enemy physical abilities and deals magic damage within a wide radius. Base success chance: 15%.		✓		✓		✓
Curse	1	Renders a target more vulnerable to "interruptions" when attacked, increasing the likelihood that queued abilities will be delayed or even cancelled. Also lowers the target's odds of interrupting enemy party actions. Base success chance: 20%.		✓	✓			✓
Cursega	3	Renders targets within a wide radius more prone to interruptions, and deals magic damage. Also lowers the targets' odds of interrupting enemy party actions. Base success chance: 15%.		✓		✓		✓
Daze	1	Stuns the target and deals magic damage. This is effectively a paralysis spell. Base success chance: 30%.		✓	✓			✓
Dazega	3	Stuns and deals magic damage within a wide radius. Base success chance: 24%.		✓		✓		✓
Dispel	2	Removes a target's most recent status enhancement and deals magic damage. Extremely useful when you face enemies who augment their natural abilities with status enhancements, though it only removes one buff per casting. Base success chance: 100%.			✓	✓	✓	✓
Death	All	Unique to Vanille. Deals magic damage in most instances, but has a 1%-base probability of killing susceptible enemies instantly. Ways to improve its effectiveness include: ◆ Cast Vigilance, Haste and Faith on Vanille. ◆ Cast Curse on the desired target. ◆ Equip her Belladonna Wand (or its upgraded equivalents). ◆ Protect her with a Sentinel to avoid interruptions. ◆ Equip accessories to gain the ATB Rate synthesized ability. ◆ Increase the Chain Bonus and Vanille's Role Level as Saboteur.					✓	

SYNERGIST ABILITIES

See page 142 for more information on status enhancements.

Name	ATB Cost	Notes	Lightning	Snow	Sazh	Hope	Vanille	Fang
Boon	AUTO	Extends the duration of a target's existing status enhancements once new buffs are bestowed. Tactically vital, this enables you to "top-up" status enhancements regularly.	✓	✓	✓	✓	✓	✓
Bravery	2	Raises the target's Strength. Causes all physical attacks to inflict more damage.	✓	✓	✓	✓		
Bravera	2	Significantly raises target's Strength for a short time.					✓	✓
Faith	2	Raises the target's Magic stat. Works in the same way as Bravery, but used primarily to augment the attacking prowess of Ravager spells, healing capacity of Medics, and offer a boost to Commandos using Ruin and Ruinga.	✓	✓	✓	✓		
Faithra	2	Significantly raises target's Magic for a short time.					✓	✓
Haste	2	Accelerates a target's ATB gauge recharge rate. One of the most useful spells available, and an essential buff during late-game play.	✓	✓	✓	✓		✓
Vigilance	2	Boosts a target's odds of interrupting enemy actions and reduces the probability that they will recoil when attacked. Acts as a counter to Curse, and increases the success rates for many abilities. Can be especially effective if bestowed on a Saboteur.	✓	✓	✓		✓	
Enfire	2	These spells add a Fire, Ice, Lightning or Water attribute to a target's attacks. A great way to exploit an enemy's elemental weaknesses.	✓		✓	✓		
Enfrost	2		✓		✓	✓		
Enthunder	2		✓		✓	✓		
Enwater	2		✓		✓	✓		
Protect	2	Raises the target's resistance to physical attacks.	✓	✓	✓	✓		
Protectra	2	Significantly raises the target's physical resistance for a short time.					✓	✓
Shell	2	Raises the target's resistance to magic attacks.	✓	✓	✓	✓		
Shellra	2	Significantly raises target's magic resistance for a short time.					✓	✓
Barfire	2	These status enhancements raise a target's resistance to the Fire, Ice, Lightning and Water elements.			✓	✓	✓	
Barfrost	2				✓	✓	✓	
Barthunder	2				✓	✓	✓	
Barwater	2				✓	✓	✓	
Veil	2	Doubles the target's status ailment resistance. An important ability when you face opponents who regularly inflict debuffs. Against such foes, it may be worthwhile to use a Synergist as party leader in order to cast Veil and Vigilance when the battle begins.				✓	✓	✓

MEDIC ABILITIES

Name	ATB Cost	Notes	Lightning	Snow	Sazh	Hope	Vanille	Fang
Cure	1	Restores the target's HP. Cure's actual restorative value is dependent on the Role Level and Magic stat of the Medic. For this reason, Hope and Vanille excel in this capacity.	✓	✓	✓	✓	✓	✓
Cura	2	Restores HP to all allied targets in range.	✓	✓	✓	✓	✓	✓
Curasa	1	Curaja restores more HP when a character is heavily wounded, but less as they approach full health (when Cure becomes more efficient in terms of ATB cost per HP points replenished).		✓	✓	✓	✓	
Curaja	2	Same as Curasa, but used on all allied targets in range.				✓	✓	
Esuna	2	Removes the target's most recently inflicted status ailment.	✓	✓	✓	✓	✓	✓
Raise	3	Revives an ally from KO. Health restoration is relatively low, so you must be ready to follow up with curative spells.	✓			✓	✓	✓

Techniques can be used at any time while the battle menu is visible, at no ATB cost, with your selection of available skills governed by your choice of leader (and, of course, progress in the Crystarium). Each Technique has a mandatory Technical Point fee, so there is a natural limit to how often you can use them.

Summon (3 TP)

Used to call the party leader's Eidolon to battle. See page 196 for more information.

Libra (1 TP)

Used to reveal data on an opponent's key characteristics, which is particularly handy if you suspect that they have a complicated arrangement of strengths and weaknesses. It will generally take two uses of Libra to unlock all information on a new foe. This Technique (and the similar Librascope item) is best used during confrontations with bosses and powerful Marks, when it could be critical that you swiftly ascertain their elemental vulnerabilities. For weaker foes, you will find that entries on the Enemy Intel page are filled automatically after a few confrontations.

Renew (2 TP)

Rescues allies from KO and restores HP to all party members – a great Technique to use in emergency situations.

Quake (1 TP)

Your only magic infused with the Earth element, this Technique attacks all enemies in a wide radius. Though the damage inflicted is not spectacular, the real purpose of Quake is to instantly Stagger multiple enemies after securing a preemptive strike. It can also be employed to maintain Chains if you are using a Paradigm with no dedicated attackers (such as Combat Clinic). Note that airborne foes usually possess an immunity to Quake.

Dispelga (1 TP)

Dispelga instantly cancels all status effects active in the current battle, removing buffs and debuffs from friend and foe alike. If your party is afflicted by a potent cocktail of status ailments – particularly if they are paralyzed by Pain and silenced by Fog – this Technique may prove to be your last chance of salvation. The fact that it could relieve your opponents of a full set of vital debuffs could be a heavy cost to pay, though. If TP is not an issue, a summon could be a better solution. You should also keep in mind that certain enemies who possess an immunity to Dispel will not be affected by this Technique, and will retain all active status enhancements and ailments.

Stopga (1 TP)

Resets party and enemy ATB gauges. This can be a life-saver when an opponent is poised to unleash a special attack that might wipe out or severely debilitate your entire battle team.

Synthesized abilities are enhancements that can be activated through special equipment combinations. The principle is simple: each piece of equipment in the game belongs to one of 29 (hidden) Synthesis Groups. By equipping more than one item of the same group (or, as a matter of fact, of the very same type), you will trigger a synthesized ability. This enhancement will be listed under the character's passive ability list at the Status and Equip screens.

Both weapons and accessories can belong to Synthesis Groups, so a character can have up to five items actively contributing to synthesized abilities, with a maximum of two synthesized abilities active at one time. Though you can set up some useful boosts during the main adventure, you will find that many of the most powerful and effective enhancements only become available later in the game.

SYNTHESIZED ABILITIES LIST

Synthesis Group	Synthesizing Items		Synthesized Ability				Description
	Weapons	Accessories	2 items	3 items	4 items	5 items	
High HP	Paladin, Winged Saint, Healer's Staff, Physician's Staff	Iron Bangle, Mythril Bangle	High HP: Power Surge				Increases damage dealt to enemies when HP is above 90%. Combine this with accessories that enable a character to strike quickly once a battle begins (such as the Aurora Scarf) to make use of this bonus before enemies can reduce the party member's HP by more than 10%. Another way to take advantage of this ability is to choose a Paradigm where a Medic is present at all times. This could be employed to inflict increased damage on enemies who are nigh-impossible to Stagger. Naturally, preemptive strikes are always a boon.
Low HP	Lifesaber, Peacemaker, Rebel Heart, Warrior's Emblem, Airwing, Skycutter, Mistilteinn, Erinye's Cane	Tungsten Bangle	Low HP: Power Surge				Increases damage dealt to enemies when HP is below 10%. Keeping such low HP is risky, and definitely not recommended for a party leader, but can work with a Sentinel. What's more, the two strongest Sentinel characters (Snow and Fang) both have high HP, and so 10% in their case turns out to be a safer and larger margin from zero than for others – especially when they're very advanced in their development.
Physical Defense	Blazefire Saber, Flamberge Gladius, Helter-skelter, Wild Bear, Feral Pride, Power Circle, Battle Standard, Ninurta, Jatayu, Binding Rod, Hunter's Rod, Bladed Lance, Glaive	Silver Bangle, Platinum Bangle, Power Wristband, Brawler's Wristband, Warrior's Wristband, Power Glove, Black Belt, General's Belt, Champion's Belt, Guardian Amulet, Shield Talisman, Hero's Amulet, Morale Talisman	Physical Wall: 5	Physical Wall: 10	Physical Wall: 20	Physical Wall: 30	Negates the first 5, 10, 20 or 30 points of damage from physical attacks. A large number of weapons fit into this Synthesis Group. This means that you may only need one other accessory, even something as rudimentary as an early Silver Bangle, to acquire a Physical Wall. Indeed, it's during the early game stages, when the characters still have HP in the hundreds rather than thousands, that this ability is excellent. It has negligible value later in the game.
Magic Defense	Edged Carbine, Razor Carbine, Vega 42s, Altairs, Deneb Duellers, Canopus AMPs, Umbra, Solaris, Hawkeye, Eagletalon, Pearlwing Staff, Brightwing Staff, Rod of Thorns, Orochi Rod, Partisan, Rhomphaia, Punisher, Banescissor Spear	Gold Bangle, Diamond Bangle, Magician's Mark, Shaman's Mark, Sorcerer's Mark, Weirding Glyph, Rune Bracelet, Witch's Bracelet, Magus's Bracelet, Auric Amulet, Soulfont Talisman, Saint's Amulet, Blessed Talisman	Magical Wall: 5	Magical Wall: 10	Magical Wall: 20	Magical Wall: 30	Same as Physical Wall, but negating the first points of damage from magic attacks. Also best used during the early stages of the story.
Damage Reduction	Pleiades Hi-Powers, Hyades Magnums, Sacrificial Circle, Indomitus, Malphas, Naberius	Titanium Bangle, Adamant Bangle	Damage Wall: 5	Damage Wall: 10	Damage Wall: 15	Damage Wall: 20	Same as Physical Wall, but negating the first points of damage from all attacks. Every weapon in this Synthesis Group has the Silk Tiger or Paper Tiger drawback to balance out their high stats, which leaves the wielder with greatly reduced HP. From this perspective, the HP bonuses of the Bangles and the Damage Wall synthesized ability should be viewed as a (rather ineffective) way of offsetting that attendant cost.
Ultimate Physic	Simurgh, Tezcatlipoca, Dragoon Lance, Dragonhorn	Kaiser Knuckles	-	-	-	Ethereal Mantle	Prevents all physical damage, but also precludes magical restoration – so you can only heal, cure status ailments and revive the character concerned with items and Eidolons. Because this synthesized ability requires five items (including a weapon), it can only be acquired by Hope and Fang.
Ultimate Magic	Feymark, Soul Blazer, Shamanic Spear, Heretic's Halberd	Magistral Crest	-	-	-	Magic Damper	Prevents all magical damage, but also precludes magical healing (so you can only heal, cure status ailments and revive the character concerned with items and Eidolons). As this synthesized ability requires five items (including a weapon), it can only be acquired by Snow and Fang. It is an extremely useful ability against enemies who do not use physical attacks (such as Raktavija – a Mark encountered during Missions 47 and 62).

Synthesis Group	Synthesizing Items		Synthesized Ability				Description
	Weapons	Accessories	2 items	3 items	4 items	5 items	
Fire Resistance	-	Ember Ring, Blaze Ring, Salamandrine Ring, Flamebane Brooch, Flameshield Earring, Fire Charm	Fire Damage: +20%	Fire Damage: +30%	Fire Damage: +50%	-	Boosts damage inflicted with the respective element. Note that there are several types of elemental resistance items within each Synthesis Group. When combined, some may create various effects all related to the same element. The obvious way to enhance these synthesized abilities is to appropriately Enfire, Enthunder, Enwater or Enfrost the user's weapons with a Synergist. The other way is to have a Saboteur cast Imperil to weaken a target against elemental attacks. The Wind Damage boost is only relevant to Ravagers, as Aero, Aerora and Aeroga are the only vehicles for this elemental bonus. Finally, the Earth Damage boost can only be exploited by a party leader who has the Quake Technique – and is arguably of little value.
Ice Resistance	-	Frost Ring, Icicle Ring, Boreal Ring, Frostbane Brooch, Frostshield Earring, Ice Charm	Ice Damage: +20%	Ice Damage: +30%	Ice Damage: +50%	-	
Lightning Resistance	-	Spark Ring, Fulmen Ring, Raijin Ring, Sparkbane Brooch, Sparkshield Earring, Lightning Charm	Lightning Damage: +20%	Lightning Damage: +30%	Lightning Damage: +50%	-	
Water Resistance	-	Aqua Ring, Riptide Ring, Nereid Ring, Aquabane Brooch, Aquashield Earring, Water Charm	Water Damage: +20%	Water Damage: +30%	Water Damage: +50%	-	
Wind Resistance	-	Zephyr Ring, Gale Ring, Sylphid Ring, Wind Charm	Wind Damage: +20%	Wind Damage: +30%	Wind Damage: +50%	-	
Earth Resistance	-	Clay Ring, Siltstone Ring, Gaian Ring, Earth Charm	Earth Damage: +20%	Earth Damage: +30%	Earth Damage: +50%	-	
Debrave Resistance	-	Giant's Glove, Warlord's Glove	Debrave Duration: -20%	Debrave Duration: -40%	Debrave Duration: -60%	-	These all reduce the duration of specific status ailments, so they're only useful against enemies who regularly cast a particular debuff. More often than not, you'll have a Synergist who can counter ailments with the opposing buff, or a Medic ready to use Esuna, so it's better to put your precious accessory slots to better use in most situations. Against some of the toughest Marks, though, these can help tremendously. Can be combined with a Goddess's Favor to enhance the overall effect.
Defaith Resistance	-	Glass Buckle, Tektite Buckle	Defaith Duration: -20%	Defaith Duration: -40%	Defaith Duration: -60%	-	
Deprotect Resistance	-	Metal Armband, Ceramic Armband	Deprotect Duration: -20%	Deprotect Duration: -40%	Deprotect Duration: -60%	-	
Deshell Resistance	-	Serenity Sachet, Safeguard Sachet	Deshell Duration: -20%	Deshell Duration: -40%	Deshell Duration: -60%	-	
Slow Resistance	-	Glass Orb, Dragonfly Orb	Slow Duration: -20%	Slow Duration: -40%	Slow Duration: -60%	-	
Poison Resistance	-	Star Pendant, Starfall Pendant	Poison Duration: -20%	Poison Duration: -40%	Poison Duration: -60%	-	
Imperil Resistance	-	Pearl Necklace, Gemstone Necklace	Imperil Duration: -20%	Imperil Duration: -40%	Imperil Duration: -60%	-	
Curse Resistance	-	Warding Talisman, Hexbane Talisman	Curse Duration: -20%	Curse Duration: -40%	Curse Duration: -60%	-	
Pain Resistance	-	Pain Dampener, Pain Deflector	Pain Duration: -20%	Pain Duration: -40%	Pain Duration: -60%	-	
Fog Resistance	-	White Cape, Effulgent Cape	Fog Duration: -20%	Fog Duration: -40%	Fog Duration: -60%	-	
Daze Resistance	-	Rainbow Anklet, Moonbow Anklet	Daze Duration: -20%	Daze Duration: -40%	Daze Duration: -60%	-	
Boost	Axis Blade, Enkindler, Antares Deluxes, Fomalhaut Elites, Otshirvani, Urubutsin	Hermes Sandals, Sprint Shoes, Whistlewind Scarf, Aurora Scarf, Nimbletoe Boots	ATB Rate: +10%	ATB Rate: +15%	ATB Rate: +20%	ATB Rate: +30%	Increases the rate at which the ATB gauge charges, and is one of the best synthesized abilities you can exploit. Even at 10%, this equates to an additional attack for every ten performed, which could make a big difference during extended confrontations. This ability stacks with the effects of Haste for blindingly fast ATB gauge recharges. With the right weapon, this accessory set-up can turn Lightning into an instrument of Chain Bonus annihilation – especially if you spam the Army of One ability.
Gestalt	Hauteclaire, Durandal, Lionheart, Ultima Weapon, Rigels, Polaris Specials, Procyons, Betelgeuse Customs, Unsetting Sun, Midnight Sun, Alicanto, Caladrius, Heavenly Axis, Abraxas, Taming Pole, Venus Gospel	Survivalist Catalog, Hunter's Friend, Speed Sash, Energy Sash, Champion's Badge	Random: Instant Chain		Gestalt/TP Boost		"Random: Instant Chain" is a great enhancement that occasionally fills a target's Chain Gauge instantly – and it's cheap, requiring just two items. It has a very low probability of success but, as there is a chance of it working with every attack and long battles can bear witness to dozens of individual command queues, the effect is likely to take place more often than you might think. When it does, it can end conflict in a flash. Naturally, you should grant this to a party member operating predominately in the Commando or Ravager roles. "Gestalt/TP Boost" makes it easier to charge the TP and Gestalt gauges in battle. This is a useful skill for both gathering the TP required to use Techniques, and also for building your Eidolon's Gestalt gauge. The four required items can include accessories that boost TP recovery through battles and kills, and the effects are cumulative.
Positive Effect	Spica Defenders, Sirius Sidearms, Vidofnir, Hresvelgr, Belladonna Wand, Malboro Wand, Pandoran Spear, Calamity Spear, Gae Bolg, Gungnir	Watchman's Amulet, Shrouding Talisman	Buff Duration: +30%	Buff Duration: +50%	Buff Duration: +70%	Buff Duration: +90%	Extends the duration of buffs such as Bravery, Protect and Haste. If your characters happen to be using weapons from this Synthesis Group for their existing and useful built-in Maintenance powers, equipping just one more Positive Effect accessory offers a 30% extension. Filling out your remaining accessory slots for 50% or higher duration times isn't an effective payoff: they could (and should) be put to much better use.
Adamancy	Organyx, Apocalypse, Aldebarans, Sadalmeliks, Tigerclaw, Wyrmfang	Cherub's Crown, Seraph's Crown, Zealot's Amulet, Battle Talisman	-	-	Vampiric Strike		Absorbs 1% of damage dealt to enemies as HP. This is one of the more interesting synthesized abilities, even though the one percent may seem like a lousy rate of return at first. Once you start encountering single enemies who have millions of hit points, you will realize that 1% represents quite a few full heals if you stick to a purely offensive role. Leaving a space for a Genji Glove (uncapped damage) is a way to maximize potential returns in the later game stages.
Independent	All ultimate weapons	Various	-				Items in this category do not support synthesized abilities.

Eidolons are "summons", a classic Final Fantasy feature that traditionally enables players to call upon powerful allies. As has been the case in recent episodes, summoning begins with a dramatic cinematic sequence, but you can skip these beautiful but lengthy cutscenes at any time by pressing SELECT/◀.

You must have 3 Technical Points (TP) to perform a summon, with the action requiring no ATB gauge segments to implement – the moment you select the option from the Techniques menu, the introductory cutscene will begin. Each Eidolon is unique to a particular character and will fight alongside them once brought into the fray. Only the current party leader's Eidolon can be called into action; to use others, change the character under your direct control before combat begins. All other party members are removed from the battlefield while an Eidolon is present, and play no further part in proceedings until it departs.

Summoning Modes

When you use a summon, your Eidolon first appears in Normal Mode and will fight alongside the party leader until the SP gauge expires, your leader is incapacitated, all enemies are defeated or, more usually, you enter Gestalt Mode. An efficient summon period should proceed in this order:

Summon Activation ➤ Normal Mode ➤ (optional Gestalt Mode) ➤ Conclusion

Normal Mode

A summoned Eidolon has its own (hidden) ATB gauge and acts of its own volition. You cannot specify which abilities it employs (though there are circumstances where an Eidolon can be influenced by your actions).

The SP gauge acts as a timer, slowly counting down the seconds until the Eidolon is dismissed. Damage dealt by enemies will deplete the Eidolon's SP gauge. The greater the injury inflicted by your opponents, therefore, the less time your Eidolon can fight in Normal Mode. If the SP gauge drops to zero, the summoned Eidolon will be dismissed from battle shortly afterwards. Note that SP cannot be replenished.

During Normal Mode, the leader can change his or her role with a Paradigm Shift. This enables you to switch to a role that will cause greatest harm to an opponent, or to increase the growth of the Chain Gauge, Chain Combo or Gestalt gauge. The combat role of the Eidolon is fixed, so changing Paradigm will only affect the leader. The Eidolon will continue to act on its own initiative.

Status enhancements can be used on an Eidolon to increase its effectiveness. In Normal Mode, the leader character is still subject to enemy attacks, so you will still need to think carefully about your tactics. If either the party leader or the Eidolon is injured, the Eidolon AI will always automatically attempt to heal. If your leader is knocked out during Normal Mode, the Eidolon will automatically revive them, then leave the battle.

GESTALT GAUGE

In Normal Mode, a purple Gestalt gauge appears in place of the party leader's TP meter in the bottom right-hand corner of the screen (Fig. 1). Filling this purple bar increases the time available to an Eidolon in Gestalt Mode. To obtain the best possible effects from a summon, then, you should aim to fill this gauge completely and leave the transition to Gestalt Mode to the very last moment.

You can activate Gestalt Mode at any time during Normal Mode. Once an Eidolon's SP gauge has reached zero, the Gestalt gauge will drain at an accelerated rate before the summon ends. If your attention has wandered during a battle, this small period of grace may enable you to quickly activate Gestalt Mode.

You can avoid an imminent attack aimed at the party leader by pressing the Gestalt Mode button before it connects, as characters are invulnerable during the transitional period between modes. This is a great way to escape a potentially fatal blow and prolong a summon that might otherwise end abruptly.

1

Gestalt Mode

Once Gestalt Mode begins, enemies cannot move or perform actions until the Eidolon departs. This also applies to any special counter-attack abilities. The Eidolon's abilities are displayed onscreen throughout Gestalt Mode. You can perform each move by using the specified buttons and Ⓛ combinations. Use ✥ to select targets. This feature is not immediately apparent, so be sure to use it to direct your attacks at specific foes.

If you do not wish to choose attacks manually, simply press ⊗/Ⓐ repeatedly to use the Autogestalt feature to have the Eidolon select moves automatically. However, a skillful player will always be able to inflict greater damage by picking their own targets and move combinations.

Displayed through both a dial and a double-digit counter in the bottom left-hand corner of the screen (Fig. 2), a timer shows how long Gestalt Mode has remaining before it expires. If you fill the Gestalt gauge in Normal Mode, the counter will start at 30 units. The dial counts down each unit of time, removing a unit from the counter when it hits base, so you will waste units if you do not queue moves and act decisively.

Each Eidolon possesses a unique "finishing" move that you should activate when approaching the last available second and that is designed to conclude each summon with a powerful attack. Using this with Ⓐ/Ⓨ will consume all remaining units on the Gestalt Mode timer and cause the Eidolon to depart. The level (and power) of the finishing move depends on how much you filled the Gestalt gauge: less than 75%, 75-99%, and 100% respectively lead to levels 1, 2, and 3.

2

Gestalt Mode: Endings & Aftereffects

The Eidolon will be released from duty and leave the battle when any one of the following conditions is met:

- **Normal Mode:** The SP gauge or Gestalt gauge have been depleted.
- **Normal Mode:** The Eidolon casts Arise to revive an incapacitated summoner.
- **Gestalt Mode:** The Gestalt Mode timer (bottom-left counter) reaches zero.
- **Gestalt Mode:** The player has used the Eidolon's finishing move (Ⓐ/Ⓨ).

Unless the battle ends during the summon, the departure of an Eidolon has a number of effects on your party and the foes they face.

Eidolon Parting Gift

Effects on Party	Effects on Enemies
All characters are revived and HP gauges fully replenished.	Chain Gauges are reset.
Full ATB charge.	Staggered enemies will be restored to their normal state.
Status ailments are healed.	Hidden enemy ATB gauges are set at zero, so they cannot attack immediately.

Eidolon Strategy

The following strategy will allow you to increase dramatically the damage caused by each summon.

1. Soften up an enemy first by raising its Chain Gauge. Remember – you don't have to worry about party members other than the leader during this phase, so you can throw caution to the wind and go for a near-suicidal all-out assault.

2. Once your main adversary is as near to being Staggered as you can manage, quickly summon the Eidolon and select a Paradigm for your leader that will enable them to increase Chains or maximize the growth of the Gestalt gauge. Build up the Gestalt gauge as a priority, then use the rest of Normal Mode to ensure that enemies are Staggered or that the Chain Bonus is suitably high. Remember that Eidolons can be enhanced with buffs in Normal Mode.

3. Just before the SP gauge expires, activate Gestalt Mode and start with moves that raise Chains even higher (such as the rapid multi-hitters like Hecatoncheir's Chain Cannons), before employing attacks that offer increased damage.

4. As the countdown comes to an end, use the final second of Gestalt Mode to initiate the special finishing move.

Alternative Uses

Though they are powerful during the earlier stages of the adventure, you will find that Eidolons become increasingly ineffective at dealing damage during later chapters, and especially so during post-story play. By the last third of the main quest, you may find that summoning consumes TP that could be more profitably spent on other techniques. The side-effect of having all Stagger conditions and Chain Gauge or Chain Bonus progress removed once the Eidolon departs also makes them less effective during battles against stronger opponents.

That said, Eidolons can still be used to extricate your party from difficult or potentially deadly situations:

- Summoning an Eidolon interrupts all enemy assaults. This is particularly expedient against bosses who "charge" dangerous special attacks, and especially if onscreen captions provide advance notice of their intentions.
- Every summon concludes with the entire party being revived, cured of ailments and restored to full HP. Later in the adventure, you could perhaps come to view Eidolons as a form of ultimate "cure-all" spell, with the added bonus of interrupting an enemy's relentless onslaught.
- Remember that you can summon an Eidolon instantly after selecting the appropriate entry in the Techniques menu. Whenever your party leader is struggling with status ailments or near to death during a long and significant battle, you should regard this option as a special "panic button".

Technical Points

There are numerous ways to increase your available TP:

- **Combat:** You earn TP by attacking enemies and increasing Chain Gauges, and by scoring high ratings – a quick five-star finish will boost the TP that you earn from a battle.
- **Thrift:** If you have Librascopes to spare, don't spend TP on Libra. A Librascope also reveals information on all enemies present during a battle, rather than a single target.
- **Items & accessories:** The first Mark mission available at the start of Chapter 11 (01 – Pond Scum) offers an Energy Sash accessory as its completion reward, which increases the TP acquired by scoring a kill in combat. The Champion's Badge accessory also helps by boosting TP gauge growth every time you win a battle. The Elixir item can be used to restore TP and HP during battle, but is far too rare and valuable to squander on general use.
- **Ethersol Shrouds:** A quick application of Ethersol prior to battle fills the TP gauge instantly.

SHIVA

- Acquired by Snow in Chapter 03.
- Shiva is actually comprised of two sisters, Stiria and Nix. They accompany Snow in battle as individual entities in Normal Mode but join to become Shiva for Gestalt Mode.
- Shiva's moves are elemental Ice attacks, but with a special property: if the target possesses elemental Ice resistance of Halved, Resistant, Immune or Absorb, this is ignored and treated instead as Normal resistance in damage calculations.
- While both sisters appear in Normal Mode, they share a common SP gauge. However, they do have separate ATB gauges.
- Enemies will target Nix (the smaller sister) and cannot attack Stiria directly. However, area-effect assaults can still hurt Stiria, causing SP depletion.

Normal Mode: Stiria

Stiria assumes a support role, acting as Medic and Synergist with a limited but effective skill set. When able and free of other tasks she will attack with elemental Ice magic. She will heal and cure Snow as a matter of priority, though. This means Snow is free to pursue a more aggressive role in combat.

Due to Stiria's priorities, having two partners in Normal Mode combat doesn't actually guarantee easier chaining. However, her magic is effective against multiple opponents, and will see use if Snow is not in need of attention.

Ability	ATB Cost	Description
Blizzard	1	Deal Ice damage to targets.
Blizzara	2	Deal Ice damage to targets in range.
Blizzaga	3	Deal Ice damage to targets within a wide radius.
Curaga	1	Restore a large amount of target's HP.
Esuna	1	Remove target's most recently inflicted status ailment.
Arise	Auto	Revive from KO with full HP and no status ailments.
Penetration	Auto	Bypass target's Fire, Ice, Lightning and Water resistances.

Normal Mode: Nix

Nix takes a Commando role in Normal Mode, dispensing physical damage with moves that emulate Launch, Ruin and Blitz. Her standard behavior is to move in close to a target, then wait for her ATB charge to fill before she launches an assault. Her special ATB Charge technique increases the rate at which her ATB gauge fills while she is waiting to attack.

Nix is the more useful sister for Snow to watch and work with when building Chains. It may be advantageous to operate as a Ravager to increase the Chain Bonus more rapidly.

Ability	ATB Cost	Description
Wheel Rap	1	Deal physical damage to target.
Flip Kick	1	Deal physical damage to target, launching it into the air if Staggered.
Wheel Grind	1	Strike target repeatedly for physical damage.
Wheel Toss	1	Attack distant target for physical damage.
Pirouette	2	Attack surrounding targets repeatedly for physical damage.
Blizzara	2	Deal Ice damage to targets in range.
ATB Charge	Auto	Store power to accelerate ATB gauge recharge.
Penetration	Auto	Bypass target's Fire, Ice, Lightning and Water resistances.

Gestalt Mode

All of Shiva's attacks are technically ranged, in the sense that the bike itself is the weapon. It can be directed at an enemy anywhere in the arena.

Ability	Cost	Move	Description
Wheelie	3	L ↑ + ⊗/A	Charge forward and deal non-elemental damage to target.
Spinfreeze	3	L ↓ + ⊗/A	Deal Ice damage to surrounding targets and launch Staggered ones into the air.
Icicle Drift	3	L ← or → + ⊗/A	Deal non-elemental damage by sliding into target.
Ice Ramp	3	◎/B	Jump off conjured ramp and deal Ice damage.
Diamond Dust	All	△/Y	Repeatedly deal Ice damage to all targets.

ODIN

- Acquired by Lightning in Chapter 04.
- Odin has the elemental affinity of Lightning.
- The name of Odin's blade is Zantetsuken, which means "Iron-cutting Sword" and is another Final Fantasy staple, as it has been both Odin's weapon and the name of his attack since Final Fantasy III.
- As with Shiva, Odin's moves are elemental attacks with a special property: if the target possesses elemental Lightning resistance of Halved, Immune or Absorb, this is ignored and treated instead as Normal resistance to Lightning.

Normal Mode

Odin operates as both a Sentinel and Commando in this mode, drawing the attention of enemies with the power of Valhalla's Call after inflicting physical damage or performing Lightning attacks.

It is possible to boost Odin's effectiveness by building Chains in Normal Mode. Against Lightning-weak enemies, try using a Paradigm that sets Lightning (the character) as a Ravager and use Thunder spells or Sparkstrike to complement Odin's sword attacks. Later in the game, Odin can be effective against large groups of Pulse Automata.

All enemies possess a "hate value" variable that influences which party member they focus on (including Eidolons). This value rises with successive attacks. Odin's abilities deliver an instant 100% "hate value" for immediate provocation of enemies. This means that Lightning is usually very safe when fighting with her Eidolon by her side.

Ability	ATB Cost	Description
Flourish of Steel	1	Repeatedly deal physical damage to targets in range.
Skyward Swing	1	Deal physical damage to surrounding targets and launch them into the air.
Seismic Strike	1	Deal physical damage to targets within a wide radius.
Crushing Blow	1	Advance and strike target for physical damage.
Thundara	1	Deal Lightning damage to targets in range.
Thundaga	1	Deal Lightning damage to targets within a wide radius.
Curaga	1	Restore a large amount of target's HP.
Arise	Auto	Revive from KO with full HP and no status ailments.
Ullr's Shield	Auto	Raise shield and defend while recharging ATB gauge.
Valhalla's Call	Auto	Force enemy damaged by Eidolon to attack Eidolon.
Penetration	Auto	Bypass target's Fire, Ice, Lightning and Water resistances.

Gestalt Mode

Odin possesses a number of low-cost moves, so you can potentially fit in more attacks than usual before the Gestalt concludes.

Against a group, the Thunderfall move spreads damage across multiple enemies, making it a great way to control crowds. Repeated use can work to suppress overwhelming numbers of lesser enemies; this is especially useful when confronting groups of opponents who can heal each other or call further enemies to the fight.

The best way to maximize Odin's damage is to build Chains, and the cheaper moves are an effective way to do that.

Ability	Cost	Move	Description
Stormblade	2	Ⓛ⬆ + ⊗/Ⓐ	Attack target with blade.
Lightning Strike	3	Ⓛ⬇ + ⊗/Ⓐ	Attack target with blade, then with Lightning.
Razor Gale	3	Ⓛ⬅ or ➡ + ⊗/Ⓐ	Attack repeatedly with blade, then with non-elemental magic.
Thunderfall	4	◎/Ⓑ	Deal Lightning damage to all enemies and launch them into the air.
Zantetsuken	All	△/Ⓨ	Attack all enemies, elevating Chain Bonuses and instantly slaying targets with low HP.

BRYNHILDR

- Acquired by Sazh in Chapter 08.
- Brynhildr has the elemental affinity of Fire.

Normal Mode

Brynhildr fulfils a role much like a Ravager. When building the Gestalt gauge, bonuses can be acquired by employing Sazh's Synergist skills. Sazh can also use status enhancements such as Enthunder or Enfrost to modify the type of shot that Brynhildr unleashes.

Brynhildr has low power, but is capable of attacking rapidly. If Sazh switches to a Ravager role to use spells and elemental weapon moves (or Commando role with Blitz) then it may be possible to increase Chains prior to Gestalt Mode.

Ability	ATB Cost	Description
Slash	1	Deal physical damage to targets in range.
Valkyrian Scythe	1	Repeatedly deal physical damage to targets in range.
Gunshot	1	Deal physical damage to target.
Pyroshot	1	Deal Fire damage to targets in range.
Cryoshot	1	Deal Ice damage to targets in range. Requires Enfrost status.
Electroshot	1	Deal Lightning damage to targets in range. Requires Enthunder status.
Hydroshot	1	Deal Water damage to targets in range. Requires Enwater status.
Pyroburst	1	Attack targets within a wide radius for Fire damage.
Cryoburst	1	Attack targets within a wide radius for Ice damage. Requires Enfrost status.
Electroburst	1	Attack targets within a wide radius for Lightning damage. Requires Enthunder status.
Hydroburst	1	Attack targets within a wide radius for Water damage. Requires Enwater status.
Curaga	1	Restore a large amount of target's HP.
Arise	Auto	Revive from KO with full HP and no status ailments.
ATB Boost	Auto	Temporarily extend ATB gauge to deliver a powerful attack.
Penetration	Auto	Bypass target's Fire, Ice, Lightning and Water resistances.

Gestalt Mode

Chainable moves repeat the damage of the previous attack, but at a reduced cost. They can be employed to boost Chain Gauge and Chain Bonus growth to increase damage.

Ability	Cost	Move	Description
Chopper Spin	2	Ⓛ ↑ + ⊗/Ⓐ	Strike target while spinning wildly. Jets deal additional damage.
Caltrop Bomb	3	Ⓛ ↓ + ⊗/Ⓐ	Scatter bombs that deal Fire damage upon detonation; jets deal additional damage.
Centrifugal Sweep	3 (1)	Ⓛ ← or → + ⊗/Ⓐ	Damage surrounding targets; jets deal additional damage; chainable by repeating input (hence second cost).
Spark Shower	3 (1)	◎/Ⓑ	Deal Fire damage to target; jets deal additional damage; chainable by repeating input (hence second cost).
Múspell Flame	All	△/Ⓨ	Engulf all enemies in roaring flames.

BAHAMUT

- Acquired by Fang in Chapter 09.
- Capable of inflicting both physical and magic damage.

Normal Mode

When building the Gestalt gauge, bonuses can be earned through Fang's combat prowess as a Sentinel (the stronger the enemy that attacks Fang – regardless of the actual damage done – the greater the bonus) or a Commando (the greater the damage that Fang deals to an enemy, the better the result).

Fang's Saboteur skills can also make a valuable contribution when used against the enemies that Bahamut attacks. Once she has acquired area-of-effect Saboteur abilities, she shouldn't have any trouble raising enemy Chains and the Gestalt gauge.

Ability	ATB Cost	Description
Dragon Claws	1	Deal physical damage to targets in range.
Whirlwind	1	Deal physical damage to surrounding targets and launch them into the air.
Umbral Vise	1	Deal heavy physical damage to target.
Inferno	1	Deal heavy magic damage to target.
Ignis	3	Deal magic damage to targets within a wide radius.
Curaga	1	Restore a large amount of target's HP.
Arise	Auto	Revive from KO with full HP and no status ailments.

Gestalt Mode

Pulsar Burst is an effective Chain builder, pummeling the enemy for many small hits. The dive moves will not always connect with ground-based enemies. Switch to a different move if you miss, and then try again from a different location.

Ability	Cost	Move	Description
Hunting Dive	2	Ⓛ⬆ + ⊗/Ⓐ	Swoop down and strike target, launching it into the air if Staggered.
Aerial Loop	2	Ⓛ⬇ + ⊗/Ⓐ	Strike target with a somersault spin, catapulting upward.
Obliterating Breath	3	Ⓛ⬅ or ➡ + ⊗/Ⓐ	Charge forward and blast target repeatedly.
Pulsar Burst	3	◎/Ⓑ	Soar upward, blasting targets within a wide radius with intense light.
Megaflare	All	△/Ⓨ	Deal massive damage to all enemies.

ALEXANDER

- Acquired by Hope in Chapter 11.
- Alexander's attacks inflict non-elemental physical damage. He has no magical attacks in Normal Mode.

Normal Mode

Alexander fulfils the role of Sentinel and Commando, complementing Hope's default specializations in protection and defense (Synergist and Medic). His Lofty Challenge acts like the Challenge and Provoke abilities, forcing enemies to attack him.

Alexander is slow to act, so he may be a little tardy in his use of Curaga when it is needed. Even slower to move, this is not an Eidolon that evades. To overcome his lack of mobility, Alexander employs ranged attacks to reach all enemies.

Alexander is ineffective at chaining without support. If you use Hope in a Ravager role to complement the Eidolon's physical attacks and cause a Stagger, the ensuing damage will be much greater.

Ability	ATB Cost	Description
Steelcrusher	1	Deal physical damage to target.
Obliterator	1	Deal heavy physical damage to target.
Soaring Uppercut	1	Deal physical damage to target and launch it into the air.
Blast Punch	1	Deal physical damage to distant target.
Explosive Fist	3	Deal physical damage to targets within a wide radius.
Lofty Challenge	1	Force enemies in range to attack Eidolon.
Curaga	1	Restore a large amount of target's HP.
Arise	Auto	Revive from KO with full HP and no status ailments.

Gestalt Mode

Alexander possesses a unique Gestalt move, sprouting fortifications that resemble a castle but prevent further movement. However, a successful attack will cause immense damage.

The position of Alexander will determine which type of attacks will be most successful. Chainable moves repeat the damage of the attack but at a reduced cost.

Ability	Cost	Move	Description
Purification	4	Ⓛ⬆ + ⊗/Ⓐ	Deal physical damage to targets in front of Eidolon and inflict Deshell.
Earthquake	4 (2)	Ⓛ⬇ + ⊗/Ⓐ	Deal proximity-based damage, launching Staggered enemies; chainable by repeating input (hence second cost).
Brutal Sanction	4 (2)	Ⓛ⬅ or ➡ + ⊗/Ⓐ	Deal magic damage to nearby and falling enemies; chainable by repeating input (hence second cost).
Retributive Blast	5	◎/Ⓑ	Damage enemies in a wide area, launching Staggered foes and inflicting Deprotect.
Divine Judgment	All	⊛/Ⓨ	Deal weakness-specific damage to all enemies.

HECATONCHEIR

- Acquired by Vanille during Chapter 11.
- Hecatoncheir has physical and magic attacks in both Normal and Gestalt Modes. His abilities include moves that mimic Launch and Blitz. He's a heavy hitter to compensate for the fact that Vanille isn't the strongest fighter.
- Hecatoncheir's attacks ignore the physical and magic defense of the target. Halved damage or Immunity is calculated as "no resistance". This rule does not apply against Protect or Shell, which are still effective against the Eidolon's attacks.
- Hecatoncheir has no Cure spell to heal Vanille.

Normal Mode

When building the Gestalt gauge, bonuses can be earned through Vanille's use of her abilities in the Saboteur role. Successful use against an enemy will grant a bonus to the gauge.

Using Vanille as Saboteur or Ravager will also help to build Chains in Normal Mode.

Ability	ATB Cost	Description
Pummel	1	Repeatedly deal physical damage to targets in range.
Aerial Tackle	1	Advance and deal physical damage to target.
Hurricane Kick	1	Deal physical damage to surrounding targets.
Force Projection	1	Deal physical damage to a distant target.
Quake	4	Deal Earth damage to targets in range.
Arise	Auto	Revive from KO with full HP and no status ailments.
Counter	Auto	Occasionally counterattack enemies after evading their attacks.
Looming Wrath	Auto	Attack any enemy that draws near.

Gestalt Mode

Chainable moves repeat the damage of the previous identical attack, but at a reduced cost.

Ability	Cost	Move	Description
Chain Cannons	1 (1)	L ↑ + ⊗/A	Repeatedly fire on target with cannons; chainable by repeating input (hence second cost).
Missile Tetrad	2 (1)	L ↓ + ⊗/A	Fire four missiles in turn at targets and surrounding enemies; chainable by repeating input (hence second cost).
Piercing Ray	3 (1)	L ← or → + ⊗/A	Blast target and interposing enemies with laser; chainable by repeating input (hence second cost).
Force Blasters	4	◎/B	Deal heavy damage to targets in range and launch them into the air.
Gaian Salvo	All	△/Y	Deal massive damage to all enemies.

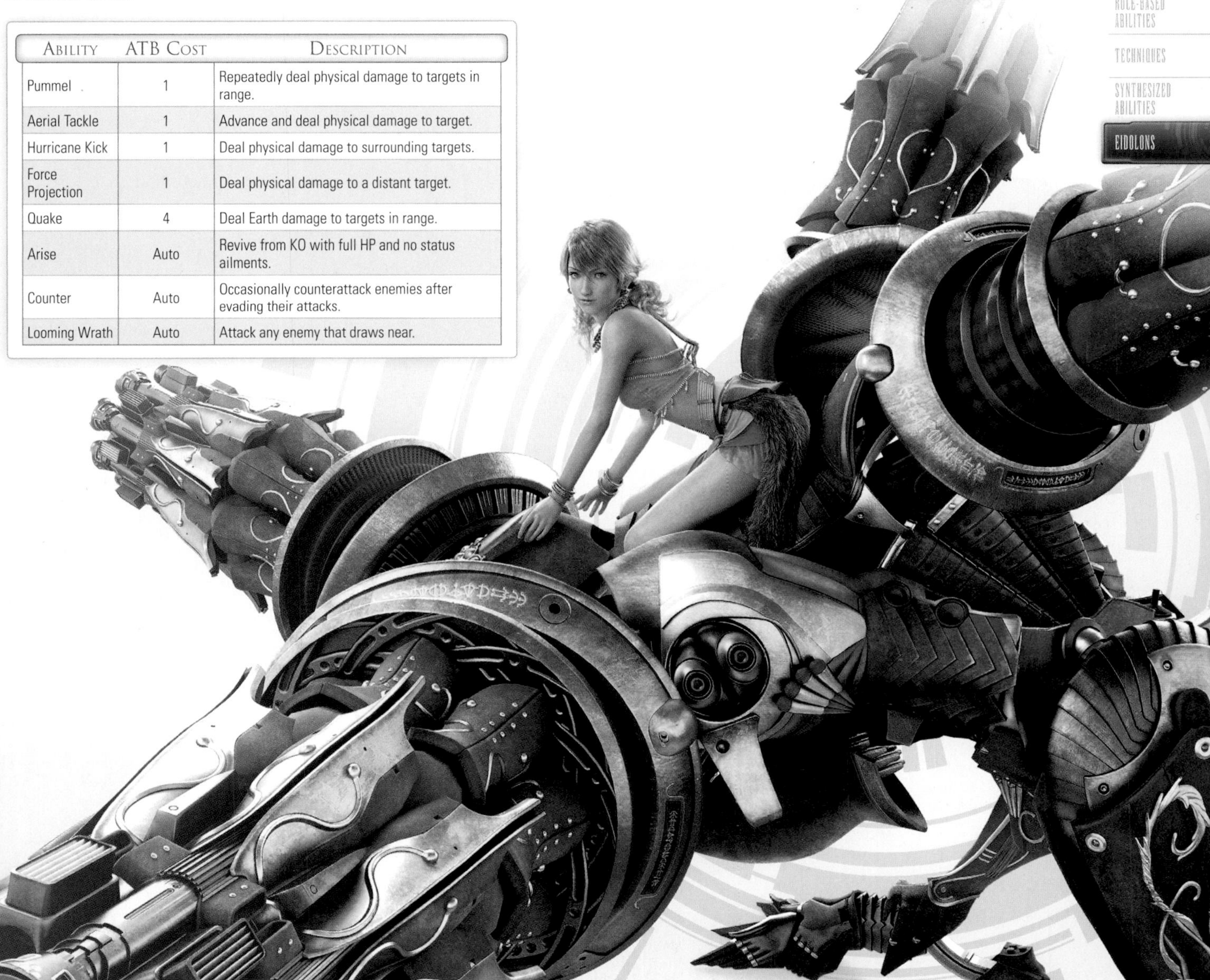

INVENTORY

Every item you equip is a tactical choice that will affect the outcome of each battle. That's why this section of the guide provides advice, complete inventory lists and statistics, including item information that is normally hidden from the player. By making more informed selections, you will create custom combinations that strengthen your characters, boost their magical powers and reveal new strategic possibilities.

CHAPTER CONTENTS

This chapter is dedicated to all items available in the game, covering both their analysis as well as how to acquire them. The actual content of each section is as follows:

Weapons (page 207) – Every weapon in the game revealed, with statistics, comparison charts of Strength and Magic potential, and tactical analysis.

Accessories (page 213) – A full list of the equipment available for your accessory slots. Records every attribute and reveals hidden details regarding function and combination.

Components (page 216) – The complete catalog of components, with information on their best use.

Upgrade (page 218) – How to improve old items and create exciting new ones, explaining the secrets of efficient combining.

Dismantle (page 220) – A breakdown of items generated through the Dismantle option, showing how to make the most beneficial returns on decommissioned kit.

Items (page 222) – Consumable items and Shrouds examined, plus an overview of all key items.

Shops (page 223) – The entire directory of vendors accessible through Save Stations, with details of their merchandise. This section includes information on obtaining e-passes to unlock all of the retail networks.

TABLE STRUCTURE

Most tables in this chapter share the same overall structure. The meaning of each column headline is detailed below. Note that Final Fantasy XIII is unusual in that it offers a subtle and complex development system for weapons and accessories. In short, you can only make sound decisions regarding the equipment you want to use if you understand the upgrade system, yet you also need to study the former carefully to really get a grip on the latter.

- **Rank** – A hidden stat that determines the experience (EXP) value of components when upgrading the item. Each weapon or accessory has a rank between 1 (lowest) and 11 (highest); the higher its rank, the lower the EXP value awarded by components.
- **Max Level** – The maximum experience level for the weapon or accessory in its current form. In the game, items that reach their maximum level display a star (★) instead of a level number.
- **Special Property** – A buff or passive ability that is conferred on the character when the item is equipped.
- **Synthesis Group** – The group of weapons and accessories with which the item should be combined to activate its synthesized ability (see page 194 for more details on these).
- **Buy/Sell Price** – The cost of acquiring the item directly from a shop, and the income derived from selling it, in Gil.
- **Availability** – Names the retail network from which the item may be purchased through the Save Station Shop option, or the creature which drops the item as spoils when defeated.
- **Catalyst** – The transformational component required to upgrade a maximum level weapon or accessory from one form to the next. In our tables, when an arrow points from one item to another, this represents such a transformation path.
- **Attribute: Min** – The item's relevant attribute (Strength, Magic, HP bonus or percentage value) at Level 1.
- **Attribute: Max** – The item's relevant attribute at maximum level.
- **Attribute: Increment** – The amount by which the attribute rises with each level increase.

As you will soon notice, each character has access to eight "families" of weapons, each including three forms (initial, intermediate and ultimate), for a total of 24 weapons per character. A party member's eight ultimate weapons are easy to recognize as they share the same name ("Omega Weapon" for Lightning, for instance).

As a general rule, initial forms can be found in Treasure Spheres or shops: however, the only way to acquire intermediate and ultimate weapons is through upgrades (see page 218 for more details). A very expensive process indeed, but one that is definitely worthwhile, as all ultimate weapons offer – among other things – a very welcome sixth ATB segment to their wielders. The only drawback is that all ultimate weapons relinquish their Synthesis Group affiliation. Special properties are retained, but you lose the benefit of synthesized abilities.

LIGHTNING'S WEAPONS

WEAPONS LIST

		Blazefire Saber	Flamberge	Omega Weapon	Axis Blade	Enkindler	Omega Weapon	Edged Carbine	Razor Carbine	Omega Weapon	Lifesaber	Peacemaker	Omega Weapon
Rank		3	5	11	5	9	11	3	5	11	5	8	11
Max Level		26	61	100	21	41	100	26	61	100	21	41	100
Special Property		-	-	-	Attack: ATB Charge	Attack: ATB Charge II	Attack: ATB Charge II	-	-	-	Improved Raise	Improved Raise II	Improved Raise II
Synthesis Group		Physical defense	Physical defense	Independent	Boost	Boost	Independent	Magic defense	Magic defense	Independent	Low HP	Low HP	Independent
Buy Price		2,000	-	-	15,000	-	-	4,600	-	-	20,000	-	-
Sell Price		1,000	4,000	12,800	7,500	19,500	34,125	2,300	9,200	29,400	10,000	26,000	45,500
Availability (shop)		Up in Arms	-	-	Plautus's Workshop	-	-	Up in Arms	-	-	Plautus's Workshop	-	-
Availability (treasure)		-	-	-	Page 56	-	-	Page 46	-	-	Page 60	-	-
Catalyst		Perovskite	Trapezohedron	-	Adamantite	Trapezohedron	-	Perovskite	Trapezohedron	-	Scarletite	Trapezohedron	-
Strength	Min	15	23	26	8	13	18	8	10	12	8	25	25
	Max	115	323	620	48	133	315	83	190	210	88	225	520
	Increment	4	5	6	2	3	3	3	3	2	4	5	5
Magic	Min	15	23	26	8	13	18	20	28	30	8	25	25
	Max	115	323	620	48	133	315	170	448	723	88	225	520
	Increment	4	5	6	2	3	3	6	7	7	4	5	5

		Gladius	Helter-skelter	Omega Weapon	Organyx	Apocalypse	Omega Weapon	Hauteclaire	Durandal	Omega Weapon	Lionheart	Ultima Weapon	Omega Weapon
Rank		4	6	11	2	4	11	4	6	11	6	8	11
Max Level		26	61	100	26	61	100	26	61	100	21	41	100
Special Property		-	-	-	Leadenstrike	Ironstrike	Ironstrike	Stagger Lock	Stagger Lock	Stagger Lock	Quick Stagger	Quick Stagger	Quick Stagger
Synthesis Group		Physical defense	Physical defense	Independent	Adamancy	Adamancy	Independent	Gestalt	Gestalt	Independent	Gestalt	Gestalt	Independent
Buy Price		7,100	-	-	280,000	-	-	20,000	-	-	28,000	-	-
Sell Price		3,550	14,200	45,440	14,000	36,400	63,700	10,000	26,000	45,500	14,000	36,400	63,700
Availability (shop)		Up in Arms	-	-	Gilgamesh, Inc.	-	-	Gilgamesh, Inc.	-	-	Plautus's Workshop	-	-
Availability (treasure)		Page 24	-	-	-	-	-	Page 84	-	-	Page 100	-	-
Catalyst		Uraninite	Trapezohedron	-	Cobaltite	Trapezohedron	-	Uraninite	Trapezohedron	-	Scarletite	Trapezohedron	-
Strength	Min	25	28	30	37	50	57	13	18	18	8	13	13
	Max	175	448	723	187	410	750	138	378	711	68	213	508
	Increment	6	7	7	6	6	7	5	6	7	3	5	5
Magic	Min	13	10	12	37	50	57	13	18	18	8	13	13
	Max	88	190	210	187	410	750	138	378	711	68	213	508
	Increment	3	3	2	6	6	7	5	6	7	3	5	5

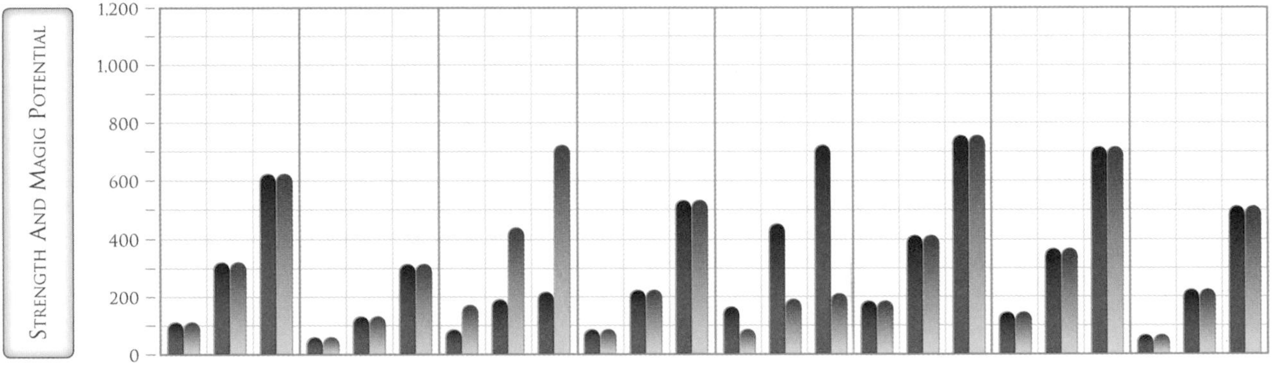

Weapon Analysis

◆ Starter weapons tend to aim for a balance of Strength and Magic, so the Blazefire Saber is particularly suited to Lightning – an all-round character who relies on a fair measure of each, switching between Commando and Ravager roles. It only lacks special properties.

◆ To emphasize and enhance just one attribute at the expense of the other, you could equip the Gladius and its upgrades for Strength (and synthesize Physical Wall) or Edged Carbine and upgrades for Magic (and synthesize Magic Wall).

◆ Hauteclaire can't inflict a Stagger on an enemy but teamwork can. Overcome its innate weakness through appropriate Paradigms and you will be free to enjoy the superior stats of this gunblade and its upgrades.

◆ Why does Organyx tower over others in both Strength and Magic? Because of an achingly slow attack rate which effectively reduces the damage that its user can inflict during a battle. Equipped with the right accessories, however, it can be accelerated or may even acquire the life-draining synthesized ability of Vampiric Strike.

◆ With similar principles of balance, the swiftness of Axis Blade and its upgrades are offset by low stats. Speed is doubtlessly their prime virtue, but what a virtue: if you combine the "Attack: ATB Charge" special property with the ATB Rate synthesized ability, you can turn Lightning into a deadly weapon.

◆ Lionheart and upgrades belong to the Synthesis Group of Gestalt items, potentially conferring some of the most interesting synthesized abilities available. Add to this some very decent raw attributes and the very useful Quick Stagger special property, and you have some of the best weapons available to Lightning.

SAZH'S WEAPONS

Name	Vega 42s	Altairs	Total Eclipses
Rank	3	5	11
Max Level	26	61	100
Special Property	-	-	-
Synthesis Group	Magic defense	Magic defense	Independent
Buy Price	2,000	-	-
Sell Price	1,000	4,000	12,800
Availability (shop)	Up in Arms	-	-
Availability (treasure)	-	-	-
Catalyst	Perovskite	Trapezohedron	-
Strength Min	12	20	20
Strength Max	137	380	812
Strength Increment	5	6	8
Magic Min	14	30	30
Magic Max	139	390	822
Magic Increment	5	6	8

Name	Spica Defenders	Sirius Sidearms	Total Eclipses
Rank	5	8	11
Max Level	21	41	100
Special Property	Augment Maintenance	Augment Maintenance II	Augment Maintenance II
Synthesis Group	Positive effect	Positive effect	Independent
Buy Price	14,500	-	-
Sell Price	7,250	18,850	32,987
Availability (shop)	Plautus's Workshop	-	-
Availability (treasure)	Page 58	-	-
Catalyst	Scarletite	Trapezohedron	-
Strength Min	6	20	20
Strength Max	46	140	713
Strength Increment	2	3	7
Magic Min	15	20	20
Magic Max	95	220	911
Magic Increment	4	5	9

Name	Deneb Duellers	Canopus AMPs	Total Eclipses
Rank	3	5	11
Max Level	26	61	100
Special Property	-	-	-
Synthesis Group	Magic defense	Magic defense	Independent
Buy Price	3,900	-	-
Sell Price	1,950	7,800	24,960
Availability (shop)	Up in Arms	-	-
Availability (treasure)	Page 32	-	-
Catalyst	Perovskite	Trapezohedron	-
Strength Min	8	14	14
Strength Max	108	374	608
Strength Increment	4	6	6
Magic Min	24	36	36
Magic Max	249	636	1,125
Magic Increment	9	10	11

Name	Rigels	Polaris Specials	Total Eclipses
Rank	4	6	11
Max Level	26	61	100
Special Property	Stagger Lock	Stagger Lock	Stagger Lock
Synthesis Group	Gestalt	Gestalt	Independent
Buy Price	19,000	-	-
Sell Price	9,500	24,700	43,225
Availability (shop)	Gilgamesh, Inc.	-	-
Availability (treasure)	Page 70	-	-
Catalyst	Uraninite	Trapezohedron	-
Strength Min	10	16	16
Strength Max	160	496	1,006
Strength Increment	6	8	10
Magic Min	15	24	24
Magic Max	165	504	1,014
Magic Increment	6	8	10

Name	Aldebarans	Sadalmeliks	Total Eclipses
Rank	2	4	11
Max Level	26	61	100
Special Property	Leadenstrike	Ironstrike	Ironstrike
Synthesis Group	Adamancy	Adamancy	Independent
Buy Price	263,000	-	-
Sell Price	13,150	34,190	59,832
Availability (shop)	Gilgamesh, Inc.	-	-
Availability (treasure)	-	-	-
Catalyst	Cobaltite	Trapezohedron	-
Strength Min	0	0	0
Strength Max	0	0	0
Strength Increment	0	0	0
Magic Min	40	60	61
Magic Max	265	660	1,150
Magic Increment	9	10	11

Name	Pleiades Hi-Powers	Hyades Magnums	Total Eclipses
Rank	3	5	11
Max Level	26	61	100
Special Property	Paper Tiger	Silk Tiger	Silk Tiger
Synthesis Group	Damage reduction	Damage reduction	Independent
Buy Price	22,000	-	-
Sell Price	11,000	28,600	50,050
Availability (shop)	Gilgamesh, Inc.	-	-
Availability (treasure)	Page 96	-	-
Catalyst	Perovskite	Trapezohedron	-
Strength Min	40	60	61
Strength Max	340	1,140	1,150
Strength Increment	12	18	11
Magic Min	0	0	0
Magic Max	0	0	0
Magic Increment	0	0	0

Name	Antares Deluxes	Fomalhaut Elites	Total Eclipses
Rank	4	6	11
Max Level	21	41	100
Special Property	Chain Bonus Boost	Chain Bonus Boost II	Chain Bonus Boost II
Synthesis Group	Boost	Boost	Independent
Buy Price	22,000	-	-
Sell Price	11,000	28,600	50,050
Availability (shop)	Plautus's Workshop	-	-
Availability (treasure)	Page 104	-	-
Catalyst	Uraninite	Trapezohedron	
Strength Min	12	16	16
Strength Max	92	216	610
Strength Increment	4	5	6
Magic Min	18	22	22
Magic Max	98	222	616
Magic Increment	4	5	6

Name	Procyons	Betelgeuse Customs	Total Eclipses
Rank	6	10	11
Max Level	21	41	100
Special Property	Stagger Maintenance	Stagger Maintenance II	Stagger Maintenance II
Synthesis Group	Gestalt	Gestalt	Independent
Buy Price	30,000	-	-
Sell Price	15,000	39,000	68,250
Availability (shop)	Plautus's Workshop	-	-
Availability (treasure)	Page 48	-	-
Catalyst	Dark Matter	Trapezohedron	-
Strength Min	14	20	26
Strength Max	94	260	620
Strength Increment	4	6	6
Magic Min	9	18	18
Magic Max	49	138	414
Magic Increment	2	3	4

Strength and Magic Potential

1,200 / 1,000 / 800 / 600 / 400 / 200 / 0

Weapon Analysis

- Augment Maintenance is intended to accentuate Sazh's skills as a Synergist. Offensive buffs such as Enfire will last 40% (80% with Augment Maintenance II) longer while a weapon with this property is equipped. For further extension, accessories of the Positive Effect Synthesis Group can be worn to bestow the synthesized ability of Buff Duration.

- The special property of Stagger Maintenance is unique to Sazh's armory. With his Procyons or Betelgeuse Customs, he can extend the time that enemies remain prone to high Chain Bonus damage by 10% (30% with Stagger Maintenance II).

- Focusing on superior Magic alone, the Aldebarans and their upgrades have the drawback of greatly reducing Sazh's attack speed. If you don't wish to synthesize the Vampiric Strike ability then there are methods for improving the problematic ATB charge rate.

- Savagely reducing your character's maximum HP in exchange for maximum firepower is certainly a sacrifice. But these are the Pleiades Hi-Powers and their variants, the most powerful handguns in the game. With the right opening strategy or measures to counteract the effects of Paper Tiger, it's a gamble that could pay off.

- Should you wish Sazh to specialize in Magic rather than Strength then the Deneb Duellers are a safer, steadier alternative to the risky Aldebarans. They will upgrade just as respectably while synthesizing the Magic Wall ability.

- Because of Sazh's importance as a support character in many Paradigms, don't ignore the Chain Bonus Boost that he receives when wielding Antares Deluxes and its upgrades.

SNOW'S WEAPONS

WEAPONS LIST

Name	Wild Bear	Feral Pride	Save the Queen	Paladin	Winged Saint	Save the Queen	Rebel Heart	Warrior's Emblem	Save the Queen	Power Circle	Battle Standard	Save the Queen
Rank	3	5	11	5	8	11	4	6	11	6	8	11
Max Level	26	61	100	21	41	100	21	41	100	26	61	100
Special Property	-	-	-	Improved Guard	Improved Guard II	Improved Guard II	Critical: Power Surge	Critical: Power Surge II	Critical: Power Surge II	-	-	-
Synthesis Group	Physical defense	Physical defense	Independent	High HP	High HP	Independent	Low HP	Low HP	Independent	Physical defense	Physical defense	Independent
Buy Price	1,800	-	-	20,000	-	-	11,000	-	-	4,500	-	-
Sell Price	900	3,600	11,520	10,000	26,000	45,500	5,500	14,300	25,025	2,250	9,000	28,800
Availability (Shop)	Up in Arms	-	-	Plautus's Workshop	-	-	Plautus's Workshop	-	-	Up in Arms	-	-
Availability (Treasure)	-	-	-	Page 52	-	-	Page 100	-	-	-	-	-
Catalyst	Perovskite	Trapezohedron	-	Scarletite	Trapezohedron	-	Uraninite	Trapezohedron	-	Scarletite	Trapezohedron	-
Strength Min	15	23	24	8	13	15	5	8	8	23	33	34
Strength Max	140	383	717	88	213	510	65	248	602	198	513	925
Strength Increment	5	6	7	4	5	5	3	6	6	7	8	9
Magic Min	15	23	24	8	13	15	10	17	17	13	5	4
Magic Max	140	383	717	88	213	510	70	257	611	38	125	202
Magic Increment	5	6	7	4	5	5	3	6	6	1	2	2

Name	Feymark	Soul Blazer	Save the Queen	Sacrificial Circle	Indomitus	Save the Queen	Unsetting Sun	Midnight Sun	Save the Queen	Umbra	Solaris	Save the Queen
Rank	4	6	11	6	8	11	3	5	11	5	9	11
Max Level	21	41	100	26	61	100	26	61	100	21	41	100
Special Property	Enfeeblement	Hindrance	Hindrance	Paper Tiger	Silk Tiger	Silk Tiger	Stagger Lock	Stagger Lock	Stagger Lock	Improved Ward	Improved Ward II	Improved Ward II
Synthesis Group	Ultimate Magic	Ultimate Magic	Independent	Damage reduction	Damage reduction	Independent	Gestalt	Gestalt	Independent	Magic defense	Magic defense	Independent
Buy Price	25,000	-	-	210,000	-	-	21,000	-	-	32,600	-	-
Sell Price	12,500	32,500	56,875	10,500	27,300	47,775	10,500	27,300	47,775	16,300	42,380	74,165
Availability (Shop)	Gilgamesh, Inc.	-	-	Gilgamesh, Inc.	-	-	Gilgamesh, Inc.	-	-	Plautus's Workshop	-	-
Availability (Treasure)	Page 74	-	-	-	-	-	Page 92	-	-	Page 64	-	-
Catalyst	Uraninite	Trapezohedron	-	Scarletite	Trapezohedron	-	Perovskite	Trapezohedron	-	Adamantite	Trapezohedron	-
Strength Min	0	0	0	41	25	30	18	23	23	13	15	14
Strength Max	0	0	0	266	565	1,020	168	503	815	73	175	410
Strength Increment	0	0	0	9	9	10	6	8	8	3	4	4
Magic Min	30	60	60	41	25	30	3	6	7	20	25	26
Magic Max	130	300	1,050	266	565	1,020	53	126	205	120	265	620
Magic Increment	5	6	10	9	9	10	2	2	2	5	6	6

Strength and Magic Potential

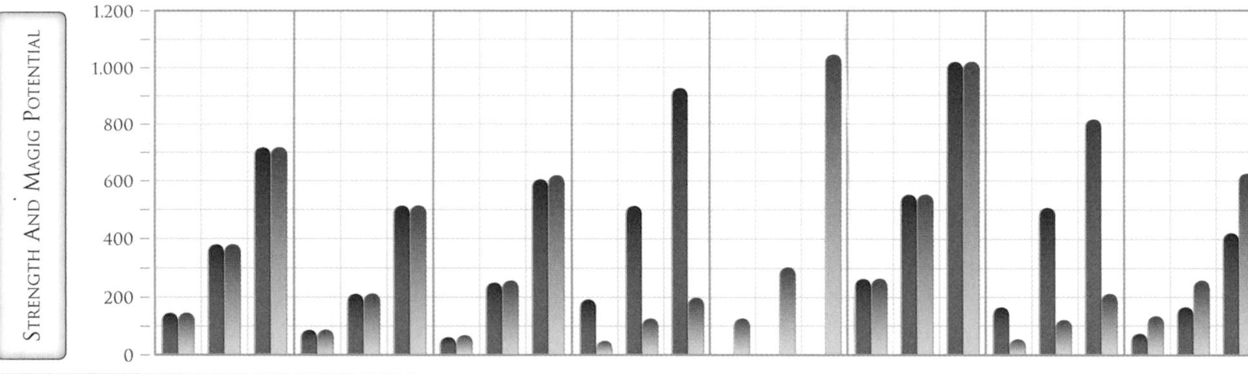

WEAPON ANALYSIS

- The default Wild Bear stays balanced through upgrades and supports Snow's capacity for elemental magic throughout. But if you just want early physical superiority for Commando punches then Power Circle boosts Strength at the expense of Magic. It also compares well with Unsetting Sun on upgrades, and without the Stagger Lock.

- Rebel Heart's Power Surge kicks in when Snow's condition drops to Critical. The smart thing to know is that the coat can be enhanced with its Synthesis Group ability for a ***second*** Critical boost on low HP, and still leave slots for other helpful recovery accessories with Critical triggers.

- Snow can acquire a greater maximum HP than any other character, but losing it to the Paper Tiger handicap remains a tactical risk later in the game. What makes it worth enduring is that Sacrificial Circle and Indomitus possess awesome power (reaching a Strength attribute of 1,020 in ultimate form), especially when you consider that they are evenly balanced in both Strength and Magic.

- Umbra and its upgrades endow the wearer with Improved Ward, a unique property that reinforces Snow's reputation as the strongest Sentinel in the party. It doesn't hurt his self-proclaimed hero status either, as his allies will benefit from greater protection against area attacks.

- You'd be forgiven for finding the "special properties" of Hindrance and Enfeeblement unappealing. You might have assumed it's the price to pay for Feymark (and its upgrades) being Snow's extreme Ravager option. But there's rather more to it, as these coats belong to the exclusive Synthesis Group of Ultimate Magic and can be equipped to confer a secret synthesized ability.

HOPE'S WEAPONS

WEAPONS LIST

Name	Airwing	Skycutter	Nue	Hawkeye	Eagletalon	Nue
Rank	4	6	11	3	5	11
Max Level	21	41	100	26	61	100
Special Property	Critical: Shield	Critical: Shield II	Critical: Shield II	-	-	-
Synthesis Group	Low HP	Low HP	Independent	Magic defense	Magic defense	Independent
Buy Price	10,000	-	-	4,400	-	-
Sell Price	5,000	13,000	28,160	2,200	8,800	22,750
Availability (shop)	Plautus's Workshop	-	-	Up in Arms	-	-
Availability (treasure)	-	-	-	Page 44	-	-
Catalyst	Uraninite	Trapezohedron	-	Perovskite	Trapezohedron	-
Strength Min	18	31	31	2	4	4
Strength Max	98	231	526	27	124	202
Strength Increment	4	5	5	1	2	2
Magic Min	12	45	45	18	26	26
Magic Max	72	205	441	193	506	917
Magic Increment	3	4	4	7	8	9

Name	Otshirvani	Urubutsin	Nue	Ninurta	Jatayu	Nue
Rank	5	8	11	3	5	11
Max Level	21	41	100	26	61	100
Special Property	Siphon Boost	Siphon Boost II	Siphon Boost II	-	-	-
Synthesis Group	Boost	Boost	Independent	Physical defense	Physical defense	Independent
Buy Price	28,200	-	-	2,800	-	-
Sell Price	14,100	36,660	64,155	1,400	5,600	17,920
Availability (shop)	Plautus's Workshop	-	-	Up in Arms	-	-
Availability (treasure)	Page 100	-	-	Page 36	-	-
Catalyst	Scarletite	Trapezohedron	-	Perovskite	Trapezohedron	-
Strength Min	6	18	18	12	18	18
Strength Max	66	178	513	137	378	612
Strength Increment	3	4	5	5	6	6
Magic Min	14	20	20	12	18	18
Magic Max	114	260	713	137	378	612
Magic Increment	5	6	7	5	6	6

Name	Vidofnir	Hresvelgr	Nue	Simurgh	Tezcatlipoca	Nue
Rank	5	8	11	4	6	11
Max Level	21	41	100	21	41	100
Special Property	Defense Maintenance	Defense Maintenance II	Defense Maintenance II	Stifled Magic	Fettered Magic	Fettered Magic
Synthesis Group	Positive effect	Positive effect	Independent	Ultimate Physic	Ultimate Physic	Independent
Buy Price	16,900	-	-	21,200	-	-
Sell Price	8,450	21,970	38,447	10,600	27,560	48,230
Availability (shop)	Plautus's Workshop	-	-	Gilgamesh, Inc.	-	-
Availability (treasure)	Page 54	-	-	Page 92	-	-
Catalyst	Scarletite	Trapezohedron	-	Uraninite	Trapezohedron	-
Strength Min	6	8	8	28	35	35
Strength Max	46	128	305	168	395	926
Strength Increment	2	3	3	7	9	9
Magic Min	14	20	20	0	0	0
Magic Max	134	300	713	0	0	0
Magic Increment	6	7	7	0	0	0

Name	Malphas	Naberius	Nue	Alicanto	Caladrius	Nue
Rank	3	5	11	4	6	11
Max Level	26	61	100	26	61	100
Special Property	Paper Tiger	Silk Tiger	Silk Tiger	Stagger Lock	Stagger Lock	Stagger Lock
Synthesis Group	Damage reduction	Damage reduction	Independent	Gestalt	Gestalt	Independent
Buy Price	198,000	-	-	18,000	-	-
Sell Price	9,900	25,740	45,045	9,000	23,400	40,950
Availability (shop)	Gilgamesh, Inc.	-	-	Gilgamesh, Inc.	-	-
Availability (treasure)	-	-	-	Page 72	-	-
Catalyst	Perovskite	Trapezohedron	-	Uraninite	Trapezohedron	-
Strength Min	30	40	40	10	14	14
Strength Max	205	520	832	110	374	608
Strength Increment	7	8	8	4	6	6
Magic Min	30	40	40	10	14	14
Magic Max	205	520	832	110	374	608
Magic Increment	7	8	8	4	6	6

Strength And Magic Potential

1,200 / 1,000 / 800 / 600 / 400 / 200 / 0

Weapon Analysis

- Hope's default Boomerang is slightly Strength-biased. For a more evenly balanced weapon with better stats, replace it with the Ninurta. However the Skycutter upgrade has "Critical: Shield II" and can exploit its synthesized ability of "Low HP: Power Surge" to improve recovery chances further whenever Hope's health dips into the red.

- Better still, plan for Hope's long term advantage as the character with strongest Magic by switching to the Hawkeye when it comes along.

- Otshirvani and upgrades can first be appreciated in a Ravager role, as they provide different strengths of the Siphon Boost property and use Hope's Fearsiphon to speed up attacks on Staggered enemies. They are also part of the Boost Synthesis Group, so accessory combinations will increase the ATB charge rate.

- If you've gone with Hawkeye, look to upgrade to Eagletalon. Long before the third and ultimate form becomes realistically available, Hope can be packing a weapon with a potential Magic attribute of 506. No special properties, but no drawbacks either.

- Vidofnir and its upgrades support Hope with magical protection, working with an initial Synergist Paradigm. Defense Maintenance extends the duration of defensive buffs by 40% (80% with Defense Maintenance II) and there is further Buff Duration available through synthesis.

- Simurgh and its upgrade may not make much sense at first: why give Hope a Strength-only weapon, no matter how powerful? The answer is that they are part of the exclusive Ultimate Physic, a very small Synthesis Group that grants a secret synthesized ability.

- If you really want to live dangerously, try out Malphas and enjoy the power before you stop to check Hope's HP.

VANILLE'S WEAPONS

WEAPONS LIST

Name	Binding Rod	Hunter's Rod	Nirvana	Tigerclaw	Wyrmfang	Nirvana
Rank	3	5	11	2	4	11
Max Level	26	61	100	26	61	100
Special Property	-	-	-	Leadenstrike	Ironstrike	Ironstrike
Synthesis Group	Physical defense	Physical defense	Independent	Adamancy	Adamancy	Independent
Buy Price	2,500	-	-	300,000	-	-
Sell Price	1,250	5,000	16,000	15,000	39,000	68,250
Availability (shop)	Up in Arms	-	-	Gilga-mesh, Inc.	-	-
Availability (treasure)	-	-	-	-	-	-
Catalyst	Perovskite	Trapezohedron	-	Cobaltite	Trapezohedron	-
Strength Min	18	22	22	23	36	36
Strength Max	168	442	715	198	516	828
Strength Increment	6	7	7	7	8	8
Magic Min	12	18	18	23	36	36
Magic Max	37	138	216	198	516	828
Magic Increment	1	2	2	7	8	8

Name	Healer's Staff	Physician's Staff	Nirvana	Pearlwing Staff	Brightwing Staff	Nirvana
Rank	5	9	11	3	5	11
Max Level	21	41	100	26	61	100
Special Property	Improved Cure	Improved Cure II	Improved Cure II	-	-	-
Synthesis Group	High HP	High HP	Independent	Magic defense	Magic defense	Independent
Buy Price	19,800	-	-	2,300	-	-
Sell Price	9,900	25,740	45,045	1,150	4,600	14,720
Availability (shop)	Plautus's Work-shop	-	-	Up in Arms	-	-
Availability (treasure)	Page 58	-	-	Page 28	-	-
Catalyst	Adamantite	Trapezohedron	-	Perovskite	Trapezohedron	-
Strength Min	8	20	28	2	3	3
Strength Max	48	180	424	27	123	201
Strength Increment	2	4	4	1	2	2
Magic Min	8	20	28	15	21	21
Magic Max	48	180	424	140	381	912
Magic Increment	2	4	4	5	6	9

Name	Rod of Thorns	Orochi Rod	Nirvana	Mistilteinn	Erinye's Cane	Nirvana
Rank	3	5	11	5	8	11
Max Level	26	61	100	21	41	100
Special Property	-	-	-	Ally KO: Power Surge	Ally KO: Power Surge II	Ally KO: Power Surge II
Synthesis Group	Magic defense	Magic defense	Independent	Low HP	Low HP	Independent
Buy Price	3,000	-	-	11,000	-	-
Sell Price	1,500	6,000	19,200	5 500	14,300	25,025
Availability (shop)	Up in Arms	-	-	Plautus's Work-shop	-	-
Availability (treasure)	Page 80	-	-	Page 104	-	-
Catalyst	Perovskite	Trapezohedron	-	Scarletite	Trapezohedron	-
Strength Min	6	16	16	5	7	7
Strength Max	131	436	709	65	167	403
Strength Increment	5	7	7	3	4	4
Magic Min	6	16	16	11	15	15
Magic Max	131	436	709	131	335	807
Magic Increment	5	7	7	6	8	8

Name	Belladonna Wand	Malboro Wand	Nirvana	Heavenly Axis	Abraxas	Nirvana
Rank	4	6	11	4	6	11
Max Level	21	41	100	26	61	100
Special Property	Improved Debuffing	Improved Debuffing II	Improved Debuffing II	Stagger Lock	Stagger Lock	Stagger Lock
Synthesis Group	Positive effect	Positive effect	Independent	Gestalt	Gestalt	Independent
Buy Price	31,200	-	-	24,000	-	-
Sell Price	15,600	40,560	70,980	12,000	31,200	54,600
Availability (shop)	Plautus's Work-shop	-	-	Gilga-mesh, Inc.	-	-
Availability (treasure)	Page 48	-	-	Page 96	-	-
Catalyst	Uraninite	Trapezohedron	-	Uraninite	Trapezohedron	-
Strength Min	5	7	7	5	7	7
Strength Max	65	167	403	80	247	403
Strength Increment	3	4	4	3	4	4
Magic Min	11	15	15	11	15	15
Magic Max	131	335	807	161	495	807
Magic Increment	6	8	8	6	8	8

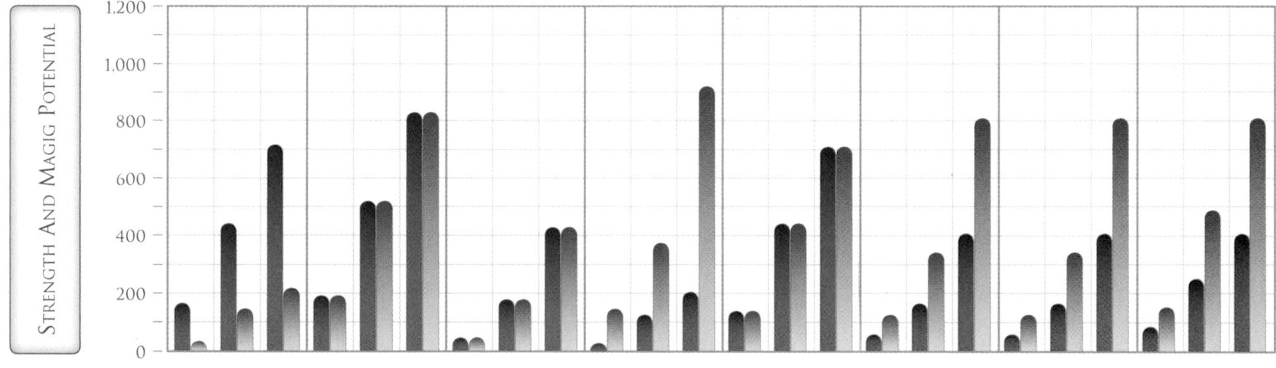

Weapon Analysis

- Vanille's default Binding Rod is also her Strength-bias weapon. You will probably prefer the Rod of Thorns, her balanced choice with no special properties.

- As a Saboteur, Ravager and Medic, Vanille is so strongly reliant on her Magic attribute that you ought to think instead about picking up her Pearlwing Staff and sticking with it as the opportunity arises.

- The Healer's Staff is the first of Vanille's role-specific choices, enhancing her capacity as a Medic by 10% (20% with Improved Cure II). Interestingly, the Staff's synthesized ability of "High HP: Power Surge" means that Vanille can increase her damage and offset the Staff's low attack power by healing herself back to over 90% HP.

- Belladonna Wand and upgrades are the tools of the Saboteur, both offering Improved Debuffing as a special property (increasing the success chance of ailments by 20%; 40% with Improved Debuffing II) and Buff Duration by synthesis.

- Mistilteinn and upgrades introduce a special property that is unique to Vanille. "Ally KO: Power Surge" boosts Strength and Magic each time a party member falls in battle. Exploiting the synthesized ability of "Low HP: Power Surge" could create a Medic with the potential to drag the team back from the brink of death, or set about unleashing revenge in a different role.

- Tigerclaw and its variants are part of the Adamancy Synthesis Group, which can synthesize the passive ability of Vampiric Strike. A Leadenstrike handicap offsets the weapon's stats with a reduced ATB charge and slow attack rate.

FANG'S WEAPONS

WEAPONS LIST

	Bladed Lance	Glaive	Kain's Lance	Dragoon Lance	Dragonhorn	Kain's Lance
Rank	3	5	11	4	6	11
Max Level	26	61	100	21	41	100
Special Property	-	-	-	Stifled Magic	Fettered Magic	Fettered Magic
Synthesis Group	Physical defense	Physical defense	Independent		Ultimate Physic	Independent
Buy Price	4,500	-	-	230,000	-	-
Sell Price	2,250	9,000	28,800	11,500	29,900	52,325
Availability (shop)	Up in Arms	-	-	Gilga-mesh, Inc.	-	-
Availability (treasure)	-	-	-	-	-	-
Catalyst	Perovskite	Trapezohedron	-	Uraninite	Trapezohedron	-
Strength Min	55	60	60	39	65	71
Strength Max	130	300	753	179	385	962
Strength Increment	3	4	7	7	8	9
Magic Min	35	17	17	0	0	0
Magic Max	85	137	314	0	0	0
Magic Increment	2	2	3	0	0	0

	Partisan	Rhomphaia	Kain's Lance	Shamanic Spear	Heretic's Halberd	Kain's Lance
Rank	3	5	11	4	6	11
Max Level	26	61	100	21	41	100
Special Property	-	-	-	Enfeeblement	Hindrance	Hindrance
Synthesis Group	Magic defense	Magic defense	Independent	Ultimate Magic	Ultimate Magic	Independent
Buy Price	6,600	-	-	23,000	-	-
Sell Price	3,300	13,200	42,240	11,500	29,900	52,325
Availability (shop)	Up in Arms	-	-	Gilga-mesh, Inc.	-	-
Availability (treasure)	Page 78	-	-	Page 106	-	-
Catalyst	Perovskite	Trapezohedron	-	Uraninite	Trapezohedron	-
Strength Min	6	10	10	0	0	0
Strength Max	31	130	307	0	0	0
Strength Increment	1	2	3	0	0	0
Magic Min	39	47	47	47	50	50
Magic Max	189	467	839	187	370	941
Magic Increment	6	7	8	7	8	9

	Punisher	Banescissor Spear	Kain's Lance	Pandoran Spear	Calamity Spear	Kain's Lance
Rank	5	8	11	5	8	11
Max Level	21	41	100	21	41	100
Special Property	Stagger: TP Charge	Stagger: TP Charge II	Stagger: TP Charge II	Improved Debilitation	Improved Debilitation II	Improved Debilitation II
Synthesis Group	Magic defense	Magic defense	Independent	Positive effect	Positive effect	Independent
Buy Price	31,000	-	-	16,200	-	-
Sell Price	15,500	40,300	70,525	8,100	21,060	36,855
Availability (shop)	Plautus's Work-shop	-	-	Plautus's Work-shop	-	-
Availability (treasure)	Page 102	-	-	Page 60	-	-
Catalyst	Scarletite	Trapezohedron	-	Scarletite	Trapezohedron	-
Strength Min	20	22	22	20	22	22
Strength Max	100	222	517	100	222	616
Strength Increment	4	5	5	4	5	6
Magic Min	31	38	38	31	38	38
Magic Max	151	318	731	151	318	830
Magic Increment	6	7	7	6	7	8

	Taming Pole	Venus Gospel	Kain's Lance	Gae Bolg	Gungnir	Kain's Lance
Rank	4	6	11	5	8	11
Max Level	26	61	100	21	41	100
Special Property	Stagger Lock	Stagger Lock	Stagger Lock	Improved Counter	Improved Counter II	Improved Counter II
Synthesis Group	Gestalt	Gestalt	Independent	Positive effect	Positive effect	Independent
Buy Price	27,000	-	-	13,100	-	-
Sell Price	13,500	35,100	61,425	6,550	17,030	29,802
Availability (shop)	Gilga-mesh, Inc.	-	-	Plautus's Work-shop	-	-
Availability (treasure)	Page 98	-	-	Page 56	-	-
Catalyst	Uraninite	Trapezohedron	-	Scarletite	Trapezohedron	-
Strength Min	23	30	30	23	30	48
Strength Max	148	390	921	103	230	642
Strength Increment	5	6	9	4	5	6
Magic Min	23	30	30	12	20	48
Magic Max	148	390	921	92	220	642
Magic Increment	5	6	9	4	5	6

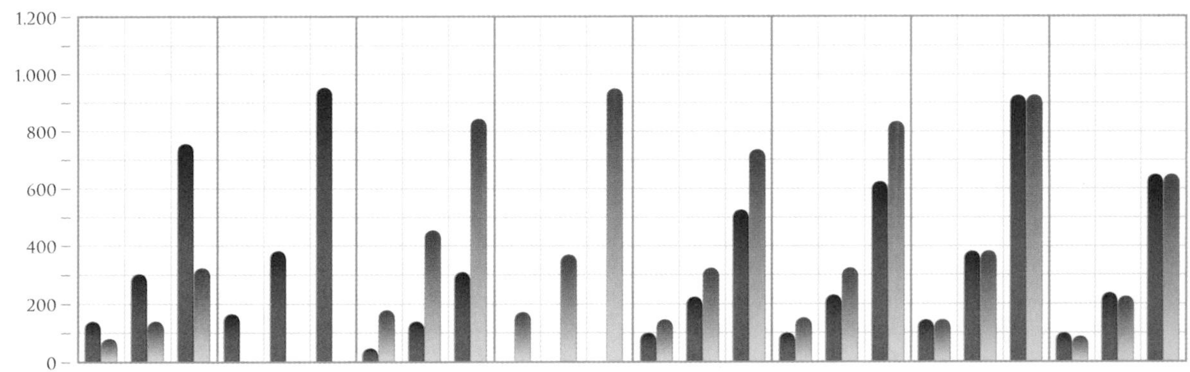

Weapon Analysis

- Fang is doubly favored when it comes to obscure synthesized abilities. Her Shamanic Spear and Heretic's Halberd belong to the Synthesis Group of Ultimate Magic, while her Dragoon Lance and Dragonhorn are members of Ultimate Physic.

- Like Vanille, Fang has role-specific supporting weapons to choose from. If Sentinel duty is likely, Gae Bolg and its upgrades will offer an Improved Counter (+40% damage; +80% with Improved Counter II) through a special property.

- No less than four of Fang's weapons belong to the Synthesis Group of Positive Effect. This can be exploited for the synthesized ability of Buff Duration, keeping Bravery and Haste in place for 30% to 90% longer than normal.

- If the Paradigm demands a Saboteur, the Pandoran Spear and upgrades boost the success rate of ebilitation by 20% (40% with Improved Debilitation II). Given that Fang can blast groups with the area-effect Saboteur spells, it's a recipe for mayhem.

- The Punisher and upgrades are interesting for Eidolon summoners and Libra users collecting Enemy Intel. "Stagger: TP Charge" partially restores Technical Points for every Staggered enemy.

- Though not strictly imbued with any specific Commando support, it is a point of play that Stagger Lock is less of a problem for Commandos than it is for Ravagers (who would lose Stagger potential against groups). That's why the Taming Pole and upgrades would be worth considering for their high potential attributes, despite drawbacks. Persuasively, they are also of the Gestalt Synthesis Group and would thus present further opportunities for recharging TP.

ACCESSORY ANALYSIS

Offensive Accessories

- HP bangles are most effective in the early game, when characters have 1,000 HP or less. They gradually lose usefulness until endgame completion, though several different synthesized abilities can be activated when equipping more than one.

- Strength-boosting accessories are among the most useful enhancements, a temporary equivalent to upgrading a weapon or spending Crystarium points. Possessing the brute force to crush an enemy before they can utter a word brusquely sidesteps the need to prepare for any spells they were intending to cast. Strength accessories will "stack" if you equip two or more at once, empowering a super-Commando and synthesizing Physical Wall. Use the Bravery buff to maximize damage.

- Magic boosters work in the same way by directly enhancing the character's attribute. Precede attacks with a Faith buff to amplify your extended Magic even further.

Defensive Accessories

- The physical resistance belts start to show their true worth when upgraded and paired to improve efficiency. Assign their damage absorption to a Sentinel and you enhance the resilience of entire Paradigms.

- Magic resistance also grows more appreciable when items are upgraded and combined. Note that it reduces damage from magic attacks but it does not guard against status ailments. This also protects against non-elemental magic, for which there are no dedicated buffs or accessories.

- Damage resistance armlets have lower upgrade limits and do not synthesize abilities; but they are economical to equip for general use, reducing the damage taken from any magic or physical assault. They will also increase the previous two resistances when combined.

Resistance Accessories

- When resistance accessories combine, you will notice they don't neatly add up: in fact, a hidden formula of diminishing returns applies. Let's say you tried to cheat Death – the enemy spell, that is – by equipping four maxed-out Seraph's Crowns. Your resistance would increase from 60% to 84%, then 94%, and finally 98%, with the last Crown making very little difference. Upgrading is generally more efficient than adding items.

- The best way to use elemental resistances is to adjust and equip for the situation. If your mission Mark shoots Lightning, break out the Fulmen Rings. Earth resistance can help to bring down mighty Oretoises. But another way to use these accessories is for their synthesized attack bonus, enhancing your own elemental affinity to deliver more damage.

- Don't miss the slot economy of the Entite Ring, which deals with all elemental damage and can be upgraded. The Twenty-sided Die can be very helpful too, but as with all Random accessories, it's a double-edged gamble.

- On the whole, debuff resistances are woefully underpowered and take up a slot that could be put to many better uses (Tetradic headgear, for one).

- The most hampering status ailments (Daze, Pain, Fog, Imperil) are a different matter, though. Equip to fight specific foes and take advantage of synthesis such as Daze Duration to prevent some frustrating battles. If slots are scarce, Ribbons and the Goddess's Favor make excellent alternatives to "single-issue" accessories.

Buff Accessories

- Auto-casting accessories activate at the start of battle, but this isn't always better than Critical accessories, so don't upgrade without thought. Each has its own application. Sprint Shoes may be ideal for an opening rush when you're aiming for five-star ratings, but Hermes Sandals are more likely to save your skin after a surprise beating.

- The Tetradic headgear benefits from buff extension powers such as Hope's Defense Maintenance weaponry, the Synergist's Role Level bonus, and the Buff Duration synthesized ability.

Misc. Accessories

- Items from the Boost Synthesis Group are among the most useful and include the Speed Sash, which not only charges your ATB gauge after kills but can be exploited for constant additional speed through synthesis.

- There are other ways of speeding up your party and improving battle ratings. Use a Whistlewind Scarf or its superb Aurora Scarf upgrade for an early strike on the enemy.

- You needn't be tempted to buy a Catalog at Moogleworks prices, as the game will give you as many as you can use (starting with a Collector Catalog in Chapter 11 (see page 94).

- The Collector, Connoisseur and Survivalist Catalogs raise the probability of item drops (normal, rare, and Shrouds respectively), increasing valuable Spoils for the whole party. The effect is not cumulative, so equipping four Catalogs of the same type is no more effective than equipping one.

- You can recover TP very quickly with the Energy Sash and Champion's Badge, which will enable you to perform techniques much more often.

Name	Rank	Max Level	Attribute			Special Property	Synthesis Group	Buy Price	Sell Price	Availability		
			Min	Max	Increment					Shop	Treasure	Catalyst
Iron Bangle	1	6	50	120	14	HP: +50	High HP	500	250	B&W Outfitters	Page 20	Millerite
Silver Bangle	2	6	100	180	16	HP: +100	Physical defense	800	400	B&W Outfitters	Page 30	Rhodochrosite
Tungsten Bangle	3	11	150	230	8	HP: +150	Low HP	1,500	750	B&W Outfitters	Page 56	Cobaltite
Titanium Bangle	4	11	200	280	8	HP: +200	Damage reduction	3,600	1,800	B&W Outfitters	-	Perovskite
Gold Bangle	5	11	250	350	10	HP: +250	Magic defense	9,000	4,500	B&W Outfitters	Page 64	Uraninite
Mythril Bangle	6	16	300	450	10	HP: +300	High HP	15,000	7,500	B&W Outfitters	Page 118	Mnar Stone
Platinum Bangle	7	21	400	600	10	HP: +400	Physical defense	48,000	24,000	Sanctum Labs	Page 84	Scarletite
Diamond Bangle	8	26	500	1,000	20	HP: +500	Magic defense	-	36,000	-	Page 132	Adamantite
Adamant Bangle	9	36	800	1,500	20	HP: +800	Damage reduction	-	50,000	-	Page 110	Dark Matter
Wurtzite Bangle	10	51	1,500	3,000	30	HP: +1,500	Independent	-	150,000	-	-	-
Power Wristband	2	6	20	60	8	Strength: +20	Physical defense	1,000	500	B&W Outfitters	Page 26	Cobaltite
Brawler's Wristband	4	11	50	120	7	Strength: +50	Physical defense	3,000	1,500	B&W Outfitters	Page 56	Uraninite
Warrior's Wristband	6	11	100	180	8	Strength: +100	Physical defense	10,000	5,000	B&W Outfitters	Page 132	Scarletite
Power Glove	8	11	150	250	10	Strength: +150	Physical defense	-	13,500	-	Page 104	Dark Matter
Kaiser Knuckles	10	11	200	300	10	Strength: +200	Ultimate Physic	-	31,500	-	-	-
Magician's Mark	2	6	20	60	8	Magic: +20	Magic defense	1,000	500	B&W Outfitters	Page 30	Cobaltite
Shaman's Mark	4	11	50	120	7	Magic: +50	Magic defense	3,000	1,500	B&W Outfitters	Page 54	Uraninite
Sorcerer's Mark	6	11	100	180	8	Magic: +100	Magic defense	10,000	5,000	B&W Outfitters	Page 129	Scarletite
Weirding Glyph	8	11	150	250	10	Magic: +150	Magic defense	-	13,500	-	Page 110	Dark Matter
Magistral Crest	10	11	200	300	10	Magic: +200	Ultimate Magic	-	31,500	-	-	-
Black Belt	3	6	10	20	2	Physical Resistance: +10%	Physical defense	4,500	2,250	B&W Outfitters	Page 36	Uraninite
General's Belt	6	11	15	25	1	Physical Resistance: +15%	Physical defense	12,000	6,000	B&W Outfitters	Page 135	Adamantite
Champion's Belt	9	11	20	30	1	Physical Resistance: +20%	Physical defense	-	18,150	-	-	-
Rune Bracelet	3	6	10	20	2	Magic Resistance: +10%	Magic defense	4,500	2,250	B&W Outfitters	Page 64	Uraninite
Witch's Bracelet	6	11	15	25	1	Magic Resistance: +15%	Magic defense	12,000	6,000	B&W Outfitters	Page 120	Adamantite
Magus's Bracelet	9	11	20	30	1	Magic Resistance: +20%	Magic defense	-	18,150	-	-	-
Royal Armlet	8	11	5	15	1	Damage Resistance: +5%	Independent	200,000	20,000	Sanctum Labs	Page 62	Dark Matter
Imperial Armlet	10	6	10	20	2	Damage Resistance: +10%	Independent	-	50,000	-	-	-
Ember Ring	2	6	20	30	2	Fire Resistance: +20%	Fire Resistance	-	1,000	-	Page 38	Cobaltite
Blaze Ring	4	6	25	35	2	Fire Resistance: +25%	Fire Resistance	-	3,000	-	Page 102	Uraninite
Salamandrine Ring	6	6	30	40	2	Fire Resistance: +30%	Fire Resistance	-	5,000	-	-	-
Frost Ring	2	6	20	30	2	Ice Resistance: +20%	Ice Resistance	-	1,000	-	Page 130	Cobaltite
Icicle Ring	4	6	25	35	2	Ice Resistance: +25%	Ice Resistance	-	3,000	-	-	Uraninite
Boreal Ring	6	6	30	40	2	Ice Resistance: +30%	Ice Resistance	-	5,000	-	-	-
Spark Ring	2	6	20	30	2	Lightning Resistance: +20%	Lightning Resistance	-	1,000	-	Page 34	Cobaltite
Fulmen Ring	4	6	25	35	2	Lightning Resistance: +25%	Lightning Resistance	-	3,000	-	Page 129	Uraninite
Raijin Ring	6	6	30	40	2	Lightning Resistance: +30%	Lightning Resistance	-	5,000	-	-	-
Aqua Ring	2	6	20	30	2	Water Resistance: +20%	Water Resistance	-	1,000	-	Page 50	Cobaltite
Riptide Ring	4	6	25	35	2	Water Resistance: +25%	Water Resistance	-	3,000	-	Page 88	Uraninite
Nereid Ring	6	6	30	40	2	Water Resistance: +30%	Water Resistance	-	5,000	-	-	-
Zephyr Ring	2	6	20	30	2	Wind Resistance: +20%	Wind Resistance	-	1,000	-	Page 80	Cobaltite
Gale Ring	4	6	25	35	2	Wind Resistance: +25%	Wind Resistance	-	3,000	-	Page 92	Uraninite
Sylphid Ring	6	6	30	40	2	Wind Resistance: +30%	Wind Resistance	-	5,000	-	-	-
Clay Ring	2	6	20	30	2	Earth Resistance: +20%	Earth Resistance	-	1,000	-	Page 80	Cobaltite
Siltstone Ring	4	6	25	35	2	Earth Resistance: +25%	Earth Resistance	-	3,000	-	-	Uraninite
Gaian Ring	6	6	30	40	2	Earth Resistance: +30%	Earth Resistance	-	5,000	-	-	-
Giant's Glove	3	6	30	45	3	Debrave Resistance: +30%	Debrave Resistance	3,000	1,500	B&W Outfitters	Page 132	Perovskite
Warlord's Glove	5	11	40	60	2	Debrave Resistance: +40%	Debrave Resistance	-	4,000	-	-	-
Glass Buckle	3	6	30	45	3	Defaith Resistance: +30%	Defaith Resistance	3,000	1,500	B&W Outfitters	-	Perovskite
Tektite Buckle	5	11	40	60	2	Defaith Resistance: +40%	Defaith Resistance	-	4,000	-	-	-
Metal Armband	3	6	30	45	3	Deprotect Resistance: +30%	Deprotect Resistance	3,000	1,500	B&W Outfitters	Page 38	Perovskite
Ceramic Armband	5	11	40	60	2	Deprotect Resistance: +40%	Deprotect Resistance	-	4,000	-	-	-
Serenity Sachet	3	6	30	45	3	Deshell Resistance: +30%	Deshell Resistance	3,000	1,500	B&W Outfitters	-	Perovskite
Safeguard Sachet	5	11	40	60	2	Deshell Resistance: +40%	Deshell Resistance	-	4,000	-	-	-
Glass Orb	3	6	30	45	3	Slow Resistance: +30%	Slow Resistance	3,000	1,500	B&W Outfitters	Page 92	Perovskite
Dragonfly Orb	5	11	40	60	2	Slow Resistance: +40%	Slow Resistance	-	4,000	-	-	-
Star Pendant	3	6	30	45	3	Poison Resistance: +30%	Poison Resistance	3,000	1,500	B&W Outfitters	Page 46	Perovskite
Starfall Pendant	5	11	40	60	2	Poison Resistance: +40%	Poison Resistance	-	4,000	-	-	-

ACCESSORIES LIST

Name	Rank	Max Level	Attribute: Min	Attribute: Max	Attribute: Increment	Special Property	Synthesis Group	Buy Price	Sell Price	Availability: Shop	Availability: Treasure	Availability: Catalyst
Pearl Necklace	3	6	30	45	3	Imperil Resistance: +30%	Imperil Resistance	3,000	1,500	B&W Outfitters	Page 129	Perovskite
Gemstone Necklace	5	11	40	60	2	Imperil Resistance: +40%	Imperil Resistance	-	4,000	-	-	-
Warding Talisman	3	6	30	45	3	Curse Resistance: +30%	Curse Resistance	3,000	1,500	B&W Outfitters	Page 52	Perovskite
Hexbane Talisman	5	11	40	60	2	Curse Resistance: +40%	Curse Resistance	-	4,000	-	-	-
Pain Dampener	3	6	30	45	3	Pain Resistance: +30%	Pain Resistance	3,000	1,500	B&W Outfitters	Page 62	Perovskite
Pain Deflector	5	11	40	60	2	Pain Resistance: +40%	Pain Resistance	-	4,000	-	-	-
White Cape	3	6	30	45	3	Fog Resistance: +30%	Fog Resistance	3,000	1,500	B&W Outfitters	Page 62	Perovskite
Effulgent Cape	5	11	40	60	2	Fog Resistance: +40%	Fog Resistance	-	4,000	-	-	-
Rainbow Anklet	3	6	30	45	3	Daze Resistance: +30%	Daze Resistance	3,000	1,500	B&W Outfitters	Page 68	Perovskite
Moonbow Anklet	5	11	40	60	2	Daze Resistance: +40%	Daze Resistance	-	4,000	-	-	-
Cherub's Crown	3	6	30	45	3	Death Resistance: +30%	Adamancy	3,000	1,500	B&W Outfitters	Page 106	Perovskite
Seraph's Crown	5	11	40	60	2	Death Resistance: +40%	Adamancy	-	4,000	-	-	-
Guardian Amulet	2	2	-	-	-	Critical: Protect	Physical defense	5,000	2,500	Magical Moments	Page 54	Perovskite
Shield Talisman	5	2	-	-	-	Auto-Protect	Physical defense	-	6,000	-	-	-
Auric Amulet	2	2	-	-	-	Critical: Shell	Magic defense	5,000	2,500	Magical Moments	Page 42	Perovskite
Soulfont Talisman	5	2	-	-	-	Auto-Shell	Magic defense	-	6,000	-	-	-
Watchman's Amulet	2	2	-	-	-	Critical: Veil	Positive effect	5,000	2,500	Magical Moments	Page 46	Perovskite
Shrouding Talisman	5	2	-	-	-	Auto-Veil	Positive effect	-	6,000	-	-	-
Hero's Amulet	2	2	-	-	-	Critical: Bravery	Physical defense	5,000	2,500	Magical Moments	Page 68	Perovskite
Morale Talisman	5	2	-	-	-	Auto-Bravery	Physical defense	-	6,000	-	-	-
Saint's Amulet	2	2	-	-	-	Critical: Faith	Magic defense	5,000	2,500	Magical Moments	Page 68	Perovskite
Blessed Talisman	5	2	-	-	-	Auto-Faith	Magic defense	-	6,000	-	-	-
Zealot's Amulet	2	2	-	-	-	Critical: Vigilance	Adamancy	5,000	2,500	Magical Moments	Page 124	Perovskite
Battle Talisman	5	2	-	-	-	Auto-Vigilance	Adamancy	-	6,000	-	-	-
Flamebane Brooch	2	2	-	-	-	Critical: Barfire	Fire Resistance	3,000	1,500	Magical Moments	Page 98	Perovskite
Flameshield Earring	5	2	-	-	-	Auto-Barfire	Fire Resistance	-	4,000	-	-	-
Frostbane Brooch	2	2	-	-	-	Critical: Barfrost	Ice Resistance	3,000	1,500	Magical Moments	Page 94	Perovskite
Frostshield Earring	5	2	-	-	-	Auto-Barfrost	Ice Resistance	-	4,000	-	-	-
Sparkbane Brooch	2	2	-	-	-	Critical: Barthunder	Lightning Resistance	3,000	1,500	Magical Moments	Page 90	Perovskite
Sparkshield Earring	5	2	-	-	-	Auto-Barthunder	Lightning Resistance	-	4,000	-	-	-
Aquabane Brooch	2	2	-	-	-	Critical: Barwater	Water Resistance	3,000	1,500	Magical Moments	Page 88	Perovskite
Aquashield Earring	5	2	-	-	-	Auto-Barwater	Water Resistance	-	4,000	-	-	-
Hermes Sandals	2	2	-	-	-	Critical: Haste	Boost	-	2,500	-	Page 133	Perovskite
Sprint Shoes	5	2	-	-	-	Auto-Haste	Boost	-	6,000	-	-	-
Tetradic Crown	4	2	-	-	-	Critical: Tetradefense	Independent	-	15,000	-	Page 108	Scarletite
Tetradic Tiara	8	2	-	-	-	Auto-Tetradefense	Independent	-	40,000	-	-	-
Whistlewind Scarf	2	2	-	-	-	ATB Advantage	Boost	1,000	500	Moogleworks	Page 62	Rhodochrosite
Aurora Scarf	3	2	-	-	-	First Strike	Boost	-	1,500	-	-	Cobaltite
Nimbletoe Boots	4	2	-	-	-	Improved Evasion	Boost	6,000	3,000	Moogleworks	-	-
Gold Watch	3	2	-	-	-	Time Extension	Independent	-	10,000	-	Page 137	-
Champion's Badge	4	2	-	-	-	Victory: TP Charge	Gestalt	-	5,000	-	Page 102	-
Survivalist Catalog	5	2	-	-	-	Shroud Scavenger	Gestalt	-	3,500	-	Page 130	Uraninite
Collector Catalog	4	2	-	-	-	Item Scavenger	Independent	100,000	50,000	Moogleworks	Page 94	Mnar Stone
Connoisseur Catalog	5	2	-	-	-	Item Collector	Independent	-	125,000	-	-	-
Hunter's Friend	5	2	-	-	-	Kill: Libra	Gestalt	-	2,500	-	Page 135	Uraninite
Speed Sash	6	2	-	-	-	Kill: ATB Charge	Gestalt	10,000	5,000	Moogleworks	Page 120	Mnar Stone
Energy Sash	7	2	-	-	-	Kill: TP Charge	Gestalt	-	7 500	-	Page 83	-
Doctor's Code	2	2	-	-	-	Improved Potions	Independent	-	2,500	-	Page 48	-
Fire Charm	5	2	-	-	-	Random: Fire Eater	Fire Resistance	-	7,500	-	Page 80	Mnar Stone
Ice Charm	5	2	-	-	-	Random: Ice Eater	Ice Resistance	-	7,500	-	Page 80	Mnar Stone
Lightning Charm	5	2	-	-	-	Random: Lightning Eater	Lightning Resistance	-	7,500	-	Page 80	Mnar Stone
Water Charm	5	2	-	-	-	Random: Water Eater	Water Resistance	-	7,500	-	Page 88	Mnar Stone
Wind Charm	5	2	-	-	-	Random: Wind Eater	Wind Resistance	-	7,500	-	Page 80	Mnar Stone
Earth Charm	5	2	-	-	-	Random: Earth Eater	Earth Resistance	-	7,500	-	Page 80	Mnar Stone
Twenty-sided Die	7	2	-	-	-	Random: Nullify Damage	Independent	-	22,500	-	Page 135	-
Growth Egg	8	2	-	-	-	CP: ×2	Independent	-	250,000	-	Page 136	-
Entite Ring	5	16	10	25	1	Elemental Resistance: +10%	Independent	120,000	60,000	Sanctum Labs	-	Uraninite
Goddess's Favor	6	2	-	-	-	Rapid Recovery	Independent	-	10	-	-	-
Ribbon	9	6	20	25	1	Resilience: +20%	Independent	-	10	-	-	Dark Matter
Super Ribbon	10	6	25	30	1	Resilience: +25%	Independent	-	10	-	-	-
Genji Glove	9	2	-	-	-	Uncapped Damage	Independent	-	10	-	Page 137	-

There are two different categories of components. Regular components have an EXP value that can be added to weapons and accessories through the Upgrade option, increasing the chosen item's level. An item that reaches its maximum potential (★) may then be transformed into a new and generally superior version by adding a specific component from the second category, called a catalyst. The transformation can only be achieved if you possess the correct type of transformational catalyst.

In the nearby table, every component is described in terms of the following qualities where applicable.

EXP value: The base EXP value of the component when used on a rank 6 item, such as Lightning's Helter-skelter for example. This average value increases or decreases with items of respectively lower and higher ranks.

Multiplier value: The component's positive or negative effect on the hidden multiplier value. An EXP Bonus of 25% (x1.25) to 200% (x3) can be applied to the EXP value of components used in upgrading, and this EXP Bonus changes whenever the multiplier value's running total crosses a threshold. See overleaf for more details.

Rank: The rank of regular components is largely irrelevant. However, the rank of a catalyst is noteworthy in that it determines the rank of the item produced by transformation.

Availability: Names the retail network from which the item may be purchased through a Save Station Shop option, or a creature which drops the item as Spoils when defeated. Components marked with a "-" can only be obtained by other means (such as in Treasure Spheres), and therefore cannot be collected in large quantities.

Buy Price/Sell Price: The cost of acquiring the item directly from a shop, and the income derived from selling it, in Gil. "Can be sold for a premium" is the descriptive hint the game uses to indicate components that will become your primary source of Gil: these "premium" components make poor quality upgrades but will generate exceptional revenue when sold.

COMPONENTS LIST

QUICKSTART
WALKTHROUGH
STRATEGY & ANALYSIS
INVENTORY
BESTIARY
EXTRAS
INTRODUCTION
WEAPONS
ACCESSORIES
COMPONENTS
UPGRADE
DISMANTLE
ITEMS
SHOPS

Organic Components

Name	EXP Value	Multiplier Value	Rank	Availability	Buy Price	Sell Price
Begrimed Claw	4	+4	1	Kaiser Behemoth	-	15
Bestial Claw	11	+10	3	Creature Comforts	80	40
Gargantuan Claw	24	+15	5	Creature Comforts	150	75
Hellish Talon	42	+24	7	Kaiser Behemoth	-	110
Shattered Bone	4	+8	2	Yaksha	-	15
Sturdy Bone	12	+14	4	Creature Comforts	80	40
Otherworldly Bone	24	+21	6	Creature Comforts	150	75
Ancient Bone	43	+31	8	Yaksha	-	110
Moistened Scale	3	+5	1	Sahagin	-	15
Seapetal Scale	11	+11	3	Sahagin	-	40
Abyssal Scale	23	+16	5	Orobon	-	75
Seaking's Beard	40	+25	7	Dagonite	-	110
Segmented Carapace	4	+7	2	Navidon	-	15
Iron Shell	13	+13	4	Creature Comforts	80	40
Armored Shell	26	+20	6	Creature Comforts	150	75
Regenerating Carapace	47	+30	8	Gurangatch	-	110
Chipped Fang	4	+7	2	Gorgonopsid	-	15
Wicked Fang	13	+13	4	Creature Comforts	80	40
Monstrous Fang	26	+20	6	Creature Comforts	150	75
Sinister Fang	47	+30	8	Uridimmu	-	110
Severed Wing	3	+6	1	Amphisbaena	-	15
Scaled Wing	10	+12	3	Creature Comforts	80	40
Abominable Wing	21	+17	5	Creature Comforts	150	75
Menacing Wings	37	+26	7	Zirnitra	-	110
Molted Tail	4	+8	2	Triffid	-	15
Barbed Tail	12	+14	4	Creature Comforts	80	40
Diabolic Tail	24	+21	6	Creature Comforts	150	75
Entrancing Tail	43	+31	8	Mushussu	-	110
Torn Leather	3	+5	1	Adroa	-	15
Thickened Hide	11	+11	3	Creature Comforts	80	40
Smooth Hide	23	+16	5	Creature Comforts	150	75
Supple Leather	40	+25	7	Adroa	-	110
Gummy Oil	5	+6	2	Alraune	-	15
Fragrant Oil	14	+12	4	Creature Comforts	80	40
Medicinal Oil	29	+19	6	Creature Comforts	150	75
Esoteric Oil	47	+29	8	Alraune	-	110
Scraggly Wool	2	+7	1	Sheep (see page 123)	-	15
Rough Wool	9	+13	3	Sheep (see page 123)	-	40
Thick Wool	19	+18	5	Sheep (see page 123)	-	75
Fluffy Wool	33	+27	7	Sheep (see page 123)	-	110
Murky Ooze	4	+8	2	Flan	-	15
Vibrant Ooze	12	+14	4	Creature Comforts	80	40
Transparent Ooze	24	+21	6	Creature Comforts	150	75
Wonder Gel	49	+31	8	Ectopudding	-	110
Fractured Horn	3	+6	1	Goblin	-	15
Spined Horn	10	+12	3	Munchkin	-	40
Fiendish Horn	21	+17	5	Goblin	-	75
Infernal Horn	37	+26	7	Borgbear	-	110
Strange Fluid	5	+6	2	Ceratosaur	-	15
Enigmatic Fluid	14	+12	4	Creature Comforts	80	40
Mysterious Fluid	29	+19	6	Creature Comforts	150	75
Ineffable Fluid	43	+29	8	Ceratosaur	-	110
Cie'th Tear	6	+10	2	Seeker	-	15
Tear of Frustration	12	+14	4	Pijavica	-	40
Tear of Remorse	24	+24	6	Seeker	-	75
Tear of Woe	49	+40	8	Vampire	-	110
Red Mycelium	6	+10	2	-	-	85
Blue Mycelium	22	+21	5	-	-	190
White Mycelium	48	+34	7	-	-	360
Black Mycelium	84	+51	8	-	-	675
Dawnlight Dew	12	+31	2	Chocobo (see page 123)	-	500
Dusklight Dew	28	+42	3	Chocobo (see page 123)	-	850
Gloomstalk	32	+46	4	Microchu	-	1,000
Sunpetal	102	+21	8	Ochu	-	1,000
Moonblossom Seed	73	+55	3	Bandersnatch	-	6,000
Starblossom Seed	230	+91	6	Bandersnatch	-	13,000
Chocobo Plume	7	+34	3	Chocobo (see page 123)	-	20
Chocobo Tail Feather	29	+58	5	Chocobo (see page 123)	-	50
Succulent Fruit	10	+55	6	-	-	1,750
Malodorous Fruit	7	+21	3	-	-	4,000
Green Needle	60	+100	7	R&D Depot	7,000	3,500
Perfume	180	+120	10	Sacrifice	-	12,500

Mechanical Components

Name	EXP Value	Multiplier Value	Rank	Availability	Buy Price	Sell Price
Insulated Cabling	65	-18	3	Lenora's Garage	280	140
Fiber-optic Cable	216	-49	6	Lenora's Garage	840	420
Liquid Crystal Lens	70	-19	3	Lenora's Garage	320	160
Ring Joint	208	-50	6	Lenora's Garage	840	420
Epicyclic Gear	66	-20	3	Lenora's Garage	320	160
Crankshaft	215	-47	6	Lenora's Garage	840	420
Electrolytic Capacitor	68	-20	3	Bulwarker	-	160
Flywheel	204	-48	6	-	-	420
Sprocket	71	-21	3	-	-	160
Actuator	220	-46	6	-	-	420
Spark Plug	62	-18	3	Pulsework Gladiator	-	140
Iridium Plug	102	-48	6	-	-	420
Needle Valve	70	-21	3	Boxed Phalanx	-	160
Butterfly Valve	232	-50	6	Ambling Bellows	-	420
Bomb Ashes	37	-8	2	Cryohedron	-	90
Bomb Fragment	82	-27	4	Lenora's Garage	430	215
Bomb Shell	206	-53	6	Circuitron	-	420
Bomb Core	551	-78	8	Cryohedron	-	600
Analog Circuit	40	-9	2	Hoplite	-	90
Digital Circuit	89	-21	4	Aquila Velocycle	-	230
Gyroscope	149	-34	5	Megrim Thresher	-	330
Electrode	434	-56	7	Vernal Harvester	-	500
Ceramic Armor	147	-35	5	Lenora's Garage	660	330
Chobham Armor	460	-54	7	Bulwarker	-	500
Radial Bearing	64	-20	3	Lenora's Garage	320	160
Thrust Bearing	200	-48	6	Pulsework Gladiator	-	420
Solenoid	220	-47	6	Hoplite	-	420
Mobius Coil	627	-81	8	Vernal Harvester	-	800
Tungsten Tube	192	-53	6	Juggernaut	-	420
Titanium Tube	565	-84	8	-	-	750
Passive Detector	188	-54	6	Lenora's Garage	840	420
Active Detector	582	-82	8	Pulsework Centurion	-	750
Transformer	42	-9	2	Tyrant	-	90
Amplifier	108	-28	4	Lenora's Garage	520	260
Carburetor	274	-55	6	Immortal	-	420
Supercharger	774	-82	8	-	-	800
Piezoelectric Element	310	-50	6	Lenora's Garage	840	420
Crystal Oscillator	845	-79	8	Megrim Thresher	-	1,000
Paraffin Oil	67	-20	3	Lenora's Garage	320	160
Silicone Oil	152	-32	5	Lenora's Garage	660	330
Synthetic Muscle	222	-49	6	-	-	420
Turboprop	768	-85	8	-	-	800
Turbojet	212	-46	6	Lenora's Garage	840	420
Tesla Turbine	823	-79	8	Anavatapta Warmech	-	900
Polymer Emulsion	43	-18	2	Lenora's Garage	200	100
Ferroelectric Film	102	-37	4	Lenora's Garage	460	230
Superconductor	400	-59	6	Lenora's Garage	840	420
Perfect Conductor	751	-83	8	Lenora's Garage	1,600	800
Particle Accelerator	4.800	-87	7	R&D Depot	10,000	5,000
Ultracompact Reactor	40.000	-100	11	R&D Depot	50,000	25,000

Premium Components

Name	EXP Value	Multiplier Value	Rank	Availability	Buy Price	Sell Price
Credit Chip	1	-1	2	Sanctum Archangel	-	500
Incentive Chip	1	-1	5	Sanctum Archangel	-	2,500
Cactuar Doll	1	-1	10	Cactuar	-	12,000
Moogle Puppet	1	-1	10	Chocobo (see page 123)	-	18,000
Tonberry Figurine	1	-1	10	Mission 41	-	28,500
Plush Chocobo	1	-1	10	Chocobo (see page 123)	-	35,000
Gold Dust	1	0	2	Chocobo (see page 123)	-	15,000
Gold Nugget	1	0	4	Chocobo (see page 123)	-	60,000
Platinum Ingot	1	0	7	Adamantortoise, Adamantoise	-	150,000

Catalysts

Name	EXP Value	Multiplier Value	Rank	Availability	Buy Price	Sell Price
Millerite	0	0	2	The Motherlode	3,000	1,000
Rhodochrosite	0	0	3	The Motherlode	8,000	2,000
Cobaltite	0	0	4	The Motherlode	17,000	3,000
Perovskite	0	0	5	The Motherlode	30,000	4,000
Uraninite	0	0	6	The Motherlode	45,000	5,000
Mnar Stone	0	0	7	The Motherlode	60,000	6,000
Scarletite	0	0	8	The Motherlode	100,000	7,000
Adamantite	0	0	9	R&D Depot	220,000	8,000
Dark Matter	0	0	10	R&D Depot	840,000	9,000
Trapezohedron	0	0	11	R&D Depot	2,000,000	10,000

Basics

Upgrading can be performed at any Save Station, becoming available after you acquire the Omni-kit Key Item in Chapter 04. That said, it's not recommended that you start upgrading until much later in the game as it takes plenty of resources to do it efficiently.

To upgrade, select the weapon or accessory you wish to improve and you will see its current level (Lv. 1, for instance) and its experience points (EXP) displayed in the Attributes panel. Now choose a component to combine with it. Regular components have an EXP value that will be added to the EXP of the item when combined. Once you have raised enough EXP to meet or exceed the next EXP target shown, your equipment will gain a level. Depending on the item, this can mean higher stats, greater damage or improved effects.

You can find components in Treasure Spheres; earn them as Spoils from battles; or buy them from shops. Shopping is the fastest way to acquire large amounts, though, and this is ultimately the key to upgrading in the most efficient manner.

Even when a weapon or accessory reaches its maximum level (★), it may be possible to upgrade it further through the use of a specific transformational catalyst. These are rare and expensive components whose sole purpose is to transform one item of equipment into a superior one. Each piece of equipment thus has a fixed development path to its fullest potential:

Advanced Tips

- Each component has a hidden multiplier value that influences the EXP Bonus applied to upgrades. As a general rule, organic components (with a claw icon by their name) gradually raise the EXP Bonus but add very few experience points to the equipment. Mechanical components (with a bolt icon) offer high EXP values but will reduce the EXP Bonus when used.

- The best way to upgrade equipment, therefore, rests in first using organic components to build the EXP Bonus to its maximum level (x3 – a 200% gain), and then spending a large quantity of a single mechanical component type in one go. This will reset the EXP Bonus, but triple the experience value gained from all of the mechanical components.

- Ideally, being cost/time-efficient when upgrading involves being able to identify the components with the right attributes, and to acquire them in great quantities – most likely from shops – up to the Inventory maximum of 99.

- The EXP value of a component will vary from item to item. This is because of another hidden value, the item's rank. The better your equipment, and thus the higher its rank, the less it will gain in EXP from the components you spend on it.

Doing the Math

The multiplier effect of each component can be found in the table on the preceding double-page spread. For example, the very first component in the list – the Begrimed Claw – is worth +4 points to the multiplier value. Further down the list, by contrast, you'll see that a Spark Plug is worth -18 points.

The game keeps track of the running total in the background, remembering the multiplier value for each item you upgrade. The item's EXP Bonus changes whenever this hidden total crosses certain thresholds, as this table shows:

MULTIPLIER VALUE THRESHOLD

Multiplier Value	EXP Bonus
0-50	x1
51-100	x1.25
101-200	x1.5
201-250	x1.75
251-500	x2
501+	x3

So, following our example, upgrading with 26 Begrimed Claws (26 x 4 = 104) would add 104 points to the multiplier value and raise the EXP Bonus to x1.5. The further addition of a single Spark Plug (-18 points) would reduce the multiplier value to 86 points, so the EXP Bonus would also drop to x1.25.

To obtain the x3 maximum from the start, you would also need 126 Begrimed Claws (126 x 4 = 504) to exceed the highest threshold. Not entirely practical, especially considering the 99 cap on inventory. The solution, therefore, is to identify the components with the highest multiplier value-to-cost ratio. These are listed here, in order of effectiveness (note that this table focuses on the most efficient upgrading agents you can buy).

MULTIPLIER: BEST SHOP COMPONENTS

Component	Multiplier Effect	Buy Price
Sturdy Bone	+14	80
Barbed Tail	+14	80
Vibrant Ooze	+14	80
Otherworldly Bone	+21	150
Diabolic Tail	+21	150
Transparent Ooze	+21	150

There are several components with a higher multiplier value, which cannot be purchased, and which take considerable time and effort to obtain in large numbers. Even if found or won, some components (like Perfume, at +120) would still be more efficiently exchanged for Gil to spend on hundreds of the components highlighted.

Sturdy Bone, Barbed Tail and Vibrant Ooze have the best cost-effective rate; use 36 of them and you get an instant x3 EXP Bonus. Otherworldly Bone, Diabolic Tail and Transparent Ooze are just behind – a slightly lower ratio per Gil, but lighter on inventory space as you only need 24 of them to reach that 200% EXP gain.

After boosting the EXP Bonus to x3, thanks to organic components, it's time to use mechanical components to actually level up the equipment. For the best results, use a large quantity of a single type in one go so that the x3 applies to every component. If you added them one by one, your x3 multiplier would soon be reduced to zero after just a few. Again, the ideal solution is to identify what components offer the best EXP value-to-cost ratio. These are listed here, in order of effectiveness:

EXP: BEST COMPONENTS

Component	Average EXP	Buy Price
Ultracompact Reactor	40,000	50,000
Supercharger	774	1,600
Particle Accelerator	4,800	10,000
Turboprop	768	1,600
Superconductor	400	840
Perfect Conductor	751	1,600
Chobham Armor	460	1,000
Bomb Core	551	1,200
Tesla Turbine	823	1,800

Ultracompact Reactors are perfect when you need huge amounts of EXP, as you'll find when you see the requirements for taking an ultimate weapon to its maximum level. Particle Accelerators are an intermediate solution – still very high EXP, but ten times lower. You will need to unlock the R&D Depot retail network to buy these items.

At this price, you should also avoid waste incurred from using more components than necessary. Work out how much EXP will be required by multiplying the number of levels to be upgraded with the average cost of each level (depending on how many levels have yet to be gained). Aim to come in as near as possible to the maximum level. Make up any final remaining difference with lesser components.

Don't be surprised by the fact that the same component may offer different EXP depending on the target equipment. The higher the rank of the item, the lower the EXP gained from the component. Ranks run from 1 to 11, lowest to highest, and the EXP values in the guide are based on Rank 6 items (average). Before you decide to upgrade a weapon, do have a look at its rank. Two weapons with a maximum level of 61, but with different ranks, will require very different total amounts of EXP.

As a general rule of thumb, upgrading an initial weapon from Lv. 1 to Lv. ★ requires approximately 50,000 EXP; upgrading an intermediate weapon from Lv. 1 to Lv. ★ requires approximately 450,000 EXP; upgrading an ultimate weapon from Lv. 1 to Lv. ★ requires approximately 1,500,000 EXP. Alternatively, trial and error with a saved game can give an equally good answer.

If you want to make precise calculations, it might help to note that every item starts with a base EXP requirement to take it to Lv. 2, and then increases the requirement by the same amount per level. For example, a Silver Bangle needs 200 EXP to level up at first, then 256 EXP, then 312 EXP, rising by 56 EXP per level. The same applies to every item, though each has its own base and increment value.

Summary: Efficient Upgrading

For players who just want a shorthand guide, here's a five-step recap of the procedure to follow:

1. Choose the piece of equipment you want to upgrade.

2. Check its rank and maximum level, then calculate the EXP amount required (or simply use our approximate EXP requirements just above).

3. Use 36 Sturdy Bones, Barbed Tails or Vibrant Oozes (or 24 Otherworldly Bones, Diabolic Tails or Transparent Oozes) to get an instant x3 EXP Bonus.

4. Follow it with the right quantity of Ultracompact Reactors, Particle Accelerators or one of the other recommended components to bring the piece of equipment directly to maximum level (★).

5. Where applicable, use the transformational catalyst required to transform the item into its superior version, then return to step 2.

Dismantle Analysis

Dismantling is only worthwhile if you dismantle fully upgraded equipment. Doing so with an item that's not at maximum level (★) is a waste. This is because the quality of raw parts generated will vary greatly according to the level of the dismantled item, and you only get the very best results with fully upgraded ★ items.

Very often, dismantling a maxed-out item leads to the return of an earlier or inferior version. However, the sale value of the dismantled parts is always smaller than the cost of upgrading the item in the first place. You cannot build to dismantle without making a huge loss.

So what's the point of the dismantle process? One answer is that it can sometimes produce rare items – the kind that can't be bought or found. Dismantling can also be exploited by a few devious methods, enabling you to multiply expensive components such as Trapezohedrons. Read the following section for a selection of particularly noteworthy tricks.

Note that there are three accessories that you should neither transform (through upgrades) nor dismantle. These are the Gold Watch, the Champion's Badge and the Survivalist Catalog. All three are very rare items, whose upgrade path leads to the Collector Catalog, an item that can be bought from the Moogleworks.

Best Dismantled Parts

TRAPEZOHEDRON MULTIPLICATION

You need at least six Trapezohedrons to make just one ultimate weapon per character, and would somehow have to fathom raising 12,000,000 Gil to buy them. But there is a trick through dismantling if you already own one Trapezohedron. Create one of the following weapons:

- **Kain's Lance** (made from the Dragoon Lance, Shamanic Spear, Punisher, Pandoran Spear or Gae Bolg)

- **Nirvana** (made from the Tigerclaw, Healer's Staff, Belladonna Wand or Mistilteinn)

Upgrade either Kain's Lance or Nirvana to maximum level (at a cost of approximately 1,500,000 Gil), and then dismantle it. You'll obtain three Trapezohedrons, tripling your initial investment, and for rather less than the 4,000,000 Gil you'd have paid in a shop. You'll even get a present of 36 Moonblossom Seeds at the same time, worth 216,000 Gil.

HOW TO OBTAIN SPRINT SHOES

Sprint Shoes and Hermes Sandals belong to the Boost Synthesis Group and both have excellent Haste and ATB: Rate potential. You can get the items you need by defeating Mission Mark 07 (Bituitus), a very easy battle with its activation Cie'th Stone obligingly nearby. This enemy drops Tetradic Crowns and Tetradic Tiaras so you can obtain several in a rather short time, especially if you equip Catalogs. Upgrade and dismantle these items to obtain, respectively, Hermes Sandals (which transform into Sprint Shoes) and Sprint Shoes.

HOW TO OBTAIN ETHERSOL

You can buy a Speed Sash from the Moogleworks retail network for 5,000 Gil and upgrade it into an Energy Sash. At maximum level, this accessory dismantles into Ethersol (along with Black Mycelium).

HOW TO OBTAIN ELIXIRS

Wondering why you've only found one? During the game, you can obtain a few Doctor's Codes (from the battle against Anima; a Treasure Sphere in the Sunleth Waterscape; and as a reward for Mission 41), an accessory of short-lived usefulness. Once fully upgraded by a mere 200 EXP, it dismantles into three Shrouds plus an almighty Elixir, a party-rescuing item for the toughest battles in the game.

HOW TO OBTAIN RIBBONS

Ribbons are rather rare items that can be upgraded to the supreme Super Ribbon. You'll win one from the Chocobo treasure-hunting mini-game, and you can get more from Flowering Cactuars in the Faultwarrens, but this requires a very advanced party. If you have 120,000 Gil to spare, though, you can buy an Entite Ring from Sanctum Labs. This can be upgraded into a Goddess's Favor accessory, which – once fully upgraded – dismantles into a Ribbon.

Dismantle

These tables reveal what dismantled parts you obtain for fully upgraded items. If you dismantle an item anything less than maxed-out, you will only get the less valuable parts in the selection, and in smaller quantities.

ACCESSORIES

Name	Dismantle
Iron Bangle	Transformer (x3), Polymer Emulsion
Silver Bangle	Transformer (x4), Polymer Emulsion
Tungsten Bangle	Amplifier (x3), Ferroelectric Film, Iron Bangle
Titanium Bangle	Amplifier (x6), Ferroelectric Film (x2), Silver Bangle
Gold Bangle	Amplifier (x9), Ferroelectric Film (x4), Tungsten Bangle
Mythril Bangle	Carburetor (x12), Superconductor (x6), Titanium Bangle
Platinum Bangle	Carburetor (x19), Superconductor (x15), Piezoelectric Element (x7), Gold Bangle
Diamond Bangle	Carburetor (x29), Superconductor (x20), Piezoelectric Element (x9), Mythril Bangle
Adamant Bangle	Supercharger (x13), Perfect Conductor (x8), Crystal Oscillator (x3), Particle Accelerator, Platinum Bangle
Wurtzite Bangle	Supercharger (x20), Perfect Conductor (x14), Crystal Oscillator (x5), Ultracompact Reactor, Diamond Bangle
Power Wristband	Transformer (x5), Ferroelectric Film
Brawler's Wristband	Amplifier (x9), Dawnlight Dew
Warrior's Wristband	Synthetic Muscle (x12), Paraffin Oil (x7), Titanium Tube
Power Glove	Synthetic Muscle (x17), Paraffin Oil (x9), Active Detector
Kaiser Knuckles	Dusklight Dew (x19), White Mycelium (x14), Silicone Oil (x8), Power Wristband
Magician's Mark	Transformer (x5), Ferroelectric Film
Shaman's Mark	Amplifier (x9), Dawnlight Dew
Sorcerer's Mark	Passive Detector (x12), Piezoelectric Element (x7), Titanium Tube
Weirding Glyph	Turboprop (x17), Piezoelectric Element (x9), Active Detector
Magistral Crest	Dusklight Dew (x19), White Mycelium (x14), Crystal Oscillator (x8), Magician's Mark
Black Belt	Thickened Hide (x9), Credit Chip
General's Belt	Smooth Hide (x9), Incentive Chip, Rhodochrosite
Champion's Belt	Supple Leather (x15), Incentive Chip (x2), Black Belt
Rune Bracelet	Barbed Tail (x9), Credit Chip
Witch's Bracelet	Diabolic Tail (x9), Incentive Chip, Rhodochrosite
Magus's Bracelet	Entrancing Tail (x15), Incentive Chip (x2), Rune Bracelet
Royal Armlet	Piezoelectric Element (x19), Cobaltite (x2)
Imperial Armlet	Crystal Oscillator (x10), Perovskite, Royal Armlet
Ember Ring	Gummy Oil (x15), Cie'th Tear
Blaze Ring	Fragrant Oil (x12), Tear of Frustration (x8), Sturdy Bone
Salamandrine Ring	Medicinal Oil (x10), Tear of Remorse (x6), Otherworldly Bone (x4), Ember Ring
Frost Ring	Moistened Scale (x15), Cie'th Tear
Icicle Ring	Seapetal Scale (x12), Tear of Frustration (x8), Spined Horn
Boreal Ring	Abyssal Scale (x10), Tear of Remorse (x6), Fiendish Horn (x4), Frost Ring

ACCESSORIES

Name	Dismantle
Spark Ring	Chipped Fang (x15), Cie'th Tear
Fulmen Ring	Wicked Fang (x12), Tear of Frustration (x8), Thickened Hide
Raijin Ring	Monstrous Fang (x10), Tear of Remorse (x6), Smooth Hide (x4), Spark Ring
Aqua Ring	Strange Fluid (x15), Cie'th Tear
Riptide Ring	Enigmatic Fluid (x12), Tear of Frustration (x8), Vibrant Ooze
Nereid Ring	Mysterious Fluid (x10), Tear of Remorse (x6), Transparent Ooze (x4), Aqua Ring
Zephyr Ring	Severed Wing (x15), Cie'th Tear
Gale Ring	Scaled Wing (x12), Tear of Frustration (x8), Barbed Tail
Sylphid Ring	Abominable Wing (x10), Tear of Remorse (x6), Diabolic Tail (x4), Zephyr Ring
Clay Ring	Begrimed Claw (x15), Cie'th Tear
Siltstone Ring	Bestial Claw (x12), Tear of Frustration (x8), Iron Shell
Gaian Ring	Gargantuan Claw (x10), Tear of Remorse (x6), Armored Shell (x4), Clay Ring
Giant's Glove	Iron Shell (x10), Gloomstalk
Warlord's Glove	Armored Shell (x9), Sunpetal (x2), Carburetor
Glass Buckle	Spined Horn (x10), Gloomstalk
Tektite Buckle	Fiendish Horn (x9), Sunpetal (x2), Carburetor
Metal Armband	Bestial Claw (x10), Gloomstalk
Ceramic Armband	Gargantuan Claw (x9), Sunpetal (x2), Carburetor
Serenity Sachet	Barbed Tail (x10), Gloomstalk
Safeguard Sachet	Diabolic Tail (x9), Sunpetal (x2), Carburetor
Glass Orb	Fragrant Oil (x10), Gloomstalk
Dragonfly Orb	Medicinal Oil (x9), Sunpetal (x2), Carburetor
Star Pendant	Vibrant Ooze (x10), Gloomstalk
Starfall Pendant	Transparent Ooze (x9), Sunpetal (x2), Carburetor
Pearl Necklace	Enigmatic Fluid (x10), Gloomstalk
Gemstone Necklace	Mysterious Fluid (x9), Sunpetal (x2), Carburetor
Warding Talisman	Sturdy Bone (x10), Gloomstalk
Hexbane Talisman	Otherworldly Bone (x9), Sunpetal (x2), Carburetor
Pain Dampener	Seapetal Scale (x10), Gloomstalk
Pain Deflector	Abyssal Scale (x9), Sunpetal (x2), Carburetor
White Cape	Thickened Hide (x10), Gloomstalk
Effulgent Cape	Smooth Hide (x9), Sunpetal (x2), Carburetor
Rainbow Anklet	Wicked Fang (x10), Gloomstalk
Moonbow Anklet	Monstrous Fang (x9), Sunpetal (x2), Carburetor
Cherub's Crown	Rough Wool (x10), Gloomstalk
Seraph's Crown	Thick Wool (x9), Sunpetal (x2), Carburetor
Guardian Amulet	Moistened Scale (x5), Piezoelectric Element
Shield Talisman	Moistened Scale (x10), Seapetal Scale (x5), Crystal Oscillator (x3)
Auric Amulet	Segmented Carapace (x5), Piezoelectric Element
Soulfont Talisman	Segmented Carapace (x10), Iron Shell (x5), Crystal Oscillator (x3)
Watchman's Amulet	Torn Leather (x5), Piezoelectric Element
Shrouding Talisman	Torn Leather (x10), Thickened Hide (x5), Crystal Oscillator (x3)
Hero's Amulet	Begrimed Claw (x5), Piezoelectric Element
Morale Talisman	Begrimed Claw (x10), Bestial Claw (x5), Crystal Oscillator (x3)
Saint's Amulet	Shattered Bone (x5), Piezoelectric Element
Blessed Talisman	Shattered Bone (x10), Sturdy Bone (x5), Crystal Oscillator (x3)
Zealot's Amulet	Gummy Oil (x5), Piezoelectric Element
Battle Talisman	Gummy Oil (x10), Fragrant Oil (x5), Crystal Oscillator (x3)
Flamebane Brooch	Chipped Fang (x7), Piezoelectric Element
Flameshield Earring	Chipped Fang (x8), Wicked Fang (x6), Crystal Oscillator (x3)
Frostbane Brooch	Murky Ooze (x7), Piezoelectric Element
Frostshield Earring	Murky Ooze (x8), Vibrant Ooze (x6), Crystal Oscillator (x3)
Sparkbane Brooch	Fractured Horn (x7), Piezoelectric Element
Sparkshield Earring	Fractured Horn (x8), Spined Horn (x6), Crystal Oscillator (x3)
Aquabane Brooch	Strange Fluid (x7), Piezoelectric Element
Aquashield Earring	Strange Fluid (x8), Enigmatic Fluid (x6), Crystal Oscillator (x3)
Hermes Sandals	Severed Wing (x7), Piezoelectric Element
Sprint Shoes	Severed Wing (x5), Scaled Wing (x6), Crystal Oscillator (x3)
Tetradic Crown	Green Needle, Guardian Amulet, Auric Amulet, Watchman's Amulet, Hermes Sandals
Tetradic Tiara	Perfume, Shield Talisman, Soulfont Talisman, Shrouding Talisman, Sprint Shoes
Whistlewind Scarf	Chocobo Plume (x5), Chocobo Tail Feather
Aurora Scarf	Chocobo Tail Feather (x8), Active Detector
Nimbletoe Boots	Chocobo Tail Feather (x5), Supercharger
Gold Watch	Credit Chip (x5), Incentive Chip (x2)
Champion's Badge	Dawnlight Dew (x8), Ethersol
Survivalist Catalog	Fortisol (x2), Aegisol (x2), Deceptisol
Collector Catalog	Incentive Chip, Succulent Fruit
Connoisseur Catalog	Incentive Chip (x2), Malodorous Fruit
Hunter's Friend	Deceptisol (x3), Librascope
Speed Sash	Chocobo Tail Feather (x40), Blue Mycelium (x10)
Energy Sash	Black Mycelium (x6), Ethersol
Doctor's Code	Fortisol, Aegisol, Ethersol, Elixir
Fire Charm	Ember Ring, Chocobo Plume (x10), Crystal Oscillator (x3)
Ice Charm	Frost Ring, Chocobo Plume (x10), Crystal Oscillator (x3)
Lightning Charm	Spark Ring, Chocobo Plume (x10), Crystal Oscillator (x3)
Water Charm	Aqua Ring, Chocobo Plume (x10), Crystal Oscillator (x3)
Wind Charm	Zephyr Ring, Chocobo Plume (x10), Crystal Oscillator (x3)
Earth Charm	Clay Ring, Chocobo Plume (x10), Crystal Oscillator (x3)
Twenty-sided Die	Titanium Tube (x5), Electrode (x5), Supercharger (x5), Incentive Chip (x3)
Growth Egg	Perfume (x2), Ultracompact Reactor, Platinum Ingot
Entite Ring	Malodorous Fruit (x4), Starblossom Seed, Perfume
Goddess's Favor	Scarletite, Perfume, Ribbon
Ribbon	Dusklight Dew (x36), Red Mycelium (x10)
Super Ribbon	Black Mycelium (x60), Starblossom Seed (x2), Ribbon
Genji Glove	Tear of Woe, Trapezohedron

WEAPONS

Name	Dismantle
Blazefire Saber	Spark Plug (x13), Tungsten Tube
Flamberge	Iridium Plug (x18), Electrolytic Capacitor (x12), Blazefire Saber
Omega Weapon	Spark Plug (x71), Tesla Turbine (x35), Perfect Conductor (x15), Ultracompact Reactor (x5), Trapezohedron
Axis Blade	Spark Plug (x7), Perovskite
Enkindler	Iridium Plug (x12), Cobaltite, Axis Blade
Omega Weapon	Iridium Plug (x51), Mobius Coil (x45), Crystal Oscillator (x28), Particle Accelerator (x6), Trapezohedron (x2)
Edged Carbine	Polymer Emulsion (x13), Actuator
Razor Carbine	Ferroelectric Film (x18), Liquid Crystal Lens (x12), Edged Carbine
Omega Weapon	Polymer Emulsion (x71), Crystal Oscillator (x35), Perfect Conductor (x15), Ultracompact Reactor (x5), Trapezohedron
Lifesaber	Polymer Emulsion (x7), Perovskite
Peacemaker	Ferroelectric Film (x12), Perovskite, Lifesaber
Omega Weapon	Ferroelectric Film (x51), Superconductor (x45), Crystal Oscillator (x28), Particle Accelerator (x6), Trapezohedron (x2)
Gladius	Spark Plug (x13), Carburetor
Helter-skelter	Iridium Plug (x18), Transformer (x12), Gladius
Omega Weapon	Spark Plug (x71), Supercharger (x35), Perfect Conductor (x15), Ultracompact Reactor (x5), Trapezohedron
Organyx	Spark Plug (x13), Millerite
Apocalypse	Iridium Plug (x18), Millerite (x2), Organyx
Omega Weapon	Iridium Plug (x61), Credit Chip (x56), Incentive Chip (x42), Perfect Conductor (x9), Platinum Ingot (x3)
Hauteclaire	Ceramic Armor (x13), Cobaltite
Durandal	Chobham Armor (x18), Cobaltite (x2), Hauteclaire
Omega Weapon	Ceramic Armor (x61), Credit Chip (x56), Incentive Chip (x42), Perfect Conductor (x9), Platinum Ingot (x3)
Lionheart	Ceramic Armor (x7), Uraninite
Ultima Weapon	Chobham Armor (x12), Uraninite, Lionheart
Omega Weapon	Chobham Armor (x51), Electrode (x45), Crystal Oscillator (x28), Particle Accelerator (x6), Trapezohedron (x2)
Vega 42s	Insulated Cabling (x13), Flywheel
Altairs	Fiber-optic Cable (x18), Liquid Crystal Lens (x12), Vega 42s
Total Eclipses	Insulated Cabling (x71), Turbojet (x35), Perfect Conductor (x15), Ultracompact Reactor (x5), Trapezohedron
Spica Defenders	Insulated Cabling (x7), Perovskite
Sirius Sidearms	Fiber-optic Cable (x12), Perovskite, Spica Defenders
Total Eclipses	Fiber-optic Cable (x51), Bomb Ashes (x45), Crystal Oscillator (x28), Particle Accelerator (x6), Trapezohedron (x2)
Deneb Duellers	Analog Circuit (x13), Crankshaft
Canopus AMPs	Digital Circuit (x18), Epicyclic Gear (x12), Deneb Duellers
Total Eclipses	Analog Circuit (x71), Mobius Coil (x35), Perfect Conductor (x15), Ultracompact Reactor (x5), Trapezohedron
Rigels	Analog Circuit (x13), Cobaltite
Polaris Specials	Digital Circuit (x18), Cobaltite (x2), Rigels
Total Eclipses	Digital Circuit (x61), Credit Chip (x56), Incentive Chip (x42), Perfect Conductor (x9), Platinum Ingot (x3)
Aldebarans	Needle Valve (x13), Millerite
Sadalmeliks	Butterfly Valve (x18), Millerite (x2), Aldebarans
Total Eclipses	Needle Valve (x61), Credit Chip (x56), Incentive Chip (x42), Perfect Conductor (x9), Platinum Ingot (x3)
Pleiades Hi-Powers	Needle Valve (x13), Rhodochrosite
Hyades Magnums	Butterfly Valve (x18), Rhodochrosite (x2), Pleiades Hi-Powers
Total Eclipses	Butterfly Valve (x61), Credit Chip (x56), Incentive Chip (x42), Perfect Conductor (x9), Platinum Ingot (x3)
Antares Deluxes	Radial Bearing (x7), Cobaltite
Fomalhaut Elites	Thrust Bearing (x12), Cobaltite, Antares Deluxes
Total Eclipses	Radial Bearing (x51), Titanium Tube (x45), Crystal Oscillator (x28), Particle Accelerator (x6), Trapezohedron (x2)
Procyons	Radial Bearing (x7), Bomb Core
Betelgeuse Customs	Thrust Bearing (x12), Bomb Shell (x6), Procyons
Total Eclipses	Thrust Bearing (x51), Bomb Fragment (x45), Crystal Oscillator (x28), Particle Accelerator (x6), Trapezohedron (x2)
Wild Bear	Spark Plug (x13), Ring Joint
Feral Pride	Iridium Plug (x18), Liquid Crystal Lens (x12), Wild Bear
Save the Queen	Spark Plug (x71), Carburetor (x35), Perfect Conductor (x15), Ultracompact Reactor (x5), Trapezohedron
Paladin	Spark Plug (x7), Silicone Oil
Winged Saint	Iridium Plug (x12), Paraffin Oil (x6), Paladin
Save the Queen	Iridium Plug (x51), Ferroelectric Film (x45), Crystal Oscillator (x28), Particle Accelerator (x6), Trapezohedron (x2)
Rebel Heart	Analog Circuit (x7), Chobham Armor
Warrior's Emblem	Digital Circuit (x12), Ceramic Armor (x6), Rebel Heart
Save the Queen	Analog Circuit (x51), Chobham Armor (x45), Crystal Oscillator (x28), Particle Accelerator (x6), Trapezohedron (x2)
Power Circle	Analog Circuit (x13), Active Detector
Battle Standard	Digital Circuit (x18), Passive Detector (x12), Power Circle
Save the Queen	Digital Circuit (x71), Synthetic Muscle (x35), Perfect Conductor (x15), Ultracompact Reactor (x5), Trapezohedron
Feymark	Tungsten Tube (x7), Thrust Bearing
Soul Blazer	Titanium Tube (x12), Radial Bearing (x6), Feymark
Save the Queen	Tungsten Tube (x51), Mobius Coil (x45), Crystal Oscillator (x28), Particle Accelerator (x6), Trapezohedron (x2)
Sacrificial Circle	Tungsten Tube (x13), Uraninite
Indomitus	Titanium Tube (x18), Uraninite (x2), Sacrificial Circle
Save the Queen	Titanium Tube (x61), Credit Chip (x56), Incentive Chip (x42), Perfect Conductor (x9), Platinum Ingot (x3)
Unsetting Sun	Ceramic Armor (x13), Rhodochrosite
Midnight Sun	Chobham Armor (x18), Rhodochrosite (x2), Unsetting Sun
Save the Queen	Ceramic Armor (x61), Credit Chip (x56), Incentive Chip (x42), Perfect Conductor (x9), Platinum Ingot (x3)
Umbra	Ceramic Armor (x7), Perovskite
Solaris	Chobham Armor (x12), Perovskite, Umbra
Save the Queen	Chobham Armor (x51), Ring Joint (x45), Crystal Oscillator (x28), Particle Accelerator (x6), Trapezohedron (x2)

Name	Dismantle
Airwing	Radial Bearing (x7), Cobaltite
Skycutter	Thrust Bearing (x12), Cobaltite, Airwing
Nue	Radial Bearing (x51), Superconductor (x45), Crystal Oscillator (x28), Particle Accelerator (x6), Trapezohedron (x2)
Hawkeye	Radial Bearing (x13), Butterfly Valve
Eagletalon	Thrust Bearing (x18), Needle Valve (x12), Hawkeye
Nue	Thrust Bearing (x71), Actuator (x35), Perfect Conductor (x15), Ultracompact Reactor (x5), Trapezohedron
Otshirvani	Gyroscope (x7), Perovskite
Urubutsin	Electrode (x12), Perovskite (x2), Otshirvani
Nue	Gyroscope (x51), Carburetor (x45), Crystal Oscillator (x28), Particle Accelerator (x6), Trapezohedron (x2)
Ninurta	Gyroscope (x13), Crankshaft
Jatayu	Electrode (x18), Epicyclic Gear (x12), Ninurta
Nue	Electrode (x71), Sprocket (x35), Perfect Conductor (x15), Ultracompact Reactor (x5), Trapezohedron
Vidofnir	Tungsten Tube (x7), Flywheel
Hresvelgr	Titanium Tube (x12), Electrolytic Capacitor (x6), Vidofnir
Nue	Tungsten Tube (x51), Fiber-optic Cable (x45), Crystal Oscillator (x28), Particle Accelerator (x6), Trapezohedron (x2)
Simurgh	Tungsten Tube (x7), Tesla Turbine
Tezcatlipoca	Titanium Tube (x12), Turbojet (x6), Simurgh
Nue	Titanium Tube (x51), Tesla Turbine (x45), Crystal Oscillator (x28), Particle Accelerator (x6), Trapezohedron (x2)
Malphas	Paraffin Oil (x13), Rhodochrosite
Naberius	Silicone Oil (x18), Rhodochrosite (x2), Malphas
Nue	Paraffin Oil (x61), Credit Chip (x56), Incentive Chip (x42), Perfect Conductor (x9), Platinum Ingot (x3)
Alicanto	Paraffin Oil (x13), Cobaltite
Caladrius	Silicone Oil (x18), Cobaltite (x3), Alicanto
Nue	Silicone Oil (x61), Credit Chip (x56), Incentive Chip (x42), Perfect Conductor (x9), Platinum Ingot (x3)
Binding Rod	Begrimed Claw (x13), Blue Mycelium
Hunter's Rod	Bestial Claw (x18), Red Mycelium (x12), Binding Rod
Nirvana	Bestial Claw (x91), Black Mycelium (x49), Perfume (x25), Starblossom Seed (x10), Trapezohedron (x2)
Tigerclaw	Bestial Claw (x13), Millerite
Wyrmfang	Gargantuan Claw (x18), Millerite (x2), Tigerclaw
Nirvana	Gargantuan Claw (x71), Menacing Wings (x60), Moonblossom Seed (x36), Tear of Woe (x10), Trapezohedron (x3)
Healer's Staff	Shattered Bone (x7), Perovskite
Physician's Staff	Sturdy Bone (x12), Perovskite, Healer's Staff
Nirvana	Sturdy Bone (x71), Seaking's Beard (x60), Moonblossom Seed (x36), Tear of Woe (x10), Trapezohedron (x3)
Pearlwing Staff	Sturdy Bone (x13), Rough Wool
Brightwing Staff	Otherworldly Bone (x18), Scraggly Wool (x12), Pearlwing Staff
Nirvana	Otherworldly Bone (x91), Fluffy Wool (x49), Perfume (x25), Starblossom Seed (x10), Trapezohedron (x2)
Rod of Thorns	Chipped Fang (x13), Tear of Remorse
Orochi Rod	Wicked Fang (x18), Tear of Frustration (x12), Rod of Thorns
Nirvana	Wicked Fang (x91), Tear of Remorse (x25), Perfume (x10), Starblossom Seed (x10), Trapezohedron (x2)
Mistilteinn	Wicked Fang (x7), Perovskite
Erinye's Cane	Monstrous Fang (x12), Perovskite, Mistilteinn
Nirvana	Monstrous Fang (x71), Entrancing Tail (x60), Moonblossom Seed (x36), Tear of Woe (x10), Trapezohedron (x3)
Belladonna Wand	Fractured Horn (x7), Cobaltite
Malboro Wand	Spined Horn (x12), Cobaltite, Belladonna Wand
Nirvana	Spined Horn (x71), Supple Leather (x60), Moonblossom Seed (x36), Tear of Woe (x10), Trapezohedron (x3)
Heavenly Axis	Spined Horn (x13), Cobaltite
Abraxas	Fiendish Horn (x18), Cobaltite (x2), Heavenly Axis
Nirvana	Fiendish Horn (x81), Chocobo Plume (x72), Green Needle (x54), Perfume (x15), Platinum Ingot (x5)
Bladed Lance	Shattered Bone (x13), Enigmatic Fluid
Glaive	Sturdy Bone (x18), Strange Fluid (x12), Bladed Lance
Kain's Lance	Sturdy Bone (x91), Esoteric Oil (x49), Perfume (x25), Starblossom Seed (x10), Trapezohedron (x2)
Dragoon Lance	Sturdy Bone (x7), Cobaltite
Dragonhorn	Otherworldly Bone (x12), Cobaltite, Dragoon Lance
Kain's Lance	Otherworldly Bone (x71), Fluffy Wool (x60), Moonblossom Seed (x36), Tear of Woe (x10), Trapezohedron (x3)
Partisan	Chipped Fang (x13), Iron Shell
Rhomphaia	Wicked Fang (x18), Segmented Carapace (x12), Partisan
Kain's Lance	Wicked Fang (x91), Regenerating Carapace (x49), Perfume (x25), Starblossom Seed (x10), Trapezohedron (x2)
Shamanic Spear	Wicked Fang (x7), Seapetal Scale
Heretic's Halberd	Monstrous Fang (x12), Moistened Scale (x6), Shamanic Spear
Kain's Lance	Monstrous Fang (x71), Menacing Wings (x60), Moonblossom Seed (x36), Tear of Woe (x10), Trapezohedron (x3)
Punisher	Fractured Horn (x7), Perovskite
Banescissor Spear	Spined Horn (x12), Perovskite, Punisher
Kain's Lance	Spined Horn (x71), Black Mycelium (x60), Moonblossom Seed (x36), Tear of Woe (x10), Trapezohedron (x3)
Pandoran Spear	Spined Horn (x7), Perovskite
Calamity Spear	Fiendish Horn (x12), Perovskite, Pandoran Spear
Kain's Lance	Fiendish Horn (x71), Wonder Gel (x60), Moonblossom Seed (x36), Tear of Woe (x10), Trapezohedron (x3)
Taming Pole	Begrimed Claw (x13), Cobaltite
Venus Gospel	Bestial Claw (x18), Cobaltite (x12), Taming Pole
Kain's Lance	Bestial Claw (x81), Chocobo Plume (x72), Green Needle (x54), Perfume (x15), Platinum Ingot (x5)
Gae Bolg	Bestial Claw (x7), Smooth Hide
Gungnir	Gargantuan Claw (x12), Thickened Hide (x3), Gae Bolg
Kain's Lance	Gargantuan Claw (x71), Supple Leather (x60), Moonblossom Seed (x36), Tear of Woe (x10), Trapezohedron (x3)

There are two categories of items to note. Consumables may be used at any time during combat, whereas Shrouds must be activated prior to battle.

Most items can be obtained from shops, though a couple are much harder to acquire. Shrouds are sometimes awarded as prizes after a battle, with a higher probability if your battle rating is low and if you equip the Survivalist Catalog accessory.

ITEMS LIST

	Name	Effect	Buy Price	Sell Price	Availability
Consumables	Potion	Restores a small amount of HP to all allies.	50	25	Unicorn Mart
	Antidote	Removes Poison from one ally.	100	50	Unicorn Mart
	Painkiller	Removes Pain from one ally.	100	50	Unicorn Mart
	Mallet	Removes Fog from one ally.	100	50	Unicorn Mart
	Holy Water	Removes Curse from one ally.	100	50	Unicorn Mart
	Wax	Removes Imperil from one ally.	100	50	Unicorn Mart
	Foul Liquid	Removes Daze from one ally.	100	50	Unicorn Mart
	Phoenix Down	Revives one ally from KO.	1,000	500	Unicorn Mart
	Elixir	Fully restores the party's HP and TP.	-	10	Dismantle (see page 220)
	Librascope	Reveals complete Enemy Intel of all foes in a battle.	10,000	500	Eden Pharmaceuticals
Shrouds	Fortisol	Casts Bravery, Faith, and Haste at the start of battle.	12,000	500	Eden Pharmaceuticals
	Aegisol	Casts Protect, Shell, Veil, and Vigilance at the start of battle.	12,000	500	Eden Pharmaceuticals
	Deceptisol	Makes the party invisible to enemy eyes.	30,000	500	Eden Pharmaceuticals
	Ethersol	Restores the party's TP.	-	500	Dismantle (see page 220)

KEY ITEMS

Once you receive a key item, it remains permanently in your inventory. You cannot use them or sell them in the traditional sense; instead, they represent items relevant to the plot or embody a new feature added to the game system.

You obtain most key items as part of the main storyline. However, there are a few optional ones that can only be acquired by fulfilling special conditions, usually within the context of a side-quest.

KEY ITEMS LIST

Name	Description
Grav-con Unit	Lightning's personal gravity control device.
Datalog	A digital journal that autonomously streams useful data.
Survival Knife	Lightning's birthday present.
Serah's Tear	Serah's crystallized teardrop.
Com Unit	A Guardian Corps communication handset.
Odin Eidolith	A crystal housing the soul of the Eidolon Odin.
Shiva Eidolith	A crystal housing the souls of the Shiva sisters, Stiria and Nix.
Brynhildr Eidolith	A crystal housing the soul of the Eidolon Brynhildr.
Alexander Eidolith	A crystal housing the soul of the Eidolon Alexander.
Hecatoncheir Eidolith	A crystal housing the soul of the Eidolon Hecatoncheir.
Bahamut Eidolith	A crystal housing the soul of the Eidolon Bahamut.
Unicorn Mart	A pass granting access to the Unicorn Mart retail network.
Eden Pharmaceuticals	A pass granting access to the Eden Pharmaceuticals retail network.
Up in Arms	A pass granting access to the Up in Arms retail network.
Plautus's Workshop	A pass granting access to the Plautus's Workshop retail network.
Gilgamesh, Inc. [1]	A pass granting access to the Gilgamesh, Inc. retail network.
B&W Outfitters	A pass granting access to the B&W Outfitters retail network.
Magical Moments	A pass granting access to the Magical Moments retail network.
Moogleworks	A pass granting access to the Moogleworks retail network.
Sanctum Labs	A pass granting access to the Sanctum Labs retail network.
Creature Comforts	A pass granting access to the Creature Comforts retail network.
The Motherlode	A pass granting access to the Motherlode retail network.
Lenora's Garage	A pass granting access to the Lenora's Garage retail network.
R&D Depot [2]	A pass granting access to the R&D Depot retail network.
Omni-kit	A kit enabling you to upgrade weapons and accessories.
Gysahl Reins [3]	Reins allowing you to ride chocobos on the Archylte Steppe.
Power Cable [4]	A power cable liberated from a transport cart in Oerba.
Trochoid Gear [4]	A gear pried from the clutches of a Cie'th in Oerba.
Metal Plate [4]	A sheet of metal originally serving as a sign in Oerba.
Battery Pack [4]	A battery pack discovered in a mill in Oerba.
Aspheric Lens [4]	A lens once used in a classroom in Oerba.

[1] Complete Mark Mission 46 (see page 135). [2] Complete Mark Mission 07 (see page 129). [3] Complete Mark Mission 14 (see page 130). [4] Part of the "Repairing Bhakti" side-quest (see page 97).

SHOPS

Save Stations grant access to an increasing number of Shops throughout the game, with only two of them requiring special conditions. These are R&D Depot and Gilgamesh, Inc., which are unlocked by completing Mark Missions 07 and 46 respectively.

UNICORN MART

Item	Buy Price (GIL)
Potion	50
Antidote	100
Painkiller	100
Mallet	100
Holy Water	100
Wax	100
Foul Liquid	100
Phoenix Down	1,000

EDEN PHARMACEUTICALS

Item	Buy Price (GIL)
Librascope	10,000
Fortisol	12,000
Aegisol	12,000
Deceptisol	30,000

UP IN ARMS

Item	Buy Price (GIL)
Blazefire Saber	2,000
Edged Carbine	4,600
Gladius	7,100
Vega 42s	2,000
Deneb Duellers	3,900
Wild Bear	1,800
Power Circle	4,500
Hawkeye	4,400
Ninurta	2,800
Binding Rod	2,500
Pearlwing Staff	2,300
Rod of Thorns	3,000
Bladed Lance	4,500
Partisan	6,600

PLAUTUS'S WORKSHOP

Item	Buy Price (GIL)
Axis Blade	15,000
Lifesaber	20,000
Lionheart	28,000
Spica Defenders	14,500
Antares Deluxes	22,000
Procyons	30,000
Paladin	20,000
Rebel Heart	11,000
Umbra	32,600
Airwing	10,000
Otshirvani	28,200
Vidofnir	16,900
Healer's Staff	19,800
Mistilteinn	11,000
Belladonna Wand	31,200
Punisher	31,000
Pandoran Spear	16,200
Gae Bolg	13,100

GILGAMESH, INC.

Item	Buy Price (GIL)
Organyx	280,000
Hauteclaire	20,000
Rigels	19,000
Aldebarans	263,000
Pleiades Hi-Powers	22,000
Feymark	25,000
Sacrificial Circle	210,000
Unsetting Sun	21,000
Simurgh	21,200
Malphas	198,000
Alicanto	18,000
Tigerclaw	300,000
Heavenly Axis	24,000
Dragoon Lance	230,000
Shamanic Spear	23,000
Taming Pole	27,000

B&W OUTFITTERS

Item	Buy Price (GIL)
Iron Bangle	500
Silver Bangle	800
Tungsten Bangle	1,500
Titanium Bangle	3,600
Gold Bangle	9,000
Mythril Bangle	15,000
Power Wristband	1,000
Brawler's Wristband	3,000
Warrior's Wristband	10,000
Magician's Mark	1,000
Shaman's Mark	3,000
Sorcerer's Mark	10,000
Black Belt	4,500
General's Belt	12,000
Rune Bracelet	4,500
Witch's Bracelet	12,000
Giant's Glove	3,000
Glass Buckle	3,000
Metal Armband	3,000
Serenity Sachet	3,000
Glass Orb	3,000
Star Pendant	3,000
Pearl Necklace	3,000
Warding Talisman	3,000
Pain Dampener	3,000
White Cape	3,000
Rainbow Anklet	3,000
Cherub's Crown	3,000

MAGICAL MOMENTS

Item	Buy Price (GIL)
Guardian Amulet	5,000
Auric Amulet	5,000
Watchman's Amulet	5,000
Hero's Amulet	5,000
Saint's Amulet	5,000
Zealot's Amulet	5,000
Flamebane Brooch	3,000
Frostbane Brooch	3,000
Sparkbane Brooch	3,000
Aquabane Brooch	3,000

MOOGLEWORKS

Item	Buy Price (GIL)
Whistlewind Scarf	1,000
Nimbletoe Boots	6,000
Collector Catalog	100,000
Speed Sash	10,000

SANCTUM LABS

Item	Buy Price (GIL)
Platinum Bangle	48,000
Royal Armlet	200,000
Entite Ring	120,000

CREATURE COMFORTS

Item	Buy Price (GIL)
Wicked Fang	80
Thickened Hide	80
Enigmatic Fluid	80
Sturdy Bone	80
Scaled Wing	80
Fragrant Oil	80
Barbed Tail	80
Bestial Claw	80
Vibrant Ooze	80
Iron Shell	80
Monstrous Fang	150
Smooth Hide	150
Mysterious Fluid	150
Otherworldly Bone	150
Abominable Wing	150
Medicinal Oil	150
Diabolic Tail	150
Gargantuan Claw	150
Transparent Ooze	150
Armored Shell	150

THE MOTHERLODE

Item	Buy Price (GIL)
Millerite	3,000
Rhodochrosite	8,000
Cobaltite	17,000
Perovskite	30,000
Uraninite	45,000
Mnar Stone	60,000
Scarletite	100,000

LENORA'S GARAGE

Item	Buy Price (GIL)
Polymer Emulsion	200
Ferroelectric Film	460
Insulated Cabling	280
Ceramic Armor	660
Passive Detector	840
Liquid Crystal Lens	320
Epicyclic Gear	320
Radial Bearing	320
Superconductor	840
Bomb Fragment	430
Fiber-optic Cable	840
Ring Joint	840
Crankshaft	840
Perfect Conductor	1,600
Piezoelectric Element	840
Turbojet	840
Paraffin Oil	320
Amplifier	520
Silicone Oil	660

R&D DEPOT

Item	Buy Price (GIL)
Green Needle	7,000
Particle Accelerator	10,000
Ultracompact Reactor	50,000
Adamantite	220,000
Dark Matter	840,000
Trapezohedron	2,000,000

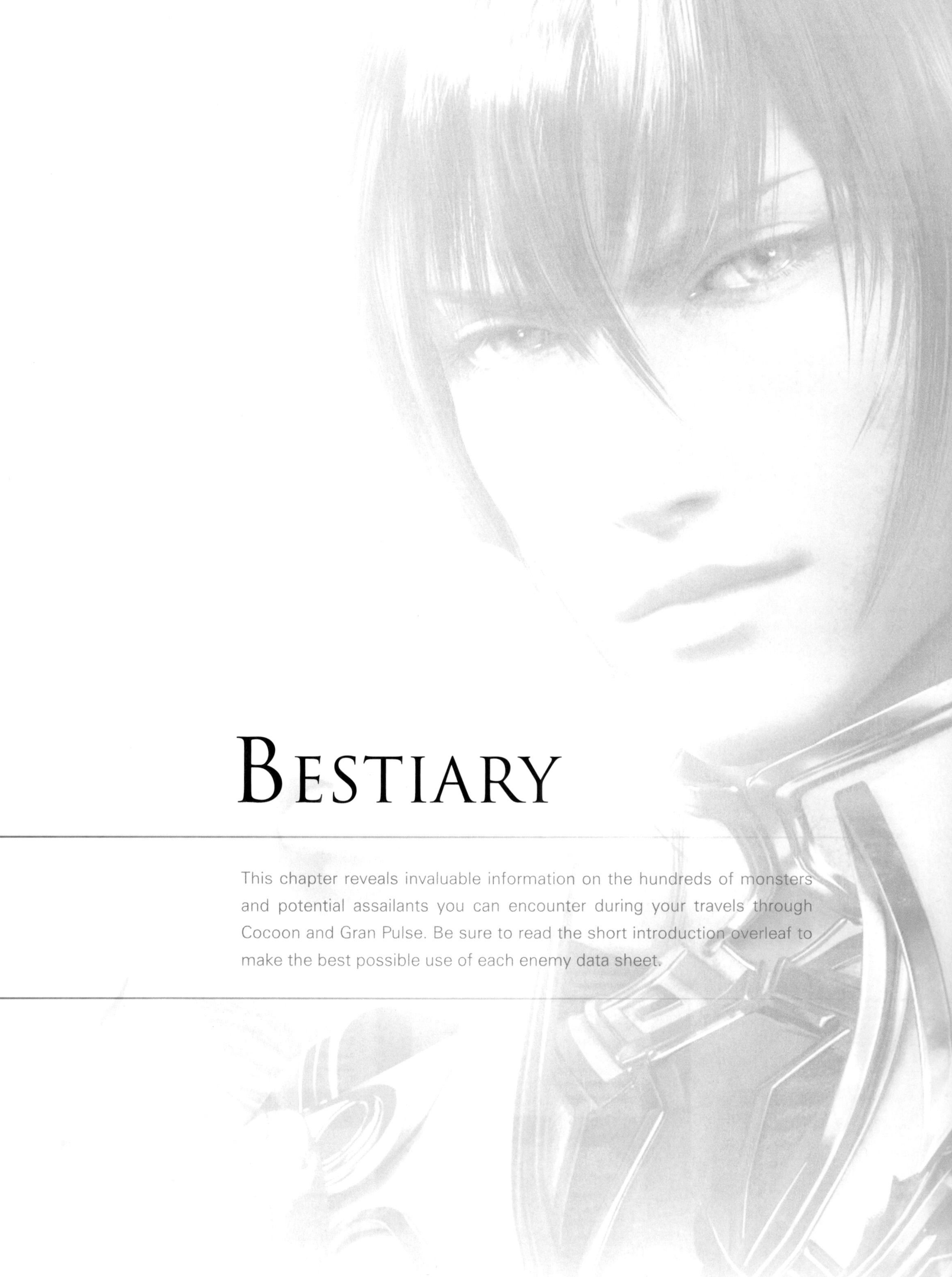

Bestiary

This chapter reveals invaluable information on the hundreds of monsters and potential assailants you can encounter during your travels through Cocoon and Gran Pulse. Be sure to read the short introduction overleaf to make the best possible use of each enemy data sheet.

ENEMY SHEET STRUCTURE

All enemy data sheets in this chapter share a standardized format for quick and easy reference. The information they contain includes the data offered by the in-game Enemy Intel files, but with many additions and revelations that the game itself does not divulge.

The meaning of each cell is as follows:

Location: The map area where you encounter the creature for the first time, and other known habitats where applicable.

Damage Affinities: The way in which the enemy reacts to the different types of damage you can inflict. The meaning of each icon is revealed here:

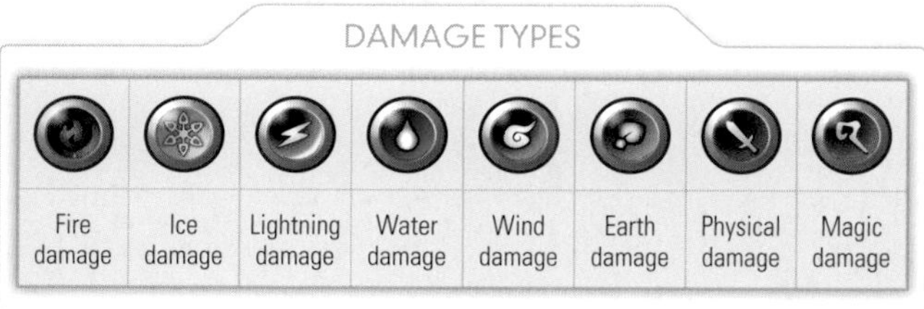

DAMAGE TYPES
Fire damage
Ice damage
Lightning damage
Water damage
Wind damage
Earth damage
Physical damage
Magic damage

There are six possible reactions to every type of attack, each corresponding to a multiplier applied to the base damage inflicted. These are as follows:

DAMAGE VULNERABILITIES

Reaction	Meaning
x2	Enemy has a weakness, damage is doubled.
-	Normal reaction, no multiplier employed.
½	Damage is halved.
1/10	Enemy resists, damage is divided by ten.
IMM	Enemy is immune to damage type.
ABS	Damage absorbed: your attacks will actually heal the target (up to 30% of the usual damage total).

HP: The amount of damage the creature can endure, in Hit Points, before it is defeated.

Magic: The Magic attribute of the enemy: the higher the number, the more damage it can deal when using magical attacks.

Strength: The Strength attribute of the enemy: the higher this is, the more damage its physical attacks will inflict.

CP: The amount of Crystogen Points each of your characters will receive for defeating the target.

Status Ailment Susceptibility: Shows, by percentage, how susceptible your opponent is to debuffs. The meaning of the icons used is as follows:

STATUS AILMENTS
Deprotect
Deshell
Imperil
Poison
Slow
Pain
Fog
Curse
Daze
Provoke
Death
Dispel

Normal Drop: The enemy's common drop, with your base chance of obtaining the item after battle. This probability can be increased by equipping a Collector Catalog.

Rare Drop: The enemy's rare drop, with your base chance of winning the item. This probability can be increased by equipping a Connoisseur Catalog and by obtaining high post-battle ratings.

Stagger: The target's Stagger Point – in other words, the size of the Chain Bonus you need to reach to cause a Stagger.

Chain Resistance: The higher this value, the longer it will take to fill the enemy's Chain Gauge.

Notes: Highlights the strengths and weaknesses of the creature.

ENEMY CLASSIFICATION

For maximum clarity, all enemies in our Bestiary are sorted in the same order as their in-game Datalog entries. The classification used is as follows:

Type	Subtype	Page
Soldiers	PSICOM Shock Troops	228
	PSICOM Hunters	228
	PSICOM Artillery	229
	PSICOM Airborne	229
	PSICOM Epopts	229
	PSICOM Elites	229
	Corps Footmen	230
	Corps Gunmen	230
Militarized Units	Drones	230
	Tilters	230
	Golems	231
	Cognispeeders	231
	Armatures	231
	Razorclaws	232
	Zwerg Droids	232
	Vespids	232
	Leeches	232
	Armadons	232
	Flan	233
	Behemoths	233
	Annihilators	233
Feral Creatures	Beasts	234
	Terraquatics	235
	Spooks	235
	Daemons	236

Type	Subtype	Page
Feral Creatures	Stalkers	237
	Armadillons	237
	Nudibranchs	237
	Wyverns	237
	Woodwraiths	238
	Oretoises	238
	Flan	239
	Behemoths	240
	Goblins	240
	Sahagin	241
	Cactuars	241
	Ochu	241
	Tonberries	242
Pulse Automata	Pulsework Soldiers	242
	Combat Engineers	242
	Centaurions	242
	Bombs	243
	Armaments	243
Cie'th	Shambling Cie'th	243
	Winged Cie'th	244
	Unusual Cie'th	245
	The Undying	245
Others	Fal'Cie	245
	L'Cie	246
	Eidolons	247

PSICOM ENFORCER

Location: The Hanging Edge, Aerorail Trussway 13-E; Lake Bresha

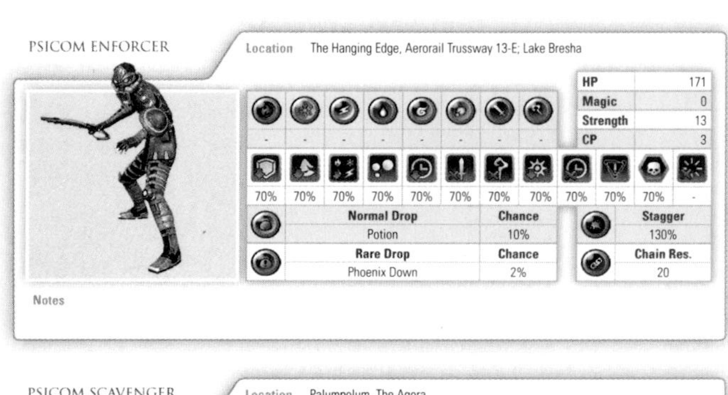

HP	Magic	Strength	CP
171	0	13	3

-	-	-	-	-	-	-	-

70%	70%	70%	70%	70%	70%	70%	70%	70%	70%	70%	-

Normal Drop	Chance	Rare Drop	Chance	Stagger	Chain Res.
Potion	10%	Phoenix Down	2%	130%	20

Notes

PSICOM TRACKER

Location: Lake Bresha, Encased in Crystal; The Vile Peaks

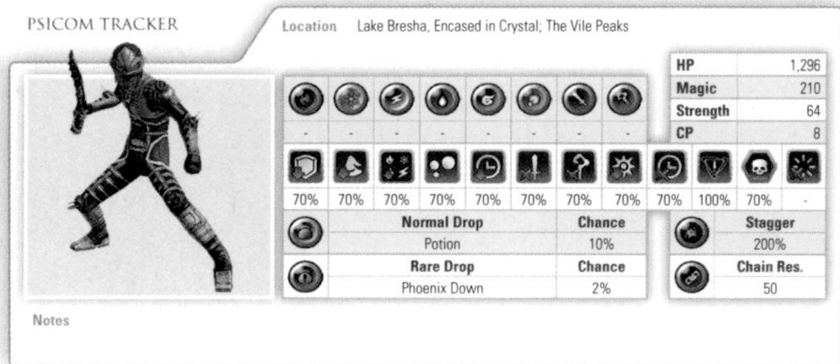

HP	Magic	Strength	CP
1,296	210	64	8

-	-	-	-	-	-	-	-

70%	70%	70%	70%	70%	70%	70%	70%	70%	100%	70%	-

Normal Drop	Chance	Rare Drop	Chance	Stagger	Chain Res.
Potion	10%	Phoenix Down	2%	200%	50

Notes

PSICOM SCAVENGER

Location: Palumpolum, The Agora

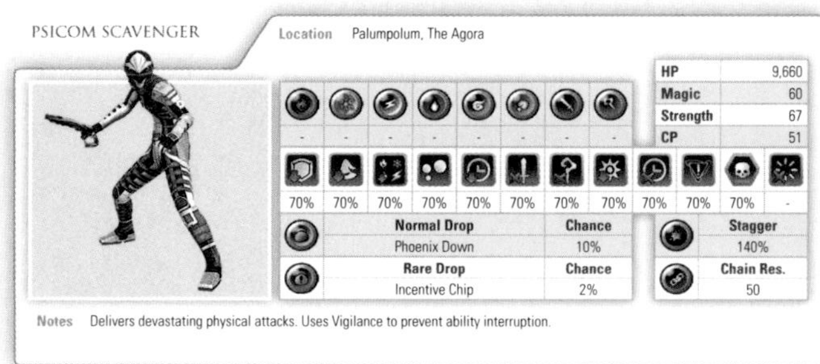

HP	Magic	Strength	CP
9,660	60	67	51

-	-	-	-	-	-	-	-

70%	70%	70%	70%	70%	70%	70%	70%	70%	70%	70%	-

Normal Drop	Chance	Rare Drop	Chance	Stagger	Chain Res.
Phoenix Down	10%	Incentive Chip	2%	140%	50

Notes: Delivers devastating physical attacks. Uses Vigilance to prevent ability interruption.

PSICOM RAIDER

Location: The Palamecia, Short-field Landing Deck

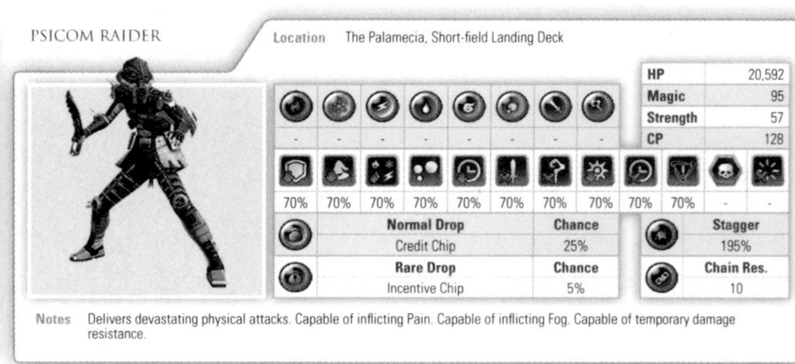

HP	Magic	Strength	CP
20,592	95	57	128

-	-	-	-	-	-	-	-

70%	70%	70%	70%	70%	70%	70%	70%	70%	70%	-	-

Normal Drop	Chance	Rare Drop	Chance	Stagger	Chain Res.
Credit Chip	25%	Incentive Chip	5%	195%	10

Notes: Delivers devastating physical attacks. Capable of inflicting Pain. Capable of inflicting Fog. Capable of temporary damage resistance.

SANCTUM SERAPH

Location: Eden, The Skywalk

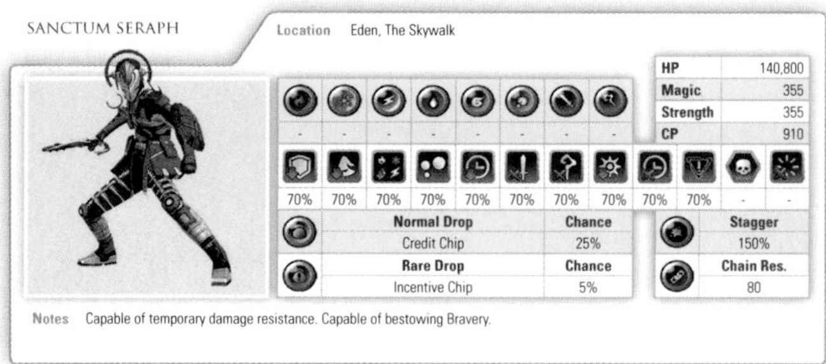

HP	Magic	Strength	CP
140,800	355	355	910

-	-	-	-	-	-	-	-

70%	70%	70%	70%	70%	70%	70%	70%	70%	70%	-	-

Normal Drop	Chance	Rare Drop	Chance	Stagger	Chain Res.
Credit Chip	25%	Incentive Chip	5%	150%	80

Notes: Capable of temporary damage resistance. Capable of bestowing Bravery.

TARGETING BEACON

Location: The Vile Peaks, Scavenger's Trail

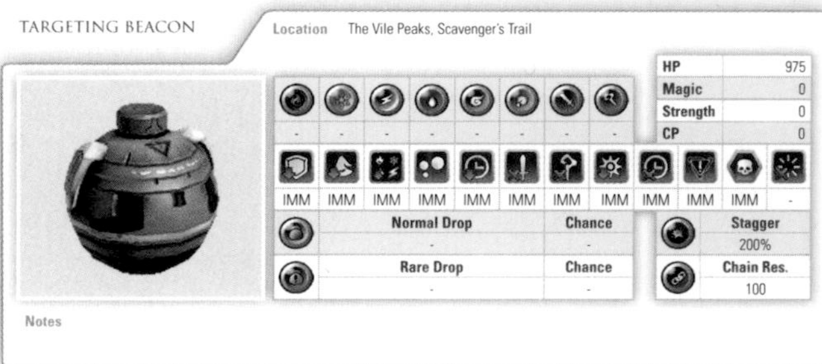

HP	Magic	Strength	CP
975	0	0	0

-	-	-	-	-	-	-	-

IMM	IMM	IMM	IMM	IMM	IMM	IMM	IMM	IMM	IMM	IMM	-

Normal Drop	Chance	Rare Drop	Chance	Stagger	Chain Res.
-	-	-	-	200%	100

Notes

TARGETING BEACON

Location: Eden

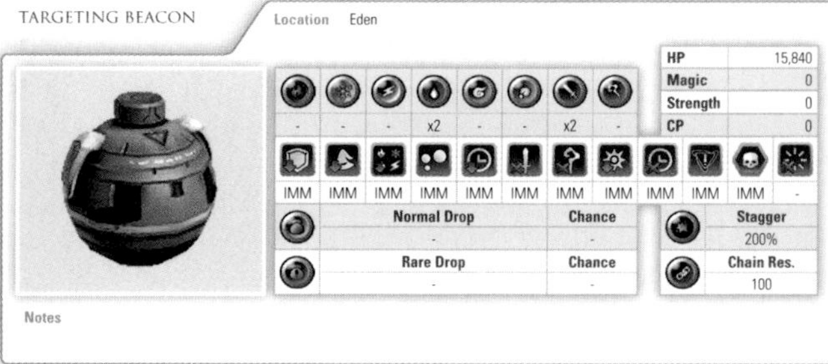

HP	Magic	Strength	CP
15,840	0	0	0

-	-	-	x2	-	-	x2	-

IMM	IMM	IMM	IMM	IMM	IMM	IMM	IMM	IMM	IMM	IMM	-

Normal Drop	Chance	Rare Drop	Chance	Stagger	Chain Res.
-	-	-	-	200%	100

Notes

PSICOM WARDEN

Location: The Hanging Edge, Aerorail Trussway 13-E; Lake Bresha

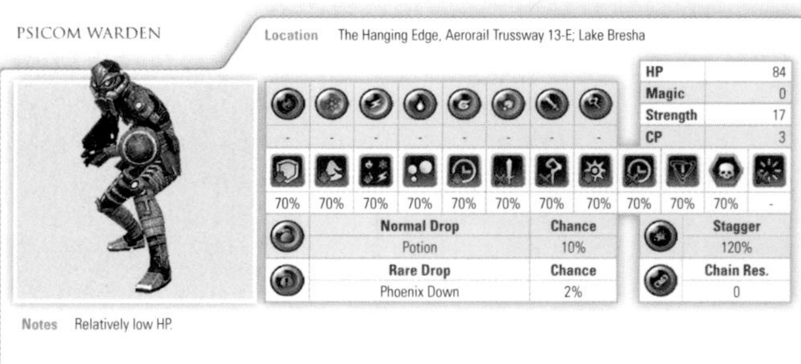

HP	Magic	Strength	CP
84	0	17	3

-	-	-	-	-	-	-	-

70%	70%	70%	70%	70%	70%	70%	70%	70%	70%	70%	-

Normal Drop	Chance	Rare Drop	Chance	Stagger	Chain Res.
Potion	10%	Phoenix Down	2%	120%	0

Notes: Relatively low HP.

PSICOM RANGER

Location: Lake Bresha, Encased in Crystal; The Vile Peaks

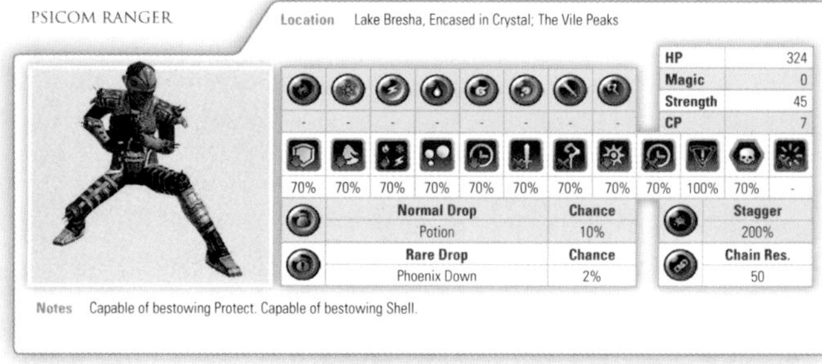

HP	Magic	Strength	CP
324	0	45	7

-	-	-	-	-	-	-	-

70%	70%	70%	70%	70%	70%	70%	70%	70%	100%	70%	-

Normal Drop	Chance	Rare Drop	Chance	Stagger	Chain Res.
Potion	10%	Phoenix Down	2%	200%	50

Notes: Capable of bestowing Protect. Capable of bestowing Shell.

PSICOM PREDATOR

Location: Palumpolum, Pedestrian Terraces

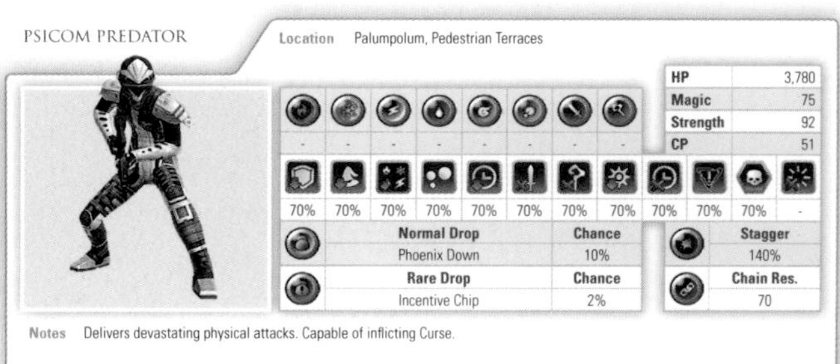

HP	Magic	Strength	CP
3,780	75	92	51

-	-	-	-	-	-	-	-

70%	70%	70%	70%	70%	70%	70%	70%	70%	70%	70%	-

Normal Drop	Chance	Rare Drop	Chance	Stagger	Chain Res.
Phoenix Down	10%	Incentive Chip	2%	140%	70

Notes: Delivers devastating physical attacks. Capable of inflicting Curse.

PSICOM INFILTRATOR

Location: The Palamecia, Short-field Landing Deck

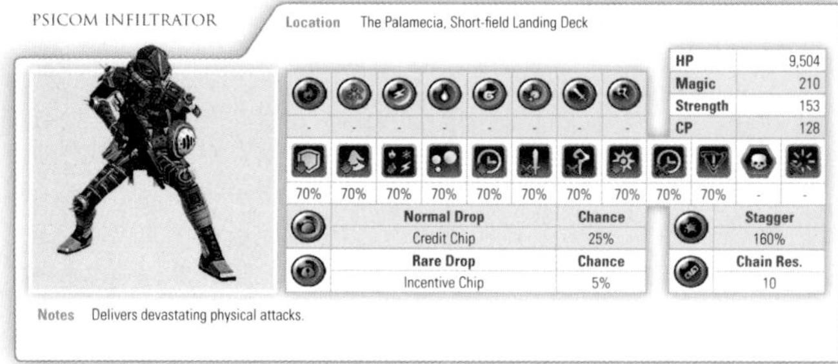

HP	Magic	Strength	CP
9,504	210	153	128

-	-	-	-	-	-	-	-

70%	70%	70%	70%	70%	70%	70%	70%	70%	70%	-	-

Normal Drop	Chance	Rare Drop	Chance	Stagger	Chain Res.
Credit Chip	25%	Incentive Chip	5%	160%	10

Notes: Delivers devastating physical attacks.

SANCTUM ARCHANGEL

Location: Eden, The Skywalk

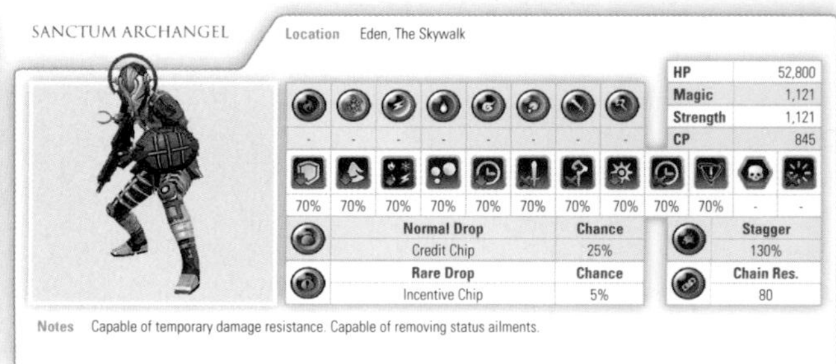

HP	Magic	Strength	CP
52,800	1,121	1,121	845

-	-	-	-	-	-	-	-

70%	70%	70%	70%	70%	70%	70%	70%	70%	70%	-	-

Normal Drop	Chance	Rare Drop	Chance	Stagger	Chain Res.
Credit Chip	25%	Incentive Chip	5%	130%	80

Notes: Capable of temporary damage resistance. Capable of removing status ailments.

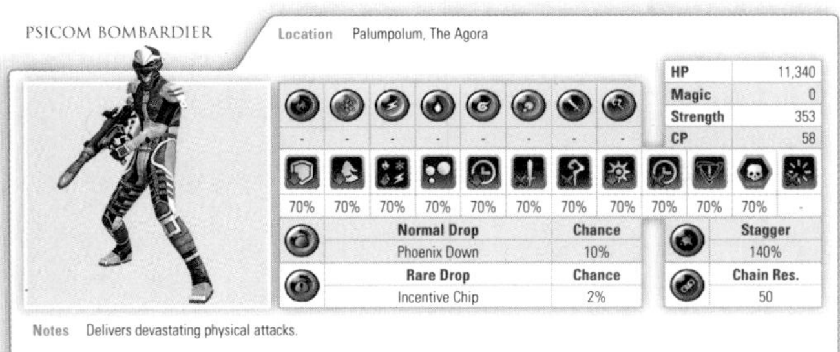

PSICOM BOMBARDIER

Location: Palumpolum, The Agora

HP	11,340
Magic	0
Strength	353
CP	58

-	-	-	-	-	-	-	-

70%	70%	70%	70%	70%	70%	70%	70%	70%	70%	70%	-

Normal Drop	Chance	Stagger
Phoenix Down	10%	140%
Rare Drop	**Chance**	**Chain Res.**
Incentive Chip	2%	50

Notes: Delivers devastating physical attacks.

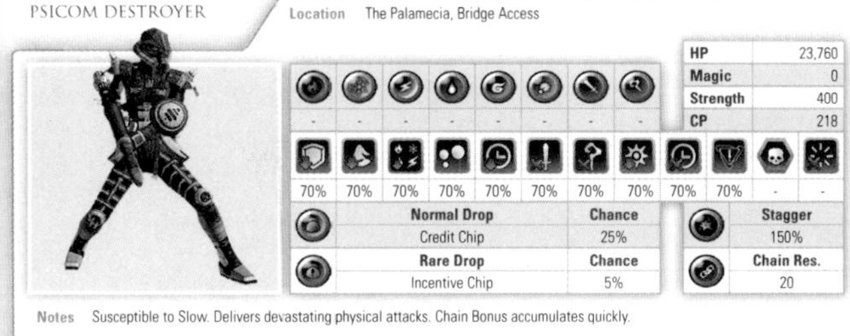

PSICOM DESTROYER

Location: The Palamecia, Bridge Access

HP	23,760
Magic	0
Strength	400
CP	218

-	-	-	-	-	-	-	-

70%	70%	70%	70%	70%	70%	70%	70%	70%	70%	-	-

Normal Drop	Chance	Stagger
Credit Chip	25%	150%
Rare Drop	**Chance**	**Chain Res.**
Incentive Chip	5%	20

Notes: Susceptible to Slow. Delivers devastating physical attacks. Chain Bonus accumulates quickly.

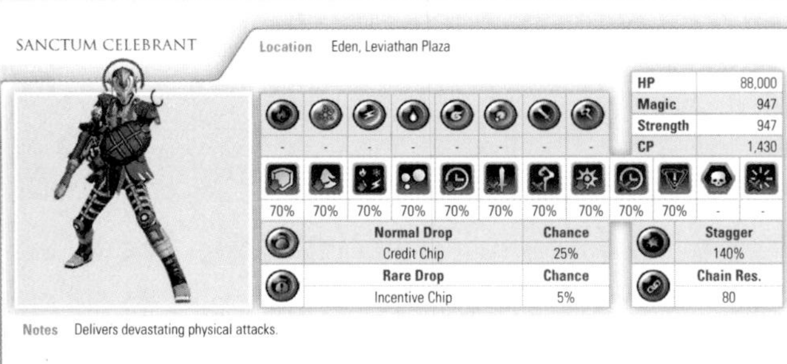

SANCTUM CELEBRANT

Location: Eden, Leviathan Plaza

HP	88,000
Magic	947
Strength	947
CP	1,430

-	-	-	-	-	-	-	-

70%	70%	70%	70%	70%	70%	70%	70%	70%	70%	-	-

Normal Drop	Chance	Stagger
Credit Chip	25%	140%
Rare Drop	**Chance**	**Chain Res.**
Incentive Chip	5%	80

Notes: Delivers devastating physical attacks.

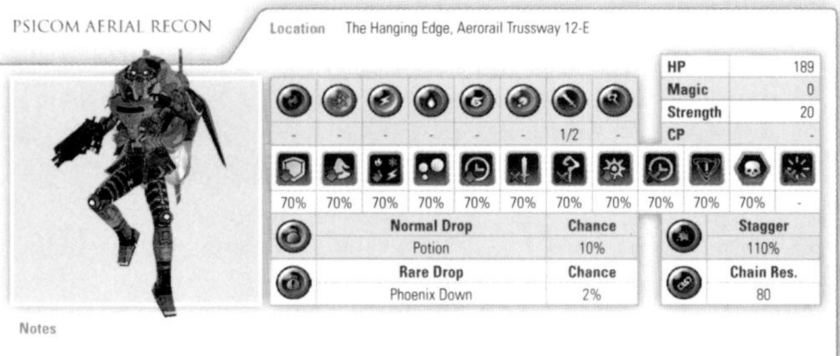

PSICOM AERIAL RECON

Location: The Hanging Edge, Aerorail Trussway 12-E

HP	189
Magic	0
Strength	20
CP	-

-	-	-	-	-	-	1/2	-

70%	70%	70%	70%	70%	70%	70%	70%	70%	70%	70%	-

Normal Drop	Chance	Stagger
Potion	10%	110%
Rare Drop	**Chance**	**Chain Res.**
Phoenix Down	2%	80

Notes

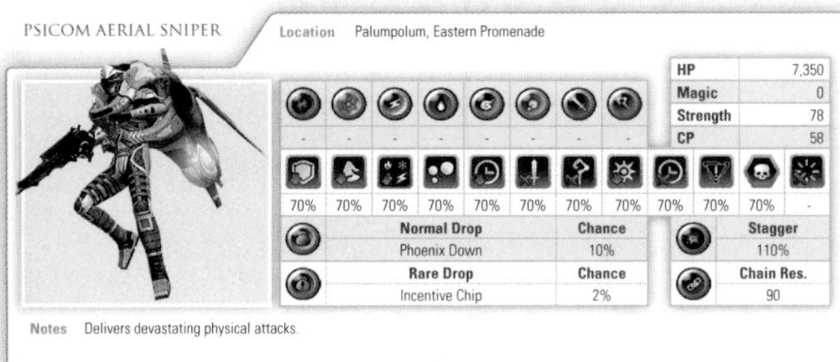

PSICOM AERIAL SNIPER

Location: Palumpolum, Eastern Promenade

HP	7,350
Magic	0
Strength	78
CP	58

-	-	-	-	-	-	-	-

70%	70%	70%	70%	70%	70%	70%	70%	70%	70%	70%	-

Normal Drop	Chance	Stagger
Phoenix Down	10%	110%
Rare Drop	**Chance**	**Chain Res.**
Incentive Chip	2%	90

Notes: Delivers devastating physical attacks.

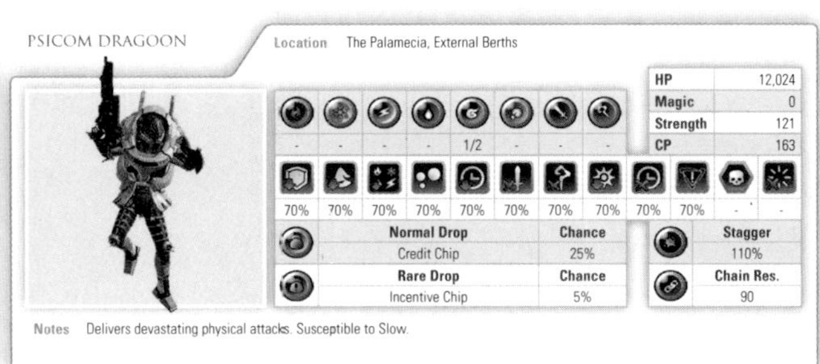

PSICOM DRAGOON

Location: The Palamecia, External Berths

HP	12,024
Magic	0
Strength	121
CP	163

-	-	-	-	1/2	-	-	-

70%	70%	70%	70%	70%	70%	70%	70%	70%	70%	-	-

Normal Drop	Chance	Stagger
Credit Chip	25%	110%
Rare Drop	**Chance**	**Chain Res.**
Incentive Chip	5%	90

Notes: Delivers devastating physical attacks. Susceptible to Slow.

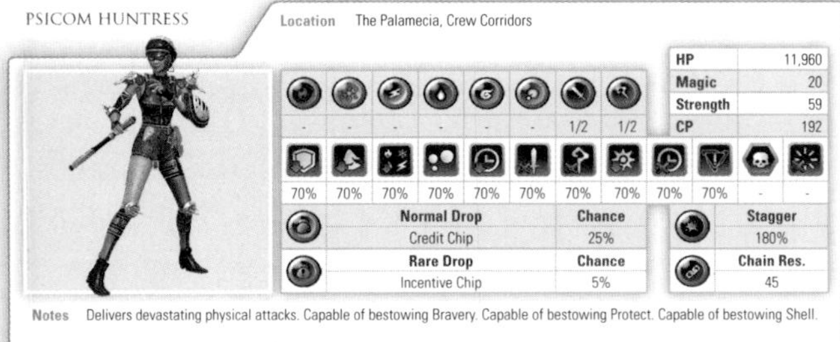

PSICOM HUNTRESS

Location: The Palamecia, Crew Corridors

HP	11,960
Magic	20
Strength	59
CP	192

-	-	-	-	-	-	1/2	1/2

70%	70%	70%	70%	70%	70%	70%	70%	70%	70%	-	-

Normal Drop	Chance	Stagger
Credit Chip	25%	180%
Rare Drop	**Chance**	**Chain Res.**
Incentive Chip	5%	45

Notes: Delivers devastating physical attacks. Capable of bestowing Bravery. Capable of bestowing Protect. Capable of bestowing Shell.

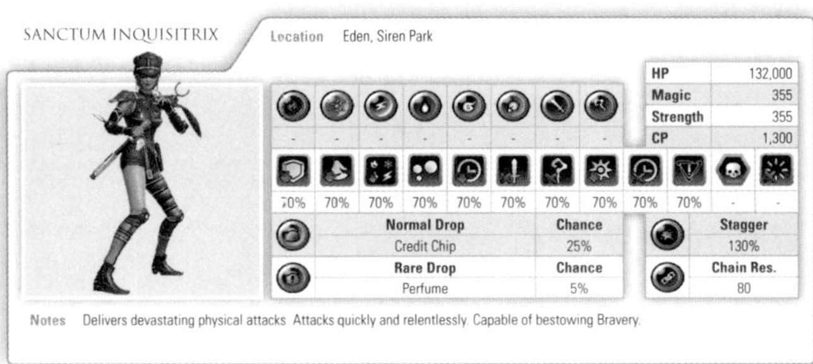

SANCTUM INQUISITRIX

Location: Eden, Siren Park

HP	132,000
Magic	355
Strength	355
CP	1,300

-	-	-	-	-	-	-	-

70%	70%	70%	70%	70%	70%	70%	70%	70%	70%	-	-

Normal Drop	Chance	Stagger
Credit Chip	25%	130%
Rare Drop	**Chance**	**Chain Res.**
Perfume	5%	80

Notes: Delivers devastating physical attacks. Attacks quickly and relentlessly. Capable of bestowing Bravery.

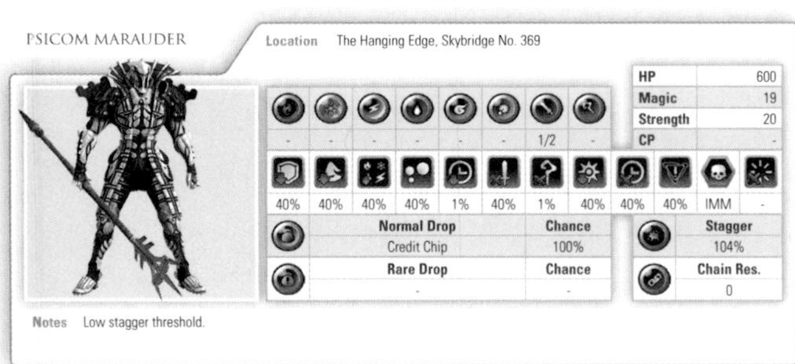

PSICOM MARAUDER

Location: The Hanging Edge, Skybridge No. 369

HP	600
Magic	19
Strength	20
CP	-

-	-	-	-	-	-	1/2	-

40%	40%	40%	40%	1%	40%	1%	40%	40%	40%	IMM	-

Normal Drop	Chance	Stagger
Credit Chip	100%	104%
Rare Drop	**Chance**	**Chain Res.**
-	-	0

Notes: Low stagger threshold.

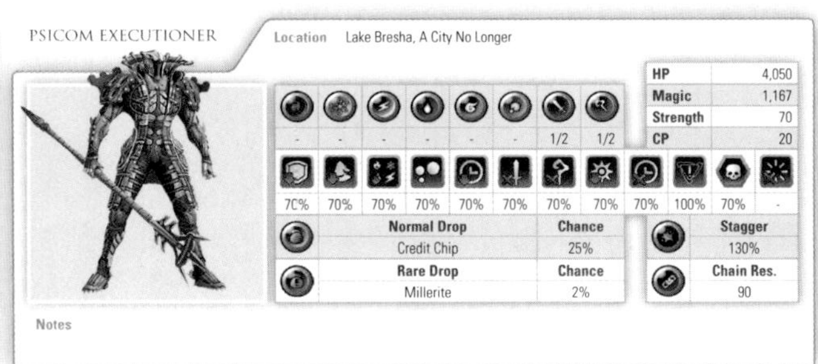

PSICOM EXECUTIONER

Location: Lake Bresha, A City No Longer

HP	4,050
Magic	1,167
Strength	70
CP	20

-	-	-	-	-	-	1/2	1/2

70%	70%	70%	70%	70%	70%	70%	70%	70%	100%	70%	-

Normal Drop	Chance	Stagger
Credit Chip	25%	130%
Rare Drop	**Chance**	**Chain Res.**
Millerite	2%	90

Notes

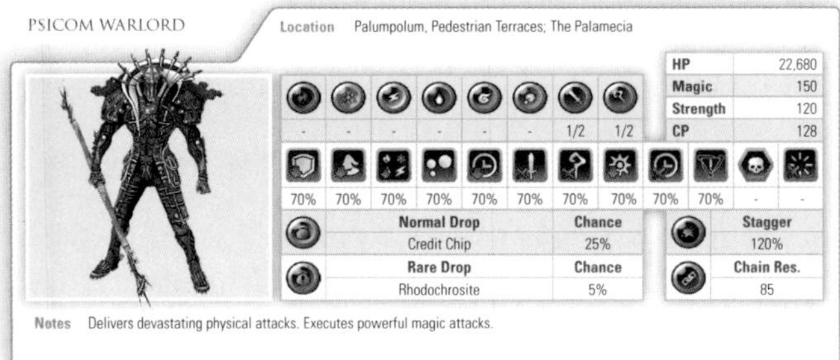

PSICOM WARLORD

Location: Palumpolum, Pedestrian Terraces; The Palamecia

HP	22,680
Magic	150
Strength	120
CP	128

-	-	-	-	-	-	1/2	1/2

70%	70%	70%	70%	70%	70%	70%	70%	70%	70%	-	-

Normal Drop	Chance	Stagger
Credit Chip	25%	120%
Rare Drop	**Chance**	**Chain Res.**
Rhodochrosite	5%	85

Notes: Delivers devastating physical attacks. Executes powerful magic attacks.

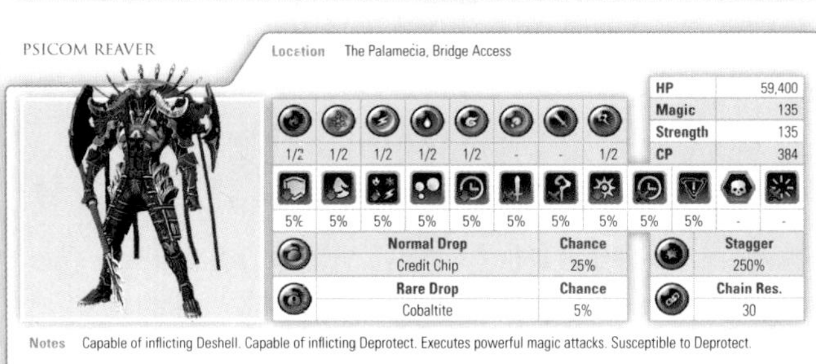

PSICOM REAVER

Location: The Palamecia, Bridge Access

HP	59,400
Magic	135
Strength	135
CP	384

1/2	1/2	1/2	1/2	1/2	-	-	1/2

5%	5%	5%	5%	5%	5%	5%	5%	5%	5%	-	-

Normal Drop	Chance	Stagger
Credit Chip	25%	250%
Rare Drop	**Chance**	**Chain Res.**
Cobaltite	5%	30

Notes: Capable of inflicting Deshell. Capable of inflicting Deprotect. Executes powerful magic attacks. Susceptible to Deprotect.

SANCTUM TEMPLAR

Location Orphan's Cradle, The Tesseracts

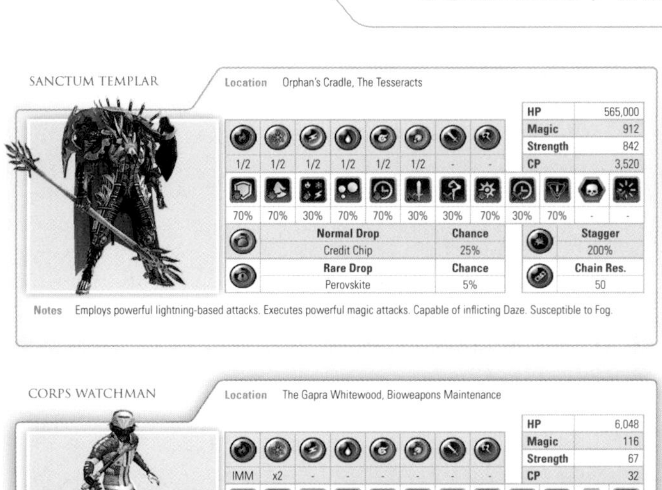

1/2	1/2	1/2	1/2	1/2	1/2	-	-

70%	70%	30%	70%	70%	30%	30%	70%	30%	70%	-	-

HP	565,000
Magic	912
Strength	842
CP	3,520

Normal Drop	Chance	Stagger
Credit Chip	25%	200%
Rare Drop	**Chance**	**Chain Res.**
Perovskite	5%	50

Notes Employs powerful lightning-based attacks. Executes powerful magic attacks. Capable of inflicting Daze. Susceptible to Fog.

CORPS REGULAR

Location The Vile Peaks, Scavenger's Trail

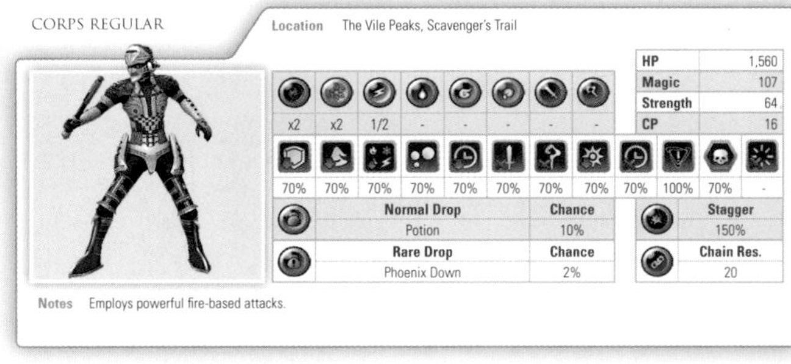

x2	x2	1/2	-	-	-	-	-

70%	70%	70%	70%	70%	70%	70%	70%	70%	100%	70%	-

HP	1,560
Magic	107
Strength	64
CP	16

Normal Drop	Chance	Stagger
Potion	10%	150%
Rare Drop	**Chance**	**Chain Res.**
Phoenix Down	2%	20

Notes Employs powerful fire-based attacks.

CORPS WATCHMAN

Location The Gapra Whitewood, Bioweapons Maintenance

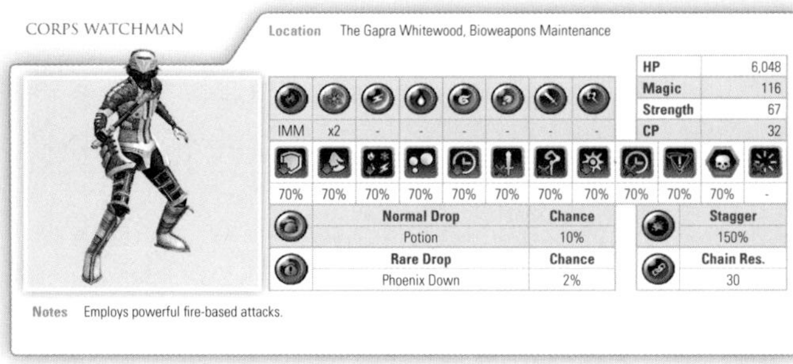

IMM	x2	-	-	-	-	-	-

70%	70%	70%	70%	70%	70%	70%	70%	70%	70%	70%	-

HP	6,048
Magic	116
Strength	67
CP	32

Normal Drop	Chance	Stagger
Potion	10%	150%
Rare Drop	**Chance**	**Chain Res.**
Phoenix Down	2%	30

Notes Employs powerful fire-based attacks.

CORPS PACIFEX

Location Palumpolum, The Metrostile

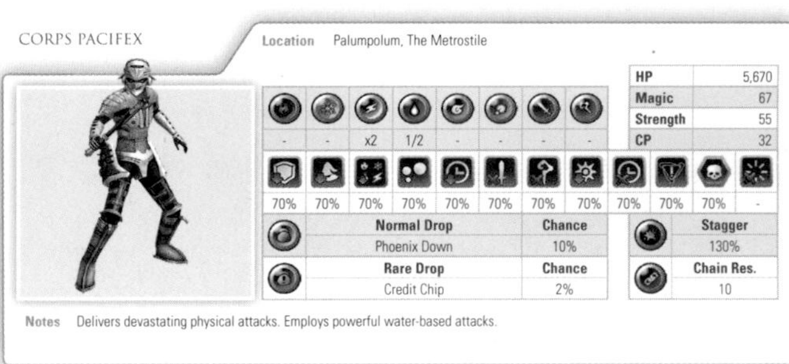

-	-	x2	1/2	-	-	-	-

70%	70%	70%	70%	70%	70%	70%	70%	70%	70%	70%	-

HP	5,670
Magic	67
Strength	55
CP	32

Normal Drop	Chance	Stagger
Phoenix Down	10%	130%
Rare Drop	**Chance**	**Chain Res.**
Credit Chip	2%	10

Notes Delivers devastating physical attacks. Employs powerful water-based attacks.

CORPS STEWARD

Location Eden, The Skywalk

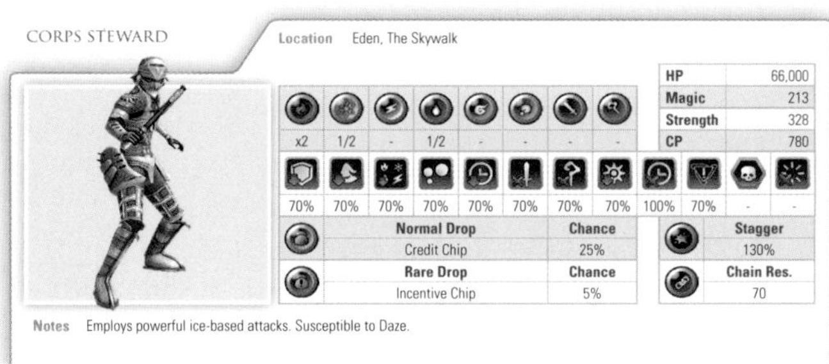

x2	1/2	-	1/2	-	-	-	-

70%	70%	70%	70%	70%	70%	70%	70%	100%	70%	-	-

HP	66,000
Magic	213
Strength	328
CP	780

Normal Drop	Chance	Stagger
Credit Chip	25%	130%
Rare Drop	**Chance**	**Chain Res.**
Incentive Chip	5%	70

Notes Employs powerful ice-based attacks. Susceptible to Daze.

CORPS GUNNER

Location The Vile Peaks, Scavenger's Trail; Nautilus Park

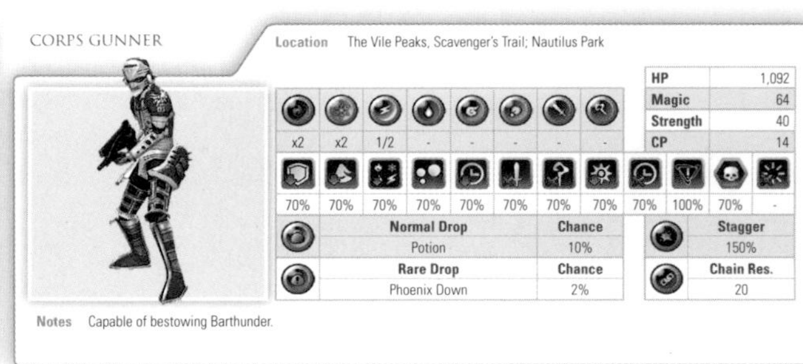

x2	x2	1/2	-	-	-	-	-

70%	70%	70%	70%	70%	70%	70%	70%	70%	100%	70%	-

HP	1,092
Magic	64
Strength	40
CP	14

Normal Drop	Chance	Stagger
Potion	10%	150%
Rare Drop	**Chance**	**Chain Res.**
Phoenix Down	2%	20

Notes Capable of bestowing Barthunder.

CORPS MARKSMAN

Location The Gapra Whitewood, Bioweapons Maintenance

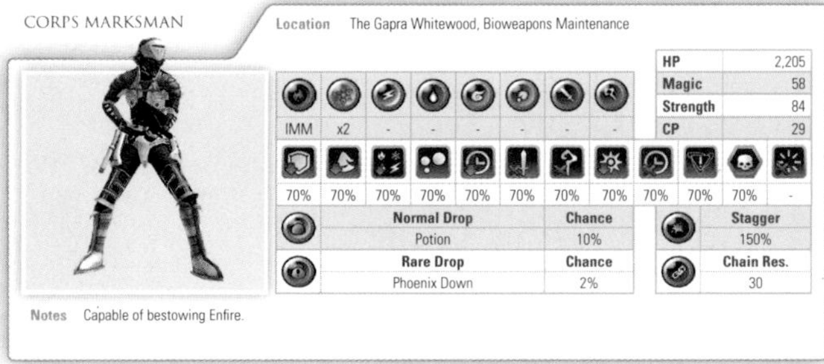

IMM	x2	-	-	-	-	-	-

70%	70%	70%	70%	70%	70%	70%	70%	70%	70%	70%	-

HP	2,205
Magic	58
Strength	84
CP	29

Normal Drop	Chance	Stagger
Potion	10%	150%
Rare Drop	**Chance**	**Chain Res.**
Phoenix Down	2%	30

Notes Capable of bestowing Enfire.

CORPS TRANQUIFEX

Location Palumpolum, The Metrostile

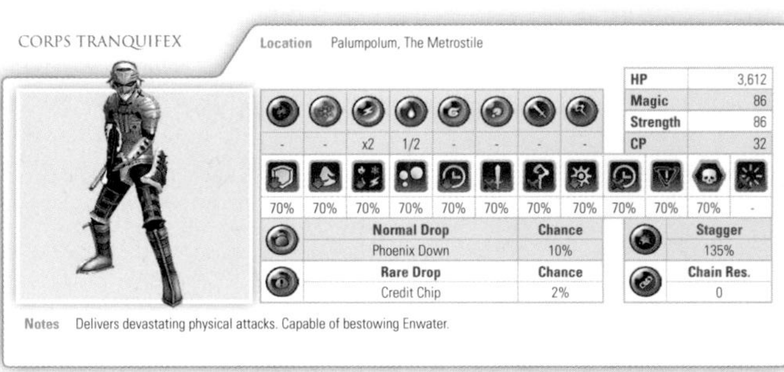

-	-	x2	1/2	-	-	-	-

70%	70%	70%	70%	70%	70%	70%	70%	70%	70%	70%	-

HP	3,612
Magic	86
Strength	86
CP	32

Normal Drop	Chance	Stagger
Phoenix Down	10%	135%
Rare Drop	**Chance**	**Chain Res.**
Credit Chip	2%	0

Notes Delivers devastating physical attacks. Capable of bestowing Enwater.

CORPS DEFENDER

Location Eden, The Skywalk

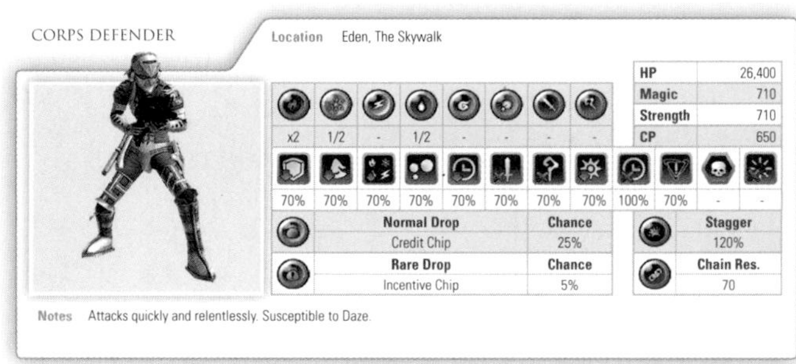

x2	1/2	-	1/2	-	-	-	-

70%	70%	70%	70%	70%	70%	70%	70%	100%	70%	-	-

HP	26,400
Magic	710
Strength	710
CP	650

Normal Drop	Chance	Stagger
Credit Chip	25%	120%
Rare Drop	**Chance**	**Chain Res.**
Incentive Chip	5%	70

Notes Attacks quickly and relentlessly. Susceptible to Daze.

WATCHDRONE

Location Lake Bresha, Encased in Crystal; The Vile Peaks

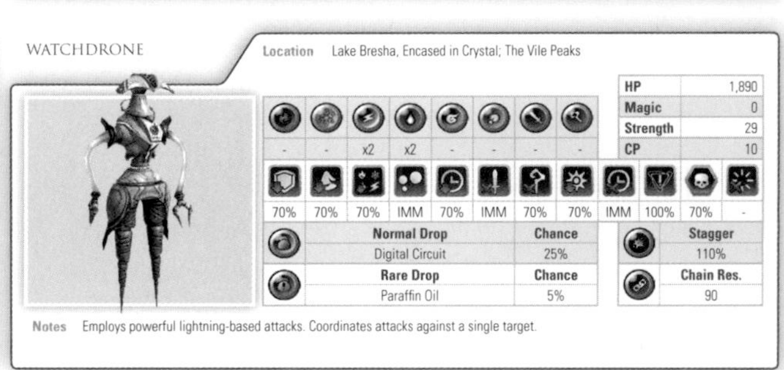

-	-	x2	x2	-	-	-	-

70%	70%	70%	IMM	70%	IMM	70%	70%	IMM	100%	70%	-

HP	1,890
Magic	0
Strength	29
CP	10

Normal Drop	Chance	Stagger
Digital Circuit	25%	110%
Rare Drop	**Chance**	**Chain Res.**
Paraffin Oil	5%	90

Notes Employs powerful lightning-based attacks. Coordinates attacks against a single target.

DECKDRONE

Location The Palamecia, External Berths

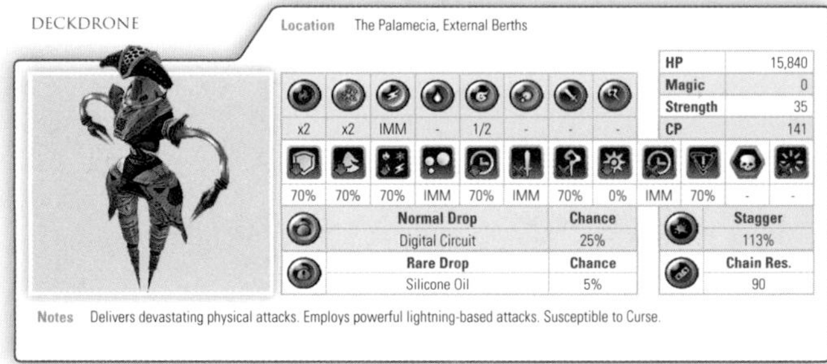

x2	x2	IMM	-	1/2	-	-	-

70%	70%	70%	IMM	70%	IMM	70%	0%	IMM	70%	-	-

HP	15,840
Magic	0
Strength	35
CP	141

Normal Drop	Chance	Stagger
Digital Circuit	25%	113%
Rare Drop	**Chance**	**Chain Res.**
Silicone Oil	5%	90

Notes Delivers devastating physical attacks. Employs powerful lightning-based attacks. Susceptible to Curse.

MYRMIDON

Location The Hanging Edge; The Pulse Vestige, Ambulatory

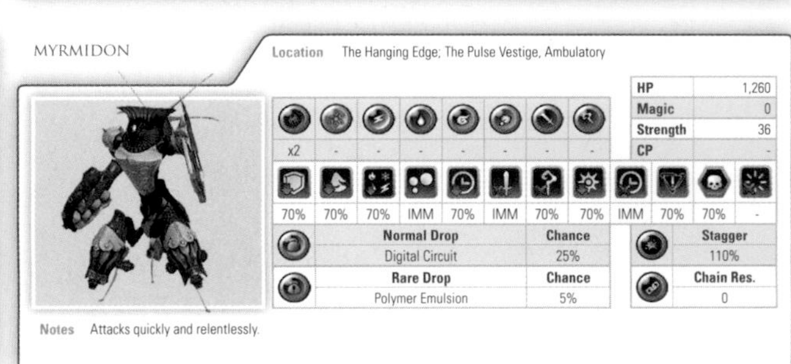

x2	-	-	-	-	-	-	-

70%	70%	70%	IMM	70%	IMM	70%	70%	IMM	70%	70%	-

HP	1,260
Magic	0
Strength	36
CP	-

Normal Drop	Chance	Stagger
Digital Circuit	25%	110%
Rare Drop	**Chance**	**Chain Res.**
Polymer Emulsion	5%	0

Notes Attacks quickly and relentlessly.

QUICKSTART
WALKTHROUGH
STRATEGY & ANALYSIS
INVENTORY
BESTIARY
EXTRAS
INTRODUCTION
CLASSIFICATION
SOLDIERS
MILITARIZED UNITS
FERAL CREATURES
PULSE AUTOMATA
CIE'TH
OTHERS

CRUSADER

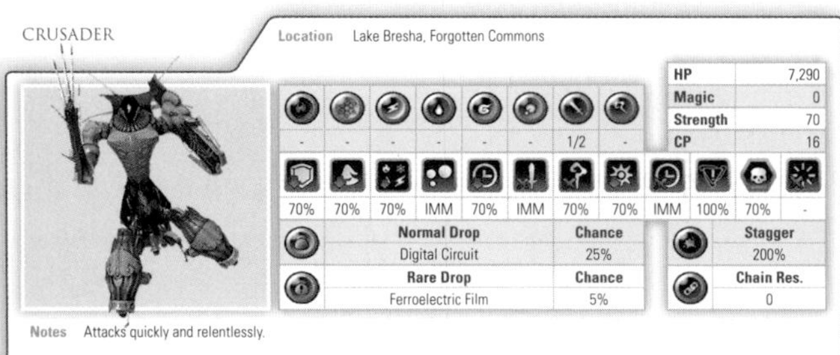

Location Lake Bresha, Forgotten Commons

-	-	-	-	-	-	1/2	-

70%	70%	70%	IMM	70%	IMM	70%	70%	IMM	100%	70%	-

HP	7,290
Magic	0
Strength	70
CP	16

Normal Drop	Chance
Digital Circuit	25%
Rare Drop	**Chance**
Ferroelectric Film	5%

Stagger
200%
Chain Res.
0

Notes Attacks quickly and relentlessly.

ORION

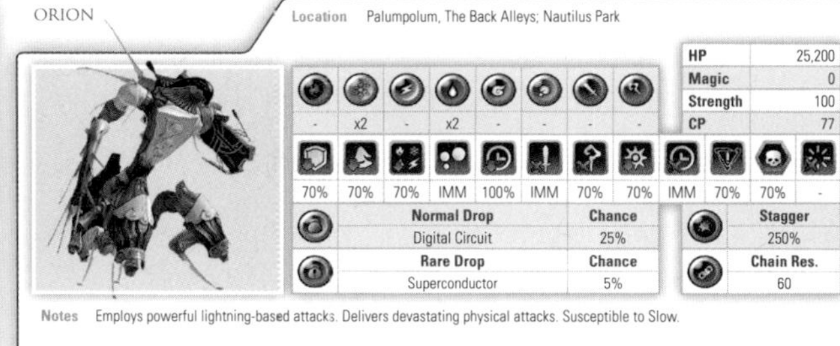

Location Palumpolum, The Back Alleys; Nautilus Park

-	x2	-	x2	-	-	-	-

70%	70%	70%	IMM	100%	IMM	70%	70%	IMM	70%	70%	-

HP	25,200
Magic	0
Strength	100
CP	77

Normal Drop	Chance
Digital Circuit	25%
Rare Drop	**Chance**
Superconductor	5%

Stagger
250%
Chain Res.
60

Notes Employs powerful lightning-based attacks. Delivers devastating physical attacks. Susceptible to Slow.

VIKING

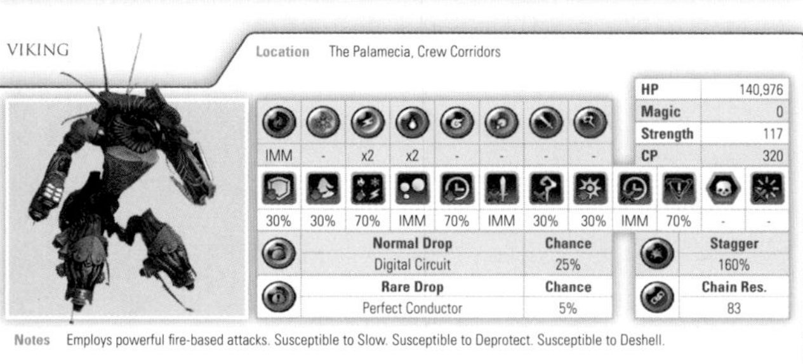

Location The Palamecia, Crew Corridors

IMM	-	x2	x2	-	-	-	-

30%	30%	70%	IMM	70%	IMM	30%	30%	IMM	70%	-	-

HP	140,976
Magic	0
Strength	117
CP	320

Normal Drop	Chance
Digital Circuit	25%
Rare Drop	**Chance**
Perfect Conductor	5%

Stagger
160%
Chain Res.
83

Notes Employs powerful fire-based attacks. Susceptible to Slow. Susceptible to Deprotect. Susceptible to Deshell.

UHLAN

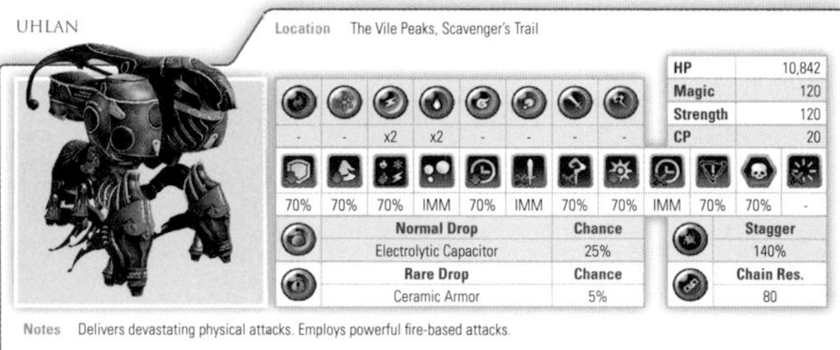

Location The Vile Peaks, Scavenger's Trail

-	-	x2	x2	-	-	-	-

70%	70%	70%	IMM	70%	IMM	70%	70%	IMM	70%	70%	-

HP	10,842
Magic	120
Strength	120
CP	20

Normal Drop	Chance
Electrolytic Capacitor	25%
Rare Drop	**Chance**
Ceramic Armor	5%

Stagger
140%
Chain Res.
80

Notes Delivers devastating physical attacks. Employs powerful fire-based attacks.

BULWARKER

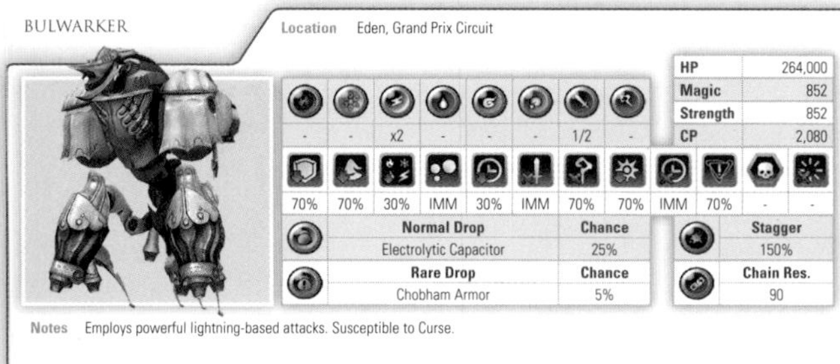

Location Eden, Grand Prix Circuit

-	-	x2	-	-	-	1/2	-

70%	70%	30%	IMM	30%	IMM	70%	70%	IMM	70%	-	-

HP	264,000
Magic	852
Strength	852
CP	2,080

Normal Drop	Chance
Electrolytic Capacitor	25%
Rare Drop	**Chance**
Chobham Armor	5%

Stagger
150%
Chain Res.
90

Notes Employs powerful lightning-based attacks. Susceptible to Curse.

CICONIA VELOCYCLE

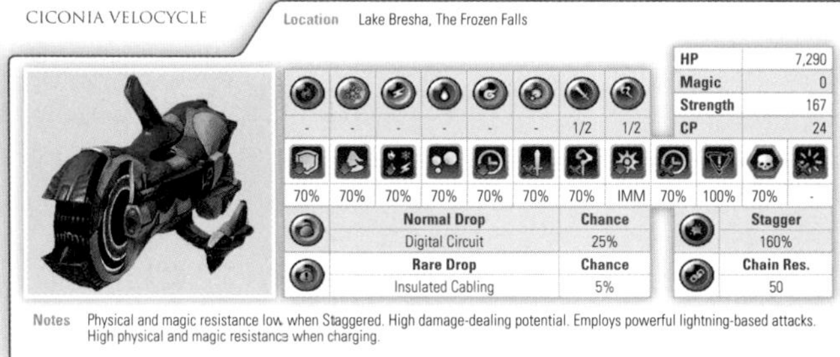

Location Lake Bresha, The Frozen Falls

-	-	-	-	-	-	1/2	1/2

70%	70%	70%	70%	70%	70%	70%	IMM	70%	100%	70%	-

HP	7,290
Magic	0
Strength	167
CP	24

Normal Drop	Chance
Digital Circuit	25%
Rare Drop	**Chance**
Insulated Cabling	5%

Stagger
160%
Chain Res.
50

Notes Physical and magic resistance low when Staggered. High damage-dealing potential. Employs powerful lightning-based attacks. High physical and magic resistance when charging.

FALCO VELOCYCLE

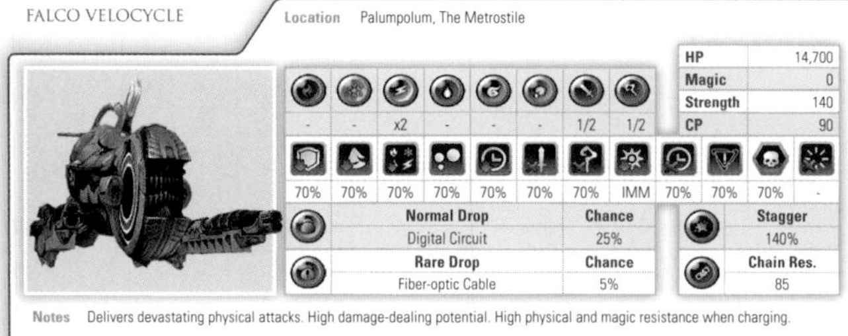

Location Palumpolum, The Metrostile

-	-	x2	-	-	-	1/2	1/2

70%	70%	70%	70%	70%	70%	70%	IMM	70%	70%	70%	-

HP	14,700
Magic	0
Strength	140
CP	90

Normal Drop	Chance
Digital Circuit	25%
Rare Drop	**Chance**
Fiber-optic Cable	5%

Stagger
140%
Chain Res.
85

Notes Delivers devastating physical attacks. High damage-dealing potential. High physical and magic resistance when charging.

MILVUS VELOCYCLE

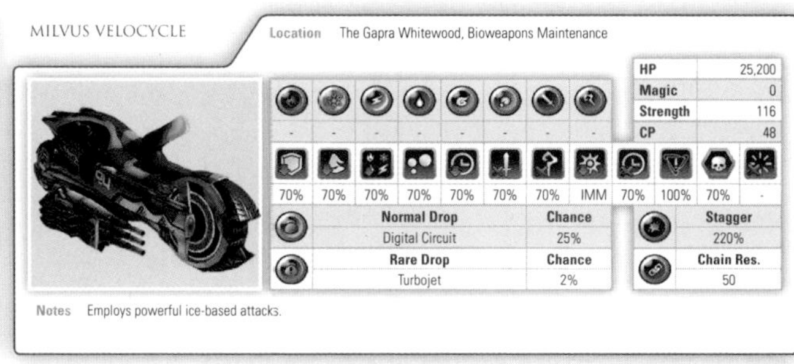

Location The Gapra Whitewood, Bioweapons Maintenance

-	-	-	-	-	-	-	-

70%	70%	70%	70%	70%	70%	70%	IMM	70%	100%	70%	-

HP	25,200
Magic	0
Strength	116
CP	48

Normal Drop	Chance
Digital Circuit	25%
Rare Drop	**Chance**
Turbojet	2%

Stagger
220%
Chain Res.
50

Notes Employs powerful ice-based attacks.

AQUILA VELOCYCLE

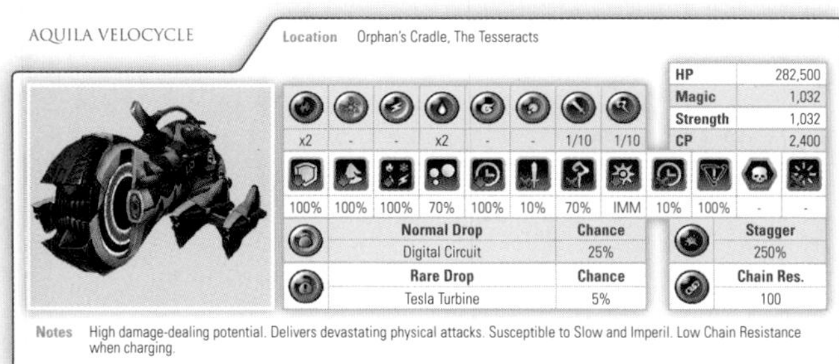

Location Orphan's Cradle, The Tesseracts

x2	-	-	x2	-	-	1/10	1/10

100%	100%	100%	70%	100%	10%	70%	IMM	10%	100%	-	-

HP	282,500
Magic	1,032
Strength	1,032
CP	2,400

Normal Drop	Chance
Digital Circuit	25%
Rare Drop	**Chance**
Tesla Turbine	5%

Stagger
250%
Chain Res.
100

Notes High damage-dealing potential. Delivers devastating physical attacks. Susceptible to Slow and Imperil. Low Chain Resistance when charging.

MIDLIGHT REAPER

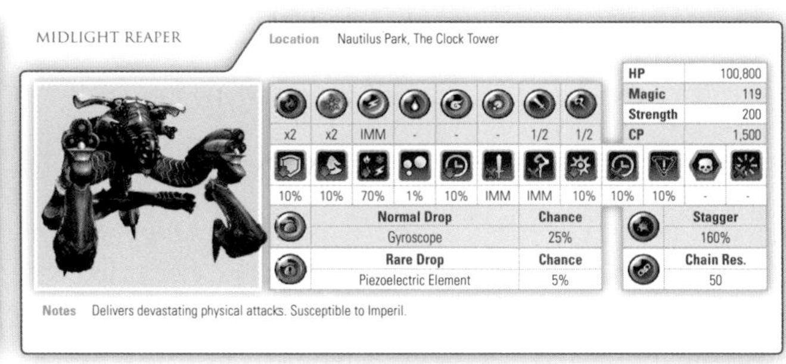

Location Nautilus Park, The Clock Tower

x2	x2	IMM	-	-	-	1/2	1/2

10%	10%	70%	1%	10%	IMM	IMM	10%	10%	10%	-	-

HP	100,800
Magic	119
Strength	200
CP	1,500

Normal Drop	Chance
Gyroscope	25%
Rare Drop	**Chance**
Piezoelectric Element	5%

Stagger
160%
Chain Res.
50

Notes Delivers devastating physical attacks. Susceptible to Imperil.

MEGRIM THRESHER

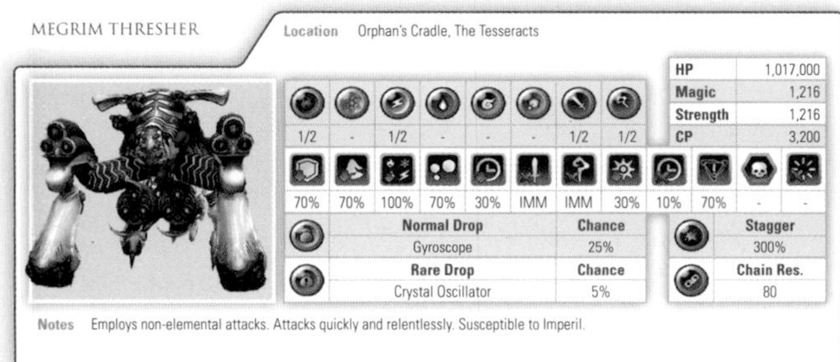

Location Orphan's Cradle, The Tesseracts

1/2	-	1/2	-	-	-	1/2	1/2

70%	70%	100%	70%	30%	IMM	IMM	30%	10%	70%	-	-

HP	1,017,000
Magic	1,216
Strength	1,216
CP	3,200

Normal Drop	Chance
Gyroscope	25%
Rare Drop	**Chance**
Crystal Oscillator	5%

Stagger
300%
Chain Res.
80

Notes Employs non-elemental attacks. Attacks quickly and relentlessly. Susceptible to Imperil.

HAVOC SKYTANK

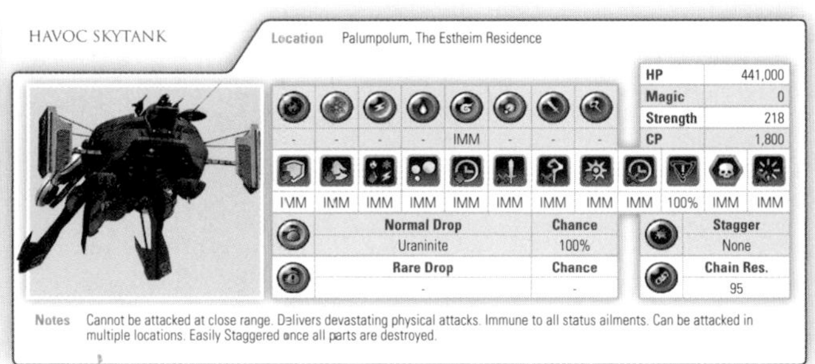

Location Palumpolum, The Estheim Residence

-	-	-	-	IMM	-	-	-

IMM	IMM	IMM	IMM	IMM	IMM	IMM	IMM	IMM	100%	IMM	IMM

HP	441,000
Magic	0
Strength	218
CP	1,800

Normal Drop	Chance
Uraninite	100%
Rare Drop	**Chance**
-	-

Stagger
None
Chain Res.
95

Notes Cannot be attacked at close range. Delivers devastating physical attacks. Immune to all status ailments. Can be attacked in multiple locations. Easily Staggered once all parts are destroyed.

HAVOC SKYTANK (TURRETS)

Location Palumpolum, The Estheim Residence

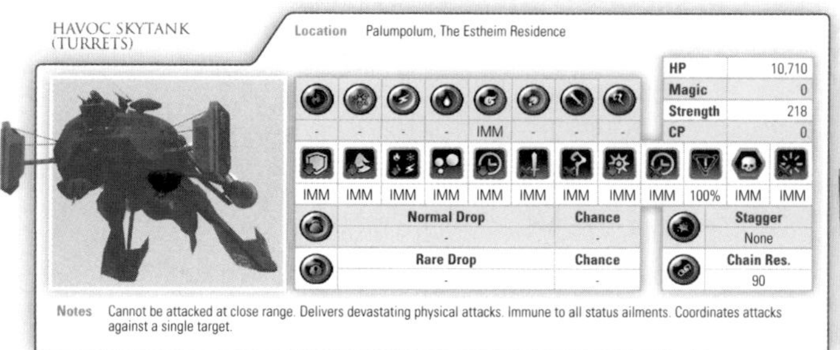

HP	Magic	Strength	CP
10,710	0	218	0

-	-	-	-	IMM	-	-	-

IMM	IMM	IMM	IMM	IMM	IMM	IMM	IMM	IMM	100%	IMM	IMM

Normal Drop	Chance	Rare Drop	Chance	Stagger	Chain Res.
-	-	-	-	None	90

Notes Cannot be attacked at close range. Delivers devastating physical attacks. Immune to all status ailments. Coordinates attacks against a single target.

HAVOC SKYTANK (HULLS)

Location Palumpolum, The Estheim Residence

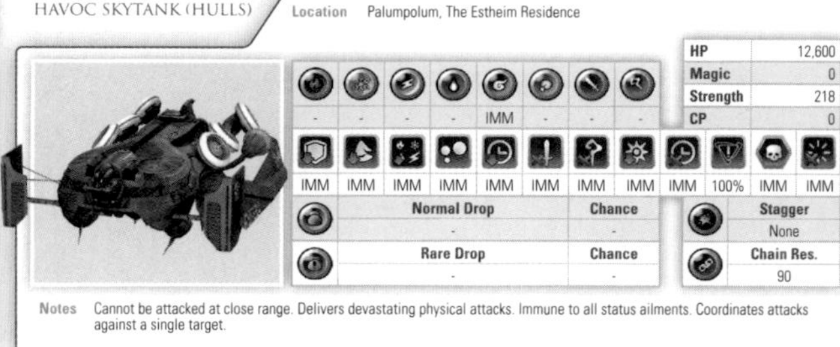

HP	Magic	Strength	CP
12,600	0	218	0

-	-	-	-	IMM	-	-	-

IMM	IMM	IMM	IMM	IMM	IMM	IMM	IMM	IMM	100%	IMM	IMM

Normal Drop	Chance	Rare Drop	Chance	Stagger	Chain Res.
-	-	-	-	None	90

Notes Cannot be attacked at close range. Delivers devastating physical attacks. Immune to all status ailments. Coordinates attacks against a single target.

PANTHERON

Location The Hanging Edge, Aerorail Trussway 12-E; The Pulse Vestige; Lake Bresha; The Vile Peaks

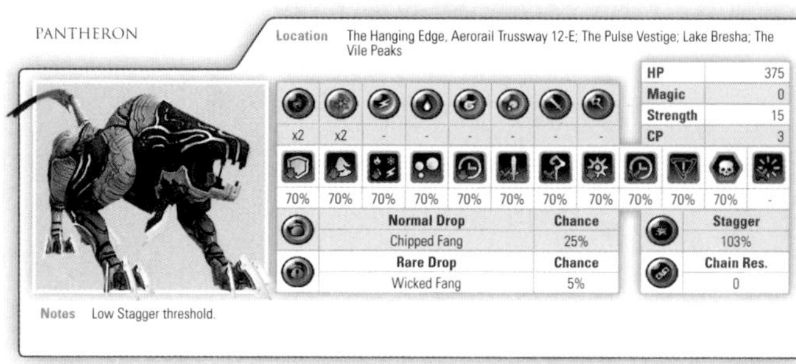

HP	Magic	Strength	CP
375	0	15	3

x2	x2	-	-	-	-	-	-

70%	70%	70%	70%	70%	70%	70%	70%	70%	70%	70%	-

Normal Drop	Chance	Rare Drop	Chance	Stagger	Chain Res.
Chipped Fang	25%	Wicked Fang	5%	103%	0

Notes Low Stagger threshold.

THEXTERON

Location The Vile Peaks, Wrack and Ruin; The Gapra Whitewood

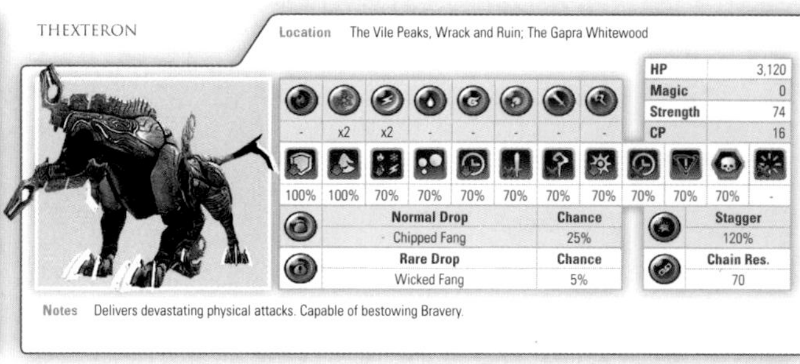

HP	Magic	Strength	CP
3,120	0	74	16

-	x2	x2	-	-	-	-	-

100%	100%	70%	70%	70%	70%	70%	70%	70%	70%	70%	-

Normal Drop	Chance	Rare Drop	Chance	Stagger	Chain Res.
Chipped Fang	25%	Wicked Fang	5%	120%	70

Notes Delivers devastating physical attacks. Capable of bestowing Bravery.

ADAMANTHERON

Location Eden, The Skywalk

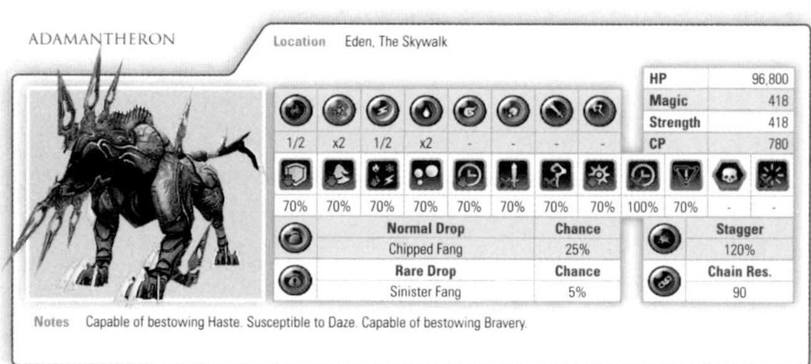

HP	Magic	Strength	CP
96,800	418	418	780

1/2	x2	1/2	x2	-	-	-	-

70%	70%	70%	70%	70%	70%	70%	70%	100%	70%	-	-

Normal Drop	Chance	Rare Drop	Chance	Stagger	Chain Res.
Chipped Fang	25%	Sinister Fang	5%	120%	90

Notes Capable of bestowing Haste. Susceptible to Daze. Capable of bestowing Bravery.

ZWERG SCANDROID

Location The Pulse Vestige, Sacrarium

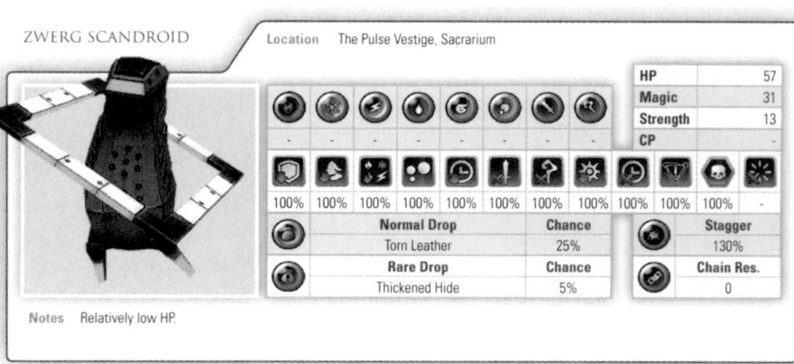

HP	Magic	Strength	CP
57	31	13	-

-	-	-	-	-	-	-	-

100%	100%	100%	100%	100%	100%	100%	100%	100%	100%	100%	-

Normal Drop	Chance	Rare Drop	Chance	Stagger	Chain Res.
Torn Leather	25%	Thickened Hide	5%	130%	0

Notes Relatively low HP.

ZWERG METRODROID

Location Nautilus Park, The Mall

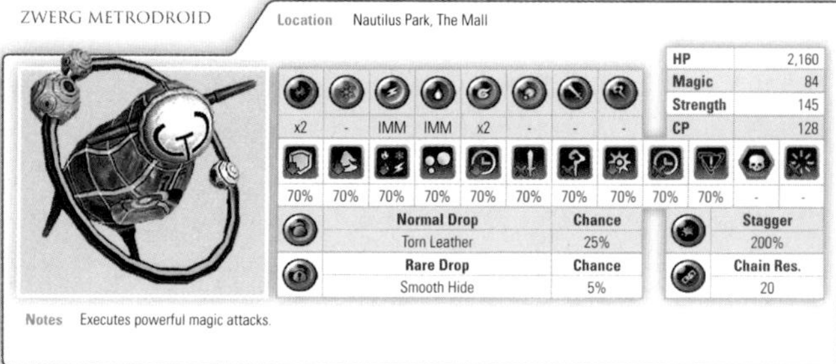

HP	Magic	Strength	CP
2,160	84	145	128

x2	-	IMM	IMM	x2	-	-	-

70%	70%	70%	70%	70%	70%	70%	70%	70%	70%	-	-

Normal Drop	Chance	Rare Drop	Chance	Stagger	Chain Res.
Torn Leather	25%	Smooth Hide	5%	200%	20

Notes Executes powerful magic attacks.

VESPID

Location The Gapra Whitewood, Canopy Wardwalks

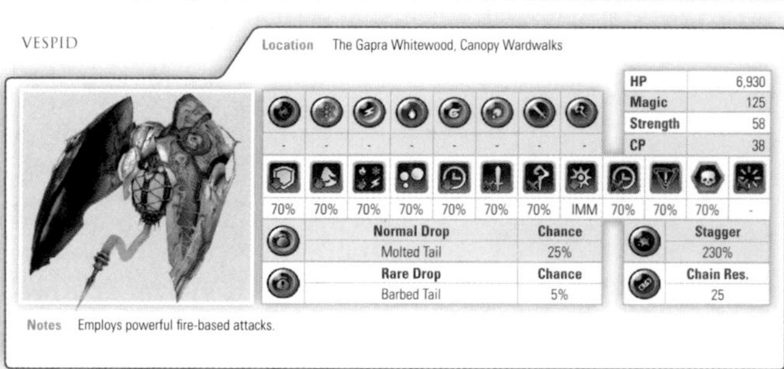

HP	Magic	Strength	CP
6,930	125	58	38

-	-	-	-	-	-	-	-

70%	70%	70%	70%	70%	70%	70%	IMM	70%	70%	70%	-

Normal Drop	Chance	Rare Drop	Chance	Stagger	Chain Res.
Molted Tail	25%	Barbed Tail	5%	230%	25

Notes Employs powerful fire-based attacks.

VESPID SOLDIER

Location The Palamecia, Rotary Shaft

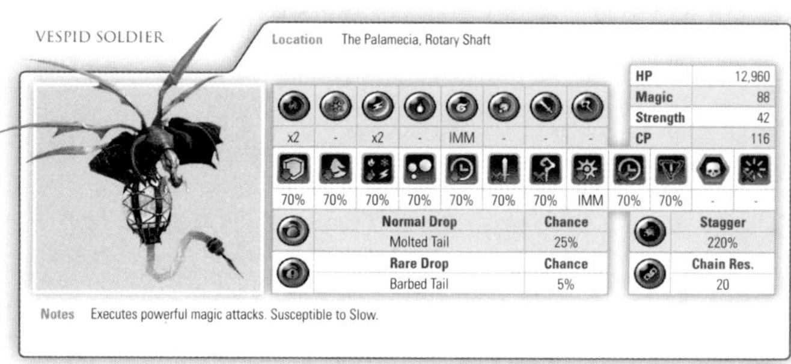

HP	Magic	Strength	CP
12,960	88	42	116

x2	-	x2	-	IMM	-	-	-

70%	70%	70%	70%	70%	70%	70%	IMM	70%	70%	-	-

Normal Drop	Chance	Rare Drop	Chance	Stagger	Chain Res.
Molted Tail	25%	Barbed Tail	5%	220%	20

Notes Executes powerful magic attacks. Susceptible to Slow.

FRAG LEECH

Location The Gapra Whitewood, Ecological Research

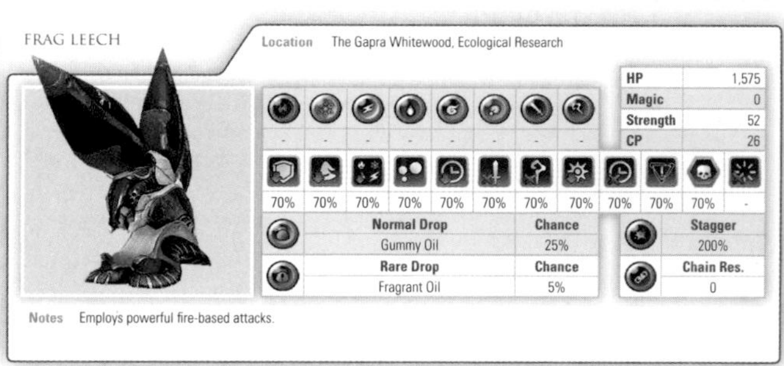

HP	Magic	Strength	CP
1,575	0	52	26

-	-	-	-	-	-	-	-

70%	70%	70%	70%	70%	70%	70%	70%	70%	70%	70%	-

Normal Drop	Chance	Rare Drop	Chance	Stagger	Chain Res.
Gummy Oil	25%	Fragrant Oil	5%	200%	0

Notes Employs powerful fire-based attacks.

LUCIDON

Location Palumpolum, Nutriculture Complex

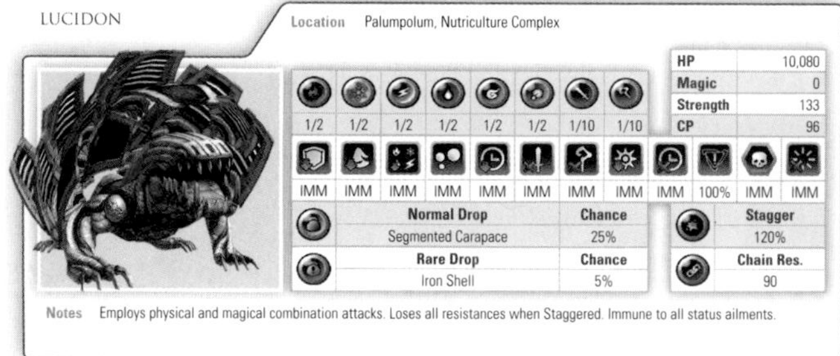

HP	Magic	Strength	CP
10,080	0	133	96

1/2	1/2	1/2	1/2	1/2	1/2	1/10	1/10

IMM	IMM	IMM	IMM	IMM	IMM	IMM	IMM	IMM	100%	IMM	IMM

Normal Drop	Chance	Rare Drop	Chance	Stagger	Chain Res.
Segmented Carapace	25%	Iron Shell	5%	120%	90

Notes Employs physical and magical combination attacks. Loses all resistances when Staggered. Immune to all status ailments.

THERMADON

Location The Palamecia, Rotary Shaft

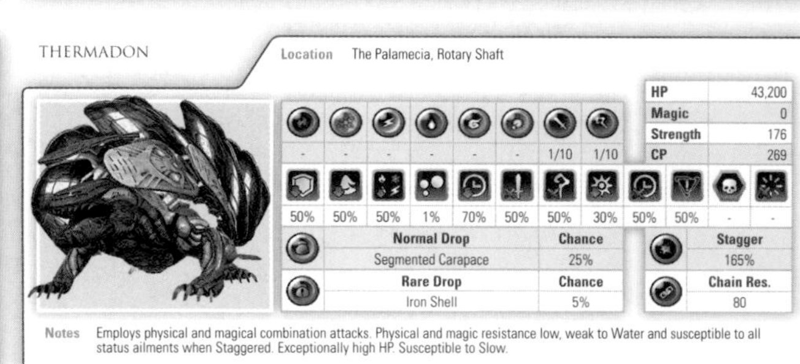

HP	Magic	Strength	CP
43,200	0	176	269

-	-	-	-	-	-	1/10	1/10

50%	50%	50%	1%	70%	50%	50%	30%	50%	50%	-	-

Normal Drop	Chance	Rare Drop	Chance	Stagger	Chain Res.
Segmented Carapace	25%	Iron Shell	5%	165%	80

Notes Employs physical and magical combination attacks. Physical and magic resistance low, weak to Water and susceptible to all status ailments when Staggered. Exceptionally high HP. Susceptible to Slow.

FLANITOR

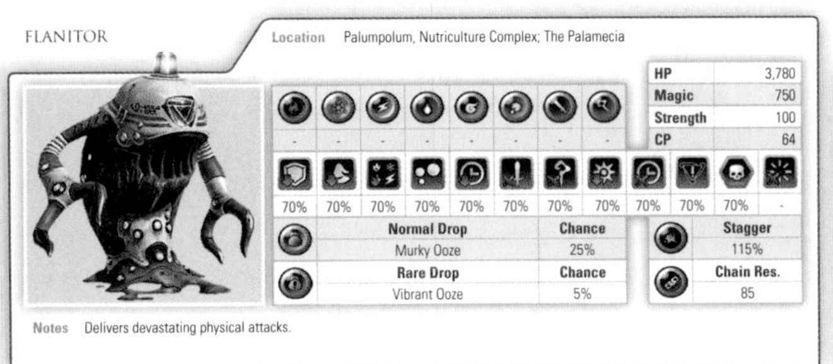

Location: Palumpolum, Nutriculture Complex; The Palamecia

HP	3,780
Magic	750
Strength	100
CP	64

-	-	-	-	-	-	-	-

70%	70%	70%	70%	70%	70%	70%	70%	70%	70%	70%	-

Normal Drop	Chance	Stagger
Murky Ooze	25%	115%
Rare Drop	**Chance**	**Chain Res.**
Vibrant Ooze	5%	85

Notes: Delivers devastating physical attacks.

FLANBORG

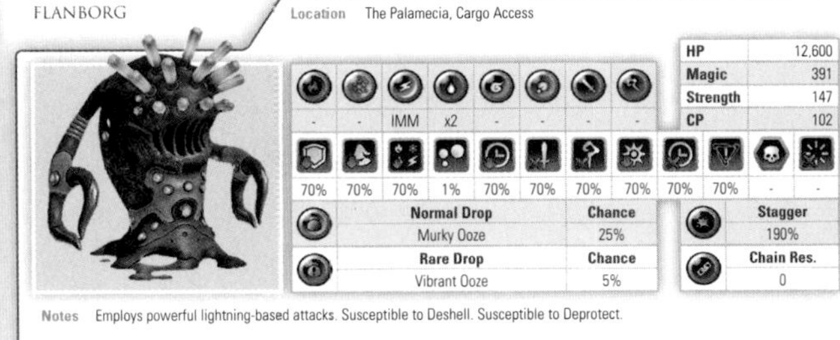

Location: The Palamecia, Cargo Access

HP	12,600
Magic	391
Strength	147
CP	102

-	-	IMM	x2	-	-	-	-

70%	70%	70%	1%	70%	70%	70%	70%	70%	70%	-	-

Normal Drop	Chance	Stagger
Murky Ooze	25%	190%
Rare Drop	**Chance**	**Chain Res.**
Vibrant Ooze	5%	0

Notes: Employs powerful lightning-based attacks. Susceptible to Deshell. Susceptible to Deprotect.

BETA BEHEMOTH

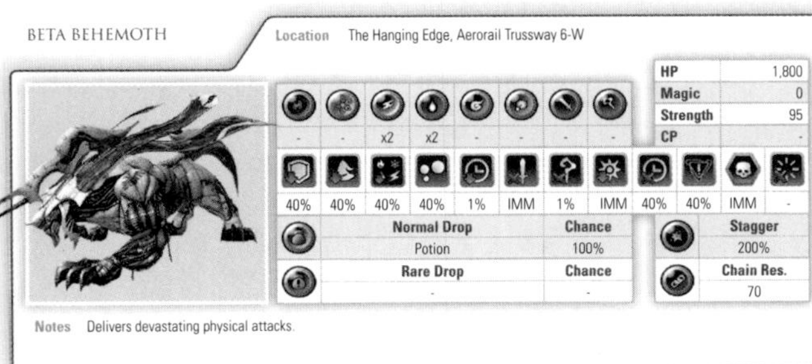

Location: The Hanging Edge, Aerorail Trussway 6-W

HP	1,800
Magic	0
Strength	95
CP	

-	-	x2	x2	-	-	-	-

40%	40%	40%	40%	1%	IMM	1%	IMM	40%	40%	IMM	-

Normal Drop	Chance	Stagger
Potion	100%	200%
Rare Drop	**Chance**	**Chain Res.**
-	-	70

Notes: Delivers devastating physical attacks.

ALPHA BEHEMOTH

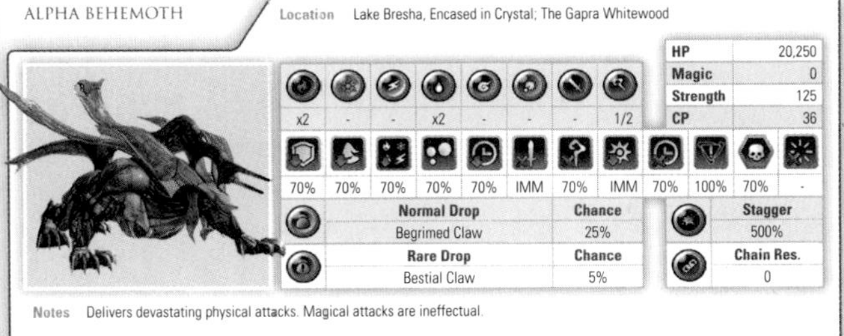

Location: Lake Bresha, Encased in Crystal; The Gapra Whitewood

HP	20,250
Magic	0
Strength	125
CP	36

x2	-	-	x2	-	-	-	1/2

70%	70%	70%	70%	70%	IMM	70%	IMM	70%	100%	70%	-

Normal Drop	Chance	Stagger
Begrimed Claw	25%	500%
Rare Drop	**Chance**	**Chain Res.**
Bestial Claw	5%	0

Notes: Delivers devastating physical attacks. Magical attacks are ineffectual.

LODESTAR BEHEMOTH

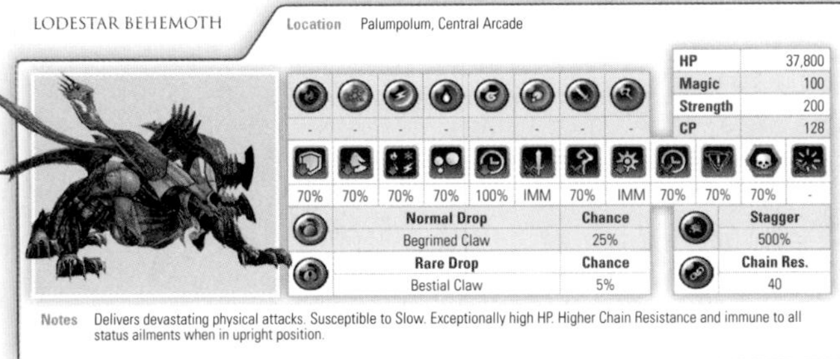

Location: Palumpolum, Central Arcade

HP	37,800
Magic	100
Strength	200
CP	128

-	-	-	-	-	-	-	-

70%	70%	70%	70%	100%	IMM	70%	IMM	70%	70%	70%	-

Normal Drop	Chance	Stagger
Begrimed Claw	25%	500%
Rare Drop	**Chance**	**Chain Res.**
Bestial Claw	5%	40

Notes: Delivers devastating physical attacks. Susceptible to Slow. Exceptionally high HP. Higher Chain Resistance and immune to all status ailments when in upright position.

PROTO-BEHEMOTH

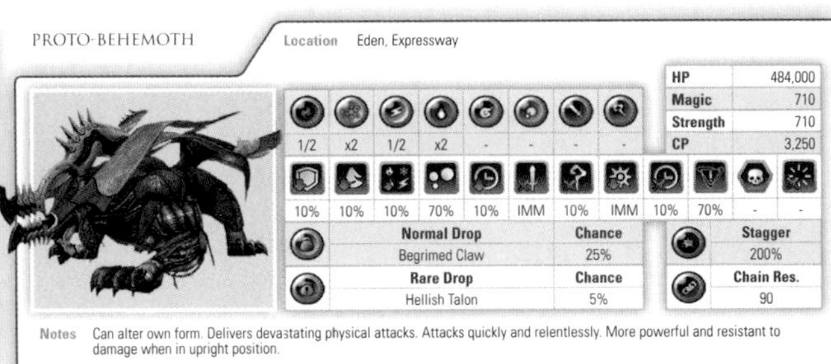

Location: Eden, Expressway

HP	484,000
Magic	710
Strength	710
CP	3,250

1/2	x2	1/2	x2	-	-	-	-

10%	10%	10%	70%	10%	IMM	10%	IMM	10%	70%	-	-

Normal Drop	Chance	Stagger
Begrimed Claw	25%	200%
Rare Drop	**Chance**	**Chain Res.**
Hellish Talon	5%	90

Notes: Can alter own form. Delivers devastating physical attacks. Attacks quickly and relentlessly. More powerful and resistant to damage when in upright position.

MANASVIN WARMECH

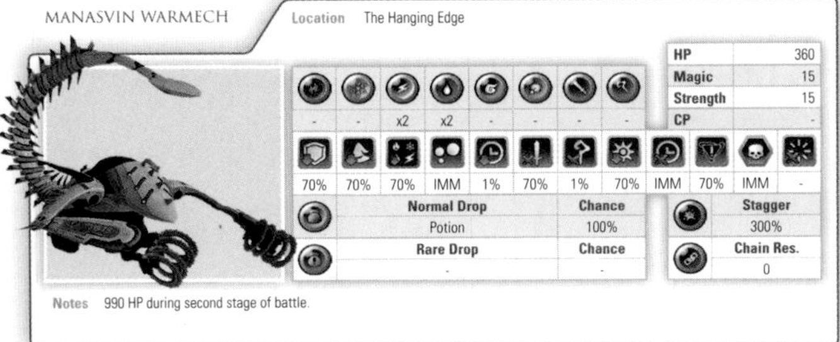

Location: The Hanging Edge

HP	360
Magic	15
Strength	15
CP	

-	-	x2	x2	-	-	-	-

70%	70%	70%	IMM	1%	70%	1%	70%	IMM	70%	IMM	-

Normal Drop	Chance	Stagger
Potion	100%	300%
Rare Drop	**Chance**	**Chain Res.**
		0

Notes: 990 HP during second stage of battle.

MANASVIN WARMECH

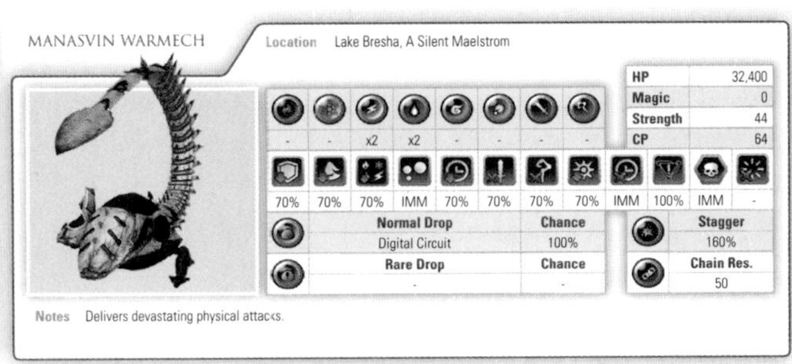

Location: Lake Bresha, A Silent Maelstrom

HP	32,400
Magic	0
Strength	44
CP	64

-	-	x2	x2	-	-	-	-

70%	70%	70%	IMM	70%	70%	70%	70%	IMM	100%	IMM	-

Normal Drop	Chance	Stagger
Digital Circuit	100%	160%
Rare Drop	**Chance**	**Chain Res.**
		50

Notes: Delivers devastating physical attacks.

ANAVATAPTA WARMECH

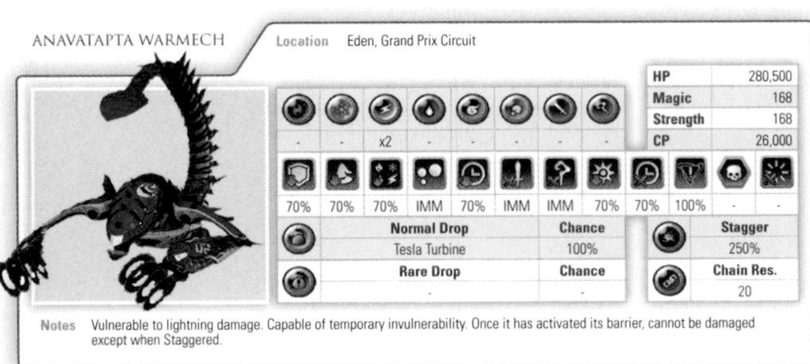

Location: Eden, Grand Prix Circuit

HP	280,500
Magic	168
Strength	168
CP	26,000

-	-	x2	-	-	-	-	-

70%	70%	70%	IMM	70%	IMM	IMM	70%	70%	100%	-	-

Normal Drop	Chance	Stagger
Tesla Turbine	100%	250%
Rare Drop	**Chance**	**Chain Res.**
		20

Notes: Vulnerable to lightning damage. Capable of temporary invulnerability. Once it has activated its barrier, cannot be damaged except when Staggered.

GARUDA INTERCEPTOR (1ST BATTLE)

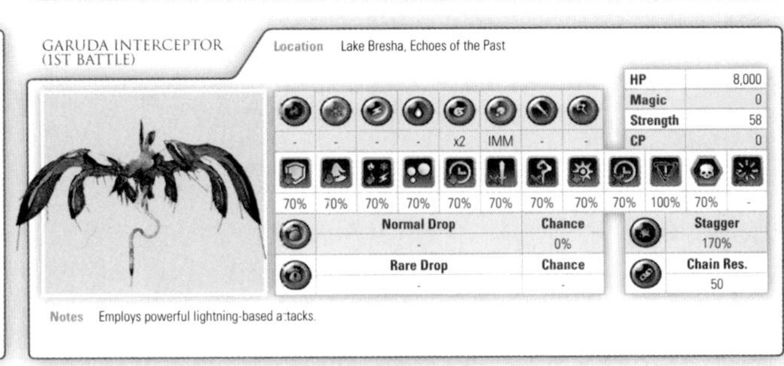

Location: Lake Bresha, Echoes of the Past

HP	8,000
Magic	0
Strength	58
CP	0

-	-	-	-	x2	IMM	-	-

70%	70%	70%	70%	70%	70%	70%	70%	70%	100%	70%	-

Normal Drop	Chance	Stagger
-	0%	170%
Rare Drop	**Chance**	**Chain Res.**
-		50

Notes: Employs powerful lightning-based attacks.

GARUDA INTERCEPTOR (2ND BATTLE)

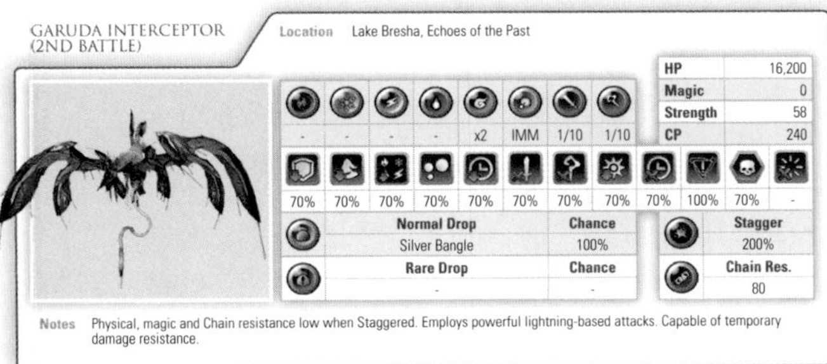

Location: Lake Bresha, Echoes of the Past

HP	16,200
Magic	0
Strength	58
CP	240

-	-	-	-	x2	IMM	1/10	1/10

70%	70%	70%	70%	70%	70%	70%	70%	70%	100%	70%	-

Normal Drop	Chance	Stagger
Silver Bangle	100%	200%
Rare Drop	**Chance**	**Chain Res.**
-		80

Notes: Physical, magic and Chain resistance low when Staggered. Employs powerful lightning-based attacks. Capable of temporary damage resistance.

KALAVINKA STRIKER (1ST BATTLE)

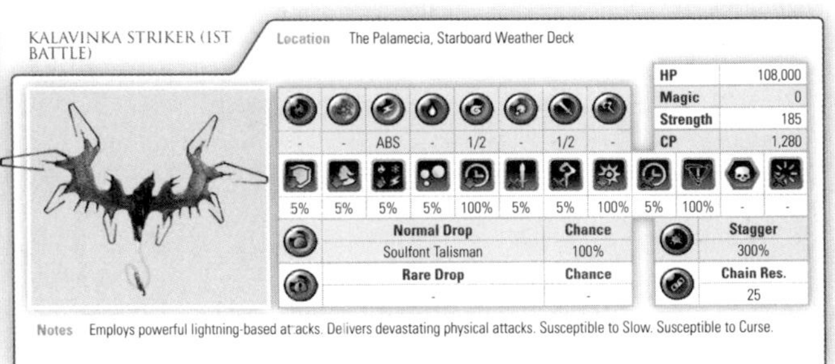

Location: The Palamecia, Starboard Weather Deck

HP	108,000
Magic	0
Strength	185
CP	1,280

-	-	ABS	-	1/2	-	1/2	-

5%	5%	5%	5%	100%	5%	5%	100%	5%	100%	-	-

Normal Drop	Chance	Stagger
Soulfont Talisman	100%	300%
Rare Drop	**Chance**	**Chain Res.**
-		25

Notes: Employs powerful lightning-based attacks. Delivers devastating physical attacks. Susceptible to Slow. Susceptible to Curse.

KALAVINKA STRIKER (2ND BATTLE)

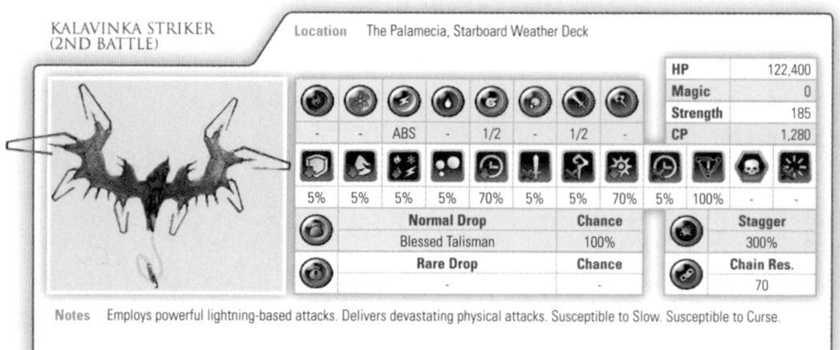

Location The Palamecia, Starboard Weather Deck

HP	Magic	Strength	CP
122,400	0	185	1,280

-	-	ABS	-	1/2	-	1/2	-

5%	5%	5%	5%	70%	5%	5%	70%	5%	100%	-	-

Normal Drop	Chance	Rare Drop	Chance	Stagger	Chain Res.
Blessed Talisman	100%	-	-	300%	70

Notes Employs powerful lightning-based attacks. Delivers devastating physical attacks. Susceptible to Slow. Susceptible to Curse.

ASTER PROTOFLORIAN

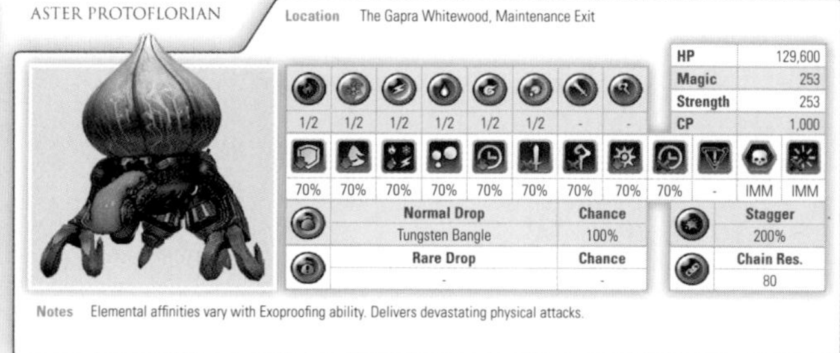

Location The Gapra Whitewood, Maintenance Exit

HP	Magic	Strength	CP
129,600	253	253	1,000

1/2	1/2	1/2	1/2	1/2	1/2	-	-

70%	70%	70%	70%	70%	70%	70%	70%	70%	-	IMM	IMM

Normal Drop	Chance	Rare Drop	Chance	Stagger	Chain Res.
Tungsten Bangle	100%	-	-	200%	80

Notes Elemental affinities vary with Exoproofing ability. Delivers devastating physical attacks.

VERNAL HARVESTER

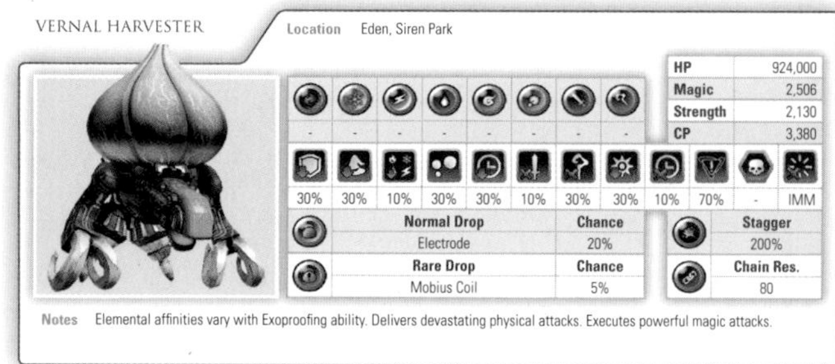

Location Eden, Siren Park

HP	Magic	Strength	CP
924,000	2,506	2,130	3,380

-	-	-	-	-	-	-	-

30%	30%	10%	30%	30%	10%	30%	30%	10%	70%	-	IMM

Normal Drop	Chance	Rare Drop	Chance	Stagger	Chain Res.
Electrode	20%	Mobius Coil	5%	200%	80

Notes Elemental affinities vary with Exoproofing ability. Delivers devastating physical attacks. Executes powerful magic attacks.

USHUMGAL SUBJUGATOR (1ST ENCOUNTER)

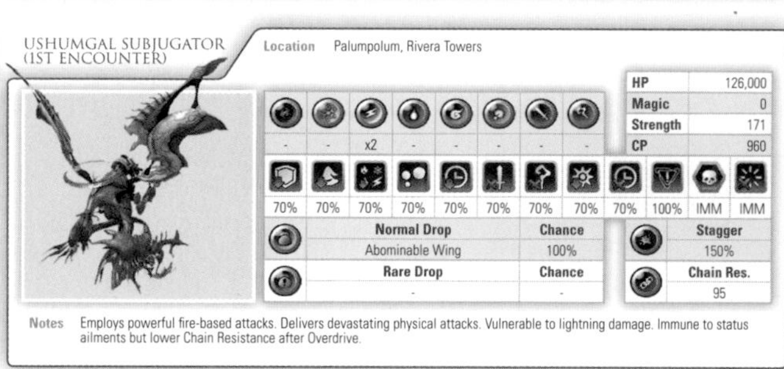

Location Palumpolum, Rivera Towers

HP	Magic	Strength	CP
126,000	0	171	960

-	-	x2	-	-	-	-	-

70%	70%	70%	70%	70%	70%	70%	70%	70%	100%	IMM	IMM

Normal Drop	Chance	Rare Drop	Chance	Stagger	Chain Res.
Abominable Wing	100%	-	-	150%	95

Notes Employs powerful fire-based attacks. Delivers devastating physical attacks. Vulnerable to lightning damage. Immune to status ailments but lower Chain Resistance after Overdrive.

USHUMGAL SUBJUGATOR (2ND ENCOUNTER)

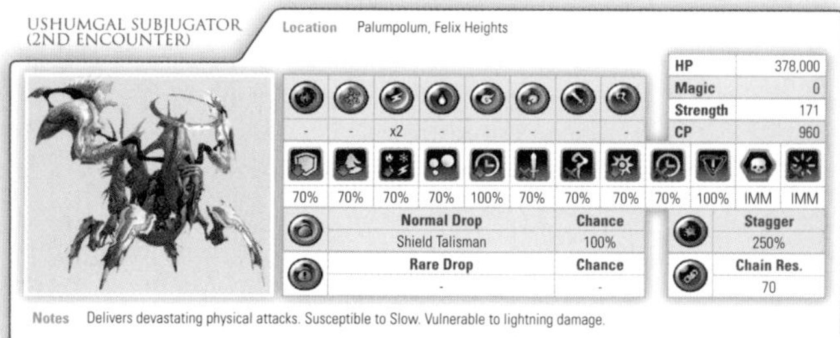

Location Palumpolum, Felix Heights

HP	Magic	Strength	CP
378,000	0	171	960

-	-	x2	-	-	-	-	-

70%	70%	70%	70%	100%	70%	70%	70%	70%	100%	IMM	IMM

Normal Drop	Chance	Rare Drop	Chance	Stagger	Chain Res.
Shield Talisman	100%	-	-	250%	70

Notes Delivers devastating physical attacks. Susceptible to Slow. Vulnerable to lightning damage.

TIAMAT ELIMINATOR

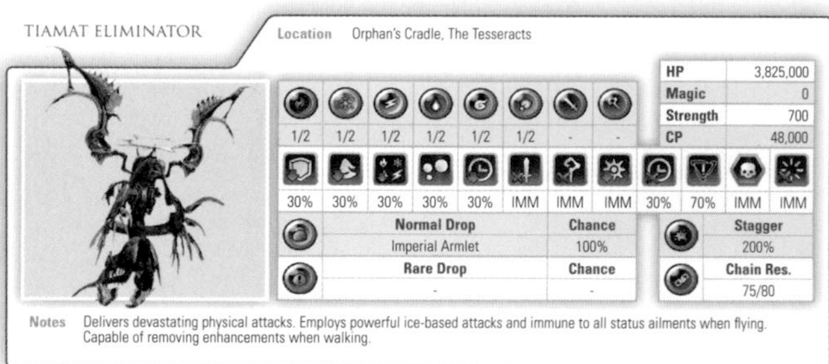

Location Orphan's Cradle, The Tesseracts

HP	Magic	Strength	CP
3,825,000	0	700	48,000

1/2	1/2	1/2	1/2	1/2	1/2	-	-

30%	30%	30%	30%	30%	IMM	IMM	IMM	30%	70%	IMM	IMM

Normal Drop	Chance	Rare Drop	Chance	Stagger	Chain Res.
Imperial Armlet	100%	-	-	200%	75/80

Notes Delivers devastating physical attacks. Employs powerful ice-based attacks and immune to all status ailments when flying. Capable of removing enhancements when walking.

THE PROUDCLAD (1ST ENCOUNTER)

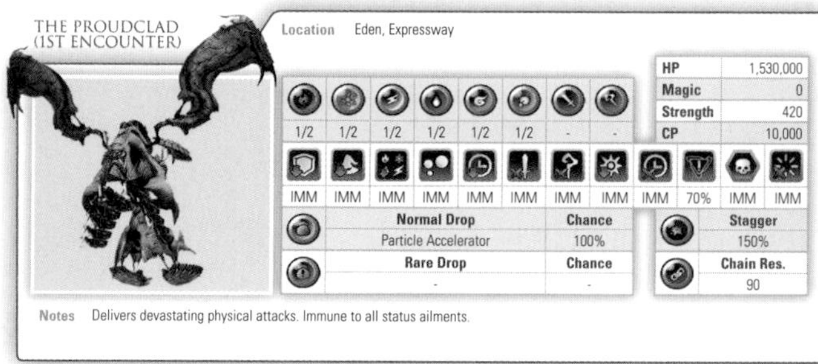

Location Eden, Expressway

HP	Magic	Strength	CP
1,530,000	0	420	10,000

1/2	1/2	1/2	1/2	1/2	1/2	-	-

IMM	IMM	IMM	IMM	IMM	IMM	IMM	IMM	IMM	70%	IMM	IMM

Normal Drop	Chance	Rare Drop	Chance	Stagger	Chain Res.
Particle Accelerator	100%	-	-	150%	90

Notes Delivers devastating physical attacks. Immune to all status ailments.

THE PROUDCLAD (2ND ENCOUNTER)

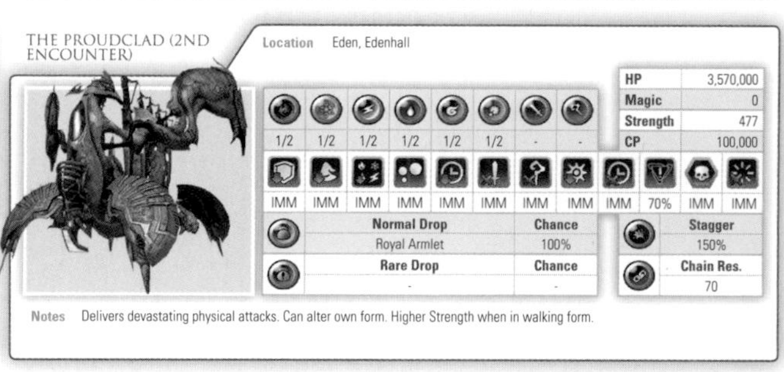

Location Eden, Edenhall

HP	Magic	Strength	CP
3,570,000	0	477	100,000

1/2	1/2	1/2	1/2	1/2	1/2	-	-

IMM	IMM	IMM	IMM	IMM	IMM	IMM	IMM	IMM	70%	IMM	IMM

Normal Drop	Chance	Rare Drop	Chance	Stagger	Chain Res.
Royal Armlet	100%	-	-	150%	70

Notes Delivers devastating physical attacks. Can alter own form. Higher Strength when in walking form.

SILVER LOBO

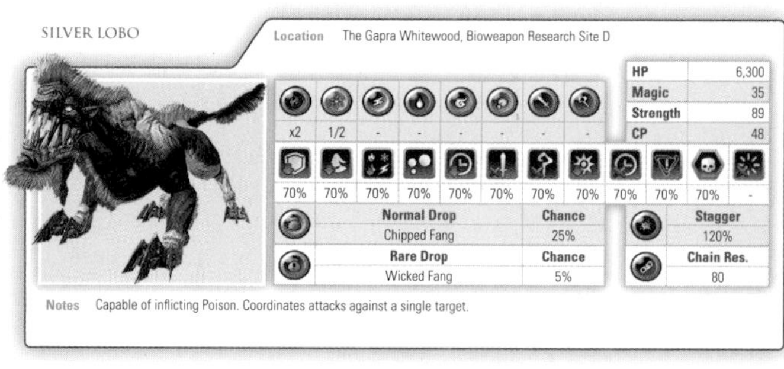

Location The Gapra Whitewood, Bioweapon Research Site D

HP	Magic	Strength	CP
6,300	35	89	48

x2	1/2	-	-	-	-	-	-

70%	70%	70%	70%	70%	70%	70%	70%	70%	70%	70%	-

Normal Drop	Chance	Rare Drop	Chance	Stagger	Chain Res.
Chipped Fang	25%	Wicked Fang	5%	120%	80

Notes Capable of inflicting Poison. Coordinates attacks against a single target.

GORGONOPSID

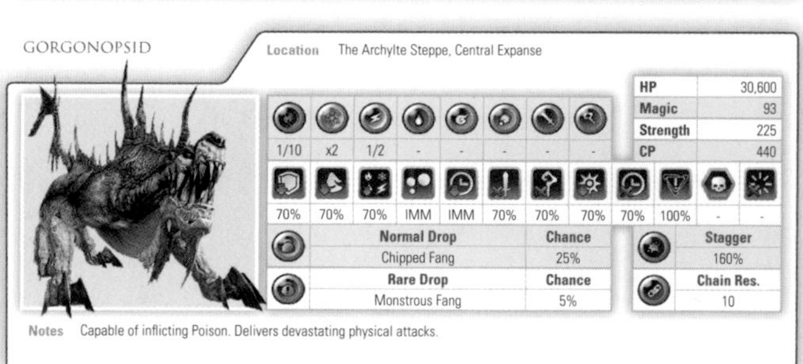

Location The Archylte Steppe, Central Expanse

HP	Magic	Strength	CP
30,600	93	225	440

1/10	x2	1/2	-	-	-	-	-

70%	70%	70%	IMM	IMM	70%	70%	70%	70%	100%	-	-

Normal Drop	Chance	Rare Drop	Chance	Stagger	Chain Res.
Chipped Fang	25%	Monstrous Fang	5%	160%	10

Notes Capable of inflicting Poison. Delivers devastating physical attacks.

URIDIMMU

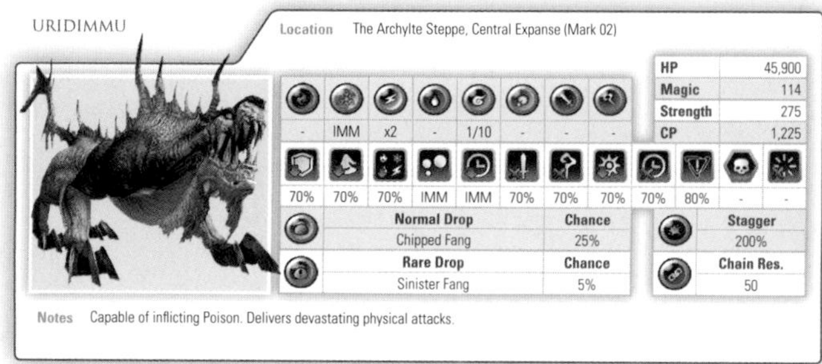

Location The Archylte Steppe, Central Expanse (Mark 02)

HP	Magic	Strength	CP
45,900	114	275	1,225

-	IMM	x2	-	1/10	-	-	-

70%	70%	70%	IMM	IMM	70%	70%	70%	70%	80%	-	-

Normal Drop	Chance	Rare Drop	Chance	Stagger	Chain Res.
Chipped Fang	25%	Sinister Fang	5%	200%	50

Notes Capable of inflicting Poison. Delivers devastating physical attacks.

AMAM

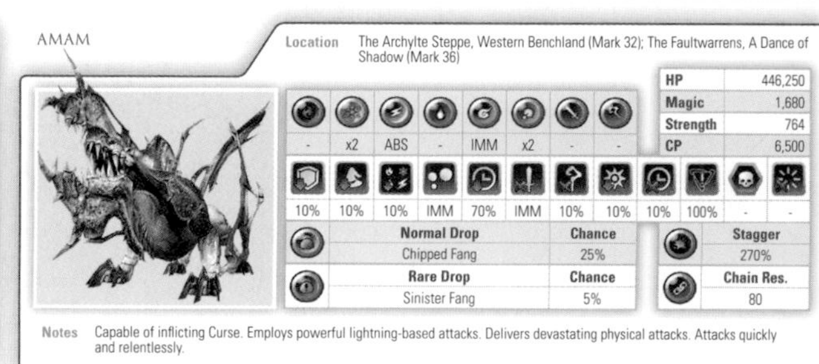

Location The Archylte Steppe, Western Benchland (Mark 32); The Faultwarrens, A Dance of Shadow (Mark 36)

HP	Magic	Strength	CP
446,250	1,680	764	6,500

-	x2	ABS	-	IMM	x2	-	-

10%	10%	10%	IMM	70%	IMM	10%	10%	10%	100%	-	-

Normal Drop	Chance	Rare Drop	Chance	Stagger	Chain Res.
Chipped Fang	25%	Sinister Fang	5%	270%	80

Notes Capable of inflicting Curse. Employs powerful lightning-based attacks. Delivers devastating physical attacks. Attacks quickly and relentlessly.

MÁNAGARMR

Location: Taejin's Tower, The Palisades

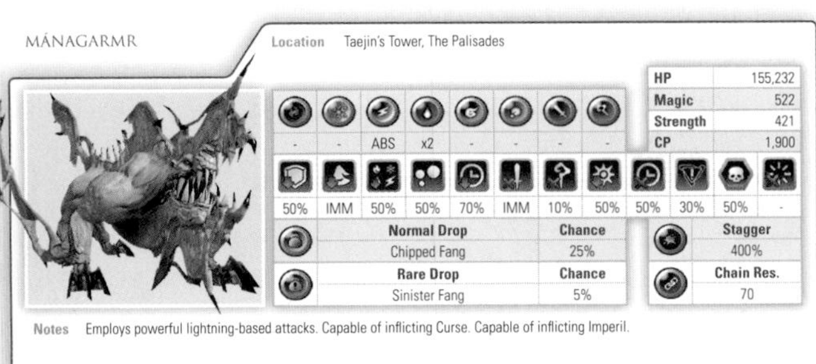

HP	Magic	Strength	CP
155,232	522	421	1,900

Elemental							
-	-	ABS	x2	-	-	-	-

Status											
50%	IMM	50%	50%	70%	IMM	10%	50%	50%	30%	50%	-

Normal Drop	Chance	Rare Drop	Chance	Stagger	Chain Res.
Chipped Fang	25%	Sinister Fang	5%	400%	70

Notes: Employs powerful lightning-based attacks. Capable of inflicting Curse. Capable of inflicting Imperil.

UGALLU

Location: Yaschas Massif, The Tsubaddran Highlands (Mark 03); Yaschas Massif, The Ascendant Scarp (Mark 56)

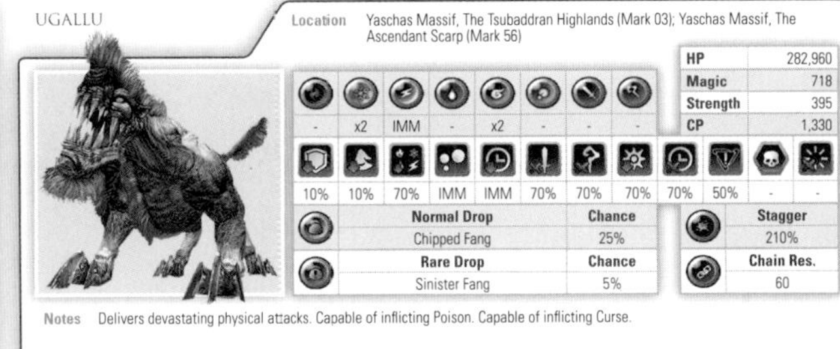

HP	Magic	Strength	CP
282,960	718	395	1,330

Elemental							
-	x2	IMM	-	x2	-	-	-

Status											
10%	10%	70%	IMM	IMM	70%	70%	70%	70%	50%	-	-

Normal Drop	Chance	Rare Drop	Chance	Stagger	Chain Res.
Chipped Fang	25%	Sinister Fang	5%	210%	60

Notes: Delivers devastating physical attacks. Capable of inflicting Poison. Capable of inflicting Curse.

MEGISTOTHERIAN

Location: The Archylte Steppe, Northern Highplain

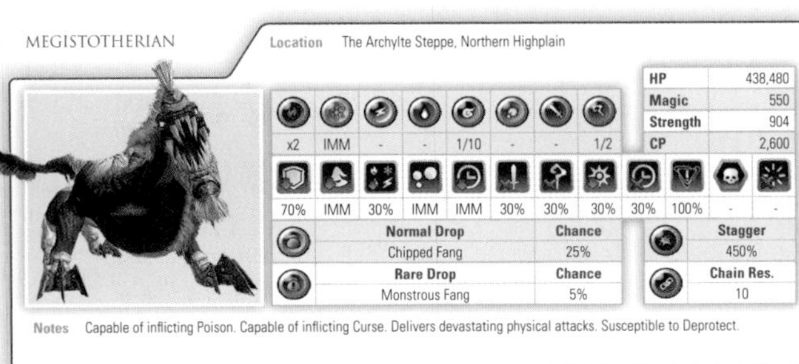

HP	Magic	Strength	CP
438,480	550	904	2,600

Elemental							
x2	IMM	-	-	1/10	-	-	1/2

Status											
70%	IMM	30%	IMM	IMM	30%	30%	30%	30%	100%	-	-

Normal Drop	Chance	Rare Drop	Chance	Stagger	Chain Res.
Chipped Fang	25%	Monstrous Fang	5%	450%	10

Notes: Capable of inflicting Poison. Capable of inflicting Curse. Delivers devastating physical attacks. Susceptible to Deprotect.

BLOODFANG BASS

Location: Lake Bresha, Encased in Crystal

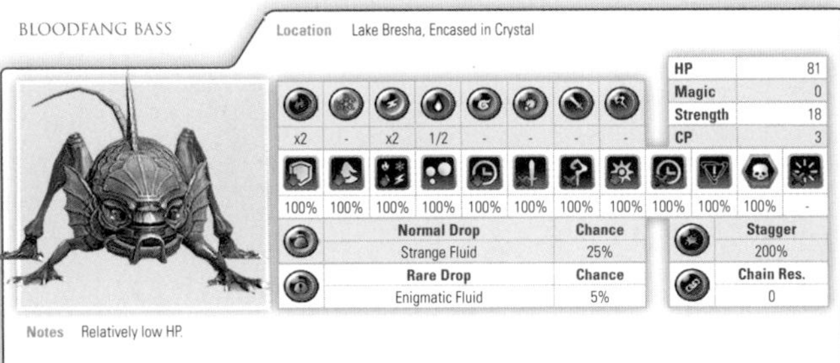

HP	Magic	Strength	CP
81	0	18	3

Elemental							
x2	-	x2	1/2	-	-	-	-

Status											
100%	100%	100%	100%	100%	100%	100%	100%	100%	100%	100%	-

Normal Drop	Chance	Rare Drop	Chance	Stagger	Chain Res.
Strange Fluid	25%	Enigmatic Fluid	5%	200%	0

Notes: Relatively low HP.

BRESHAN BASS

Location: Lake Bresha, Amid Timebound Waves

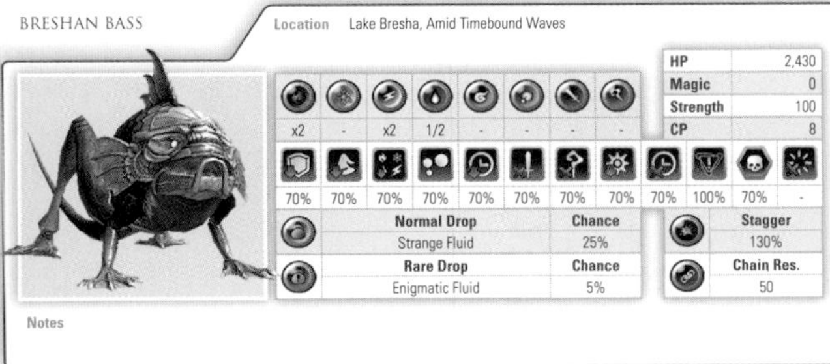

HP	Magic	Strength	CP
2,430	0	100	8

Elemental							
x2	-	x2	1/2	-	-	-	-

Status											
70%	70%	70%	70%	70%	70%	70%	70%	70%	100%	70%	-

Normal Drop	Chance	Rare Drop	Chance	Stagger	Chain Res.
Strange Fluid	25%	Enigmatic Fluid	5%	130%	50

Notes

HEDGE FROG

Location: The Sunleth Waterscape, The Old Growth

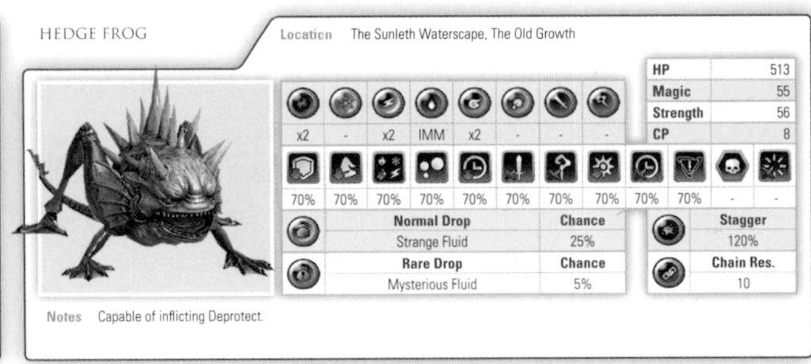

HP	Magic	Strength	CP
513	55	56	8

Elemental							
x2	-	x2	IMM	x2	-	-	-

Status											
70%	70%	70%	70%	70%	70%	70%	70%	70%	70%	-	-

Normal Drop	Chance	Rare Drop	Chance	Stagger	Chain Res.
Strange Fluid	25%	Mysterious Fluid	5%	120%	10

Notes: Capable of inflicting Deprotect.

MUD FROG

Location: The Sunleth Waterscape, Rain-spotted Vale

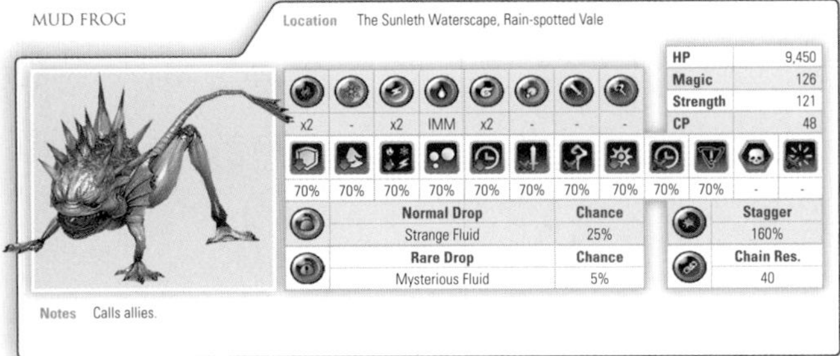

HP	Magic	Strength	CP
9,450	126	121	48

Elemental							
x2	-	x2	IMM	x2	-	-	-

Status											
70%	70%	70%	70%	70%	70%	70%	70%	70%	70%	-	-

Normal Drop	Chance	Rare Drop	Chance	Stagger	Chain Res.
Strange Fluid	25%	Mysterious Fluid	5%	160%	40

Notes: Calls allies.

CERATOSAUR

Location: Sulyya Springs, Subterranean Lake; Oerba, Village Proper (Mark 28)

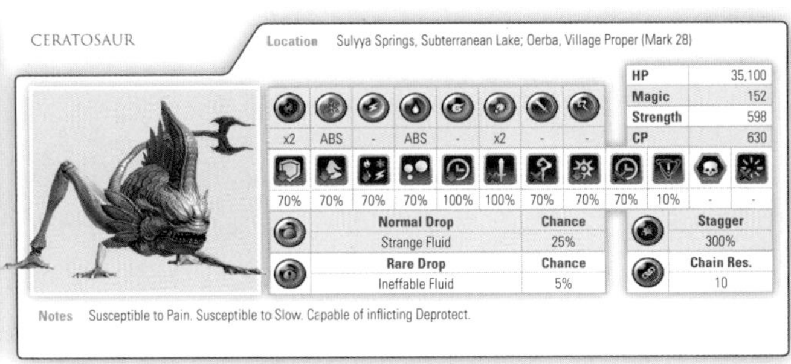

HP	Magic	Strength	CP
35,100	152	598	630

Elemental							
x2	ABS	-	ABS	-	x2	-	-

Status											
70%	70%	70%	70%	100%	100%	70%	70%	70%	10%	-	-

Normal Drop	Chance	Rare Drop	Chance	Stagger	Chain Res.
Strange Fluid	25%	Ineffable Fluid	5%	300%	10

Notes: Susceptible to Pain. Susceptible to Slow. Capable of inflicting Deprotect.

CERATORAPTOR

Location: Sulyya Springs, Subterranean Lake

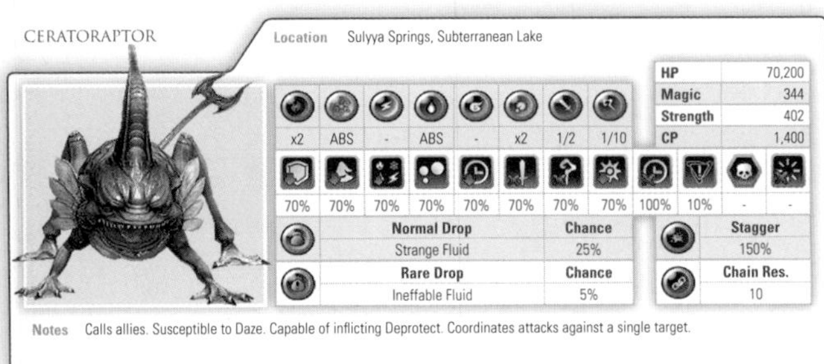

HP	Magic	Strength	CP
70,200	344	402	1,400

Elemental							
x2	ABS	-	ABS	-	x2	1/2	1/10

Status											
70%	70%	70%	70%	70%	70%	70%	70%	100%	10%	-	-

Normal Drop	Chance	Rare Drop	Chance	Stagger	Chain Res.
Strange Fluid	25%	Ineffable Fluid	5%	150%	10

Notes: Calls allies. Susceptible to Daze. Capable of inflicting Deprotect. Coordinates attacks against a single target.

GREMLIN

Location: The Vile Peaks, Scrap Processing; The Sunleth Waterscape

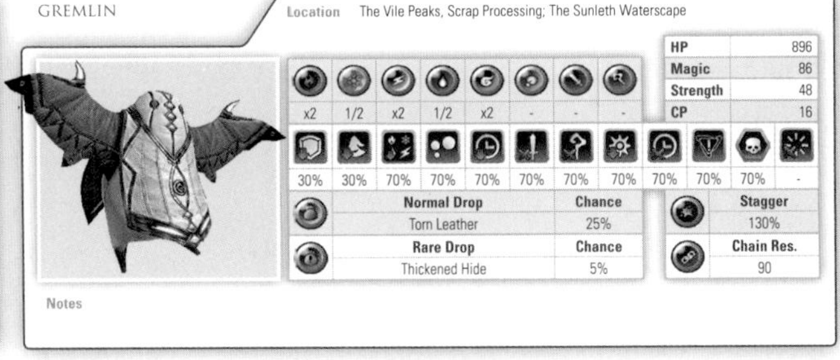

HP	Magic	Strength	CP
896	86	48	16

Elemental							
x2	1/2	x2	1/2	x2	-	-	-

Status											
30%	30%	70%	70%	70%	70%	70%	70%	70%	70%	70%	-

Normal Drop	Chance	Rare Drop	Chance	Stagger	Chain Res.
Torn Leather	25%	Thickened Hide	5%	130%	90

Notes

GARCHIMACERA

Location: The Sunleth Waterscape, Rain-spotted Vale

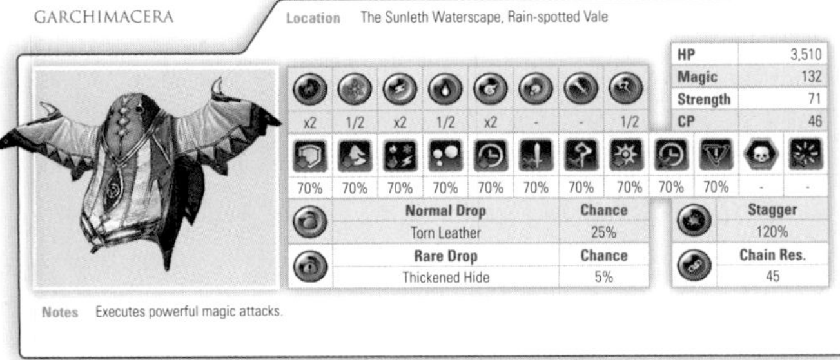

HP	Magic	Strength	CP
3,510	132	71	46

Elemental							
x2	1/2	x2	1/2	x2	-	-	1/2

Status											
70%	70%	70%	70%	70%	70%	70%	70%	70%	70%	-	-

Normal Drop	Chance	Rare Drop	Chance	Stagger	Chain Res.
Torn Leather	25%	Thickened Hide	5%	120%	45

Notes: Executes powerful magic attacks.

IMP

Location: The Fifth Ark, Inner Conduit

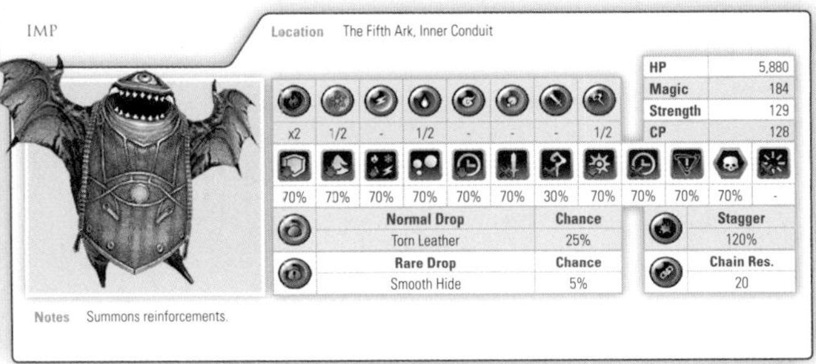

HP	Magic	Strength	CP
5,880	184	129	128

Elemental							
x2	1/2	-	1/2	-	-	-	1/2

Status											
70%	70%	70%	70%	70%	70%	30%	70%	70%	70%	70%	-

Normal Drop	Chance	Rare Drop	Chance	Stagger	Chain Res.
Torn Leather	25%	Smooth Hide	5%	120%	20

Notes: Summons reinforcements.

AHRIMAN

Location The Fifth Ark, Inner Conduit

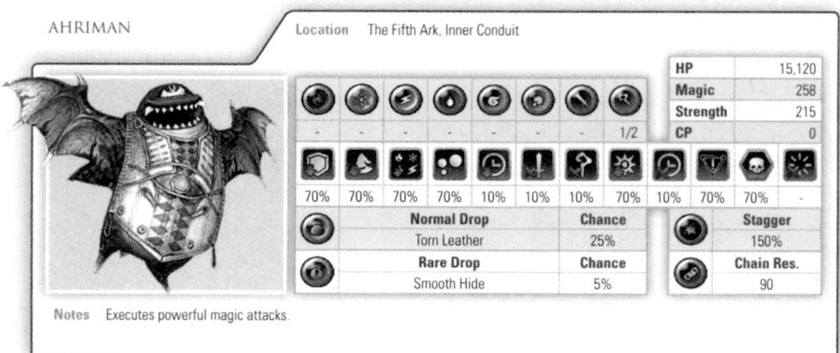

HP	Magic	Strength	CP
15,120	258	215	0

-	-	-	-	-	-	-	1/2

70%	70%	70%	70%	10%	10%	10%	70%	10%	70%	70%	-

Normal Drop	Chance	Stagger
Torn Leather	25%	150%
Rare Drop	**Chance**	**Chain Res.**
Smooth Hide	5%	90

Notes Executes powerful magic attacks.

LEYAK

Location The Archylte Steppe, Western Benchland; Yaschas Massif

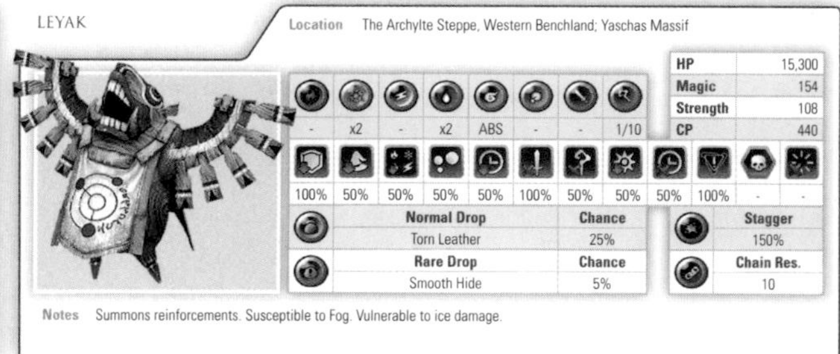

HP	Magic	Strength	CP
15,300	154	108	440

-	x2	-	x2	ABS	-	-	1/10

100%	50%	50%	50%	50%	100%	50%	50%	50%	100%	-	-

Normal Drop	Chance	Stagger
Torn Leather	25%	150%
Rare Drop	**Chance**	**Chain Res.**
Smooth Hide	5%	10

Notes Summons reinforcements. Susceptible to Fog. Vulnerable to ice damage.

RANGDA

Location The Archylte Steppe, Western Benchland; Yaschas Massif

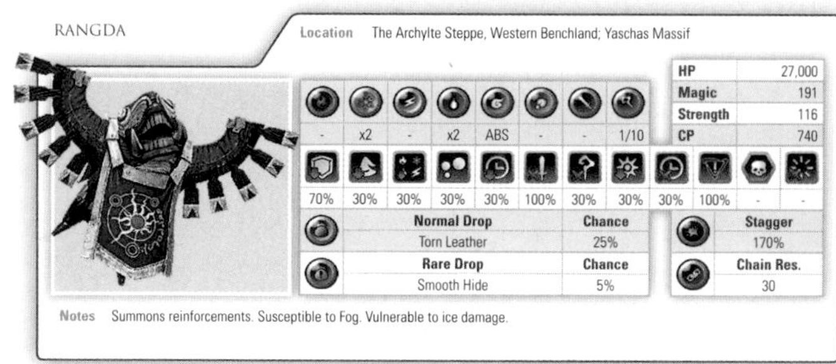

HP	Magic	Strength	CP
27,000	191	116	740

-	x2	-	x2	ABS	-	-	1/10

70%	30%	30%	30%	30%	100%	30%	30%	30%	100%	-	-

Normal Drop	Chance	Stagger
Torn Leather	25%	170%
Rare Drop	**Chance**	**Chain Res.**
Smooth Hide	5%	30

Notes Summons reinforcements. Susceptible to Fog. Vulnerable to ice damage.

ADROA

Location Yaschas Massif, The Ascendant Scarp (Mark 04); The Archylte Steppe, Central Expanse (Mark 11)

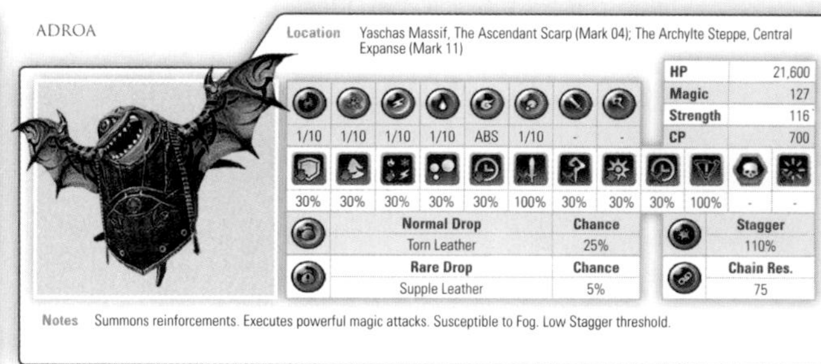

HP	Magic	Strength	CP
21,600	127	116	700

1/10	1/10	1/10	1/10	ABS	1/10	-	-

30%	30%	30%	30%	30%	100%	30%	30%	30%	100%	-	-

Normal Drop	Chance	Stagger
Torn Leather	25%	110%
Rare Drop	**Chance**	**Chain Res.**
Supple Leather	5%	75

Notes Summons reinforcements. Executes powerful magic attacks. Susceptible to Fog. Low Stagger threshold.

VERDELET

Location The Faultwarrens, Via Lunae (Mark 38); The Faultwarrens, Via Solis (Mark 40); The Faultwarrens, Titan's Throne (Mark 48)

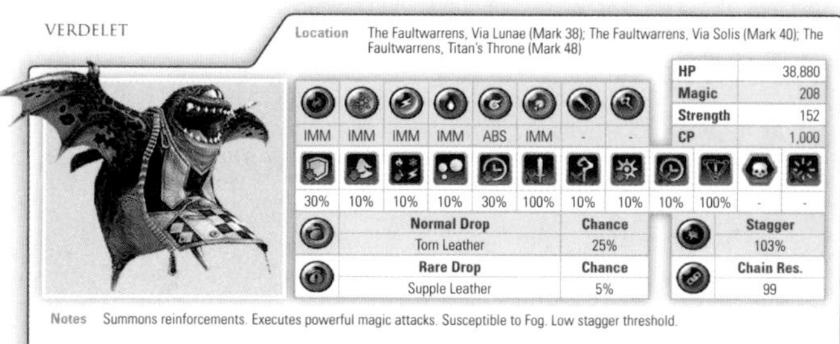

HP	Magic	Strength	CP
38,880	208	152	1,000

IMM	IMM	IMM	IMM	ABS	IMM	-	-

30%	10%	10%	10%	30%	100%	10%	10%	10%	100%	-	-

Normal Drop	Chance	Stagger
Torn Leather	25%	103%
Rare Drop	**Chance**	**Chain Res.**
Supple Leather	5%	99

Notes Summons reinforcements. Executes powerful magic attacks. Susceptible to Fog. Low stagger threshold.

INCUBUS

Location The Vile Peaks, Munitions Necropolis

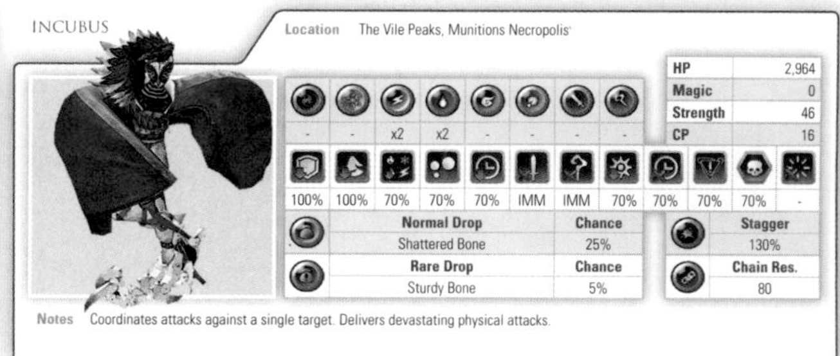

HP	Magic	Strength	CP
2,964	0	46	16

-	-	x2	x2	-	-	-	-

100%	100%	70%	70%	70%	IMM	IMM	70%	70%	70%	70%	-

Normal Drop	Chance	Stagger
Shattered Bone	25%	130%
Rare Drop	**Chance**	**Chain Res.**
Sturdy Bone	5%	80

Notes Coordinates attacks against a single target. Delivers devastating physical attacks.

SUCCUBUS

Location The Vile Peaks, Munitions Necropolis

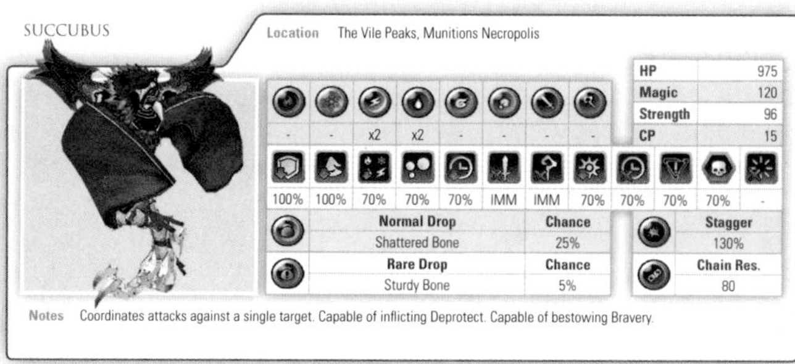

HP	Magic	Strength	CP
975	120	96	15

-	-	x2	x2	-	-	-	-

100%	100%	70%	70%	70%	IMM	IMM	70%	70%	70%	70%	-

Normal Drop	Chance	Stagger
Shattered Bone	25%	130%
Rare Drop	**Chance**	**Chain Res.**
Sturdy Bone	5%	80

Notes Coordinates attacks against a single target. Capable of inflicting Deprotect. Capable of bestowing Bravery.

SKATA'NE

Location The Fifth Ark, High Conflux; Mah'habara

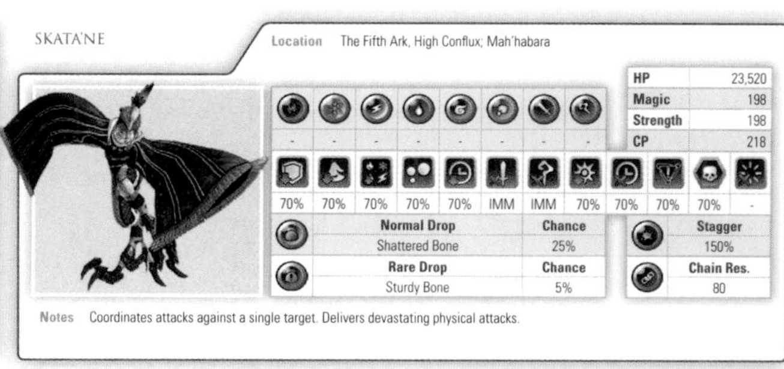

HP	Magic	Strength	CP
23,520	198	198	218

-	-	-	-	-	-	-	-

70%	70%	70%	70%	70%	IMM	IMM	70%	70%	70%	70%	-

Normal Drop	Chance	Stagger
Shattered Bone	25%	150%
Rare Drop	**Chance**	**Chain Res.**
Sturdy Bone	5%	80

Notes Coordinates attacks against a single target. Delivers devastating physical attacks.

STIKINI

Location The Fifth Ark, High Conflux

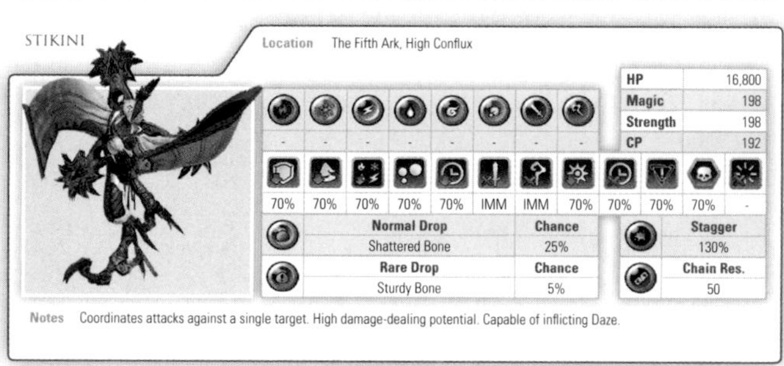

HP	Magic	Strength	CP
16,800	198	198	192

-	-	-	-	-	-	-	-

70%	70%	70%	70%	70%	IMM	IMM	70%	70%	70%	70%	-

Normal Drop	Chance	Stagger
Shattered Bone	25%	130%
Rare Drop	**Chance**	**Chain Res.**
Sturdy Bone	5%	50

Notes Coordinates attacks against a single target. High damage-dealing potential. Capable of inflicting Daze.

YAKSHA

Location Taejin's Tower, Fourth Tier; Mah'habara, An Asylum from Light

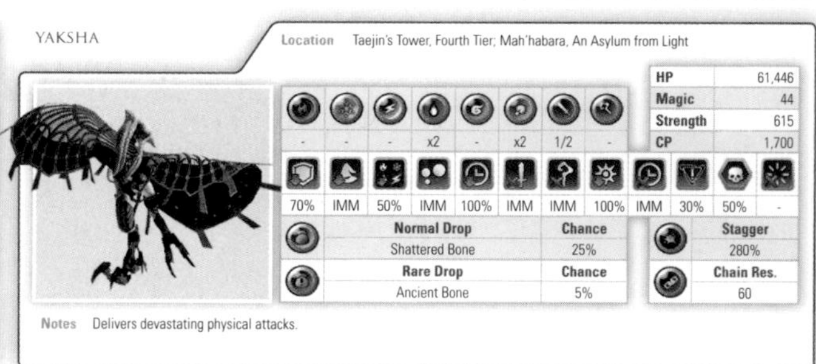

HP	Magic	Strength	CP
61,446	44	615	1,700

-	-	-	x2	-	x2	1/2	-

70%	IMM	50%	IMM	100%	IMM	IMM	100%	IMM	30%	50%	-

Normal Drop	Chance	Stagger
Shattered Bone	25%	280%
Rare Drop	**Chance**	**Chain Res.**
Ancient Bone	5%	60

Notes Delivers devastating physical attacks.

YAKSHINI

Location Taejin's Tower, Fifth Tier; Mah'habara, An Asylum from Light

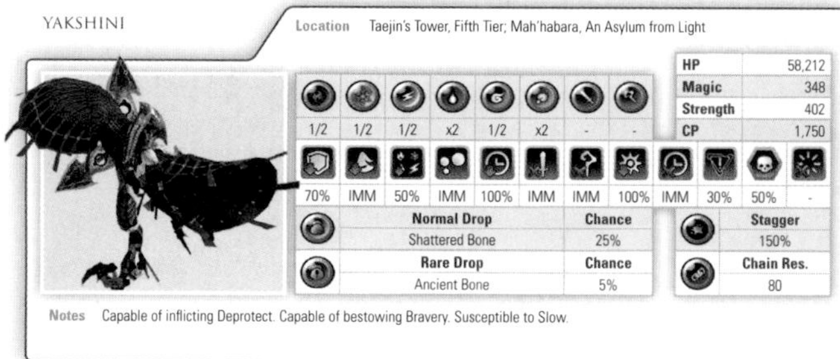

HP	Magic	Strength	CP
58,212	348	402	1,750

1/2	1/2	1/2	x2	1/2	x2	-	-

70%	IMM	50%	IMM	100%	IMM	IMM	100%	IMM	30%	50%	-

Normal Drop	Chance	Stagger
Shattered Bone	25%	150%
Rare Drop	**Chance**	**Chain Res.**
Ancient Bone	5%	80

Notes Capable of inflicting Deprotect. Capable of bestowing Bravery. Susceptible to Slow.

RAKSHASA

Location Vallis Media, Atzilut's Tears (Mark 08)

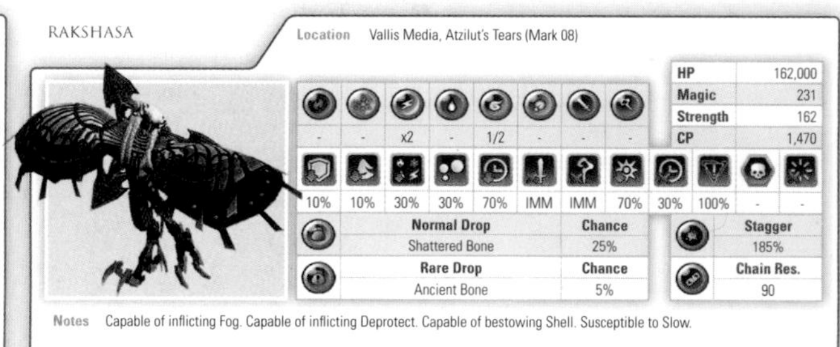

HP	Magic	Strength	CP
162,000	231	162	1,470

-	-	x2	-	1/2	-	-	-

10%	10%	30%	30%	70%	IMM	IMM	70%	30%	100%	-	-

Normal Drop	Chance	Stagger
Shattered Bone	25%	185%
Rare Drop	**Chance**	**Chain Res.**
Ancient Bone	5%	90

Notes Capable of inflicting Fog. Capable of inflicting Deprotect. Capable of bestowing Shell. Susceptible to Slow.

BARBED SPECTER

Location: The Gapra Whitewood, Field Trial Range N

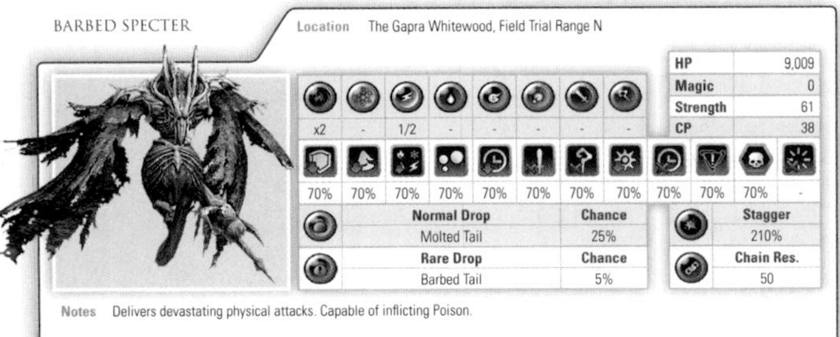

HP	Magic	Strength	CP
9,009	0	61	38

x2	-	1/2	-	-	-	-	-

70%	70%	70%	70%	70%	70%	70%	70%	70%	70%	70%	-

Normal Drop	Chance
Molted Tail	25%
Rare Drop	**Chance**
Barbed Tail	5%

Stagger	Chain Res.
210%	50

Notes: Delivers devastating physical attacks. Capable of inflicting Poison.

TRIFFID

Location: Yaschas Massif, The Tsubaddran Highlands; The Archylte Steppe, Aggra's Pasture

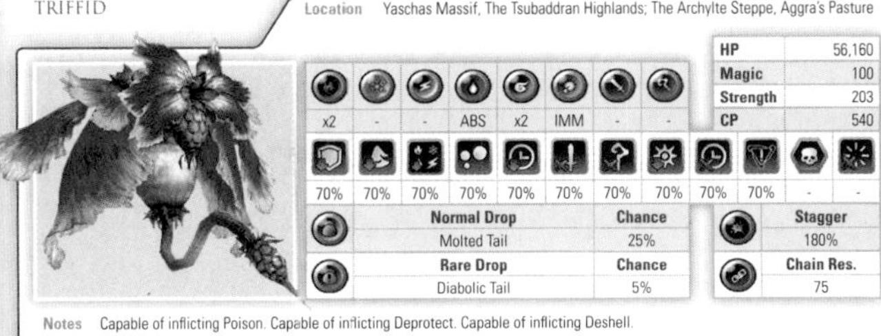
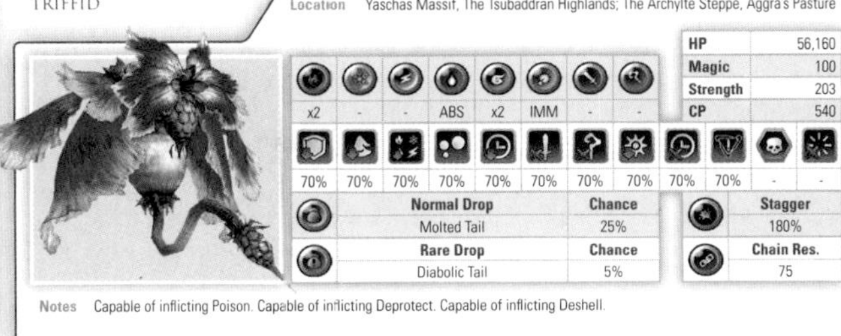

HP	Magic	Strength	CP
56,160	100	203	540

x2	-	-	ABS	x2	IMM	-	-

70%	70%	70%	70%	70%	70%	70%	70%	70%	70%	-	-

Normal Drop	Chance
Molted Tail	25%
Rare Drop	**Chance**
Diabolic Tail	5%

Stagger	Chain Res.
180%	75

Notes: Capable of inflicting Poison. Capable of inflicting Deprotect. Capable of inflicting Deshell.

MUSHUSSU

Location: Taejin's Tower, Fifth Tier (Mark 24)

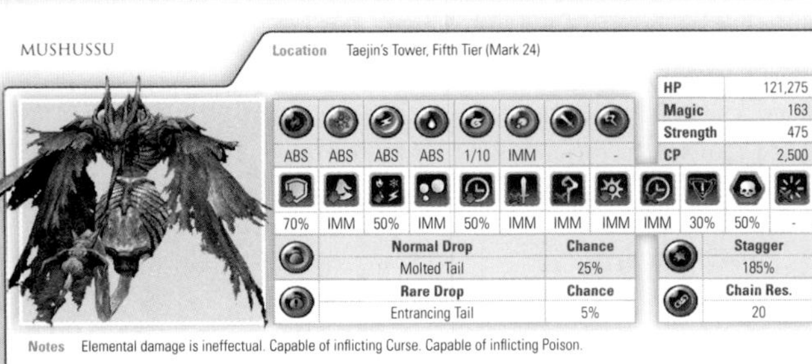

HP	Magic	Strength	CP
121,275	163	475	2,500

ABS	ABS	ABS	ABS	1/10	IMM	-	-

70%	IMM	50%	IMM	50%	IMM	IMM	IMM	IMM	30%	50%	-

Normal Drop	Chance
Molted Tail	25%
Rare Drop	**Chance**
Entrancing Tail	5%

Stagger	Chain Res.
185%	20

Notes: Elemental damage is ineffectual. Capable of inflicting Curse. Capable of inflicting Poison.

SCALEBEAST

Location: The Sunleth Waterscape, A Shimmering Sky

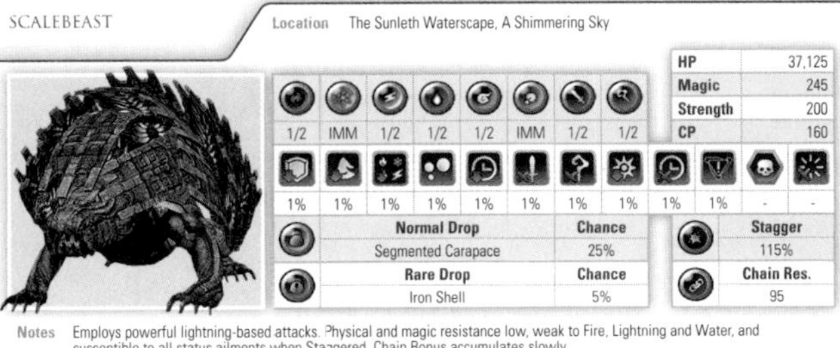

HP	Magic	Strength	CP
37,125	245	200	160

1/2	IMM	1/2	1/2	1/2	IMM	1/2	1/2

1%	1%	1%	1%	1%	1%	1%	1%	1%	1%	-	-

Normal Drop	Chance
Segmented Carapace	25%
Rare Drop	**Chance**
Iron Shell	5%

Stagger	Chain Res.
115%	95

Notes: Employs powerful lightning-based attacks. Physical and magic resistance low, weak to Fire, Lightning and Water, and susceptible to all status ailments when Staggered. Chain Bonus accumulates slowly.

NAVIDON

Location: The Archylte Steppe, Eastern Tors

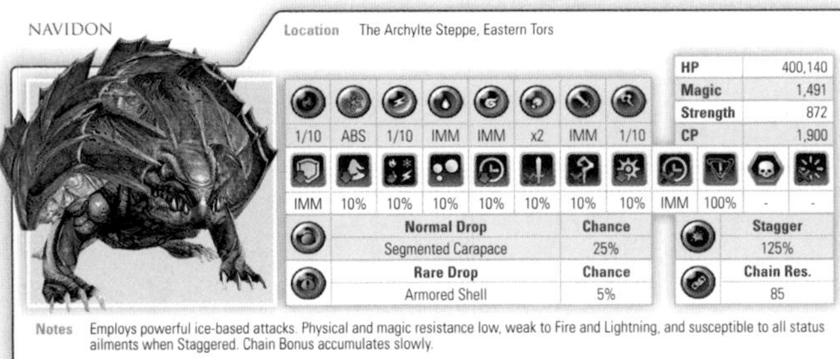

HP	Magic	Strength	CP
400,140	1,491	872	1,900

1/10	ABS	1/10	IMM	IMM	x2	IMM	1/10

IMM	10%	10%	10%	10%	10%	10%	10%	IMM	100%	-	-

Normal Drop	Chance
Segmented Carapace	25%
Rare Drop	**Chance**
Armored Shell	5%

Stagger	Chain Res.
125%	85

Notes: Employs powerful ice-based attacks. Physical and magic resistance low, weak to Fire and Lightning, and susceptible to all status ailments when Staggered. Chain Bonus accumulates slowly.

GURANGATCH

Location: Taejin's Tower, Second Tier (Mark 23); The Faultwarrens, Primeval Crossroads (Mark 35)

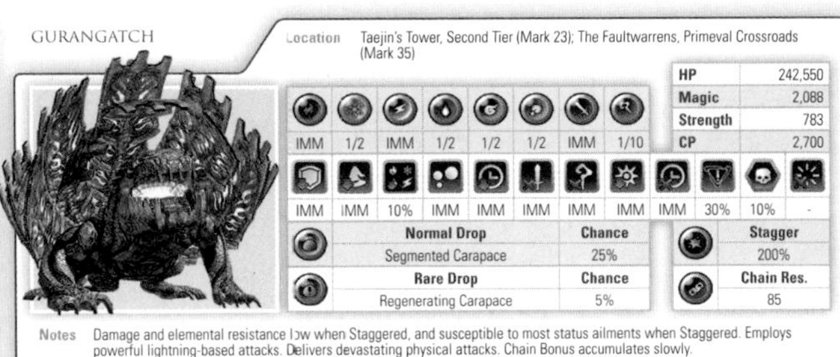

HP	Magic	Strength	CP
242,550	2,088	783	2,700

IMM	1/2	IMM	1/2	1/2	1/2	IMM	1/10

IMM	IMM	10%	IMM	IMM	IMM	IMM	IMM	IMM	30%	10%	-

Normal Drop	Chance
Segmented Carapace	25%
Rare Drop	**Chance**
Regenerating Carapace	5%

Stagger	Chain Res.
200%	85

Notes: Damage and elemental resistance low when Staggered, and susceptible to most status ailments when Staggered. Employs powerful lightning-based attacks. Delivers devastating physical attacks. Chain Bonus accumulates slowly.

CRAWLER

Location: The Gapra Whitewood, Bioweapon Research Site D

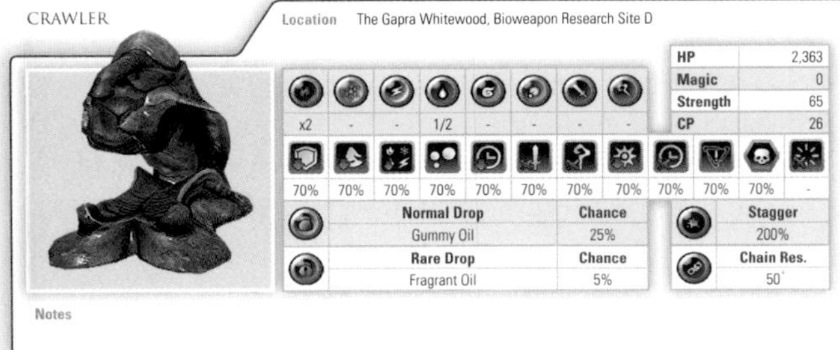

HP	Magic	Strength	CP
2,363	0	65	26

x2	-	-	1/2	-	-	-	-

70%	70%	70%	70%	70%	70%	70%	70%	70%	70%	70%	-

Normal Drop	Chance
Gummy Oil	25%
Rare Drop	**Chance**
Fragrant Oil	5%

Stagger	Chain Res.
200%	50

Notes

NOCTILUCALE

Location: The Fifth Ark, Lower Traverse

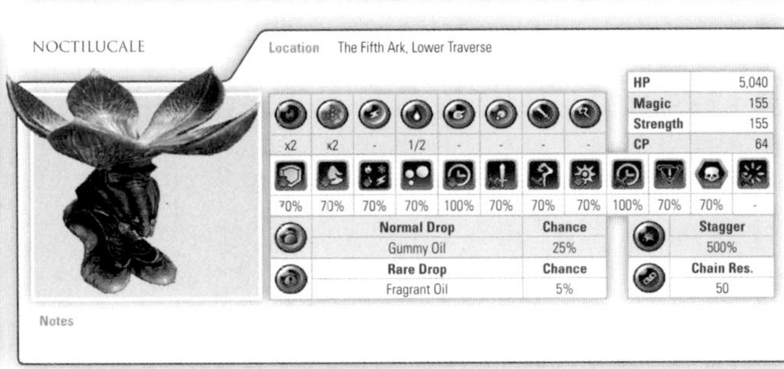

HP	Magic	Strength	CP
5,040	155	155	64

x2	x2	-	1/2	-	-	-	-

70%	70%	70%	70%	100%	70%	70%	70%	100%	70%	70%	-

Normal Drop	Chance
Gummy Oil	25%
Rare Drop	**Chance**
Fragrant Oil	5%

Stagger	Chain Res.
500%	50

Notes

ALRAUNE

Location: Vallis Media, Fingers of Stone; Yaschas Massif

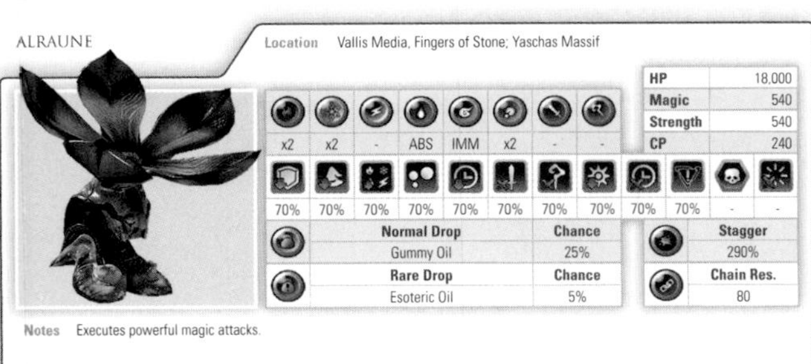

HP	Magic	Strength	CP
18,000	540	540	240

x2	x2	-	ABS	IMM	x2	-	-

70%	70%	70%	70%	70%	70%	70%	70%	70%	70%	-	-

Normal Drop	Chance
Gummy Oil	25%
Rare Drop	**Chance**
Esoteric Oil	5%

Stagger	Chain Res.
290%	80

Notes: Executes powerful magic attacks.

RAFFLESIA

Location: The Faultwarrens, A Dance of Light (Mark 37)

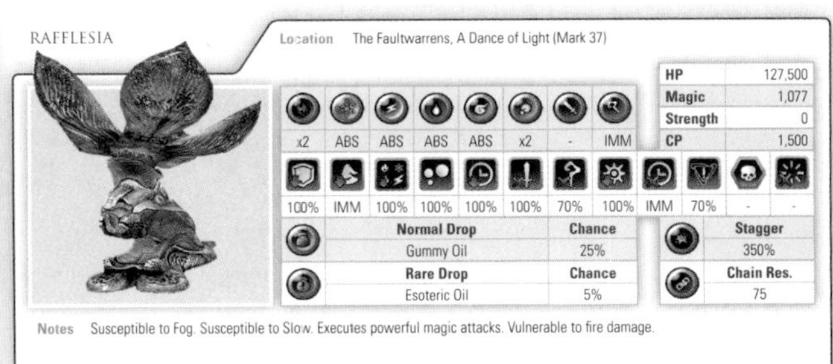

HP	Magic	Strength	CP
127,500	1,077	0	1,500

x2	ABS	ABS	ABS	ABS	x2	-	IMM

100%	IMM	100%	100%	100%	100%	70%	100%	IMM	70%	-	-

Normal Drop	Chance
Gummy Oil	25%
Rare Drop	**Chance**
Esoteric Oil	5%

Stagger	Chain Res.
350%	75

Notes: Susceptible to Fog. Susceptible to Slow. Executes powerful magic attacks. Vulnerable to fire damage.

WYVERN

Location: The Sunleth Waterscape, Rain-spotted Vale

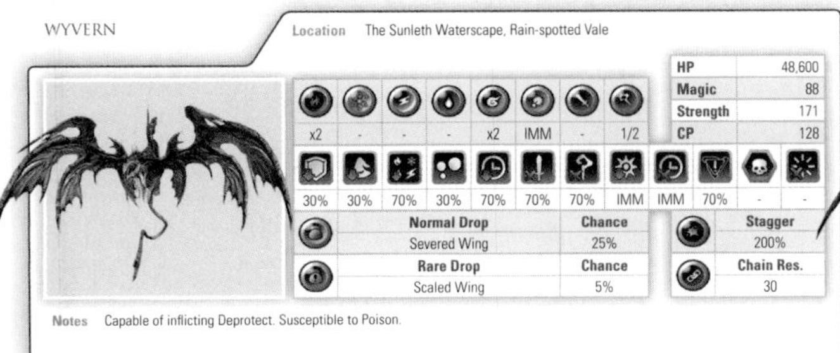

HP	Magic	Strength	CP
48,600	88	171	128

x2	-	-	-	x2	IMM	-	1/2

30%	30%	70%	30%	70%	70%	70%	IMM	IMM	70%	-	-

Normal Drop	Chance
Severed Wing	25%
Rare Drop	**Chance**
Scaled Wing	5%

Stagger	Chain Res.
200%	30

Notes: Capable of inflicting Deprotect. Susceptible to Poison.

SVAROG

Location: Yaschas Massif, The Ascendant Scarp

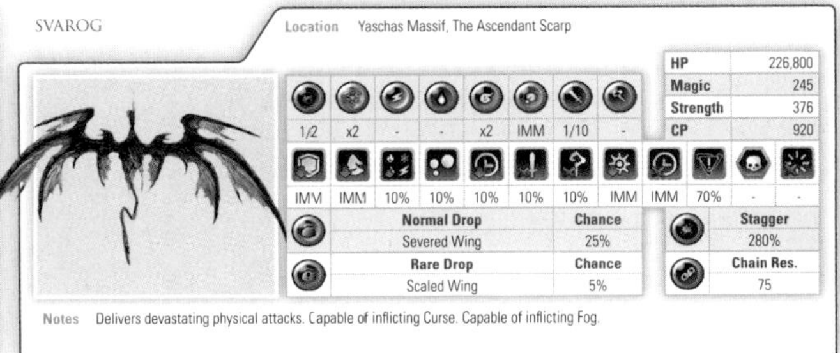

HP	Magic	Strength	CP
226,800	245	376	920

1/2	x2	-	-	x2	IMM	1/10	-

IMM	IMM	10%	10%	10%	10%	10%	IMM	IMM	70%	-	-

Normal Drop	Chance
Severed Wing	25%
Rare Drop	**Chance**
Scaled Wing	5%

Stagger	Chain Res.
280%	75

Notes: Delivers devastating physical attacks. Capable of inflicting Curse. Capable of inflicting Fog.

AMPHISBAENA

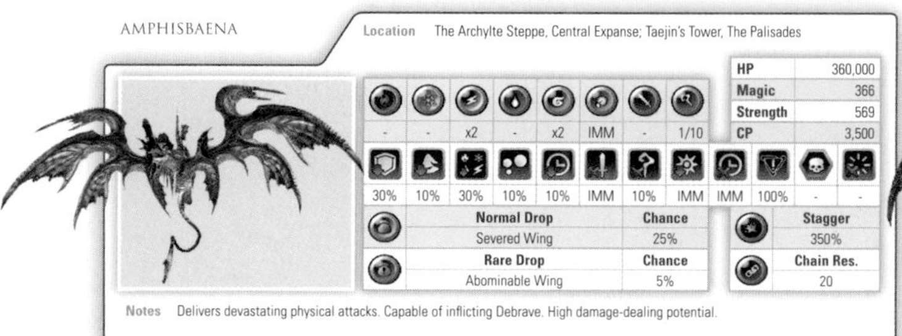

Location The Archylte Steppe, Central Expanse; Taejin's Tower, The Palisades

HP	360,000
Magic	366
Strength	569
CP	3,500

-	-	x2	-	x2	IMM	-	1/10

30%	10%	30%	10%	10%	IMM	10%	IMM	IMM	100%	-	-

Normal Drop	Chance	Stagger
Severed Wing	25%	350%
Rare Drop	**Chance**	**Chain Res.**
Abominable Wing	5%	20

Notes Delivers devastating physical attacks. Capable of inflicting Debrave. High damage-dealing potential.

ZIRNITRA

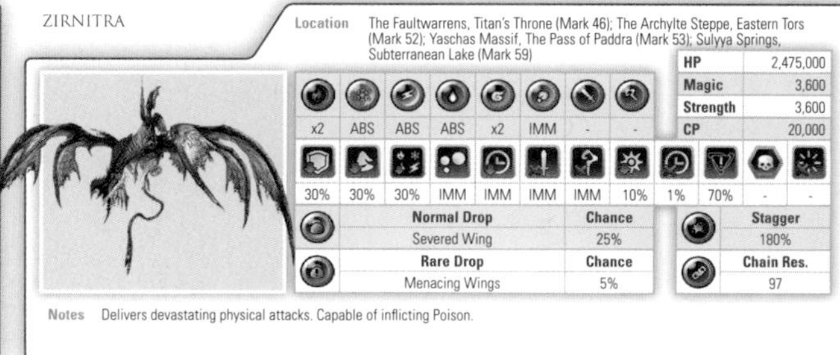

Location The Faultwarrens, Titan's Throne (Mark 46); The Archylte Steppe, Eastern Tors (Mark 52); Yaschas Massif, The Pass of Paddra (Mark 53); Sulyya Springs, Subterranean Lake (Mark 59)

HP	2,475,000
Magic	3,600
Strength	3,600
CP	20,000

x2	ABS	ABS	ABS	x2	IMM	-	-

30%	30%	30%	IMM	IMM	IMM	IMM	10%	1%	70%	-	-

Normal Drop	Chance	Stagger
Severed Wing	25%	180%
Rare Drop	**Chance**	**Chain Res.**
Menacing Wings	5%	97

Notes Delivers devastating physical attacks. Capable of inflicting Poison.

ENKI

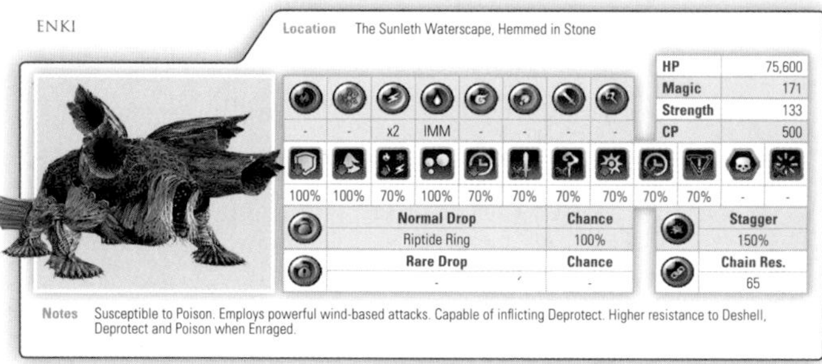

Location The Sunleth Waterscape, Hemmed in Stone

HP	75,600
Magic	171
Strength	133
CP	500

-	-	x2	IMM	-	-	-	-

100%	100%	70%	100%	70%	70%	70%	70%	70%	70%	-	-

Normal Drop	Chance	Stagger
Riptide Ring	100%	150%
Rare Drop	**Chance**	**Chain Res.**
-	-	65

Notes Susceptible to Poison. Employs powerful wind-based attacks. Capable of inflicting Deprotect. Higher resistance to Deshell, Deprotect and Poison when Enraged.

ENLIL

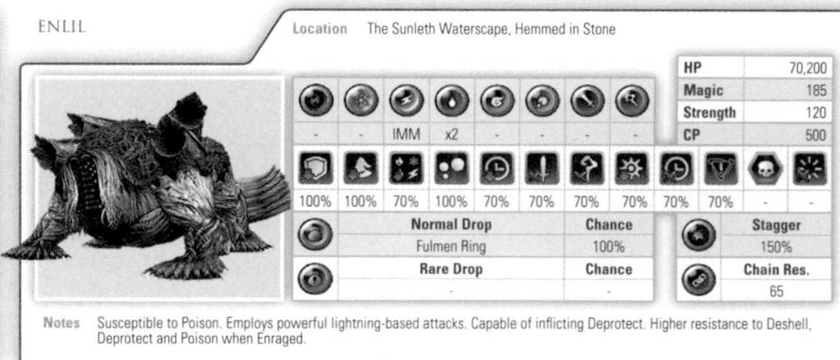

Location The Sunleth Waterscape, Hemmed in Stone

HP	70,200
Magic	185
Strength	120
CP	500

-	-	IMM	x2	-	-	-	-

100%	100%	70%	100%	70%	70%	70%	70%	70%	70%	-	-

Normal Drop	Chance	Stagger
Fulmen Ring	100%	150%
Rare Drop	**Chance**	**Chain Res.**
-	-	65

Notes Susceptible to Poison. Employs powerful lightning-based attacks. Capable of inflicting Deprotect. Higher resistance to Deshell, Deprotect and Poison when Enraged.

BANDERSNATCH

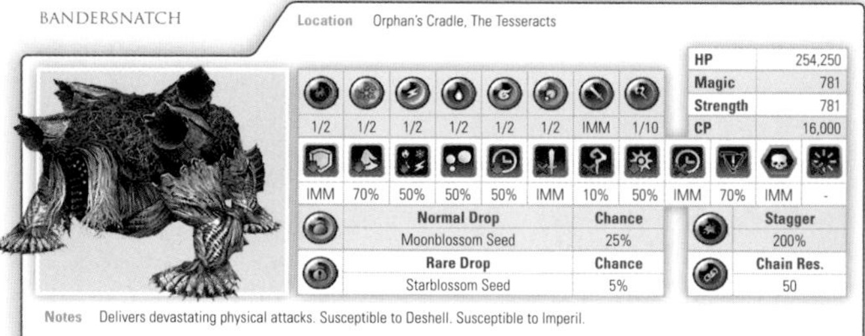

Location Orphan's Cradle, The Tesseracts

HP	254,250
Magic	781
Strength	781
CP	16,000

1/2	1/2	1/2	1/2	1/2	1/2	IMM	1/10

IMM	70%	50%	50%	50%	IMM	10%	50%	IMM	70%	IMM	-

Normal Drop	Chance	Stagger
Moonblossom Seed	25%	200%
Rare Drop	**Chance**	**Chain Res.**
Starblossom Seed	5%	50

Notes Delivers devastating physical attacks. Susceptible to Deshell. Susceptible to Imperil.

JABBERWOCKY

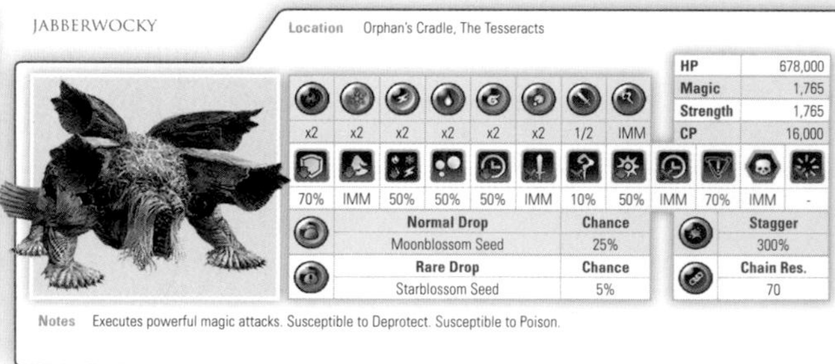

Location Orphan's Cradle, The Tesseracts

HP	678,000
Magic	1,765
Strength	1,765
CP	16,000

x2	x2	x2	x2	x2	x2	1/2	IMM

70%	IMM	50%	50%	50%	IMM	10%	50%	IMM	70%	IMM	-

Normal Drop	Chance	Stagger
Moonblossom Seed	25%	300%
Rare Drop	**Chance**	**Chain Res.**
Starblossom Seed	5%	70

Notes Executes powerful magic attacks. Susceptible to Deprotect. Susceptible to Poison.

ADAMANTORTOISE

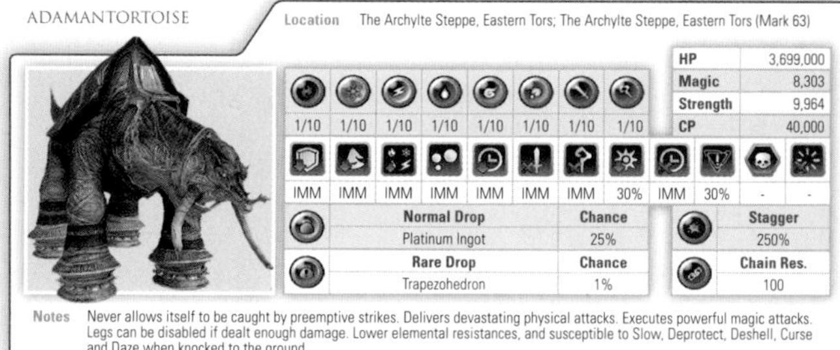

Location The Archylte Steppe, Eastern Tors; The Archylte Steppe, Eastern Tors (Mark 63)

HP	3,699,000
Magic	8,303
Strength	9,964
CP	40,000

1/10	1/10	1/10	1/10	1/10	1/10	1/10	1/10

IMM	IMM	IMM	IMM	IMM	IMM	IMM	30%	IMM	30%	-	-

Normal Drop	Chance	Stagger
Platinum Ingot	25%	250%
Rare Drop	**Chance**	**Chain Res.**
Trapezohedron	1%	100

Notes Never allows itself to be caught by preemptive strikes. Delivers devastating physical attacks. Executes powerful magic attacks. Legs can be disabled if dealt enough damage. Lower elemental resistances, and susceptible to Slow, Deprotect, Deshell, Curse and Daze when knocked to the ground.

ADAMANTORTOISE (LEGS)

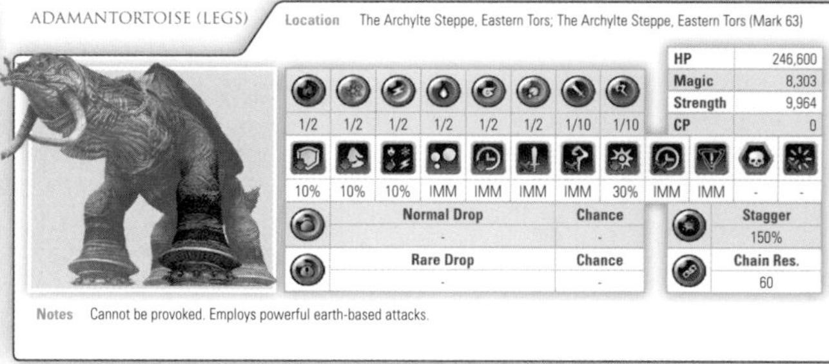

Location The Archylte Steppe, Eastern Tors; The Archylte Steppe, Eastern Tors (Mark 63)

HP	246,600
Magic	8,303
Strength	9,964
CP	0

1/2	1/2	1/2	1/2	1/2	1/2	1/10	1/10

10%	10%	10%	IMM	IMM	IMM	IMM	30%	IMM	IMM	-	-

Normal Drop	Chance	Stagger
-	-	150%
Rare Drop	**Chance**	**Chain Res.**
-	-	60

Notes Cannot be provoked. Employs powerful earth-based attacks.

ADAMANCHELID

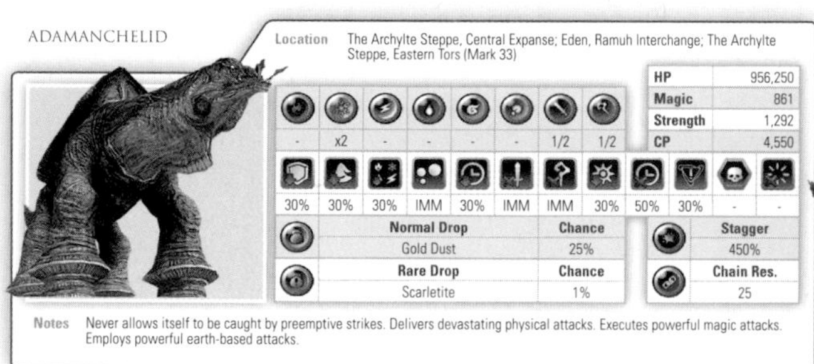

Location The Archylte Steppe, Central Expanse; Eden, Ramuh Interchange; The Archylte Steppe, Eastern Tors (Mark 33)

HP	956,250
Magic	861
Strength	1,292
CP	4,550

-	x2	-	-	-	-	1/2	1/2

30%	30%	30%	IMM	30%	IMM	IMM	30%	50%	30%	-	-

Normal Drop	Chance	Stagger
Gold Dust	25%	450%
Rare Drop	**Chance**	**Chain Res.**
Scarletite	1%	25

Notes Never allows itself to be caught by preemptive strikes. Delivers devastating physical attacks. Executes powerful magic attacks. Employs powerful earth-based attacks.

ADAMANTOISE

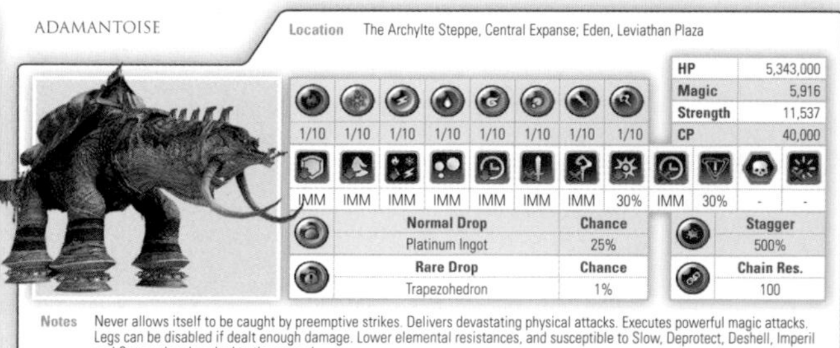

Location The Archylte Steppe, Central Expanse; Eden, Leviathan Plaza

HP	5,343,000
Magic	5,916
Strength	11,537
CP	40,000

1/10	1/10	1/10	1/10	1/10	1/10	1/10	1/10

IMM	IMM	IMM	IMM	IMM	IMM	IMM	30%	IMM	30%	-	-

Normal Drop	Chance	Stagger
Platinum Ingot	25%	500%
Rare Drop	**Chance**	**Chain Res.**
Trapezohedron	1%	100

Notes Never allows itself to be caught by preemptive strikes. Delivers devastating physical attacks. Executes powerful magic attacks. Legs can be disabled if dealt enough damage. Lower elemental resistances, and susceptible to Slow, Deprotect, Deshell, Imperil and Curse when knocked to the ground.

ADAMANTOISE (LEGS)

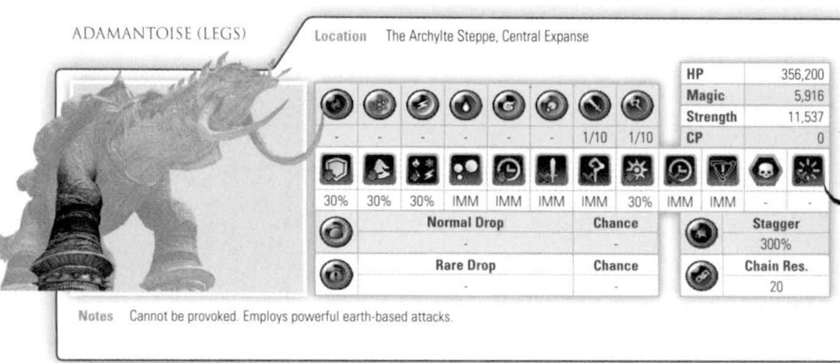

Location The Archylte Steppe, Central Expanse

HP	356,200
Magic	5,916
Strength	11,537
CP	0

-	-	-	-	-	-	1/10	1/10

30%	30%	30%	IMM	IMM	IMM	IMM	30%	IMM	IMM	-	-

Normal Drop	Chance	Stagger
-	-	300%
Rare Drop	**Chance**	**Chain Res.**
-	-	20

Notes Cannot be provoked. Employs powerful earth-based attacks.

LONG GUI

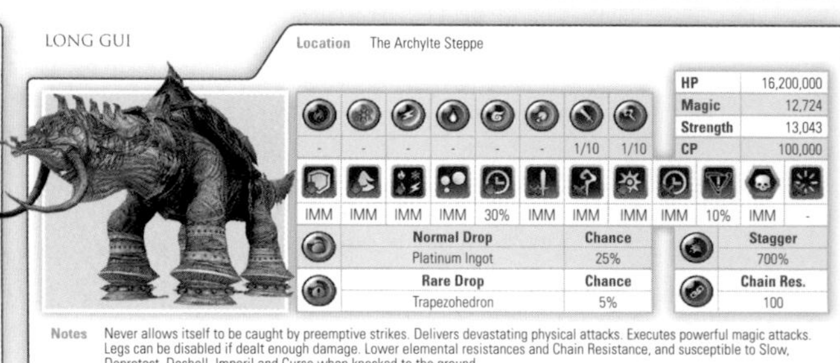

Location The Archylte Steppe

HP	16,200,000
Magic	12,724
Strength	13,043
CP	100,000

-	-	-	-	-	-	1/10	1/10

IMM	IMM	IMM	IMM	30%	IMM	IMM	IMM	IMM	10%	IMM	-

Normal Drop	Chance	Stagger
Platinum Ingot	25%	700%
Rare Drop	**Chance**	**Chain Res.**
Trapezohedron	5%	100

Notes Never allows itself to be caught by preemptive strikes. Delivers devastating physical attacks. Executes powerful magic attacks. Legs can be disabled if dealt enough damage. Lower elemental resistances and Chain Resistance, and susceptible to Slow, Deprotect, Deshell, Imperil and Curse when knocked to the ground.

QUICKSTART
WALKTHROUGH
STRATEGY & ANALYSIS
INVENTORY
BESTIARY
EXTRAS
INTRODUCTION
CLASSIFICATION
SOLDIERS
MILITARIZED UNITS
FERAL CREATURES
PULSE AUTOMATA
CIE'TH
OTHERS

LONG GUI (LEGS)

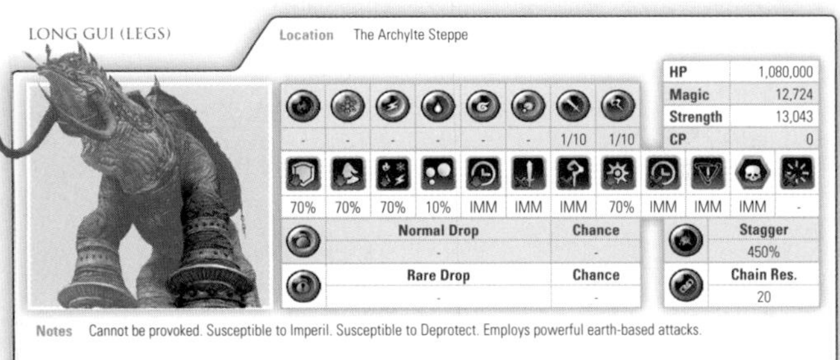

Location: The Archylte Steppe

HP	Magic	Strength	CP
1,080,000	12,724	13,043	0

-	-	-	-	-	-	1/10	1/10

70%	70%	70%	10%	IMM	IMM	IMM	70%	IMM	IMM	IMM	-

Normal Drop	Chance	Stagger
-	-	450%
Rare Drop	**Chance**	**Chain Res.**
-	-	20

Notes: Cannot be provoked. Susceptible to Imperil. Susceptible to Deprotect. Employs powerful earth-based attacks.

SHAOLONG GUI

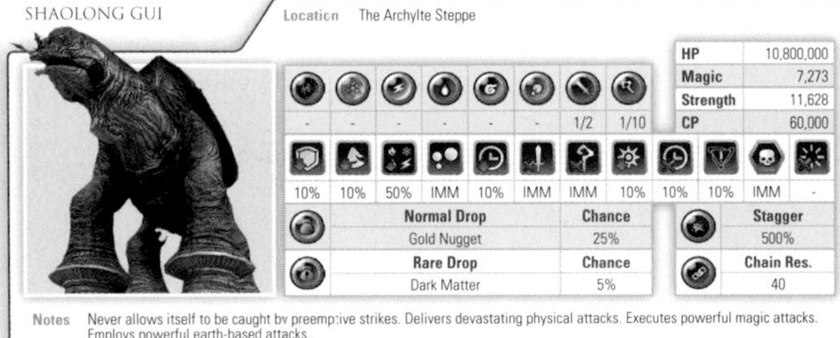

Location: The Archylte Steppe

HP	Magic	Strength	CP
10,800,000	7,273	11,628	60,000

-	-	-	-	-	-	1/2	1/10

10%	10%	50%	IMM	10%	IMM	IMM	10%	10%	10%	IMM	-

Normal Drop	Chance	Stagger
Gold Nugget	25%	500%
Rare Drop	**Chance**	**Chain Res.**
Dark Matter	5%	40

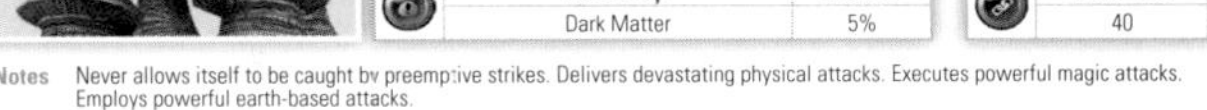

Notes: Never allows itself to be caught by preemptive strikes. Delivers devastating physical attacks. Executes powerful magic attacks. Employs powerful earth-based attacks.

FLAN

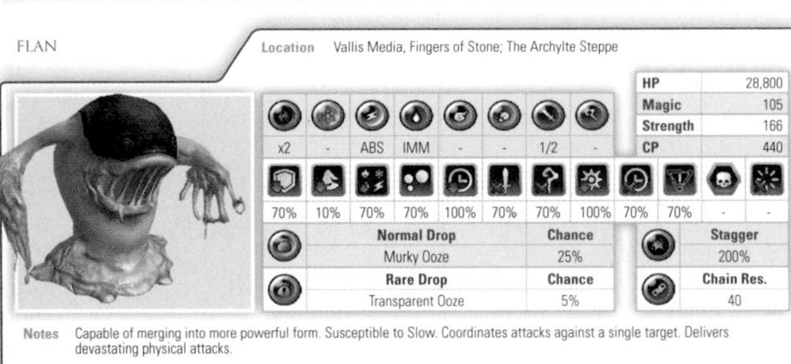

Location: Vallis Media, Fingers of Stone; The Archylte Steppe

HP	Magic	Strength	CP
28,800	105	166	440

x2	-	ABS	IMM	-	-	1/2	-

70%	10%	70%	70%	100%	70%	70%	100%	70%	70%	-	-

Normal Drop	Chance	Stagger
Murky Ooze	25%	200%
Rare Drop	**Chance**	**Chain Res.**
Transparent Ooze	5%	40

Notes: Capable of merging into more powerful form. Susceptible to Slow. Coordinates attacks against a single target. Delivers devastating physical attacks.

DIRE FLAN

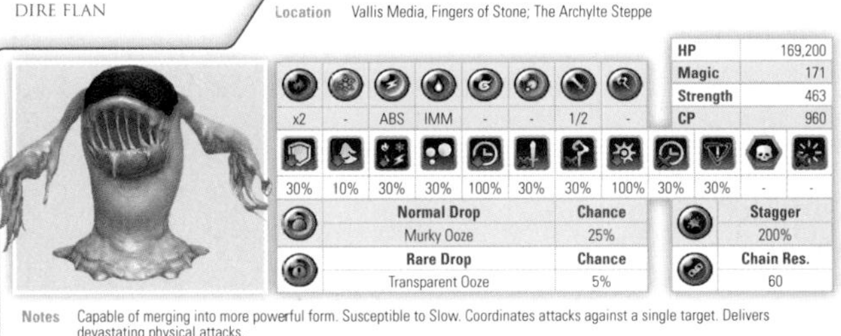

Location: Vallis Media, Fingers of Stone; The Archylte Steppe

HP	Magic	Strength	CP
169,200	171	463	960

x2	-	ABS	IMM	-	-	1/2	-

30%	10%	30%	30%	100%	30%	30%	100%	30%	30%	-	-

Normal Drop	Chance	Stagger
Murky Ooze	25%	200%
Rare Drop	**Chance**	**Chain Res.**
Transparent Ooze	5%	60

Notes: Capable of merging into more powerful form. Susceptible to Slow. Coordinates attacks against a single target. Delivers devastating physical attacks.

MONSTROUS FLAN

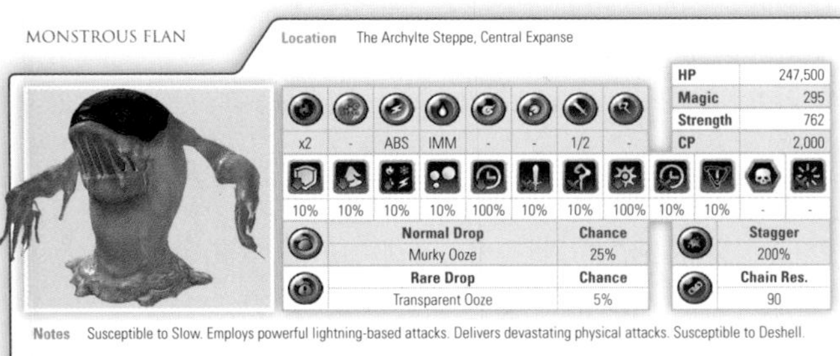

Location: The Archylte Steppe, Central Expanse

HP	Magic	Strength	CP
247,500	295	762	2,000

x2	-	ABS	IMM	-	-	1/2	-

10%	10%	10%	10%	100%	10%	10%	100%	10%	10%	-	-

Normal Drop	Chance	Stagger
Murky Ooze	25%	200%
Rare Drop	**Chance**	**Chain Res.**
Transparent Ooze	5%	90

Notes: Susceptible to Slow. Employs powerful lightning-based attacks. Delivers devastating physical attacks. Susceptible to Deshell.

RUST PUDDING

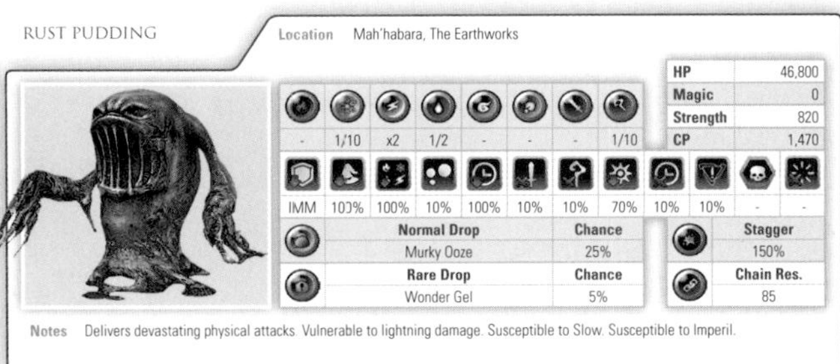

Location: Mah'habara, The Earthworks

HP	Magic	Strength	CP
46,800	0	820	1,470

-	1/10	x2	1/2	-	-	-	1/10

IMM	100%	100%	10%	100%	10%	10%	70%	10%	10%	-	-

Normal Drop	Chance	Stagger
Murky Ooze	25%	150%
Rare Drop	**Chance**	**Chain Res.**
Wonder Gel	5%	85

Notes: Delivers devastating physical attacks. Vulnerable to lightning damage. Susceptible to Slow. Susceptible to Imperil.

FERRUGINOUS PUDDING

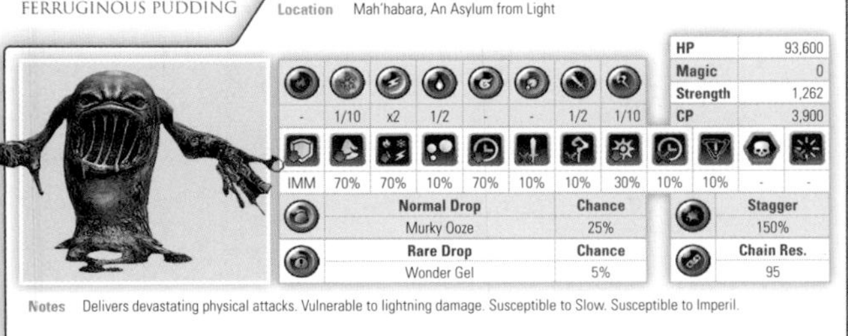

Location: Mah'habara, An Asylum from Light

HP	Magic	Strength	CP
93,600	0	1,262	3,900

-	1/10	x2	1/2	-	-	1/2	1/10

IMM	70%	70%	10%	70%	10%	10%	30%	10%	10%	-	-

Normal Drop	Chance	Stagger
Murky Ooze	25%	150%
Rare Drop	**Chance**	**Chain Res.**
Wonder Gel	5%	95

Notes: Delivers devastating physical attacks. Vulnerable to lightning damage. Susceptible to Slow. Susceptible to Imperil.

CORROSIVE CUSTARD

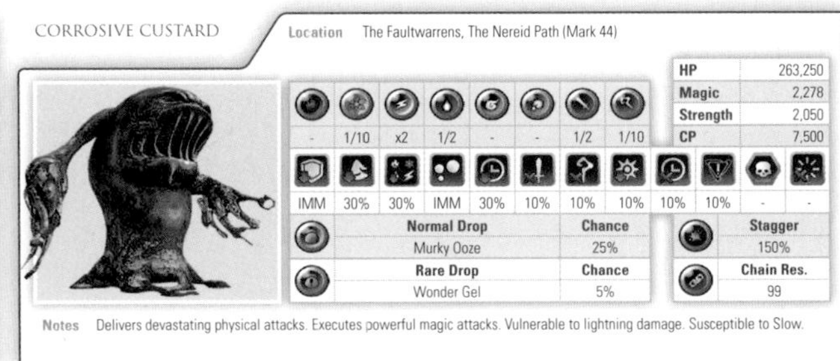

Location: The Faultwarrens, The Nereid Path (Mark 44)

HP	Magic	Strength	CP
263,250	2,278	2,050	7,500

-	1/10	x2	1/2	-	-	1/2	1/10

IMM	30%	30%	IMM	30%	10%	10%	10%	10%	10%	-	-

Normal Drop	Chance	Stagger
Murky Ooze	25%	150%
Rare Drop	**Chance**	**Chain Res.**
Wonder Gel	5%	99

Notes: Delivers devastating physical attacks. Executes powerful magic attacks. Vulnerable to lightning damage. Susceptible to Slow.

FLANDRAGORA

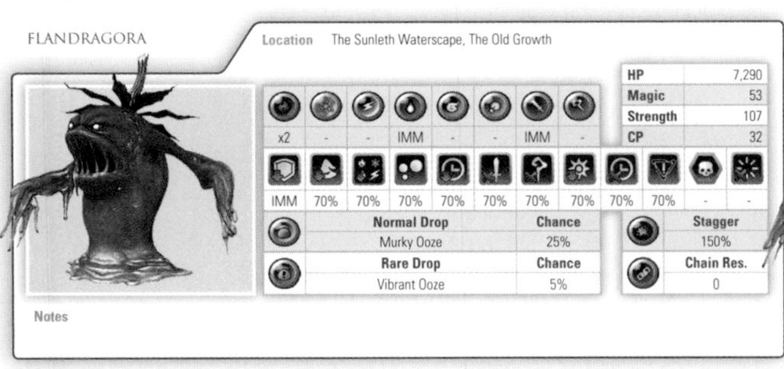

Location: The Sunleth Waterscape, The Old Growth

HP	Magic	Strength	CP
7,290	53	107	32

x2	-	-	IMM	-	-	IMM	-

IMM	70%	70%	70%	70%	70%	70%	70%	70%	70%	-	-

Normal Drop	Chance	Stagger
Murky Ooze	25%	150%
Rare Drop	**Chance**	**Chain Res.**
Vibrant Ooze	5%	0

Notes:

HYBRID FLORA

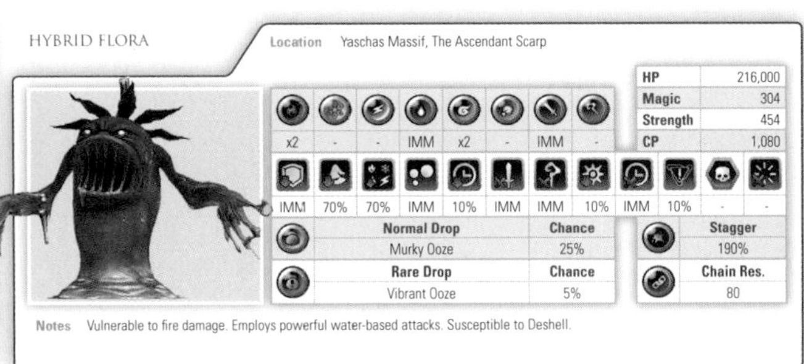

Location: Yaschas Massif, The Ascendant Scarp

HP	Magic	Strength	CP
216,000	304	454	1,080

x2	-	-	IMM	x2	-	IMM	-

IMM	70%	70%	IMM	10%	IMM	IMM	10%	IMM	10%	-	-

Normal Drop	Chance	Stagger
Murky Ooze	25%	190%
Rare Drop	**Chance**	**Chain Res.**
Vibrant Ooze	5%	80

Notes: Vulnerable to fire damage. Employs powerful water-based attacks. Susceptible to Deshell.

PHOSPHORIC OOZE

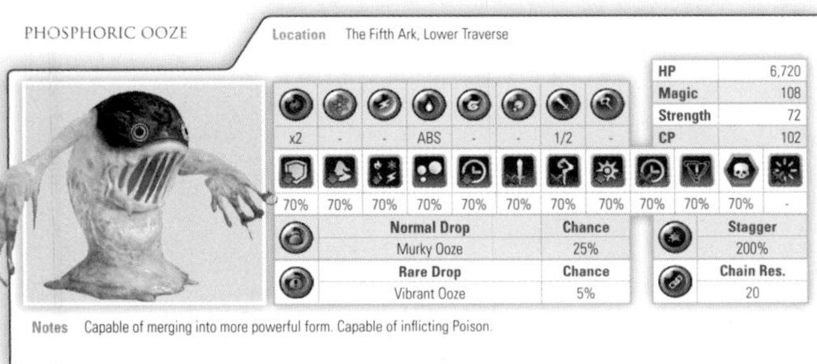

Location: The Fifth Ark, Lower Traverse

HP	Magic	Strength	CP
6,720	108	72	102

x2	-	-	ABS	-	-	1/2	-

70%	70%	70%	70%	70%	70%	70%	70%	70%	70%	70%	-

Normal Drop	Chance	Stagger
Murky Ooze	25%	200%
Rare Drop	**Chance**	**Chain Res.**
Vibrant Ooze	5%	20

Notes: Capable of merging into more powerful form. Capable of inflicting Poison.

ALCHEMIC OOZE

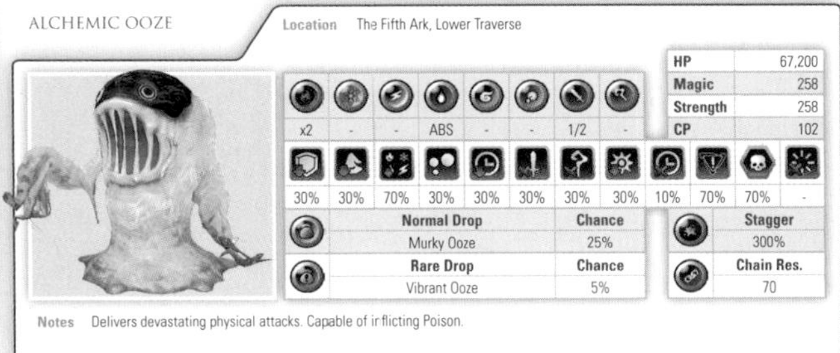

Location: The Fifth Ark, Lower Traverse

HP	Magic	Strength	CP
67,200	258	258	102

x2	-	-	ABS	-	-	1/2	-

30%	30%	70%	30%	30%	30%	30%	30%	10%	70%	70%	-

Normal Drop	Chance	Stagger
Murky Ooze	25%	300%
Rare Drop	**Chance**	**Chain Res.**
Vibrant Ooze	5%	70

Notes: Delivers devastating physical attacks. Capable of inflicting Poison.

GELATITAN

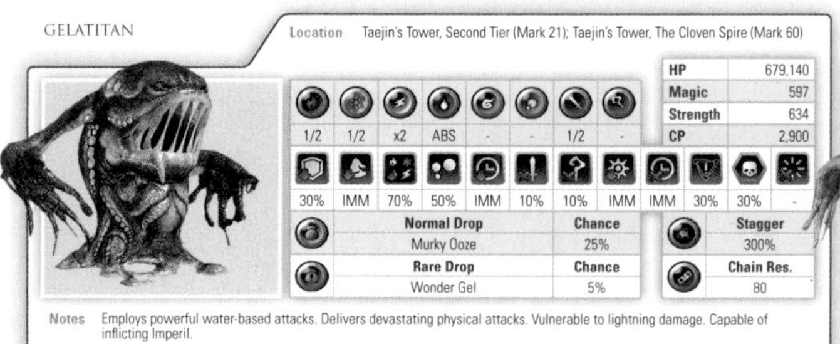

Location Taejin's Tower, Second Tier (Mark 21); Taejin's Tower, The Cloven Spire (Mark 60)

HP	Magic	Strength	CP
679,140	597	634	2,900

1/2	1/2	x2	ABS	-	-	1/2	-

30%	IMM	70%	50%	IMM	10%	10%	IMM	IMM	30%	30%	-

Normal Drop	Chance	Rare Drop	Chance	Stagger	Chain Res.
Murky Ooze	25%	Wonder Gel	5%	300%	80

Notes Employs powerful water-based attacks. Delivers devastating physical attacks. Vulnerable to lightning damage. Capable of inflicting Imperil.

ECTOPUDDING

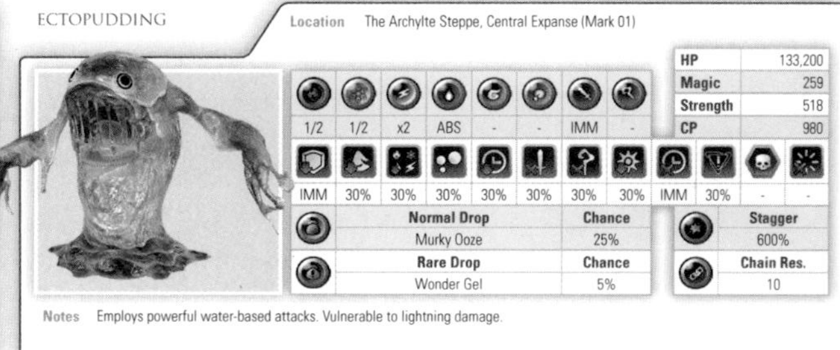

Location The Archylte Steppe, Central Expanse (Mark 01)

HP	Magic	Strength	CP
133,200	259	518	980

1/2	1/2	x2	ABS	-	-	IMM	-

IMM	30%	30%	30%	30%	30%	30%	30%	IMM	30%	-	-

Normal Drop	Chance	Rare Drop	Chance	Stagger	Chain Res.
Murky Ooze	25%	Wonder Gel	5%	600%	10

Notes Employs powerful water-based attacks. Vulnerable to lightning damage.

FERAL BEHEMOTH

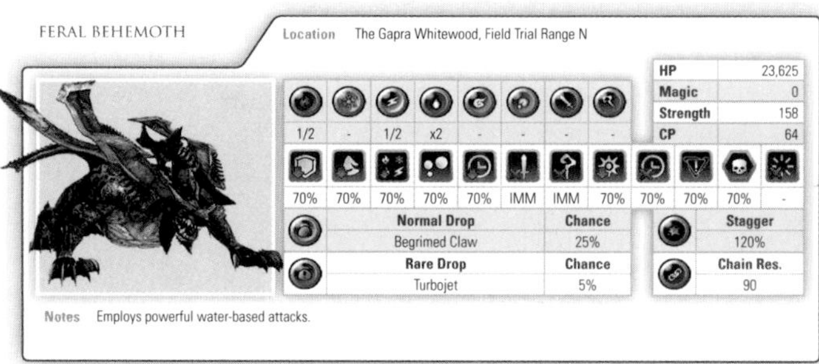

Location The Gapra Whitewood, Field Trial Range N

HP	Magic	Strength	CP
23,625	0	158	64

1/2	-	1/2	x2	-	-	-	-

70%	70%	70%	70%	70%	IMM	IMM	70%	70%	70%	70%	-

Normal Drop	Chance	Rare Drop	Chance	Stagger	Chain Res.
Begrimed Claw	25%	Turbojet	5%	120%	90

Notes Employs powerful water-based attacks.

GREATER BEHEMOTH

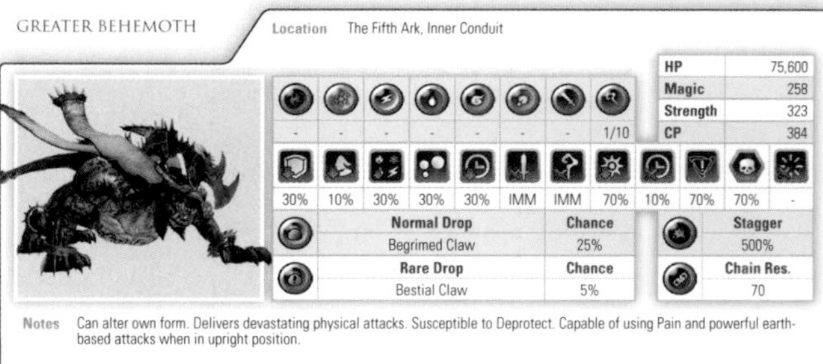

Location The Fifth Ark, Inner Conduit

HP	Magic	Strength	CP
75,600	258	323	384

-	-	-	-	-	-	-	1/10

30%	10%	30%	30%	30%	IMM	IMM	70%	10%	70%	70%	-

Normal Drop	Chance	Rare Drop	Chance	Stagger	Chain Res.
Begrimed Claw	25%	Bestial Claw	5%	500%	70

Notes Can alter own form. Delivers devastating physical attacks. Susceptible to Deprotect. Capable of using Pain and powerful earth-based attacks when in upright position.

KAISER BEHEMOTH

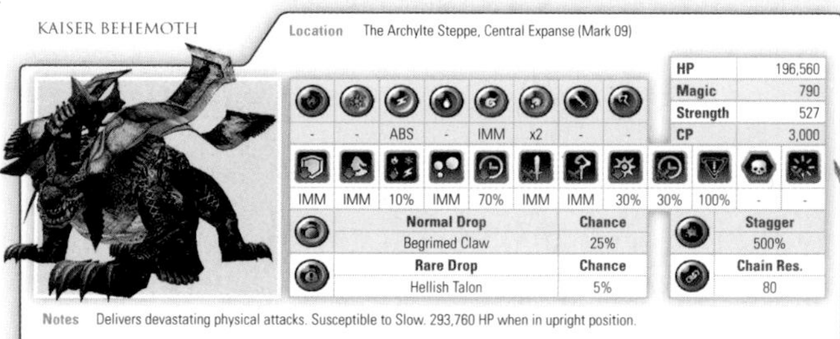

Location The Archylte Steppe, Central Expanse (Mark 09)

HP	Magic	Strength	CP
196,560	790	527	3,000

-	-	ABS	-	IMM	x2	-	-

IMM	IMM	10%	IMM	70%	IMM	IMM	30%	30%	100%	-	-

Normal Drop	Chance	Rare Drop	Chance	Stagger	Chain Res.
Begrimed Claw	25%	Hellish Talon	5%	500%	80

Notes Delivers devastating physical attacks. Susceptible to Slow. 293,760 HP when in upright position.

BEHEMOTH KING

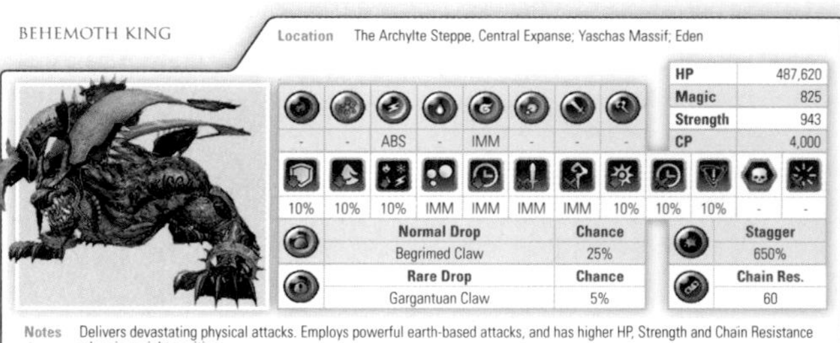

Location The Archylte Steppe, Central Expanse; Yaschas Massif; Eden

HP	Magic	Strength	CP
487,620	825	943	4,000

-	-	ABS	-	IMM	-	-	-

10%	10%	10%	IMM	IMM	IMM	IMM	10%	10%	10%	-	-

Normal Drop	Chance	Rare Drop	Chance	Stagger	Chain Res.
Begrimed Claw	25%	Gargantuan Claw	5%	650%	60

Notes Delivers devastating physical attacks. Employs powerful earth-based attacks, and has higher HP, Strength and Chain Resistance when in upright position.

HUMBABA

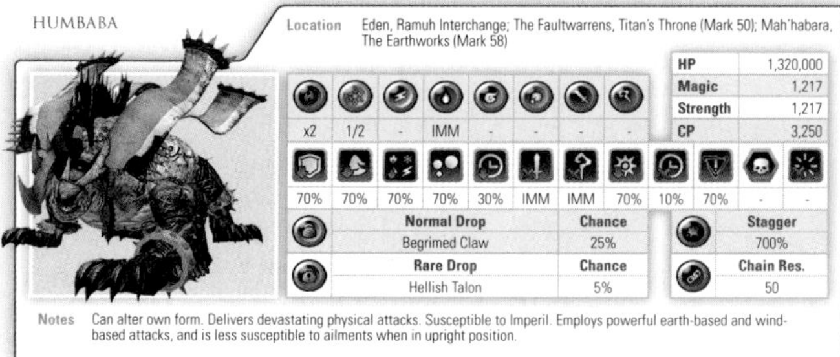

Location Eden, Ramuh Interchange; The Faultwarrens, Titan's Throne (Mark 50); Mah'habara, The Earthworks (Mark 58)

HP	Magic	Strength	CP
1,320,000	1,217	1,217	3,250

x2	1/2	-	IMM	-	-	-	-

70%	70%	70%	70%	30%	IMM	IMM	70%	10%	70%	-	-

Normal Drop	Chance	Rare Drop	Chance	Stagger	Chain Res.
Begrimed Claw	25%	Hellish Talon	5%	700%	50

Notes Can alter own form. Delivers devastating physical attacks. Susceptible to Imperil. Employs powerful earth-based and wind-based attacks, and is less susceptible to ailments when in upright position.

GOBLIN

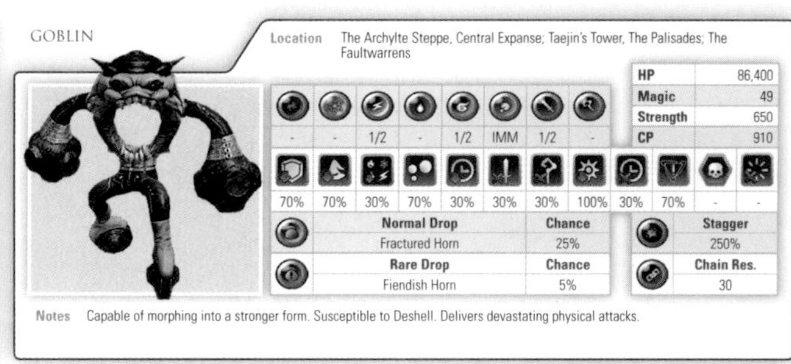

Location The Archylte Steppe, Central Expanse; Taejin's Tower, The Palisades; The Faultwarrens

HP	Magic	Strength	CP
86,400	49	650	910

-	-	1/2	-	1/2	IMM	1/2	-

70%	70%	30%	70%	30%	30%	30%	100%	30%	70%	-	-

Normal Drop	Chance	Rare Drop	Chance	Stagger	Chain Res.
Fractured Horn	25%	Fiendish Horn	5%	250%	30

Notes Capable of morphing into a stronger form. Susceptible to Deshell. Delivers devastating physical attacks.

GOBLIN CHIEFTAIN

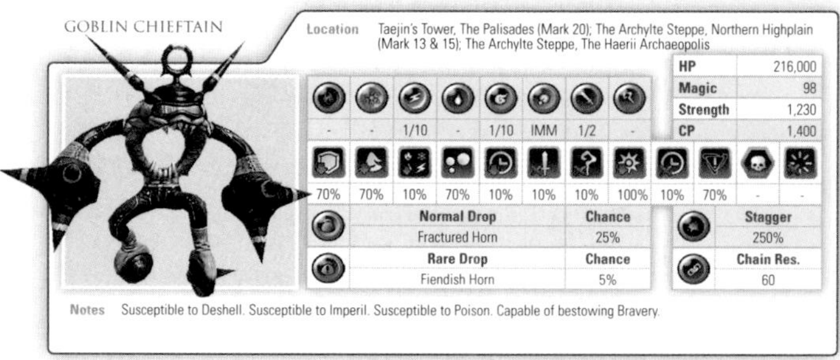

Location Taejin's Tower, The Palisades (Mark 20); The Archylte Steppe, Northern Highplain (Mark 13 & 15); The Archylte Steppe, The Haerii Archaeopolis

HP	Magic	Strength	CP
216,000	98	1,230	1,400

-	-	1/10	-	1/10	IMM	1/2	-

70%	70%	10%	70%	10%	10%	10%	100%	10%	70%	-	-

Normal Drop	Chance	Rare Drop	Chance	Stagger	Chain Res.
Fractured Horn	25%	Fiendish Horn	5%	250%	60

Notes Susceptible to Deshell. Susceptible to Imperil. Susceptible to Poison. Capable of bestowing Bravery.

MUNCHKIN

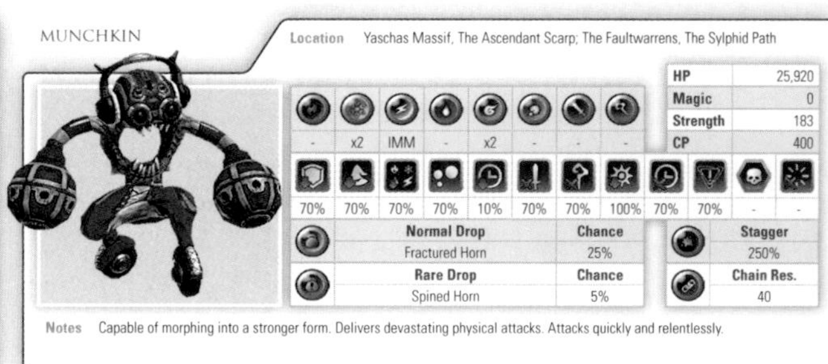

Location Yaschas Massif, The Ascendant Scarp; The Faultwarrens, The Sylphid Path

HP	Magic	Strength	CP
25,920	0	183	400

-	x2	IMM	-	x2	-	-	-

70%	70%	70%	70%	10%	70%	70%	100%	70%	70%	-	-

Normal Drop	Chance	Rare Drop	Chance	Stagger	Chain Res.
Fractured Horn	25%	Spined Horn	5%	250%	40

Notes Capable of morphing into a stronger form. Delivers devastating physical attacks. Attacks quickly and relentlessly.

MUNCHKIN MAESTRO

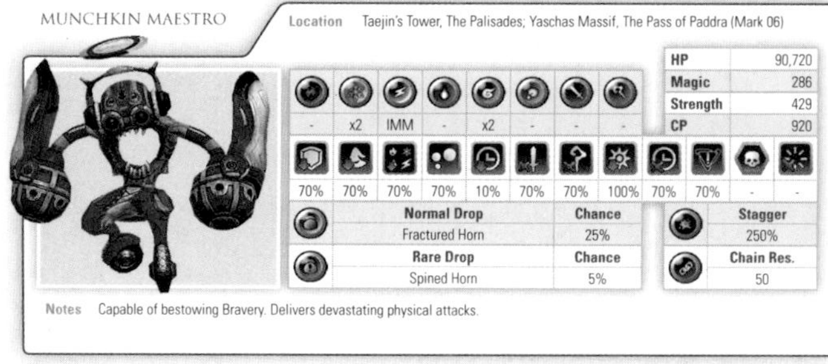

Location Taejin's Tower, The Palisades; Yaschas Massif, The Pass of Paddra (Mark 06)

HP	Magic	Strength	CP
90,720	286	429	920

-	x2	IMM	-	x2	-	-	-

70%	70%	70%	70%	10%	70%	70%	100%	70%	70%	-	-

Normal Drop	Chance	Rare Drop	Chance	Stagger	Chain Res.
Fractured Horn	25%	Spined Horn	5%	250%	50

Notes Capable of bestowing Bravery. Delivers devastating physical attacks.

BORGBEAR

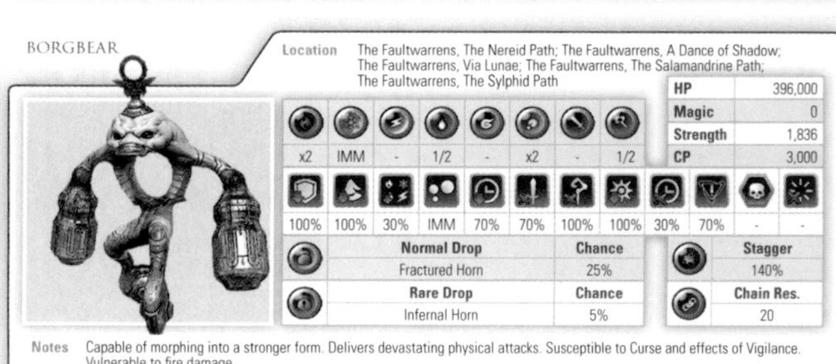

Location The Faultwarrens, The Nereid Path; The Faultwarrens, A Dance of Shadow; The Faultwarrens, Via Lunae; The Faultwarrens, The Salamandrine Path; The Faultwarrens, The Sylphid Path

HP	Magic	Strength	CP
396,000	0	1,836	3,000

x2	IMM	-	1/2	-	x2	-	1/2

100%	100%	30%	IMM	70%	70%	100%	100%	30%	70%	-	-

Normal Drop	Chance	Rare Drop	Chance	Stagger	Chain Res.
Fractured Horn	25%	Infernal Horn	5%	140%	20

Notes Capable of morphing into a stronger form. Delivers devastating physical attacks. Susceptible to Curse and effects of Vigilance. Vulnerable to fire damage.

BORGBEAR HERO

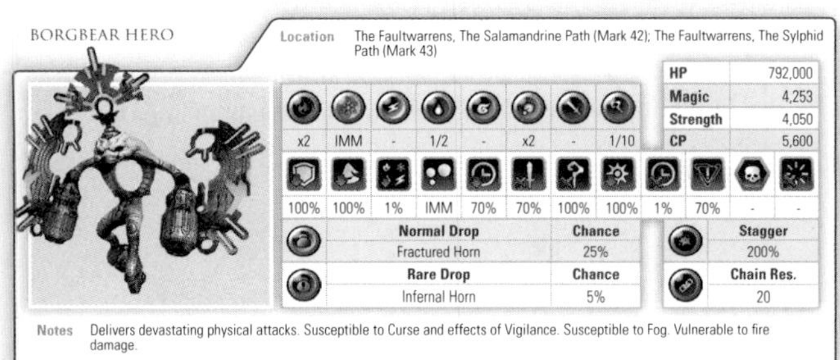

Location The Faultwarrens, The Salamandrine Path (Mark 42); The Faultwarrens, The Sylphid Path (Mark 43)

HP	Magic	Strength	CP
792,000	4,253	4,050	5,600

x2	IMM	-	1/2	-	x2	-	1/10

100%	100%	1%	IMM	70%	70%	100%	100%	1%	70%	-	-

Normal Drop	Chance	Rare Drop	Chance	Stagger	Chain Res.
Fractured Horn	25%	Infernal Horn	5%	200%	20

Notes Delivers devastating physical attacks. Susceptible to Curse and effects of Vigilance. Susceptible to Fog. Vulnerable to fire damage.

SAHAGIN

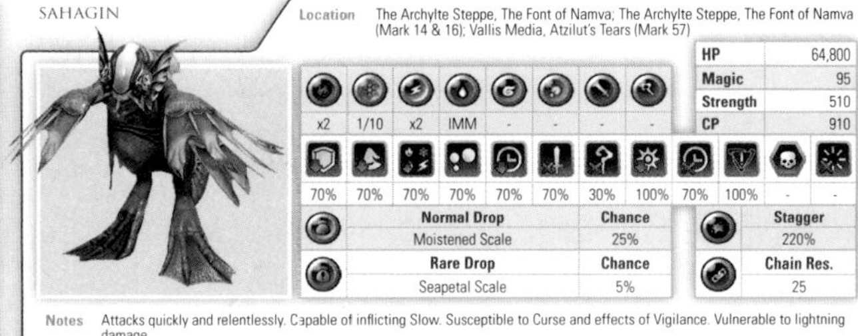

Location The Archylte Steppe, The Font of Namva; The Archylte Steppe, The Font of Namva (Mark 14 & 16); Vallis Media, Atzilut's Tears (Mark 57)

HP	Magic	Strength	CP
64,800	95	510	910

x2	1/10	x2	IMM	-	-	-	-

70%	70%	70%	70%	70%	70%	30%	100%	70%	100%	-	-

Normal Drop	Chance	Rare Drop	Chance	Stagger	Chain Res.
Moistened Scale	25%	Seapetal Scale	5%	220%	25

Notes Attacks quickly and relentlessly. Capable of inflicting Slow. Susceptible to Curse and effects of Vigilance. Vulnerable to lightning damage.

DAGONITE

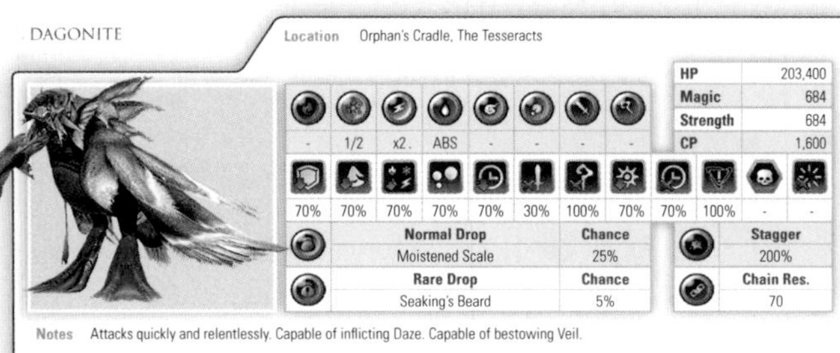

Location Orphan's Cradle, The Tesseracts

HP	Magic	Strength	CP
203,400	684	684	1,600

-	1/2	x2	ABS	-	-	-	-

70%	70%	70%	70%	70%	30%	100%	70%	70%	100%	-	-

Normal Drop	Chance	Rare Drop	Chance	Stagger	Chain Res.
Moistened Scale	25%	Seaking's Beard	5%	200%	70

Notes Attacks quickly and relentlessly. Capable of inflicting Daze. Capable of bestowing Veil.

OROBON

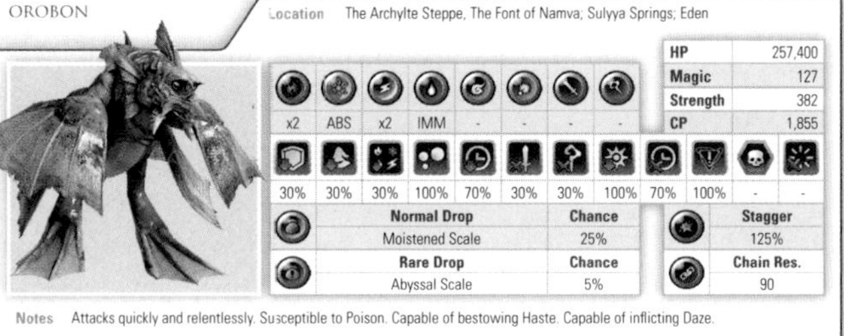

Location The Archylte Steppe, The Font of Namva; Sulyya Springs; Eden

HP	Magic	Strength	CP
257,400	127	382	1,855

x2	ABS	x2	IMM	-	-	-	-

30%	30%	30%	100%	70%	30%	30%	100%	70%	100%	-	-

Normal Drop	Chance	Rare Drop	Chance	Stagger	Chain Res.
Moistened Scale	25%	Abyssal Scale	5%	125%	90

Notes Attacks quickly and relentlessly. Susceptible to Poison. Capable of bestowing Haste. Capable of inflicting Daze.

CACTUAR

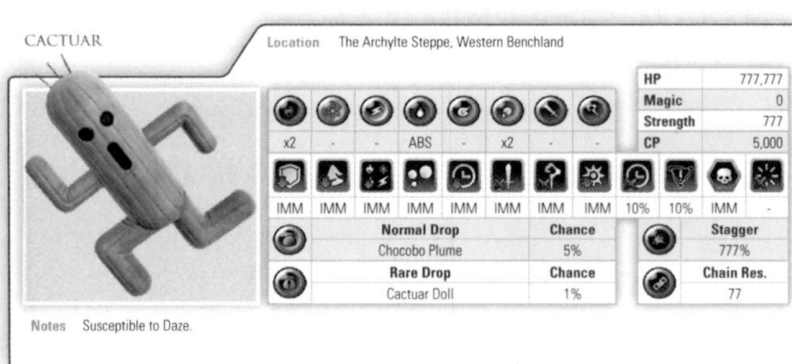

Location The Archylte Steppe, Western Benchland

HP	Magic	Strength	CP
777,777	0	777	5,000

x2	-	-	ABS	-	x2	-	-

IMM	IMM	IMM	IMM	IMM	IMM	IMM	IMM	10%	10%	IMM	-

Normal Drop	Chance	Rare Drop	Chance	Stagger	Chain Res.
Chocobo Plume	5%	Cactuar Doll	1%	777%	77

Notes Susceptible to Daze.

GIANT CACTUAR

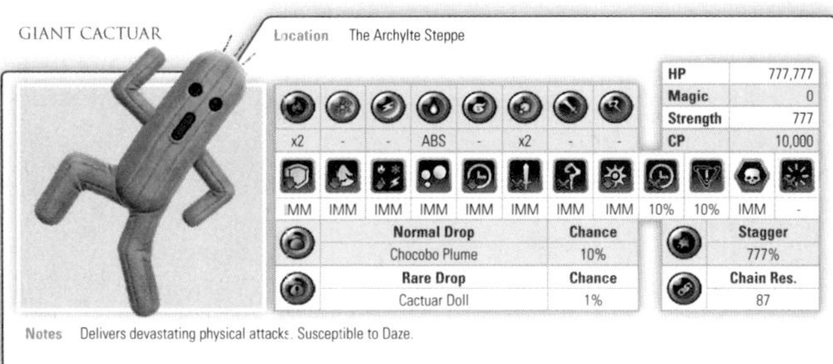

Location The Archylte Steppe

HP	Magic	Strength	CP
777,777	0	777	10,000

x2	-	-	ABS	-	x2	-	-

IMM	IMM	IMM	IMM	IMM	IMM	IMM	IMM	10%	10%	IMM	-

Normal Drop	Chance	Rare Drop	Chance	Stagger	Chain Res.
Chocobo Plume	10%	Cactuar Doll	1%	777%	87

Notes Delivers devastating physical attacks. Susceptible to Daze.

CACTUAR PRIME

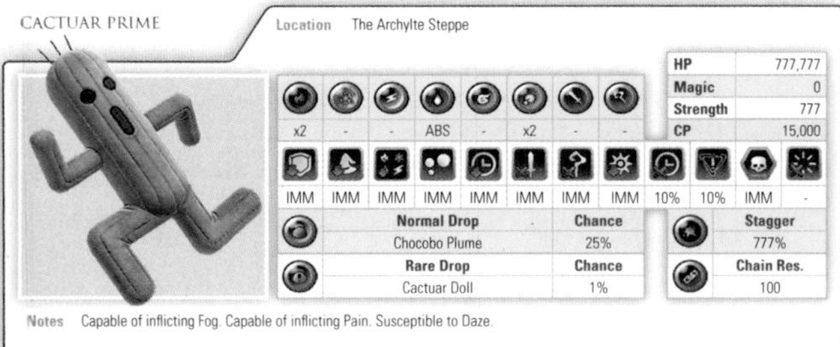

Location The Archylte Steppe

HP	Magic	Strength	CP
777,777	0	777	15,000

x2	-	-	ABS	-	x2	-	-

IMM	IMM	IMM	IMM	IMM	IMM	IMM	IMM	10%	10%	IMM	-

Normal Drop	Chance	Rare Drop	Chance	Stagger	Chain Res.
Chocobo Plume	25%	Cactuar Doll	1%	777%	100

Notes Capable of inflicting Fog. Capable of inflicting Pain. Susceptible to Daze.

GIGANTUAR

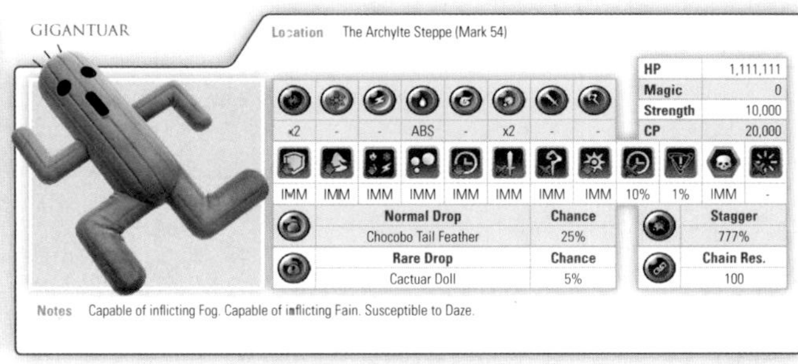

Location The Archylte Steppe (Mark 54)

HP	Magic	Strength	CP
1,111,111	0	10,000	20,000

x2	-	-	ABS	-	x2	-	-

IMM	IMM	IMM	IMM	IMM	IMM	IMM	IMM	10%	1%	IMM	-

Normal Drop	Chance	Rare Drop	Chance	Stagger	Chain Res.
Chocobo Tail Feather	25%	Cactuar Doll	5%	777%	100

Notes Capable of inflicting Fog. Capable of inflicting Pain. Susceptible to Daze.

FLOWERING CACTUAR

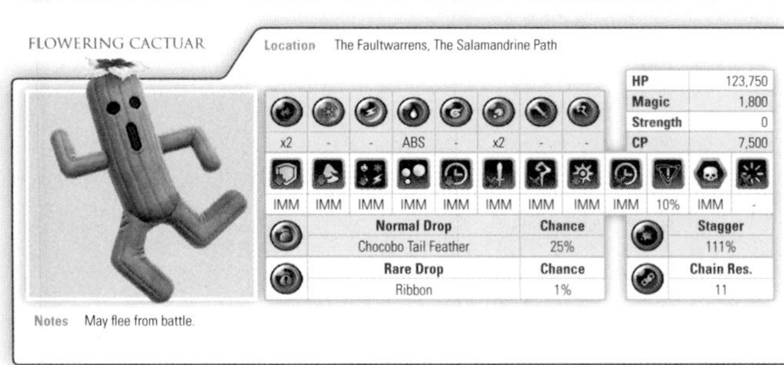

Location The Faultwarrens, The Salamandrine Path

HP	Magic	Strength	CP
123,750	1,800	0	7,500

x2	-	-	ABS	-	x2	-	-

IMM	IMM	IMM	IMM	IMM	IMM	IMM	IMM	IMM	10%	IMM	-

Normal Drop	Chance	Rare Drop	Chance	Stagger	Chain Res.
Chocobo Tail Feather	25%	Ribbon	1%	111%	11

Notes May flee from battle.

OCHU

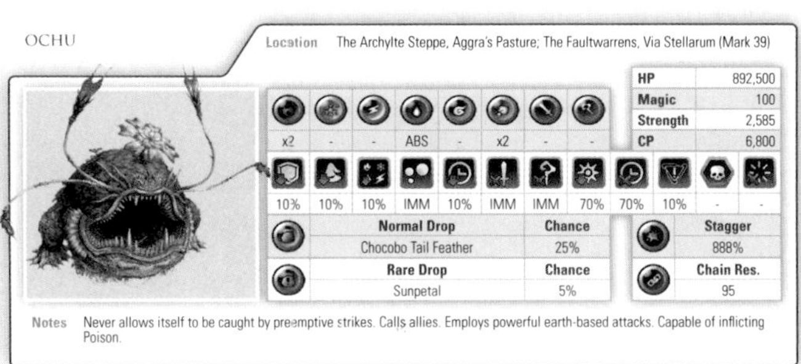

Location The Archylte Steppe, Aggra's Pasture; The Faultwarrens, Via Stellarum (Mark 39)

HP	Magic	Strength	CP
892,500	100	2,585	6,800

x2	-	-	ABS	-	x2	-	-

10%	10%	10%	IMM	10%	IMM	IMM	70%	70%	10%	-	-

Normal Drop	Chance	Rare Drop	Chance	Stagger	Chain Res.
Chocobo Tail Feather	25%	Sunpetal	5%	888%	95

Notes Never allows itself to be caught by preemptive strikes. Calls allies. Employs powerful earth-based attacks. Capable of inflicting Poison.

MICROCHU

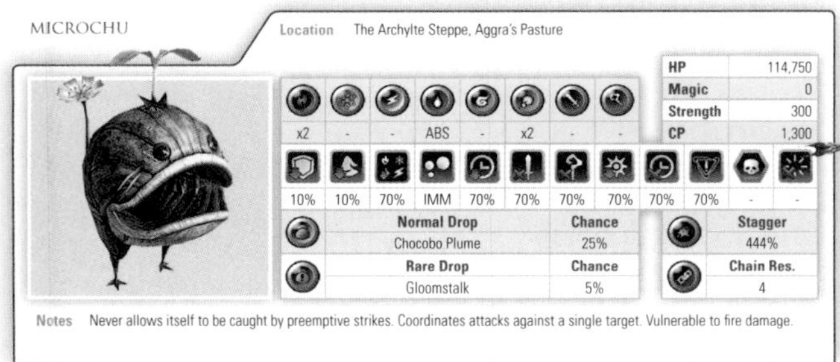

Location The Archylte Steppe, Aggra's Pasture

HP	Magic	Strength	CP
114,750	0	300	1,300

x2	-	-	ABS	-	x2	-	-

10%	10%	70%	IMM	70%	70%	70%	70%	70%	70%	-	-

Normal Drop	Chance	Rare Drop	Chance	Stagger	Chain Res.
Chocobo Plume	25%	Gloomstalk	5%	444%	4

Notes Never allows itself to be caught by preemptive strikes. Coordinates attacks against a single target. Vulnerable to fire damage.

NEOCHU

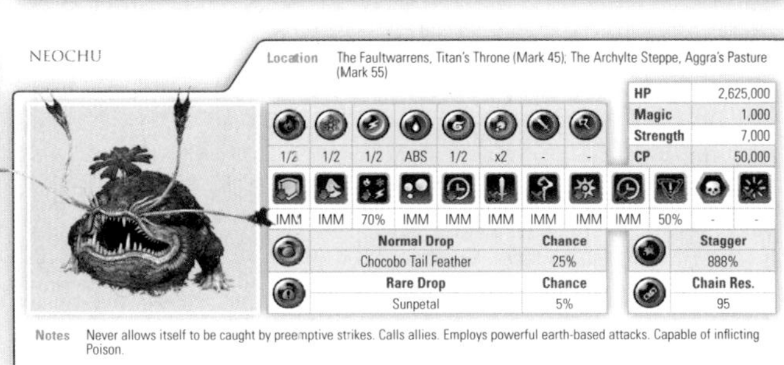

Location The Faultwarrens, Titan's Throne (Mark 45); The Archylte Steppe, Aggra's Pasture (Mark 55)

HP	Magic	Strength	CP
2,625,000	1,000	7,000	50,000

1/2	1/2	1/2	ABS	1/2	x2	-	-

IMM	IMM	70%	IMM	IMM	IMM	IMM	IMM	IMM	50%	-	-

Normal Drop	Chance	Rare Drop	Chance	Stagger	Chain Res.
Chocobo Tail Feather	25%	Sunpetal	5%	888%	95

Notes Never allows itself to be caught by preemptive strikes. Calls allies. Employs powerful earth-based attacks. Capable of inflicting Poison.

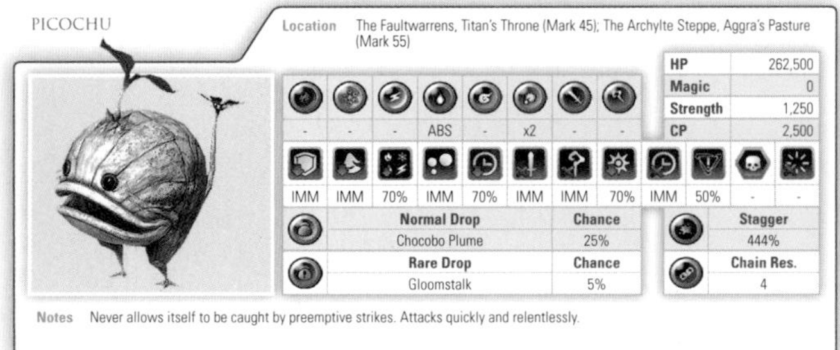

PICOCHU

Location The Faultwarrens, Titan's Throne (Mark 45); The Archylte Steppe, Aggra's Pasture (Mark 55)

HP	Magic	Strength	CP
262,500	0	1,250	2,500

-	-	-	ABS	-	x2	-	-

IMM	IMM	70%	IMM	70%	IMM	IMM	70%	IMM	50%	-	-

Normal Drop	Chance	Stagger
Chocobo Plume	25%	444%
Rare Drop	**Chance**	**Chain Res.**
Gloomstalk	5%	4

Notes Never allows itself to be caught by preemptive strikes. Attacks quickly and relentlessly.

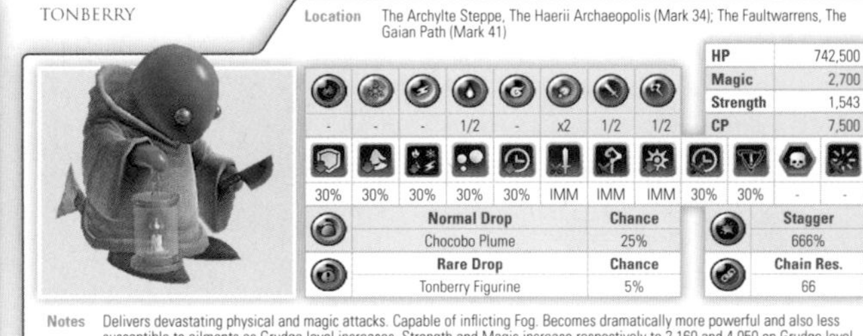

TONBERRY

Location The Archylte Steppe, The Haerii Archaeopolis (Mark 34); The Faultwarrens, The Gaian Path (Mark 41)

HP	Magic	Strength	CP
742,500	2,700	1,543	7,500

-	-	-	1/2	-	x2	1/2	1/2

30%	30%	30%	30%	30%	IMM	IMM	IMM	30%	30%	-	-

Normal Drop	Chance	Stagger
Chocobo Plume	25%	666%
Rare Drop	**Chance**	**Chain Res.**
Tonberry Figurine	5%	66

Notes Delivers devastating physical and magic attacks. Capable of inflicting Fog. Becomes dramatically more powerful and also less susceptible to ailments as Grudge level increases. Strength and Magic increase respectively to 2,160 and 4,050 on Grudge level 1; 5,940 and 9,963 on Grudge level 2; 10,395 and 14,945 on Grudge level 3; 14,033 and 26,154 on Grudge level 4.

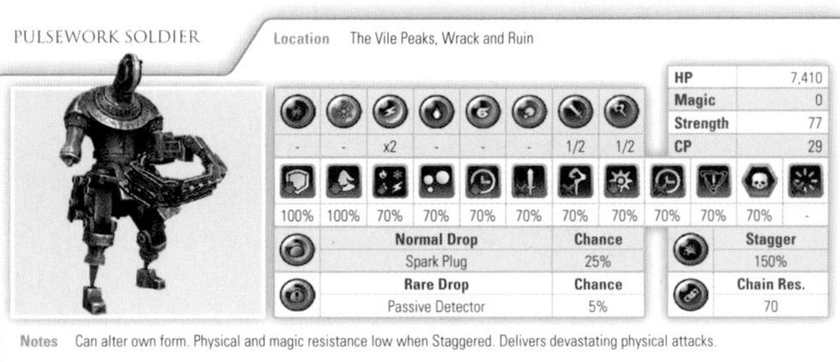

PULSEWORK SOLDIER

Location The Vile Peaks, Wrack and Ruin

HP	Magic	Strength	CP
7,410	0	77	29

-	-	x2	-	-	-	1/2	1/2

100%	100%	70%	70%	70%	70%	70%	70%	70%	70%	70%	-

Normal Drop	Chance	Stagger
Spark Plug	25%	150%
Rare Drop	**Chance**	**Chain Res.**
Passive Detector	5%	70

Notes Can alter own form. Physical and magic resistance low when Staggered. Delivers devastating physical attacks.

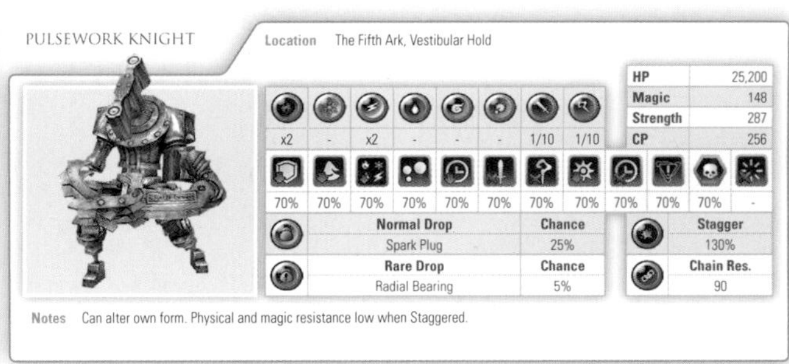

PULSEWORK KNIGHT

Location The Fifth Ark, Vestibular Hold

HP	Magic	Strength	CP
25,200	148	287	256

x2	-	x2	-	-	-	1/10	1/10

70%	70%	70%	70%	70%	70%	70%	70%	70%	70%	70%	-

Normal Drop	Chance	Stagger
Spark Plug	25%	130%
Rare Drop	**Chance**	**Chain Res.**
Radial Bearing	5%	90

Notes Can alter own form. Physical and magic resistance low when Staggered.

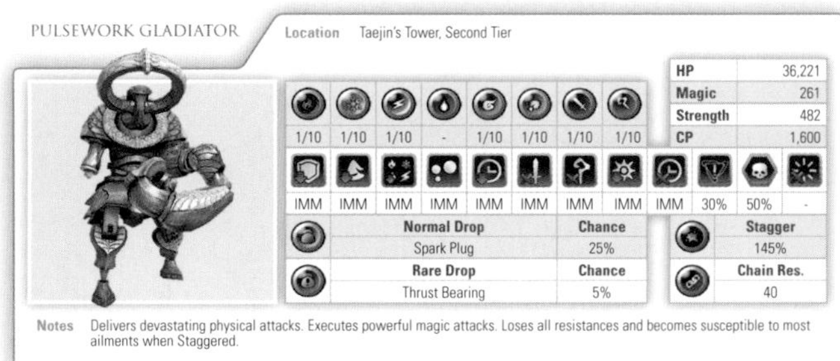

PULSEWORK GLADIATOR

Location Taejin's Tower, Second Tier

HP	Magic	Strength	CP
36,221	261	482	1,600

1/10	1/10	1/10	-	1/10	1/10	1/10	1/10

IMM	IMM	IMM	IMM	IMM	IMM	IMM	IMM	IMM	30%	50%	-

Normal Drop	Chance	Stagger
Spark Plug	25%	145%
Rare Drop	**Chance**	**Chain Res.**
Thrust Bearing	5%	40

Notes Delivers devastating physical attacks. Executes powerful magic attacks. Loses all resistances and becomes susceptible to most ailments when Staggered.

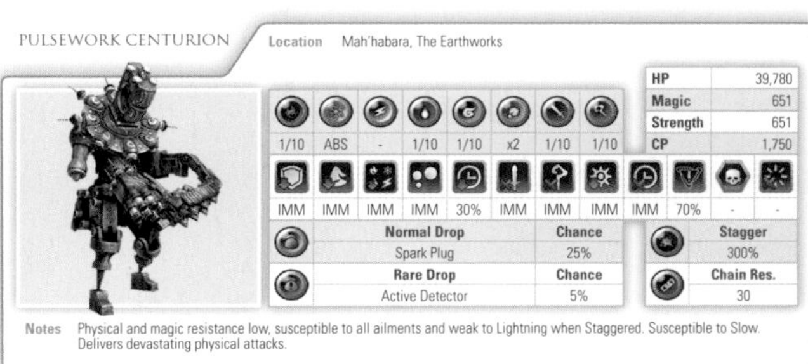

PULSEWORK CENTURION

Location Mah'habara, The Earthworks

HP	Magic	Strength	CP
39,780	651	651	1,750

1/10	ABS	-	1/10	1/10	x2	1/10	1/10

IMM	IMM	IMM	IMM	30%	IMM	IMM	IMM	IMM	70%	-	-

Normal Drop	Chance	Stagger
Spark Plug	25%	300%
Rare Drop	**Chance**	**Chain Res.**
Active Detector	5%	30

Notes Physical and magic resistance low, susceptible to all ailments and weak to Lightning when Staggered. Susceptible to Slow. Delivers devastating physical attacks.

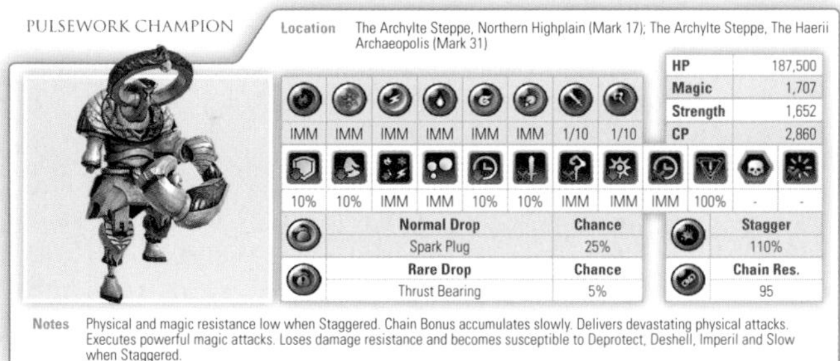

PULSEWORK CHAMPION

Location The Archylte Steppe, Northern Highplain (Mark 17); The Archylte Steppe, The Haerii Archaeopolis (Mark 31)

HP	Magic	Strength	CP
187,500	1,707	1,652	2,860

IMM	IMM	IMM	IMM	IMM	IMM	1/10	1/10

10%	10%	IMM	IMM	10%	10%	IMM	IMM	IMM	100%	-	-

Normal Drop	Chance	Stagger
Spark Plug	25%	110%
Rare Drop	**Chance**	**Chain Res.**
Thrust Bearing	5%	95

Notes Physical and magic resistance low when Staggered. Chain Bonus accumulates slowly. Delivers devastating physical attacks. Executes powerful magic attacks. Loses damage resistance and becomes susceptible to Deprotect, Deshell, Imperil and Slow when Staggered.

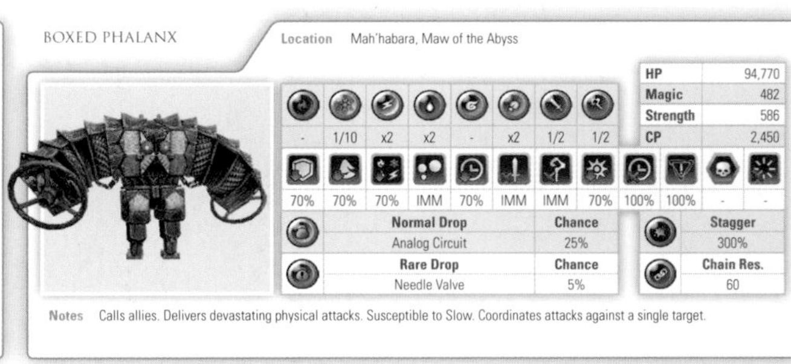

BOXED PHALANX

Location Mah'habara, Maw of the Abyss

HP	Magic	Strength	CP
94,770	482	586	2,450

-	1/10	x2	x2	-	x2	1/2	1/2

70%	70%	70%	IMM	70%	IMM	IMM	70%	100%	100%	-	-

Normal Drop	Chance	Stagger
Analog Circuit	25%	300%
Rare Drop	**Chance**	**Chain Res.**
Needle Valve	5%	60

Notes Calls allies. Delivers devastating physical attacks. Susceptible to Slow. Coordinates attacks against a single target.

HOPLITE

Location Mah'habara, Maw of the Abyss

HP	Magic	Strength	CP
33,638	315	494	770

-	1/10	x2	-	-	x2	-	-

50%	50%	10%	IMM	100%	10%	10%	10%	100%	10%	-	-

Normal Drop	Chance	Stagger
Analog Circuit	25%	270%
Rare Drop	**Chance**	**Chain Res.**
Solenoid	5%	80

Notes Susceptible to Daze. Vulnerable to lightning damage.

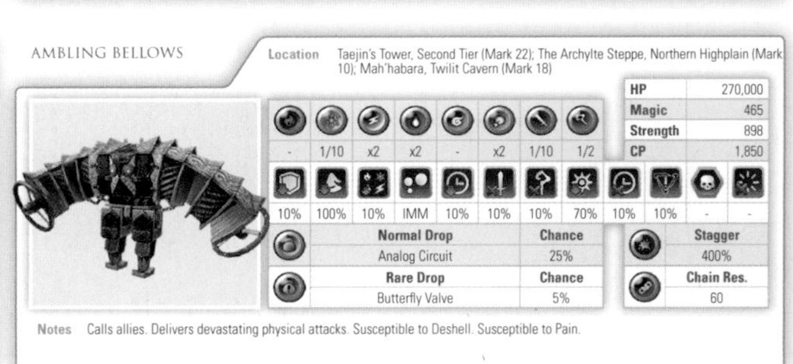

AMBLING BELLOWS

Location Taejin's Tower, Second Tier (Mark 22); The Archylte Steppe, Northern Highplain (Mark 10); Mah'habara, Twilit Cavern (Mark 18)

HP	Magic	Strength	CP
270,000	465	898	1,850

-	1/10	x2	x2	-	x2	1/10	1/2

10%	100%	10%	IMM	10%	10%	10%	70%	10%	10%	-	-

Normal Drop	Chance	Stagger
Analog Circuit	25%	400%
Rare Drop	**Chance**	**Chain Res.**
Butterfly Valve	5%	60

Notes Calls allies. Delivers devastating physical attacks. Susceptible to Deshell. Susceptible to Pain.

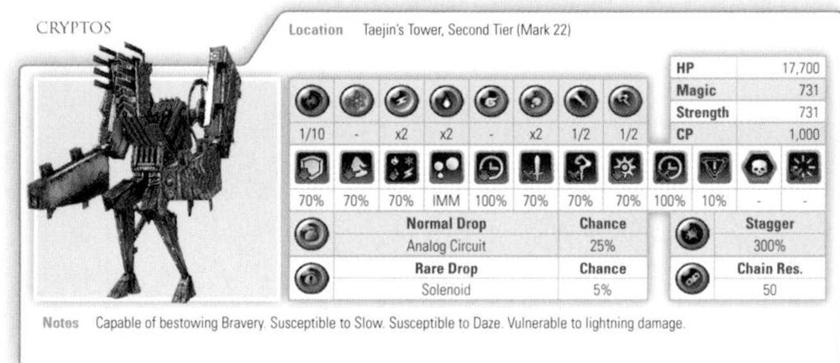

CRYPTOS

Location Taejin's Tower, Second Tier (Mark 22)

HP	Magic	Strength	CP
17,700	731	731	1,000

1/10	-	x2	x2	-	x2	1/2	1/2

70%	70%	70%	IMM	100%	70%	70%	70%	100%	10%	-	-

Normal Drop	Chance	Stagger
Analog Circuit	25%	300%
Rare Drop	**Chance**	**Chain Res.**
Solenoid	5%	50

Notes Capable of bestowing Bravery. Susceptible to Slow. Susceptible to Daze. Vulnerable to lightning damage.

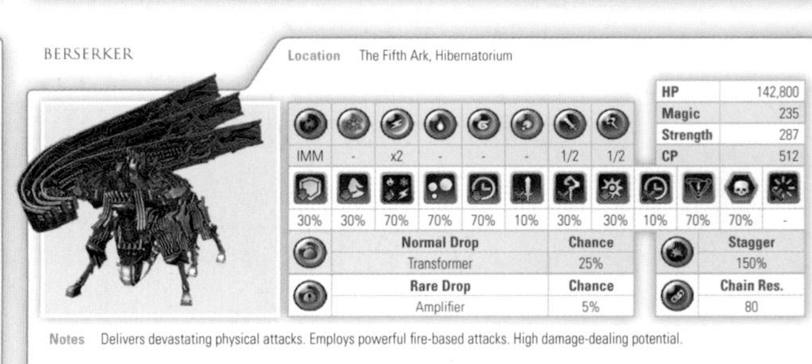

BERSERKER

Location The Fifth Ark, Hibernatorium

HP	Magic	Strength	CP
142,800	235	287	512

IMM	-	x2	-	-	-	1/2	1/2

30%	30%	70%	70%	70%	10%	30%	30%	10%	70%	70%	-

Normal Drop	Chance	Stagger
Transformer	25%	150%
Rare Drop	**Chance**	**Chain Res.**
Amplifier	5%	80

Notes Delivers devastating physical attacks. Employs powerful fire-based attacks. High damage-dealing potential.

CENTAURION BLADE (BERSERKER)

Location: The Fifth Ark, Hibernatorium

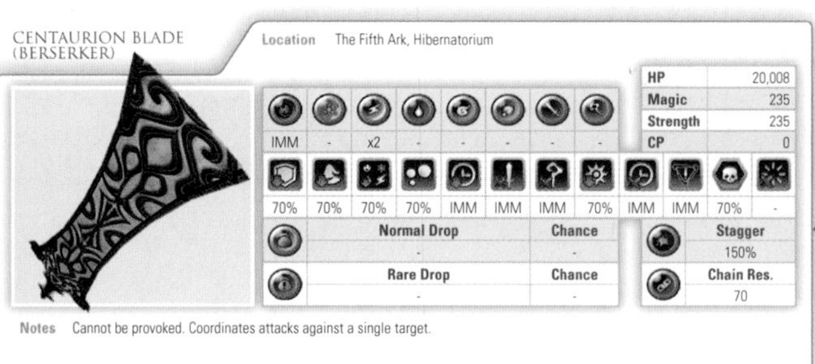

Elemental resistances	IMM	-	x2	-	-	-	-	-

Status	70%	70%	70%	70%	IMM	IMM	IMM	70%	IMM	IMM	70%	-

HP	Magic	Strength	CP
20,008	235	235	0

Normal Drop	Chance	Rare Drop	Chance	Stagger	Chain Res.
-	-	-	-	150%	70

Notes: Cannot be provoked. Coordinates attacks against a single target.

TYRANT

Location: Taejin's Tower, Fifth Tier; Eden; Mah'habara; The Faultwarrens, Titan's Throne (Mark 49)

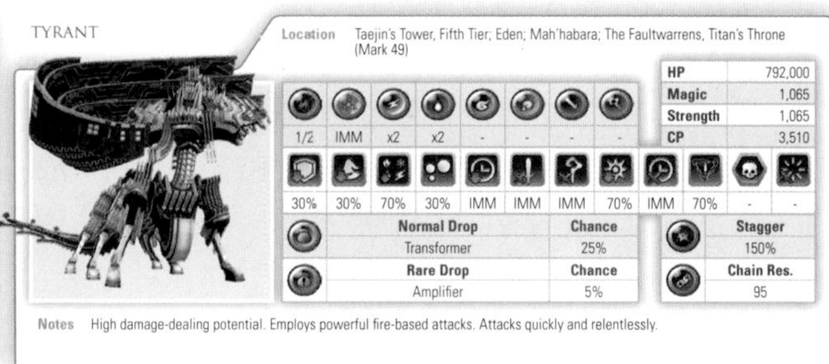

Elemental resistances	1/2	IMM	x2	x2	-	-	-	-

Status	30%	30%	70%	30%	IMM	IMM	IMM	70%	IMM	70%	-	-

HP	Magic	Strength	CP
792,000	1,065	1,065	3,510

Normal Drop	Chance	Rare Drop	Chance	Stagger	Chain Res.
Transformer	25%	Amplifier	5%	150%	95

Notes: High damage-dealing potential. Employs powerful fire-based attacks. Attacks quickly and relentlessly.

CENTAURION BLADE (TYRANT)

Location: Taejin's Tower, Fifth Tier; Eden; Mah'habara; The Faultwarrens, Titan's Throne (Mark 49)

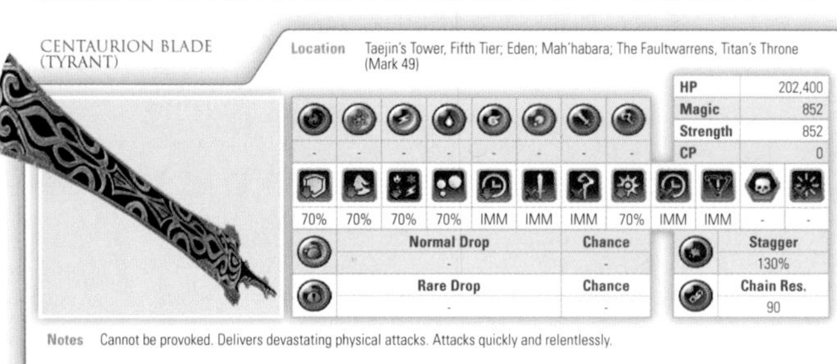

Elemental resistances	-	-	-	-	-	-	-	-

Status	70%	70%	70%	70%	IMM	IMM	IMM	70%	IMM	IMM	-	-

HP	Magic	Strength	CP
202,400	852	852	0

Normal Drop	Chance	Rare Drop	Chance	Stagger	Chain Res.
-	-	-	-	130%	90

Notes: Cannot be provoked. Delivers devastating physical attacks. Attacks quickly and relentlessly.

IMMORTAL

Location: Orphan's Cradle, The Tesseracts

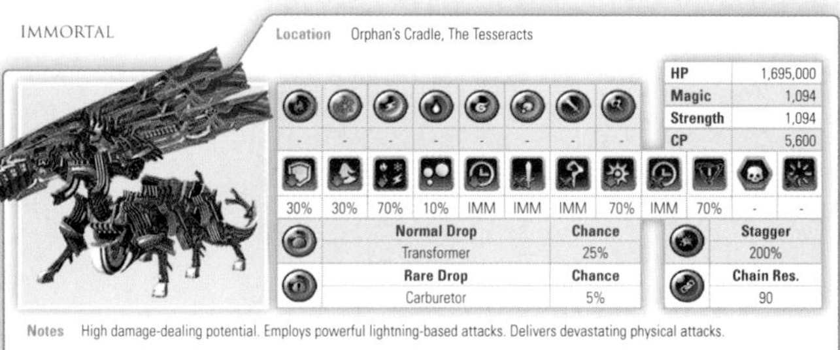

Elemental resistances	-	-	-	-	-	-	-	-

Status	30%	30%	70%	10%	IMM	IMM	IMM	70%	IMM	70%	-	-

HP	Magic	Strength	CP
1,695,000	1,094	1,094	5,600

Normal Drop	Chance	Rare Drop	Chance	Stagger	Chain Res.
Transformer	25%	Carburetor	5%	200%	90

Notes: High damage-dealing potential. Employs powerful lightning-based attacks. Delivers devastating physical attacks.

CENTAURION BLADE (IMMORTAL)

Location: Orphan's Cradle, The Tesseracts

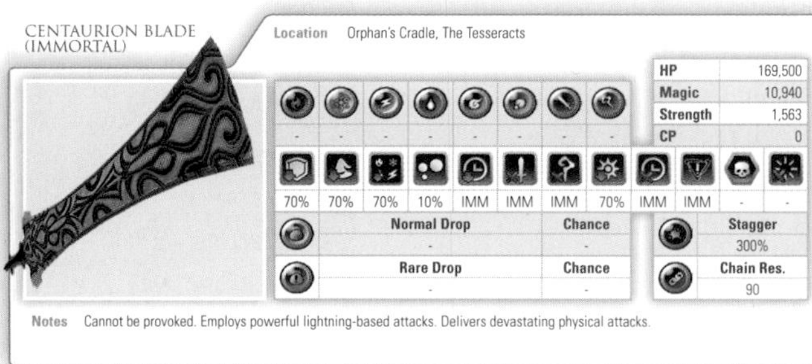

Elemental resistances	-	-	-	-	-	-	-	-

Status	70%	70%	70%	10%	IMM	IMM	IMM	70%	IMM	IMM	-	-

HP	Magic	Strength	CP
169,500	10,940	1,563	0

Normal Drop	Chance	Rare Drop	Chance	Stagger	Chain Res.
-	-	-	-	300%	90

Notes: Cannot be provoked. Employs powerful lightning-based attacks. Delivers devastating physical attacks.

BOMB

Location: The Vile Peaks, Scrap Processing

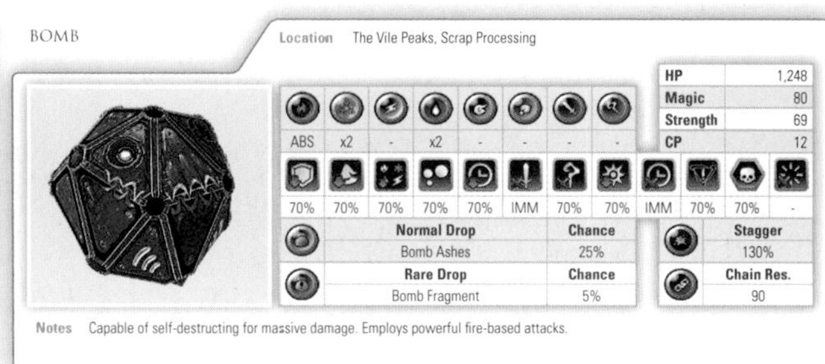

Elemental resistances	ABS	x2	-	x2	-	-	-	-

Status	70%	70%	70%	70%	70%	IMM	70%	70%	IMM	70%	70%	-

HP	Magic	Strength	CP
1,248	80	69	12

Normal Drop	Chance	Rare Drop	Chance	Stagger	Chain Res.
Bomb Ashes	25%	Bomb Fragment	5%	130%	90

Notes: Capable of self-destructing for massive damage. Employs powerful fire-based attacks.

CIRCUITRON

Location: The Fifth Ark, Vestibular Hold

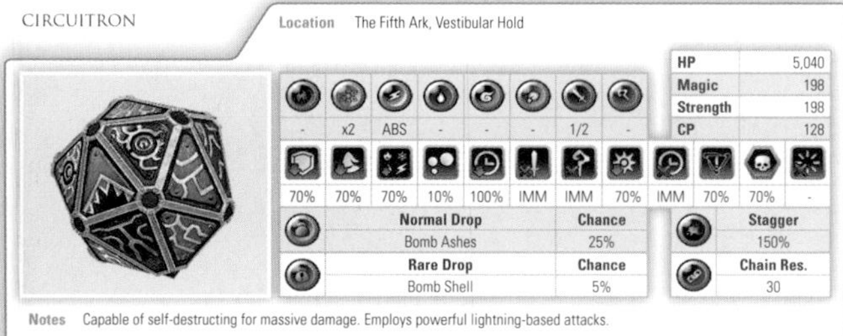

Elemental resistances	-	x2	ABS	-	-	-	1/2	-

Status	70%	70%	70%	10%	100%	IMM	IMM	70%	IMM	70%	70%	-

HP	Magic	Strength	CP
5,040	198	198	128

Normal Drop	Chance	Rare Drop	Chance	Stagger	Chain Res.
Bomb Ashes	25%	Bomb Shell	5%	150%	30

Notes: Capable of self-destructing for massive damage. Employs powerful lightning-based attacks.

CRYOHEDRON

Location: Mah'habara, Maw of the Abyss

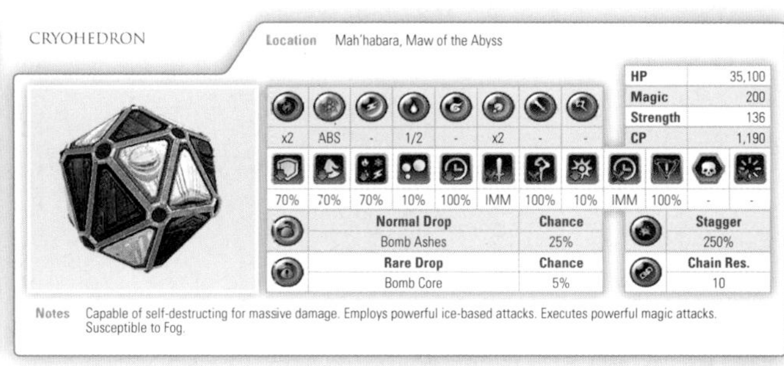

Elemental resistances	x2	ABS	-	1/2	-	x2	-	-

Status	70%	70%	70%	10%	100%	IMM	100%	10%	IMM	100%	-	-

HP	Magic	Strength	CP
35,100	200	136	1,190

Normal Drop	Chance	Rare Drop	Chance	Stagger	Chain Res.
Bomb Ashes	25%	Bomb Core	5%	250%	10

Notes: Capable of self-destructing for massive damage. Employs powerful ice-based attacks. Executes powerful magic attacks. Susceptible to Fog.

DREADNOUGHT (1ST BATTLE)

Location: The Vile Peaks, Devastated Dreams

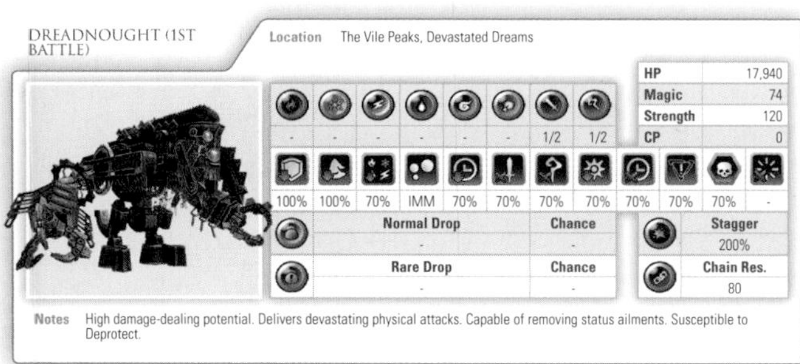

Elemental resistances	-	-	-	-	-	-	1/2	1/2

Status	100%	100%	70%	IMM	70%	70%	70%	70%	70%	70%	70%	-

HP	Magic	Strength	CP
17,940	74	120	0

Normal Drop	Chance	Rare Drop	Chance	Stagger	Chain Res.
-	-	-	-	200%	80

Notes: High damage-dealing potential. Delivers devastating physical attacks. Capable of removing status ailments. Susceptible to Deprotect.

DREADNOUGHT (2ND BATTLE)

Location: The Vile Peaks, Devastated Dreams

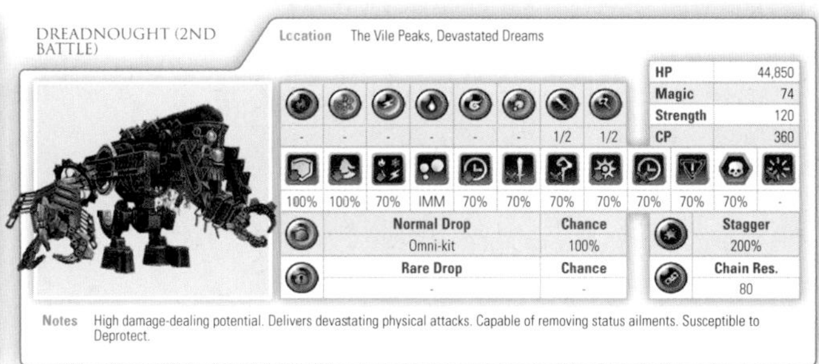

Elemental resistances	-	-	-	-	-	-	1/2	1/2

Status	100%	100%	70%	IMM	70%	70%	70%	70%	70%	70%	70%	-

HP	Magic	Strength	CP
44,850	74	120	360

Normal Drop	Chance	Rare Drop	Chance	Stagger	Chain Res.
Omni-kit	100%			200%	80

Notes: High damage-dealing potential. Delivers devastating physical attacks. Capable of removing status ailments. Susceptible to Deprotect.

JUGGERNAUT

Location: Mah'habara, Maw of the Abyss; Eden, Leviathan Plaza; Taejin's Tower, The Palisades (Mark 29); Oerba, Village Proper (Mark 61)

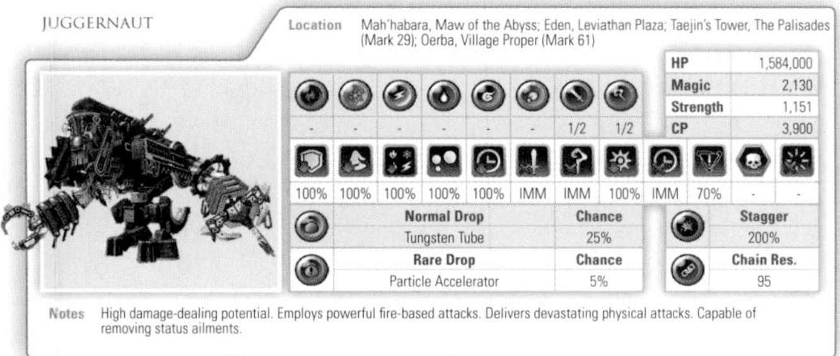

Elemental resistances	-	-	-	-	-	-	1/2	1/2

Status	100%	100%	100%	100%	100%	IMM	IMM	100%	IMM	70%	-	-

HP	Magic	Strength	CP
1,584,000	2,130	1,151	3,900

Normal Drop	Chance	Rare Drop	Chance	Stagger	Chain Res.
Tungsten Tube	25%	Particle Accelerator	5%	200%	95

Notes: High damage-dealing potential. Employs powerful fire-based attacks. Delivers devastating physical attacks. Capable of removing status ailments.

GHOUL

Location: The Pulse Vestige, Oblatorium; Lake Bresha

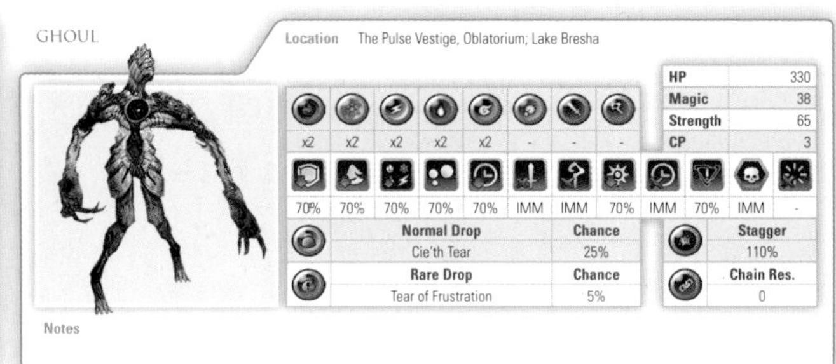

Elemental resistances	x2	x2	x2	x2	x2	-	-	-

Status	70%	70%	70%	70%	70%	IMM	IMM	70%	IMM	70%	IMM	-

HP	Magic	Strength	CP
330	38	65	3

Normal Drop	Chance	Rare Drop	Chance	Stagger	Chain Res.
Cie'th Tear	25%	Tear of Frustration	5%	110%	0

Notes:

CIE'TH

GHAST

Location The Pulse Vestige, Ambulatory; Lake Bresha

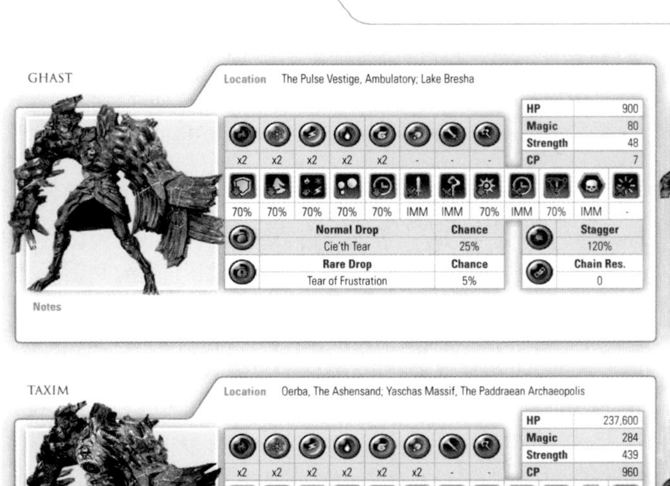

HP	900
Magic	80
Strength	48
CP	7

x2	x2	x2	x2	x2	-	-	-

70%	70%	70%	70%	70%	IMM	IMM	70%	IMM	70%	IMM	-

Normal Drop	Chance	Stagger
Cie'th Tear	25%	120%
Rare Drop	**Chance**	**Chain Res.**
Tear of Frustration	5%	0

Notes

STRIGOI

Location Mah'habara, Abandoned Dig; The Archylte Steppe, The Haerii Archaeopolis

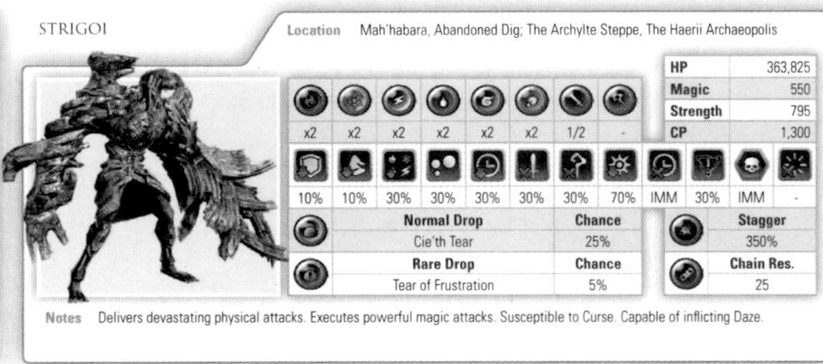

HP	363,825
Magic	550
Strength	795
CP	1,300

x2	x2	x2	x2	x2	x2	1/2	-

10%	10%	30%	30%	30%	30%	30%	70%	IMM	30%	IMM	-

Normal Drop	Chance	Stagger
Cie'th Tear	25%	350%
Rare Drop	**Chance**	**Chain Res.**
Tear of Frustration	5%	25

Notes Delivers devastating physical attacks. Executes powerful magic attacks. Susceptible to Curse. Capable of inflicting Daze.

TAXIM

Location Oerba, The Ashensand; Yaschas Massif, The Paddraean Archaeopolis

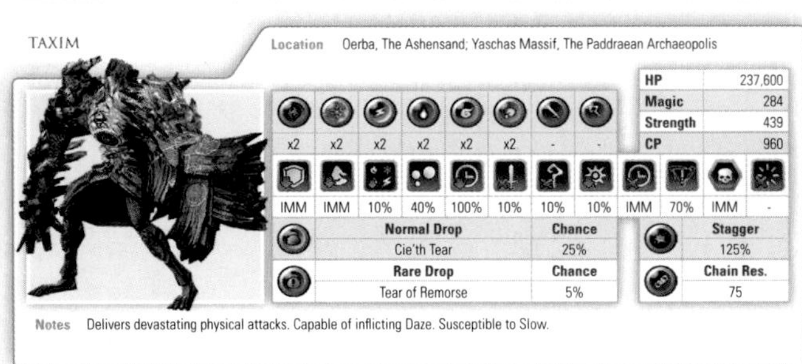

HP	237,600
Magic	284
Strength	439
CP	960

x2	x2	x2	x2	x2	x2	-	-

IMM	IMM	10%	40%	100%	10%	10%	10%	IMM	70%	IMM	-

Normal Drop	Chance	Stagger
Cie'th Tear	25%	125%
Rare Drop	**Chance**	**Chain Res.**
Tear of Remorse	5%	75

Notes Delivers devastating physical attacks. Capable of inflicting Daze. Susceptible to Slow.

VAMPIRE

Location Taejin's Tower, Sixth Tier; Oerba; Eden

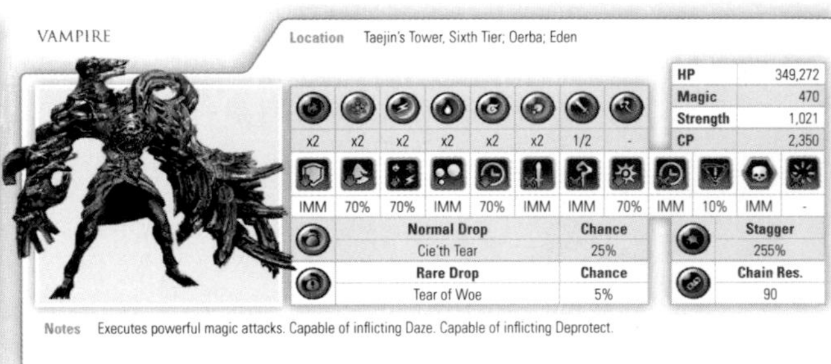

HP	349,272
Magic	470
Strength	1,021
CP	2,350

x2	x2	x2	x2	x2	x2	1/2	-

IMM	70%	70%	IMM	70%	IMM	IMM	70%	IMM	10%	IMM	-

Normal Drop	Chance	Stagger
Cie'th Tear	25%	255%
Rare Drop	**Chance**	**Chain Res.**
Tear of Woe	5%	90

Notes Executes powerful magic attacks. Capable of inflicting Daze. Capable of inflicting Deprotect.

SACRIFICE

Location Eden, Edenhall; Orphan's Cradle

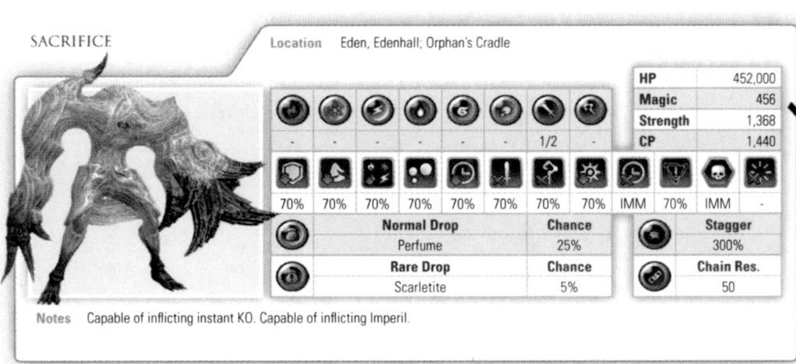

HP	452,000
Magic	456
Strength	1,368
CP	1,440

-	-	-	-	-	-	1/2	-

70%	70%	70%	70%	70%	70%	70%	70%	IMM	70%	IMM	-

Normal Drop	Chance	Stagger
Perfume	25%	300%
Rare Drop	**Chance**	**Chain Res.**
Scarletite	5%	50

Notes Capable of inflicting instant KO. Capable of inflicting Imperil.

WIGHT

Location The Pulse Vestige, Anima's Throne

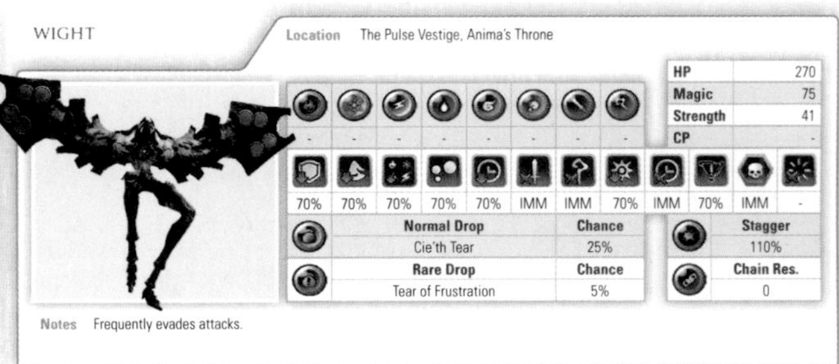

HP	270
Magic	75
Strength	41
CP	-

-	-	-	-	-	-	-	-

70%	70%	70%	70%	70%	IMM	IMM	70%	IMM	70%	IMM	-

Normal Drop	Chance	Stagger
Cie'th Tear	25%	110%
Rare Drop	**Chance**	**Chain Res.**
Tear of Frustration	5%	0

Notes Frequently evades attacks.

PIJAVICA

Location The Archylte Steppe, The Haerii Archaeopolis

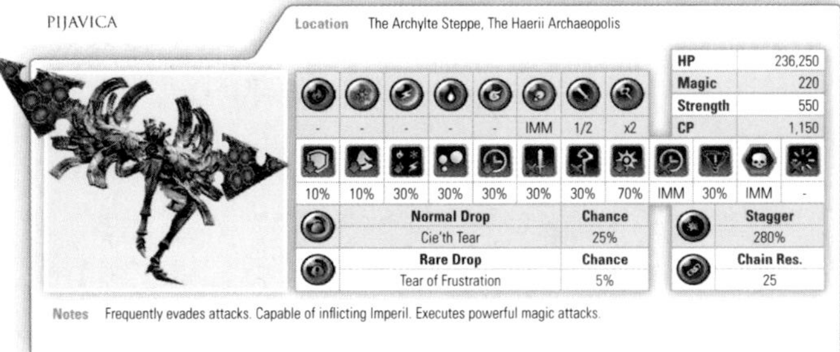

HP	236,250
Magic	220
Strength	550
CP	1,150

-	-	-	-	-	IMM	1/2	x2

10%	10%	30%	30%	30%	30%	30%	70%	IMM	30%	IMM	-

Normal Drop	Chance	Stagger
Cie'th Tear	25%	280%
Rare Drop	**Chance**	**Chain Res.**
Tear of Frustration	5%	25

Notes Frequently evades attacks. Capable of inflicting Imperil. Executes powerful magic attacks.

NELAPSI

Location Yaschas Massif, The Paddraean Archaeopolis

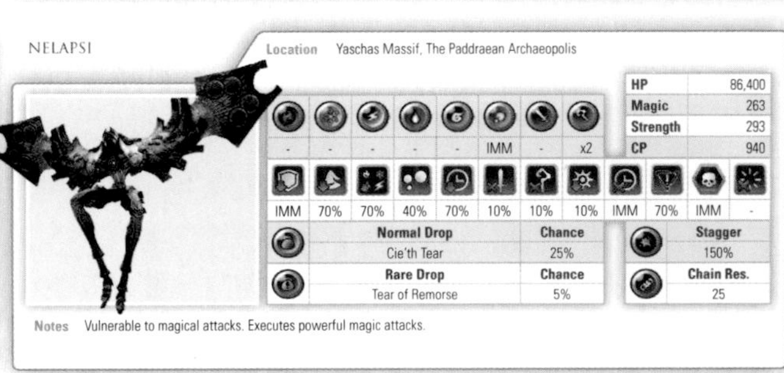

HP	86,400
Magic	263
Strength	293
CP	940

-	-	-	-	-	IMM	-	x2

IMM	70%	70%	40%	70%	10%	10%	10%	IMM	70%	IMM	-

Normal Drop	Chance	Stagger
Cie'th Tear	25%	150%
Rare Drop	**Chance**	**Chain Res.**
Tear of Remorse	5%	25

Notes Vulnerable to magical attacks. Executes powerful magic attacks.

VARCOLACI

Location Taejin's Tower, Fourth Tier; Oerba; Eden

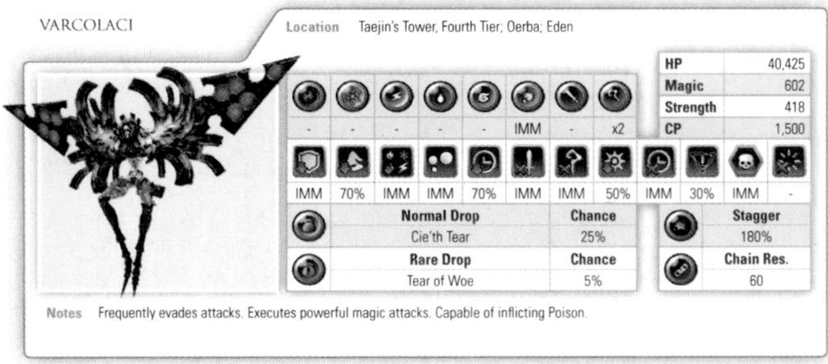

HP	40,425
Magic	602
Strength	418
CP	1,500

-	-	-	-	-	IMM	-	x2

IMM	70%	IMM	IMM	70%	IMM	IMM	50%	IMM	30%	IMM	-

Normal Drop	Chance	Stagger
Cie'th Tear	25%	180%
Rare Drop	**Chance**	**Chain Res.**
Tear of Woe	5%	60

Notes Frequently evades attacks. Executes powerful magic attacks. Capable of inflicting Poison.

EDIMMU

Location Yaschas Massif, The Tsumitran Basin (Mark 05)

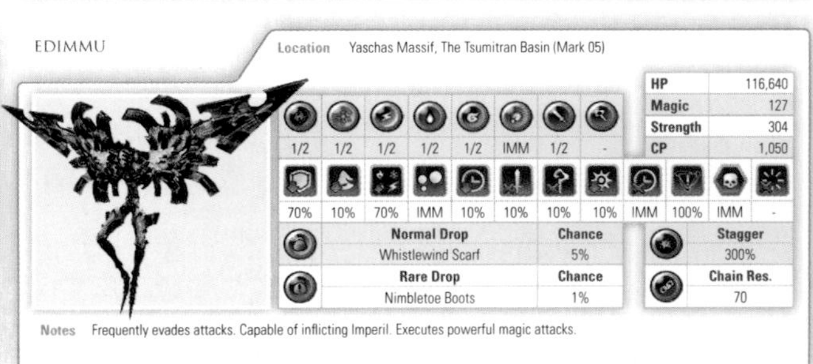

HP	116,640
Magic	127
Strength	304
CP	1,050

1/2	1/2	1/2	1/2	1/2	IMM	1/2	-

70%	10%	70%	IMM	10%	10%	10%	10%	IMM	100%	IMM	-

Normal Drop	Chance	Stagger
Whistlewind Scarf	5%	300%
Rare Drop	**Chance**	**Chain Res.**
Nimbletoe Boots	1%	70

Notes Frequently evades attacks. Capable of inflicting Imperil. Executes powerful magic attacks.

CHONCHON

Location Taejin's Tower, Sixth Tier; Oerba

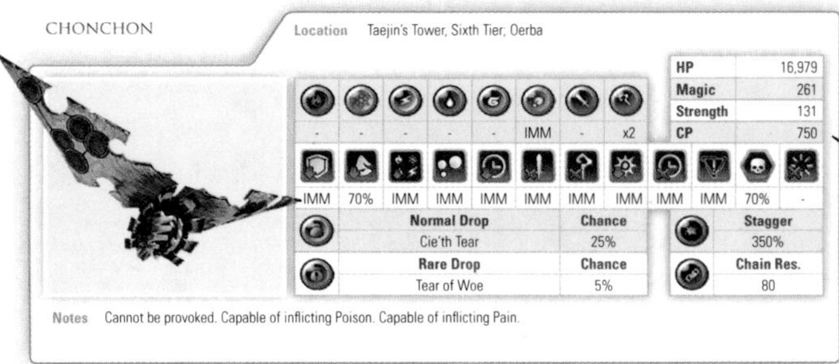

HP	16,979
Magic	261
Strength	131
CP	750

-	-	-	-	-	IMM	-	x2

IMM	70%	IMM	IMM	IMM	IMM	IMM	IMM	IMM	IMM	70%	-

Normal Drop	Chance	Stagger
Cie'th Tear	25%	350%
Rare Drop	**Chance**	**Chain Res.**
Tear of Woe	5%	80

Notes Cannot be provoked. Capable of inflicting Poison. Capable of inflicting Pain.

PENANGGALAN

Location Taejin's Tower, Sixth Tier (Mark 26)

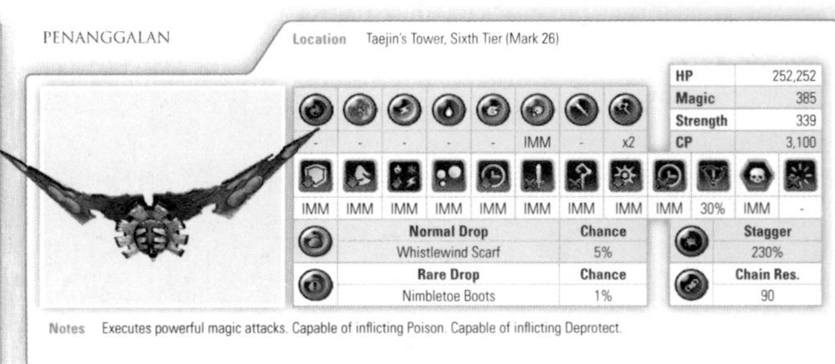

HP	252,252
Magic	385
Strength	339
CP	3,100

-	-	-	-	-	IMM	-	x2

IMM	IMM	IMM	IMM	IMM	IMM	IMM	IMM	IMM	30%	IMM	-

Normal Drop	Chance	Stagger
Whistlewind Scarf	5%	230%
Rare Drop	**Chance**	**Chain Res.**
Nimbletoe Boots	1%	90

Notes Executes powerful magic attacks. Capable of inflicting Poison. Capable of inflicting Deprotect.

VETALA

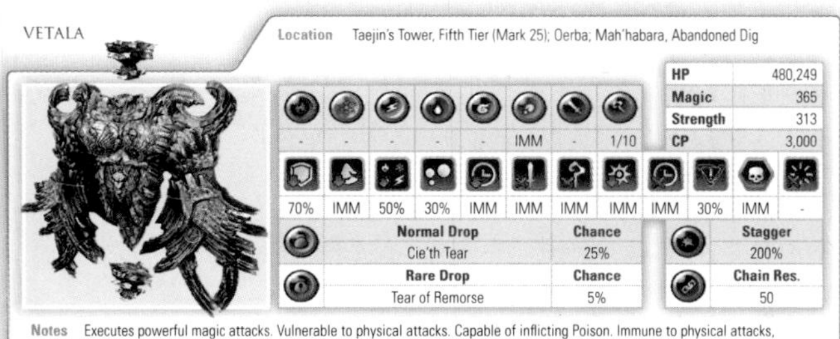

Location Taejin's Tower, Fifth Tier (Mark 25); Oerba; Mah'habara, Abandoned Dig

HP	Magic	Strength	CP
480,249	365	313	3,000

-	-	-	-	-	IMM	-	1/10

70%	IMM	50%	30%	IMM	IMM	IMM	IMM	IMM	30%	IMM	-

Normal Drop	Chance	Rare Drop	Chance	Stagger	Chain Res.
Cie'th Tear	25%	Tear of Remorse	5%	200%	50

Notes Executes powerful magic attacks. Vulnerable to physical attacks. Capable of inflicting Poison. Immune to physical attacks, Deprotect and Earth, and halves other elemental damage when Inertial Barrier is active.

RAKTAVIJA

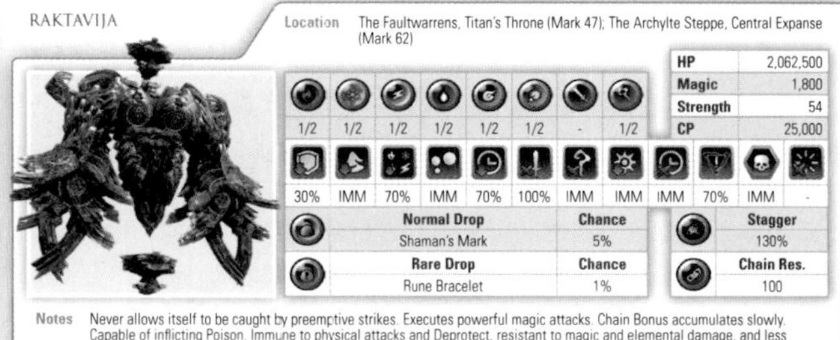

Location The Faultwarrens, Titan's Throne (Mark 47); The Archylte Steppe, Central Expanse (Mark 62)

HP	Magic	Strength	CP
2,062,500	1,800	54	25,000

1/2	1/2	1/2	1/2	1/2	1/2	-	1/2

30%	IMM	70%	IMM	70%	100%	IMM	IMM	IMM	70%	IMM	-

Normal Drop	Chance	Rare Drop	Chance	Stagger	Chain Res.
Shaman's Mark	5%	Rune Bracelet	1%	130%	100

Notes Never allows itself to be caught by preemptive strikes. Executes powerful magic attacks. Chain Bonus accumulates slowly. Capable of inflicting Poison. Immune to physical attacks and Deprotect, resistant to magic and elemental damage, and less susceptible to Imperil, Slow and Fain when Inertial Barrier is active.

SEEKER

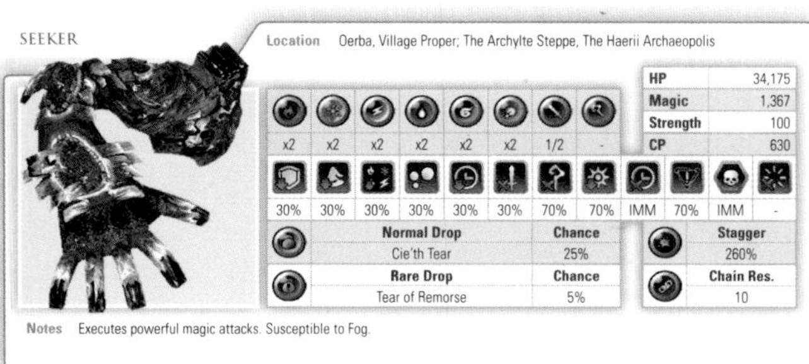

Location Oerba, Village Proper; The Archylte Steppe, The Haerii Archaeopolis

HP	Magic	Strength	CP
34,175	1,367	100	630

x2	x2	x2	x2	x2	x2	1/2	-

30%	30%	30%	30%	30%	30%	70%	70%	IMM	70%	IMM	-

Normal Drop	Chance	Rare Drop	Chance	Stagger	Chain Res.
Cie'th Tear	25%	Tear of Remorse	5%	260%	10

Notes Executes powerful magic attacks. Susceptible to Fog.

MITHRIDATES

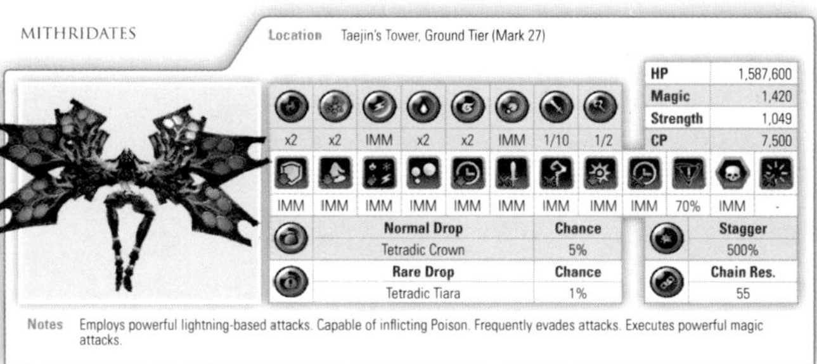

Location Taejin's Tower, Ground Tier (Mark 27)

HP	Magic	Strength	CP
1,587,600	1,420	1,049	7,500

x2	x2	IMM	x2	x2	IMM	1/10	1/2

IMM	IMM	IMM	IMM	IMM	IMM	IMM	IMM	IMM	70%	IMM	-

Normal Drop	Chance	Rare Drop	Chance	Stagger	Chain Res.
Tetradic Crown	5%	Tetradic Tiara	1%	500%	55

Notes Employs powerful lightning-based attacks. Capable of inflicting Poison. Frequently evades attacks. Executes powerful magic attacks.

BITUITUS

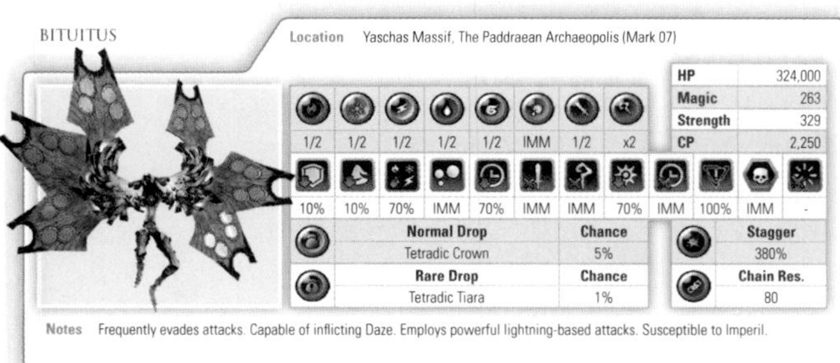

Location Yaschas Massif, The Paddraean Archaeopolis (Mark 07)

HP	Magic	Strength	CP
324,000	263	329	2,250

1/2	1/2	1/2	1/2	1/2	IMM	1/2	x2

10%	10%	70%	IMM	70%	IMM	IMM	70%	IMM	100%	IMM	-

Normal Drop	Chance	Rare Drop	Chance	Stagger	Chain Res.
Tetradic Crown	5%	Tetradic Tiara	1%	380%	80

Notes Frequently evades attacks. Capable of inflicting Daze. Employs powerful lightning-based attacks. Susceptible to Imperil.

GEISERIC

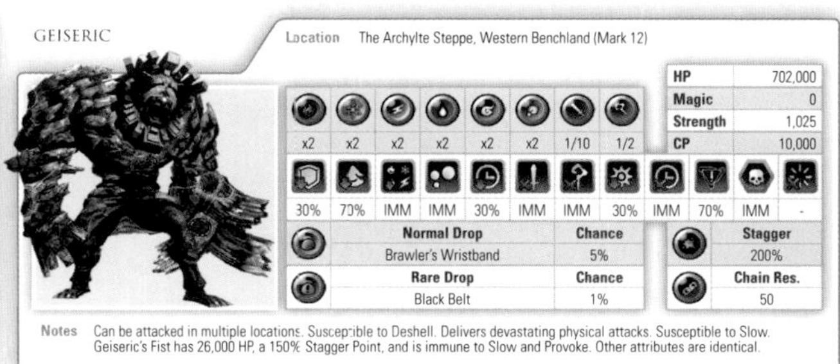

Location The Archylte Steppe, Western Benchland (Mark 12)

HP	Magic	Strength	CP
702,000	0	1,025	10,000

x2	x2	x2	x2	x2	x2	1/10	1/2

30%	70%	IMM	IMM	30%	IMM	IMM	30%	IMM	70%	IMM	-

Normal Drop	Chance	Rare Drop	Chance	Stagger	Chain Res.
Brawler's Wristband	5%	Black Belt	1%	200%	50

Notes Can be attacked in multiple locations. Susceptible to Deshell. Delivers devastating physical attacks. Susceptible to Slow. Geiseric's Fist has 26,000 HP, a 150% Stagger Point, and is immune to Slow and Provoke. Other attributes are identical.

SYPHAX

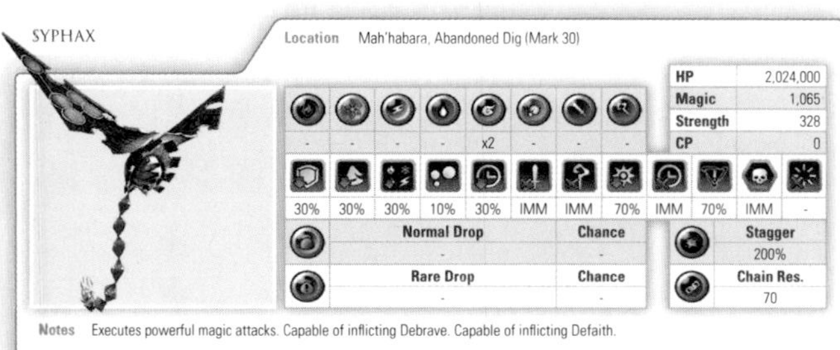

Location Mah'habara, Abandoned Dig (Mark 30)

HP	Magic	Strength	CP
2,024,000	1,065	328	0

-	-	-	-	x2	-	-	-

30%	30%	30%	10%	30%	IMM	IMM	70%	IMM	70%	IMM	-

Normal Drop	Chance	Rare Drop	Chance	Stagger	Chain Res.
-	-	-	-	200%	70

Notes Executes powerful magic attacks. Capable of inflicting Debrave. Capable of inflicting Defaith.

NUMIDIA

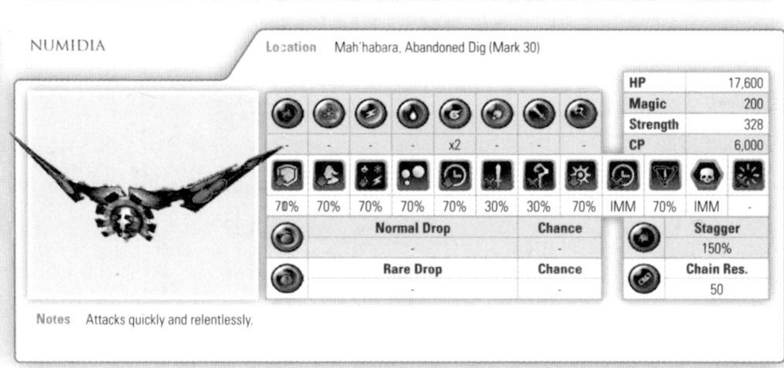

Location Mah'habara, Abandoned Dig (Mark 30)

HP	Magic	Strength	CP
17,600	200	328	6,000

-	-	-	-	x2	-	-	-

70%	70%	70%	70%	70%	30%	30%	70%	IMM	70%	IMM	-

Normal Drop	Chance	Rare Drop	Chance	Stagger	Chain Res.
-	-	-	-	150%	50

Notes Attacks quickly and relentlessly.

ATTACUS

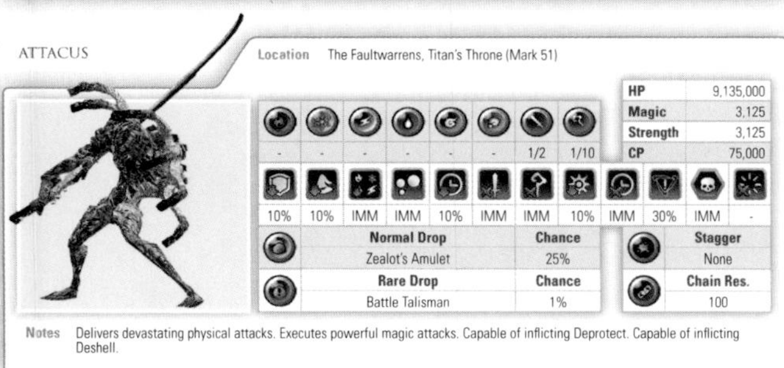

Location The Faultwarrens, Titan's Throne (Mark 51)

HP	Magic	Strength	CP
9,135,000	3,125	3,125	75,000

-	-	-	-	-	-	1/2	1/10

10%	10%	IMM	IMM	10%	IMM	IMM	10%	IMM	30%	IMM	-

Normal Drop	Chance	Rare Drop	Chance	Stagger	Chain Res.
Zealot's Amulet	25%	Battle Talisman	1%	None	100

Notes Delivers devastating physical attacks. Executes powerful magic attacks. Capable of inflicting Deprotect. Capable of inflicting Deshell.

WLADISLAUS

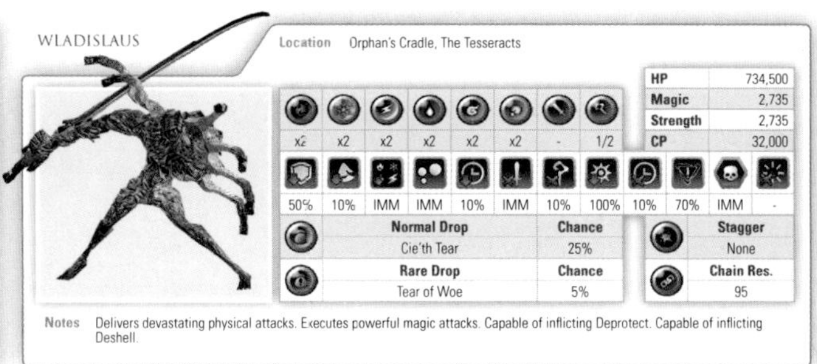

Location Orphan's Cradle, The Tesseracts

HP	Magic	Strength	CP
734,500	2,735	2,735	32,000

x2	x2	x2	x2	x2	x2	-	1/2

50%	10%	IMM	IMM	10%	IMM	10%	100%	10%	70%	IMM	-

Normal Drop	Chance	Rare Drop	Chance	Stagger	Chain Res.
Cie'th Tear	25%	Tear of Woe	5%	None	95

Notes Delivers devastating physical attacks. Executes powerful magic attacks. Capable of inflicting Deprotect. Capable of inflicting Deshell.

VERCINGETORIX

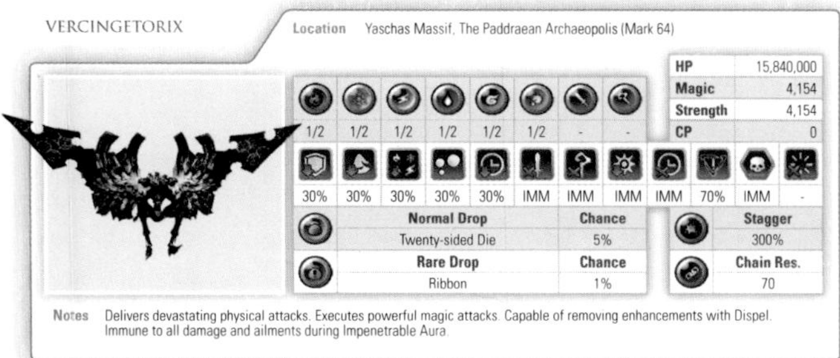

Location Yaschas Massif, The Paddraean Archaeopolis (Mark 64)

HP	Magic	Strength	CP
15,840,000	4,154	4,154	0

1/2	1/2	1/2	1/2	1/2	1/2	-	-

30%	30%	30%	30%	30%	IMM	IMM	IMM	IMM	70%	IMM	-

Normal Drop	Chance	Rare Drop	Chance	Stagger	Chain Res.
Twenty-sided Die	5%	Ribbon	1%	300%	70

Notes Delivers devastating physical attacks. Executes powerful magic attacks. Capable of removing enhancements with Dispel. Immune to all damage and ailments during Impenetrable Aura.

ANIMA

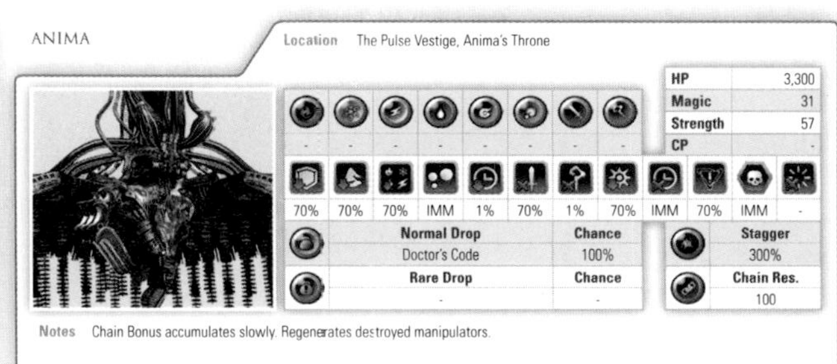

Location The Pulse Vestige, Anima's Throne

HP	Magic	Strength	CP
3,300	31	57	-

-	-	-	-	-	-	-	-

70%	70%	70%	IMM	1%	70%	1%	70%	IMM	70%	IMM	-

Normal Drop	Chance	Rare Drop	Chance	Stagger	Chain Res.
Doctor's Code	100%	-	-	300%	100

Notes Chain Bonus accumulates slowly. Regenerates destroyed manipulators.

ANIMA (MANIPULATORS)

Location The Pulse Vestige, Anima's Throne

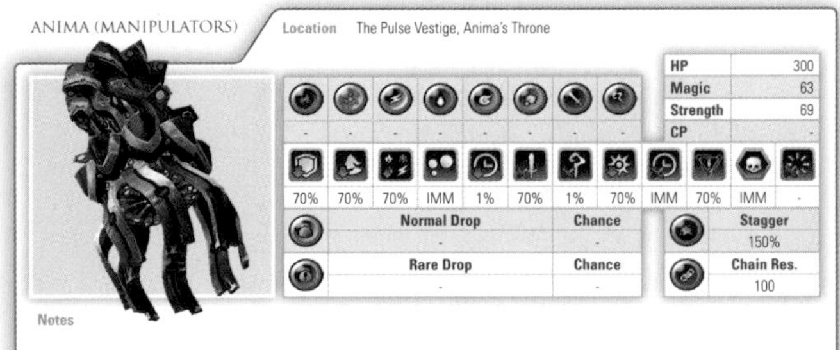

HP	Magic	Strength	CP
300	63	69	-

-	-	-	-	-	-	-	-

70%	70%	70%	IMM	1%	70%	1%	70%	IMM	70%	IMM	-

Normal Drop	Chance	Rare Drop	Chance	Stagger	Chain Res.
-	-	-	-	150%	100

Notes

DAHAKA

Location Taejin's Tower, The Cloven Spire

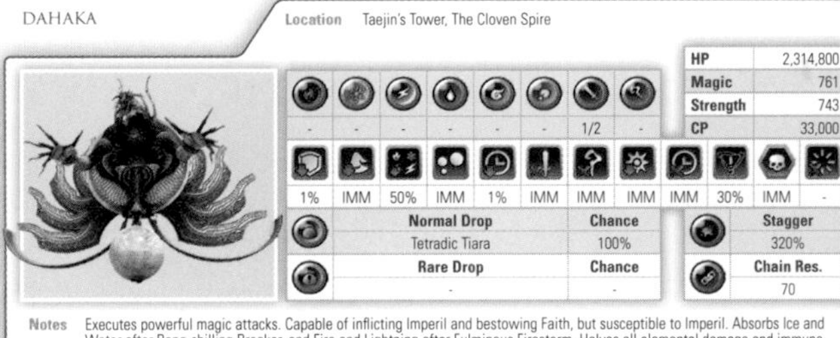

HP	Magic	Strength	CP
2,314,800	761	743	33,000

-	-	-	-	-	-	1/2	-

1%	IMM	50%	IMM	1%	IMM	IMM	IMM	IMM	30%	IMM	-

Normal Drop	Chance	Rare Drop	Chance	Stagger	Chain Res.
Tetradic Tiara	100%	-	-	320%	70

Notes Executes powerful magic attacks. Capable of inflicting Imperil and bestowing Faith, but susceptible to Imperil. Absorbs Ice and Water after Bone-chilling Breaker, and Fire and Lightning after Fulminous Firestorm. Halves all elemental damage and immune to all ailments after Diluvial Plague. Susceptible to Deprotect, Imperil and Slow when Staggered.

BARTHANDELUS

Location The Palamecia, Bridge Access

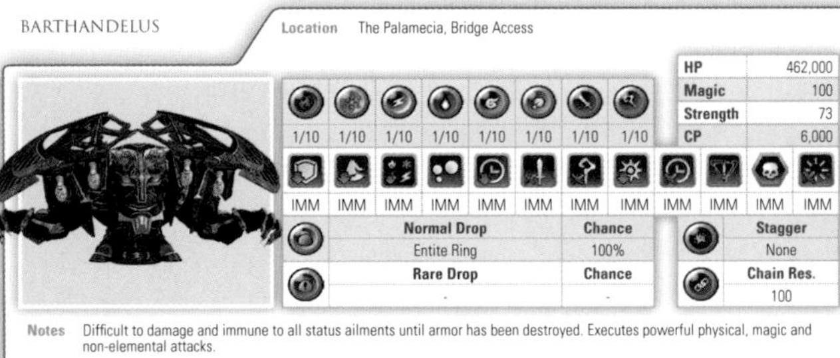

HP	Magic	Strength	CP
462,000	100	73	6,000

1/10	1/10	1/10	1/10	1/10	1/10	1/10	1/10

IMM	IMM	IMM	IMM	IMM	IMM	IMM	IMM	IMM	IMM	IMM	IMM

Normal Drop	Chance	Rare Drop	Chance	Stagger	Chain Res.
Entite Ring	100%	-	-	None	100

Notes Difficult to damage and immune to all status ailments until armor has been destroyed. Executes powerful physical, magic and non-elemental attacks.

BARTHANDELUS (LEFT AILETTE)

Location The Palamecia, Bridge Access

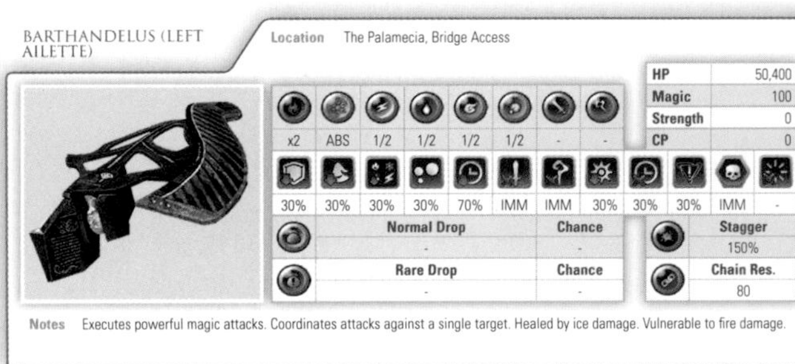

HP	Magic	Strength	CP
50,400	100	0	0

x2	ABS	1/2	1/2	1/2	1/2	-	-

30%	30%	30%	30%	70%	IMM	IMM	30%	30%	30%	IMM	-

Normal Drop	Chance	Rare Drop	Chance	Stagger	Chain Res.
-	-	-	-	150%	80

Notes Executes powerful magic attacks. Coordinates attacks against a single target. Healed by ice damage. Vulnerable to fire damage.

BARTHANDELUS (LEFT PAULDRON)

Location The Palamecia, Bridge Access

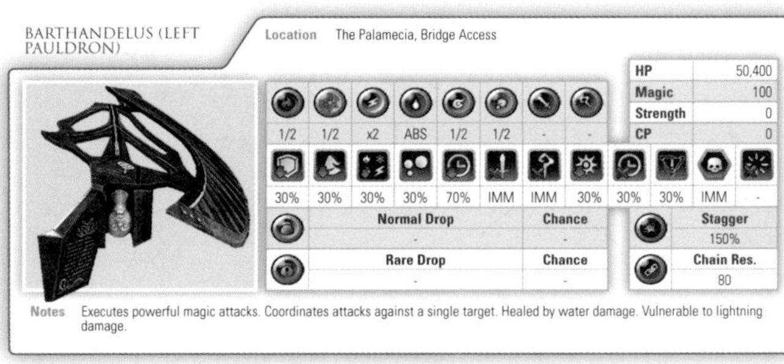

HP	Magic	Strength	CP
50,400	100	0	0

1/2	1/2	x2	ABS	1/2	1/2	-	-

30%	30%	30%	30%	70%	IMM	IMM	30%	30%	30%	IMM	-

Normal Drop	Chance	Rare Drop	Chance	Stagger	Chain Res.
-	-	-	-	150%	80

Notes Executes powerful magic attacks. Coordinates attacks against a single target. Healed by water damage. Vulnerable to lightning damage.

BARTHANDELUS (RIGHT AILETTE)

Location The Palamecia, Bridge Access

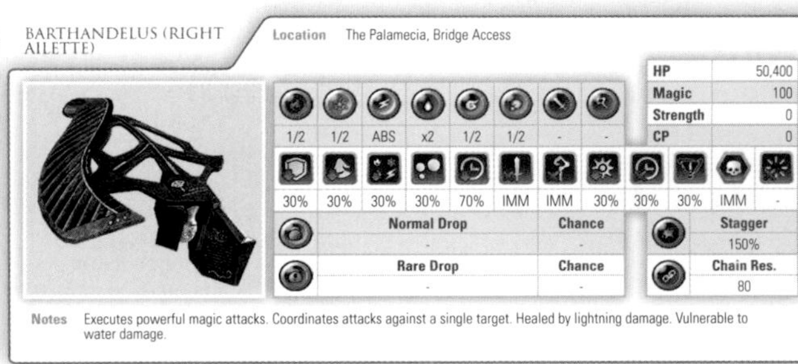

HP	Magic	Strength	CP
50,400	100	0	0

1/2	1/2	ABS	x2	1/2	1/2	-	-

30%	30%	30%	30%	70%	IMM	IMM	30%	30%	30%	IMM	-

Normal Drop	Chance	Rare Drop	Chance	Stagger	Chain Res.
-	-	-	-	150%	80

Notes Executes powerful magic attacks. Coordinates attacks against a single target. Healed by lightning damage. Vulnerable to water damage.

BARTHANDELUS (RIGHT PAULDRON)

Location The Palamecia, Bridge Access

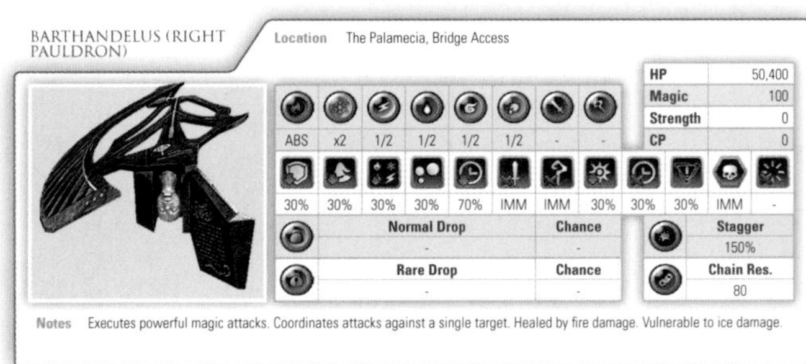

HP	Magic	Strength	CP
50,400	100	0	0

ABS	x2	1/2	1/2	1/2	1/2	-	-

30%	30%	30%	30%	70%	IMM	IMM	30%	30%	30%	IMM	-

Normal Drop	Chance	Rare Drop	Chance	Stagger	Chain Res.
-	-	-	-	150%	80

Notes Executes powerful magic attacks. Coordinates attacks against a single target. Healed by fire damage. Vulnerable to ice damage.

BARTHANDELUS

Location Oerba, Rust-eaten Bridge

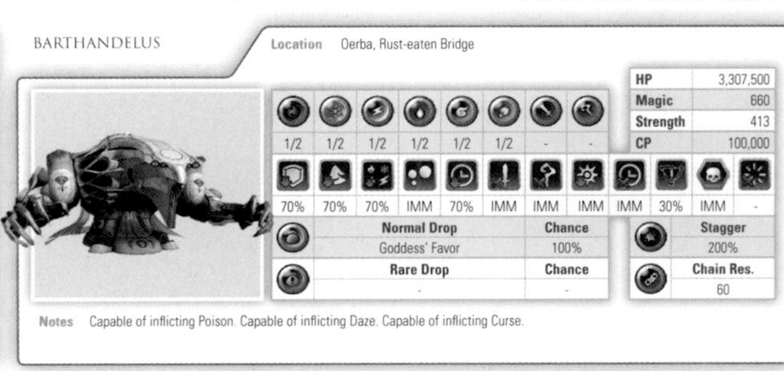

HP	Magic	Strength	CP
3,307,500	660	413	100,000

1/2	1/2	1/2	1/2	1/2	1/2	-	-

70%	70%	70%	IMM	70%	IMM	IMM	IMM	IMM	30%	IMM	-

Normal Drop	Chance	Rare Drop	Chance	Stagger	Chain Res.
Goddess' Favor	100%	-	-	200%	60

Notes Capable of inflicting Poison. Capable of inflicting Daze. Capable of inflicting Curse.

BARTHANDELUS

Location Orphan's Cradle, The Narthex

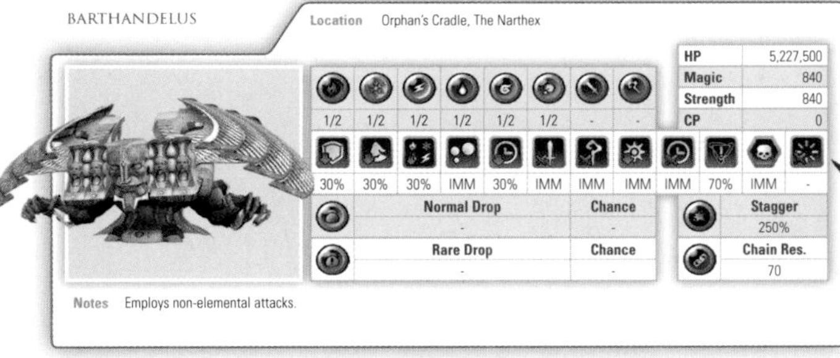

HP	Magic	Strength	CP
5,227,500	840	840	0

1/2	1/2	1/2	1/2	1/2	1/2	-	-

30%	30%	30%	IMM	30%	IMM	IMM	IMM	IMM	70%	IMM	-

Normal Drop	Chance	Rare Drop	Chance	Stagger	Chain Res.
-	-	-	-	250%	70

Notes Employs non-elemental attacks.

ORPHAN (FIRST BATTLE)

Location Orphan's Cradle, The Narthex

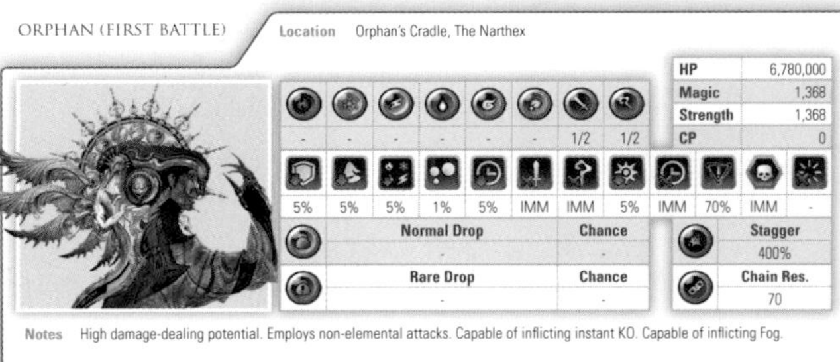

HP	Magic	Strength	CP
6,780,000	1,368	1,368	0

-	-	-	-	-	-	1/2	1/2

5%	5%	5%	1%	5%	IMM	IMM	5%	IMM	70%	IMM	-

Normal Drop	Chance	Rare Drop	Chance	Stagger	Chain Res.
-	-	-	-	400%	70

Notes High damage-dealing potential. Employs non-elemental attacks. Capable of inflicting instant KO. Capable of inflicting Fog.

ORPHAN (SECOND BATTLE)

Location Orphan's Cradle, The Narthex

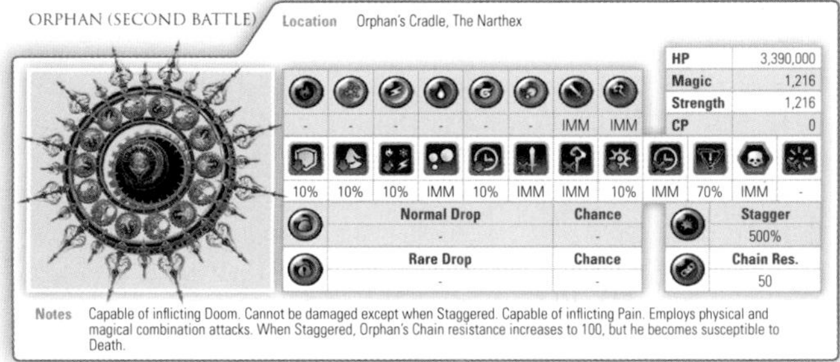

HP	Magic	Strength	CP
3,390,000	1,216	1,216	0

-	-	-	-	-	-	IMM	IMM

10%	10%	10%	IMM	10%	IMM	IMM	10%	IMM	70%	IMM	-

Normal Drop	Chance	Rare Drop	Chance	Stagger	Chain Res.
-	-	-	-	500%	50

Notes Capable of inflicting Doom. Cannot be damaged except when Staggered. Capable of inflicting Pain. Employs physical and magical combination attacks. When Staggered, Orphan's Chain resistance increases to 100, but he becomes susceptible to Death.

CID RAINES

Location The Fifth Ark, Inner Conduit

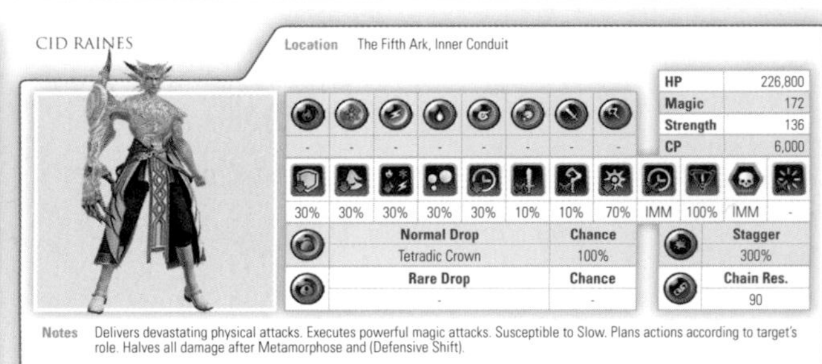

HP	Magic	Strength	CP
226,800	172	136	6,000

-	-	-	-	-	-	-	-

30%	30%	30%	30%	30%	10%	10%	70%	IMM	100%	IMM	-

Normal Drop	Chance	Rare Drop	Chance	Stagger	Chain Res.
Tetradic Crown	100%	-	-	300%	90

Notes Delivers devastating physical attacks. Executes powerful magic attacks. Susceptible to Slow. Plans actions according to target's role. Halves all damage after Metamorphose and (Defensive Shift).

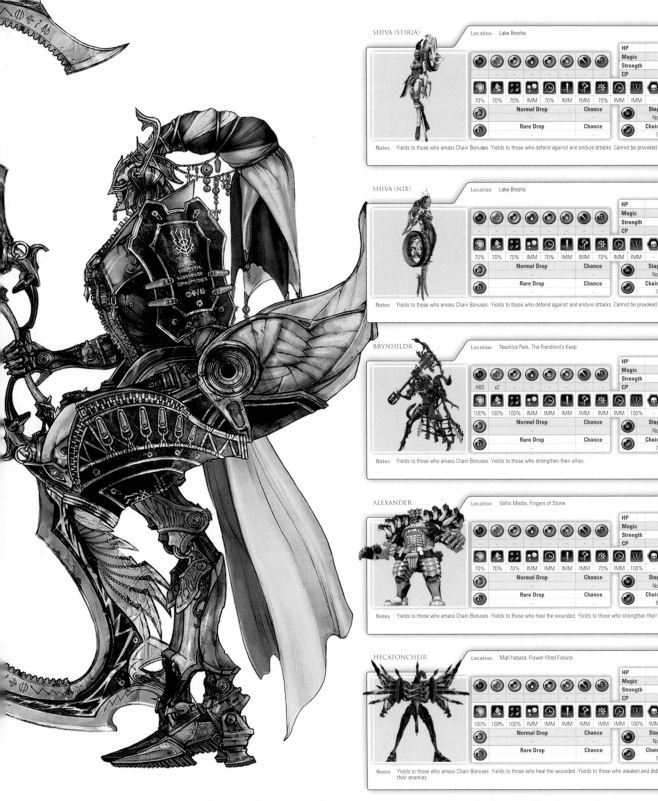

SHIVA (STIRIA)

Location Lake Bresha

HP	-
Magic	1,000
Strength	50
CP	0

-	-	-	-	-	-	-	-

70%	70%	70%	IMM	70%	IMM	IMM	70%	IMM	IMM	-	-

Normal Drop	Chance	Stagger
-	-	None
Rare Drop	**Chance**	**Chain Res.**
-	-	70

Notes Yields to those who amass Chain Bonuses. Yields to those who defend against and endure attacks. Cannot be provoked.

SHIVA (NIX)

Location Lake Bresha

HP	-
Magic	60
Strength	55
CP	0

-	-	-	-	-	-	-	-

70%	70%	70%	IMM	70%	IMM	IMM	70%	IMM	IMM	-	-

Normal Drop	Chance	Stagger
-	-	None
Rare Drop	**Chance**	**Chain Res.**
-	-	70

Notes Yields to those who amass Chain Bonuses. Yields to those who defend against and endure attacks. Cannot be provoked.

BRYNHILDR

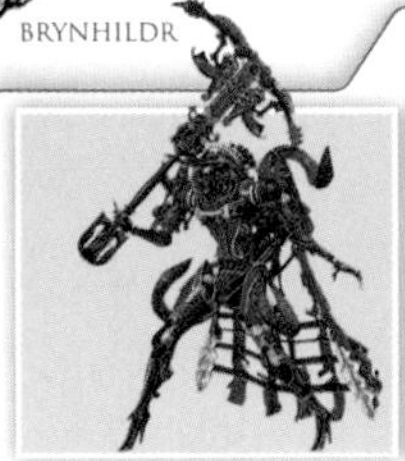

Location Nautilus Park, The Fiendlord's Keep

HP	-
Magic	128
Strength	116
CP	0

ABS	x2	-	-	-	-	-	-

100%	100%	100%	IMM	IMM	IMM	IMM	IMM	IMM	100%	-	-

Normal Drop	Chance	Stagger
-	-	None
Rare Drop	**Chance**	**Chain Res.**
-	-	70

Notes Yields to those who amass Chain Bonuses. Yields to those who strengthen their allies.

ALEXANDER

Location Vallis Media, Fingers of Stone

HP	-
Magic	850
Strength	850
CP	0

-	-	-	-	-	-	-	-

70%	70%	70%	IMM	IMM	IMM	IMM	70%	IMM	100%	-	-

Normal Drop	Chance	Stagger
-	-	None
Rare Drop	**Chance**	**Chain Res.**
-	-	85

Notes Yields to those who amass Chain Bonuses. Yields to those who heal the wounded. Yields to those who strengthen their allies.

HECATONCHEIR

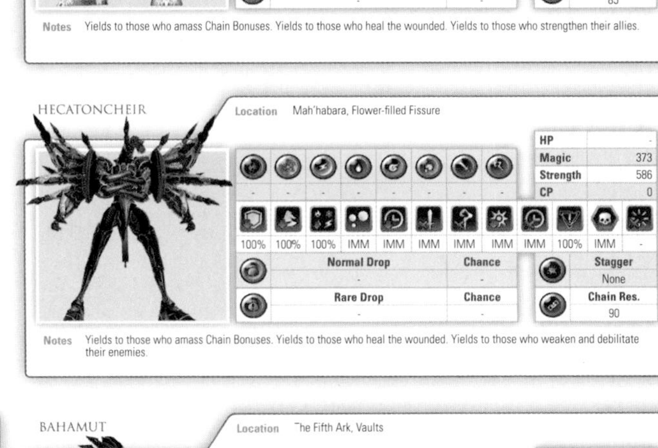

Location Mah'habara, Flower-filled Fissure

HP	-
Magic	373
Strength	586
CP	0

-	-	-	-	-	-	-	-

100%	100%	100%	IMM	IMM	IMM	IMM	IMM	IMM	100%	IMM	-

Normal Drop	Chance	Stagger
-	-	None
Rare Drop	**Chance**	**Chain Res.**
-	-	90

Notes Yields to those who amass Chain Bonuses. Yields to those who heal the wounded. Yields to those who weaken and debilitate their enemies.

ODIN

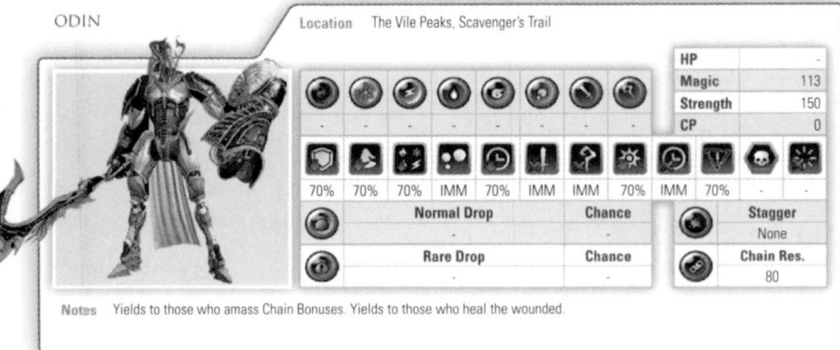

Location The Vile Peaks, Scavenger's Trail

HP	-
Magic	113
Strength	150
CP	0

-	-	-	-	-	-	-	-

70%	70%	70%	IMM	70%	IMM	IMM	70%	IMM	70%	-	-

Normal Drop	Chance	Stagger
-	-	None
Rare Drop	**Chance**	**Chain Res.**
-	-	80

Notes Yields to those who amass Chain Bonuses. Yields to those who heal the wounded.

BAHAMUT

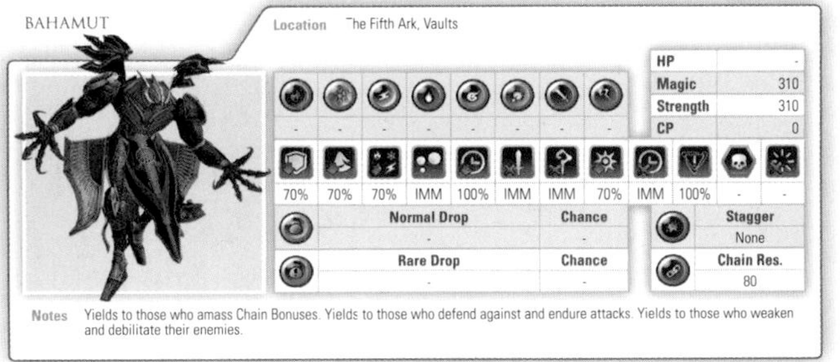

Location The Fifth Ark, Vaults

HP	-
Magic	310
Strength	310
CP	0

-	-	-	-	-	-	-	-

70%	70%	70%	IMM	100%	IMM	IMM	70%	IMM	100%	-	-

Normal Drop	Chance	Stagger
-	-	None
Rare Drop	**Chance**	**Chain Res.**
-	-	80

Notes Yields to those who amass Chain Bonuses. Yields to those who defend against and endure attacks. Yields to those who weaken and debilitate their enemies.

EXTRAS

This short final chapter offers checklists of all side-quests and optional adventures in Final Fantasy XIII, and a dedicated guide to unlocking Trophies and Achievements. A word of warning: the pages that follow contain frequent **spoilers**. If you have yet to complete the main storyline, we strongly suggest that you read no further.

The following tables are designed to act as checklists that will enable you to track your overall progress in FFXIII and identify tasks you have missed, with page references leading to further information and advice elsewhere in the guide.

SIDE-QUESTS CHECKLIST

Name	Description	Page
Pulse Armament minigame	Minigame where you can obtain rewards by defeating certain amounts of Pulsework Soldiers in the Vile Peaks.	41
Scrap Processing secrets	You can access secret areas on the Scrap Processing map (in the Vile Peaks) to reach two additional Treasure Spheres.	43
Nutriculture Complex secret platforms	There are two secret platforms in the Nutriculture Complex (Palumpolum) that you can reach to find Treasure Spheres.	53
The Archylte Steppe secret areas	The Archylte Steppe is packed with optional adventures, unlockable features and opportunities for exploration.	120
Mark missions	Interacting with Cie'th Stones enables you to begin special missions where you hunt very specific enemies known as "Marks".	82, 128
Mah'habara secret areas	After you ride the Atomos to Sulyya Springs, you have the option to get straight back on and backtrack to Mah'habara, where new map areas are unlocked.	126
Taejin's Tower Seventh Tier	After defeating Dahaka on top of the Cloven Spire, you can access a secret Seventh Tier where you can find a Collector Catalog and rotate the floor (a prerequisite to complete a Mark mission).	94
Repairing Bhakti	If you locate five special parts, all found within Oerba village, you can repair Bhakti and obtain rewards.	97, 127
The Tesseracts secrets	In Orphan's Cradle, when you reach the Tesseracts level with hexagonal platforms, the warp gate at the center leads to four hidden Treasure Spheres.	111
Chocobo secrets	You can ride chocobos on the Archylte Steppe to reach otherwise inaccessible areas.	122
Chocobo treasure hunting	Chocobos can also be used to dig up hidden treasures on the Archylte Steppe.	123
Vallis Media secret areas	After fighting the Alexander Eidolon in Vallis Media, you can return there to explore new (and entirely optional) areas.	117
Yaschas Massif secret areas	The Yaschas Massif is a large optional area that you can visit after you reach the Archylte Steppe in Chapter 11.	118
The Archylte Steppe secret sheep	You can find herds of sheep on the Archylte Steppe, and obtain wool as a reward.	123
The Faultwarrens secret areas	The Faultwarrens is a maze of small map areas connected by a collection of Mark missions known as the Titan's Trials.	124

MARK MISSIONS CHECKLIST

#	Cie'th Stone Location	Mark Location	Mark	Class	Reward	Secondary Reward	Page
01	The Archylte Steppe – Central Expanse	The Archylte Steppe – Central Expanse	Ectopudding	D	Energy Sash	Bomb Core (x3)	129
02	The Archylte Steppe – Central Expanse	The Archylte Steppe – Central Expanse	Uridimmu	D	Cobaltite	Bomb Shell (x3)	129
03	The Archylte Steppe – Central Expanse	Yaschas Massif – Tsubaddran Highlands	Ugallu	D	Platinum Bangle	Bomb Core (x3)	129
04	Yaschas Massif – Tsubaddran Highlands*	Yaschas Massif – The Ascendant Scarp	Adroa	D	Pearl Necklace	Bomb Shell (x3)	129
05	Yaschas Massif – The Ascendant Scarp	Yaschas Massif – Tsumitran Basin	Edimmu	D	Sorcerer's Mark	Bomb Core (x5)	129
06	Yaschas Massif – Paddraean Archaeopolis*	Yaschas Massif – The Pass of Paddra	Munchkin Maestro	C	Fulmen Ring	Bomb Shell (x3)	129
07	Yaschas Massif – Paddraean Archaeopolis	Yaschas Massif – Paddraean Archaeopolis	Bituitus	C	R&D Depot Pass	Bomb Core (x5)	129
08	Vallis Media – Base Camp	Vallis Media – Atzilut's Tears	Rakshasa	C	Collector Catalog	Bomb Shell (x3)	130
09	The Archylte Steppe – Central Expanse*	The Archylte Steppe – Central Expanse	Kaiser Behemoth	C	Rhodochrosite	Bomb Core (x3)	130
10	The Archylte Steppe – Central Expanse	The Archylte Steppe – Northern Highplain	Ambling Bellows	C	Superconductor (x4)	Thrust Bearing (x3)	130
11	The Archylte Steppe – Northern Highplain	The Archylte Steppe – Central Expanse	Adroa	C	Frost Ring (x2)	Bomb Shell (x3)	130
12	The Archylte Steppe – Arid Strath	The Archylte Steppe – Western Benchland	Geiseric	C	Royal Armlet	Bomb Core (x5)	130
13	The Archylte Steppe – Central Expanse	The Archylte Steppe – Northern Highplain	Goblin Chieftain	C	Cobaltite	Bomb Shell (x4)	130
14	The Archylte Steppe – Western Benchland	The Archylte Steppe – Font of Namva	Sahagin	C	Gysahl Reins	Bomb Shell (x3)	130
15	The Archylte Steppe – Central Expanse	The Archylte Steppe – Northern Highplain	Goblin Chieftain	C	Survivalist Catalog	Bomb Shell (x4)	130
16	The Archylte Steppe – Eastern Tors	The Archylte Steppe – Font of Namva	Sahagin	B	Rhodochrosite	Bomb Shell (x4)	132
17	The Archylte Steppe – Northern Highplain*	The Archylte Steppe – Northern Highplain	Pulsework Champion	B	Perfect Conductor (x3)	Piezoelectric Element (x4)	132
18	Mah'habara – Twilit Cavern*	Mah'habara – Twilit Cavern	Ambling Bellows	C	Sorcerer's Mark	Piezoelectric Element (x4)	131
19	Sulyya Springs – Ceiling of Sky*	Sulyya Springs – Subterranean Lake	Uridimmu	C	Cobaltite	Bomb Shell (x5)	131
20	Taejin's Tower – The Palisades*	Taejin's Tower – The Palisades	Goblin Chieftain	C	Rhodochrosite	Bomb Shell (x5)	131
21	Taejin's Tower – Second Tier	Taejin's Tower – Second Tier	Gelatitan	C	Speed Sash	Bomb Shell (x4)	131
22	Taejin's Tower – Second Tier	Taejin's Tower – Second Tier	Ambling Bellows	C	Particle Accelerator (x3)	Electrode (x3)	131
23	Taejin's Tower – Second Tier	Taejin's Tower – Second Tier	Gurangatch	B	Warrior's Wristband	Bomb Shell (x4)	132
24	Taejin's Tower – Fifth Tier	Taejin's Tower – Fifth Tier	Mushussu	B	Moonblossom Seed (x6)	Moonblossom Seed	132
25	Taejin's Tower – Sixth Tier	Taejin's Tower – Fifth Tier	Vetala	B	Cobaltite	Bomb Core (x6)	132
26	Taejin's Tower – Fifth Tier	Taejin's Tower – Sixth Tier	Penanggalan	B	Diamond Bangle	Bomb Core (x6)	132
27	Taejin's Tower – The Cloven Spire	Taejin's Tower – Ground Tier	Mithridates	B	Blaze Ring	Bomb Core (x6)	132
28	Oerba – Village Proper*	Oerba – Village Proper	Ceratosaur	C	Giant's Glove	Bomb Shell (x5)	132
29	Mah'habara – Maw of the Abyss	Taejin's Tower – The Palisades	Juggernaut	B	Uraninite	Mobius Coil (x3)	133
30	The Archylte Steppe – Haerii Oldroad	Mah'habara – Abandoned Dig	Syphax	B	Uraninite	Bomb Core (x6)	133
31	The Archylte Steppe – Haerii Archaeopolis*	The Archylte Steppe – Haerii Archaeopolis	Pulsework Champion	B	Perfect Conductor (x3)	Crystal Oscillator (x2)	133
32	Vallis Media – Earthen Bosom	The Archylte Steppe – Western Benchland	Amam	B	Glass Buckle	Bomb Shell (x5)	133
33	The Archylte Steppe – Haerii Archaeopolis	The Archylte Steppe – Eastern Tors	Adamanchelid	B	White Cape	Bomb Shell (x5)	133
34	The Archylte Steppe – Way of the Ancients	The Archylte Steppe – Haerii Archaepolis	Zenobia	B	Hermes Sandals	Bomb Core (x7)	133
35	Faultwarrens – Truthseeker's Rise	Faultwarrens – Primeval Crossroads	Gurangatch	C	Witch's Bracelet	Bomb Shell (x5)	133
36	Faultwarrens – Primeval Crossroads	Faultwarrens – A Dance of Shadow	Amam	C	Uraninite	Bomb Shell (x6)	134
37	Faultwarrens – Primeval Crossroads	Faultwarrens – A Dance of Light	Rafflesia	C	Star Pendant	Bomb Shell (x5)	134
38	Faultwarrens – A Dance of Shadow	Faultwarrens – Via Lunae	Verdelet	B	Diamond Bangle	Bomb Shell (x5)	134
39	Faultwarrens – A Dance of Shadow/A Dance of Light	Faultwarrens – Via Stellarum	Ochu	C	Siltstone Ring	Moonblossom Seed (x2)	134
40	Faultwarrens – A Dance of Light	Faultwarrens – Via Solis	Verdelet	B	Zealot's Amulet	Bomb Shell (x5)	134
41	Faultwarrens – Via Lunae	Faultwarrens – Gaian Path	Tonberry	A	Doctor's Code	Tonberry Figurine	134
42	Faultwarrens – Via Lunae/Via Stellarum	Faultwarrens – Salamandrine Path	Borgbear Hero	B	Witch's Bracelet	Bomb Core (x7)	134
43	Faultwarrens – Via Stellarum/Via Solis	Faultwarrens – Sylphid Path	Borgbear Hero	B	Speed Sash	Bomb Core (x7)	134
44	Faultwarrens – Via Solis	Faultwarrens – Nereid Path	Corrosive Custard	A	General's Belt	Bomb Shell (x7)	135
45	Faultwarrens – Gaian Path	Faultwarrens – Titan's Throne	Neochu	A	Hunter's Friend	Moonblossom Seed (x3)	135
46	Faultwarrens – Salamandrine Path	Faultwarrens – Titan's Throne	Zirnitra	A	Gilgamesh, Inc. Pass	Bomb Core (x10)	135
47	Faultwarrens – Salamandrine Path	Faultwarrens – Titan's Throne	Raktavija	B	Mnar Stone	Bomb Core (x10)	135
48	Faultwarrens – Sylphid Path	Faultwarrens – Titan's Throne	Verdelet	A	Twenty-sided Die	Bomb Shell (x10)	135
49	Faultwarrens – Sylphid Path	Faultwarrens – Titan's Throne	Tyrant	A	Particle Accelerator (x7)	Crystal Oscillator (x2)	135
50	Faultwarrens – Nereid Path	Faultwarrens – Titan's Throne	Humbaba	B	Scarletite	Bomb Core (x7)	136
51	Faultwarrens – Sylphid Path/Gaian Path/ Salamandrine Path/Nereid Path	Faultwarrens – Titan's Throne	Attacus	A	Genji Glove	Bomb Core (x10)	136
52	The Archylte Steppe – Western Benchland	The Archylte Steppe – Eastern Tors	Zirnitra	A	Gale Ring	Bomb Core (x7)	136
53	Mah'habara – An Asylum from Light	Yaschas Massif – The Pass of Paddra	Zirnitra	A	Blaze Ring	Bomb Core (x10)	136
54	The Archylte Steppe – Northern Highplain	The Archylte Steppe – Eastern Tors	Gigantuar	B	Cactuar Doll	Chocobo Plume (x2)	136
55	Oerba – Deserted Schoolhouse (Roof)	The Archylte Steppe – Aggra's Pasture	Neochu	A	Growth Egg	Moonblossom Seed (x2)	136
56	The Archylte Steppe – Eastern Tors	Yaschas Massif – The Ascendant Scarp	Ugallu	C	Rhodochrosite	Bomb Shell (x5)	131
57	The Archylte Steppe – Eastern Tors	Vallis Media – Atzilut's Tears	Sahagin	C	Uraninite	Bomb Shell (x5)	131
58	The Archylte Steppe – Eastern Tors	Mah'habara – The Earthworks	Humbaba	C	Speed Sash	Bomb Shell (x5)	131
59	The Archylte Steppe – Eastern Tors	Sulyya Springs – Subterranean Lake	Zirnitra	A	Energy Sash	Bomb Core (x6)	136
60	The Archylte Steppe – Eastern Tors	Taejin's Tower – The Cloven Spire	Gelatitan	A	Mnar Stone	Bomb Core (x7)	137
61	The Archylte Steppe – Eastern Tors	Oerba – Village Proper	Juggernaut	A	Royal Armlet	Crystal Oscillator (x2)	137
62	The Archylte Steppe – Eastern Tors	The Archylte Steppe – Central Expanse	Raktavija	A	Genji Glove	Bomb Core (x10)	137
63	Sulyya Springs – Subterranean Lake	The Archylte Steppe – Eastern Tors	Adamantortoise	A	Genji Glove	Gold Nugget	137
64	Oerba – Rust-eaten Bridge	Yaschas Massif – Paddraean Archaeopolis	Vercingetorix	A	Gold Watch	Bomb Core (x10)	137

* Cie'th Waystone

Final Fantasy XIII features a challenging range of Trophies and Achievements. Some are relatively simple and merely acknowledge your progress in the main storyline, while others have been designed to reward very specific feats. Unlocking the full complement on PS3 or Xbox 360 is no trivial undertaking, so use the following guide to both plan and track your progress.

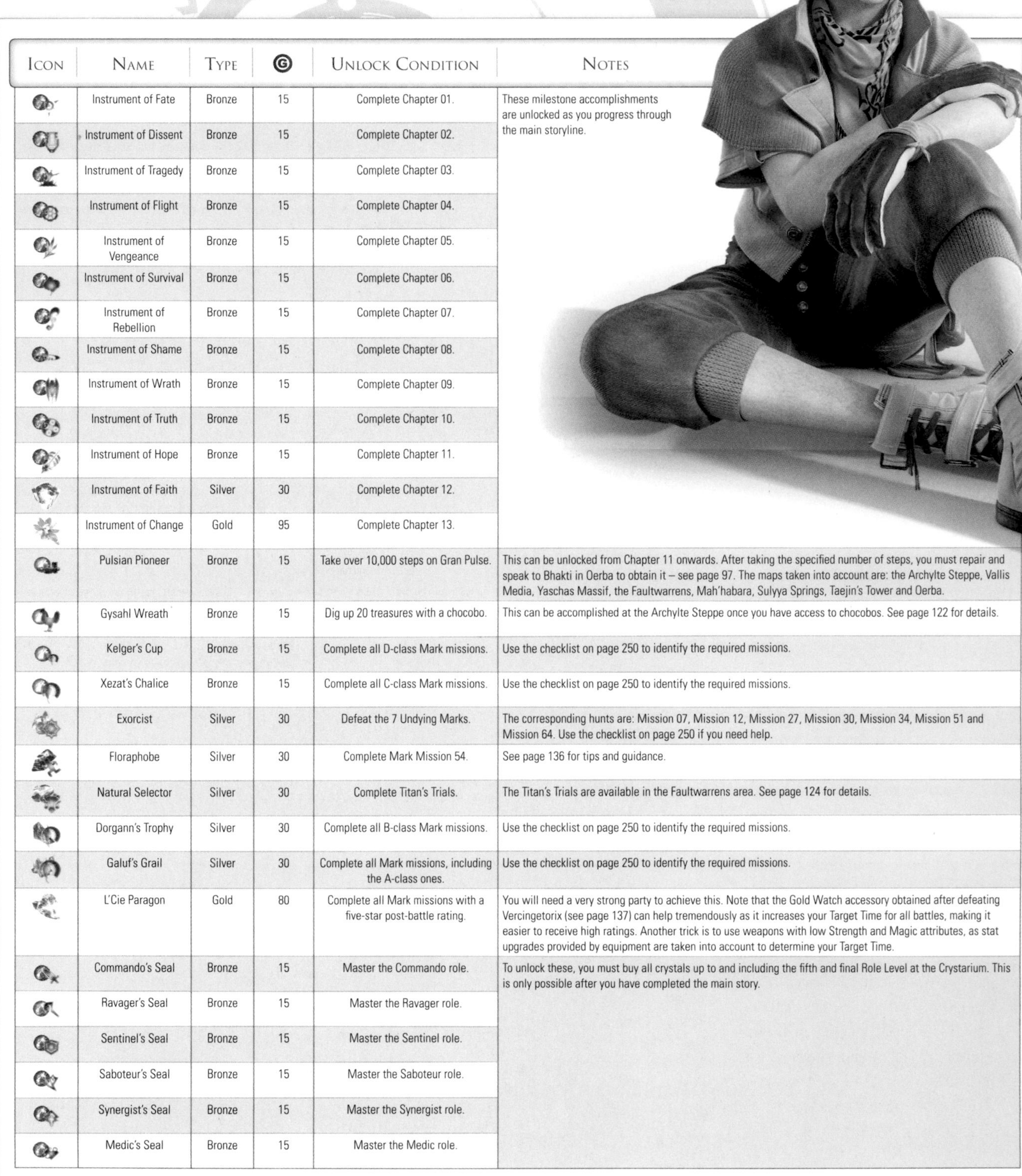

Icon	Name	Type	G	Unlock Condition	Notes
	Instrument of Fate	Bronze	15	Complete Chapter 01.	These milestone accomplishments are unlocked as you progress through the main storyline.
	Instrument of Dissent	Bronze	15	Complete Chapter 02.	
	Instrument of Tragedy	Bronze	15	Complete Chapter 03.	
	Instrument of Flight	Bronze	15	Complete Chapter 04.	
	Instrument of Vengeance	Bronze	15	Complete Chapter 05.	
	Instrument of Survival	Bronze	15	Complete Chapter 06.	
	Instrument of Rebellion	Bronze	15	Complete Chapter 07.	
	Instrument of Shame	Bronze	15	Complete Chapter 08.	
	Instrument of Wrath	Bronze	15	Complete Chapter 09.	
	Instrument of Truth	Bronze	15	Complete Chapter 10.	
	Instrument of Hope	Bronze	15	Complete Chapter 11.	
	Instrument of Faith	Silver	30	Complete Chapter 12.	
	Instrument of Change	Gold	95	Complete Chapter 13.	
	Pulsian Pioneer	Bronze	15	Take over 10,000 steps on Gran Pulse.	This can be unlocked from Chapter 11 onwards. After taking the specified number of steps, you must repair and speak to Bhakti in Oerba to obtain it – see page 97. The maps taken into account are: the Archylte Steppe, Vallis Media, Yaschas Massif, the Faultwarrens, Mah'habara, Sulyya Springs, Taejin's Tower and Oerba.
	Gysahl Wreath	Bronze	15	Dig up 20 treasures with a chocobo.	This can be accomplished at the Archylte Steppe once you have access to chocobos. See page 122 for details.
	Kelger's Cup	Bronze	15	Complete all D-class Mark missions.	Use the checklist on page 250 to identify the required missions.
	Xezat's Chalice	Bronze	15	Complete all C-class Mark missions.	Use the checklist on page 250 to identify the required missions.
	Exorcist	Silver	30	Defeat the 7 Undying Marks.	The corresponding hunts are: Mission 07, Mission 12, Mission 27, Mission 30, Mission 34, Mission 51 and Mission 64. Use the checklist on page 250 if you need help.
	Floraphobe	Silver	30	Complete Mark Mission 54.	See page 136 for tips and guidance.
	Natural Selector	Silver	30	Complete Titan's Trials.	The Titan's Trials are available in the Faultwarrens area. See page 124 for details.
	Dorgann's Trophy	Silver	30	Complete all B-class Mark missions.	Use the checklist on page 250 to identify the required missions.
	Galuf's Grail	Silver	30	Complete all Mark missions, including the A-class ones.	Use the checklist on page 250 to identify the required missions.
	L'Cie Paragon	Gold	80	Complete all Mark missions with a five-star post-battle rating.	You will need a very strong party to achieve this. Note that the Gold Watch accessory obtained after defeating Vercingetorix (see page 137) can help tremendously as it increases your Target Time for all battles, making it easier to receive high ratings. Another trick is to use weapons with low Strength and Magic attributes, as stat upgrades provided by equipment are taken into account to determine your Target Time.
	Commando's Seal	Bronze	15	Master the Commando role.	To unlock these, you must buy all crystals up to and including the fifth and final Role Level at the Crystarium. This is only possible after you have completed the main story.
	Ravager's Seal	Bronze	15	Master the Ravager role.	
	Sentinel's Seal	Bronze	15	Master the Sentinel role.	
	Saboteur's Seal	Bronze	15	Master the Saboteur role.	
	Synergist's Seal	Bronze	15	Master the Synergist role.	
	Medic's Seal	Bronze	15	Master the Medic role.	

Icon	Name	Type	G	Unlock Condition	Notes
	Limit Breaker	Silver	30	Deal 100,000 damage with a single attack.	This is best done with a highly developed Commando – Fang is naturally the best choice. The following tips will help: • Use fully upgraded equipment – we recommend a weapon with very high Strength, three Kaiser Knuckles and a Genji Glove. The Genji Glove is essential as it removes a damage cap that would otherwise render this feat impossible. • Cast Bravera on Fang. • You can further improve the damage you deal by Staggering the enemy and driving its Chain Bonus up to 999%. Lightning's Army of One ability can help here. • If Fang can hit a target as it is about to recover from a Stagger, the Smite and Scourge Auto-abilities can further increase the damage. • If Fang's HP is near maximum, the Adrenaline Auto-ability will make her even more powerful. An alternative method is to summon Bahamut with Fang and use his Megaflare Lv.3 finishing move in Gestalt Mode.
	Adamant Will	Silver	30	Defeat a Long Gui.	This enemy can be found on the Archylte Steppe after you have completed Mission 51. It is extremely tough, so you will need a supremely advanced party. The following tips will enable you to triumph against this creature. • Use Shrouds before the battle. • Use Infiltration (SAB + SAB + SAB) to weaken both legs. • Use Relentless Assault to disable the legs. • Use Infiltration (SAB + SAB + SAB) to weaken the knocked down Long Gui. Ensure that Poison is active. • Use Relentless Assault to Stagger and inflict maximum damage on your target. • Switch to Tortoise (SEN + SEN + SEN) as the creature climbs back to its feet to better resist the powerful attacks that follow. • Heal with Salvation (MED + MED + MED) and refresh your buffs with Rapid Growth (SYN + SYN + SYN). • In case of an emergency, summon your Eidolon. This will not only instantly disable both legs, but also heal your party. • If you have Elixirs in your inventory, these can be used to turn the tide of the battle. As they both fully heal the party and restore your TP gauge, they will enable you to summon your Eidolon one more time. This will provide you with another free knockdown and full healing for your party.
	Master's Seal	Silver	30	Fully develop all characters.	You must complete all roles at the Crystarium for every character. This will require an enormous amount of time spent power-leveling your party to unlock. The Growth Egg accessory will help with this task. See page 144 for tips on where you can farm CP with relatively little effort.
	Treasure Hunter	Gold	80	Collect all items available in the game.	This includes all weapons (though only one ultimate weapon per character is necessary) and accessory upgrades. These do not need to be in your inventory at the same time – you simply need to have owned each object type once. Refer to the Inventory chapter (page 204) for a complete list of all weapons, accessories, components and items. The title is awarded to you when you speak to Bhakti (see page 127).
	Loremaster	Gold	80	Reveal the full attributes of 100 enemies.	You will probably obtain this later in the main storyline. If not, hunt for opponents with incomplete Enemy Intel pages and use Libra or Librascopes until you reach the required total.
	Superstar	Gold	80	Defeat Orphan in his second form and obtain a five-star post-battle rating.	This is easy if you return to fight Orphan with a well-developed party after completing most Mark missions. Again, using low-level weapons and equipping the Gold Watch accessory (obtained after defeating Vercingetorix) will increase your allocated Target Time for this battle. See page 115 for a detailed strategy. Note that Orphan's second form is susceptible to Death while Staggered.
	Ultimate Hero (PS3 only)	Platinum	-	Acquire all Trophies.	-

BONUS THEMES & GAMER PICTURES

You can activate one of seven XMB Themes (PS3 only) or Gamer Pictures (Xbox 360 only) via the "Extras" menu available at FFXIII's title screen. Each of these is unlocked by obtaining specific Trophies or Achievements, as revealed in the accompanying table.

Theme/ Gamer Picture	Unlock Condition
 Lightning	Obtain the Superstar Trophy/Achievement.
 Snow	Obtain the L'Cie Paragon Trophy/Achievement.
 Sazh	Obtain the Loremaster Trophy/Achievement.
 Vanille	Obtain the Instrument of Faith Trophy/Achievement.
 Hope	Obtain the Instrument of Change Trophy/Achievement.
 Fang	Obtain the Treasure Hunter Trophy/Achievement.
 Serah	Obtain all Trophies/Achievements.

Trivia and Miscellany

Whenever you are hunting treasures while riding a chocobo (see page 123), there is a simple tip that can save you a lot of time: the bird always looks in the direction of the buried item. Combine this with other visual cues, and you will find treasures with little effort.

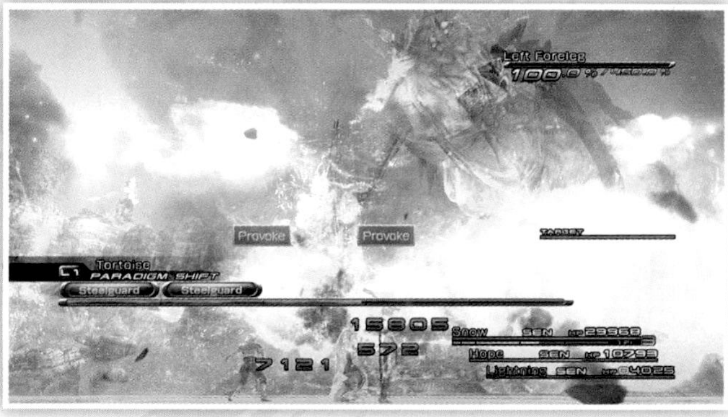

With a very advanced party, it is possible to get Snow to enter a "perfect defense" state. Equip him with his Winged Saint weapon or Save the Queen upgrade (for the Improved Guard II ability); your three active party members must have reached Role Level 5 as Sentinels. Paradigm Shift to Tortoise (SEN + SEN + SEN), and have Snow perform Steelguard or Mediguard. Any attack aimed at him during that time will inflict only 1% damage or less.

You can find a picture of Vanille and Fang on the table in the Dilapidated Dwelling zone in Oerba, proof of their past existence on Gran Pulse.

Secret Alphabets

There are two secret alphabets that appear in the game – one for Cocoon and another for Gran Pulse. These are revealed here, along with translations of instances where they can actually be encountered.

Cocoon Alphabet

Upper-case Character	Lower-case Character	Meaning
		A
		B
		C
		D
		E
		F
		G
		H
		I
		J
		K
		L
		M
		N
		O
		P
		Q
		R
		S
		T
		U
		V
		W
		X
		Y
		Z

Cocoon Cypher	Meaning	Cocoon Cypher	Meaning
	1		6
	2		7
	3		8
	4		9
	5		0

This can be seen on Lightning's weapon and reads "LIGHTNING".

This appears above the entrance to the bar in Bodhum and reads "BEACH HOUSE".

The access screen to the "B&W OUTFITTERS" shop.

GRAN PULSE ALPHABET*

Character	Meaning
	A
	B
	C
	E
	F
	G
	H
	L
	M
	N
	O
	R
	S
	T
	U
	Y

* This alphabet does not include the letters D, I, J, K, P, Q, V, W, X, and Z.

These sign boards in Oerba read "CARGO" and "SCHOOL".

Get close enough and you will see "BEHEMOTH" written on the shoulder of a Greater Behemoth.

Study Fang's weapon and you can read "OERBA" and "FANG" on it.

Funnily enough, the game over screen actually reads "GAME OVER".

If you are looking for specific information, this alphabetical listing is just what you need. To avoid any potential spoilers, note that all entries that link to pages featuring sensitive information are written in **red**.